AN

INQUIRY

INTO

THE PRINCIPLES AND POLICY

OF THE

GOVERNMENT

OF

THE UNITED STATES

———

BY JOHN TAYLOR

OF CAROLINE COUNTY, VIRGINIA

———

THE LAWBOOK EXCHANGE, LTD.
Clark, New Jersey

ISBN 978-1-886363-46-5 (hardcover)
ISBN 978-1-61619-320-1 (paperback)

Lawbook Exchange edition 1998, 2013

The quality of this reprint is equivalent to the quality of the original work.

THE LAWBOOK EXCHANGE, LTD.

33 Terminal Avenue
Clark, New Jersey 07066-1321

*Please see our website for a selection of our other publications
and fine facsimile reprints of classic works of legal history:*
www.lawbookexchange.com

Library of Congress Cataloging-in-Publication Data
Taylor, John, 1753-1824.
   An inquiry into the principles and policy of the government of the
United States / by John Taylor
     p. cm.
   Originally published: Fredericksburg : Green and Cady, 1814.
   Includes bibliographical references and index.
   ISBN 1-886363-46-3   (cloth : alk. paper)
   1. United States—Politics and government. I. Title.
JK181.157   1998
320.973'09'034—dc21   98-11147
                                                           CIP

Printed in the United States of America on acid-free paper

AN

INQUIRY

INTO

THE PRINCIPLES AND POLICY

OF THE

GOVERNMENT

OF

THE UNITED STATES

———

BY JOHN TAYLOR

OF CAROLINE COUNTY, VIRGINIA

———

NEW HAVEN

YALE UNIVERSITY PRESS

1950

FIRST PUBLISHED IN 1814
THIS NEW EDITION PUBLISHED IN 1950

PRINTED IN GREAT BRITAIN
BY WESTERN PRINTING SERVICES LTD
BRISTOL

CONTENTS

INTRODUCTION BY ROY FRANKLIN NICHOLS   *page* 7

DISTRICT OF VIRGINIA, TO WIT   30

TO THE PUBLICK   31

I. ARISTOCRACY   35

II. THE PRINCIPLES OF THE POLICY OF THE UNITED STATES, AND OF THE ENGLISH POLICY   94

III. THE EVIL MORAL PRINCIPLES OF THE GOVERNMENT OF THE UNITED STATES   165

IV. FUNDING   230

V. BANKING   267

VI: THE GOOD MORAL PRINCIPLES OF THE GOVERNMENT OF THE UNITED STATES   354

VII. AUTHORITY   447

VIII. THE MODE OF INFUSING ARISTOCRACY INTO THE POLICY OF THE UNITED STATES   477

IX. THE LEGAL POLICY OF THE UNITED STATES   501

INTRODUCTION

I

LIBERTY and authority exist side by side in some modern states but they are uneasy neighbours. Where should the line between them be drawn? When does liberty become licence? When does authority become tyranny? The great social and political changes beginning to be so apparent in the seventeenth and eighteenth centuries stirred the intellectual world to a great debate on this basic problem in political science, a debate which still rages. Active minds in both Europe and America were ceaselessly at work on the great question. The inquiring bent of the European mind and the unprecedented experiments across the Atlantic gave the contribution of publicists in the New World an unusual significance. Europe was watching America and America was instructing Europe.

John Taylor of Caroline County was a Virginia planter who lived through much of this ferment and was particularly jealous of liberty and fearful of power. In 1814 he published his *Inquiry into the Principles and Policy of the Government of the United States* and established his fame as a political theorist of note. His *Inquiry* reflects the intellectual power and breadth of the eighteenth century.

The eighteenth, and the seventeenth century preceding it, were periods charged with great energy in Europe. There political revolution changed man's concepts of freedom and government. A flood of inventions started an industrial revolution which was to re-order men's lives and alter their thinking. Europe was expanding and planting new settlements in far-off wildernesses, which in turn were to contribute a mass of new folkways to alter the behaviour patterns of mankind.

. Few centuries have produced thinkers of wider interests and greater enthusiasm for truth than the more outstanding of the eighteenth-century philosophers, particularly in France and Great Britain. They were anticipating a new heaven which was to descend upon earth to demonstrate how men of virtue could lead

7

society along highways of progress ever nearer the goal of perfection. Many of the eighteenth-century citizens of the Enlightenment, like the men of ancient Athens, preferred nothing so much as hearing some new thing; they felt intense interest in American happenings. For their part, the new Americans were growing more and more to feel that they had the answer to some of society's problems, particularly those touching politics.

The atmosphere in which Taylor grew up was decidedly influenced by European relationships of a complex sort. The nature of his thinking, the reasons for his conclusions and his contributions to political theory can be grasped only by placing them in their setting of European-American interchange; for Taylor, like all his fraternity, had the patterns of his thought drawn by the hand of experience.

II

After European intellectuals of the eighteenth century became aware of what was happening in America, they provoked a controversial interchange which was one of the ostensible motives stirring Taylor to write. As they awoke to the fact that America was a laboratory of ideas which might be extremely useful to them, there was much discussion of the true nature of government, of rights and privileges and of the measure and distribution of power. The variety of new governments now being set up in America perhaps might work out some of these problems.

Various philosophers studied and wrote about the work in America. Abbé Raynal published a *Philosophical and Political History of European Settlements and Commerce in the Two Indies* (1770 and many subsequent editions) wherein he sought to show how horribly Europeans were interfering in a society which had great possibilities.[1] Others like Chastellux, Mably and Brissot de Warville either read about the New World or visited it and then made their thoughts the texts for published admonitions to Europe to take note. Statesmen, like Turgot, studied American achievement to gain light on the problems of European statecraft.

The philosophers and humanitarians were examining everything American with peculiar zeal and their research was encouraging. These observant Europeans were finding the New World a place of superior virtue, despite heartless European cruelty and exploita-

[1] See also François Jean de Chastellux, *Voyage de M. le chevalier de Chastellux en Amérique* [Cassel] (1785.)

tion. Here dwelt 'the noble savage', the American Indian who was imparting some of his rugged strength and social understanding to the white race coming to his shores.

Work had been going on in this laboratory for nearly a century and a half, particularly in the thirteen British colonies on the North American mainland. These colonies on the Atlantic shore had a most favourable environment for social advance in the stimulating climate of the north temperate zone. Economically they were likewise fortunate, for moderate effort would yield an adequate living with a surplus as a spur to wealth-getting. But the most favouring circumstances for institutional achievement were political. The situation in the homeland and in the colonies combined to make possible superior institutions.

The colonies had been planted at a time when Great Britain was at a stage of energetic expansion. The exploits of the Elizabethan Age were followed by the Puritan Revolution, and Englishmen seemingly were on their mettle. Some of that energy was turned to colonial founding. Religious zealots, sturdy adventurers and wealth-hungry enterprisers saw in America the place for their hearts' desires. They came across the seas to a wilderness which demanded resourcefulness or death; they had the requisite resourcefulness.

From their religious, economic and political heritage in England they drew their institutional patterns and then adjusted them as new frontier experiences prescribed. They created governments which were composites of the religious congregation and synod, the stock company, and the British government under which they had been reared. They adopted the doctrines of the Puritan and the Glorious Revolutions and grew more and more independent in their practice of self-government.

In the years following 1689 the colonial bodies politic were called upon to exercise their powers of government at the same time they participated in a series of general European wars which tested them and taught them both their own competence and the uncertain quality of the strength and efficiency of the mother country. The British Government appeared to the colonials as neglectful, inept at management and, through many of its military and political agents, supercilious, disagreeable and insulting. By the time the Seven Years War came to its end in 1763, the thirteen colonies had come of age, though the British Government, like many parents, seemed unable to grasp the implications of the fact.

A*   9

The powers of self-government, and the freedom to exercise them, by this time had been so long enjoyed that they led to another political experiment. They had come to be accepted as matters of the colonists' rightful prerogative. When the home government, at the close of an exhausting war, strove to balance the budget and reorganize the empire administratively, the colonials resisted. Throughout the colonies, certain politicos feared interference with their controls, merchants were worried about taxes and loss of profits and property, and citizens in general saw curtailment of rights and liberties which had become precious to them.

- The British Government of that day was lacking in understanding and was befuddled by the peculiarly complicated politics played by the Old Whigs, the Bloomsbury Gang and the King's Friends. Also, the various ministries of the 1760's had to operate in a period of demoralization such as often follows wars. Many people were at loose ends in an economic depression; and colonial governments, like the British ministry, were confronted with unbalanced budgets and heavy taxes.

Apprehension, accident, bad administration, use of military force, rising indignation, clever propaganda and leadership, plus the great separation in time and space between London and the colonies all made their contribution. The result was that a series of energetic colonial groups led by persons who had gained political experience in running the various legislatures and local governments became active in protesting against the 'tyranny' and 'unconstitutional' taxation which their spokesmen so eloquently described. The efforts of the home government to cope with them were inept and futile, no statesman arose with sufficient wisdom to meet the situation and the result was a Declaration of Independence backed by military force. The language of these protests and of the Declaration as it was drafted by Jefferson, Franklin, Adams, Sherman and their associates was that of the political philosophers of this and the preceding centuries. The natural rights theory, the concept of a government of law, the necessity of popular consent to acts of rulers, and the right of revolution, all were beautifully phrased.

The philosophical world, particularly in Paris, looked on with keen interest and a widespread approval. This favourable attention was not lessened by French resentment at their own recent defeat and by a desire to see the British power weakened by dissension and secession. American emissaries, particularly Franklin, were received in France with enthusiasm, supplies and money were provided and enthusiasts for the cause of liberty enlisted. Here was an opportunity for those who believed in the new theories of social and political progress to have a hand in the laboratory experiment, and young zealots like Lafayette, and also some canny adventurers, threw in their lot with the colonists. Statesmen and politicians watched successive events transpire and at an opportune moment the French Government, playing power politics, recognized the colonies as a republic and implemented a military alliance. Philosophical enthusiasm and power politics were tightly tangled in a pattern which can be explained according to the predilections of him who seeks to interpret it.

The laboratory technicians were constantly at work during this War for Independence and their product was extensive. Besides the Declaration of Independence they must prepare fourteen other statements to carry out their will and at the same time to 'enlighten a candid world'. Each colony must write its social contract or constitution, and some of them were elaborate. They must proclaim and safeguard liberty; they must anticipate and destroy possible tyrannies. So they exalted the legislatures which were the representatives of the people, and sharply curbed the executives. Further, the representatives of the thirteen republics must create a confederation, must make a reality of the idea of a United States of America. They drafted the Articles of Confederation, a contract for the perpetual union of the thirteen sovereign republics.

The writing of these documents illustrated difficulties which have been present from the beginning of international co-operation. One difficulty was the lack of acquaintance among the leaders of the various colonies. The delegates to the 'Continental Congress', which began meeting in 1774, were like delegates to other conferences and congresses before and since. Most of them had never met, they came from communities which had grown up independently and which had different habits and customs. The men from New England represented a tradition of religious, economic and other cultural attitudes and activities quite different from those of the southern colonies. These strangers had to learn to trust each other enough to make mutual concessions.

Another difficulty, and one noted particularly by some European observers, especially Turgot, was the creation of authority. From the meeting of the first Continental Congress there had been a concern about power. The ex-colonials were enthusiastic about rights and liberties and suspicious of power, of possible tyrants. Who was to have power and could anyone be trusted with it? From the beginning it was agreed that as little authority as possible should be permitted and the disposition of that little was dominated by political expediency.

All this dread of power worked to produce a rather naïve and unrealistic concept of the problem of confederation. The authors of the Articles assumed that, if they continued their Congress of emissaries without establishing any executive authority, a system of committees could manage foreign affairs and the armed forces, just as they had during the War for Independence, and that most other functions of government could be left to the states. Furthermore they assumed that the states would contribute quotas of funds on request, and therefore they gave the Confederation no levy power. Furthermore they permitted no changes in fundamental law save by a unanimous vote of the states; on all matters each state had one vote, regardless of the size of its population, just as though they were nations in a diplomatic conference.

It was not long before certain weaknesses in this confederation became apparent. The states, absorbed in their own problems, failed to give the financial support requested and quarrelled among themselves. The new confederacy was flouted abroad by other powers, its borders were harassed by unfriendly neighbours —Spanish and French as well as British—in league with the Indian tribes; and within, there were alarming signs of civil disorder endangering life and property. Some of the friends of the experiment, at home and abroad, began to be gravely concerned. Within the Confederation men like Washington, Hamilton, Madison and Wilson, and observers abroad like Turgot, saw that a vital cause of the trouble was the failure to endow the Confederation with power. Jealousy and the naïve disregard for the need of power had not safeguarded liberty so much as they had produced weakness.

Confronted by the problem, certain of the American leaders went about the task of creating power in true eighteenth-century fashion. They secured authorization of a special 'constitutional convention' to study the situation and to produce a plan. They were 'rational men of virtue' and they would apply the techniques of the Enlightenment. Several delegates to the conference made elaborate preparations. They conducted intensive research in the works of the historians and philosophers and made digests of the experiences of all governments, particularly federations. They refreshed themselves in Montesquieu, and their discussions within and without the convention hall centred round this research. They worked out an eighteenth-century rationalization of fact and theory and produced a well-conceived logical document for themselves and their posterity.

This document was more the product of Anglo-American experience, and less of research and reason, than its authors probably realized, a generalization which should be axiomatic in political science. The British Government and those of the colonies had, generally speaking, three branches: executive, legislative and judicial; the legislative branch was generally bicameral. As this form had been blessed by Montesquieu, it was a natural choice. The resulting Constitution not only supplied the needed power, by creating an executive and granting more functions to the legislative branch, but it provided also a neat system of checks and balances to prevent that power from becoming absolute.

The confederation concept was modified, in the light of unhappy recent experience and of the study of other such experiments. Counsels were divided. Some persons, despite experience and research, wanted to continue the loose federation idea. Others advocated a strong, centralized, national republic. The result was a compromise; a federal system in which the states surrendered more power than some of their leaders thought safe, while the advocates of national strength had to be content with a division of power which they thought weakening.

Form and function were easier to derive than the solution of the question of participation. Who was to be responsible for the operation of the system? The new document spoke in the name of the people, 'We, the people', but it was apparent that those of the people who were to have the responsibility were limited in number. Neither the judiciary nor the executive branch could be chosen by popular vote. The judges were to be appointed and the executive, in line with the theory of the founders, was to be chosen by a special college of experts elected for the purpose. The upper house of the legislative arm—the Senate—was to be selected by the legislatures of the states. Only the lower house of that branch was to come directly from the people and the 'people' in each instance were only those to whom the several states entrusted the franchise. This privilege varied; the lower houses of the state legislatures were generally chosen by male voters who usually must own property or pay taxes. In some cases the upper houses were designed to represent more substantial elements in the state population. The new federal constitution, like some of the state constitutions, was designed to ensure a stable government in which people of property should have the greater responsibility. The Constitution may be described as a counter-revolutionary document, proposed for the purpose of stabilizing the forces let loose during the achievement of independence. Some of the most conspicuous leaders of the Revolution had no part in it and a few opposed it.

This document was duly presented to the state legislatures which had commissioned the authors of it. They arranged for its ratification though in some instances over great opposition, particularly by those who feared that it had given sufficient power to the new federal government to create a new tyranny. No popular vote was· ever taken, so it can never be known whether it was favoured by a voting majority of the people. It was acquiesced in by those who were not fully convinced and even by those who opposed it most vigorously.

III

It was one thing to secure acceptance of the new frame, it was another to put it into operation. Here another struggle for power ensued, where the same love of liberty and fear of tyranny emerged. The friends of the Constitution assumed the task of putting it into operation with little experience to guide them. They knew instinctively that they must give positions of trust only to those who favoured the order and that they must gain power and the respect of their opponents. Public confidence they concluded could only be based upon a show of strength and strength began with adequate money and credit. The finances of the new nation were in a chaotic and demoralizing condition, so that the first charge must be to secure the means to pay the debts and current running expenses of the new government.

A stroke of genius was needed and it was forthcoming. President Washington had chosen Alexander Hamilton to be Secretary of the Treasury and he produced the much-needed plans. He was an admirer of the system of British public finance with its skilful use of the national debt and the Bank of England as auxiliaries of the Exchequer and he proposed a similar scheme to the new Congress. He would fund the Confederation debt, assume the debts of the states and create a Bank of the United States with the new government as minority stockholder. Hamilton's projects appealed to those who wanted strength and power in the new government.

All did not go smoothly. Power is frightening to many people, particularly when it is exercised by strangers who live in other regions and who seemingly have interests which may be conflicting, or ideas which may be unpalatable. When the new government was being put into operation the greater part of the republic was rural; ninety-five per cent of the population lived in isolated hamlets or on lonely farmsteads, a population widely scattered. This meant that a large number of the people had no contacts beyond the few available to farmers. They knew little of the outside world except as news came to them by the meagre newspapers, by the few available books and pamphlets or by the rumours that were carried from mouth to mouth. Some few had correspondence and learned from letters, but mail service was poor and such means of communication not frequently used by the great mass of the people who could not easily engage in letter writing, even had they had anyone to whom to write. The result was that there was a large number of uninformed people who could easily become concerned over matters but vaguely understood, just as three decades before a large number had been concerned by the imperial policies after the Seven Years War.

Power was growing up in distant places, in the cities which they had never seen. In New York, in Philadelphia and Boston a new power was arising which might easily be feared in much the same terms as the British Government once had been feared. The new government had now the authority to tax, with the means to grant subsidies to the favoured at the expense of the population. It was also a government which might send officers to enforce unpopular laws which in turn might possibly be backed by military force. Most politicians in the state capitals were never certain that this new central government might not grow stronger at their expense and lower their prestige and perquisites. It was thus inevitable that there should arise expressions of fear and protest. This protest had to have a vocabulary and, as is usual, the protesters adopted words and ideas which were current, which had a familiar sound and struck familiar chords.

The language of protest had been polished in England, where the tradition of such resistance went back to the days of the Magna Carta and had been vastly reinforced recently in the seventeenth century. The troubled years of the Puritan and Glorious Revolutions had brought naturally to the lips of Englishmen certain words which can be summed up by the terms 'rights' and 'liberties'. They feared tyranny and had come to regard it as their duty to curb and, if necessary, liquidate tyrants. The 'immemorial rights of Englishmen' were precious possessions which were more frequently lauded than defined. This vocabulary was fresh in American minds, as it had been used vigorously during the recent War for Independence. When the colonists defied King George III they had formulated their defiance in the terms of the Lockeian political science and psychology, and they then submitted their formula in print as a matter of duty for the information of that 'candid world' of theirs. Most of the state constitutions contained a bill of rights drawn largely from English sources and the omission of such provisions from the federal Constitution had been a powerful weapon in the hands of those opposed to its ratification. In fact, the addition of a bill of rights to the Constitution, in the guise of the first ten amendments to it, had to be promised before ratification could be secured.

When Washington, Hamilton and their Federalist associates set out to develop the power of the central government, it was very easy for their opponents to employ the language of the Revolutionary tradition in vigorous protest against what they envisioned as tyranny, proclaiming that their rights were in danger. To be sure, there was no king, and Washington was sufficiently revered and trusted by most men to make unprofitable the general charge that he was seeking the crown. Yet Jefferson was convinced, or said he was, that Hamilton was trying to persuade the General to become a monarch. The Jeffersonians were wont to accuse the Federalist party, as a group, of having monarchistic preferences. Furthermore, the fact that Hamilton and Washington had set themselves to an elaborate task of debt financing and fiscal organization, particularly in the form of a bank, laid them open to attack for the economic policies of their new federal government.

This line of attack had a very widespread appeal, because of the physiographic, ethnographic and economic variety within the new republic. Physiographically the United States could be divided into several sections. Peculiarities of soil and climate meant that sections such as New England, the Middle States and the South had each its own environment which would encourage different ways of living and different social customs. Ethnographically, distribution was very uneven; the few cities were located predominantly in the more northerly region. In the south the people were scattered over large and small farms having a minimum of communication with their neighbours, with other states or with the world at large. Economically, also, there were sharp contrasts; the commercial and general business activity was largely within the northern states, concentrated in Philadelphia, .New York, Boston and their few municipal contemporaries. Outside of these cities few people knew anything of commerce and much less of banking and stock corporation activity. In the South the rural economy was maintained in part by Negro slave labour which produced an economic and social organization markedly different from the rest of the country.

These numerous and deeply felt differences, plus the fact that most people lived isolated lives without much means of communication, made it possible for politicians to utilize local situations, to capitalize interests and prejudices and to develop a propaganda along simple lines of thought and emotion.

The opposition to the policies of the Federalists for putting the new government into operation began, first in New York and later in Philadelphia, among active men closely associated in the Washington Administration, and in the two houses of Congress. Here individual differences, incompatible personalities and rival ambitions worked, as they always do, to divide co-operating groups. Within Washington's official family were Jefferson and Hamilton, brilliant men who rubbed each other the wrong way. As Hamilton was quicker and more dynamic and had greater influence with Washington he seems to have given Jefferson something akin to a feeling of inferiority; this feeling in the breast of the latter scarcely hindered his growing belief that the political policy of the Administration was dangerous.

In Congress, men of different temperaments, ideas and backgrounds were becoming acquainted with their duties and each other. In the association with each other they were inevitably exchanging likes and dislikes, and forming cliques. In this process, sectionalism continued to play a role, as it had done in the Continental Congress of Revolutionary days and under the Articles of Confederation. Men from New England, the Middle States and the South, while they had much in common, represented different ways of life which would naturally be reflected in their legislative behaviour. Therefore, when the Washington Administration presented its fiscal policy there was bound to be a contest based upon personal and environmental differences. Those who for one reason or another wished to block or modify the new policies would appeal to and capitalize these differences. Likewise they would make use of certain ideas which were then current.

Jefferson and Madison took the lead in opposition to the Administration and therefore in the founding of partisan organization in the new republic. At first they had been willing to follow Washington and Hamilton in supporting the fiscal policies because they felt, with all the Administration, that the government must have credit and funds. Jefferson had gone so far as to intervene to secure reluctant Virginia votes in Congress. However, as his relations with Hamilton, in Washington's official family, grew more complex and as he saw that these fiscal policies were very profitable to certain northern speculators and business groups, he began to wonder. He soon discovered that the southern and indeed the rural regions in general were getting very little direct benefit nor were they sharing much in the profits. For his part, Madison began to take the lead in a Congressional bloc that was critical of the Hamiltonian policies.

Foreign relations were also complicating this growing partisanship. The French Revolution had begun almost simultaneously with the Washington Administration and had immediately aroused great interest in the United States. There seemed to be a bond between the two nations forged by the Enlightenment; many Frenchmen had been connected, sympathetically, with the American Revolution. The philosophers had watched it intently, the enthusiasts like Lafayette had participated in it, and the politicians had aided it. Then Franklin had taken Paris by his wit, wisdom and charm, combined with a delightful eccentricity of manner and an eye for the ladies. Jefferson, too, had been stationed there. Mably had written his *Observations sur le gouvernement et les lois des États-Unis d'Amérique* and Brissot de Warville had been to America and was now talking and writing of his experiences though his book was not to come out until the French Revolution was further advanced.[1]

Americans remembered all this and many rejoiced that their republicanism was spreading to France. The great monarchy was yielding to the force of American virtue. What a compliment!

[1] Amsterdam, 1784. See also Jean Pierre Brissot de Warville, *Nouveau voyage dans les États-Unis de l'Amérique Septentrionale fait en 1788* (Paris, 1791).

American Revolutionary documents and constitutions had been translated and were being read. What a triumph of human reason! The United States was prepared to encourage France as she embarked on the unfamiliar waters of constitutionalism in search of liberty. But the halcyon days did not last long. The French became more radical; heads, even crowned ones, fell, the Christian religion was abandoned in favour of a godless rationalism and the forces of world politics began to operate. England and France were at war.

These developments divided American public opinion. When France, beset by her enemies, notably Great Britain, called upon the new republic for aid under the treaty of 1778 the issue was placed squarely before the American Government and public. By this time a reaction against France had set in. The excesses of the Revolutionaries in destroying life, property and religion had not gone unnoticed and many pious and conservative people shuddered. Also the commercial and financial ties between London and the United States had been resumed profitably and war would sunder them. Furthermore, the new republic had practically abandoned its armament and had neither force nor money with which to go to war. Washington and his Administration, including Jefferson, friend of France though he was, decided that neutrality was the only course. Nevertheless Jefferson resented this decision as a further evidence of favour to England, which he knew was Hamilton's interest; and it did not improve their relationships. Other friends of France who resented neutrality might be rallied against Washington.

Altogether Jefferson had excellent material out of which to build party organization: fear of profiteers, of corruption and of Britain, the prejudices of rural taxpayers, friendship for liberty and for France. He began a skilful mobilization. There were no modern conveniences for political organization but he proceeded in methodical fashion. He talked to many. He wrote to leaders in the various states. He sought to stimulate men to assume leadership. He travelled, ostensibly for recreation, but he knew whom to visit. He made friends among the local editors and subsidized an organ from State Department funds. Thus he and Madison and his friends spread their ideas. They set up little formal machinery. They held no great conventions, no meetings of delegates. But there was constant letter writing; and at such gatherings as sessions of state legislatures everywhere, at sittings of county courts in the South and at town meetings in New England, friends of Jefferson met, conferred and decided to endorse candidates for office. Gradually the idea grew that the administration of the federal government was in the hands of monarchists and reactionary friends of the rich who were careless or disdainful of rights and liberties.

IV

. These experiences became the guiding influence in the growth of John Taylor's ideas and the key to his philosophy. He had been born in 1753 and was coming into manhood in the stirring birth years of the American Revolution.[1] His father died when he was three and he was brought up by a kinsman, Edmund Pendleton. His guardian was a lawyer and politician, judge and legislator. Young Taylor was sent to William and Mary College and afterwards studied law with Pendleton. He became a practising attorney at the age of twenty-one in 1774, just as the Revolution was brewing.

He had been educated, not only in the classics and in the law, but likewise in politics and political theory. From 1760 to 1776, Virginia had been talking politics, seeking to define its various relations with Great Britain and with the British Government. From Patrick Henry's speech in the Parsons' Cause, until Richard Henry Lee's resolutions in the Continental Congress and Thomas Jefferson's report on the Declaration of Independence, the anvils in the smithy of ideas were ringing with heavy blows from mighty hammers. Pendleton was one of those at work at the forges and Taylor in his most impressionable years was ably tutored in the revolutionary philosophy of rights and liberties.

Taylor served in the Virginia militia and in the Continental army during much of the war and emerged from the last Virginia campaign as a lieutenant-colonel. Furthermore he was a member of the Virginia legislature during the most perilous period of the struggle. He was not only indoctrinated with republicanism but he had practical experience in putting these doctrines into effect.

After the struggle was over Taylor married the daughter of a wealthy lawyer-planter, John Penn, signer of the Declaration of Independence. Taylor, like most of his neighbours now that the peaceful days had come, settled down to farm and practise law. He and his wife bought and inherited several plantations and he

[1] Avery O. Craven, 'John Taylor' in *Dictionary of American Biography*, XVII; Henry H. Simms, *Life of John Taylor* (Richmond, Va., 1932).

was as ardent an agriculturist as he had been a revolutionary. Also he was fond of reading and kept up with the times, and then there was always the Virginia planters' dash of politics to add zest to life. He was one of the republican oligarchy of lawyer-planters who ruled the counties of Virginia and either went to the legislature or chose those who were to go. He was the friend of Jefferson and since boyhood the companion of James Madison.

Taylor was not in any official position at the time that the question of ratification of the Constitution was in the public eye, so he did not participate actively in this contest. However, he was doubtful about the document because it contained no bill of rights. He did not follow Washington, with whom he seems to have had no particular contact at any time. His real activity in politics waited until 1792, when he was appointed Senator to fill an unexpired term. Appearing in the then capital city of Philadelphia while the heat generated by Hamilton's financial policies ran high, he became convinced that there was danger to the Republic from the creation of a monied interest, and he published a pamphlet, *A Definition of Parties, or the Political Effects of the Paper System Considered*, which exposed what he felt approached corruption. The promoters of Hamilton's plan, said the author, were receiving a profit which they did not deserve and which they would secure at the expense of the taxpayers.

From this time forward Taylor worked with Thomas Jefferson in building up the party which was to curb the Federalists, christened the Democratic-Republican party. His term in the Senate was brief, lasting less than two years, after which he returned to Virginia though not entirely to private life. He was a Presidential elector supporting Jefferson in 1796 and shortly afterwards he entered the Virginia legislature. In the meantime the interests of the Federalists had not been confined to establishing a strong central government and a sound credit; difficulties connected with the European war had led the Federalist administration of John Adams to take repressive measures in the interests of public security. Fearing particularly the intrigues of foreigners and the attacks which the Republican friends of France were making upon the government, Congress enacted laws, the Alien and Sedition Acts, which empowered the Federal government to suppress certain types of freedom of expression and political activity.

Jefferson and his friends saw, not only that these acts were really dangerous to the spirit of liberty, but also that they would make good political ammunition. Thereupon they proceeded to use them effectively. They began a propaganda attacking the Federalists as violating the Constitution, destroying liberty and favouring Great Britain. In true eighteenth-century fashion they decided that they must put their views in writing. So John Taylor introduced into the Virginia legislature the famous series of resolutions which he suggested to Jefferson and which Madison composed, denouncing the Federal administration for tyrannical laws and calling upon the states to interpose, to arrest them as violations of the Constitution. These pronouncements, together with a similar series passed by the Kentucky legislature, became popularly known as the 'Virginia and Kentucky Resolutions' and became the political platform of Jefferson's party.

The appeal of Jeffersonian principles, the astuteness of Jefferson as leader, the ineptitude of the Federalists and the weakness bred of twelve years of power produced the downfall of the Federalists in 1800 and the accession of Jefferson to the Presidency. During this administration Taylor returned to the Senate, again for a brief time, 1803–1804. Here he undertook to defend the Chief Executive, even accepting the Louisiana Purchase. However, the party of Jefferson was not to be wholly harmonious and he, like Washington, found that he could not keep the Virginians in line. There were rivals for the succession. Jefferson favoured Madison but James Monroe, coming back from a futile mission to Great Britain with a grievance, soon joined those opposing the elevation of Madison. This anti-Madison faction varied in different states but represented a common desire seemingly to express dissatisfaction with Jefferson's methods of political management. These schismatics were generally known as 'Tertium Quids', i.e. neither Jeffersonians nor Federalists, but something else.

· John Taylor found himself among the Tertium Quids as he was coming to the belief that Jefferson was not true to Republican ideals and that it was necessary to speak out. Colonel Taylor in fact had been engaged, in rather desultory fashion, for nearly twenty years in formulating an eighteenth-century inquiry into the reason for things political. Scarcely realizing that it pertained to a century which was past, he nevertheless felt it was time to bring this long analysis to a close and give it to the public. He may have wanted it to be campaign material for the Presidential election of 1812, but so large was the work and so slow the printer that it did not appear until 1814.

V

This *Inquiry*, being a reflection of late eighteenth-century political science, can best be understood in the light of the political philosophy of the time. It fitted into a sequence of polemic writing which had started during the Revolution. The progress of the struggle for independence and effective government in America had stimulated a mass of writing, both theoretical and practical, since Europe's political philosophers and statesmen, particularly in France, had been keenly interested in various aspects of the contest. The efforts at constitution-making by the states and the Confederation received careful attention and editions in French translation were printed as early as 1778. The French statesman, Turgot, studied them and wrote a criticism of these constitutions that year which was published after his death in 1784. He concentrated particularly on division of power and the checks and balances which were the pride of American constitution-making. He felt that an effective state must have its powers concentrated in one sovereign body, not divided. From other quarters there was criticism that these states were not democratic and that the will of the people could be too easily checked or circumvented.[1] Then in 1786 a civil disturbance over mortgage foreclosures in Massachusetts, known as Shays Rebellion, gave emphasis to such strictures.

These criticisms moved John Adams, then American minister at the Court of St. James's, to take up his pen. When he was so moved, nothing could stop him, and the result was a three-volume work, *A Defence of the Constitutions of Government of the United States of America.*[2] In this heavy opus he sought to answer Turgot's criticism and also a work, *The Excellency of a Free State*, by an Englishman of radical leanings, Marchamont Nedham. He surveyed a great variety of governments, related their history at length and came to certain conclusions. Mankind, he decided, was naturally unfitted to rule itself and therefore not to be trusted; governments must be so organized as to check man's depraved tendencies. The various types of government devised so far were unsatisfactory. Aristocratic or monarchical governments tended to be despotic. Demo-

[1] Richard Price, *Observations on the Importance of the American Revolution and the Means of Making it a Benefit to the World* (London, 1784), contains letter of Turgot to Price, Paris, Mar. 22, 1788.

[2] John Adams, *A Defence of the Constitutions of Government of the United States* (Phila., 1787).

cracy, which Adams believed to be the worst of governments, led to the despotism of the mob or its leaders, or to anarchy.

The only way to produce good government was to unite these types in a balanced form, with a strong executive, checked by a legislature representing the aristocratic and the democratic elements in its two houses. It was hoped that in this way the best people, the natural aristocrats, the well-born, rich, talented and virtuous could be given a reasonable predominance in government, checked always by the representatives of the mass in one of the houses of the legislature.

This system of checks and balances was described by Adams in the first volume of his book which was ready in time to be in the hands of some of those making the Constitution in 1787. A similar system was devised and incorporated in that instrument, not because of Adams' eloquence, but because colonial and British experience had directed the thoughts of the drafters in that channel.

Their work raised apprehensions among many who thought the new system might curtail liberty; and so three of the most gifted of the advocates of the Constitution undertook to urge its adoption in a series of essays printed in the newspapers, known as the Federalist papers. They, likewise, had recourse to history and showed that government without authority was ineffective and productive of anarchy. A government must have power and at the same time must allow mankind the enjoyments of rights and liberty; the federal republic with its representative system was designed to do just that. The checks and balances would prevent any faction, interest or pressure group from getting undue control. The central, federal power was to be a stabilizing influence, not an oppressive instrument.

The arguments of Adams and of the authors of the Federalist long disturbed Taylor and men of his sympathies. His experience with the new government from 1789 to 1811 only confirmed him in a growing apprehension that something of great value to the world, which America had produced, was being perverted. He felt impelled to work out a counter-philosophy which should commend itself to his fellowmen and give them a platform on which to rally in their effort to awaken the American people to a sense of danger. So, twenty-seven years after John Adams' volumes appeared, Taylor published his large book, the *Inquiry*, which was ostensibly in great part a refutation of Adams' philosophy.

Taylor was neither an orderly thinker nor a concise writer. Also, whether consciously or unconsciously, he distorted Adams' meaning. The latter was defending the type of government devised by certain states like Massachusetts before the Federal Constitution was drafted while Taylor argues as though he were describing the new national instrument. Also he was very slow and evidently started and stopped many times. His work therefore has changes of mood. It reflected his disagreement with Adams in 1787–88, his fear of Hamilton in 1790–93, his opposition to the Federalists, 1797–1801, and his disappointment in Jefferson in 1806–09. He also made use of ideas which he had published in pamphlet form and thoughts he had uttered in legislative chambers. As the most casual reader will see it is verbose, repetitive and disorganized. Also it is naïve and unsophisticated in some respects; its author was the victim of the simplicity of social thought and the inadequacy of the social knowledge of the famous century of the Enlightenment.

Yet the *Inquiry* is surprisingly wise and clear-sighted. Taylor had read widely among the philosophers; Aristotle, Machiavelli, Locke, Sidney, Adam Smith, Malthus, the Physiocrats, Rousseau, Montesquieu and Godwin were known to him. He had devised a political theory which has a familiar sound to those who have walked with the eighteenth-century philosophers. This farmer-politician was a devotee of the cult of Arcadian virtues—a very natural choice for him to make.

Man, he believed, was not depraved, he was dominated by moral qualities which might be either good or evil. Therefore it was essential that government should be devised to direct man in the path of virtue, to stimulate his good rather than his evil impulses. To this end government should be one of laws, not of men. Laws could be made on the basis of moral principles but men might well be dynamic zealots, demagogues who could not be trusted. Men in power would probably be guided by self-interest, would build support by granting special favours and thus would produce an unjust distribution of property and a class of parasites.

Taylor's reading of history, too, was quite extensive and he emerged from it with a deep conviction that power is corrupting. Throughout the development of the human race, despotism had appeared constantly, based upon superstition, force or unjust seizure of property. Priestly classes supporting divinely created monarchs, feudal aristocracies and their royal suzerains, and more recently stock-jobbing capitalists who supported kings and on occasion assumed titles of nobility, these, so far, had been the sum total of the results of man's experience with government—with one exception: the United States.

This republic was the first attempt made to found a government on good moral principles. It had a government of law, no men were to be given much opportunity to feel the corrupting hand of power, for each community, or state, was to manage its own affairs and leave little to be done by the new federal government. The men, i.e. the officials, in this central government would be balanced by the men, i.e. the voters, in the local communities who in frequent elections would check any tendencies among those in the federal government to succumb to the lure of power. The United States, he asserted, was not a government of aristocrats and monarchs with only feeble checks by popular representatives in one house of Congress. Rather it was a government of plain men with little power in federal office, jealously watched by other plain men who came frequently to the polls to check. These same voters would also serve as the militia, so there would be no standing army to be useful in any abuse of power. Thus virtuous rational Arcadians, intelligent voters and sturdy militia men who peacefully cultivated their broad acres and kept up with the times, would preserve the moral principles upon which the new government was founded.

Such was the moral achievement in political science which Taylor believed the founders had desired. But, he lamented, it had soon been perverted. Men like Adams with his cult of aristocracy, men like Hamilton with their corrupt schemes of unjust property distribution at the expense of the Arcadians, were dangerous. All history had shown that those in office sought to take not only power but wealth. Hamilton by his plans for funding the debt, establishing a bank and enacting a protective tariff had enriched speculators, stock jobbers, and parasites at the expense of the land-holding taxpayers. This group was ready to support the central government in ever greater usurpations and injustices.

Not only must such schemes be guarded against eternally by a party alive to Republican virtues, such as Jefferson and his associates had led to power in 1800, but there were more subtle dangers. Federal power, even in the hands of virtuous Arcadians, was corrupting. The noble Jefferson had fallen a victim of it, his administration had been autocratic and centralizing and not too unfriendly to speculative interests.

His safeguards against such perils were Spartan. He would shorten the terms of the president and senators, no executive should be eligible for re-election. The irresponsibility of the judiciary should be checked. There must be strict virtue and adherence to moral principles. Those in power must sternly put aside the temptation to favour a few or to distribute wealth by law. Government must protect, not distribute property. The federal government must be self-denying, exercise only a minimum of authority and leave the responsibilities of rule largely to the citizens of the states where Republican virtue could be better exercised by free Arcadians. They would be immune from the temptation of power, dwelling on their own farms, progressing by their own efforts towards that perfection which Taylor believed education and individual effort could achieve.

In one sense of course this is a very imperfect and simple philosophy, assuming as it did the continued prevalence of rural social organization and economy. Taylor grasped few of the dynamic potentialities of the mechanization of life and industry. Nor were the evidences of evil, which he saw in Hamilton's efforts to create sound credit and to encourage adequate industry, as convincing as he claimed. Subsidy was inevitable in a new undeveloped country; working against it was like Canute's gesture against the tide. Also centralization was necessary, as Jefferson learned even if Taylor did not. Taylor's understanding of the complexities of human behaviour was no clearer than those current in the Enlightenment.

On the other hand there is a decidedly modern note in all this, one which is typically American. Taylor may be said to be the first Muckraker. He anticipated the Populists, the Progressives and the New Dealers of a later day. He saw the evil of an alliance between government and business interests. He would drive the money changers from the temple. His strictures on the activities of banking corporations have the same basic meaning as those against railroads, trusts and utility-holding companies of a much later date. His attacks on the paper-holders, whom, he charged, Hamilton wished to enrich, were similar to later denunciations of bond-holders, 'bankers', and malefactors of great wealth. His demand for strict regard for moral principles, and that those in office hold themselves bound by public trust to resist and overcome temptation, has been repeated by statesmen and reformers in every crisis since. These pleas for public morality are universals that bear no mark of any century but are prized in all.

27

So Colonel John Taylor wrote his book. A Virginia farmer, lawyer and politician, he assumed attitudes which had been typical of his time and residence. His political thinking was dominated by his situation in life and he evolved or accepted theories which accorded with his circumstances. When he was in the Senate and of the minority party he thought as the minority thought. When he returned to the Senate as one of the majority he, like Jefferson, put aside these scruples and proceeded unfettered. When he left the Senate a second time and saw his influence less than formerly, he again had doubts and even worried about Jefferson's consistency. The evolution of Taylor's thought illustrates very well a fact that political theorists have been known to neglect, namely that political theory is seldom the exercise in pure reason which its author believes it to be, but rather a reflection of some very practical experiences in the intriguing field of political endeavour and ambition.

Taylor's writing continued after the publication of the *Inquiry*. In the next ten years he went back to the Senate for a brief term (1822–27) and published several more tracts, *Construction Construed, and Constitutions Vindicated* (1820) *New Views of the Constitution of the United States* (1823) and *Tyranny Unmasked* (1822). He continued to see the dangers which government would create for itself by subsidy to business. He fought the protective tariff and the Bank of the United States and stressed even more vigorously the theory of a limited federal government and the paramount rights of the states. His various writings, never widely read, were used by others who could speak more coherently than he could write. They were translated into vigorous oratory, particularly by Calhoun and by other politicians and publicists who were becoming more and more concerned over the relation of the southern states to the Federal government. No small part of the oratorical contests which had so much to do with the coming of the Civil War were fought with the ideas of Taylor. But the Arcadian philosophy of a rural era could not solve the problems of a multiplying population in an age of cities and machines. Alas for the Arcadian dream of rural felicity!

The *Inquiry* was lost sight of for many years. It was never reprinted and was hard to secure as early as the 1830's. Not until the twentieth century did it come to life. Then, when a more realistic school of historians and political scientists were seeking a 'New History', much of the old story was reassessed. In the United States, the public, aided by Gladstone and Lord Bryce, had accepted an idealized view of the nature of the American constitutions and the impulses of its founders. Charles A. Beard was not satisfied and went to Treasury records, pamphlets and the correspondence of the founders and produced an 'economic interpretation'. He showed, as Taylor had done, how profitable had been the operation of the new constitution under the guidance of Hamilton's policies. He noted Taylor's penetration in detecting this over a century before and proclaimed Taylor's work one of the 'two or three really historic contributions to political science which have been produced in the United States'.[1] Historians and political theorists have done much in recent years to explore Taylor's thought and bring him forth as the 'Philosopher of Jeffersonian Democracy', the 'most fruitful of Republican intellects'.[2]

This plain Virginia farmer, it is now recognized, made a significant contribution to the debate over the limits of liberty and authority. Though he was weak in his understanding of the inevitability of some of the trends which he feared yet he was strong in his perception of the evils that threatened the American government and in his sturdy faith that public morality is essential in a democracy.

ROY FRANKLIN NICHOLS

[1] Charles A. Beard, *Economic Origins of Jeffersonian Democracy* (N.Y., 1915), p. 323.
[2] Eugene T. Mudge, *The Social Philosophy of John Taylor of Caroline* (N.Y., 1939); Benjamin F. Wright, Jr., 'The Philosopher of Jeffersonian Democracy', *Am. Pol. Sci. Rev.*, XXII, 870–92; Albert J. Beveridge, *Life of John Marshall* (Boston, 1916–19), IV, 58 *n*.

DISTRICT OF VIRGINIA, To wit:

BE IT REMEMBERED, That on the fifteenth day of November, in the thirty-eighth year of the Independence of the United States of America, JOHN TAYLOR, of the said District, hath deposited in this Office, the Title of a Book, the right whereof he claims as Author, in the words following, to wit: . . .

'An Inquiry into the Principles and Policy of the Government of the United States, comprising nine sections, under the following heads: . . . I. Aristocracy. II. The Principles of the Policy of the United States, and of the English Policy. III. The Evil Moral Principles of the Government of the United States. IV. Funding. V. Banking. VI. The Good Moral Principles of the Government of the United States. VII. Authority. VIII. The Mode of infusing Aristocracy into the Policy of the United States. IX. The Legal Policy of the United States. By JOHN TAYLOR, of Caroline county, Virginia.'

In conformity to the Act of the Congress of the United States, entitled 'An Act for the encouragement of Learning, by securing the copies of Maps, Charts, and Books, to the Authors and Proprietors of such copies during the times therein mentioned;' and also to an Act, entitled 'An act supplementary to an Act, entituled, "An Act for the encouragement of Learning, by securing the copies of Maps, Charts, and Books, to the Authors and Proprietors of such copies, during the times therein mentioned;" and extending the benefits thereof to the arts of Designing, Engraving, and Etching historical and other prints.'

* * * * * *
* SEAL *
* * * * * *

WILLIAM MARSHALL
Clerk of the District of Virginia

TO THE PUBLICK

This book being written for your use, and subject to your judgement, the means, motives and habits of the author ought to be disclosed, lest its imperfections should be ascribed to his cause, instead of his bias or inability.

Having arrived at manhood just before the commencement of the revolutionary war, the ardour of that controversy, a considerable intercourse with many of the chiefs who managed it, a service of three years in the continental army, of twelve in legislative bodies, and an experience of our policy both in poverty and affluence, inspired him with the opinions he has endeavoured to sustain. At the age of forty, his circumstances, which had been ruined by military expenses and the depreciation of paper money, having been repaired by the practice of the law, a desire of being more useful, induced him to devote the residue of his life in a private station, to the advancement of academical, agricultural, and political knowledge. These essays contain the result of his endeavours as to the last; and whatever may be their fate, he is not conscious of having written a single sentence from a bad motive.

Upon the appearance of Mr. Adams's defence of the American constitutions, and of the essays signed Publius, but entitled the Federalist, he imbibed an opinion, that both had paid too much respect to political skeletons, constructed with fragments torn from monarchy, aristocracy and democracy, called, in these essays, the numerical analysis; and too little to the ethereal moral principles, alone able to bind governments to the interest of nations. Subsequent occurrences induced him to conclude, that a confidence in that analysis, inspired by these books, had deadened the public attention to the only means for preserving a free and moderate government. And the following essays (in which the reader will not find Mr. Adams's erudition, nor the elegant style of Publius, because the author was not master of them) are the contemporaneous suggestions of these occurrences or of experience, designed to portray human nature in a political state, and to explain the moral principles capable of foretelling its actions, and controlling its vices.

Monarchy, aristocracy and democracy, appeared to the author to be inartificial, rude, and almost savage political fabricks; and the idea of building a new one with the materials they could afford, seemed like that of erecting a palace with materials drawn from Indian cabins. He thought that these respectable commentators, in making the attempt, had allowed little or nothing new or pre-eminent to the policy of the United States; had overlooked both the foundation and the beautiful entablature of its pillars: and had left mankind still enchanted within the magick circle of the numerical analysis.

Believing that the true value and real superiority of our policy consisted in its good moral principles; that these principles were the only worthy object of national affection, and the only just solution of the ill success of other governments and of the wonderful prosperity of our own; that by transplanting it upon the British substratum, maxims and measures destructive to ours, however calculated for their political system, would be introduced; that the danger of this approximation was greatly augmented, by the respect which the English form of government attracts as the work of our gallant ancestors, the source of our affection for liberty, and the solitary rival of our own; that the belief of such an affinity, would enable legislation to draw the confines of the two forms of government so near together, that a step or even a stumble might pass from one to the other; and that a disclosure of the contrariety in their principles, might become a beacon against an exchange of good and lasting moral principles, for cobweb and fluctuating numerical balances; the author of these essays concluded, that the next age ought not to be deluded, by the silence of its predecessors, into a belief that this affinity was generally allowed.

Although the elevation of the British form of government, produced by a few moral principles, violently and of course clumsily thrust under it at different times, constituted the American observatory at the epoch of the revolution; from whence, through the telescope, necessity, new principles were discovered, now confirmed by the distinct experience of each state for periods, exceeding, when united, the duration of any one of the modifications of the British government: yet the non-existence of the supposed affinity is at once disclosed by the few words 'balance of orders and judicial independence.' The first, indigenously implying a sovereignty of orders of men, and the second a judicial dependence upon that sovereignty; transplanted, balance is applied to powers without sovereignty, and independence to confer a judicial power never thought of in England.

By the British policy, the nation and the government is considered as one, and the passive obedience denied to the king conceded to the government, whence it alters its form and its principles, without any other concurrence than that of its parts; whereas, by ours, the nation and the government are considered as distinct, and a claim of passive obedience by the latter, would of course be equivalent to the same claim by a British king.

Instead of an affinity, a deep rooted contrariety appeared to the author of these essays to exist, in the reliance of one policy upon political law and national opinion, and of the other upon official power, for the control of official power. It seemed to him as unphilosophical to suppose that official power could be mixed with human nature without changing its qualities, as that alcohol would not change the qualities of water; and that to moderate official power by official power, was something like weakening alcohol with alcohol. On the other hand, he could not discern how publick opinion could perform the office expected of it, unless it was well instructed in those good moral principles, capable of distinguishing between laws or measures consonant to the nature of our policy, and those flowing from avarice, party zeal, ambition, or the errour of its supposed affinity to the British.

The human mind, buoyed up to the zenith of hope upon the billows of the French revolution, sunk with its wreck into the gloom of despair; and philosophers seem inclined to abandon a successful experiment, because they have been obliged to disgorge extravagant theories. It is necessary for the happiness and safety of the people of the United States, to revive political discussion, both to enable them to defeat the frauds of factions, and lest it be inferred from the despotism of France, that the government of their rival is the last refuge from oppression. The great danger of artisans and agriculturists lies in the legal depredations of the various parties actuated by exclusive interests, natural to the British policy, such as a court interest, a military interest, a stock interest, and various other separate interests, whose business it is to get what they can from the rest of the nation. Like the armies of Bonaparte, all such parties subsist upon contributions, and repay them with arrogance and contempt. By such parties, or by enlisting under some statesman or general, agriculture and arts have been universally degraded from political influence, and subjected to a tutelage formed to plunder them.

A few texts are selected from Mr. Adams's defence of the constitutions of the United States, because its candour furnished the best materials for a distinct exhibition of certain subjects; and the inviolable obligation of freely examining his doctrines, was not inconsistent with a high opinion of his virtue and talents.

The author has only to add, that he has nothing to plead in excuse of the imperfections of these essays, but his incapacity, and that a common sentinel may awaken an army. He has devoted to them the occasional spare time of a busy life, during twenty years. Their revision and publication was deferred, until age had abated temporal interests and diminished youthful prejudices; so that they are almost letters from the dead. And he offers them near the end of his life, as an oblation to those political principles, for which he was indebted for much happiness in his passage through it.

It is necessary to inform the publick that these essays were written before the 17th day of November, 1811, when the contract was made for printing them; to disclose the reason, why no use has been made of any subsequent event.

THE AUTHOR

Section the First

ARISTOCRACY

M<small>R</small>. A<small>DAMS</small>'s political system, deduces government from a natural fate; the policy of the United States deduces it from moral liberty. Every event proceeding from a motive, may, in a moral sense, be termed natural. And in this view, 'natural' is a term, which will cover all human qualities. Lest, therefore, the terms 'natural and moral' may not suggest a correct idea of the opposite principles, which have produced rival political systems, it is a primary object to ascertain the sense in which they are here used.

Man, we suppose to be compounded of two qualities, distinguishable from each other; matter and mind. By mind, we analyze the powers of matter; by matter we cannot analyze the powers of mind. Matter being an agent of inferior power to mind, its powers may be ascertained by mind; but mind being an agent of sovereign power, there is no power able to limit its capacity. The subject cannot be an adequate menstruum for its own solution. Therefore, as we cannot analyze mind, it is generally allowed to be a supernatural quality.

To the human agencies, arising from the mind's power of abstraction, we apply the term 'moral;' to such as are the direct and immediate effect of matter, independent of abstraction, the terms 'natural or physical.' Should Mr. Adams disallow the application of this distinction to his theory, by saying, that when he speaks of natural political systems, he refers both to man's mental and physical powers, and includes whatever the term 'moral' can reach; I answer, that it is incorrect to confound in one mass the powers of mind and body, in order to circumscribe those of mind, by applying to the compound, the term 'natural,' if it is impossible for mind to limit and ascertain its own powers.

Whether the human mind is able to circumscribe its own powers, is a question, between the two modern political parties. One (of which Mr. Adams is a disciple) asserts that man can ascertain his own moral capacity, deduces consequences from this postulate, and erects thereon schemes of government—right, say they, because natural. The other, observing that those who affirm the doctrine, have never been able to agree upon this natural form of government; and that human nature has been perpetually escaping from all forms; considers government as capable of unascertained modification and improvement, from moral causes.

To illustrate the question; let us confront Mr. Adams's opinion 'that aristocracy is natural, and therefore unavoidàble,' with one 'that it is artificial or factitious, and therefore avoidable.' He seems to use the term 'natural' to convey an idea distinct from moral, by coupling it with the idea of fatality. But moral causes, being capable of human modification, events flowing from them, possess the quality of freedom or evitation. As the moral efforts, by which ignorance or knowledge are produced, are subjects themselves of election, so ignorance and knowledge, the effects of these moral effects, are also subjects of election; and ignorance and knowledge are powerful moral causes. If, therefore, by the term 'natural' Mr. Adams intended to include 'moral,' the idea of 'fatality' is inaccurately coupled with it; and if he resigns this idea, the infallibility of his system, as being natural, must also be resigned.

That he must resign his political predestination, and all its consequences, I shall attempt to prove, by shewing, that aristocracies, both ancient and modern, have been variable and artificial; that they have all proceeded from moral, not from natural causes; and that they are evitable and not inevitable.

An opinion 'that nature makes kings or nobles' has been the creed of political fatalists, from the commencement of the sect; and confronts its rival creed 'that liberty and slavery are regulated by political law.' However lightly Mr. Adams may speak of Filmer, it is an opinion in which they are associated, and it is selected for discussion, because by its truth or falsehood, the folly or wisdom of the policy of the United States is determined.

In the prosecution of these objects, frequent use will be made of the word 'aristocracy,' because the ideas at present attached to it, make it more significant than any other.

Mr. Adams rears his system upon two assertions: 'That there are only three generical forms of government; monarchy, aristocracy and democracy, of which all other forms are mixtures; and that every society naturally produces an order of men, which it is impossible to confine to an equality of rights.' Political power in

36

one man, without division or responsibility, is monarchy; the same power in a few, is aristocracy; and the same power in the whole nation, is democracy. And the resemblance of one system of government to either of these forms, depends upon the resemblance of a president or a governor to a monarch; of an American senate, to an hereditary order; and of a house of representatives, to a legislating nation.

Upon this threefold resemblance Mr. Adams has seized, to bring the political system of America within the pale of the English system of checks and balances, by following the analysis of antiquity; and in obedience to that authority, by modifying our temporary, elective, responsible governors, into monarchs; our senates into aristocratical orders; and our representatives, into a nation personally exercising the functions of government.

Whether the terms 'monarchy, aristocracy and democracy,' or the one, the few, and the many, are only numerical; or characteristic, like the calyx, petal and stamina of plants; or complicated, with the idea of a balance; they have never yet singly or collectively been used to describe a government, deduced from good moral principles.

If we are unable to discover in our form of government, any resemblance of monarchy, aristocracy or democracy, as defined by ancient writers, and by Mr. Adams himself, it cannot be compounded of all, but must be rooted in some other political element; whence it follows, that the opinion which supposes monarchy, aristocracy and democracy, or mixtures of them, to constitute all the elements of government, is an error, which has produced a numerical or exterior classification, instead of one founded in moral principles.

By this error, the moral efforts of mankind, towards political improvement, have been restrained and disappointed. Under every modification of circumstances, these three generical principles of government, or a mixture of them, have been universally allowed to comprise the whole extent of political volition; and whilst the liberty enjoyed by the other sciences, has produced a series of wonderful discoveries; politics, circumscribed by an universal opinion (as astronomy was for centuries) remained stationary from the earliest ages, to the American revolution.

It will be an effort of this essay to prove, that the United States have refuted the ancient axiom, 'that monarchy, aristocracy and democracy, are the only elements of government,' by planting theirs in moral principles, without any reference to those elements; and that by demolishing the barrier hitherto obstructing the progress of political science, they have cleared the way for improvement.

Mr. Adams's system promises nothing. It tells us that human nature is always the same: that the art of government can never change; that it is contracted into three simple principles; and that mankind must either suffer the evils of one of these simple principles; as at Athens, Venice, or Constantinople; or those of the same principles compounded, as at London, Rome, or Lacedemon. And it gravely counts up several victims of democratic rage, as proofs, that democracy is more pernicious than monarchy or aristocracy. Such a computation is a spectre, calculated to arrest our efforts, and appal our hopes, in pursuit of political good. If it be correct, what motives of preference between forms of government remain? On one hand, Mr. Adams calls our attention to hundreds of wise and virtuous patricians, mangled and bleeding victims of popular fury; on the other, he might have exhibited millions of plebeians, sacrificed to the pride, folly and ambition of monarchy and aristocracy; and, to complete the picture, he ought to have placed right before us, the effects of these three principles commixed, in the wars, rebellions, persecutions and oppressions of the English form, celebrated by Mr. Adams as the most perfect of the mixed class of governments. Is it possible to convince us, that we are compelled to elect one of these evils? After having discovered principles of government, distinct from monarchy, aristocracy or democracy, in the experience of their efficacy, and the enjoyment of their benefits; can we be persuaded to renounce the discovery, to restore the old principles of political navigation, and to steer the commonwealth into the disasters, against which all past ages have pathetically warned us? It is admitted, that man, physically, is 'always the same;' but denied that he is so, morally. Upon the truth or error of this distinction, the truth or error of Mr. Adams's mode of reasoning and of this essay, will somewhat depend. If it is untrue, then the cloud of authorities collected by him from all ages, are irrefutable evidence, to establish the fact, that political misery is unavoidable; because man is always the same. But if the moral qualities of human nature are not always the same, but are different both in nations and individuals; and if government ought to be constructed in relation to these moral qualities, and not in relation to factitious orders; these authorities do not produce a conclusion so deplorable. The variety in the kinds and degrees of political misery, is alone conclusive evidence of distinct degrees of moral character, capable of unknown moral efforts.

Supposing that none of Mr. Adams's quotations had been taken from poetical and fabulous authors; that no doubt could exist of the truth of those furnished by ancient historians; and that they had not been dexterously selected to fit an hypothesis; yet their whole weight would have depended upon the similarity of moral circumstances, between the people of America, and those of Greece, Italy, Switzerland, England, and a multitude of countries, collected from all ages into our modern theatre.

Do the Americans recognize themselves in a group of Goths, Vandals, Italians, Turks and Chinese? If not, man is not always morally the same. If man is not always morally the same, it is not true that he requires the same political regimen. And thence a conclusion of considerable weight follows, to overthrow the groundwork of Mr. Adams's system; for by proving, if he had proved it, that his system was proper for those men, and those times, resorted to by him for its illustration, he proves that it is not proper for men and times of dissimilar moral characters and circumstances.

The traces of intellectual originality and diversity; the shades and novelties of the human character, between the philosopher and the savage; between different countries, different governments, and different eras; exhibit a complexity, which the politician and philologist have never been able to unravel. Out of this intellectual variety, arises the impossibility of contriving one form of government, suitable for every nation; and also the fact, that human nature, instead of begetting one form constantly, demonstrates its moral capacity, in the vast variety of its political productions.

Having apprized the reader, by these general remarks, of the political principles to be vindicated or assailed in this essay; and that an effort will be made to prove, that the policy of the United States is rooted in moral or intellectual principles, and not in orders, clans or casts, natural or factitious; this effort must be postponed, until the way is opened to it, by a more particular review of Mr. Adams's system. To this, therefore, I return.

He supposes 'that every society must *naturally* produce an aristocratical order of men, which it will be impossible to confine to an equality of rights with other men.' To determine the truth of this position, an inquiry must be made into the mode by which these orders have been produced in those countries, placed before us by Mr. Adams, as objects of terror or imitation.

In order to understand the question correctly, it is proper to hear Mr. Adams state it himself. Throughout his book, it is constantly appearing, as constituting the great principle upon which his system is founded; but here it can only appear in a quotation, selected as concise, explicit and unequivocal.

'These sources of inequality,' says he, 'which are common to every people, and can never be altered by any, *because they are founded in the constitution of nature;* this *natural* aristocracy among mankind, has been dilated on, because it is a fact essential to be considered in the constitution of a government. It is a body of men which contains the greatest collection of *virtues and abilities* in a free government: *the brightest ornament and glory of a nation; and may always be made the greatest blessing of society, if it be judiciously managed in the constitution.* But if it is not, it is always the most dangerous; nay, it may be added, it never fails to be the destruction of the commonwealth. What shall be done to guard against it? There is but one expedient yet discovered, to avail the society of all the benefits from this body of men, which they are capable of affording, and at the same time prevent them from undermining or invading the public liberty; *and that is to throw them all, or at least the most remarkable of them, into one assembly together, in the legislature;* to keep all the executive power entirely out of their hands, as a body; *to erect a first magistrate over them, invested with the whole executive authority;* to make them dependant on that executive magistrate for all public executive employments; to give that magistrate a negative on the legislature, by which he may defend both himself and the people from all their enterprises in the legislature; and to erect on the other side of them, an impregnable barrier against them, *in a house of commons fairly, fully, and adequately representing the people,* who shall have the power of negativing all their attempts at encroachments in the legislature, and of withholding both from them *and the crown* all supplies, by which they may be paid for their services in executive offices, or even the public service carried on to the detriment of the nation.'*

This is the text on which it is proposed to comment; incidentally considering several of the arguments, by which its doctrine is defended, without the formality of frequent quotations. It contains the substance of Mr. Adams's system, and is evidently the English form of government, excepting an equal representation of the people, in the proposed house of commons.

* Adams's Def. vol. 1, pp. 116–117., 3d Philadelphia edition.

The position first presenting itself is, 'that an aristocracy is the work of nature.' A position equivalent to the antiquated doctrine, 'that a king is the work of God.' A particular attention will be now paid to this point, because Mr. Adams's theory is entirely founded upon it.

Superior abilities constitutes one among the enumerated causes of a natural aristocracy. This cause is evidently as fluctuating as knowledge and ignorance; and its capacity to produce aristocracy, must depend upon this fluctuation. The aristocracy of superior abilities will be regulated by the extent of the space, between knowledge and ignorance. As the space contracts or widens, it will be diminished or increased; and if aristocracy may be thus diminished, it follows that it may be thus destroyed.

No certain state of knowledge, is a natural or unavoidable quality of man. As an intellectual or moral quality, it may be created, destroyed and modified by human power. Can that which may be created, destroyed and modified by human power, be a natural and inevitable cause of aristocracy?

It has been modified in an extent, which Mr. Adams does not even compute, by the art of printing, discovered subsequently to almost the whole of the authorities which have convinced Mr. Adams, that knowledge, or as he might have more correctly asserted, ignorance, was a cause of aristocracy.

The peerage of knowledge or abilities, in consequence of its enlargement by the effects of printing, can no longer be collected and controlled in the shape of a noble order or a legislative department. The great body of this peerage must remain scattered throughout every nation, by the enjoyment of the benefit of the press. By endowing a small portion of it with exclusive rights and privileges, the indignation of this main body is excited. If this endowment should enable a nation to watch and control an inconsiderable number of that species of peerage produced by knowledge, it would also purchase the dissatisfaction of its numberless members unjustly excluded; and would be a system for defending a nation against imbecility, and inviting aggression from strength, equivalent to a project for defeating an army, by feasting its vanguard.

If this reasoning is correct, the collection of that species of natural aristocracy (as Mr. Adams calls it) produced by superior abilities, into a legislative department, for the purpose of watching and controlling it, is now rendered impracticable, however useful it might have been, at an era when the proportion between knowledge and ignorance was essentially different; and this impracticability is a strong indication of the radical inaccuracy of considering aristocracy as an inevitable natural law. The wisdom of uniting exclusive knowledge by exclusive privileges, that it may be controlled by disunited ignorance, is not considered as being an hypothetical question, since this aristocratical knowledge cannot now exist.

Similar reasoning applies still more forcibly to the idea of nature's constituting aristocracy, by means of exclusive virtue. Knowledge and virtue both fluctuate. A steady effect, from fluctuating causes, is morally and physically impossible. And yet Mr. Adams infers a natural aristocracy, from the error, that virtue and knowledge are in an uniform relation to vice and ignorance; sweeps away by it every human faculty, for the attainment of temporal or eternal happiness; and overturns the efficacy of law, to produce private or public moral rectitude.

Had it been true, that knowledge and virtue were natural causes of aristocracy, no fact could more clearly have exploded Mr. Adams's system, or more unequivocally have dissented from the eulogy he bestows on the English form of government. Until knowledge and virtue shall become genealogical, they cannot be the causes of inheritable aristocracy; and its existence, without the aid of superior knowledge and virtue, is a positive refutation of the idea, that nature creates aristocracy with these tools.

Mr. Adams has omitted a cause of aristocracy in the quotation, which he forgets not to urge in other places; namely, exclusive wealth. This, by much the most formidable with which mankind have to contend, is necessarily omitted, whilst he is ascribing aristocracy to nature; and being both artificial and efficacious, it contributes to sustain the opinion, 'that as aristocracy is thus artificially created, it may also be artificially destroyed.'

Alienation is the remedy for an aristocracy founded on landed wealth; inhibitions upon monopoly and incorporation, for one founded on paper wealth. Knowledge, enlisted by Mr. Adams under the banner of aristocracy, deserted her associate by the invention of alienation, and became its natural enemy. Discovering its hostility to human happiness, like Brutus, she has applied the axe to the neck of what Mr. Adams calls her progeny; and instead of maintaining the exclusiveness of wealth, contributes to its division by inciting competition, and assailing perpetuities. How suc-

ARISTOCRACY

cessfully, let England illustrate. She, no longer relying upon nature for an aristocracy, is perpetually obliged to repair the devastations it sustains from alienation; the weapon invented by knowledge; by resorting to the funds of paper systems, pillage, patronage and hierarchy, for fresh supplies.

The reader will be pleased to recollect the question in debate. Mr. Adams asserts, that an aristocratical body of men is necessary, as being natural. Having thus gotten it, he admits that it will be ambitious and dangerous to liberty. Being ambitious and dangerous, he infers, that it ought to be controlled. And this, he says, can only be effected by a king over it, and a house of commons under it; thus placing it between two fires, on account of its strength, danger and ambition.

The entire hypothesis rests upon a single foundation, 'that aristocracy is natural and inevitable;' and therefore this groundwork ought to be well examined.

The contrivance for erecting a system, by asserting and setting out from the will of God, or from nature, is not new. Most of those systems of government, to which Mr. Adams refers us for instruction, resorted to it; and therefore the propriety of reviving the principle, upon which these ancient systems were generally or universally founded, to revive its effects, must be admitted. 'It is the will of Jupiter,' exclaimed some artful combination of men. 'The will of Jupiter is inevitable,' responded the same combination to itself; and ignorance submitted to a fate, manufactured by human fraud.

Whenever it is impossible to prove a principle, which is necessary to support a system, a reference to an inevitable power, calling it God or nature, is preferable to reasoning: because every such principle is more likely to be exploded, than established by reasoning. For instance; it would be difficult to convince us, that we ought to erect an aristocracy spontaneously; the folly of which, Mr. Adams unwarily admits, by insisting upon the great danger to be apprehended from it, to enhance the merit of his system, in meeting this danger with a king and a house of commons. And therefore the short and safe expedient is, to tell us that nature has settled the question, by declaring that we shall have an aristocracy; being induced to believe and concede this, the difficulty is over; and the whole system, bottomed upon the concession, becomes irrefutable.

Hence have been derived, the sanctity of oracles, the divinity of

43

kings, and the holiness of priests; and now that these bubbles have become the scoff of common sense, experiment is to decide, whether there remains in America a stock of superstition, upon which can be ingrafted, 'an aristocracy from nature.'

Should it grow upon this stem, Mr. Adams is not entitled to the reputation of an inventor. He states the origin of the thought, in speaking of the aristocracies of Greece. These, he says, had the address to persuade the people, that they deduced their genealogies from the Gods; of course their titles to aristocratical preeminences were of divine origin, and inheritable quality. But Mr. Adams's system, it must be admitted, improves upon the idea, in relying upon some perpetual operation of nature, as a less fortuitous resource for an aristocracy, than the amorous adventures of heathen deities.

In old times, kings as well as nobles were believed to be heavenborn. But Mr. Adams confines the procreative power of nature to an aristocracy, and thus makes room for the human invention of a king and a house of commons, to check and discipline nature's unkindness. So Filmer might have acquired political fame, by proposing a house of lords and a house of commons, as checks upon his divine or natural king.

A short review of a few of the aristocracies quoted by Mr. Adams, will exhibit the affinity between the ancient idea of a divine, and Mr. Adams's, of a natural aristocracy.

In speaking of the aristocracies of Greece, he observes, that they derived themselves from some of the heathen deities, taking great care to retain the priesthood and religious mysteries in their own hands; and that these precautions had great influence towards restraining democratical innovations, by inspiring the lower orders with fear and veneration for their superiors.

Here then is the origin of a Grecian aristocracy. Was it founded in fraud, or begotten by the Gods, as it asserted? A divine origin is not contended for by Mr. Adams; he deduces it from a deception; yet if Jupiter and his associates had maintained their influence to this day, aristocracy would not have renounced its parentage: but the degradation or modern chastity of the heathen deities, compelled it to adopt another ancestor more analogous to modern theology, and whose progeny was not likely to fail. The election has fallen on nature; and the new question, 'whether aristocracy is fraudulent or natural,' has, from this circumstance, become the substitute of the old, 'whether it was fraudulent or divine.'

The Grecian commonalty were never easy, even under this heaven-born aristocracy. Bound in the chains of superstition, and blinded by the mist of ignorance, something was still telling them that it was not right; something was still urging them to correct an evil of which they were sensible. It was thy inspiration, Oh! divine nature! Thou didst unfold to man glimmerings of truth, even in ages of superstition and ignorance! And yet thou art arraigned as the author of aristocracy, which thou art for ever inciting thy children to destroy!

The struggle between aristocracy and democracy in Greece, is repeatedly urged by Mr. Adams, to prove the advantage of balancing them against each other in our legislatures. But it was previously incumbent upon him to have proved, both that the Grecian aristocracy was natural and unavoidable, and also that our state of manners and knowledge is so exactly theirs, that we cannot avoid a similar aristocracy; namely, one of divine blood; before these precedents, any more than magna charta, could be made useful in his mode, to modern liberty. He was unable to do this. We know that man, yoked to obedience by superstition, and half bereft of his faculties by ignorance, was yet impatient under aristocracy; though he believed it to be the offspring of the Gods: the inference which presents itself is, that, enlightened by the effects of printing, he will not easily be subjected by one, which he knows to be the offspring of men.

An opposition to aristocratical power seems to have been constantly coeval with an advance of national information. It began in Greece, appeared at Rome, and has continued the companion of mental improvement, down to the present day. As knowledge advanced in England, this opposition gained ground, and at length a victory, before that wise and natural aristocracy discovered its danger.

By the natural coalition between knowledge and an enmity to aristocracy, that of England was substantially annihilated, whilst its forms remained. The nobility have ceased to be feared, because they have ceased to be powerful; and the prohibition of ennobled orders in America, is the formal effect of their previous substantial destruction, by the progress of knowledge in England.

Knowledge and commerce, by a division of virtue, of talents, and of wealth among multitudes, have annihilated that order of men, who in past ages constituted 'a natural aristocracy,' (as Mr. Adams thinks) by exclusive virtue, talents and wealth. This ancient object of terror has shrunk into a cypher; whilst a single executive, proposed by Mr. Adams as its check, has become, by the aid of patronage and paper, a political figure, at the head of a long row of decimals.

From the tyranny of aristocracy, Mr. Adams takes refuge under the protection of a king, and considers him as so essentially the ally and protector of the people, as positively to declare, that, 'instead of the trite saying, "no bishop, no king," it would be a much more exact and important truth to say, no people, no king, and no king, no people; meaning, by the word king, a first magistrate, possessed exclusively of executive power.'*

Throughout his system, Mr. Adams infers a necessity for a king, or (what is the same thing) of a 'first magistrate, possessed exclusively of executive power,' from the certainty of a natural aristocracy. But if aristocracy is artificial and not natural, it may be prevented, by detecting the artifice: and by preventing aristocracy (the only cause for a king) the king himself becomes useless. His utility, according to Mr. Adams's system, consists in checking aristocratical power; but if no such power naturally exists, it would evidently be absurd to create a scourge (as Mr. Adams allows it to be) merely as a cause for a king.

In order to illustrate the opinion, that the aristocracy exhibited to us by Mr. Adams, as creating a necessity for his system, is only a ghost, let us turn our eyes for a moment towards its successor.

As the aristocracies of priestcraft and conquest decayed, that of patronage and paper stock grew; not the rival, but the instrument of a king; without rank or title; regardless of honor; of insatiable avarice; and neither conspicuous for virtue and knowledge, or capable of being collected into a legislative chamber. Differing in all its qualities from Mr. Adams's natural aristocracy, and defying his remedy, it is condensed and combined by an interest, exclusive, and inimical to public good.

Why has Mr. Adams written volumes to instruct us how to manage an order of nobles, sons of the Gods, of exclusive virtue, talents and wealth, and attended by the pomp and fraud of superstition; or one of feudal barons, holding great districts of unalienable country, warlike, high spirited, turbulent and dangerous; now that these orders are no more? Whilst he passes over in silence the aristocracy of paper and patronage, more numerous, more burdensome, unexposed to public jealousy by the badge of title, and not

* Adams's Def. vol. 1, p. 87.

too honorable or high spirited to use and serve executive power for the sake of pillaging the people. Are these odious vices, to be concealed under apprehensions of ancient aristocracies, which, however natural, are supplanted by this modern one?

This subject will hereafter be resumed, as possessing in every view, a degree of importance, beyond any political question at this era affecting the happiness of mankind. Then having previously attempted to prove that even the titled aristocracy of England, is no longer an order, requiring the combined efforts of a king and a people to curb; I shall proceed to shew, that a new political feature has appeared among men, for which Mr. Adams's system does not provide; and that England itself cannot now furnish materials for a government conformable to her theory, because her theory was calculated for a nation less advanced in the division of knowledge and lands, and in the arts of patronage and paper. Now we will return to the subject of a natural aristocracy.

Mr. Adams, with particular approbation, uses the Spartan government, as an illustration of his hypothesis. The wisdom of Lycurgus, he observes, was evinced by a mixture of monarchical, aristocratical, and democratical principles; and the prudent manner in which he adjusted them, appeared by its continuance for eight hundred years. Conceding the Spartan experiment to be a correct emblem of the system it is used to exemplify, it is only important to be understood, for the sake of beholding in fact, the results to be expected from this system itself.

The kings of Sparta held a relation to the Spartans or nobles, somewhat similar to that existing between the kings, and what is called 'the monied interest' in England. No vestige of a demo-cratical balance was discernible during the operation of this ad-mired mixture. On the contrary, Sparta was the constant patron of the aristocratical factions throughout Greece, and finally ruined it, by a treacherous league with the Persians, entered into under the pretence of freeing tributary cities, but with the design of ad-vancing the interest of aristocratical factions in neighbouring states. Does this form of government earn the eulogy, of being the best in Greece, because it produced its ruin, by leaguing itself with absolute monarchy?

Lycurgus, by the influence of a bought and lying oracle, placed the government in the hands of a minority, excused this minority from labour and taxes, and supported it by the labour of the majority. The Helots, who were the slaves of the government but

47

not of individuals, filled the place of every majority, however denominated, subjected to the will of an aristocracy. All the difference is, that the Spartan aristocracy obtained of its Helots, subsistence and leisure for itself, by the goad and the lash; and the aristocracy of paper and patronage, obtains of theirs, wealth and luxury, by war, sinecure and taxation. This emblem of Mr. Adams's system, commenced in fraud; flourished, a tyrant; and died, a traitor; and although Lycurgus divided the Spartan aristocracy into several bodies; distributed it into different chambers; and placed at its head, dependant chiefs; impartiality will only behold an organization of an aristocratical minority for self security, however an eagerness to establish a system, may transform it into the effigy of an entire nation.

How exactly emblematical this precedent is of the English government! A minority organized, not to preserve, but to suppress, popular influence. Such is the effect of aristocratical orders, according to the examples adduced in their defence.

More intricate sections of an aristocratical interest existed at Venice, than at Sparta or London. Were these also contrived to check that interest, for the sake of advancing the democratic interest, or for its own safety?

It does not appear, whether Lycurgus left the number of his aristocracy, to be regulated by the efforts of the Heathen Gods or of nature; but neither the oracle, the Gods, or nature could keep it alive. It became naturally extinct before the artificial cords of superstition, which bound its victims to obedience, were broken.

Nor is duration, evidence of political perfection. Such an argument includes with equal complacency, the despotisms of the Roman Empire, of China, of France and of Turkey; the aristocracy of Venice, and the hierarchies of Judea and modern Rome.

The aristocracy of Sparta owed its origin to an oracle, that of Rome, to a king. Whilst we see Lycurgus, of the royal family and near the throne, and Romulus, himself a king, creating an aristocracy in antient times; and modern kings, almost universally doing the same thing; it suggests a doubt, whether kings and noble orders, are really the enemies and rivals of each other; and it is a doubt of importance, because the single effect beneficial to a nation, expected by Mr. Adams himself from his system, is, that its king will defend the people against its nobility.

It is admitted that patricians and barons have destroyed kings, and disclosed an enmity to royalty. It is equally true, that aristocratical orders are at this day their friends and instruments. A correct theory could only be formed upon an estimate of both facts; Mr. Adams endeavours to establish his upon one. Armies have frequently exhibited an enmity to generals and kings; ought armies therefore to be considered as checks upon their ambition, and balances of their power?

By comparing the causes of the antient enmity with those of the modern affection of noble orders for royalty, we obtain a result, accounting for these phenomena, fatal to Mr. Adams's theory.

Clientage, clanship, and feudality, have sown various countries with petty kings, under various titles, and these have been inspired with enmity to a great king, and a great king with an enmity to these, by a mutual interest to annoy each other; but now that clanship is melted down into one mass of civilization, and baronies into private estates, petty kingship is annihilated, and noble orders are completely sensible, that ribbon, livery and escutcheon, are not means for assaulting kings, equivalent to subjects, castles and principalities.

Admitting monarchy to be an evil, the ratio of the evil must be increased or diminished by its quantity, and it was evidently the comparative interest of the people to diminish the number of kings, for the sake of contracting the oppressions of monarchy. In England, one king, would be less mischievous than one hundred. This motive actuated the people to assist the great king to destroy the little kings; and ambition, not the popular interest, induced the great king to avail himself of this assistance. But when the petty monarchies, which had excited the jealousy, and produced the coalition, of one king and the people, were destroyed, this jealousy transferred itself to the allies. Having acquired a complete victory, they became objects of danger to each other and resorted to mutual precautions. Representation, invented by the crown to destroy the barons, was used by the people against the crown; and is now used by the crown against the people. The conquered nobility, reduced from sovereigns to subjects, became the chief disciples of royal patronage; and having lost the power of annoying the king, revenged itself upon the people, by uniting with the king to annoy them.

The result we obtain from this short history, is, that noble orders, divested of royalties, and reduced to the degree of subjects, are the instruments of kings; but that such orders, chiefs of clans, and possessed of dominions, are inimical to a monarchy, sufficiently powerful to suppress their own. Thus these phenomena are reconciled, and the alliance between kings and nobles in some cases, and their enmity in others accounted for. When the reasons inducing kings to destroy barons and to create lords are understood, the interest of the people to aid them in the first work, and to oppose them in the second, will be discerned; and Mr. Adams's system must sustain the shock of admitting, that a king cannot be a good remedy against the evils of any species of aristocracy, created by himself for an instrument, not for a check of monarchical power.

The aristocratical varieties just described, evince a factitious origin; and the frauds practised by the Roman aristocracy for self-preservation, in common with its Grecian predecessor, acknowledge a similar ancestry. It usurped the dignities of government, monopolized public property, enriched itself by conquest and by forcing the people to borrow at exorbitant usury of itself, to supply the loss of labour whilst fighting for the lands it monopolized, assumed the priesthood, practised upon the vulgar superstition, and impressed an idea that its progeny was well born, by prohibiting the connubial intercourse between itself and inferior orders. Nature needed not these arbitrary and fraudulent helps, in manufacturing aristocracy, had she been its parent.

And what was the fate of this Roman aristocracy, thus entrenched behind law, religion and robbery? It was modified occasionally by popular lucid intervals, until the people, wearied with its injuries and frauds, took refuge from the oppression of five hundred tyrants under that of one. Then this ancient aristocracy merged in a despotism, and for centuries remained in a state of abeyance. Why may not a modern aristocracy merge in the principle of representation? The peerage of England, like the conscript athers under an Emperor, being in this state of abeyance, so little requires Mr. Adams's king and commons to control it, that it would naturally became extinct, except for the nourishment of royal patronage.

Mr. Adams's hypothesis, being evidently borrowed from the English model, we will view that model with more attention than will be devoted to other forms of government.

For the sake of perspicuity, I shall call the ancient aristocracy, chiefly created and supported by superstition, 'the aristocracy of the first age;' that produced by conquest, known by the title of the feudal system, 'the aristocracy of the second age;' and that erected by paper and patronage, 'the aristocracy of the third or present age.' If aristocracy is the work of nature, by deserting her accustomed constancy, and slily changing the shape of her work, she has cunningly perplexed our defensive operations: to create the aristocracy of the first age, she used Jupiter; of the second, Mars; and of the third, Mercury. Jupiter is dethroned by knowledge; the usurpations of Mars are scattered by commerce and alienation; and it only remains to detect the impostures of Mercury.

And in order to avoid the confusion, arising from a complication of ideas, it is necessary to remind the reader, that Mr. Adams does not use the terms 'natural aristocracy' in relation to a fluctuating superiority in mind or body; but in relation to a superiority, capable of being collected into a legislative chamber, and permanently transmitted by descent. To this latter idea he limits his meaning, by illustrating it with the British system. Therefore superiorities in mind or body, must be excluded from a correct survey of Mr. Adams's natural aristocracy; for these would still adhere to the wisest or tallest individual, and not to the issue of an hereditary nobility.

England furnishes a perfect view of the aristocracies of the second and third age; and it is probable that a modification of the aristocracy of the first age, existed there also in the times of the Druids; but we shall only use the example of England for the illustration of the two others.

In France, the aristocracy of the second age, had become so feeble, that it fell, almost without a struggle; and being more numerous and wealthy than the same species of aristocracy in England, its imbecility furnishes a suspicion, that its English correlative does not substantially exist.

A real aristocracy is allowed to be formidable and dangerous; but the qualities, necessary to create an aristocracy according to Mr. Adams, should appear in the English peerage, to defend the precaution of monarchy; just as a danger of war, could only defend the bitter precaution of a standing army.

Reader, pause, and recollect several of the ingredients compounding aristocracy, in the opinion of Mr. Adams. Do you behold them in the English peerage? Do you behold an exclusive mass of virtue, almost inducing you to exclaim 'these are the sons of the Gods?' Do you behold an exclusive mass of talents, compelling you to acknowledge 'that these are sages qualified to govern?' Do you behold an exclusive mass of wealth, purchasing and converting into armies, clients and followers? Or do you behold a band of warriors inured to hardships, skilled in war, and inspiring fear and love? Truth compels you to acknowledge, that you cannot discern a solitary particle of these qualities, so essential to aristocracy according to Mr. Adams. And will you, against an acknowledgment which you cannot withhold, concur with Mr. Adams in believing, that such a body of men as the English nobility, ought to be placed in a legislative branch, that it may be guarded by a king and a house of commons?

Place the democracy of England on one side, and the nobility on the other; engage them in hostilities, and view the combat. Let the warfare be moral or physical. Still the combat would be like that between the universe and an atom. The king, without his aristocracy of the third age, would be but a feather on either side. This fact was experimentally settled in France. The French nobility civil and hierarchical, were more numerous, and exceeded the English in every aristocratical ingredient mentioned by Mr. Adams; yet with the king at its head, it was hardly felt as a power by the democracy, and would not have been felt, except for the combination of kingdoms by which it was aided. Is there then any real cause of apprehension in the fallen peerage of England?

Suppose the people of England should attempt to abolish monarchy. Both the aristocracy of the present age, and the nobility would arrange themselves in its defence. Which would be most formidable? The remnant or hieroglyphick of the feudal system, would indeed display a ridiculous pomp, and imbecile importance; it would appear armed with title, ribbon and symbol, and evince its weakness by tottering under shadows. But the real aristocracy of the present age; neither begotten by the Gods, the curse of conquest, nor the offspring of nature; the aristocracy of patronage and paper would draw out its fleets, armies, public debt, corporate bodies and civil offices. Which species of aristocracy, I ask again, would be the strongest auxiliary for despotism, and the most dangerous enemy to the nation? And yet Mr. Adams has written three volumes, to excite our jealousy against the aristocracy of motto and blazon, without disclosing the danger from the aristocracy of paper and patronage; that political hydra of modern invention, whose arms embrace a whole nation, whose ears hear every sound, whose eyes see all objects, and whose hands can reach every purse and every throat.

The faint traces discernible in England, of the aristocracy of the second age, evidently disclose a revolution in its qualities, which must have been produced by a cause; and when we perceive, that the present nobility no longer awaken the jealousy of the king, or attract the attention of the people, it behoves us to ascertain this cause, in order to understand what aristocracy is; and to distinguish between that which is nominal and that which is real; between a Chilperic, and a Charles Martel.

The circumstances which constituted the cause of this revolution, disclose the wounds which destroyed the aristocracy of the second age, and the impossibility of its existence, whilst these circumstances remain. Its essence consisted of chivalry, principality, sovereignty, splendor, munificence and vassalage; its shadow, of title. Of all these constituents, except the last, it has been stript by subjecting it to a competition with talents, and exposing it to the effects of commerce and alienation. Plebeians are now the compeers of these titled patricians in wealth, and they, the compeers of Plebeians in subjection to law; and the equalising spirit of knowledge has exalted one class, and reduced the other, to the common standard of mortal men.

An endeavour to record the magnanimity, ambition and consequence, exhibited by the British peerage, would conduct us precisely to the era of the change, at which the history would stop of itself, in defiance of the historian; it would terminate where the history of patronage and paper begins, because one form of aristocracy supplants another; and it would pass on from the dead to the living, as in the case of any other succession. Thence forward, the English peerage gradually sunk into the aristocracy of the third age; it became the creature of patronage, and the subject of paper; and although it is seen on account of a legislative formulary, it is as little regarded by the nation, as a butterfly by a man in agony. Its number is recruited from the corps raised and disciplined by the system of patronage and paper; and the claims it once possessed to superior knowledge, virtue, wealth and independence, have been long since immolated at the shrines of printing, alienation and executive power.

Nor does Great Britain possess the materials for reviving the aristocracy of the first or second age, or erecting one in any respect correspondent to that contemplated by Mr. Adams's political scheme. If this assertion is established, his hypothesis is destroyed. It is therefore allowable to bring it again into view, that an argument so important, may be better understood.

Every society, in Mr. Adams's opinion, will naturally produce a class of men minor in number, but superior to the major class in virtue, abilities and wealth; and hence, important, dangerous and ambitious. That they may be watched and controlled, they must be thrown into a separate legislative body, and balanced by a king on one side, and a house of Commons on the other; otherwise they will usurp the government.

This assertion depends upon a plain computation. Can a class of men, capable of being condensed in a legislative chamber, under the eye of the king and the Commons, be found in Great Britain, possessing more virtue, wisdom and wealth, than the rest of the nation; or even a portion sufficiently exclusive, to render it important, dangerous and ambitious? And if such a class could have been found, would not its importance and ambition presently become victims to printing, alienation and commerce?

If it be admitted, that the mass of virtue, wisdom and wealth, remaining with the people of Great Britain, infinitely exceeds that collected into the present house of lords, Mr. Adams's system contains the palpable error, of providing against the importance, danger and ambition of a diminutive portion of the virtue, wisdom and wealth of a nation, and of not providing against the importance, danger and ambition of the great mass of these qualities. This great mass, it may be answered, will be prevented from doing harm to the nation, by the representative principle to be found in the house of commons. If that principle is capable of managing the great mass of virtue, wisdom and wealth, it is also capable of managing an inconsiderable portion of this mass; and hence results the propriety of an elective, and the impropriety of an hereditary senate, upon Mr. Adams's own principles.

In this argument, Mr. Adams's definition of aristocracy is adhered to; he makes it to consist in a dangerous share of virtue, wisdom and wealth, held by a number of individuals, so few, as to be capable of constituting a legislative branch. The difference between us is, that his computation to make out a fact analogous to his system, must refer to the period of feudal aristocracy; mine takes the fact now existing, as the best foundation for political inferences, to be now applied.

But his definition undoubtedly possesses a considerable share of truth, and suggests an observation extremely plain. The possession by a few, of the major part of the whole stock of renown, talents or wealth, within the compass of a society, was the moral cause which supported the aristocracies of the first and second ages; when the

cause ceased, the effects ceased also; and the aristocracies of superstition and the feudal system disappeared. But this effect may be
revived by reviving its cause. A monopoly by a few, of renown,
talents or wealth, may be reproduced, by superstition, conquest or
fraud; and the question is, whether this would be advisable, for the
sake of trying the efficacy of his system.

We must turn our eyes once more towards England, in order to
illustrate the necessity for this reproduction, as the only means of
erecting an aristocracy. We see there a chamber of nobility. But
where is its exclusive renown? Vanished with superstition and entails. Where are its exclusive talents? Buried by the art of printing
in the same grave with ignorance. Where is its exclusive wealth?
Pouring through the sluices of dissipation, opened by alienation
and commerce. And where is its heroism? Consecrated in the
temple of luxury. These elements of aristocracy are gone, and the
spectre only remains, to assail our fears in behalf of the system I am
contesting. But the system of patronage and paper has reproduced
a monopoly of wealth. What! have Pylades and Orestes at length
quarrelled, and does one adhere to the English peerage, whilst the
other deserts to this English system?

This apparition of aristocracy is not however devoid of malignity, arising from its privilege of uttering legislative incantations.
As to that kind of ambition which impels heroes to the perpetration of crimes; as to those enterprises which disturb nations, and
excite the jealousy of kings; the innocence of the English nobility is
incontestable. Therefore these nobles are no longer jealous of the
king, nor the king of them. And however speciously the system of
king, lords and commons, is attempted to be filtered by the supposition of a mutual jealousy; however correctly the fact might
have warranted such a supposition, when English lords were
feudal barons; now that they are only titled courtiers, mutual harmony, the probable effect, is equally warranted by the actual fact.
King, lords and commons are melted up together by the aristocracy of the third age, retaining, like Cerberus, three mouths, and
yet possessing all the defects of political power collected into one
body, so ably demonstrated by Mr. Adams; and the unhappy
English are exposed to all the oppressions of a substantial aristocracy existing in the monopolies of paper and patronage, and to
all the evils of a legislative power in the ghost of an unsubstantial
one.

We are ready to acknowledge that extraordinary virtue, talents and wealth united, will govern, and ought to govern; and yet it is denied that this concession is reconcileable with the system of king, lords and commons. If a body of men which possesses the virtue, talents and wealth of a nation, ought to govern; it follows, that a body of men, which does not possess these attributes, ought not to govern.

The aristocracy of Rome for instance, did, at certain periods, possess a greater proportion of virtue, talents and wealth, than can be found in any cast or order of men at present, among commercial nations; which, and not the house of lords in England, Mr. Adams must have had in his eye, when in speaking of an aristocracy, he utters the following expressions, 'it is the brightest ornament and glory of a nation, and may always be made the greatest blessing of society, if it be judiciously managed in the constitution;' unless he can shew us, that the English house of lords merits this eulogy.

Plebeian ignorance was both the cause and justification of the Roman aristocracy. That might have been a worse magistrate, than patrician knowledge; and the magic circle drawn by superstition around the conscript fathers, might have been necessary to restrain the excesses of a rude nation inclosed within a single city. But this supplies no argument in favor of an aristocracy, in societies not of national aggregation, but of national dispersion; not of national ignorance, but of national intelligence; not sustained by superstition, but by a common interest.

Similar causes produced the feudal aristocracy. The conquering tribes were moving cities and colonising armies; and hereditary privileges were preferred to national annihilation. The feudal commanders, compared with their ignorant vassals, possessed that superiority in renown, talents and wealth, which might have produced the feudal system, as the moral effect of these moral causes. Such a form of government might have been the best which these moving cities, these tribes or these armies could bear, and yet execrable for a nation, not in the same moral state.

Having thus conceded to Mr. Adams, that wherever a few possess the mass of the renown, virtue, talents and wealth of a nation, that they will become an aristocracy, and probably ought to do so; it would be a concession, strictly reciprocal, to admit, that wherever no such body is to be found, an aristocracy ought not to be created by legal assignments of wealth and poverty. As the first species of minority will govern, because of the power arising from such monopolies only, so no other species can, without these sources of power. Where its sources are, power will be found; and hence the great mass of wealth, created by the system of paper and patronage, has annihilated the power of the didactick and titled peerage of England; because it has not a sufficient mass of virtue, renown, talents or wealth, to oppose against stock and patronage.

The aristocracies of the first and second ages were indebted for their power to ignorance, fraud and superstition; now reason, sincerity and truth, are demanded by the human mind. It disdains to worship a pageant or fear a phantom, and is only to be guided by views of interest or happiness. This change in the human character indicates an impossibility of reviving the principles which sustained the aristocracies of the first and second age, when mankind believed in the Gods of a pantheon, and in the prophetic powers of convulsed women.

Talents and virtue are now so widely distributed, as to have rendered a monopoly of either, equivalent to that of antiquity, impracticable; and if an aristocracy ought to have existed, whilst it possessed such a monopoly, it ought not also to exist, because this monopoly is irretrievably lost. The distribution of wealth produced by commerce and alienation, is equal to that of knowledge and virtue, produced by printing; but as the first distribution might be artificially counteracted, with a better prospect of success than the latter, aristocracy has abandoned a reliance on a monopoly of virtue, renown and abilities, and resorted wholly to a monopoly of wealth, by the system of paper and patronage. Modern taxes and frauds to collect money, and not ancient authors, will therefore afford the best evidence of its present character.

· A distribution of knowledge, virtue and wealth, produced public opinion, which ought now to govern for the reason urged by Mr. Adams in favour of aristocracy. It is the declaration of the mass of national wealth, virtue and talents. Power, in Mr. Adams's opinion, ought to follow this mass in the hands of a few, because it is the ornament of society. It is unimportant whether an aristocracy is a natural, physical or moral effect, if its cause, by means, natural, physical or moral, may be lost or transferred. Whenever the mass of wealth, virtue and talents, is lost by a few and transferred to a great portion of a nation, an aristocracy no longer retains the only sanctions of its claim; and wherever these sanctions deposit themselves, they carry the interwoven power. By spreading themselves so generally throughout a nation, as to be no longer compressible into a legislative chamber, or inheritable by the aid of perpetuity and superstition, these antient sanctions of aristocracy, become the modern sanctions of public opinion. And as its will (now the rightful sovereign upon the self-same principle, urged in favor of the best founded aristocracy) can no longer be obtained through the medium of an hereditary order, the American invention of applying the doctrine of responsibility to magistrates, is the only one yet discovered for effecting the same object, which was effected by an aristocracy, holding the mass of national virtue, talents and wealth. This mass governed through such an aristocracy. This mass cannot now govern through any aristocracy. This mass has searched for a new organ, as a medium for exercising the sovereignty, to which it is on all sides allowed to be entitled; and this medium is representation.

When the principles and practice of the American policy come to be considered, one subject of inquiry will be, whether public opinion, or the declaration of the mass of national virtue, talents and wealth, will be able to exercise this its just sovereignty, in union with the system of paper and patronage. If not, it is very remarkable, that this system, denominated the aristocracy of the third age, is equally inimical to Mr. Adams's principles and to mine. We both assign political power to the mass of virtue, talents and wealth in a nation. He only contends for an aristocracy from a supposition that it must possess this mass, and be the only organ of its will; I acknowledge the sovereignty of these qualities, deny their residence in a minority compressible into an aristocracy, and contend for a different organ. In order to discover whether the aristocracy of paper and patronage, is a good organ for expressing the will of the sovereign we have agreed upon, let us return to England, and consider, whether the revolution, which finally destroyed the aristocracy of the second age, and established that of the third, has placed the government in the hands of the wealth, virtue and talents of the nation, or subjected it to the influence of public opinion.

If you had seen the vulture preying upon the entrails of the agonized Prometheus, would you have believed, though Pluto himself had sworn it, that the vulture was under the control of Prometheus? If you could not have believed this, neither can you believe, that the concubinage between a government, and the system of paper and patronage, is an organ of national opinion, or of the wealth, virtue and talents of the nation, and not a conspiracy between avarice and ambition; because, it is as impossible that a

58

nation should derive pleasure from a government founded in the principle of voraciousness, as the man from the laceration of his bowels.

It has been said, that paper and office are property; and as by their means, a minority may bring into its coffers, the whole profit of national labour, so it ought to be considered as the nation. Had Prometheus fattened by being fed upon by the vulture, it would have given some colour to this ingenious deception.

Again it has been said, that the system of paper and patronage encourages commerce, agriculture, manufactures and conquest; it aggravated the misery of Prometheus, that his liver was made to grow for the gratification of a harpy, without appeasing its voracity.

The difficulty of producing a correct opinion of the cause and consequences of the new-born aristocracy of paper and patronage, surpasses the same difficulty in relation to the aristocracies of the first and second ages, as far as its superior importance. The two last being substantially dead, their bodies may be cut up, the articulation of their bones exposed, and the convolution of their fibres unravelled; but whenever the intricate structure of the system of paper and patronage is attempted to be dissected, we moderns surrender our intellects to yells uttered by the living monster, similar to those with which its predecessors astonished, deluded, and oppressed the world for three thousand years. The aristocracy of superstition defended itself by exclaiming, the Gods! the temples! the sacred oracles! divine vengeance! and Elysian fields!—and that of paper and patronage exclaims, national faith! sacred charters! disorganization! and security of property!

Let us moderns cease to boast of our victory over superstition and the feudal system, and our advancement in knowledge. Let us neither pity, ridicule or despise the ancients, as dupes of frauds and tricks, which we can so easily discern; lest some ancient sage should rise from his grave, and answer, 'You moderns are duped by arts more obviously fraudulent, than those which deceived us. The agency of the Gods was less discernible, than the effects of paper and patronage. We could not see, that the temporal and eternal pains and pleasures, threatened and promised by our aristocracy, could not be inflicted or bestowed by it; you see throughout Europe the effects of your aristocracy. Without your light, oracles were necessary to deceive us; with the help of printing, and two detections, you are deceived by aristocracy in a third form, although it pretends neither to the divinity nor heroism claimed by its two first forms. And under these disadvantages, the impositions of our aristocracy were restrained within narrower bounds than those of yours. Did any aristocracy of the first age, extend its annual spoliation from one to thirty-five millions of pounds sterling, in less than a century?'

Whenever one fraud is detected, ambition and avarice have hitherto invented another. The aristocracy of the second age, being weakened in England, by the wars between the houses of York and Lancaster, Henry the seventh seized the opportunity of breaking its power. The four succeeding kings, (excluding Edward) uncontrolled by the remaining aristocracy, though more warlike and wealthy than the present; or by the degree of knowledge, virtue and wealth among the people; were so completely despotic, as to be even able to modify religion, according to the suggestions of their amours, their bigotry, or their minions. The barons were conquered, and knowledge, virtue and wealth, had not been sufficiently dispersed to create the sovereignty of public opinion. So that during these four reigns, society remained in an anomalous state, between the suppression of an aristocracy, and the acquisition of knowledge, virtue and wealth by the people, from printing and commerce. Charles the first lost his life, because he either did not mark the progress of this acquisition, or had not liberality enough to yield to it. His son, less magnanimous than his father, escaped a similar fate by the national weariness of bigotry, fraud and tyranny united; and by practising in some degree the system of corruption. William of Orange farther advanced this baleful system; and Sir Robert Walpole completely organized the aristocracy of the present age, for the purpose of corrupting those, whom the progress of knowledge had enlightened.

From Henry the eighth to that time, the nobility had been but slightly felt as a political power; and Walpole's project for the modern aristocracy, substantially annihilated them. During this interval, superstition, ignorance and feudal power were declining. By their aid, minorities had oppressed nations. By their aid, minorities had erected themselves into the aristocracies of the first and second ages; and patronage and paper became the substitute for these forms of aristocracy, because avarice and ambition, having discovered that man could no longer be made subservient to their designs by means of his ignorance, saw the necessity of obtaining the same subserviency by means of his avarice.

We discern but two kinds of aristocracy; that which is the tyrant itself, and that which is the instrument of the tyrant. The ancient feudal and hierarchical aristocracies of England were tyrants themselves. The modern nobles and bishops; the patronage and stock interests; the generals and titulars of Bonaparte, and the mandarins of China, are instruments of tyranny. The same reasons inducing the people to unite with kings against aristocracies, which were themselves tyrants, ought to determine them to assail such as are the instruments of kings. Independent of kings, they are universally the first kind of evil; dependent on them, the second. But mankind are distracted by an host of political doctors, who utter prejudices imbibed from obsolete cases or existing interests. The whole college agree that the British policy is afflicted with some inveterate distemper, but each doctor asserts his favorite limb to be sound; and whilst the aggregate by one opinion pronounces it to be in the agonies of death, the same aggregate by many opinions pronounces it to be in perfect health. Funding, banking, patronage, charter, mercenary armies and partial bounties, are each admired as a panacea by some one; even corruption is defended as a happy expedient for managing the house of commons; and doctor Balance, venerable with the rest of antiquity, excites universal astonishment by declaring with unaffected gravity, that a nobility endowed with enormous wealth, virtue and talents, is only wanting to renovate it throughout. Such doctors are labouring to patch up a policy for the United States, out of the self-same limbs, with an animal thus compounded, lying in convulsions before their eyes.

The advantage of studying the anatomy of a dead body, is the knowledge of a living one. In like manner, the usefulness of our observations in relation to the aristocracies of the first and second ages, consists in opening our way towards that of the third. A knowledge of this last, is capable of a beneficial application; whereas a knowledge of the aristocracies of superstition and the feudal system, abstracted from the light they may reflect on that of paper and patronage, is only a steril amusement.

And it was also necessary to lay the ghost of the feudal aristocracy, now conjured up only as a decoy to draw the publick attention from its regenerated body, to come fairly to the objects of this essay; among which, an investigation of the system of paper and patronage occupies a chief place.

Preparatory to this, a political analysis is offered to the reader, as a key to the system of reasoning, subsequently to be pursued.

It has already been observed, that government is founded in

moral, and not in natural or physical causes. Now the moral qualities of man, being only good and evil, every form of government must be founded in that principle of the two, which prevails, like every other human action of a moral nature. This analysis is anterior to that of monarchy, aristocracy and democracy, and is capable of displaying the true character of every government, of each of its sections, and of all its measures; objects to which the numerical analysis is utterly incompetent.

For instance: A government, a section of it, or a measure, founded in an evil moral principle, such as fraud, ambition, avarice or superstition, must produce correspondent effects, and defeat the end of government; but resting upon a good moral principle, such as honesty, self-government, justice and knowledge, its effects will also be good, and conformable to the duty and office of government. Whereas the numerical analysis cannot with certainty enable us to foresee the character of a government, because it has no reference to moral causes or effects, good or evil. An absolute monarch, guided by the good moral qualities of man, may produce national happiness; and so any other anomalous case under the numerical analysis, may serve to perplex the science of politicks; because the publick happiness ensuing from it, instead of being attributed to the accidental preponderance of the good class of moral qualities, in the monarch, the aristocracy, or the democracy, is too often attributed to numerical classification. By exploding this analysis, and substituting that of government, bottomed upon good or evil moral principles, human happiness will less frequently fluctuate with the characters of individuals.

The reader will be often reminded of these principles, which are now to be applied to the aristocracy of paper and patronage.

This being suggested by, or founded in, the evil moral qualities of avarice and ambition, must inevitably produce evil effects; because a system is merely a moral being, and a moral demon cannot be a saint. Under either member of the numerical classification, a nation has a chance for happiness, however inconsiderable, because men may be guided by good moral principles; but none under the vicious system of paper and patronage, because an evil moral principle cannot produce good moral effects. That a system, founded like this, upon evil moral principles, is incapable of amelioration from the personal virtues of magistrates, is proved by its steady unfluctuating course of effects in England, where its rigorous consistency, and growing severity, is neither interrupted nor softened in the smallest degree by the virtues of individuals. Martial law and stock law, are naturally and necessarily tyrants, but a man may be a tyrant or a patriot. If a political system, founded in evil moral principles, proceeds consistently and certainly in the dispensation of evil to nations, without sustaining impediments from the virtues even of its administrators; is it not conceivable, that one founded in good moral principles, is discoverable, capable of dispensing good, independently also of the vices of its administrators? One as free from evil qualities, as that of paper and patronage is from good, would probably effect so desirable an object.

An enumeration of the effects of the system of paper and patronage, will disclose the consistency, between causes and effects in the moral world, the vast political influence of this system, and its operation upon human happiness. The first, is that of its enabling a minor interest, to guide and subsist upon a major interest.

It is not the mode by which this is effected, but the effect, which causes oppression. It is the same thing to a nation whether it is subjected to the will of a minority, by superstition, conquest, or patronage and paper. Whether this end is generated by errour, by force, or by fraud, the interest of the nation is invariably sacrificed to the interest of the minority.

If the oppressions of the aristocracies of the first and second ages, arose from the power obtained by minorities, how has it happened, that a nation which has rejoiced in their downfall, should be joyfully gliding back into the same policy? How happens it, that whilst religious frauds are no longer rendered sacred, by calling them oracles, political fraud should be sanctified, by calling it national credit? Experience, it is agreed, has exploded the promises of oracles; does it not testify also to those of paper stock?

Paper stock always promises to defend a nation, and always flees from danger. America and France saved themselves by physical power, after danger had driven paper credit out of the field. In America, so soon as the danger disappeared, paper credit loudly boasted of its capacity to defend nations, and though a deserter, artfully reaped the rewards due to the conqueror. In France, it transferred to fraud and avarice the domains which ought to have aided in defending the nation, or to have been restored to the former owners.

Paper credit is a disciple of the doctrine, that truth is best ascertained by the sword. The utmost exertion it has ever made to enlighten the mind, was by this instrument. And the crusade against

France, in preference to leaving to the arbitrament of man's intellectual powers, an estimate of fair experience, is a proof that it only counts its own interest, and forgets the evils it inflicts. Otherwise, could paper credit have inflicted upon Britain all the calamities of a war, to be closed by her ruin, or by a debt of several hundred millions of pounds sterling, merely to prevent the French from forming a government for France?

Had there existed in England, a single chaste organ for expressing and enforcing the public interest, this crusade to guide opinion, would have been escaped by England, as it was by America; and if no such organ did exist, to what but the system of patronage and paper was it owing? It is therefore a menstruum, capable of dissolving the several sections of a government, however divided, into one interest or centre; and of infusing the most unprincipled avarice and ambition into the mass.

Sinecure, armies, navies, offices, war, anticipation and taxes, make up an outline of that vast political combination, concentrated under the denomination of paper and patronage. These, and its other means, completely enable it to take from the nation as much power and as much wealth, as its conscience or its no conscience will allow it to receive; and lest the capacity of public loaning to transfer private property should be overlooked, it has proceeded in England to the indirect sale of private real property. If a land tax is sold for a term amounting to the value of the land, a proprietor is to buy his own land at its value, or admit of a co-proprietor, to whom he must pay that value by instalments; and thus a paper system can sell all the lands of a nation. If national danger should occur after this sale, it can only be met by the people; and the purchaser from a paper system, of an exemption from the land tax to-day, must be again taxed or fight for his land to-morrow. The case of this individual is precisely that of every nation, made use of directly or indirectly to enrich a paper system; it is perpetually at auction, and never receives any thing for itself; because, however ingeniously a paper system can manage artificial danger for its own emolument, it is neither able nor willing to meet real danger; and however rich it is made by a nation, the nation must still defend itself, or perish.

This catastrophe has already arrived in Britain. Swindled out of endless wealth, by the vauntings of paper credit, of its will and ability to defend liberty and property; that hapless nation sees itself taxed and impressed, to increase the penalty of its own credulity, and to protect that which promised to yield protection; its annual taxes beget annual additions to permanent debt, and its endless war with France was commenced by the fears of its paper system, however this war may have gradually changed its ground.

The effect of opposite interests, one enriched by and governing the other, correctly follows its cause. One interest is a tyrant, the other its slave. In Britain, one of these interests owes to the other above ten hundred millions of pounds sterling, which would require twelve millions of slaves to discharge, at eighty pounds sterling each. If the debtor interest amounts to ten millions of souls, and would be worth forty pounds sterling round, sold for slaves, it pays twelve and an half per centum on its capitation value, to the creditor interest, for the exclusive items of debt and bank stock. This profit for their masters, made by those who are called freemen, greatly exceeds what is generally made by those who are called slaves. But as nothing is calculated except two items, by including the payments for useless offices, excessive salaries, and fat sinecures, it is evident that one interest makes out of the other, a far greater profit than if it had sold this other, and placed the money in the most productive state of usance.

Such is the freeman of paper and patronage. Had Diogenes lived until this day, he would have unfledged a cock once more, and exhibited him as an emblem, not of Plato's man, but of a freeborn Englishman. Had Sancho known of a paper stock system, he would not have wished for the government of an island inhabited by negroes. Has Providence used this system to avenge the Africans, upon the Europeans and Americans?

Whatever destroys an unity of interest between a government and a nation, infallibly produces oppression and hatred. Human conception is unable to invent a scheme, more capable of afflicting mankind with these evils, than that of paper and patronage. It divides a nation into two groups, creditors and debtors; the first supplying its want of physical strength, by alliances with fleets and armies, and practising the most unblushing corruption. A consciousness of inflicting or suffering injuries, fills each with malignity towards the other. This malignity first begets a multitude of penalties, punishments and executions, and then vengeance.

A legislature, in a nation where the system of paper and patronage prevails, will be governed by that interest, and legislate in its favour. It is impossible to do this, without legislating to the injury of the other interest, that is, the great mass of the nation. Such a legislature will create unnecessary offices, that themselves or their relations may be endowed with them. They will lavish the revenue, to enrich themselves. They will borrow for the nation, that they may lend. They will offer lenders great profits, that they may share in them. As grievances gradually excite national discontent, they will fix the yoke more securely, by making it gradually heavier. And they will finally avow and maintain their corruption, by establishing an irresistible standing army, not to defend the nation, but to defend a system for plundering the nation.

An uniform deception resorted to by a funding system, through legislative bodies, unites with experience in testifying to its uniform corruption of legislatures. It professes that its object is to pay debts. A government must either be the fraudulent instrument of the system, or the system a fraudulent instrument of a government; or it would not utter this falsehood to deceive the people.

This promise is similar to that of protecting property. It promises to diminish, and accumulates; it promises to protect, and invades. All political oppressors deceive, in order to succeed. When did an aristocracy avow its purpose? Sincerity demanded of that of the third age, the following confession: 'Our purpose is to settle wealth and power upon a minority. It will be accomplished by national debt, paper corporations, and offices, civil and military. These will condense king, lords and commons, a monied faction, and an armed faction, in one interest. This interest must subsist upon another, or perish. The other interest is national, to govern and pilfer which, is our object; and its accomplishment consists in getting the utmost a nation can pay. Such a state of success can only be maintained by armies, to be paid by the nation, and commanded by this minority; by corrupting talents and courage; by terrifying timidity; by inflicting penalties on the weak and friendless, and by distracting the majority with deceitful professions. That with which our project commences, is invariably a promise to get a nation out of debt; but the invariable effect of it is, to plunge it irretrievably into debt.'

The English system of paper and patronage, has made these confessions by the whole current of its actions for a century, and laboured to hide them by its words. That guilt should eternally endeavour to beguile, is natural. Is it also natural, that innocence should eternally be its dupe? Is it the character of virtue, in spite of common sense, to shut her eyes upon truth, and open her ears to falsehood?

A nation exposed to a paroxysm of conquering rage, has infinitely the advantage of one, subjected to this aristocratical system. One is local and temporary; the other is spread by law and perpetual. One is an open robber, who warns you to defend yourself; the other a sly thief, who empties your pockets under a pretence of paying your debts. One is a pestilence, which will end of itself; the other a climate deadly to liberty.

After an invasion, suspended rights may be resumed, ruined cities rebuilt, and past cruelties forgotten; but in the oppressions of the aristocracy of paper and patronage, there can be no respite; so long as there is any thing to get, it cannot be glutted with wealth; so long as there is any thing to fear, it cannot be glutted with power; other tyrants die; this is immortal.

A conqueror may have clemency; he may be generous; at least he is vain, and may be softened by flattery. But a system founded in evil moral qualities, is insensible to human virtues and passions, incapable of remorse, guided constantly by the principles which created it, and acts by the iron instruments, law, armies and tax gatherers. With what prospect of success, reader, could you address the clemency, generosity or vanity of the system of paper and patronage? Wherefore has no one tried this hopeless experiment? Because clemency, generosity and vanity, are not among the moral qualities which constitute the character of an evil moral system.

The only two modes extant of enslaving nations, are those of armies and the system of paper and patronage. The European nations are subjected by both, so that their chains are doubly riveted. The Americans devoted their effectual precautions to the obsolete modes of title and hierarchy, erected several barriers against the army mode, and utterly disregarded the mode of paper and patronage. The army mode was thought so formidable, that military men are excluded from legislatures, and limited to charters or commissions at will; and the paper made so harmless, that it is allowed to break the principle of keeping legislative, executive and judicative powers separate and distinct, to infuse itself into all these departments, to unite them in one conspiracy, and to obtain charters or commissions for unrestricted terms, entrenched behind publick faith, and out of the reach, it is said, of national will; which it may assail, wound and destroy with impunity. This jealousy of armies, and confidence in paper systems, can only be justified, if the following argument in its defence is correct.

'An army of soldiers have a separate interest from the nation,

67

because they draw their subsistence from it, and therefore they will combine for their own interest against the national interest; but an army of stockjobbers have no such separate interest, and will not combine. Soldiers admitted into the legislature, would legislate in favour of soldiers; but stockjobbers will not legislate in favour of stockjobbers. Soldiers may use our arms to take our money; but stockjobbers cannot use our money to take our arms. Soldiers may adhere to a chief in preference to the nation, as an instrument for gratifying their avarice and ambition upon the nation; but stockjobbers have no avarice nor ambition to be gratified, and will not therefore adhere to a chief for that purpose. Soldiers are dangerous, because they assail the liberty of a nation by open force; stockjobbers harmless, because they do it by secret fraud. All are jealous of soldiers, and therefore they will not be watched; few are jealous of stockjobbers, and therefore they will be watched. Many instances have occurred of the oppressions by the army system; one instance only of a perfect capacity in the paper system for oppression can be adduced; and as that has lasted only a single century, it would be precipitate to detect and destroy the aristocracy of paper and patronage, in less time than was requisite to detect and destroy those of superstition and the feudal system.'

Alas! is it true, that ages are necessary to understand, whilst a moment will suffice to invent, an imposture? Is it true, that the example of their venerable ancestor, groaning for a century under the oppressions of this modern system of aristocracy, is incapable of awakening the Americans; and that they themselves must also become a beacon for the benefit of a more enlightened era? Cæsar profited by the failure of Marius, in the art of enslaving his country; will no nation ever profit by the failure of another in the art of preserving its liberty?

Let us drop the subject for a moment, and consider whether we ought to reject truth, because it is plainly told? Because Marcus Aurelius was despotick, should we therefore speak tenderly of despotism? Because Washington was a soldier, should we therefore speak tenderly of standing armies? And because we see around us stockjobbers whom we love, ought we therefore to speak tenderly of paper systems? A despot may condemn tyranny; a soldier may condemn standing armies; and a stockjobber may condemn paper systems. In reasoning boldly against the system of paper and patronage, no private reputation is attacked, more than that of

Marcus Aurelius would be, by reasoning against despotism; or Washington's, by reasoning against standing armies. To insinuate truth only, is to betray it. Veracity in terms cannot be censurable, if veracity in matter is entitled to approbation. The discharge of a duty, cannot require an apology, and without making one, I will proceed.

A paper system proposes to fulfil its promise of defending a nation, by giving it credit; from which credit, it infers an increase of national strength. Let us ascertain what national strength is, before we hastily conclude, that it can be created by a stock system. It consists of people and revenue. If by any means a nation was deprived of half its people, would this add to its strength? If by a paper system, it is deprived of half its revenue, can this either add to its strength? Revenue, like people, is subject to numerical limits. Suppose the people of Britain are able to pay a revenue of forty millions sterling, but that thirty are appropriated to the use of the system of paper and patronage: Are not three fourths of their strength gone, so far as it consists of revenue? But Great Britain with her ten millions of free revenue can borrow two hundred millions. If strength is to be measured by the power of borrowing, she could have borrowed four times as much, had her whole revenue been free, and consequently would have been four times as strong.

Strength arising from revenue, is relative. If the free revenue of Great Britain is ten millions, and the whole revenue of a rival nation fifteen, all of which is free, then the rival nation would possess more money and more credit, capable of being applied to national use, than Great Britain with an actual revenue of forty millions, thirty whereof were enslaved.

Hence it is obvious, that debt, so far from being either strength or credit, is a diminution of both; and that freedom from debt, is the only genuine source of national strength depending on revenue.

England and France are rival nations. If England was bound to pay to France the whole amount of the annual interest of her debt, it would obviously increase the strength and credit of France, and diminish those of England. This proves, that it is the receiver and not the payer, who obtains an addition of strength and credit. And it also furnishes a complete illustration of the effect of the system of paper and patronage, upon the real productive interests of society. The unproductive but subsisting interests of this system, and the productive and taxed interests of society, may be called

69

natural enemies, with more justice than France and England. If the payment by England of thirty millions annually to France would subject England to France, will not the payment by the productive and taxed interests, of the same sum to their natural enemy, the unproductive interest, subject them also to their natural enemy? This demonstrates, that strength is gained by the receiver, and not by the payer; and displays the certainty with which the system of paper and patronage will subject a nation, under pretence of enabling it to defend itself.

Hereafter, the doctrine of anticipation will be considered: but this machine cannot shake our arguments to prove that a nation is weakened, and consequently enslaved by debt, unless the power of anticipation is infinite like debt, and increases with it; which will hardly be asserted.

But if this anticipating resource, did naturally swell with debt, still an indebted nation, would be in a state of subjection. New anticipations are exclusively governed by old anticipations; to borrow, recourse must be had to the monied interest, and the funds or old anticipations, united with paper corporations, constitute that interest. A nation therefore which depends upon anticipation, must be governed by that interest which governs anticipation; so that it cannot will and judge for itself, like a poorer nation, which is independent of anticipation.

Thus whilst a paper system pretends to make a nation rich and potent, it only makes a minority of that nation rich and potent, at the expense of the majority, which it makes poor and impotent. Wealth makes a nation, a faction or an individual, powerful; and therefore if paper systems extracted the wealth they accumulate from the winds, and not from property and labour, they would still be inimical to the principles of every constitution, founded in the idea of national will; because the subjection of a nation to the will of individuals or factions, is an invariable effect of great accumulation of wealth; but when the accumulation of a minority, impoverishes a majority, a double operation, doubly rivets this subjection.

The delusion of all paper projects is at once detected by turning upon them their own doctrine. All boast of doing good to a nation. Suppose a nation was to decline this beneficence, and propose to reward it, by doing good to paper projects, exactly in the same way they propose to benefit the nation; that is, by taking from the owners of stock, their income, and consigning over to them the taxes and the credit attached to the debtor, with the blessing of a paper circulation; the credulity which believes, that these institutions do really impose upon nations debt and taxes, direct and indirect, from motives of public good, would be presently cured by the faltering tongues, the wan faces, and the distressing lamentations, which a proposition for this exchange would produce. These paper projects which pretend to be blessings to nations, would be deprecated as curses by themselves, if the case was thus altered.

It is said that paper systems being open to all, are not monopolies. He who has money, may buy stock. All then is fair, as every man (meaning however only every monied man) may share in the plunder.

Every man may enlist in an army, yet an army may enslave a nation. A monopoly may be open to a great number, yet those who do engage in it, may imbibe the spirit of faction; but it cannot be open to all, because no interest, which must subsist upon a nation, can consist of that nation; as I cannot fatten myself by eating myself. If every citizen should go into an army, it would transform that army into the nation itself, and its pay and subsistence would cease; in like manner the profits of paper, were they generally or universally distributed, would cease; because each citizen would be his own paymaster. Had the objection been as true in practice as it is plausible in theory, these answers suffice to prove, that it would have converted paper aristocracies into paper democracies.

The reason, however, for this apparent common power of becoming a stockjobber, consists in the constant necessity felt for recruits by every species of aristocracy. The Mamelukes of Egypt have sufficient penetration to discover this. No individual, nor an inconsiderable number of individuals, can enslave a nation. A despot raises soldiers by bounties. This system is also recruited by bounties. The soldier sometimes deserts, or takes part with the nation, after his bounty is spent; but the bounty of paper systems is so contrived, that it is perpetually going on, and annually repeated; so that the aristocracy of an oppressive system, never deserts or takes part with the nation, as the army of an oppressive prince has sometimes done.

Where avarice and ambition beat up for recruits, too many are prone to enlist. Kings, ministers, lords and commons will be obliged to command the army, and share in the plunder, or submit to be cashiered. The makers and managers of aristocracy, gamble with a certainty of winning, for a stake extorted and increased by

71

themselves. If they deposit their penny, they draw a pound, and augment their power. The system of paper and patronage, freights annual galleons for a government and a faction, at a national mine called industry; and bestows on the people such blessings, as those enjoy who dig up the ores of Peru and Mexico. The receivers of the profit drawn from this mine, reap wealth and power; the earners reap armies, wars, taxes, monopolies, faction, poverty and ten hundred millions of debt. This is an English picture. America hopes that her governors and citizens are neither ambitious nor avaricious, and upon this solid hope, is committing the custody of her liberty to the same system. Oh! America, America, thou art the truly begotten of John Bull! It is not proposed to follow this system throughout its deleterious effects upon the morals of private citizens. But if it is capable of corrupting publick officers, or government itself, a remark to exhibit its superior malignity over the aristocracies of the first and second ages, cannot be suppressed. The manners and principles of government, are objects of imitation, and influence national character. The aristocracy of the first age, exhibited sanctity, veneration for the Gods, and moral virtues, to the publick view; not unuseful in their operation, and particularly so in times of ignorance; that of the second, the virtues of generosity, honour and bravery, not unuseful in softening barbarism into civilization, by the magnanimity and even the folly of chivalry: but what virtues for imitation appear in the aristocracy of the present age? Avarice and ambition being its whole soul, what private morals will it infuse, and what national character will it create? It subsists by usurpation, deceit and oppression. A consciousness of fraud, impels it towards perpetration. By ever affecting, and never practising sincerity, it teaches a perpetual fear of treachery, and a perpetual effort to insnare. Its end is distrust and fraud, which convert the earth into a scene of ambuscade, man against man. Its acquisitions inflict misery, without bestowing happiness; because they can only feed a rapacity which can never be satisfied, and a luxury which cannot suppress remorse. In relation to private people, this system may only encourage idleness, teach swindling, ruin individuals, and destroy morals; but allied to a government, it presents a policy of such unrivalled malignity, as only to be expressed by saying, 'the government is a speculator upon the liberty and property of the nation.'

A pamphlet written by Doctor Johnson, to disprove the principles which produced the independence of America, comprises in its title, 'taxation no slavery,' the whole argument to which the system of paper and patronage, finally flees for refuge. Taxation is not liberty. But the distinction is obvious. It lies plainly between taxes imposed for the benefit of a nation, or for the benefit of a minority; between those designed to defend, or to enslave. Taxation to enrich a minority or aristocracy, is robbery; to endow it gradually with power, treason.

It is strange, that it is so difficult to distinguish between honest and fraudulent taxes, imposed by a minor interest on the publick interest, and so easy to discern the real design of taxes imposed by one nation upon another. In the latter case, monopoly is clearly understood to be an indirect mode of taxation. The United States know, that the monopoly of their commerce by the English, was a tribute; but they refuse to know, that the monopoly of a circulating medium by banking, is also a tribute. Useless offices, established here by the English government, were clearly perceived to be a tribute; but useless offices established by our own government are denied to be so. Pretexts for taxation invented by England, were detected by dullness herself; but pretexts invented at home, seem to deceive the keenest penetration.

And yet correct reasoning must conclude, that if one nation, by means of a monopoly, can impoverish another; a combination or corporate body, may also impoverish the rest of a nation, by the same means. That a monopoly which enriches, will correspondently impoverish, unless it produces or creates; that if Britain possessed the privilege of furnishing America with bank paper, at the annual profit of eight per centum, it would have constituted a tax, enriching Britain and impoverishing America—co-extensively with her former commercial monopoly; that if this privilege would have enriched the English at our expense, it must also equally enrich stockholders, at the expense of those who are not stockholders; that if national indigence is gradually produced by a subjection to a foreign monopoly, the indigence of the mass of a nation, will be produced by a domestick monopoly, profitable, but unproductive; and that if a nation has a moral right to liberate itself from an indirect tribute to another nation, it has also a moral right to liberate itself from a similar tribute to a domestick combination; unless it is a moral duty heroically to withstand evils imposed by foreigners, for the purpose of penitentially embracing them when imposed by natives. If these effects of the contemplated monopoly are true, they terminate inevitably in the aristocracy of the third age.

Doctor Johnson's maxim could never convince us, that taxation by banking, funding systems, protecting duties or patronage, was no slavery, if the profits arising from such institutions were re-received by English capitalists: does the substitution of a different receiver, alter the case? If not, 'taxation' is 'slavery,' however moderate the tax may be, when the object of the tax is not the publick benefit, but to enrich and impoverish individuals, and thereby undermine the principles necessary to preserve national liberty.

As to oppressive taxation, there are few cases capable of justifying it; and none, those excepted, wherein it repels a greater evil than itself. Admit that it expels tyranny; it is itself a tyrant. Admit that tyranny will obliterate moral virtues, and replenish the mind with vices; oppressive taxation will do it also. A nation oppressed by taxes, can never be generous, benevolent or enlightened. If the lion was burdened like the ass, he would presently become cowardly, and stupid. But oppressive taxation, by law and monopoly, direct and indirect, to create or sustain the system of paper and patronage, proposes nothing retributory for reducing a people to the condition of asses, except an aristocracy to provide for them a succession of burdens.

Hereditary aristocracy, supported by perpetuities, is preferable to a paper and patronage aristocracy, because its taxation would be less oppressive, since its landed estate would furnish it with opulence and power; whereas eternal and oppressive taxation is necessary to supply the aristocracy of paper and patronage, with these vital qualities.

As a government is melted by law, into the aristocracy of the third age, the ligaments which united it with the nation, are gradually broken; and a consciousness of this, gradually drives the government, for defending itself against the people, into war, armies, corruption, debt, charters, bounties, and every species of patronage for which a pretext can be invented; and a sinking fund cloaks its drift, as proclamations did that of Lewis the fourteenth, declaring, previously to his inundating Europe with Christian blood, his anxiety to prevent its effusion.

When this process is managed by a government, it proves that the government is welded to that interest which the process advances; it substantially destroys the English theory; divides a nation into two interests, and cooks one in the modes most delicious to the appetite of the other. Such is the essential evil of every species of bad government, by whatever name distinguished. A particular interest thus quartered upon the general interest, has never failed to harass a nation: a government is good, when it is coupled to the general interest; and bad, when it is coupled to a particular interest of any kind, whether military, hierarchical, feudal, or stock.

It is admitted by Mr. Adams, that an order of men having great wealth, will acquire a correspondent degree of power. If this wealth consists of land, it may be measured and balanced. Suppose a nation should establish a landed nobility, and should conclude that the possession of one third of the lands, would confer a share of wealth on this order so unequal, as to make it unmanageable, and of course despotick; this nation might restrict their landed order to one fourth of all the lands in the state, concluding that the three fourths divided among all other orders, might suffice to check the power arising from condensing one fourth in one interest. This is what Lord Shaftesbury means by 'a balance of property.' But if an order of paper and patronage is erected, (remember that nothing makes an order but one interest,) in what manner is its power to be checked by a balance of property? The wealth of paper and patronage is daily growing, wherefore it cannot be measured or limited; it is therefore impossible to balance it; and yet without this balance of property, the power which clings to wealth, will destroy liberty, even in the opinion of the English theorists. According to Mr. Adams's principles, this syllogism presents itself. Exorbitant wealth will obtain a degree of power dangerous to society, if not checked or balanced; paper systems will bestow exorbitant wealth, to check or balance which, no means have been invented; therefore, paper systems are dangerous to society.

Not land, but its profit, constitutes wealth and power. By taxation, the profit arising from land may be apportioned between the possession, and the system of paper and patronage; or it may be wholly transferred to the system. If then an order, such as the late nobility and clergy of France, by an income consisting of the profit of one third of the lands of France, attracted a degree of power oppressive to the nation; does it not evidently follow, whenever the system of paper and patronage, has acquired one third of the profit produced by all the lands of a nation, that it will also acquire the oppressive degree of power, interwoven with that degree of wealth?

Although I am considering this system in relation to Britain, an ignorance of any rule by which to compute the profit of all the land of that island, compels me to refer to America for an illustration of the last observation.

All the exports from the United States, may probably amount to the whole profit yielded by land, allowing subsistence to the possessors, which forms no part of rent or profit. This amount has never extended to sixty millions of dollars annually, yet for the purpose of including the whole, we will estimate the annual profit of land at that sum. If the interest of paper and patronage received twelve millions annually from direct taxation, and eight millions annually from indirect, by bounties and the circulation of bank paper, then this system would possess that degree of wealth, which rendered the former civil and religious nobility of France, dangerous and oppressive; and it would be obvious, that a system, which had so rapidly absorbed one third of the profit of the land in the United States, possessed a capacity of extending that third to a moiety, or even beyond a moiety, as in England; and that as no mode of collecting a dangerous degree of wealth into one interest, with equal rapidity, had ever yet appeared, there is none so alarming to a nation, or which so loudly demanded the application of Mr. Adams's or Lord Shaftesbury's idea of a balance of property.

To display the celerity with which this system collects wealth, and changes forms of government, it is only necessary to recollect, that the mode of monopolizing wealth by conquest, required above six hundred years to destroy the Roman Republick; whereas the system of paper and patronage, by changing the nature of the English government in less than a century, has verified the savage opinion, that certain conjurers by hieroglyphical representations, could take away life; it transfers property and kills governments by a like graphical art. It paints as many pounds or dollars upon paper as it pleases, which transfers money and power from the holders of land and industry, to the holders of the paper. Let casuists decide between the morality of taking away life in the mode of the Indian conjurer, and taking away property and liberty in the mode of the paper conjurer.

Is it on account of this sorcery, that the aristocracy of the third age considers painting as one of the fine arts, and devotes its whole philosophy to a taste for this species of it? The aristocracies of superstition and ennobled orders, by cultivating the circle of the · sciences, checked their passions, and humanized their rule; this cultivates a science to take away the property of its friends, like that used by a savage to take away the life of his foe. The savage passion of vengeance is however appeased, by the death of the father, and thirsts not for the blood of the son; but the passion which seeks property by hieroglyphical representation, is never appeased, and what it takes from one generation, only whets its malignity towards the next. Is this sorcery really preferable to the ancient modes of aristocracy?

It is universally agreed that power is attracted by wealth. Ten hundred millions of pounds sterling, being a great sum of wealth, must therefore attract some share of power to the paper interest of England. Whatever it attracts was not bestowed by the English form of government, and is of course an unconstitutional and revolutionary acquisition. This must be admitted, or it must be proved, that great wealth acquired by a particular interest, does not attract power. If the system of paper and patronage, will destroy the principles of limited monarchy without changing its forms, either by amalgamating king, lords and commons, or by creating a new power, may it not also destroy the principles of a republican government, and leave its form also standing?

United interests, or an aggregation of wealth by one interest, are equally at enmity with Mr. Adams's system of a balance of power and property; and if the system of paper and patronage produces both or either, his cannot exist a moment in communion with that. An unconquerable enmity in theory and principle, would crown an attempt to foster both these systems, with several ludicrous inconsistencies. Mr. Adams's system requires an illustrious, high-spirited, enlightened, virtuous and wealthy house of Lords; and the system of paper and patronage would fill it with the spawn of stockjobbing and corruption. How long will it require to purge off the contaminations of the father before the son will be well born? Or will not the system of paper and patronage recontaminate faster, than the generative process can purify, so as to prevent Mr. Adams from ever collecting the necessary qualities in his noble senate? Without superior qualities, his system does not contend for superior distinction; but it is notorious that the system of paper and patronage peoples the two houses of parliament in England, and so completely moulds their character, that all sorts of men, make the same sort of lords and commons.

We may conceive the manner in which the aristocracy of the third age is consolidated with a government, by supposing the territory to be represented by a multitude of landscapes, which the

77

government could transfer with the lands they represented, just as it transfers wealth by pictures of money. Would not the individuals who administered the government, take to themselves some of these landscapes? Would they not purchase accomplices and protectors with others? and would not this unjust mode of taking away lands, presently generate a centre of power and interest, infinitely more oppressive than Turgot's centre, so justly censured by Mr. Adams?

If the system of paper and patronage has made any impression upon the English theory, it behoved Mr. Adams accurately to have explained this impression, before he made use of that theory in his defence of the American constitutions. Without this explanation, we are at a loss to know whether the object of his reference and admiration is the ancient theory or modern practice: Whether it is the king, lords and commons of the fourteenth or of the eighteenth century.

Had this explanation appeared, his arguments would have been better understood, and the practicability of his system more easily estimated; nor could he possibly have escaped some coincidence of opinion with the principles of this essay, except by proving that the system of paper and patronage had made no impression on the English theory. Otherwise, by applauding the old theory, he must have coincided in a disapprobation of the new system of paper and patronage, because it corrupts this old theory; or if he applauded the new system, he must have condemned the old theory destroyed by it. He could not have justified the new system of paper and patronage, without surrendering his idea of checks and balances, or discovering checks and balances in this new system.

The checks and balances of the old English theory and the new English system, seem to have little or no relation to each other. The former consisted of king, lords and commons. The two first were weights, by reason of domains, manors, prerogatives and tenures; the last, from the confidence of the people attracted by responsibility. These weights or checks and balances, no longer exist. Bidders for loans and dealers in omnium, constitute the most ponderous weight next to the king, and the vibrations of stock possess ten fold the power of the house of lords. The nearest approach towards the idea of checks and balances made by the invention of paper and patronage, is by dividing a nation into two weights, one consisting of the government, stockjobbers and office holders; the other of the people. It places pecuniary voraciousness

78

in one scale, and Promethean patience in the other; and with these weights, produces a political system, as wide from one founded in a balance among kings, lords and commons, according to Mr. Adams's explanation of it, as can be imagined.

Without discriminating between the English theory, unattended by the system of paper and patronage, or influenced by it, Mr. Adams arranges the Roman, Lacedemonian, and other governments, in the class of mixed forms, together with the English; as being of a similar nature, and yielding similar inferences. If from this alliance, we are compelled for the sake of maintaining the consistency of Mr. Adams's arguments, to consider him as referring to the old English theory, the old practice, and the old balances, it follows, that his whole political system is built with materials which have vanished; and that it is as imaginary and romantick gravely to talk of patricians, plebeians, and feudal barons at this day, as it would be to propose the restoration of oracles, or the revival of chivalry.

To bring this argument within the full view of the reader, was one design for devoting so much time to the explanation of the new English system of paper and patronage; because, if it is proved, that this has made a material impression upon the balances of the old theory, it follows, that the English form of government has undergone a revolution; that the new system of paper and patronage, corrupts and destroys the old system of checks and balances; that if the American forms of government are, as Mr. Adams asserts, founded in the old theory of checks and balances, they are exposed to destruction by this new foe, which has evinced its power over that old theory, by undermining it in England; that Mr. Adams's argument is eminently defective, in having overlooked the destroyer of his favourite theory of checks and balances; and that this new enemy to human liberty must be met by some other form of government; that composed of checks and balances modified according to the old theory, having become its victim, after a feeble resistance.

To prove that the new English practice is inconsistent with the old English theory, let us consider the declaration of Mr. Adams, 'that among the ancient forms of government, the Lacedemonian approached nearest to the English,' wherefore he bestows on it particular commendations. Our evidence results from a comparison between the present English form of government and the Lacedemonian.

By one, money was despised; of the other, it is the God. One inspired heroism; the other avarice. One taught nobles to fight for their country; the other, to become the sycophants of a king. In one, the legislature controlled two kings; in the other, one king corrupts two legislative bodies. One inspired a love of country; the other, a derision of patriotism. One taught frugality and temperance; the other, profusion and luxury. In short, one disclosed the few virtues natural to the aristocracies of the first and second ages; the other, all the vices natural to the aristocracy of the third.

That forms of government mould manners, will not be denied; and as the manners of the Spartans and the modern English, bear no similarity to each other, it follows that the principles of their governments were also essentially different. To assert, that the principles were the same, but the effects different, would destroy the only solid ground of reasoning, namely, that similar causes will produce similar effects; and deprive us of the entire motive for a preference between forms of government.

If this difference exists, between the principles and manners of the Spartans and the modern English, the resemblance between the English and Spartan governments seen by Mr. Adams, must have arisen from a comparison of the Spartan, not with the present English government, because between these there is no resemblance, but with that which was compounded of an hierarchy rendered powerful by superstition, of an honest legislature, and of a frugal, warlike and hardy nobility, able to control and punish kings.

By classing the English with the Spartan, and other mixed forms of government, it is obvious that Mr. Adams, throughout his book, has only considered that era of the English government, in which its form has some resemblance to the ancient governments with which he compares it; and that he has wholly omitted to consider the present English aristocracy of paper and patronage, or the present English government; since that, neither in its causes or effects, has any resemblance to a single ancient form of government, from which Mr. Adams has drawn his illustrations.

Throughout his system, Mr. Adams deduces his aristocracy from oracles, a supposed descent from the Gods, or a superiority of virtue and talents; and his essential effort is to ascertain the best mode of checking it. These are the aristocracies of the first and second ages; and if his mode of checking them is well contrived, it might have been useful to Lycurgus and Solon, to the Italian republicks, and to nations of the ancient and middle ages. But would it therefore follow, that the same check or balance will secure the liberty of nations against the modern mode of invading it? Will his system check corruption, restrain patronage, control armies, and limit the draughts of avarice upon national wealth and labour? Behold England, if his system exists there, and answer the question. If it does not exist there, it follows, that Mr. Adams's system is irrelative to the existing case, or to the subject which he professed to consider, and which I profess to consider; namely, the nature of the existing American and English forms of government. In drawing his comparison, Mr. Adams refers to a landed aristocracy; I refer to an aristocracy of paper and patronage. Let us endeavour to discover which of us is fencing with a shadow.

Perhaps the discovery may be made by the following questions. Would a dissertation upon the system of paper and patronage, have explained Mr. Adams's system of checks and balances to the people of Greece? If not, can a dissertation upon checks and balances, explain the effects of a system of paper and patronage to the present age? Suppose an author in the fifteenth century, had proved the system of paper and patronage to be right, and inferred, that the feudal aristocracy, or the then existing English government, was therefore the best in the world; would it not have been precisely analogous to an inference, that the now existing English government, under the system of paper and patronage, is also proved to be the best form in the world, by proving the feudal system of the fifteenth century to have been so? In fact, we all see a distinction between the English governments of the fifteenth and the eighteenth centuries: where does it lie, except between the systems of checks and balances, and of paper and patronage? One is the feudal, the other the monied aristocracy. For which does Mr. Adams contend? It would be a whimsical event, if the landed interest of the United States, should be induced by Mr. Adams's compliments to the landed aristocracy of the second age, to erect the paper aristocracy of the third. That by being convinced of its own natural right to be a master, it should be induced to become a slave. And that the praises bestowed on its own virtues, should make it blind to the vices of corruption and avarice, nourished by the aristocracy of paper and patronage. Will it be just to punish a wish to erect a landed aristocracy, by making the landed interest a dupe and a victim? If so, Mr. Adams's dissertation may have the merit of an avenger. For it will hereafter be shewn, that the English system, though it is able to introduce into the United States, the aristocracy of paper and patronage, is unable to introduce a landed aristocracy; and that the landed interest has no alternative, under our circumstances, but that of supporting an equal, free government, or becoming a slave to the system of paper and patronage. Where indeed could we find an interest, for the landed interest of the United States to mount in the form of an aristocracy?

Not less whimsical would it be, if the system of paper and patronage, which has substantially destroyed a landed aristocracy in England, should create one here; particularly if our form of government (as Mr. Adams believes) is similar to the English, which has proved either a feeble foe or a convenient instrument to a monied aristocracy.

Hereafter, when our constitution is considered, the competency of its security against the aristocracy of paper and patronage, or that of the present age, will be computed; and then it is not meant to shrink from the consideration of this species of aristocracy, in reference to the United States; on the contrary, an effort will be made to place it in several points of view, inadmissible, whilst considering it in relation to England.

At present, supposing that the paper and patronage system of England, is a modern political power of vast force; that it has corrupted or supplanted the old English form of government; that its oppressions overspread the land; that its principles are vicious, and its designs fraudulent; we will proceed to inquire what ought to be done.

Superstition and noble orders were defended by the strongest sanctions within the scope of human invention. Penalties, temporal and eternal; splendour, pomp and honour; united to terrify, to dazzle, to awe and to flatter the human mind: and the real or external virtues of charity and meekness, hospitality and nobleness of mind, induced some to love that, which most hated, and all feared. Yet the intellect of the last age pierced through the delusions, behind which the oppressions of hierarchy and nobility had taken shelter.

We pity the ancients for their dullness in discovering oppressions, so clearly seen by ourselves now that they are exploded. We moderns; we enlightened Americans; we who have abolished hierarchy and title; and we who are submitting to be taxed and enslaved by patronage and paper, without being deluded or terrified by the promise of heaven, the denunciation of hell, the

82

penalties of law, the brilliancy and generosity of nobility, or the pageantry and charity of superstition.

A spell is put upon our understandings by the words 'publick faith and national credit,' which fascinates us into an opinion, that fraud, corruption and oppression, constitute national credit; and debt and slavery, publick faith. This delusion of the aristocracy of the present age, is not less apparent, than the ancient divinity of kings, and yet it required the labours of Locke and Sidney to detect that ridiculous imposture.

Publick faith is made with great solemnity to mount the rostrum, and to pronounce the following lecture:

'Law enacted for the benefit of a nation, is repealable; but law enacted for the benefit of individuals, though oppressive to a nation, is a charter, and irrepealable. The existing generation is under the tutelage of all past generations, and must rely upon the responsibility of the grave for the preservation of its liberty. Posterity, being bound by the contracts of its ancestry, in every case which diminishes its rights, man is daily growing less free by a doctrine which never increases them. A government intrusted with the administration of publick affairs for the good of a nation, has a right to deed away that nation for the good of itself or its partisans, by law charters for monopolies or sinecures; and posterity is bound by these deeds. But although an existing generation can never reassume the liberty or property held by its ancestor, it may recompence itself by abridging or abolishing the rights of its descendant.'

Such is the doctrine which has prevented the eye of investigation from penetrating the recesses of the aristocracy of the present age. It simply offers the consolation of softening injuries to ourselves by adding to the wretchedness of our descendants. By this artifice, (the offspring of interest and cunning,) whenever men cut off their shackles with the sword, they are riveted on again by the pen. A successful war, to avenge a small and temporary injury, is made to gain a great and lasting calamity. Victory over enemies is followed by defeat from friends. And an enemy destroyed abroad, is only the head of an hydra, which produces two at home. This is not exaggeration, if the idea of the aristocracy of paper and patronage is not chimerical. And thence occur these curious questions: Can the United States kill one Englishman or Frenchman, without converting two at least of their own citizens, into members of this aristocracy? Which would be most dangerous and burdensome to the union, one of these foreigners abroad, or two of these aristocrats at home?

The best argument in favour of the mortgage of a nation to a faction, is, that it is a purchase; an argument however, which does not extend to the family of law charters in general. A few of a nation, have bought the nation. Cæsar by plunder and rapine, amassed the means of buying or corrupting the Roman government; was his title to despotism over the Roman people therefore sound? If Jugurtha had been rich enough to buy Rome, ought the nation to have submitted to the sale, because the bargain was made with the government? If a freeman has no right to enslave his child by selling him, can one generation sell another? And if one generation has no right to sell another, can a government which exercises the double character of seller and buyer, in erecting the aristocracy of the present age, transform the most atrocious iniquity into political or moral rectitude, by writing in its forehead 'publick faith?' Then let us acquit every thief, who assumes for his motto the words 'honest man.'

This kind of faith and honesty, have invented the opinion 'that policy and justice require a law, beneficial to 'individuals at the expense of a nation, to exist for the period prescribed;' to sustain which, it is necessary to reverse the elemental political maxim 'that the good of the whole, ought to be preferred to the good of a few.' Government is erected for the purpose of carrying this maxim into execution, by passing laws for the benefit of a nation; and shall a violation of the purpose of its institution, by passing laws injurious to a nation, in creating or fostering the aristocracy of paper and patronage, be cleansed of its guiltiness, because individuals have become the accomplices of the government?

A law or a contract, prescribing an immoral action, is void. No sanction can justify murder, perjury or theft. Yet the murder of national liberty, the perjury of a traitorous government, and the theft of national wealth, by the gradual introduction of the aristocracy of the third age, are varnished into a gloss by a cunning dogma, capable even of dazzling men, so excessively honest as to put other men to death for petty thefts, committed to appease hunger or cover nakedness.

The same mouth will solemnly assert, that the principles of equity annul every contract, which defrauds an individual; and that justice or policy requires a catalogue of law charters which defraud a nation, to exist and have their effect.

This is owing to the artful conversion of good words, into knavish dogmas. It is not new, to see errour take refuge under the garb of truth. Superstition has in all ages called itself religion. Thus law charters, with the faithless design of enslaving a nation by the introduction of the aristocracy of the present age, crouch behind the good and honest words 'publick faith and national credit,' to prevent a nation from destroying that, which is destroying it. And they succeed; because we are as unsuspicious that a false and fraudulent dogma, is hidden under fair language, as that a well dressed gentleman indicates a thief.

To come at truth, we ought not to stop at a verbal investigation. We must consider whether the effects of every law and every measure, by whatever names the law or measure are called, are on the side of virtue or vice.

An irrepealable law charter is a standing temptation to governments to do evil, and an invitation to individuals to become their accessaries; by its help, a predominant party may use temporary power, to enact corporate or individual emoluments for itself, at the national expense. Successive parties will repeat the same iniquity; and even the outs or opposition will be corrupted, to do obeisance at the shrine of the dogma, that they also may reap of the fruit it bestows, when a nation shall fall into their hands; which upon every change of administration, will have its hopes of reform gratified, by new pillages under the sanctions of publick faith and national credit.

This modern system of law charters, is founded in the same design, with the ancient system of a social compact. Under the sanction of social compact, governments have formerly tyrannised over nations. Under the sanction of law charters, governments now buy a faction, rob nations of enormous wealth, and soar beyond responsibility. The inviolability of a social compact was the old dogma; the inviolability of law charters is the new; for effecting the same end. The last is however an engine in the hands of avarice and ambition, of power far superior to the first. It is able to corrupt and pillage a nation without limit. The first was an opinion unable to purchase partisans; the last offers every thing to its disciples, which can gratify pernicious passions, and meets arguments with bribes. Thus a nation, which won self-government by exploding the doctrine of the antiquated compact dogma, may lose it again in the modern law charter dogma; and thus a nation, which thought it morally wrong to suffer slavery from troops hired by clothes, pay and rations, may be persuaded that it is morally right to suffer slavery from troops hired by dividends, interest upon stock, and protecting duty bounties.

As the English began to emerge from Gothic ignorance, the idea of liberty by compact, and not of natural right, led them to extort charters from their princes; but wofully is the doctrine of deriving a right to liberty from charters, turned upon this gallant nation. By allowing them to bestow, it was discovered that they could destroy. Such as diminish, and not those which enlarge national freedom, have become the sacred charters. The errour of parchment liberty, has made liberty the creature of parchment. A government, good or bad, can easily take away that liberty by charters, which was created by charters. Before the idea of deriving liberty from charter or compact became fashionable, the evils produced by bad governments were temporary; now, slavery, as liberty condescended to be, is created by charters, so as to perpetuate these evils, and to hem in the efforts of patriotism so narrowly, as to destroy the effect of virtue in office.

By admitting that donations of publick property by a government to individuals, should irrevocably transform it into private property, it is obvious that the stock of publick rights will be continually whittled away. Tyranny is only a partial disposition of publick rights, in favour of one or a few. The system of paper and patronage, bottomed upon charters and commissions, enables avarice and ambition to draw more extensively upon the national stock, than any system hitherto invented. It can convert publick property into private, with unexampled rapidity, or transfer wealth and power from the mass of a nation to a few. Its guilt is made its sanction. Neither 'private nor publick property' is allowed to be a sanction against the frauds and invasions of paper and patronage, until the fraud or invasion is committed; and then 'private property' (good words, as are 'publick faith and national credit') is converted into a dogma for the protection of this fraud and invasion. Titles, tythes, feudal services, monasteries, South Sea and Mississippi projects, funding and banking systems, sinecure offices, and every species of fraud, monopoly and usurpation, call the pillages of private property, private property, and generally contrive to make it so by laws or armies.

But in the eye of justice, property, publick or private, cannot be transferred by fraud. A nation erects a government for the publick benefit and does not empower it to bring about the aggrandisement of itself, and its faction, to the publick detriment. If this is effected by a transfer of property, publick or private, the transfer is fraudulent, and void; because the nation never empowered the government, by that or any other mode, to injure its liberty or happiness. The principles of moral rectitude, do not forbid a nation to resume power, usurped by a government; nor property, chartered away to individuals, by fraudulent laws; because otherwise they could not resume just rights, since power and law are the vehicles in which these rights are constantly taken away.

The ideas annexed to the words 'publick faith, national credit and private property' in England, may be correct in reference to the English civil policy, and erroneous in relation to the civil policy of the United States. Monopoly is the leading principle of their political, religious, and mercantile systems; everything the reverse of monopoly, constitutes our political, religious and mercantile systems. The king, with his annual million, his prerogatives, and his patronage, made up of fleets, armies, offices, and corruption; a house of inheritable legislation, without responsibility, entrenched behind the crown, and flanked with privileges; a house of commons, purchasers of diplomas bestowing an exclusive power to tax and to receive; a hierarchy, tythe gatherers and test makers; mercantile corporations, masters of kingdoms and islands; a bank of England, which can make it unlawful to pay its own debts; a funding system, mortgaging the nation for more money than the world possesses; a multitude of places obsolete, except as to fees and salaries; and a variety of rights and privileges, exercised by corporations, trades, companies and districts—form a vast mass of monopoly, which in a multitude of ways incorporates with itself the talents and power of the nation, and has therefore annexed ideas to the words 'publick faith, national credit and private property' adapted to nourish and not destroy itself.

If the English ideas of these expressions, have been inculcated by the most complicated and wide spreading system of monopoly which has ever existed; and if this system would not have inculcated such ideas, had they been unfriendly to its ambition and avarice; it follows, that their construction of these expressions being suggested by and friendly to a system of monopoly and aristocracy, must be unfriendly to a system, at enmity with monopoly and aristocracy.

Fraud and ambition can never succeed, except by subtilty. Hence they seize upon our virtues by plausible phrases, and manage nations by prejudices they themselves plant. By these phrases and prejudices they rear and nurture a multitude of opinions, which concur in advancing their designs and interest. Could fraud and ambition be compelled to substitute sincerity in the place of this subtilty, they would acknowledge that the invariable result of their doctrines, is, the sacrifice of a nation to the ambition and avarice of a few; but an acknowledgment of this end, would explode all their arguments, however specious; and repeal all their laws, however sanctioned. It is the felicity of the United States, to commence a government at a period, when the aristocracies of the first, the second, and the third ages, have all sincerely and unequivocally displayed their end and purpose, by effects. The purpose of the ideas annexed in England, to the words 'publick faith,' 'national credit' and 'charter' is displayed in the state of the people; this, and not the brilliancy of the government or the splendour of individuals, is the object which an honest politician will contemplate. The wealth found by Khouli Khan in Delhi, and the riches collected by Nabobs, were no proofs of the happiness of Hindostan, or the goodness of its government.

Nations, by false dogmas, have been restrained from defending their liberties, and armies have paid their lives for their prejudices. The sacred nature of law charters, is the sword of their enemies at the threats of the bigoted Israelites on their sabbath day. They are extended to periods, within which the grantees may acquire so much wealth, and corrupt such a proportion of talents, as to secure a continuance. The question is, shall the nation destroy charters, or charters destroy the nation? The dogma declares charters to be sacred, and forbids the nation to resist until they have acquired an irresistible maturity. Even the Jews, obstinate as they were, at length discovered fighting on the sabbath day to be preferable to death; but the enlightened nations of Europe, who laugh at their sabbatism, piously believe, that there is a charm in the words charter, credit and publick faith; making slavery preferable to a fair and free government.

A gradual monopoly of lands and wealth, overturned the Roman Republick. By assailing it in time, it might have been suppressed. The murder of the Gracchi is a proof, that usurpation can only be corrected in its infancy, and that fraudulent acquisitions will perpetuate any crime for self-defence. But this system of monopoly was suffered to proceed to maturity, and the commonwealth was poisoned by the miasma it diffused. It was a consequence of the Roman conquests which avenged the injured nations; but do the Americans equally merit the vengeance of the English system of paper and patronage, for having vindicated their liberty against it?

The idea annexed by this system of monopoly to private property, requires a nation to sacrifice itself for the benefit of an individual. This is a new principle of moral rectitude, which fraud only could suggest, and folly alone adopt. Heretofore, individuals who sacrificed themselves for a nation, have been celebrated as performing an act of heroick virtue. Heretofore, a suppression of personal appetites, for the sake of advancing public good, has been thought a species of morality, highly meritorious; and a destruction of publick good, to gratify personal appetites, a species of immorality, highly vicious. Place in one scale publick liberty and happiness; in the other, the gratifications of individuals by the system of paper and patronage, with the label 'private property' fixed upon these gratifications: morality, it is agreed, ought only to determine which scale should preponderate. Will she too be the dupe of a fraudulent dogma, and a treacherous badge? Will she too devote a nation to oppression and misery, to feed the lusts of individuals, under the influence of a superstitious sanction? A crocodile has been worshipped, and its priesthood have asserted, that morality required the people to suffer themselves to be eaten by the crocodile; to encourage them, the people might also have been told, that the crocodile would die in time, and that then, they would be no longer eaten. In this species of morality the people believed, and whenever the old crocodile was about to expire, a young one was put in his place, and the people continued to be eaten. Law charters are a family of those crocodiles.

Publick faith is the moral principle, called upon to defend monopoly and law charter, under the name of private property. Let us consider what this sanction is in a free government. If the government should solemnly, by law, enter into a contract with a number of individuals, the object of which was to diminish the liberty and wealth of the people, by increasing the power and wealth of the government and these individuals, does publick faith require from the nation a fulfilment of this contract? If the question is answered in the negative, a correct definition of publick faith, must comprise both a faithfulness to the publick good, and also a faithfulness in contracts with individuals; nor can these two duties be made inconsistent with each other by publick faith, without admitting it to be a principle of a double character, sometimes good and sometimes bad. Because, if it compels the performance of one duty, by the breach of another; and if the duty required to be fulfilled, is trivial, compared with that required to be infringed; it would bestow on publick faith a mixed character, and even a prevalence of evil. Publick faith then, considered as a good moral principle, must either include and reconcile, a loyalty both to the publick good and to contracts with individuals; or if the former is not a duty imposed by publick faith, it must be a duty of superior and superseding obligation.

The construction of publick faith by monopoly, avarice and ambition, is precisely the reverse of this. They confine it to a fulfilment of every species of contract made by a government with individuals, especially if entered into for the purpose of gratifying themselves at the expense of a nation; and thus limited, consider it as the most sacred of all duties. And so far are these glossographers, from considering publick faith as a good moral principle, that they make it enforce contracts, entered into for every conceivable vicious purpose; from those of betraying nations, armies, cities and forts, down to those of perjury, theft and assassination. Under this construction, whenever the publick good and a contract with an individual come in conflict, publick faith is made to decide, that the contract shall prevail; and thus its definition will come out, 'national duty to suffer oppression, and lose its liberty, by laws, charters or contracts, made by a government for that purpose, provided they convey an interest to individuals.' So soon as it is thus changed from a good to a vicious principle, its effects change also. From being a pledge of publick good, it becomes the protector of political fraud; it compels a nation to be an accomplice in its own ruin; it takes from it the right of self-preservation; and it becomes the modern subterfuge of the modern aristocracy.

Hitherto, in comparing the duty of a government to a nation, and to a law charter, the comparison has been exhibited in the most favourable light for the latter, by forbearing to insist upon any degree of criminality in a faction, which accepts of a charter from a government, injurious to a nation. It is, however, questionable, whether the priesthood were innocent, which executed the evil of hierarchy; or the barons, who sustained that of the feudal aristocracy; or the solicitors and holders of sinecure offices; or those who pilfer a nation by means of a law charter. If their accomplices are not guilty, tyrants themselves must be innocent.

Individuals may be aiders and abetters in projects replete with publick evil, without discerning their tendency; but the rarity of this case is evinced, by the tacit compact and union produced by such projects. This compact and union, disclose a thorough knowledge of the interest on one side, and the injury on the other, because it is the plain effort of profit; and a fear of losing profit can only be inspired by a conviction of committing an injury in its acquisition. This fear makes every individual who is conscious of drawing wealth from a nation unjustly, the friend and encomiast of the strongest power he can find; because power is the only protector of injustice. And if he cannot find a power strong enough to protect injustice, he will exert himself to erect one. When such a power exists, the more unfaithful it is to the publick good, the more its publick faith will be celebrated by those who receive the benefit of its unfaithfulness. Lewis the fourteenth, an ignorant, fanatical and tyrannical prince, was celebrated even by philosophers, because he robbed the French nation, to give them pensions.

Individuals, who do not derive their acquisitions from projects replete with public evil, are never formed into a tacit compact or union, because, being unconscious of drawing gain from a nation unjustly, they have nothing to fear. Being unconscious of injustice, they are not naturally the friends and encomiasts of a power, strong enough to protect injustice. And deriving no benefit from the unfaithfulness of a government to the publick good, they will not celebrate a government for it. In order to see the force of this comparison, it is only necessary to conceive a society consisting of two classes, one made up of agriculturists, professions, trades and commerce, all unconnected with banking, funding and patronage; the other, of a funding system, bank charters, pensions and patronage. Which class would be the disciple and parasite of despotism? If this is discernible, the consequence of erecting this modern species of aristocracy is also discernible.

The exact similarity in nature and principle, between laws or charters establishing funding systems, banks, or sinecure profit of any kind; and laws or charters establishing privileged orders or endowed hierarchies; appears in their common union with, and devotion to, a power capable of protecting injustice.

It is still objected 'that unless laws, beneficial to individuals, though injurious to a nation, are supported, confidence in government will be destroyed, and national credit, lost.' The doctrine amounts to this: 'that it is good policy in a nation, to make a few individuals its masters or owners, to excite an inclination in these few individuals to lend it money, for a handsome premium and high interest.' And this policy is literally pursued, by establishing a certain number of paper systems and charters, for drawing money from the nation directly or indirectly, in order to enable a few to lend a part of this money to the nation.

To this item of the value of a confidence 'that laws and charters, injurious to a nation, but beneficial to individuals, will be maintained,' must be added a corruption of manners, arising from the traffick between a government and a faction, for the objects of gratifying the ambition of one dealer, and the avarice of the other; and the customary violent and wretched parties, between the commencement of this confidence and its catastrophe.

On the other hand, a confidence that laws and charters injurious to a nation, will be repealed, whenever their pernicious tendency is discovered, will prevent the destructive evils generated by a contrary opinion; will enable honest governments to correct the frauds of knavish; and will check or even cure the malevolence of factions. And one effect of inestimable value flowing from this latter confidence, would be the detection and overthrow of an insidious sanction, under cover of which the modern aristocracy of paper and patronage, is fast fettering modern nations.

The analysis of aristocracy, by the first, the second, and the third ages, has been used for the purpose of a distinct arrangement of the arguments adduced to explain the superstitious, feudal, and fiscal modes of enslaving nations, by placing the powers in the hands of a minority; an effect, however produced, denominated aristocracy throughout this essay. But it is not intended to insinuate, that the causes of aristocracy have generally acted singly; on the contrary, they more frequently unite.

It was necessary thoroughly to understand the most prominent causes of aristocracy, before we proceeded to a closer examination of our civil policy, and Mr. Adams's principles; in order to keep in mind that we have never seen a venerated and wealthy hierarchy, an army stronger than the nation, an endowed, titled and privileged order of men, or an incorporated, enriched or united faction, without having at the same time seen the aristocracy of the first, the second, or the third age. By recollecting this testimony, derived from universal experience, an inference, equivalent to mathematical certainty, 'that such ends will eternally flow from such means,' will unavoidably present itself.

Few would deny these premises or the inference, if it was proposed to revive oracles or feudal services. These causes of aristocracy are distinctly seen, because they do not exist. They have no counsel in court. They are, therefore, better understood than when they flourished. But both the premises and the inference are denied when they implicate the aristocracy of paper and patronage. This cause of aristocracy is not seen, because it does exist; and the more oppressive it shall become, the greater will be the difficulty of discovering its existence. The two first are exposed naked to our view; and the third, disguised in the garb of republicanism, and uttering patriotick words, joins the mob in kicking them about, by way of diverting the publick attention from itself. An opinion that aristocracy can only exist in the form of a hereditary order, or a hierarchy, is equivalent to an opinion, that the science of geometry can only be illustrated by a square or a triangle.

Section the Second

THE PRINCIPLES OF THE POLICY
OF THE UNITED STATES,
AND OF THE ENGLISH POLICY

B<small>EFORE</small> we proceed to the consideration of the policy of the United States, it is necessary to discover a political analysis, founded in some moral principle; because government is as strictly subject to the moral, as a physical being is to the physical laws of nature. Persons are not principles; and hence the operations of monarchy, aristocracy and democracy (governments founded in persons) are fluctuating; generally evil, but sometimes good; whereas the effects of a moral principle are ever the same. Mr. Adams, however, adopts the ancient analysis of governments, asserts that it comprises all their generical forms, and adds 'that every society naturally produces an order of men, which it is impossible to confine to an equality of rights;' and he erects his system upon the foundations of this ancient analysis, and of a natural or unavoidable aristocracy. If society cannot exist without aristocracy, (as it cannot, if aristocracy is natural to society,) then democracy and monarchy cannot be generical forms of government, unless they can exist without society or with aristocracy. This disagreement between the ancient analysis, and a system bottomed upon it, at the threshold of their association; and Mr. Adams's idea that one of his generical forms of government was a natural consequence of society, without contending that the others were, excited doubts of the correctness of that analysis. If monarchy, aristocracy and democracy are all natural or generical forms of government, nature has determined on Mr. Adams's mixed government, and his labours in favour of her will, were superfluous; but if either of these forms is artificial, it could not be natural or generical, and an invention of one form by the human intellect, is no proof that it is unable to invent another. The terms monarchy, aristocracy and democracy, convey adequate ideas of

94

particular forms of government, but they are insufficient for the purpose of disclosing a government which will certainly be free and moderate, since the effects of each depend on the administration of wise and good, or of weak and wicked men: and all are therefore founded in the same principle, however differing in form. This both suggests a doubt of the soundness of the ancient analysis, and a solution of the phenomenon 'that all these natural or generical forms of government should produce bad effects.' The effects of these three forms are bad, because they are all founded on one principle, namely, an irresponsible undivided power; and that principle is bad. We want an analysis, distinguishing governments in point of substance, and not limited to form.

The moral qualities of human nature are good and evil. An analysis founded in this truth, however general, can alone ascertain the true character, and foretell the effects, of any form of government, or of any social measure. Every such form and measure must have a tendency to excite the good or the evil moral qualities of man; and according to its source, so will be its tendency with moral certainty.

The strongest moral propensity of man, is to do good to himself. This begets a propensity to do evil to others, for the sake of doing good to himself. A sovereignty of the people, or self-government, is suggested by the first moral propensity; responsibility, division, and an exclusion of monarchy and aristocracy, by the second.

Self love, being the strongest motive to do evil to others, as well as good to ourselves, will operate as forcibly to excite an individual or a faction to injure a nation for advancing self good, as to excite a nation to preserve its own happiness. Therefore, whilst national self government, is founded in the strongest moral quality for producing national good; every other species of government, is founded in the strongest moral quality for producing national evil.

The objection to this analysis is, that nations may oppress individuals or minorities. An imperfection does not destroy comparative superiority; and should one be found in a form of government bottomed upon the quality of a nation's love for itself, it will not diminish the defects of forms, bottomed upon the self love of individuals or minorities, if these are as likely to oppress majorities, as majorities are to oppress these.

The quality, self love, stimulates in proportion to the good or gratification in view. This prospect to an individual or minority, having power to extract good or gratification from a nation, must

95

be infinitely more alluring, than to a nation, having power to extract good or gratification from an individual or a minority; and as the excitement to injure others, for gratifying ourselves, will be in proportion to the extent of the gratification, it follows, that an individual or minority will be infinitely more likely to oppress a nation for self gratification, than a nation, for the same end, to oppress an individual or minority.

The certainty with which moral inferences flow from moral causes, is illustrated by a computation of the cases, in which the quality of self love, has induced nations to oppress individuals, or individuals to oppress nations. The anomaly of a nation's becoming a tyrant over an individual, would be nearer to the character of prodigy, than even that of monarchy or aristocracy, preferring national good or gratification, to its own.

It is from the want of some test, to determine whether a form of government, or law, is founded in the good or evil qualities of man, that the disciples of monarchy, aristocracy and democracy, have entered into the field of controversy, with so much zeal. Each, though blinded to the defects of the system he defends, from education, habit, or a supposed necessity of enlisting under one, clearly discerns the defects of the system espoused by his adversary; and despises him for a blindness, similar to his own. That monarchy, aristocracy and democracy will all make men miserable, is universally assented to, by two out of the three members of this analysis itself; and a contrary effect from either, is allowed by two to one to be out of the common course of events. A violation of the relation between cause and effect, awakens the admiration of mankind, whenever a good moral effect proceeds from a government founded in evil moral qualities.

It is not enough for the illustration of our analysis, that a good effect from either monarchy, aristocracy or democracy, is by this majority considered as a phenomenon; a few reasons, accounting for it according to the principles of that analysis, will be added.

Monarchy and aristocracy, have the strongest tendency of any conceivable human situation, to excite the evil moral quality, or propensity, of injuring others for our own benefit, both by the magnitude of the temptation, and the power of reaching it. A long catalogue of evil moral qualities, are included in this. These forms of government are therefore founded in the evil moral qualities of man, and it is unnatural that evil moral qualities, should produce good moral effects.

96

Mr. Adams allows that evil consequences unavoidably arise from monarchy and aristocracy, by endeavouring to provide against them. The probable success of his endeavour will appear, by concisely reciting their cause. It consists in a degree of power capable of exciting evil moral qualities, craving self gratification at the expense of others. Nothing can prevent this excitement, but a removal of the power; and if the power is removed, the principle of monarchy or aristocracy is destroyed, though the name should remain. Mr. Adams's remedy can only remove the cause or leave the cause. If it remains, the effects follow. Our state governours would not be monarchs or despots, if they were called kings; because they want the degree of power necessary to excite and bring into action, the evil moral qualities of monarchs or despots. Henry the eighth would have been a monarch or despot, though he had been called governour, because he possessed that degree of power. His species of government was founded in evil, and that of the States in good moral qualities.

Democracy is not less calculated to excite evil moral qualities of one kind, than monarchy and aristocracy of another. By democracy is meant, a nation exercising personally the functions of government. Turbulence, instability, injustice, suspicion, ingratitude, and excess of gratitude, are among the evil moral qualities, which this form of government has a tendency to excite. Democracy, therefore, is a form of government founded in evil moral qualities.

All these forms of government were intended to be destroyed in America, and a government, founded in the good moral qualities of man to be erected; that is, one which would cautiously avoid to excite his evil qualities, and carefully attempt to suppress them if they should appear.

Democracy was destroyed by election; and one errour of Mr. Adams consists in proposing to bring into the field monarchy and aristocracy, after their plebeian foe no longer exists. As election has destroyed democracy, election, responsibility and division of power, were intended also to destroy monarchy and aristocracy. And if democracy may be destroyed, or at least filtered of its evil moral qualities by election, why may not monarchy and aristocracy be destroyed or filtered of their evil qualities likewise by election, responsibility and a division of power? Or if for the sake of a balance of orders, it would be adviseable to revive monarchy and aristocracy in their natural malignancy, ought not democracy to be also revived in its natural malignancy, to make out a complete system of checks and balances, in conformity to the ideas of Aristotle, who is quoted by Mr. Adams?

Aristotle, and all the ancient authors, by the term 'democracy,' intended to describe a nation, legislating, judging and sometimes even executing in person. Such is the form of government to which is ascribed all the evils of democracy, and which has in reality produced those evils. And Mr. Adams has transplanted all these evils from this ancient democracy into his book, as charges against the elective and responsible system of America; with what degree of justice, will depend upon a resemblance between our system, and a nation exercising political and civil power within the walls of Athens or Rome. The democracy of Athens, and our policy, were founded in principles exactly opposite to each other. One was calculated to excite a multitude of evil moral qualities, which the other will suppress, by representation, responsibility and division. An imperfect representation in England, suppressed the evil effects attached to the Athenian democracy, and though imperfect, evinced the excellence of the principle of representation, by moderating the malignancy of monarchy and aristocracy. Had democracy, monarchy and aristocracy, according to the ancient ideas annexed to these terms, been mingled and balanced, a government would have been produced, which may be contemplated, by placing an English king at the head of the democracy and aristocracy of Rome. By the addition of one good principle to two bad ones, the paroxysms of good, and the predominance of evil, under the English form, are accounted for. And by removing the evil principles, monarchy and aristocracy, to make room for division and responsibility; as the evil principle, democracy, has been removed by representation; mankind will probably escape the calamities inflicted by these evil principles, on the English nation.

The inherent evil nature of monarchy, aristocracy and democracy, can only furnish a solution of the fact, testified by all history, 'that each separately, any two, and the three however mingled, have uniformly produced evil effects, which have driven mankind into a multitude of exchanges and modifications.' From all, disappointment has issued, because good effects could not be extracted from evil principles. At length, all philosophers, politicians and learned men have been taught by experience to unite in one opinion. They universally agree, that monarchy, aristocracy and democracy, acting separately, will produce evil to nations; they agree, that any two will operate oppressively; and they also agree that the three, however blended, excluding the modern idea of representation, will also operate oppressively. Is it then possible, that the ancient analysis of political systems, which separately or combined, presented only a form of government now universally acknowledged to be bad, could have been correct?

From a belief that a political analysis does exist, capable of arranging all forms of government into two classes; one rooted in good, and the other in evil moral qualities; and that monarchy, aristocracy and democracy, singly or united, belong to the latter class; the idea has been brought before the reader preparatory to arguments designed to prove, that the civil policy of the United States must be assigned to the first class; that it is of course at enmity with Mr. Adams's mixture of monarchy, aristocracy and representation; but that certain of its details and laws, are at enmity with its essential principles, for want of some distinct analysis as a test to ascertain their nature and effects. A position contended for is, 'that political temptations, which propel to vice, are founded in evil moral principles.'

The reader is solicited for the last time, to keep in mind, that in this essay, the term 'democracy' means 'a government administered by the people,' and not 'the right of the people to institute a government, nor the responsibility of magistrates to the people.' The contrast of the ancient analysis between its three forms of government, is imperfect unless democracy is thus understood, since the two terms opposed to it, are used to specify governments, as numerically administered. Monarchy and aristocracy mean, governments administered by one or a few, and not a right in one or a few to institute a government, and make it responsible to the institutor. Democracy also meant, a government administered by the people personally. The distinction is considered as useful, for relieving the mind from an association, between the sovereignty of the people, and the evils produced by a nation's exercising the functions of government.

Let us now take up the thread of this essay. I have endeavoured to prove that aristocracy is artificial and not natural; that the aristocracies of superstition and landed wealth, have been destroyed by knowledge, commerce and alienation; that a new aristocracy has arisen during the last century from paper and patronage, of a character so different from titled orders, as not to be compressible within Mr. Adams's system; and that his system is evidently defective, in having silently past over this powerful aristocracy, now existing in England.

By the civil policy of the United States, I mean the general and state constitutions, as forming one system. Most of the state constitutions existed when Mr. Adams wrote, and no new principles have been introduced by those since created. The differences among them all, consist only in modifications of the same principles. As immaterial is the anachronism of applying Mr. Adams's reasoning to the general constitution, because if his system is inimical to that, it must have been more so to the state constitutions he professed to defend; as in that, the executive and senatorial lines are drawn with a stronger pencil than in those.*

Mr. Adams's system simply is, 'that nature will create an aristocracy, and that policy ought to create a king, or a single, independent executive power, and a house of popular representatives, to balance it.'

Let one of the state constitutions speak for the rest. That of Massachusetts declares, that 'all men are born free and equal.' That 'no man, or corporation, or association of men, have any other title to obtain advantages, or particular and exclusive privileges, distinct from those of the community, than what arises from the consideration of services, rendered to the publick. And this title being, *in nature*, neither hereditary, nor transmissible to children, or descendants, or relations by blood, the idea of a man born a magistrate, law giver or judge, is absurd and unnatural.' 'That the people have the sole and exclusive right of governing themselves.' That 'government is instituted for the common good, for the protection, safety, prosperity, and happiness of the people; and not for the profit, honour, or private interest of any one man, family, or class of men.' And that 'in order to prevent those, who are vested with authority, from becoming oppressors, the people have a right, at such periods, and in such manner, as they shall establish by their frame of government, to cause their publick officers to return to private life; and to fill up vacant places, by certain and regular elections and appointments.' Two principles are clearly expressed by them all; one, that every person in authority is responsible and removable; the other, that talents, virtue, and political power, are not inheritable.

These principles are precisely levelled at the opinions, that

* Adams's Def. v. 3, 187 & 426.

monarchy is divine, and nobility natural; the first asserted by Filmer, the last by Mr. Adams. And they treat the idea of hereditary power, contended for by Mr. Adams, as '*absurd and unnatural.*'*

The constitutions build their policy upon the basis of human equality—'all men are born free and equal;' and erect the artificial inequalities of civil government, with a view of preserving and defending the natural equality of individuals. Mr. Adams builds his policy upon the basis of human inequality by nature—'aristocracy is natural;' and proposes to produce an artificial level or equality, not of individuals, but of orders, composed of individuals naturally unequal. Yet the disciples of the balance, accuse the republicans of levelism.

It is necessary to affix a correct idea to the term 'equality,' contended for by the constitutions, and denied by Mr. Adams. They do not mean an equality of stature, strength or understanding, but an equality of moral rights and duties. The constitutions admit of no inequality in these moral rights and duties, excepting that produced by temporary and responsible power, conferred 'for the common good.' Mr. Adams contends for a natural inequality of moral rights and duties, in contending for a natural aristocracy. The constitutions establish the inequalities of temporary and responsible power, with a view of maintaining an equality of moral rights and duties among the individuals of society; and Mr. Adams proposes orders, with a view of maintaining his natural inequality among men, by balancing or equalising the rights of orders.

The constitutions consider a nation as made of individuals; Mr. Adams's system, as made of orders. Nature, by the constitutions, is considered as the creator of men; by the system, of orders. The first idea suggests the sovereignty of the people, and the second refutes it; because, if nature creates the ranks of the one, the few and the many, the nation must be compounded of these ranks; and one rank, politically, is the third part of a nation. These ranks composing the nation, have of course a power to alter the form of government at any time, without consulting the people, because the people do not constitute the nation. An illustration of this idea has several times occurred in the English practice of Mr. Adams's system.

By most of the constitutions, a plural executive is created; by a few, a qualified negative upon laws is given to the executive power; but in all, that power is made subordinate to the legislative power.

* Mr. Adams calls Filmer's notions 'ABSURD AND SUPERSTITIOUS.'—Vol. 1, 7.

Mr. Adams declares, that a single executive, having an unqualified negative upon the laws, and power sufficient to defend himself against the other two branches of the legislature, is essential to his system.

In short, Mr. Adams's system is bottomed upon a classification of men; our constitutions, upon an application of moral principles to human nature. He arranges men into the one, the few and the many, and bestows on the one and the few, more power than he gives to the many, to counterbalance numerical or˙ physical strength; our constitutions divide power with a view to the responsibility of the agent, and jealous of the danger of accumulating great power in the hands of one or a few, because all history proves that this species of condensation begets tyranny, bestow most power on their most numerous functionary.

Mr. Godwin, in his 'Political Justice,' v. 2. p. 180, asserts that 'scarcely any plausible argument can be adduced in favour of what has been denominated by political writers a division of power.' This authoritative decision seems to have been made, without any consideration of the ground upon which a division of power is justified in this essay. Mr. Adams confines a division of power, to a division of orders of men; Mr. Godwin extends it to a division of orders of power, such as legislative, executive and judicative; but this essay, considering a classification of power into orders, as little less erroneous than a classification of men, extends the idea of its division to the counteraction of monopoly in any form, by a man, an order or a government, in a degree sufficient to excite ambition, avarice or despotism. This idea of a division of power is consonant to the policy of the United States, as is evinced by the responsibility of the executive, the allotments of power to the state and the general governments, and the reservations from the powers of both, retained by the people; and is distinct from the ideas both of Mr. Adams and Mr. Godwin. The latter gentleman's opinions in favour of a division of property, and against a division of power, are inconsistent, if a monopoly of either, will beget a monopoly of both; if wealth attracts power, and power wealth. The same principles dictate a distribution of both; and the same effects flow from an accumulation of either. A law of primogeniture in respect to power, is similar to a law of primogeniture in respect to property. The objection to both is comprised in their enmity to the principle of division. This subject will occur again in a subsequent part of this essay.

Let us pause, and take a glance at the title of Mr. Adams's treatise. Why was it called 'a defence of the constitutions of government of the United States of America?' It assails the principle, upon which these constitutions are founded; it asserts doctrines which they condemn; and it justifies a system of government which would be a revolution of them all. If this unsuitable title, arose from an incapacity to distinguish between the principles of our policy, and those of a system of balanced orders, the errour is pardonable, and only destroys the authority of the treatise; but if it was an artifice, to mask under a pretended affection for our principles of government, an attack upon them, the erudition of the treatise will not be able to conceal, nor the freedom of political disquisition to justify, the insincerity of such an intention.

To prove the correctness of this criticism, it is necessary to return more particularly to Mr. Adams's treatise, for the purpose of elucidating its drift beyond the possibility of misapprehension. Thus also we shall advance in a knowledge of the policy of the United States, and of that of England; which are important objects of this essay.

The pretext for Mr. Adams's treatise, appears in the first page of the first volume, in the following extract of a letter from Mr. Turgot, to Doctor Price: 'that he is not satisfied with the constitutions which have hitherto been formed for the different States of America. That by most of them *the customs of England are imitated,* without any particular motive. Instead of collecting all authority into one centre, *that of the nation,* they have established different bodies, *a body of representatives,* a *council,* and a *governour,* because there is in England a house of commons, a house of lords, and a king. They endeavour to *balance these different powers,* as if this equilibrium, which in England may be a necessary check to the enormous influence of royalty, could be of any use in republicks founded upon the equality of all the citizens, and as if *establishing different orders of men was not a source of divisions and disputes.'*

Against this charge, Mr. Adams exhibits a defence for the constitutions in a mode entirely new. He labours to prove that every word of it is true, and that the balance of power, and orders of men, spoken of by Mr. Turgot, have been borrowed by us from England, and do in fact constitute the only good form of government.

The task of proving the charge untrue, would have been much easier. I will concisely endeavour to do so, before I proceed in the examination of the use Mr. Adams has made of it.

A celebrated author has pronounced in a tone of great authority, that 'government is in all cases an evil.'* This assertion, and Mr. Turgot's misconception, are founded in the same errour; that of contemplating monarchy, aristocracy and democracy, as an analysis comprising every form of government. These being all founded in evil moral principles, would produce evil effects, and Mr. Godwin beholding this fact, pronounces 'that government is in all cases an evil,' because he had not conceived any other elements of governments, except those of monarchy, aristocracy and democracy; and these producing much evil, his remedy is to destroy government itself. But had he considered, that government could not be an evil, if it was founded in principles which would excite the good moral qualities of human nature, he would have searched for some such form, capable of excluding monarchy, aristocracy and democracy, all of which produce evil, because of their tendency to excite man's evil qualities.

The same analysis led Mr. Turgot into a misconception of the principles of our policy. Supposing us to be tied down to a form compounded of the whole analysis, or of one or two members of it, and preferring democracy to a mixed government, he concluded that our governments were compounded of the whole analysis, because he could not discern the object of his preference; and in not being able to discern democracy among our state constitutions, Mr. Turgot justifies the idea, which supposes that the evil 'democracy' is as capable of remedy, as the evils 'monarchy and aristocracy,' and that it is actually removed by our system of government.

Mr. Turgot, not seeing the object of his preference, hastily concluded our policy to have copied the English; and founds his conclusion in an opinion, that it makes state governours kings, balances powers, and establishes orders of men. All this is obviously erroneous. We have less of monarchy and aristocracy in our policy, both of which he pretends to see, than of democracy, which he could not see. Instead of balancing power, we divide it and make it responsible, to prevent the evils of its accumulation in the hands of one interest. And such is the force of this principle of dividing power, to excite the good, and suppress the evil qualities of man, that among several hundred state governours who have already existed, not one instance has appeared of kingly qualities, of usurpation, or of war between neighbouring states. Why have the state governments escaped the evils of monarchy? For the same

* Godwin on Pol. Jus: v. 2, 211.

reason that they have escaped those of aristocracy and democracy. This example of the good moral conduct of their governours, testifies to the correctness of our analysis. Instead of monarchy, which excites evil qualities, our division (not a balance) of power, renders it responsible, and brings good qualities out of governours; and instead of a tumultuary nation, election, by division also, is filtered of its worst vice, and brings good qualities out of the mass of the people. Whereas a balance of power or a balance of orders (for it will amount to the same thing) has constantly produced a spirit as bitter as the animosity between rival clans, and caused distraction and misery, until the latter becomes permanent in a despotism, begotten by the predominance of one order or of one power.

Mr. Turgot's errour in supposing our constitutions to have been formed by the English model, and his condemnation of such an imitation, afforded an opportunity precisely fitted for Mr. Adams's purpose. He assumes our defence against the condemnation, and assails Mr. Turgot's preference for collecting all authority into one centre. In justifying us against Turgot's condemnation for having copied the English system, it was incumbent on Mr. Adams to prove that system to be the most perfect model of civil policy; in endeavouring to effect this, he was enabled to make some use of our prepossessions, by scattering in his first volume a few compliments to our constitutions; these however are bestowed upon them as copies, but like copies, they are presently forgotten in the admiration excited by the original.

Turgot condemns a balance of power, and different orders of men, and approves of collecting all authority into one centre, the nation. Mr. Adams tacitly admits our constitutions to be artificers of this balance and these orders, converts Turgot's centre into a single chamber of representatives, engages these phantoms in hostility, and astounds us with history, anecdote, poetry and fable, to prove— what? That Mr. Turgot was mistaken in supposing that there were political orders created by our constitutions? No. To prove that such orders naturally existed, and that no good government could be formed, except by balancing power among such orders.

Whether Mr. Turgot approves or not, of concentrating all power in a single house of representatives, is immaterial; except that Mr. Adams, by supposing him to do so, has very artificially interwoven, an assault upon that idea, a vindication of a mixed or limited monarchy, and a few slight compliments to our constitutions. He uses the constitutions as a weak ally in carrying on the war against Turgot's centre of power, places the system of limited monarchy in the van of the battle, and gives it all the credit of conscious victory.

Turgot's idea of 'collecting all authority into one centre,' 'that of the nation,' might possibly have extended to national sovereignty only, without condemning a distribution of power among publick functionaries by a moderate scale; but Mr. Adams, by making that centre to consist of one house of representatives, seized upon the strongest ground for exhibiting representative government in distortion. To render monarchy most hateful, all power ought to be exhibited in the hands of a single man; so to render representation hateful, the best exhibition, is all power in the hands of a single house. We caricature what we wish to make odious, and adorn what we wish to recommend. Thus Mr. Adams contrasts republicanism in its most hideous, with monarchy, in its most becoming dress. One he adorns with his checks and balances, his jealousy among orders, and his patrician virtues; and tells no tale of woe produced by its vices: the other he places in a centre of monopoly, from whence she is made to hurl legislative, executive and judicial destruction on friends and enemies. It is admitted that the object of his embellishment, might possibly be some relief against the monster disfigured for its foil.

But the question so important to America, is not to be thus eluded. Because Mr. Turgot has charged us with having established governments, bottomed upon the English system of balancing classes of power, and creating orders of men; and because Mr. Adams has defended our governments against this charge, not by denying it, but by endeavouring to prove that system to be the best; it does not follow that our political policy is really that of the English. It only results from the charge and defence, that Mr. Turgot condemned and Mr. Adams approved of the English policy. And although Mr. Adams has been pleased to engage that policy in hostilities with Turgot's phantasm, of concentrating all power in one chamber of representatives, (if such an opinion is justly ascribed to him) a victory on either side can furnish no conclusion or inference applicable to the civil policy of the United States. That consists neither of Mr. Adams's orders and balance, nor of Turgot's chamber. It stands aloof, and like a giant looks down without interest on this pigmy war. Shall one of the pigmies, because he has beaten the other, be considered as having also obtained a victory over the giant?

The question is not to be eluded. Whether Mr. Turgot's chamber, or Mr. Adams's orders and balances, constitute the best form of government, is not a question with which the United States have any concern; and that is the question discussed by Mr. Adams. If he has gained a victory over Turgot, it is not a victory also over the policy of the United States, unless that policy is Turgot's, though disclaimed by him; nor is our policy entitled to any share of his laurels, unless it is, as Turgot asserted, the English policy.

However disguised, the true question is discernible. It simply is, whether the existing form of government of the United States, or the English limited monarchy is preferable. It is in this question that we are interested. This question has not been discussed by Mr. Adams, in mauling Turgot's chamber with his balances. But we ought to acquire a thorough knowledge of the English system and its principles, and of our own system and its principles, to discover wherein they differ, and to bestow with justice the contested preference. Much of our labour has already been appropriated towards this important object; more is yet necessary. At present we will proceed in our endeavours to ascertain with preciseness the opinion of the author upon whose work we are commenting.

Mr. Adams's second volume commences with the following motto: 'As for *us Englishmen*, thank heaven we have a better sense of government delivered to us from our ancestors. We have the notion of a publick, and a constitution; how a legislature, and how an executive is moulded; we understand weight and measure in this kind, and can reason justly on the *balance of power and property. The maxims we draw from hence, are as evident as those of mathematicks.* Our increasing knowledge, shows every day what common sense is in politicks.'*

In a motto, an author condenses his opinion and his subject to the utmost of his power. This combines a strong idea of the English system, with a stronger approbation of it. No preference can be stronger than one founded in mathematical evidence; and no room remains for farther political discovery, after mathematical demonstration. If the English system possesses this degree of perfection, it excels ours by the confession of our constitutions, in provisions for their own improvement.

Shaftesbury wrote this sentence, about a century past, when the system of paper and patronage was neither understood nor felt in

* In the edition of 1757, the words are 'us Britons.'—Extracted from Shaftesbury's Charact. v. 1, part 3d, sec. 1, p. 83.

England, and when a portion of the landed wealth of the nobility remained, sufficient to bestow some importance upon that order. What does he say produced these mathematical political maxims of the English system? 'A balance of power and property:' power and property are the indissoluble companions by which the system was regulated. If property and nobility became divided, would power and nobility continue united? Neither the actual nor comparative wealth of the English nobility is now what it was a century past. Paper systems, patronage and commerce, have overturned the balance which furnished Shaftesbury's mathematical political maxims. And as according to these maxims, power with mathematical certainty will follow property, so the existence of the aristocracy of paper and patronage, contended for by this essay, is established upon Lord Shaftesbury's principles, and by Mr. Adams's motto.

When Lord Shaftesbury wrote, the balance of property in England was created on the part of the king, by the domains annexed to his office, by certain pecuniary acquisitions derived from prerogative, by some patronage, and by an annuity for life; and on the part of the nobility, by the extent and value of their manors. Now, the last weight, is no longer in the scale; and the first, has become ponderous. Is the balance between these two orders, even without taking into the account the new weight created by paper and patronage, what it was a century past? If not, will different weights, a new or a broken balance, supply Mr. Adams with the same mathematical maxims of government, which Shaftesbury, mathematically also, extracted from a different balance?

Both these authors unequivocally affirm the necessity of a balance of property, whereon to establish the balance of power constituting the English system. Let us apply this awful acknowledgment to the situation of the United States, without suffering political prejudice to suspend our judgments. Does this balance of property, indispensable to the British and Mr. Adams's system, in the opinion of Shaftesbury and Mr. Adams, exist here? If not, with what propriety has Mr. Adams contended that his system, was the system of the United States? Of his, this balance of property is the essence; of theirs, it forms no part.

The admitted necessity of a balance of property, for the existence of Mr. Adams's system, unfolds visibly to every politician, however superficial, that his system cannot exist without it; and the mode of introducing a balance of property here, is then to be considered.

By two ways only, has it ever been effected in England. First, by royal domains and feudal baronies. Secondly, by a million annuity, executive patronage, and the paper system. To effect this balance of property here in the first mode, it would be necessary to strip a sufficient number of landholders of their property, for the purpose of creating a landed king, and a landed aristocracy; but as this mode of making a balance of property among orders, would be too direct to be safe, the observation only furnishes a conclusive proof, that a landed aristocracy can never be created in the United States, as a member of Mr. Adams's system.

The other mode of coming at this balance, is to transfer property to the system of paper and patronage. And this being the only practicable mode, those who calculate that the system of balancing power and property, will bestow on them an unequal share of both, will use it as the only means of advancing that system. This would create a monopoly of property, not by taking the lands from the owners directly, but by taking their profits indirectly, with charters of profit, stock and patronage. By this mode, the president must be endowed with the patronage and the annual million of the king of England, to bestow on him the wealth necessary to form one order, and a monied aristocracy must be raised by such pretexts as may occur, to create another.

The motto therefore proposes two questions for the reader's consideration. One, whether this English system of balancing power and property, as existing when Shaftesbury wrote, or at this time, is the system of the United States; the other, whether it would be wise or just in the United States, to exchange their system for it.

To determine the first question, the fact will suffice. That, as stated by Lord Shaftesbury, and contended for by Mr. Adams, simply is, that an allotment of property and power is necessary among the one, the few and the many, to sustain or create, the English or Mr. Adams's system of government. And it is explicitly declared, that this allotment must amount to a balance or an equality. Hence, it is obvious, that the orders consisting of the one and the few, must each be endowed with a portion of power and property equal to that bestowed on the order consisting of the many. Therefore the system can neither subsist or be introduced without a vast accumulation of power and property in the individual and the minor order. Such is the fact on one side. On the other, it is a fact equally undeniable, that it is the policy of the United States to divide, and not to accumulate power and property. It follows that the system of balancing power and property in the hands of orders, is not the system of the United States.

To determine the second question, the argument of this essay must be estimated. Here it is only necessary to remark, that the wisdom of an exchange of our system for Mr. Adams's, will often be affirmed or denied by the dictates of self interest. Requiring as it does, that two thirds of the power and property of the nation, should be transferred to the one, and the few, it is probable that those who expect a share of this acquisition, so wonderfully adapted to solicit the exertions of ambition and avarice, will attempt to persuade us, that the exchange would be wise; on the contrary, as the order of the many, must furnish nearly the whole of the power and property necessary to bring up the two other orders to a balance with itself, it is as probable, that no individual, who understands the subject, and believes that he will be a member of the order to be despoiled, will approve of the exchange. He will see, that to make orders equal in power and property, is to make individuals unequal; and that it would be simply a case of dividing twelve millions of children belonging to one man, into three orders, of one, of about one hundred and fifty, and of eleven millions nine hundred and ninety nine thousand, eight hundred and forty nine; and of bestowing one third of the inheritance upon each order. It is very conceivable that the individuals who composed the two first orders, might be very well pleased with the system of such a balance of power and property, and that those belonging to the third, would have no great cause to rejoice. Nor would a child of the multitude, be easily convinced of the justice and wisdom of the system of balancing power and property, by a difference in the mode of effecting it; whether this was done by the force of the feudal system, or the fraud of paper and patronage, would make no difference in the consequences to him. He would therefore prefer the inequalities produced by talents and industry, to the system of levelling orders.

We will now proceed with our quotations, to exhibit a few of the amplifications of this motto to be found throughout Mr. Adams's second and third volumes, his unqualified approbation of its doctrine, and his unsuccessful efforts to compress the policy of the United States within its tenour.

'When it is found in experience, and appears probable in theory, that so simple an invention as a separate executive, with power to defend itself, is a full remedy against the fatal effects of dissentions between nobles and commons, why should we still finally hope that simple governments, or mixtures of two ingredients only, will produce effects which they never did, and we know never can? Why should the people be still deceived with insinuations, that these evils arose from the destiny of a particular city, when we know that destiny common to all mankind?'*

It is obvious that Mr. Adams is here contemplating monarchy, aristocracy and democracy, and not moral principles, as the only ingredients of government; and that in his division of power, he thinks it necessary to assign to the executive order (which he in other places limits to a single person) a quota, sufficient to enable him to defend himself against the plebeian order. In the United States, the executive power is dependent on the people. The quota of power cannot by his system be given, without a correspondent balance of wealth. The wealth then of Mr. Adams's executive order, must also balance the wealth of the plebeian order.

The assertion, that neither one nor two of these ingredients, can produce effects correspondent to our hopes, though exactly as true, as that a mixture of all three will equally disappoint us, positively affirms the necessity of this mixture; and when coupled with the deception into which such hopes have seduced the people, acknowledges, both that- the policy of the United States did not embrace this mixture, and that it was an experiment unpromising in theory, and forbidden by experience. The treatise is addressed to the people of the United States; no other people who could come to a knowledge of it, entertained an enmity in 1786, against kings and nobles; the deprecated deception and the political errour, alleged in the extract, to exist, must therefore exclusively refer to the publick opinion of the people of the United States, and to the texture of their governments. And thus are justified by the admission of Mr. Adams, the opinions asserted in this essay; that our policy is not the English; and that Mr. Adams, instead of defending it, as he proposed, has, under colour of refuting Turgot's project of a single centre of power, laboured to establish its inferiority to the English system.

'Here was the *best possible opportunity* for introducing the *most perfect form*, by giving the executive power to one of the Medici, the

---

* Adams's Def. v, 2, 53. The third Philadelphia edition is quoted throughout this essay.

power of the purse to the people, and the legislative power to both, together with the *nobility*.'*

The *best possible opportunity* in this extract spoken of, was a conjuncture in the history of Florence, at which the people expelled an usurper or a monarch of the Medicean family, and attempted to establish a popular government. That conjuncture was analogous to our expulsion of a monarch of the Guelph family. The Florentine conjuncture, says Mr. Adams, afforded the best possible opportunity for introducing the *most perfect form* of government, namely that of king, lords and commons. And the king was to be taken from the usurping and expelled family.

The last extract consisted of a positive declaration, that limited monarchy was the most perfect form of government, and a positive opinion as to the best conjuncture for introducing it. The following is of a similar character.

'The sovereign or rather the first magistrate of this monarchical republick, is the king of Prussia. Without descending to a particular account, of this *princely* republick, let me refer you to the Dictionaire de la Martiniere, and to Faber, printed at the end of the sixth volume of it, and to Coxe's sketches, and to conclude with hinting at a few features of this *excellent* constitution. None but natives are capable of holding any office, civil or military, excepting that of governor. The three *estates* shall be assembled every year. The magistrates and officers of justice shall hold their employments during good behaviour; nor is the king the judge of ill behaviour. The *king* at his accession takes an *oath* to maintain all rights, liberties, franchises, and customs, written or unwritten. The king is considered as resident only at Neuchattel, and therefore when absent can only address the citizens through his governour and the council of state. No citizen can be *tried out of the country* or otherwise than by the judges. *The prince confers nobility*, and nominates to the principal offices of state, civil and military. *The prince in his absence is represented by a governor of his own appointing.* He convokes the three estates.'†

It is not intended to insult the reader by pointing out the several eulogies upon monarchy and orders in this extract, nor is it hardly necessary to draw his attention to a repetition of an idea similar to that furnished by the preceding. In that, the reward of an usurping family, by placing one of it on a throne, would, it was said, have been good policy; and that the era of its expulsion, was the best

* Adams's Def. v. 2, 163. † Ibid., v. 2, 446 & 448.

possible opportunity for this experiment. In this, a government of orders, in which the king is absent, is said to be an 'excellent constitution.' Added to the absence of the king, the exclusion from office of all except natives, three estates assembled annually, a coronation oath, a fiction to acquire the presence of the king, trial within the country, a right in the prince to confer nobility and appoint officers, and a locum tenens king called governor, comprise every feature of the Neuchattel constitution, urged to convince us of its excellence.

I remember to have seen a book nearly contemporary with Mr. Adams's defence, written by a Sir John Dalrymple, an Englishman, containing a proposition for a reunion between England and the United States, upon terms nearly similar to the constitution of Neuchattel, celebrated by Mr. Adams. And had these two gentlemen been appointed plenipotentiaries to treat of this proposal, the ônly point for discussion which seems to have been left unsettled by the extract and Dalrymple's book, would have been, whether Neuchattel, in Switzerland, as divided from Prussia by land, was more commodiously situated for a Prussian, than the United States, for an English king.

As to the preferable form of government, no disagreement could have happened between the negociators, unless the following quotations are really eulogies upon our own policy.

'But there is a form of government which produces a love of law, liberty and country, instead of disorder, irregularity and a faction; which produces as much and more independence of spirit, and as much undaunted bravery; as much esteem of merit in preference to wealth, and as great simplicity, sincerity and generosity to all the community, as others do to a faction; which produces as great a desire of knowledge, and infinitely better faculties to pursue it; which besides *produces security of property*, and the desire and opportunities for commerce, which the others obstruct. *Shall any one hesitate then to prefer such a government to all others?* A constitution in which *the people reserve to themselves the absolute control of their purses, one essential branch of the legislature*, and the inquest of grievances and state crimes, will always produce patriotism, bravery, simplicity and science; and that infinitely better for the order, security, and tranquillity they will enjoy, *by putting the executive power in one hand*, which it becomes their interest, *as well as that of the nobles*, to watch and control.'*

* Adams's Def. v. 2, 387 & 388.

This quotation contains the precise opinion, which it is the design of this essay to controvert. Dismissing Turgot's phantom of a single house of representatives, Mr. Adams considers the people as an order, electing only one branch of the legislature, having no control over a single executive, and aided by nobles to watch and control this monarch; for when the people have made a king to check nobles, these nobles are to join the people in checking the king. And the approbation of such a form of government is as unbounded, as the censure of every other is unequivocal. That, he asserts, will produce a long string of blessings; others, specified calamities of great magnitude. Not a single defect is ascribed to the object of the eulogy, nor a single perfection to any other form. The words cannot be tortured to bring our policy within the sphere of the eulogy, nor to exclude it from that of the censure. And the English system is unequivocally preferred *without hesitation to all others*.

A single remark only will be made upon this encomium. The system of orders is said to produce security of property. But the system requires that property must be balanced among the three orders, or no balance of power can remain. 'Wealth,' says Mr Adams, 'is the machine for governing the world.' How can this balance of property be introduced or maintained, without invading property, for the indispensable purpose of enriching a king and some other interest, to make two orders? It must be invaded by force or fraud. The frauds of superstition first collected the wealth, which created and fed an aristocratical interest; then it was acquired by the force of the feudal system; and now it is drawn from the people by the frauds of paper and patronage. Can any one hesitate to prefer the security of property under the system of the United States, to such security as this?

'A science certainly comprehends all the principles in nature which belong to the subject. The principles in nature which relate to government cannot all be known, without a knowledge of the history of mankind. *The English constitution is the only one which has considered and provided for all cases that are known to have generally, indeed to have always happened in the progress of every nation; it is therefore the only scientifical government.*'*

'Whenever the people have had any share in the executive, or more than one third part of the legislative, they have always abused it, and rendered property insecure.'†

* Adams's Def. v. 3, 368.   † Ibid., v. 3, 391.

'But a *mixed government* produces and necessitates constancy in all its parts; *the king* must be constant to preserve his *prerogatives*; the senate must be constant to preserve their share; and the house theirs.'*

'It is therefore the true policy of the common people to place the whole executive power in one man, to make him *a distinct order* in the state, from whence arises an inevitable *jealousy* between him and the gentlemen.'†

Mr. Adams's third volume‡ contains a reference to the parties under our present general government, by the terms 'constitutionalist and republican;' and in the same volume§ it is said, 'that Lewis the 16th had the unrivalled glory of admitting the people to a share in the government;' an observation for which no ground existed, previously to the establishment of the present general constitution. This volume must therefore have been written or revised after the existence of that constitution; of course, that instrument is entitled to share with the constitutions proposed by the title page to be defended, in the censures of these several quotations.

One of these is an adjudication assigning literally to the 'English constitution' the utmost conceivable political perfection; and to every other, a specified comparative inferiority, with a considerable portion of actual worthlessness. 'The English constitution is the only one which has considered and provided for all cases known to have always happened in the progress of every nation.' Comparative preference could not have been more strongly expressed. 'It is the only scientific government.' A stronger expression of contempt for other forms of government could not have been used by a philosopher.

The confinement of the people to an influence over a third part of the legislature, the monarchical executive, and the independent senate, having the prerogatives of an order, are vital principles of the English system, and applauded; and that applause is an express censure of those vital principles of our policy, which extend the influence of the people far beyond the English limit, erect responsible executives short of monarchical power, and exclude the idea of prerogatived senatorial orders.

The meaning of the term 'mixed,' frequently used in Mr. Adams's treatise, is defined by the third quotation so precisely, that the loosest imagination will be unable to misconstrue the author as

* Adams's Def. v. 3, 453.　　† Ibid., v. 3, 460.
‡ Ibid., p. 187.　　§ Ibid., p. 426.

115

intending by that expression to include the policy of the United States. He limits it to a mixture of ranks or orders, made up of king, lords and commons. A division of powers without an establishment of orders, is not then an object of Mr. Adams's contemplation, when he uses this term.

Jealousy is often mentioned by Mr. Adams as the best effect of his system of balancing orders. In the last quotation, the jealousy of the common people against gentlemen, is used as a motive to propel them towards a king, for the purpose of acquiring this cardinal effect of the balances; namely, jealousy between the king and the gentlemen.

It has been stated, that a mixture of orders belonged to the class of governments founded in the evil qualities of man; and it is repeatedly asserted by Mr. Adams, that its fruit is jealousy. This is a tender term to convey an idea of the distrust, hatred and implacability, which have ever guided orders, possessed of the share of power and wealth required by Mr. Adams's system. The calamities he details, are collected from experiments of mixed orders, and display the consequences of the evil quality of jealousy, and the prospect of its becoming the fountain of good. This jealousy is graduated by the approach towards the object, on the attainment of which the perfection of Mr. Adams's system depends; and the exact adjustment of a balance of power and wealth between political orders, begets the utmost degree of its malignity; it becomes deadly, like that between two pretenders to the throne. It produces effects, like those produced in England, by a balance of wealth and power between the crown and the nobility. As equality in wealth and power, or a perfect political balance, is the utmost excitement of jealousy, so it is stifled by subordination; and the farther a form of government recedes from Mr. Adams's point of perfection, the less it is exposed to the discord of a rivalry for dominion. As the violent struggles between the crown and nobles in England, demonstrate the consequences of an attainment of Mr. Adams's political balance; so their long intermission demonstrates the consequences of a recession from his point of perfection. It is simply the question whether two or three kings are better than one, on account of the jealousy with which the one case will be blessed, and its absence from the second. The policy of the United States, by acknowledging the sovereignty of the people without a balance or a rival power, and by establishing a subordination to their opinion, has rejected the quality of jealousy, contended for by its defender.

Mr. Adams's book abounds with the evils inflicted on mankind by the contention of orders, but it omits to display the evils of their union in England; it opposes to its own facts a theory for their management, but omits to add that it has never succeeded; and it allows to nations a capacity for instituting and keeping in repair, an intricate equilibrium of power and wealth among orders, but denies that they are capable of self government.

The quotations demonstrate the enmity between the policy of the United States, and Mr. Adams's system; and a view of the general structure of his treatise, will establish its strict concurrence with the tenor of the quotations. Republicks, or governments without a monarch, are represented as detestable; and the more popular they are, the more detestable are they represented. Our policy is slightly mentioned in the first volume, thrown into the back ground throughout the second, and spoken of in the third as an experiment unlikely to succeed. As Turgot's project of a single body of men exercising all power, is made the pretext for a collateral attack upon our policy in the first volume, Nedham's 'Excellency of a free state, or the right constitution of a commonwealth,' is resorted to for opening a direct attack upon it in the third. Turgot was unfriendly to orders, and Nedham wrote to keep out a dethroned king; Mr. Adams assails them both.

Marchamont Nedham wrote about one hundred and fifty years past. Political science at that time depended upon ancient experiments, and the disciples of democracy, aristocracy or monarchy, would of course be now exposed to many just criticisms, furnished by the defects of each form, as then understood and practised. But Nedham's treatise, and the American revolution, united in assailing the same limited monarchy, in the destruction of which, one failed and the other succeeded; and Mr. Adams selects the unsuccessful combatant against the same foe, takes the side of the victorious enemy, and fights the battle over again. Limited monarchy is made to insult over Nedham's commonwealth, after having subdued it; and the commonwealth of the United States, is not allowed to take the field against limited monarchy which that has subdued. Monarchy shrinks from an avowed controversy with an erect enemy, and is by Mr. Adams decreed a new triumph over a fallen one. However it may accord with the rules of war, to undermine the main fortress by getting possession of a weak outwork, it is questionable whether this military mode of reasoning, will be considered as the right road to truth.

The policy of the United States ought not to be forced into an alliance with either Turgot's or Nedham's project. It is itself the Champion, ready to engage the English system, fairly and openly, hand to hand; nor ought the ghosts of these speculations, the one forgotten and the other unknown, to have been conjured up, for the purpose of transfixing that policy, under pretence of striking at shadows, and claiming for monarchy a victory whilst it flees from the contest.

The war is carried on with shadows; and by the help of definition, an attempt is made even to transfer the arms of these shadows to their adversary. If this can be effected, the chief weapon, the distinguishing superiority of our policy, is also lost. Let us return to Mr. Adams.

'In the science of legislation, there is a confusion of languages, as if men were but lately come from Babel. Scarcely any two writers, much less nations, agree in using words in the same sense. Such a latitude, it is true, allows a scope for politicians to speculate, like merchants with false weights, by making the same word adored by one party and execrated by another.'*

Two extracts will be selected, to show how far Mr. Adams has fulfilled the confidence which this just observation is calculated to inspire; one, containing a definition of a republick, the other of representation. Definition is indeed a false or a true weight. It discloses truth, or hides errour. It is a criminal, varnishing over law, to conceal his crime; or an unprejudiced judge, seeking for a true construction. It is a torture of words to suit a system, and deceive the superficial; or a mode of removing the mistakes arising from words, and extending our ideas to things. And it is as likely to complain of the unintelligible jargon produced by a want of precision in terms, when it purposes to deceive by this jargon, as a Jew is to complain of false weights, when he offers his sweated coin.

'Others again, more rationally, define a republick to signify only a government, in which all men, rich and poor, magistrates and subjects, officers and people, masters and servants, the first citizen and the last, are *equally subject to the laws. This indeed appears to be the true, and only true definition of a republick.*'†

'An uncertainty of law' is a 'glorious' object to avaricious lawyers. 'An uncertainty of republicanism,' would be an object, not less desirable to ambitious politicians. A definition, which produces uncertainty as to what republicanism is, will excite and aid

* Adams's Def. v. 3, 157, 158.   † Ibid., v. 3, 159.

the views of ambition, just as an uncertainty of law excites and aids the views of avarice. It is therefore highly important to consider this definition of Mr. Adams.

The analysis contended for in this essay, divides governments into two classes, distinguished by the moral elements, good and evil. And the terms 'republick and commonwealth,' have been used to convey an idea of a government, which, being founded in good moral principles, or principles both exciting good and re-straining evil qualities, will produce publick, common, or national benefit. But if 'the subjection of all to law' constitutes a republick, this idea of the term must be surrendered, and we must look out for some other, by which to make the reader comprehend the idea, of a form of government founded in good moral principles, and producing publick, common or national benefit.

A code of laws may be good or bad; and if bad, it is morally im-possible that a subjection to such a code, can constitute a govern-ment founded in good moral principles. But according to Mr. Adams, equal subjection to any code of laws, constitutes a defini-tion of a republick; if so, it follows, that this term gives us no idea of the principles or operation, of any government; and is equally pertinent to describe those calculated to dispense evil to the pub-lick, as those calculated to dispense good.

Law may be enacted by a faction, to strip a nation, and enrich itself; and the faction may find an interest in subjecting to law, the individuals composing itself, equally with other citizens. The Doge and nobility of Venice, the East-India company and stock faction of England, are evidences of this assertion.

A code of laws may operate partially, in such modes, as the establishment of privileged orders or hierarchies; or by frittering away publick rights by law charters, to individuals or corporations, so as to reduce the majority of the nation to misery and wretched-ness. Yet the bishop would be subject to law in receiving his benefice and his tythes, the labourer, in paying them; a nobility is subject to law in exercising its privileges; a corporation, in growing rich by the aid of its charter; a bank, in collecting from a nation, usury upon nominal money; and a king, in receiving a million, and expending thirty millions annually in corruption and patronage, at the national expense. Here are kings, bishops, nobility and cor-porations, all subject to law; but the laws are partial, unjust and oppressive.

There is no difficulty in framing laws, so as to oppress one portion of a community for the benefit of another; and yet every citizen may be subject to the laws, whilst the subjection of some will consist of acquisition or benefit, and of others, of loss or injury; and thus property to a vast amount may be annually transferred. Some may be combined in a priesthood, to aid a government in oppressing others; privileges may be conferred on some, to the injury and degradation of others; some may by law be excused from publick duties, so as to increase them upon others, as in the exemption of the nobility and clergy under the French monarchy from certain taxes; and some may by laws be enabled even to corrupt the government at the cost and charges of the people, as the paper and the executive orders of England.

. In all these cases, and in a multitude of others which will occur to the reader, an equal subjection to the law, constitutes the only true and genuine republick, according to Mr. Adams; a definition equivalent to an assertion, that it is not the justice or partiality, the moderation or oppressiveness of laws, which furnish an idea of liberty or slavery, of a republick, or a tyranny, but merely the execution of law, bad or good, just or unjust.

According to this definition, all forms of government, which produce a particular effect of government, that is, 'an equal subjection to the laws,' instantly become republicks, how widely soever they may differ in structure or principles; and the same form, may sometimes be a republick, and sometimes not, as fluctuations in the equal execution of law are produced, by the passions of individuals, or the arts of factions, without any change in the structure of the government. So soon as it is settled, that effects are to alter the names of causes, without altering their nature or form, the term 'republick' can no longer convey an idea of a government, unless it is in operation; because, as the title of every form to that epithet, would depend upon its effect in producing 'an equal subjection to law,' so until this effect appears in the operation of a government, it could never be known, whether it was a republick, an aristocracy or a monarchy. Politicians, to the inquiry 'what kind of government are you erecting?' must answer like the painter spoken of by Cervantes, who being asked what he was painting, replied, 'a cock or a fox, just as it happens.'

A partial execution of law by one party or faction upon another, would produce an unequal subjection to law, which must be detected and destroyed, to bring back such an erring government within the terms of the definition. It deprives us of the vernacular idea annexed to the phrases 'republick and monarchy,' and for the question 'is this a republick or a monarchy?' substitutes an inquiry, 'whether all the citizens are equally subject to the laws?'

Without having seen the definition, an Englishman being asked, under what form of government he lived, would have answered, 'a monarchy;' and to the same question, an American would have answered 'a republick.' But this new dialect may make such answers improper. In England, the government party say 'the laws govern.' According to the definition, these monarchists must allow that their government is republican, and themselves republicans; in America, the party which called itself republican, believed that the sedition law was partially executed, so as to produce an unequal subjection to law; by the definition, this party must then have denied that our form of government was republican, whilst they were avowing an affection for it because it was so. We cannot therefore discern, how this definition is calculated to diminish the confusion of political dialect, or to establish an accurate idea of the term 'republick,' capable of becoming a fixed standard against the fraudulent use of it by ambition and deceit. Let us examine if more certainty and perspicuity is displayed in the following quotation.

'An *hereditary* limited monarch is the *representative* of the whole nation, for the management of the executive power, *as much* as an house of representatives, as one branch of the legislature, and as guardian of the publick purse; and *a house of lords* too, or a standing senate, represents the nation for other purposes, viz.: as a watch set upon both the representatives and the executive power. *The people are the fountain and original of the power of kings and lords, governours and senates*, as well as the *house of commons*, or *assembly of representatives*; and if the people are sufficiently enlightened to see all the dangers that surround them, they will *always be represented by a distinct personage* to manage the whole executive power; *a distinct senate to be guardians of property against levellers for the purposes of plunder*, to be a repositary of the national tradition of publick maxims, customs and manners, and to be controllers in turn both *of Kings and their ministers on one side, and the representatives of the people on the other*, when either discover a disposition to do wrong; and a distinct house of representatives, to be the guardians of the publick purse, and to protect the people in their turn, against both *kings* and *nobles*.'*

Having sunk republicanism in subjection to law, Mr. Adams

* Adams's Defence, v. 3. 367.

here sinks representation in hereditary orders. By the definition of 'republick' any form of government may constitute it; and by this definition of representation, hereditary power in every shape, is as much a representative power, as that elected by the people. Let us consider whether this definition tends to introduce an unambigu-.ous political dialect, and to secure the people against deception.

It was said, that Mr. Adams had attempted, by definition, to rob of their arms the shadows of his enmity, and to transfer these arms to their adversary; and that if this could be effected, the chief weapons and distinguishing superiorities of our policy would be also lost. These shadows, are Turgot's chamber and Nedham's commonwealth; the reality upon which this attempt will bear, is the policy of the United States.

The distinguishing superiorities of our policy, are, the sovereignty of the people; a republican government, or a government produ-cing publick or national good; and a thorough system of responsible representation. All these, Mr. Adams transplants into his system of monarchy and privileged orders, from the policy of the United States, as Mahomet transplanted several of the best principles of Christianity into his system of religion. 'The people,' says he, 'are the fountain and original of the power of *kings, lords, governours* and *senates,* as well as the house of commons, or assembly of representa-tives.' Thus he seizes upon our principle of 'the sovereignty of the people' and appropriates it to the use of his system of kings and lords. He asserts that, *an hereditary limited monarch and a house of lords are as much the representatives of the nation as an house of representatives elected by the people.* Thus he seizes upon our principle of responsible representation, and bestows that also upon his system of kings and lords. And not contented with depriving our policy of these de-fences, and bestowing them upon a rival policy, to which they do not belong, he even robs it of its name, by defining a republick to be only 'an equal subjection to law,' and transfers that also to monarchy:—Leaving the policy of the United States, without principles, and without a name, by which it may be spoken of, or distinguished from the English system. Is this 'a language of Babel,' or one calculated to be understood? Is it calculated to furnish ambitious politicians 'with false weights,' or to come at truth?

In his effort to humour the publick opinion of the United States, in favour of 'national sovereignty and representation,' Mr. Adams lost sight of that, to prove the existence of 'a natural aristocracy.'

One of these doctrines asserts 'that the people are sovereign,' or in Mr. Adams's words, 'the fountain and original of the power of kings and lords;' the other, 'that nature creates an order above and independently of the people.' And to complete the confusion arising from thus confounding contradictory principles, Mr. Adams in the last quotation, has arranged kings and governours, lords and senators, in the class of representatives, and thus after taking from us words, takes away objects also, by which we may know our system of government, from that of king, lords and commons.

If the system of *balancing power and property*, contended for by Mr. Adams, would not be exploded by a disingenuous defence; an effort to convince the people of the United States, that their policy is the English system, ought to have no more influence upon the question, than an effort to convince the English nation, that their system was the policy of the United States. Considering such attempts as rather designed to ridicule, than mislead ignorance or prepossession, I will exhibit the essential difference between the two forms of government, in a view, heretofore transiently noticed, and hereafter to be impressed, as occasions occur.

In the last quotation, Mr. Adams recommends his noble, distinct or permanent Senate, 'as guardians of *property against levellers*;' and in a previous quotation he observes, that 'whenever the people have had any share in the executive, or more than *one third part* of the legislative, they have *always abused it*, and rendered *property insecure*:'—Thus excluding the people from any share in the executive, and any influence over the Senate, (although the king and the nobility are, as he says, their representatives,) as the only means of protecting property or checking levellers.

The love of property possesses almost an unbounded influence over the human mind. It is therefore an engine to which avarice and ambition will forever resort to effect their purposes; and every institution designed to make the mass of a nation poorer by enriching itself, will invariably avow a contrary intention, for the purpose of inducing the nation to fall into the snare. This is sometimes baited, with a pretence, that the people will be abundantly reimbursed in heaven, for the money drawn from them to enrich a hierarchy; at others, with the delusion, that they are reimbursed for the wealth drawn from them to enrich paper corporations, by an enhanced price for their labour; even for such products as are priced by a foreign demand.

The fear of losing property, is as strong as the hope of obtaining it. For this reason, the grossest abuses artfully ally themselves with real and honest property; and endeavour to excite its apprehension, when attempts are made to correct them, by exclaiming against the invasion of property and against levelism, and by deceiving the publick with fraudulent epithets.

These, we shall endeavour to prove, are precisely the grounds taken by Mr. Adams, when he boldly charges all nations, having any share in their own government beyond a third part of the legislative power, with 'rendering property insecure;' when he proposes a noble senate, as 'guardians of property;' and when he endeavours to draw upon those who approve of extending the power of the people beyond his limitation, the odium attached to the epithet 'levellers.' And we shall endeavour to prove, that the charges of levelism, and rendering property insecure, so repeatedly and profusely urged against republican principles throughout his book, do really recoil upon himself, and adhere to his own system.

The 'safety of property' is the very point, by which it is allowed that the reader ought to be determined, in bestowing a preference upon our policy or the English system. Our manners do not thirst for blood; it is the thirst of avarice and ambition for wealth and power, that we have to withstand.

To understand the question, we ought previously to settle a satisfactory idea of property. Here it is probable that a disagreement will occur, between the disciples of corporation, monopoly and orders, and myself. It is acknowledged, that I do not include under the idea of property, any artificial establishment, which subsists by taking away property; such as hierarchical, kingly, noble, official and corporate possessions, incomes and privileges; and that I consider those possessions as property, which are fairly gained by talents and industry, or are capable of subsisting, without taking property from others by law.

If this definition is correct, an invasion of property constitutes the essential quality of Mr. Adams's system. A king, a nobility and a hierarchy, cannot subsist without property, and this property must be taken away in some mode from others. The system requires a balance of property, as the only mode of balancing power; or, to use the epithet applied by Mr. Adams to those who differ from him, property and power must be levelled among three orders, and this level must be kept up, or the system falls into ruin. Therefore the supposed two orders cannot preserve a political existence, without constantly receiving the profits of two thirds of the property in a nation. This requires a regular system for invading private property to sustain a government consisting of balanced orders. A nation must toil like Sisyphus, whilst an invisible power must eternally defeat their labours, to keep this indispensable balance steady.

Nobility, separate interests or orders, have in all ages taken root and flourished, in an invasion of property. Some mode by which this is effected, will occur as an indissoluble adjunct to every such order or interest; as in the fraudulent division of conquered lands, which reared and fed the Roman patricians and feudal barons; in the sale of indulgences and other frauds of superstition, which reared and fed the popish hierarchy: and in the system of paper and patronage, which reared and feeds the English monied interest, and allies it with the crown, from a consciousness of delinquency in its perpetual invasion of property.

Supposing the charge exhibited against governments, under the national control, to be true; and admitting that they do tend towards levelism; it would then become necessary to compute, which species of levelism, that of dividing property between three orders according to Mr. Adams's system, or that of dividing property among all the individuals of a nation according to the supposed tendency, would produce the most injustice or misery. The first kind of levelism, requires a perpetual balance, only to be obtained and supported, by an artificial transfer (either fraudulent or forcible) of two thirds of the national income, to two orders consisting of very few persons. This involves a perpetual invasion of the property of the order, comprising almost the whole nation, to the extent of two thirds. And an impoverishment of individuals, with all its calamities upon mind and body, follows such an invasion, to a vast extent; suffered, not for the purpose of supplying the wants of the two orders, or doing them any good, but merely for the political object of establishing a balance of power upon this balance of property.

The *guardianship of property* derived from the system of orders, must be paid for according to its essential principles, by two thirds of the property of the people; a price, one would think, which ought to secure fidelity in discharging the trust. Instead of this, the system does not admit of the remaining third being rendered more valuable by industry. For should the third left in the hands of the people, be improved up to the value of the two thirds, transferred to the other two orders, it would destroy the balance of power. Hence the system requires the acquisitions of industry to be taken away and transferred, as they appear, to keep up its vital principle of 'a balance of property.'

This is effected in England by the aid of paper and patronage. The portion of property held by the people, began to grow as soon as perpetuities were abolished, and excited the efforts of avarice and ambition, to transfer to themselves the acquisitions of industry; to effect this object, recourse was had to the fraud of paper and patronage, so well calculated to goad on industry, and to pillage her gains. The levelism of property among three orders, created by perpetuities, domains, prerogatives, and tenures (which constituted the essence of the feudal system), had been destroyed by the acquisitions of the popular order, and in its place was invented what may be called 'the perpetual level of property,' by the perpetual motion of paper patronage and taxation. It was a discovery of the political longitude for hereditary and stock navigators. This perpetual motion, being regulated by these navigators, they can accelerate or retard its velocity, so as to maintain a perpetual level, by a regular transfer of the profit of labour and industry, from the mass of a nation, to themselves, an inconsiderable section of it. Thus, in fact, reducing Mr. Adams's orders to two only, those who lose property and those who receive it; and producing the tyranny which he justly contends will result from one order governing another.

This attempt to level or balance property among orders, has been concealed in all ages, by charging those who oppose it with an intention of equalising, levelling or balancing property among individuals; a species of levelism which has seldom appeared in any shape, would be temporary if attempted, and is impracticable.

If levelism, balancing or equality was practicable, (for the words are the same, however, as Mr. Adams observes, they may be made to be *adored by one party and execrated by another,*) the merits of the different modes would appear by extending an idea already stated. By the system for equalising property among orders, one child gets a third of the whole, one hundred and fifty another third, and eleven millions nine hundred and ninety nine thousand, eight hundred and forty nine children, the remaining third; by that for equalising property among individuals, each child would receive an equal share. The first system of equality, by a distribution excessively oppressive upon individuals, excites ambition, avarice, and universal malignity, and all the train of evil moral qualities annexed to luxury and poverty; the second system of equality, would produce all the evils of sloth and ignorance.

It is admitted that a greater portion of a nation will receive a share, by the paper and patronage system for levelling property, on account of the necessity of extending corruption to defend a fraud, relatively to the extension of knowledge; and that this multiplication of chances for a share, operates as a spur to labour and industry, as the efforts of twelve millions of persons would be more vigourously excited by the enrichment of fifty thousand than of one hundred and fifty individuals. But the more avarice is thus excited, the more oppression becomes necessary to obtain the means of its gratification; an idea furnishing the ground for a comparison between the feudal and the paper aristocracy.

Whether the reader shall hold in most detestation the system of levelling property among orders or among individuals, is unimportant to the question proposed for his consideration. And the subject is only submitted to him that he may discern the ingenuity of the first species of iniquity, in endeavouring to crouch from his eye behind the second. Conscious that it is the policy of the United States to protect property against both these modes of invading it, the mode of balancing it among orders, artfully endeavours to excite an odium against that policy, by charging it with a tendency towards the mode of balancing it among individuals, hoping that a recoil of publick opinion from one species of iniquity, may throw the nation into the other.

The source of the charge excites distrust. It is brought forward by the system of levelling property among orders. The accusers are the witnesses. And if these accusers and witnesses succeed, their reward is a real two thirds of the wealth and power of the United States, for defeating an ideal balance of property among individuals. The people are gravely advised by Mr. Adams, to transfer two thirds of their property to two orders, and to keep themselves by perpetual taxation, under a perpetual incapacity of recovering it, for the preservation of the balance of power among orders, lest they themselves should adopt the visionary project of balancing property among individuals. A perpetual balance of property among orders, is the remedy proposed against a transitory project for balancing it among individuals. The temptations exciting a division of property among individuals, are feeble; hence it has no advocates, and hence in our present circumstances, it never will have advocates. Those exciting its division among orders, are powerful; hence it has advocates, and hence the danger of property lurks behind that project.

Property, like liberty, is only to be secured upon the broad basis of publick will. When hereditary orders or separate interests, tell a nation that it is an enemy to its own liberty, but that liberty will be safe in their care, it is done with a design to rob the nation of liberty; and when these hereditary orders or separate interests tell a nation, that property can only be made secure by investing them with two thirds of it, it is done to rob the nation of property.

A specifick balance of property among orders, or separate interests, in the present state of commerce and manners, cannot be effected, by assigning to each order or interest a third part of the land held by a nation; and hence it is obvious, that a landed order, or aristocracy, cannot be established. As land itself cannot be thus balanced, the only remaining mode of effecting this indispensable object to the system of orders, is taxation. Those who receive the transfers of wealth made by taxation, and not those who supply them, must constitute the order or separate interest. *A* cannot be made a nobleman by giving property to *B*. Many conclusions ensue. The objects of paper and patronage in England, receive the benefit of the balance of property, produced by taxation—the modern mode of managing this balance; therefore those objects, and not the titled nobility, constitute the real order or separate interest in England. Property is balanced by taxing land and labour, not by a division of land; and therefore land cannot be the basis of an aristocracy. Like all other property, it loses by the balance of property maintained by taxation; and it is the order which gains, and not that which loses, which invariably constitutes the aristocracy. An aristocracy, therefore, by the modern mode of creating it, cannot consist of a landed interest, a manufacturing interest, a professional interest, or of any species of interest, that excepted which receives the property annually collected by taxation, charters and privileges. It is the share of property received, which conveys the share of power, and produces the balance of both. Corruption, charters, patronage, pensions and paper systems, are the channels through which the property annually balanced by taxation, is distributed. Therefrom the distributees derive a power, enabling them to do what a titled order would in vain attempt; to defend themselves and their king or factor, against all other interests and orders.

Let us now proceed to consider the examples in relation to his system, drawn by Mr. Adams from the governments of the middle age.

Mr. Adams affects to despise theory, and to prove all his conclusions by experience. Without estimating the difference between the savage and the civilized; the superstitious and the enlightened; a city and a great country; he reasons as if every situation and all circumstances, moral and physical, demanded the same political regimen. The manners, the colour, and the social qualities, of the brute creation, are changed by education; is reason condemned to persist in errours, from which instinct has in some degree escaped? His examples are extracted in the second and third volumes, at great length, from the Italian republicks. To be guided by these, we must shut our eyes upon the day light shining around, and dive after our character and capacity into the caverns of antiquity. Can any ingenuity induce us to believe, that a picture of human depravity and ignorance, during the middle age, is our picture? In considering this rosary of causes, it will hardly be overlooked, that Mr. Adams has been as evidently a theorist, as in assigning power to title, and forgetting to assign it to wealth.

These cases are confined to the thirteenth, fourteenth and fifteenth centuries. We relinquish the use of the deep ignorance with which these centuries had been overspread by the recent irruptions and conquests of barbarians, and will endeavour to reason in a mode more conclusive.

Mr. Adams considers Florence as affording an experiment of the most weight. He enumerates sundry evils endured by that city, and infers that his system would have prevented them. The inference is drawn, not from a comparison between the government of Florence, and other forms existing at the same period, which might have furnished probable conclusions; but from a comparison between governments which existed at periods extremely distant from each other. Parallels between contemporaries, will be allowed to furnish a sounder inference. His history of Florence commences in the year 1245. The parliament of England received the shape of king, lords and commons, as far back as that year; indeed, an act of parliament appears to have been pleaded, made in the reign of William the conqueror. From hence to the end of the fifteenth century, when Mr. Adams's history of Italian miseries ends, the balance of power and property in England among orders, was more consonant to his theory than at present. The representation of the plebeian order, was more equal at that time than now; because inhabited and not depopulated boroughs were represented. Property was placed by perpetuities in a settled state of division and balance among orders; this division and balance is now superseded by its division through commerce and alienation among individuals, and by the balance of taxation between payers and receivers. The titled order then held a real share of power, attracted by their share of property; now, power is attracted from title by a richer order or interest.

Here was strong ground for a sober inquirer after truth. The contemporary evils generated by the king, lords and commons of England, and by the Italian republicks, ought to have been minutely detailed and compared. Then the preponderating mass might have been discovered; and then similar evils might have been referred to some common cause.

The feuds and wars among the barons, between these and the kings, between the kings and the people, between pretenders to the crown, between the nation and its neighbours; catalogues of executions, murders, confiscations, banishments; seizures of church lands and monasteries; changes of religion and persecutions, begotten by amours, or bigotry; and all the effects of prerogative, privilege and feudal tenure, ought to have been made to face the calamities of the Italian republicks, to enable us to determine which were most hideous.

These calamities brought face to face, would have exhibited a resemblance not to be obliterated. And the chief distinction between them, would have consisted of more art, civilization and knowledge, among the Italians than among the English, infused by their greater portion of republicanism. From the resemblance, however, would have resulted an illustration of an analysis which supposes, that evil moral effects are produced by monarchy, aristocracy or democracy, either simple or mixed. The democracies, aristocracies, monarchies and mixtures, both of England and Italy, produced evil effects. In both countries ranks or orders existed during the three centuries to which Mr. Adams confines himself.

Admitting an exchange of forms of government to have taken place, between England and Italy, an exchange of contemporary evils or effects might have also followed; and it is not improbable but that Italy would have made the worst of the bargain. Her little republicks, would have been converted into little kingdoms; and the rivalry and ambition of neighbouring commonwealths, would have been exchanged for the rivalry and ambition of neighbouring kings. The little commonwealths existed more centuries, than the kingdoms would have done years; if we may judge by the invariable fate of a cluster of small kings..Is not this a proof of the superior excellence or moderation, of the republican, to the monarchical principle?

The numerous disunited territorial divisions of Italy, was the substratum for her republican experiment; a territorial union, of the English experiment for balancing property and orders. Italy was distracted by the mutual annoyance of jealous neighbours, and the intrigues of the Pope and the Emperour. England was strong in its extent, fortified by nature, and less exposed to foreign influence. Under these disadvantages, during the three centuries we are estimating, Italy outstript England in arts, knowledge and wealth; and probably saved the science and civilization of the world, from being lost in those ages of darkness. Her evils were inferior to those of England, under the pressure of greater local difficulties; and her prosperity greater, with fewer local advantages. But the tincture of republicanism was infinitely stronger in the Italian forms of government, than in the English.

There existed however, it must be admitted, a strong resemblance between the evils suffered by both, which excites a reasonable suspicion, that these evils flowed from some cause, also common to both. The structure of the governments was dissimilar, therefore this structure could not have been the cause. But a similarity existed between England and Italy, in two material circumstances during these centuries; ignorance and nobility. England and Italy were both in a state of turbulence and misery during the contemplated period. The balances of England, would therefore have been an ineffectual experiment to cure the calamities of Italy; and the mixed republicanism of Italy, as ineffectual to cure the calamities of England. The evil moral causes, ignorance and nobility, being common to both countries, would still have produced evil effects, had they been transposed.

From the termination of the fifteenth century, the two chief calamities which had previously afflicted Europe, diminished in malignancy. Printing gradually mitigated the effects of ignorance; and commerce and alienation, gradually destroyed the balance of property and power among orders. To defend noble or privileged orders by a comparison between Italy, before the discovery of printing and under a feudal monopoly of land, and England, enlightened by that art, and relieved from this monopoly, is reasoning thus: As England, after the power and influence of her nobility were destroyed by alienation and the diffusion of knowledge, became happier than Italy, whilst afflicted with powerful noble orders, therefore noble orders are blessings.

The amelioration of the human condition, though general to Europe, was not precisely the same in each country. It seems in a great measure to have been graduated by the thermometer of nobility, and to have proceeded with celerity or tardiness, in proportion to the imbecility or strength of noble orders.

In Russia and Poland, the nobility long retained property and power, and the people, oppression and misery. In France and Germany, the nobility retained more of its property and power, than in England, and the people were more oppressed. In England nobility received the first and hardest blow, and she suddenly overtook and surpassed several countries in prosperity, which were previously ahead of her. And in the revolution of France, the abolition of nobility, made room for a wonderful national energy and superiority, which will not be forgotten by politicians.

The history of England supports these ideas. The reign of king John ended in 1216, and that of Henry the seventh in 1509, so that the collection of Italian troubles made by Mr. Adams, is contemporary with the troubles of England during the reigns of John, Henry 3d, Edward 1st, Edw. 2d, Edw. 3d, Richard 2d, Henry 4th, 5th and 6th, Edw. 4th, Rich. 3d, and Henry 7th.

During these reigns, the nobility were rich and powerful, and the troubles of England, dreadful and unremitting. Henry the seventh began to break their power by diminishing their property, and the situation of the nation began to mend. As commerce and alienation proceeded in this work, the situation of the nation grew better; and since the new project of annually balancing property by taxation, has been substituted for the old project of a specifick landed balance, the parish poor and the publick debt, the poverty and the luxury, the vices and the wretchedness of the nation have all increased.

Powerful and wealthy orders, in no country under any form of government, have existed in union with national happiness; a system therefore, which proposes so to balance them, as to compel them to be subservient to it, is not experimental, and only a theory. Let us consider, whether it is entitled even to the weight of naked theory.

If Mr. Adams's theory existed in England at any period, before the sixteenth century, it did not produce effects which can invite us to adopt it; and afterwards, the political progress of England received its direction from the assaults made upon the power and property of the nobility by Henry the seventh, and by alienation, commerce, paper and patronage. The system therefore is made worse than naked theory, by inimical experience. The miseries of the first period, were suddenly diminished, and the effects of the second gradually produced, by successful combatants against nobility, the corner stone of his system.

The animation of defending it, by the experience of the Italian republicks, is still more remarkable than the use made of the experience of England. The history of Florence, says Mr. Adams, is the history of them all. This is only a detail of the treasons and oppressions of a turbulent nobility. We hear constantly of the Buondelmonti, Uberti, Amadei, Donati, Cherchi, Neri, Bianchi, Medicei, Albigi, and others, with their castles; of publick calamities originating in the ambition, wickedness or folly of a nobleman; of confederations between orders, and between noble families; and of efforts and concessions on the part of the people to restrain these disorders. Whilst these disorders are ascribed to the nobility, Mr. Adams imputes them to the people; merely because they did not try exactly, as he thinks, his balance of orders; and felicitating his country in having discovered a remedy for these disorders, he is willing to rebuild castles for nobles, or to erect the more impregnable fortress of paper and patronage for aristocracy, to evince the dexterity with which the calamities endured by Florence from nobility, may be averted from the United States. Nobility was the source of evil to Florence; Florence therefore furnishes no experiment, shewing nobility to have been a source of good. A system to convert nobility into a blessing, is worse than theory, if experience exhibits it as a curse. A few other quotations from the book of experience are necessary to fix its character.

'Machiavel,' says Mr. Adams, 'informs him, that the government of Florence was fallen into great disorder and misrule; for the Guelph nobility, being the majority, were grown so insolent, and stood in so little awe of the magistracy, that though many murders and other violences were daily committed, yet the criminals daily escaped with impunity, through favour of one or the other of the nobles.'*

* Adams's Def. v. 2, 18.

133

'But the behaviour of the nobility was quite the contrary,' says Machiavel, 'for as they always disdained the thoughts of equality, even when they lived a private life, so now they were in the magistracy, they thought to domineer over the whole city, and every day produced fresh instances of their pride and arrogance; which exceedingly galled the people, when they saw they had deposed one tyrant to make room for a thousand.'

'All this,' says Mr. Adams, 'one may safely believe to be exactly true, but what then? Why, they ought to have separated the nobles from the commons, and made each independent of the other.'*

These nobles were tried 'in private life and in the magistracy,' in both they retained the vicious qualities of the vicious principle, nobility. True, says Mr. Adams, but they were not tried according to my theory. Many attempts in various modes, some approaching to his theory, were unsuccessfully made in Italy to gratify or purify the principle, nobility; all failed; it continued to exhibit vicious qualities. At this period, the nobles in England were separated from and independent of the house of commons, and that house of the nobles; yet the vicious qualities of nobility caused a multitude of disorders. Mr. Adams admits the insolence of nobility, and the disorders it produces; his remedy to cure insolence and ambition, is power and wealth.

The nobles of Poland, were rich and powerful; they ruined their country, rather than soften the condition of the people. Those of Russia receive districts with the inhabitants as donations from an emperour. But, says Mr. Adams, 'hereditary kings and nobles are as much representatives of the people as those they elect.' In Russia they represent them as part of their estates. Thus the feudal English barons represented the people, whilst possessed of their baronies; now, by selling them to the crown. We see in all instances, that nobility, with great wealth and power, is a tyrant; with little, a traitor; and that orders or interests, subsisting on the people, invariably oppress or sell them; for how can they otherwise subsist?

Mr. Adams allows wealth to be the great machine for governing the world, and yet he makes no distinction between a rich order or interest, and a poor one. He has seen a rich nobility in Poland overbalance both a king and a people. He has seen a rich nobility, clergy and king in the late monarchy of France, overbalancing the people. He has seen rich barons dethroning poor kings, and poor ones the creatures of rich kings. It is in vain to say that these poor

* Adams's Def. v. 2, 46.

nobles have a share in the legislature, if they have neither property nor influence, to restrain or balance the wealth and influence of the king, with his army, and his patronage. A constitution, which divides rights among orders, giving to one a share, but no power to defend it; and to another a share, with power to encroach, to menace and to corrupt, will be as defective, as one which should bestow all power upon an individual, or a single assembly, with an injunction not to abuse it.

These arguments tend to show, that a balance of orders cannot exist without a balance of property among these orders, as Lord Shaftesbury and Mr. Adams unite in asserting. Concurring with these authors, two inferences of importance present themselves.

One, that as a balance or equality of landed property cannot subsist in community with the present state of knowledge, commerce and alienation; and as a balance or equality of power, cannot subsist without a balance of property, so the system of equalising power and property between a confederation of orders, if established, could only sustain its perfection during the moment of transit over the true balance, which might occur in the flight of property on the wings of commerce, alienation and knowledge, from the minor to the numerous order. The same effects could not possibly result from the gas of a balance of property, as from a real balance itself.

The other is still more important. As no balance of specifick property among confederated orders, can exist in communion with the present state of knowledge, commerce and alienation, taxation becomes the only engine for distributing and balancing property; and must arrange society into the two orders of payers and receivers. The latter being the enriched, must govern the impoverished order; and being a minority, is by nature an aristocracy. Though a king, a titled and a plebeian order may continue to exist, the three nominal orders, are absorbed by the two real, and the evils follow, allowed by Mr. Adams to be invariable consequences of two orders.

The history of England demonstrates these remarks. The nobility were oppressive, whilst they held an over proportion of property, by laws for perpetuating inheritances; and the monied aristocracy has become more oppressive by laws for transferring to it an over proportion of property, not through manors, but through taxation. The poison of perpetuities is lodged in the property secured to a separate interest, not in the mode of securing it; nor can it be rendered innoxious, by the title of noble, clerical or stock. Had the feudal barons exchanged their perpetual inheritances, for the perpetual income of stock and patronage, their power would never have been broken, whilst this new species of perpetuity lasted.

This view of the subject accounts for the former and present conduct of the English nobility. Whilst their property gave them power, they despised the system of taxation and patronage, civil commotion was the fruit of their arrogance and ambition, and feudal tenures and services fed their avarice. But when their property was diminished, and the king became the annual dispenser of a treasury perpetually replenished by loaning and taxation, then this nobility were converted into the courtiers of the crown, and the satellites of its usurpations. They fell under an influence, equivalent to an annual distribution by the king, of ancient baronies, among the partisans of monarchy. Yet the United States have pointed their constitutional artillery against the aristocracies of superstition and the feudal system, after reason had destroyed the first, and knowledge, commerce and alienation, the second. Did they fear or love the living foe, the aristocracy of paper and patronage bottomed upon perpetual taxation? or were they deceived at the formation of their constitutions, because it joined in trampling upon the dead bodies of its predecessors? They will no longer hesitate in discerning, that the project of equalising property among titled orders, is as impracticable in communion with knowledge, commerce and alienation, or with the system of paper and patronage, as is the project of equalising it among individuals, in communion with human mortality; that both must remain speculative theories, rebutted by experience, until perpetuities are re-established, or immortality without fecundity is bestowed on mankind; and that, excluding the idea of either, the election of the United States is confined to a distribution of property by industry and talents, or according to the avarice of a separate and minor portion of the society, by perpetual taxation, paper currencies and the arts of patronage. The feudal perpetuities cost the nation nothing; stock perpetuities are erected wholly at their expense. Is it better to entail stock on the nation to make an aristocracy, or to allow fathers to entail their lands on their sons for the same purpose?

Mr. Adams frequently endeavours to apply historical facts to his theory or the English system; these applications could not be past over, nor could the justifications of the American policy which his own facts furnished, be omitted. Our business proceeds either by shewing the insufficiency of the evidence, in favour of balancing property and power among confederated orders; the impossibility of introducing and supporting such a balance now, if it ever did exist; or the preference of our policy to that. We are not deviating therefore from the subject, in deviating somewhat from our quotations. To these let us return.

The evidence of Machiavel, 'that the nobles were the cause of the publick calamities which afflicted Italy' is admitted by Mr. Adams to be true. It is then admitted, that nobility distracted Italy for three centuries; that it caused innumerable publick calamities; and that ultimately it usurped tyrannical power, almost over every Italian republick. This is the evidence. It was said that the evidence adduced in favour of nobility by Mr. Adams, was against it.

But this is only the evidence acknowledged by Mr. Adams to be true. He omitted to acknowledge, that under the operation of the system of king, lords and commons in England, nobility were turbulent and tyrannical, as long as their property was nailed to them by entails, and that they gradually sunk into parasites of royalty, after the nail was drawn. Nobility, whenever it has appeared, has proved itself to be an evil moral principle by its effects. Experience is in full opposition to Mr. Adams's theory. And the question is, whether the United States will overlook experience, to make one more attempt to convert nobility into a good moral principle, for the sake of satisfying Mr. Adams's ardour.

Mr. Adams's collection of Italian calamities, comes down but a few years lower than 1495. We have ascribed them partly to ignorance, believing that ignorance is an evil principle, which enables nobility to afflict human nature with additional misery. But Mr. Adams, without considering the different degrees of knowledge and ignorance, existing six centuries past and at this time, uniformly considers his theory as a complete panacea for every political body, whatever may be its malady.

And yet he says that 'in 1495 a man appeared in Florence, who declared that God had constituted him his ambassador to Florence, with full power and express orders to declare his will; and this egregious impostor regulated the government.'*

Mr. Adams believes that his theory was calculated to regulate the government of a society, in a state of manners and ignorance, adapted for the practices of an egregious impostor. Supposing him

* Adams's Def. v. 2. 144.

right in this opinion, some reason ought to have been given, why a system, suitable to a national inclination for imposition and fraud, would also be suitable for an enlightened people. Until this is done, it is evident, that if the experiments of the Italian republicks, prove, as Mr. Adams asserts, that his theory would have been suitable to a state of ignorance and manners, similar to the Florentine; it is by no means a consequence, that it is suitable also for a state of knowledge and manners similar to the American. Degrees of infatuation may exist, for which imposition is the only remedy; and it does not follow, that by proving a thing to be a remedy for infatuation, that it would be useful where there is no infatuation. Without illustrating the ignorance and infatuation of Italy by a history of the crusades, we will pass on to the following quotation.

'The quarrel between Frederick the emperour, and Gregory the Pope, revived in Bologna the party distinctions of Guelphs and Ghibellines, drawn from Germany in the time of Henry the fourth. Not only some cities favoured the emperour, and others the pontiff, but in the city of Bologna, the citizens arrived to that degree of extreme madness, that, in hatred of each other, they strove to deprive each other of their lives and fortunes together. Sons became enemies to their fathers, and brothers to brothers; and, as if it was not enough to shed their own blood, like mad dogs, they proceeded to demolish houses, and to burning the cities, the trees and the corn. This diabolical pestilence produced such an aversion to each other, that they studied to distinguish themselves in all things: in their clothes, in the colours they wore, in their actions, their speech, their walk, their food, their salutations, their drink, their manner of cutting bread, in folding their napkins, in the cut of their hair, and innumerable other extravagances equally whimsical. A plague truly horrible, a flame wholly inextinguishable, which proved the extinction of so many noble families, and the ruin of so many miserable cities.'*

This picture of the effects of orders, is urged by Mr. Adams in favour of orders. He ascribes the calamities of Italy to the popular forms of their governments, and tells us at the same time, that they were owing to an Emperour, a Pope, and a nobility. Here then are all his orders, and one more than he contends for; but one which will always be resorted to as an engine, in a rivalship between two others. A hierarchy is an engine which hereditary orders play upon

* Adams's Def. v. 2, 405. 406.

each other, or upon the people. We find that the experiments of Italy were made with the one, the few, the many, and an established church. It was said, that they bore a strong resemblance to Mr. Adams's theory, and the English system.

Let us suppose that Mr. Adams had written against orders, and in favour of the policy of the United States. Would he have considered the calamities in which the Italian republicks were involved by an Emperour, a Pope and a nobility, as justifying or condemning our policy in excluding a king, a metropolitan, and hereditary orders? Would the effects stated in the extract, of a jealousy among such orders, have been urged by him to prove, that they were a curse, or a blessing? Would he have advised the United States, after recapitulating the human miseries begotten by a jealousy of orders, in every instance of their existence, to surrender their peace and happiness, merely to try whether this evil principle, from which horrours innumerable have proceeded, might be made to produce good? No, he would have demonstrated, that no politician, no theorist, no moral alchymist, has skill able to change the nature of good and evil, and to reverse the moral laws of the Deity. And he would have warned us pathetically against suffering our governments to be modelled upon such a calculation, even though the projector should declare himself to be an ambassador from God.

Nothing can more evidently display an imagination heated beyond the temperature of impartial reason, than a resort to contradiction in supporting a project.

Mr. Adams tells us that 'there were in Italy, in the middle age, *one hundred or two of cities,* all independent republicks, and all constituted in the same manner. The history of one is, under different names and various circumstances, the history of all.' He addresses two volumes of examples, drawn from republicks consisting of single cities, as evidence to extensive countries; and, rejecting even the idea, that extensive territory, national strength, and national safety, would alone have obviated many misfortunes to which these little republicks were liable, he positively assures us, that human nature is always the same, and that therefore governments consisting of single cities, furnish correct precedents for the direction of numerous nations and extensive countries. Only promising, that the same argument would prove the propriety of teaching a great and free people how to govern themselves, by examples drawn from armies, crowded in dangerous garrisons, under their general, officers and chaplains, we will proceed directly to the alleged inconsistency.

Nedham, in his 'right constitution of a commonwealth,' had drawn arguments from the democratical cantons of Switzerland, which Mr. Adams thus disposes of.

'There is not even a colour in his favour in the democratical cantons of Switzerland—narrow spots or barren mountains, where the people live on milk; nor in St. Marino or Ragusa: no precedents, surely, for England or American States, where the people are numerous and rich, the territory capacious, and commerce extensive.'*

All Mr. Adams's evidence, in his two last volumes, is drawn (Nieuchattel excepted, a narrow principality in Switzerland itself,) out of little republicks, composed of single cities, less than many cantons of Switzerland, in times of ignorance and superstition, and when the state of poverty was such, that it was a great distinction to own a horse. 'No precedents, surely, for England or American States, where the people are numerous and rich, the territory capacious, and the commerce extensive.' And thus he very correctly overturns, and disallows the whole evidence upon which his two last volumes are built.

He does more; he acknowledges an erroneous mode of reasoning in defence of his theory, in having wholly omitted to estimate the influence of physical or moral circumstances upon political experiments, and in hastily concluding human nature under all to be the same; by admitting the decisive force of such circumstances.

In the quotation, extent of territory, population, wealth and commerce, are expressly stated as affecting forms of government, and such an influence is even insinuated as likely to ensue from a milk diet. Still stronger differences ought to have occurred to Mr. Adams, between his Italian cities and American states. Their relative situation as to knowledge and ignorance, superstition and religion, privileged orders and equality, are differences, infinitely stronger than those, admitted of themselves sufficiently strong to destroy evidence similar to his own.

To contend both for the propriety and absurdity of the same evidence, by arguments urged for one object, and refuted for another, discloses an impetuosity in speculation, which ought at least to awaken an apprehension, that hereditary orders are more likely to repeat the crimes which Mr. Adams allows them to have

* Adams's Def. v, 3, 355.

committed, than to be converted into blessings by a balance of property and power.

Had not Mr. Adams's evidence been inapplicable both to the moral and physical situation of the United States, it is brought forward in a mode better calculated to excite passion and prejudice, than reason and reflection. A mass of errour, rage and ambition; of tragical catastrophe, soliciting sympathy by naming the persons of the drama; and of demolished castles, mangled limbs, and putrid carcasses, is exhibited. But truth can only be discovered by considering the evidence on both sides. Another mass of these disgusting materials, labelled 'Behold the effects of monarchy and aristocracy,' might have saved the United States the humiliation of having their credulity experimentally removed. Or was it necessary to excite an abhorrence of republican governments, to prepare the mind for a patient contemplation even of the modest monarchy, called limited?

A search among the relicks of antiquity, for principles of which to form a modern government, requires a contemporaneous estimate. The superiority of the republican policy of the United States over the ancient monarchies of Persia and Macedonia, is an argument precisely as strong in favour of popular governments, as would have been the superiority of the present monarchy of Britain, over the republicks of Athens, Rome, Carthage and of Italy, in favour of monarchy, supposing Mr. Adams to have established it. In both cases the argument would be inconclusive. But although results of inconclusive authority only can arise from a comparison between ancient and modern governments; yet a comparison of ancient governments with each other, will furnish strong indications of preference and superiority between political principles.

These indications uniformly appear on the side of the popular principle; and the nearer the forms of government approached to the policy of the United States, the stronger are the indications of superiority. As rivals of Rome and Carthage, the contemporary monarchies are almost imperceptible; and above an hundred generations, almost forgetting what the rest of the world did at that time, have transmitted to us an admiration of the little Athenian democracy, which we shall hand down to a fathomless posterity.

But let us come to the world we live in; to a world, not guided by superstition but by religion. Instead of diving after wisdom into the gloom of antiquity, when men made gods, let us leave Mr. Adams in possession of his opinion, that under truth or superstition, under the Deity or Jupiter, the human character is the same. And leaving divines also to felicitate themselves on the inutility of their labours, which this doctrine admits, let us bring into comparison the existing competitors for pre-eminence. These are the first among republicks, and the first among monarchies.

If the comparison commences from the first settlement of the United States, several centuries of prosperity and good order present themselves under the colonial form of government. How can this prosperity and good order be accounted for? By the absence of jealous and rival orders; by the absence of the system of balancing power and property between such orders; by the absence of the system of paper and patronage, for perpetuating property to one interest at the expense of another; and by the absence of a nominal king. The errours in the form of the colonial government slept, because these evils were not present to awaken them; and the solitary good principle it possessed, operated under a sufferance, arising from the inattention of the evil principles united with it. Election sufficed to produce colonial prosperity and good order, and silently formed the national character and love of liberty, which sustained a furious war almost devoid of any other resource.

At length monarchy, aristocracy, and taxation, awakened. Mr. Adams's hereditary representation and our elective representation, appeared to be principles exactly opposite, in producing opposite effects. His hereditary orders, and the system of paper and patronage, took one side, and the elective principle the other. Hereditary orders and the people, here, as in Rome and Italy, quarrelled. Had a portion of these orders, and the projects of banking and funding, been mingled with the elective system at the commencement of these hostilities, they would have destroyed its efficacy, in like manner as nobility has uniformly destroyed the efficacy of the elective principle, wherever it has been mingled with it; and as a paper influence has destroyed its efficacy in England. And as election has never produced equal beneficial effects, in communion with nobility or with paper and patronage, as when disunited from them in the instance of the United States, it probably never will.

In addition to the colonial prosperity, under the substantial auspices of the elective principle, that which we have experienced subsequently to the revolution is no theory, no hypothesis; it is plain matter of fact, of above thirty years standing. In every modification of their governments, the United States have adhered to it. When have we seen the people perpetrating the atrocious crimes charged to popular governments, plundering property, banishing merit, or tearing asunder the limbs of innocence? Where are wars, tumults, oppression, prosecutions and corruption, proceeding from the people? If these calamities have not appeared under our policy, we ought to conclude that they proceeded in former times from the causes which we have excluded; or that the human character has undergone a moral change, which secures a nation, if it will govern itself, against any danger from itself.

From the facts established by the experience of the United States, turn to the contemplation of those established by the experience of the English system of hereditary orders, paper and patronage, during the same period. Estimate the wars, entered into for the purpose of instructing Europe in political metaphysicks, or for the sake of these orders. Estimate the taxes, the tythes, the poor houses, the prisons, the fleets, the armies, the banishments to colonise a wilderness under martial law, the bastiles of state criminals, the well tenanted gibbets, the national debt, and the patronage and corruption which guides and poisons every publick measure.

If it be urged, that commotions have appeared under our system; without stopping to inquire, whether they ought to be ascribed to that, or to the arts of its rival system, it suffices to exhibit as a counterpoise to our bloodless wars, and comical excursions, the commotions in Ireland, marked by devastation and slaughter.

It cannot be omitted, that Connecticut underwent no change of government by the revolution. Here, more power has been condensed for centuries in representatives frequently elected, than is enjoyed by representatives in any other state of the Union. The happiness and good order of Connecticut, during the long operation of her popular form of government, infinitely exceeds the happiness and good order of England during the same, or any other period. Privileged orders had no influence in Connecticut, and whatever happiness and prosperity she enjoyed, was owing to the elective principle. The continued efficacy of election for two centuries in this instance, unconnected with privileged orders, accounts for its inefficacy in their presence. This remark is farther warranted, by the contemporary appearance of party malevolence and a paper system in the United States. So soon as an imitation of the English policy for dividing the nation into the two orders of payers and receivers, began to operate, the rivalry of orders, and the avarice of interest, began to make their accustomed efforts, to destroy the good effects of election.

Of the disgust against it, which they excite themselves, these vicious principles will be the first to take advantage. Mr. Adams has already seriously informed us, that hereditary kings and nobles are as much the representatives of the nation, as those they elect; and the following quotation will enforce the argument, accounting for the inefficacy of election in communion with privileged or separate interests; because it displays the intemperate enmity entertained by their disciples to the elective principle.

'If the elections are in a large country like England, for example, or one of the United States of America, where various cities, towns, boroughs, and corporations are to be represented, each scene of election will have two or more candidates, and two or more parties, each of which will study its sleights and projects, disguise its designs, draw in tools, and worm out enemies. We must remember, that every party, and every individual, is now struggling for a share in the executive and judicial power as well as legislative, for a share in the distribution of all honours, offices, rewards and profits. Every passion and prejudice of every voter will be applied to; every flattery and menace, every trick and bribe that can be bestowed, and will be accepted, will be used; *and what is horrible to think of,* that candidate or that agent *who has fewest scruples;* who will *propagate lies and slanders* with most confidence and secrecy; who will *wheedle, flatter and cajole;* who will *debauch the people by treats, feasts and diversions* with the least hesitation, and *bribe with the most impudent front,* which can consist with hypocritical concealment, will draw in tools and worm out enemies the fastest; *unsullied honour, sterling integrity, real virtue, will stand a very unequal chance. When vice, folly, impudence and knavery, have carried the election one year, they will acquire, in the course of it, fresh influence and power to succeed the next.* In the course of the year, the delegate in an assembly that disposes of all commissions, *contracts* and *pensions,* has many opportunities to reward his friends among his constituents, and punish his enemies. The son or other relation of one friend has a commission given him in the *army,* another in the *navy,* a third a benefice in the *church,* a fourth in the customs, a fifth in the excise; *shares in loans and contracts* are distributed among his friends, by which they are enabled to increase their own and his dependents and partisans, or, in other words, to draw in more instruments and parties, and worm out their opposites. All this is so easy to comprehend, so obvious to sight, and so certainly known in universal experience, that it is astonishing that our author should have ventured to assert, that such a government kills the canker-worm faction.'*

The reader will be pleased to remark, that Mr. Adams has had his eye fixed upon the operation of election in England, whilst he is giving its character. The enumerated modes of corruption, were most of them exclusively practised in England when he wrote this extract; and the means of practising the greater part, did not even exist in the United States. Presently, we shall exhibit extracts, wherein Mr. Adams recommends hereditary orders as the refuge from the vices of election. He is obliged to bend his eye towards England, to get the contour of a detestable picture of election, and places it before our eyes, to induce us to introduce the policy of England. He will not see, that our elective system is more perfect than the English, because it is less corrupted by the very policy, which has furnished the ideas for his invective; but the United States will never be charmed to fly down the gaping throat of a dreadful monster, in order to escape its malignancy. They will behold this character of election when united with hereditary orders, or separate interests, as a confession of the enmity and inconsistency of the two principles, and of the certain corruption of the first, by an alliance with the second.

It will not be denied, that the elective system of the United States, is chargeable with several of the vices imputed to election by Mr. Adams; but it does not follow, that we ought to surrender it for a system exposed to them all. The use, which republicanism ought to make of the charge, is, to awaken her sons to the necessity of removing these vices. Their danger is imminent, when they are already made the ground of a treatise in recommendation of hereditary orders, as preferable to the vices of election. Nor does the difficulty of rendering the elective system more perfect in America, seem to be insurmountable, when it is recollected, that the whole catalogue of vices ascribed to it by Mr. Adams, arises from a capacity in the delegate to acquire or dispose of money and offices. The effects of this capacity prove it to be an evil political principle, exciting the evil moral qualities of human nature. It is capable of removal from legislative delegates, and if it produces the effects ascribed to it by Mr. Adams, it ought to be removed. But this subject belongs to the defects of the constitution of the United States.

Let us, therefore, return to a contemplation of Mr. Adams's

* Adams's Def. v. 3, 275.

invective against election. It is a mode of attack, precisely similar to that used against popular governments. To discredit the one, a vast collection of evils is made, arising under a vast variety of governments, whether produced by the form of the government, or by other causes. To discredit the other, a picture is drawn of all the vices of election, acting with orders. 'It is horrible to think of,' says Mr. Adams. His horrour might have been considerably augmented, by collecting into a mass all the vices of human nature, which would have completely rounded up the doctrine 'that republicanism was a hell, election its turbulence, and men its devils.'

Human reason must turn on preference, not on perfection. If election is exploded, shall we be requited for its loss by the virtual representation of kings and nobles; or by surrendering our government to paper and patronage? These are the objects, with which we must compare election, before we are seduced to give it up for a system more defective, because Mr. Adams contends, that, like every thing human, it is imperfect. Admitting it to be so, it is unnecessary in imitation of Mr. Adams's mode of reasoning, to enrage our readers with a collection of the follies, oppressions and cruelties, committed by the fools, tyrants and madmen, to which hereditary representation has exposed the world; to prove that hereditary representation is more defective than actual election.

America has experienced both. Hereditary representation assailed her liberty and happiness; elected representation defended them. She has seen hereditary representation destroying the existence of the Irish nation; whilst elected representation, though unequal and corrupted, made some stand for it. There, hereditary representation disclosed that kind of responsibility, which Congress would disclose by a law for uniting these States with England; and had hereditary representation existed at the peace, a king like that enjoyed by Ireland, of the Neuchattel species, would probably have been one of its fruits.

Our quotation must be recollected to understand the remarks it suggests. It may be thus condensed. 'In such countries as England and America, election will produce every species of villainy; the greatest rascals will succeed; and being once elected, will retain their power.'

Mr. Adams does not perceive, that his eagerness for hereditary orders, has here again entangled him in an inconsistency. For their sake he labours to inculcate an abhorrence of election, without recollecting, that he relies upon it for one branch of his own theory.

146

Will he say, that election, united with hereditary orders, will be purged of its bad qualities? That it is abominable, applied to a senate, governour or president; but admirable, applied to a house of commons? And will he, by escaping from the inconsistency through these assertions, pass final sentence upon our policy in the opprobrious epithets of the extract?

But Mr. Adams cannot be permitted to avail himself of these assertions; and therefore his disapprobation of election, must stand, unqualified and unequivocal. It cannot be conceded as true, that election in England exhibits fewer vices, than in the United States; or that the elected order of that country, are less corrupt than the elected functionaries of this. If, therefore, he explodes the whole of our policy by discrediting election, he also explodes so much of his as depends upon the same principle, and leaves to his own theory, nothing that he commends, hereditary representation excepted.

It is not by inconsistent railings and unbounded applauses, that we are edified. It is not by magnifying the defects of election, and conceding its benefits, that we can estimate its value. Had a fair comparison been drawn between the state of election, in the United States and in England, a vast superiority in point of purity, would have appeared on the side of the United States. If so, frequency and purity of election, are in concord; and nobility and purity of election, in discord.

The idea and origin of election, have been generally, if not universally, defective, until the American revolution. In England, it is to this day a remnant of feudality, planted by prerogative. It is derived, not from the inherent natural right of self government, but from the gratuitous donation of a feudal monarch.

Ambition and avarice have been perpetually forming combinations, and practising devices for depriving men of their rights. Hence ensue struggles for redress; in the progress of which, if the usurpers find it prudent to relax, they artfully deal out these relaxations, not as rights independent of their pleasure, but as meritorious acts of grace and favour.

Accordingly, election or self government being a right fatal to usurpation, whenever some portion of it could no longer be withheld from the people, usurpers have laboured to defeat it, first, by restricting it to the idea of an indulgence; and, secondly, by contaminating it with destructive modifications.

The struggles between the people and nobles of Rome; the indulgence and modification of suffrage; the mode of voting, so as to bestow the .decision on wealth or poverty; the inveterate parties created by this division; and the vast indefinite powers retained by the senate; were artifices of hereditary orders to contaminate election and defeat its effects.

By stratagem, also, has election been managed in England. It was an indulgence of the kings. It was bestowed without rule, according to the suggestions of royal interest or ambition. And it is retained in its present corrupt state, to destroy its efficacy. It discloses no principle of right or justice, in origin, modification or practice.

Why then has Mr. Adams estimated the elective principle by the examples of Rome and England, where it was bottomed upon notorious fraud? In America, the principle is better understood: it feels the dignity of a right; we have no hereditary orders (its natural enemy) to poison it; and it enjoys the power of exercising its will. The difference in parentage between truth and errour; and in nurture, between fraud and honesty, are both so essential, as to justify expectations from the elective principle, which that principle, modelled by patrician craft, monarchical despotism, or paper frauds, does not inspire.

Much contention and ingenuity has arisen out of the question, whether society is natural or factitious. If society is natural, then natural rights may exist in, and be improved and secured by a state of society. Payne contends for the natural rights of man; Adams for the natural rights of aristocracy. If society is factitious, those who make it, can regulate rights. Society must be composed of, or created by individuals, without whom, it can neither exist nor act. Society exclusively of individuals, is an ideal being, as metaphysical as the idea of a triangle. If a number of people should inclose themselves within a triangle, they would hear with great astonishment, that they had lost the power of changing the form of the inclosure; and that the dead figure of the triangle governed living beings, instead of living beings who created that figure, governing it. So by the magick of avarice and ambition, the word society is severed from a nation, and converted into a metaphysical spectre, auspicious only to the tyrants of society. But the United States have detected the crafty absurdity; and Mr. Adams has expressly conceded to nations, a natural right to modify their governments. It is true he attempts to satisfy this right by the idea of hereditary representatives; allowing the existence of the right of self government, but attempting to evade its effect.

148

Thus the doctrine of distinguishing society from the individuals composing it, is ingeniously concealed under the notion of hereditary representation, so as to render the concession, that all societies have a right to modify their governments, nominal and ineffectual. As we have seen the principle of election artfully destroyed, by the hereditary orders of Rome and England; so here, the principle of society, namely, the right of self government, whilst it is allowed, is also annihilated by the idea of a representation of society by these same hereditary orders. For no sooner are these orders created, than they become the magick representatives of the people, according to Mr. Adams, and use the term society as an incantation, with which to transfer the rights of associated man, to associated orders. Upon the doctrines, that man has no natural rights, but that aristocratical orders, as the progeny of nature, have, is suspended the controversy between the political systems which divide mankind.

Mr. Adams, by allowing that all societies have a natural right to modify their governments, admits that some cannot possess more of this right than others; and that one generation cannot possess a natural right to violate the same natural right of another, by substituting rights of orders for the rights of society. Whenever this violation is submitted to, the natural right of a society to modify its government, acknowledged by Mr. Adams, merges in a factitious right of orders to do so; and thus this right is defeated, just as election was defeated at Rome and in England.

For Mr. Adams's concession of the right of self government to all societies, attended by his system of orders, is only the admission of a right so momentary and evanescent, as to be lost in the instant of its exercise, and as to subject all generations to the will of one.

Between election, and the conceded right of self government, the connection must be indissoluble, or the concession will be nugatory and deceptious; and, therefore, it is by no means wonderful, that artificial orders, which constitute the most successful mode of destroying the right of self government, should employ every artifice to frustrate the only means of maintaining it; or that Mr. Adams, the champion of these orders, should treat election with a severity, only equalled by the severity with which he has treated republican governments; extracting his character of both from corruptions caused by his own orders. Election does not yet engage two orders of rich and poor in perpetual hostilities in the United States; but all ranks vote individually, interwoven and commixed;

nor is it yet corrupted by commissions in armies, navies or churches, by loans or contracts, or by unequal representation and purchase. These are the corruptions, invented by political orders to destroy the efficacy of election, and these orders are the remedies proposed by Mr. Adams, for the evils of their own invention.

As in England, the national right of self government, is ever seized by orders; accordingly Judge Blackstone declares that 'the parliament may change the nature of the government, without consulting the people;' because the orders composing it, consider themselves as composing the society, and the people as no longer entitled to the right of modifying their government, allowed by Mr. Adams to every society. Of this allowance, the futility in communion with orders, is thus demonstrated by the practice and principles of Mr. Adams's theory, in the instance of England.

By deducing election from the grace and favour of hereditary chiefs, and by the artifice of compounding society of orders, and not of individuals, the usurpation of a right to modify the government without consulting a nation, is also produced; it is this usurpation, which enslaves societies, under the sanction of society; thus the orders of Denmark abolished election, and made the monarch despotick; pretending to constitute the society, they usurped the power of modifying the government, and enslaved the society. So acted the orders of Ireland. So acted the orders of England, in changing the succession of the crown; and in appointing representatives for the people for four years, by a law extending the time of service from three to seven.

It was one effort of the first part of this essay, to prove that aristocracy in every form, was artificial; but if a reader can be found who dissents from that opinion, none will deny that hereditary orders are so. They are an effect of society, as much as hereditary estates in land. Both arise from laws. Society is paramount to law; law, therefore, cannot transfer social or national rights from its creator, society, to its creature, hereditary orders. An exclusive right to form or alter a government is annexed to society, in every moment of its existence; and therefore a direct or indirect exercise of it by a government, a combination or an individual, is a badge of usurpation, and a harbinger of despotism.

This doctrine is admitted by the acknowledgment of Mr. Adams, that hereditary orders are the representatives of the nation; an acknowledgment, however, artfully bottomed upon the theory, that all governments, are the representatives of nations; and defeated by betraying in practice national rights to these theoretical representatives.

It appears that hereditary orders have uniformly destroyed the doctrine of representation, by originating election from erroneous principles; by corrupting it with treacherous modifications; and by fraudulently constituting themselves into the society; a power above responsibility. Of all the mischiefs produced by them, experience testifies to none with more constancy, than their successful operations to destroy the efficacy of election. Mr. Adams depends upon this efficacy to control hereditary orders, whilst experience tells him, that these orders have invariably destroyed the efficacy itself. Yet he builds his theory upon experience. He himself testifies to the vices of election; yet he relies upon its virtue to correct the vices of hereditary orders; he sees the vices of election produced by these orders themselves, and he proposes a remedy, in the continuance of the cause. Experience uniformly tells him, that hereditary orders, and a fair representation of a real responsibility, have never subsisted together; and he subjoins to his theory the novel and mystical idea, that hereditary orders are representatives of the nation, which they have never admitted themselves, to reinstate a representation instead of that arising from election, which they corrupt and destroy.

The admonitions of experience cannot be mistaken by deliberation and prudence. They consist on the one hand, in the uniform corruption or destruction of election and representation by hereditary orders; on the other, in a long course of beneficial effects in the United States from election and representation, where there are no such orders. Mr. Adams has viewed the elective system through the first perspective, and shuts his eyes upon the second. From the first he collects its character, and disgusted with vices, reflected from the English system itself, he proposes by introducing that system, to remedy the elective system of the United States.

Nedham had said 'that the people, by representatives successively chosen, were the best guardians of their own liberties.'* And that 'the life of liberty, and the only remedy against self interest, lies in succession of powers and persons.'† In answer to which, Mr. Adams observes, 'If this is so, the United States of America have taken the most effectual measures to secure that life and that remedy, in establishing annual elections of their governours, senators and representatives. This will probably be allowed to be as

* Adams's Def. v. 3, 213. † Adams's Def. v. 3, 282.

perfect an establishment of a succession of powers and persons, as human laws can make: but in what manner annual elections of governours and senators will operate, remains to be ascertained. It should always be remembered, that this is not the first experiment that was ever made in the world of elections to great offices of state: how they have operated in every great nation, and what has been their end, is very well known. Mankind have universally discovered that chance was preferable to a corrupt choice, and have trusted Providence rather than themselves. First magistrates and senators had better be made *hereditary* at once, *than that the people should be universally debauched and bribed, go to loggerheads, and fly to arms regularly every year.* Thank heaven! Americans understand calling conventions; and if the time should come, as it is very possible it may, when *hereditary descent* shall become a less evil than *annual fraud and violence*, such a convention may still prevent the first magistrate from becoming absolute, as well as hereditary.'*

Nedham had also said 'that it is but reason that the people should see that none be interested in the supreme authority, but persons of their own election, and such as must in a short time, return again into the same condition with themselves.' In answer to which, Mr. Adams observes, that 'the Americans have agreed with this writer in this sentiment. This hazardous experiment they have tried, and if elections are soberly made, it may answer very well; but if parties, factions, drunkenness, bribes, armies and delirium, come in, *as they always have done sooner or later*, to embroil and decide every thing, the people must again have recourse to conventions, and find a remedy. Neither *philosophy* nor *policy* has yet discovered any other cure, than by *prolonging the duration of the first magistrate and senators*. The evil may be lessened and *postponed*, by elections *for longer periods of years, till they come for life*; and if this is not found an adequate remedy, there will remain no other but to make them *hereditary*. The delicacy or the *dread of unpopularity*, that should induce any man to conceal *this important truth* from the full view and contemplation of the people, would be a weakness, if not a vice.'†

The reader now perceives the necessity of considering election, as operating independently, or under the influence of hereditary orders; because if it is more vicious in the latter situation than in the former, Mr. Adams's proposal to amend a less vicious elective system, by substituting for it one more so, is undoubtedly precipi-

* Adams's Def. v. 3, 282, 283.   † Adams's Def. v. 3, 296.

tate and erroneous. Election has been universally in the supposed vicious state, previously to the experiment of the United States, and from this vicious state Mr. Adams has drawn his inferences. At this moment it exists in the United States unconnected, and in England, connected, with hereditary orders; in the two situations between which a distinction has been attempted. The utmost pitch of his remedy is to exchange our elective and representative vices, for those of England. Election in England, being derived from an erroneous source, and corrupted by the artifices of hereditary power, is of course more vicious and less efficient than in America; and being an object of contempt on account of its vices, it attracts but a small share of national confidence, and forms but an inconsiderable obstacle to the tyranny and oppression of monarchy and aristocracy; in fact we shall hereafter endeavour to prove, that it is modified into an instrument for their use.

If it was true, therefore, as Mr. Adams asserts, 'that the manner in which annual elections of governours and senators will operate in the United States remained to be ascertained,' yet, as the utter corruption of election by hereditary power, does not remain to be ascertained, neither philosophy nor policy have yet discovered, that a certain and malignant evil, was preferable to a possible good.

Philosophy, unbiased by affections superseding a love of wisdom, has seldom or never given her suffrage in favour of hereditary power, nor will she shut her eyes upon the elective experiment of the United States, although Mr. Adams in policy is pleased to assert, that it remains to be made. It has been made upon some hundreds of governours, and thousands of senators. Is nothing ascertained? Will an equal number of kings and lords act upon the political theatre, without ascertaining also the value of the hereditary principle?

The quotations place 'corrupt choice' in contrast with 'chance;' and 'debauchery, bribery and annual civil war,' with 'hereditary government.' The treatise, ascribes to aristocracy 'virtue, wisdom and usefulness,' and one of the extracts ascribes to election, the utmost degree of profligacy. Such a mode of reasoning is fictitious, because it suppresses all the shade of the hereditary principle, and all the light of the elective; and presenting a picture of each, which excludes the most striking features of both, by deforming one and embellishing the other, it excessively obstructs our efforts to draw a correct comparison between them. Yet these fictions really terrified Mr. Adams to such a degree, as to draw from him an ejaculation for the discovery of conventions, which would enable the Americans to take refuge from the 'annual fraud and violence' of election, under 'hereditary descent;' and invigorated his mind against the 'dread of unpopularity,' to announce 'the important truth,' that 'hereditary first magistrates and senators' were the final 'remedy' against the vices of the elective system.

Mr. Adams frequently strikes with such incautious fury at his adversary, as to wound himself. It was before remarked, that the profligacy he ascribes to election, would corrupt his own theory, as well as ours, had it merited his censures; and now it is very remarkable, that he flies to a 'convention' as a remedy against 'election.' Differing with all other politicians, he makes virtue the principle of hereditary power; vice, of elective power; and yet this vice is his resource, for the creation of this virtue.

Again. Mr. Adams considers a concentration of power in a single body of representatives, as a political errour of unequalled magnitude; yet he proposes to collect this very body, by the resource, so corrupt in his opinion, and confides in it to introduce his theory, which he is fascinated to believe, would be an act of the highest publick benefit. A single body of representatives, says he, is a political monster, yet it has already done great good in America; '*thank heaven*, Americans understand calling conventions;' and it may, therefore, do one good thing more, that is, destroy all the good things it has hitherto done, and establish 'hereditary descent.' Thus allowing to the elective principle the utmost perfection, after having sunk all its useful faculties in an invective. But both the one and the other is done for the sake of an hypothesis.

The case of conventions will furnish the strongest arguments in favour of election, and many hints in relation to the organization of legislative bodies, of which it is probable, a very beneficial use will at some future period be made.

Conventions are creatures of election; of election, made upon the widest scale; they have been so successfully practised in America, as to awaken Mr. Adams's piety; they have probably prevented, and have never excited civil war; they have justified none of the charges exhibited against election, and have begotten all the political happiness enjoyed in the United States, for nearly the last thirty years. This is an operation of election, through the organ of a single chamber.

Why has this operation been so completely consistent, both in war and peace, in danger and safety, in producing order and happiness? On the contrary, why has the same principle, election, as Mr. Adams proves by a multitude of examples, produced in most cases (excepting the United States) confusion, civil war, riot and crimes? Mr. Adams in commemorating the discovery of conventions, ought to have remarked and explained the reason of these different effects from the same principle.

The solution of the difficulty justifies one ground taken in defence of our elective system. Election, as heretofore practised, was of spurious birth, and corrupted by rivals. Here, privileged orders and hierarchies did not exist to corrupt it, and it drew its origin from a society composed of people, and not of orders. Heretofore election was the martyr of arts and obloquies invented and practised by its enemies; and it only remains for us to determine, whether we will become the bubbles of examples, produced by frauds, of which the ancients were the victims.

The wonderful virtue and chastity of election and representation in the case of conventions, may be owing in a degree, to something different in the constitution of that species of power, from the constitution of an ordinary legislature. The chief differences usually existing are, that members of conventions are chosen by a greater number of electors, for a shorter space, and have no opportunities of acquiring or bestowing publick money or publick offices. To opposite causes, Mr. Adams ascribes the evils incident to a single chamber of representatives; these evils do not appear in conventions, because the causes are absent; a fact presenting a new illustration of our political analysis. As in the case of our governours, power is bestowed, so as to awaken the good and suppress the evil qualities of human nature; so the case of conventions proves the safety and utility of a single house of representatives, organized so as to suppress, and not to solicit, avarice and ambition.

An elective system, therefore, will be either good or bad, as it is calculated to suppress or excite the good or evil qualities of mankind; and its nature may be ascertained by applying to it the political analysis contended for in this essay. Election by irritated and inimical clans, arranged into factions, as at Rome; which places a nation in the hands of a minority, or exposes it to sale, as in England; or which exalts representation above responsibility, and enables it to invade or abridge the publick liberty, as in France; is founded in an evil principle, and will excite evil qualities. The cases of Cæsar, Cromwell, Bonaparte, and numberless others, are illustrations. Election, which enables a legislature to convey office or wealth to themselves, directly or indirectly, will also convey evil qualities into the bosom of representation. And election, subjected to the arts of an interest distinct from and inimical to the nation, will generate the evils of lying, cheating, bribery, and several others enumerated by Mr. Adams. But election founded in good moral principles, will produce good effects. The cases of conventions and governours are eminent proofs of the correctness of this idea. Conventions have frequently disclosed virtuous sentiments, and seldom or never vicious. But they were not elected by inimical orders or interests, by minorities, or by bargain and sale; the representative was not placed beyond responsibility, or enabled to usurp despotick authority; nor was his avarice or ambition awakened, by making his election and representation the channel, for bringing office or money to himself. This subject so radically important to the United States, will demand a further consideration.

Here, I shall only add, that the experiment proposed by Mr. Adams, is extremely hazardous; it is not to correct, but to destroy two thirds of our elective system, and to corrupt the remaining third by hereditary orders. This is proposed to be effected by election itself, on its widest ground. If the elective and representative system, should be persuaded to destroy two thirds of itself, is it not questionable, whether the substituted hereditary principle, will be equally ready to submit to annihilation, should the experiment be unfortunate? Will a privileged order, once invested with power, follow the example of election and representation, by becoming a felo de se? The national repentance which succeeds the establishment of orders of monopolies, gains only derision, and an aggravation of the evil; none of the instruments of oppression are ever relinquished without civil war; and should they be introduced into the United States, we may certainly pronounce, that no other politician will have an opportunity of again congratulating this country on the discovery of conventions, until he has seen it drenched in blood. An attempt to persuade the elective system to yield to the hereditary, is an acknowledgment of its virtue; and the constant refusal of the hereditary to hear or suffer reasoning against itself, manifests its vice. Goodness, and not wickedness, is attempted to be made the victim of scepticism.

The recourse to conventions for the introduction of a government, bottomed upon the idea, that aristocracy is natural, surrenders the foundation of the whole theory. Is that natural which may or may not be created by a mode both novel and artificial? This mode consists of an expression of national will, by representation, and admits the right of national self government to be natural. Is aristocracy, so obviously inconsistent with this right, also natural? The reference to election and representation for obtaining national will, in the momentous affair of changing the form of government, concedes, that it can be obtained in no other way. If election and representation exclusively merit national confidence, when the consignment of power is greatest, why are they to be distrusted in inferiour agencies?

In 1789, the admiration of Mr. Adams in contemplating the effects of our policy, broke forth with fervour and solemnity, in an inaugural address to the creatures of that policy; and therefore it is probable, that he had relinquished his wish to destroy it by a convention previously expressed. The following extract from that address is not printed at the end of his treatise.

'I should be destitute of sensibility, if upon my arrival in this city, and presentation to this legislature, and especially to this senate, I could see, without emotion, so many of those characters, of whose virtuous exertions I have so often been a witness—from whose countenances and examples I have ever derived encouragement and animation—whose disinterested friendship has supported me in many intricate conjunctures of publick affairs, at home and abroad: Those celebrated defenders of the liberties of this country, whom *menaces could not intimidate, corruption seduce, nor flattery allure. Those intrepid assertors of the rights of mankind, whose philosophy and policy have enlightened the world, in twenty years, more than it was ever before enlightened in many centuries, by ancient schools, or modern universities.'*

This eulogy is bestowed on our policy, as it had operated previously to the existence of the present general government, under the auspices of election and representation. It would be quite unphilosophical to assert, that Americans were insensible to the influence of intimidation, corruption and flattery; and therefore it must have been owing to our system of government, that its agents were uninfluenced by these vices. This is conceivable, by recollecting that our principle of division prevented an accumulation of power, capable of intimidating; that the system of paper and patronage did not exist to corrupt; and that we had no monarchy or aristocracy, to corrupt election and buy despotism with publick money. It does not weaken the force of these observations to urge that Mr. Adams chiefly refers in this part of the extract, to the arts and

157

practices of the English system, in assailing ours. For he thereby debases that, and exalts ours, by allowing one to be a system, fitted for these vicious practices, and the other, fitted to resist them; and he also admits that effects ensued, in the absence of causes propelling to these vices, differing from those which their presence produces; of course such causes were not interwoven with our government.

Our own governments, however, were exclusively the evidence of the following declaration; 'those intrepid assertors of the rights of mankind, whose philosophy and policy have enlightened the world, in twenty years, more than it was ever before enlightened in many centuries, by ancient schools or modern universities.' In what did this modern light, or the previous darkness consist? Will a mixture of the ignorance of many centuries, with this enlightened policy, so recently invented, obscure, or render it more splendid? In short, why has Mr. Adams, neglecting the wonderful discoveries of this modern philosophy in favour of human rights, arrayed against it a cloud of quotations, chiefly collected from the deepest tints of ancient obscurity? Was it to explain, impress and accelerate a philosophy and policy, which had advanced more rapidly in twenty years than the philosophy and policy comprising his references had in twenty centuries?

The old school of monarchy, aristocracy and democracy is at issue with the new school, of modifying government with an aspect to moral qualities, and not to numerical orders. Mr. Adams's efforts and praises appear on the side of the new school; his treatise, and his proposal to extinguish the light of our policy, so dazzling in 1789, on the side of the old; like the strokes of father and son taking different sides in a civil war to save the estate, though felt by the parties, they balance each other in the controversy.

It is necessary to understand thoroughly the ground of the controversy between 'the philosophy and policy' of the United States, and of 'ancient schools and modern universities,' to discover wherein the darkness of the one, and the light of the other, called the old, and the new school, consisted. For this purpose, let us divest our minds of all perplexing modifications of the one, the few and the many; of political terms tortured by construction; and of every analysis hitherto suggested, and endeavour to enlighten the controversy by considering, whether a government must not be founded in one or more simple elements, capable of ascertaining its nature, with great exactness.

These consist, we believe, of fraud, force and reason; the term reason, being considered as conveying an idea of a nation governed by its own will, or of self government. The element of the Roman government was first fraud, and then force. The fraud consisted of the use made of superstition, and of the privileges, pillage and usurpations of the nobility. The indignation excited by this element, was artfully managed by Julius and Augustus, to substitute the element of force for that of fraud. The government was called a republick, both before and after its elemental principle had changed; and yet neither of its elemental principles resembled the element of reason, national will or self government.

The catalogue of Italian republicks exhibits but one case resembling the Roman, which these little governments were frequently attempting to imitate. A variety exists in occasional acquisitions of superiority by the people; but these left the government upon its old element, because noble orders still existed; or because the division of election was wanting to prevent tumult and violence; or because election conveyed so much power as to induce the officer to practice fraud or force. So long as feudal tenure, superstition and ignorance flourished in England, the element of its government was a mixture of fraud and force. And here is an instance, similar to which, many might be quoted, of a change in the form, without any in the element of the government. Executive power, armies and patronage have beaten feudality out of the field, and the fraud of superstition is superseded by the fraud of paper stock; yet the elements of the government are unchanged.

Now if the elements of these governments, are not the elements of ours, then it is inferred, that the element of ours is not that of any government ancient or modern; because none can be adduced, not deeply participating of the same elements, with the governments quoted.

This brings us to the principles of the old and the new school; one founds government in the elements of force and fraud, by always bestowing power, so as to induce it to rest on those elements; the other bestows power, so as to secure its dependence on national will, and compels it to consult national reason. The essential difference of the principles of these two schools, causes the terms and phrases of the old to perplex rather than edify, the disciples of the new; because, when governments are founded on different elements, it is incorrect to reason upon their theory or effects, as if there was a similitude between them. A similitude exists between force and fraud, as being both vicious; these are proper subjects for comparison; but between force or fraud, and reason or self government, no similitude exists; because they possess no common quality. The very system of reasoning, therefore, pursued by Mr. Adams throughout his treatise, is erroneous, as being founded in comparison instead of contrast. No inference, which is the result of a comparison between dissimilar objects, can be relied on; whereas, the more dissimilar objects are, the more forcible will every argument be, which results from contrast.

Contrast alone is capable of producing the old and the new political schools, in fair competition; comparison, on the other hand, is the most dangerous weapon, with which the old can avenge its malevolence upon the new, for being 'an intrepid asserter of the rights of man.' For what can so completely blast the laurels with which Mr. Adams has himself exultingly crowned the American patriots, as the doctrine, that our new principles of policy, are similar to the old?

Let us apply the test of contrast to a few details, and if they will bear it, we may conclude with confidence, that no such ill boding similitude exists.

Upon our policy superstition has no influence; upon the ancient, its impression was powerful. In the first, there are no hereditary or privileged orders; in the second, they abounded. By the first, power is made responsible by division; in the second, either the use of division was unknown, or it was ineffectually applied. The first is enabled by the art of printing, to use the knowledge of a nation; the second used its ignorance. Formerly, the oracles of the Pythia, the flight of birds, the pecking of chickens, and the driving of nails into the capitol, were the arguments offered by governments to nations; now, reasoning, and not miracle, is used to beget opinion. Then, democracy being galled by the injuries of orders, upon casually breaking her fetters, disclosed the fury which oppression inspires; now, the democracy of the United States, if it is one, seeing only compeers, and suffering only the gentle chastening inflicted by herself, has for many years displayed rather the docility of an elephant, than the ferocity of a tiger.

Reasoning from contrast, and not from comparison, would also have disclosed with greater perspicuity, the differences between existing governments. Thus it would have unavoidably appeared, that in Europe, the elements of government continue to be force and fraud. The fraud and force of superstition, were overthrown by being discovered; wherefore it was necessary to invent a fraud, wider in its influence, and a force, physically stronger; this was done by paper and patronage and by standing armies.

The policy of the United States has laboured to prevent the introduction of force by armies, and of fraud by corruption; and to secure an allegiance of the government to the understandings of the people, and not an allegiance of the people by force or fraud, to the will of the government. Evincing that reason, and not fraud or force, is its element.

Governments, whose elements are fraud or force, will naturally excite the evil qualities of human nature; and those whose element is reason, can only excite its good. And if every government must rely for continuance, either on force or fraud, or on reason; it follows that every government must be founded in good or in evil moral principles.

To defend the elements of force and fraud, it has been said, 'that man is naturally vicious, and his own worst enemy; and that this self-malignity disqualifies him for self government, and can only be restrained by force or fraud.'

The analysis contended for, admits that human nature is compounded of good and evil qualities, and hence it is not merely allowed, but strenuously contended throughout this essay, that government ought to be modelled with a view to the preservation of the good and the control of the evil. All nations have published their concurrence in this opinion, by establishing and enforcing municipal law, for the purpose of restraining private vices; and all (the United States excepted) have hitherto failed to discover a code of political law, calculated to restrain publick vices. By publick vices and political law, I mean, injuries committed by governments against nations, and regulations to prevent or punish them.

As the vices, the virtues, the passions and the interests of mankind are multiplied by civilization, the necessity for multiplying both kinds of law, gradually increases. In an indigent or savage state, few laws, municipal or political, suffice; because few interests exist to awaken our evil propensities. Therefore simple and unlimited forms of government, and few municipal laws, universally accompany such a state of society. But whenever society advances in the arts of civilization, and the interests of men are multiplied by wealth and commerce, the number and complexity of municipal laws must be increased, to meet the case of a new moral character. It is equally necessary to suppress the simple forms of government,

F . 161

which required no restraints, where there were no temptations; and to invent new political laws, analogous also to this new moral character, in order to counteract the force of these new temptations.

In every state of society, the vices of the individuals who administer the government, will, in relation to publick duties, be as great, and probably much greater, than will be the vices of those who do not administer it, in relation to private duties. Solicitations and excitements to avarice and ambition, will be offered to publick officers by the view of a rich nation, constituting temptations to vice, superior to any which can occur in private life. Therefore, political law should not only keep pace with municipal law, to provide for this new state of society; but the former ought to outstrip the latter in energy, in the same proportion as the violations of publick duties are likely to outstrip those of private, by reason of the superiority of the temptation.

The effects of this temptation, are seen in the history of most nations, to be exactly graduated by their cause. In a poor nation, the temptation being small, publick duties are seldom violated; and such violations are more frequent and more wicked, as a nation increases in opulence; proving that the appetite of the individuals who exercise a government, for gratifications arising from a breach of duty, is within the power of a poor nation, and beyond the power of a rich one, to satisfy.

The political elements, force and fraud, are begotten by national opulence, because nations have only provided new municipal laws to control the private vices produced also by this opulence; and have neglected to provide new political laws against the more injurious publick vices arising from the same cause. For private vices, they have provided the prison and the gallows; for publick vices, wealth and power. Can these contradictory remedies for similar evils be both effectual?

The United States, beholding this as an erroneous policy; and despairing of producing good manners, or a regard for private duties, by infusing into government the 'strongest solicitations to disregard publick duties; endeavour to secure the morality of government, as the best security against the licentiousness of the people. They forbear to excite ambition and avarice by hereditary orders, or separate interests; and provide against both, by election, responsibility and division of power. They exclude the vicious moral qualities, fear and superstition, as elements of government;

and select for its basis, the most perfect moral quality of human nature.

It is as true, that a government may be vicious, as that a people may be vicious. By all hereditary systems, the people are placed extremely within the power of the government, and the government extremely without the power of the people; and a dereliction of the idea of political law, is considered as necessary to the existence of strong or rigorous municipal law. The utmost proposed by such systems is, to submit in despair to the effects of a vicious government, for the sake of curbing the vices of the people.

But the United States have aimed at a policy, possessing a capacity for regulating publick, as well as private duties; considering that government as weak, which can only regulate the latter; and that as strong, which is able to regulate both. For this purpose, they are cautious to bestow on each officer and department of government, only that portion of power, necessary to fulfil the annexed functions; to make these officers and departments, all dependent upon the nation or a section of it; and to enable the government to enforce the laws upon the individuals of the society. A policy by which the nation is considered as the executive of political law, and the avenger of violations of publick duties; and the government as the executive of municipal law, and the avenger of violations of private duties.

The contrast between this policy and the English, both in energy and perfection, is evident and forcible. One is able to prevent or punish the crimes which governments meditate or commit against nations, and also those committed by individuals; the other is unable to prevent or punish the first class of crimes, and even to punish the second, except by exciting the first. If the element of a government is force or fraud, it is obvious that the most pernicious class of crimes, namely, those perpetrated against nations by governments, are excited and not prevented or punished. But our policy provides both against the great injuries to which nations are liable from governments, and the small injuries which individuals may suffer from each other; conceiving a government to be weak and defective, however it may defend individuals against robbery and murder, which is unable to defend nations against oppression and despotism; and one to be stronger and more perfect, which, instead of exciting great crimes, for the purpose of punishing small, provides against both. A code of political law, too feeble to enforce publick duties, or to restrain publick offences, will

163

form an ambitious and avaricious government; and the vicious moral qualities of such a government, will corrupt the manners of the people; but an energetick code of political law, by producing political morality, will re-act wholesomely upon private manners by the channels of influence and imitation. A policy which fosters publick, in order to control private vices, is in contrast with one, which enforces publick duties, as an inducement to general good manners. One submits to the justice it dispenses, the other punishes the crimes it creates.

The indissoluble ligament between cause and effect, is evidently on the side of the possibility of training a government by moral principles. That moral causes are able to control the moral nature of man, and that in the form of government, they have universally controlled it, are the sources from whence the reasoning of this essay is deduced. If the surprising regularity with which the characters of governments have been graduated by their principles, and the astonishing force of these principles in corrupting or purifying the characters of magistrates, had only been demonstrated in the persons of American governours and hereditary monarchs, it ought to invigorate the human mind to keep possession of the ground it has already gained, and to push its discoveries still farther into the political terra incognita.

Section the Third

THE EVIL MORAL PRINCIPLES OF THE GOVERNMENT OF THE UNITED STATES

Let us venture to explore this country. Moral principles constitute the criterion for estimating the nature of a form of government. The number or arrangement of its administrators are such evidences of its nature, as the number and arrangement of a parterre of flowers, are of their botanical characters. Each species of the ancient analysis is bad. An analysis, which neither discloses the best, or even a good form of government, is suspicious, and excites a doubt, whether one of its evils, or a mixture of all three, is the true remedy against another. If the numerical analysis of government was superseded by one composed of principles, our attention would be attracted towards those principles. Mankind would estimate them, and discover which would infuse good, and which bad qualities. This classification of principles, would enable them to class governments, with equal precision; and the oscillation between forms, all bad, would cease.

The first part of this essay was appropriated to the establishment of a correct idea of aristocracy, and to unfolding the principles of the most eminent forms of government, ancient and modern, quoted by Mr. Adams; and the second, to an exhibition of the wide and substantial difference between these principles, and those of our policy; of Mr. Adams's inaccuracy in coercing the policy of the United States within the pale of the English balances, by the help of the old numerical analysis; and of the influence of moral principles upon the nature of governments. If such an influence exists, nothing can be more important to a nation than to understand it.

As the progress in political knowledge cannot be continued, except by an unremitting vigilance to discover interpolations of bad political principles among good, several sections will be appropriated to that object; reserving the pleasure of commemorat-

165

ing the beauties of our policy, as a compensation for discharging this irksome duty.

A dissection of our operating policy, however unpleasant, must be useful. We are indebted to the knife of the anatomist for a knowledge of the human body; this knowledge would have been infinitely more necessary, had men made men; without it, all human constitutions would have been rendered unsound, by mismatching their parts. Men do make governments, and have universally created unsound political bodies, by patching together hereditary orders and election, or separate interests and election; not perceiving, that one of these qualities has never failed to poison or maim the other.

But before we proceed to the proposed criticism, the test for detecting the nonconformity of any part to the element of our policy, must be again brought before the reader. It must be thoroughly understood to estimate our remarks. This consists of a political analysis built upon the moral foundation, that men are naturally both virtuous and vicious; and that they possess a power of regulating motives, or electing principles, which will cultivate either virtue or vice. Upon this ground, government is concluded to be a moral agent, which will be actuated by good or evil moral qualities; and that its qualities will certainly correspond with the principles by which it is created.

An eminent author, contends for a moral necessity, and a passive obedience to motives, uncontrollable by the agent. This essay proceeds upon an opinion, that man can regulate motives, and enjoys a volition, adequate to the election of virtue, and the rejection of vice. Mr. Godwin allows man to owe duties. He ought, says that author, to deliver truth 'with a spirit of universal kindness, with no narrow resentments or angry invectives.'* If he is the passive instrument of motives beyond his control, and deprived of volition, is it not unreasonable to require of him duties which he has no power to fulfil?

He farther observes, 'that man is not originally vicious.'† What then made him so? His motives impelled him to commit evil. Whence came these motives? If they followed man naturally, the assertion is untenable; if not, they must be artificial or factitious, voluntary and subject to election. Again. 'Ambition is common to all men.'‡ Is this vice, both universal, and also not natural or original? If it is factitious or voluntary, why may not the factitious

* God. Po. Jus. v. 1, 245.　　† v. 2, 203.　　‡ v. 1, 328.

principle of dividing power, so confidently condemned by Mr. Godwin, control it? But whether it is voluntary or involuntary, it may be inflamed, regulated or suppressed by motives. If a man is merely the automaton of motives, a nation may operate upon the individuals who are publick agents, by a set of motives calculated to impel to virtue or vice. Division and responsibility will impel to virtue; aggregated or undivided power will impel to vice. And if the doctrine of necessity and a passive obedience to motives is true, mankind only have to expose their governours to such as excite to good, and to shield them against those which excite to evil.

It is certainly true, that man is invariably guided by motives; and though it may be questioned, whether an individual has a power of creating or controlling his own motives, yet it cannot be denied, that others are able to influence him by motives which they can regulate. Those who compose governments or laws, may infuse into them motives to excite avarice and ambition, or liberality and patriotism.

But however metaphysicians may amuse the learned, by arguments in relation to fate and free will, politicians ought to be guided by the obvious and active qualities of human nature. In supposing moral events to be capable of regulation by causes which men can govern, such as knowledge, division of wealth and power, and responsibility; and in supposing the moral qualities of man to be good and evil, and that either one or the other may be excited; there is no deviation from the ostensible phenomena of human nature. And as government is exercised by man, all its virtues and vices must be human; wherefore, there does not seem more difficulty in ascertaining the principles or qualities which will constitute a good or a bad government, than in ascertaining those which will constitute a good or a bad man; nor more impropriety in reducing all governments to the two classes, of those founded in good, and those founded in evil moral principles, than in reducing all men to the two classes of good and bad. Bad or good principles may be infused into governments by constitutions, with more certainty than into men by education; and therefore a government corrupted by an infusion of bad principles, can more justly complain of the nation for making it wicked, than the nation can complain of the government for making it miserable.

It was not the policy nor intention of the United States to excite the evil qualities of ambition or avarice, but to suppress them; nor to form a government compounded of parts, some of which would be calculated to excite these qualities, so as to produce a perpetual spirit of discord and uneasiness, similar to what passes in that man's mind, whose virtues and vices are in a state of warfare with each other.

. Yet, it would have been wonderful, in the first experiment to erect a government upon good moral principles and the right of self-rule, if no oversight had happened. It would have been more wonderful, if no impression had been made by a depreciated debt, which from pebbles in the ocean of society, might, by a species of political diving, be made pearls in the hands of individuals. It might have been known, that patronage and power in a president, to a certain extent, would destroy division and responsibility; but the extent to which it could be carried under the constitution, might not have been foreseen. It might have been known, that an accumulation of vast wealth in few hands, by any means whatever, would create a faction or aristocracy, which would absorb power correspondent to that wealth, and gradually exchange the principles of our government for force and fraud; but such an accumulation might not have been intended.

That part of our policy called 'the constitution of the United States,' was suggested by the considerations of union and peace, of uniformity in commercial regulations, and of a revenue for general purposes. To alter or destroy our political morality or self government, and to substitute for it the principle of force or fraud, was not a motive for creating the constitution of the United States, expressed by any state convention, avowed by any individual, or conceived by the people.

On the contrary, apprehensions, lest some parts of the general constitution might on trial be found to incline from our good political elements towards those of force and fraud, were assuaged by special amendments to prevent it; and by a multitude of arguments to prove, that as titled orders were forbidden, legislative appropriations of money required, armies subjected to a duennial provision, and religion and the liberty of the press secured, self government and these elements were placed upon impregnable ground.

If, on trial, it is discovered, that the slightest inclination does exist, in any of its parts, towards the elements of force or fraud, these parts violate the national intention, and ought to be revised; because a tendency towards a political point, if unobstructed, will arrive at that point. Accumulation and permanence of power or wealth, arouse and excite certain evil moral qualities, which perpetually strive to govern by the principles of force and fraud; and so far from being instruments calculated to maintain governments founded in good moral principles and self government, they are instruments calculated for their destruction.

The executive power of the United States is infected, as we shall endeavour to shew, with a degree of accumulation and permanence of power, sufficient to excite evil moral qualities. The form of an executive power constituted no motive for the general government, nor will an alteration in that form, defeat or counteract the ends intended to be obtained. Amendments, which will secure the fundamental principles of our policy, and the essential objects of the general constitution itself, may be resorted to with safety, and are the best resources against their loss.

To prove that the form of executive power was not a recommendation of the general constitution, it need only be observed, that it is not copied by a single state. The governours of nine states, comprising a majority of the people, are annually chosen, and are ineligible after certain terms; those of the other states are chosen for two and three years, one excepted; and a multitude of other important differences exist, between the modification of executive power, under the general and the state constitutions.

The continuance of these differences, proves, that the form of executive power under the general constitution, was suffered for the sake of acquiring those of its objects, which the nation had in view; and that this form, had it been proposed alone and unconnected with other principles, would have been rejected by every state in the union.

It is therefore proper to consider, whether the executive power of the United States is so moulded, as to be calculated for awakening man's evil moral qualities, and for propelling us towards the political elements of force and fraud; because the principles of our policy ought not to be contaminated and destroyed by its details.

Experience having ascertained, that executive power in most state forms, does not awaken individual ambition and avarice for the annoyance of society; and executive power in the general form, having been created by the merit of other articles of the general constitution, it is time to consider, whether we shall persevere in applying the principles of division, responsibility and rotation, to state executives, commanding little patronage, little military power, and little territory, and continue to relax from them in the case of the general executive, guiding a patronage, a military force and a territory of great extent. Whether we shall adhere to the inconsistency of sustaining innumerable fortresses to defend our liberty in a quarter where it cannot be assaulted; and of levelling most of them with the ground, in that, whence danger is imminent.

Election is almost the only barrier opposed to executive ambition in the United States. Alone, it has universally been insufficient. Marius, Sylla, Pompey, Cæsar, Cromwell and Bonaparte were elected. The English House of Commons, and the French legislatures under several forms, were elected. Election furnished in all these cases, the means for introducing or exercising tyranny. By conveying too much power, or consolidating within a narrow compass, the power it did convey, it awakened or excited ambition and avarice. The terrors of impeachment, attainder, banishment or death, were added to election in these instances; and these threats only accelerated the transition from patriotism to power, as the fortress for guilt. Monarchs elect their civil and military officers, but seldom trust to their power of election, though strengthened by a perpetual power of removal, for safety. They are cautious not to accumulate power, or to continue great power for a long time in the same hands. They divide it. They discontinue and exchange the most dangerous officers. If they neglect these precautions, they are dethroned. The people have fewer means of detecting ambitious designs than monarchs; national sovereignty must therefore be dethroned, if it relaxes from precautions, necessary to preserve the sovereignty of monarchs.

It is the insufficiency of election, exclusively, to secure political liberty, which has suggested to mankind a multitude of other expedients; and Mr. Adams, concurring with experience as to this insufficiency, proposes the theory of orders, and the practice of a division of power among these orders, as an additional security.

The necessity of applying the principle of division to power, to keep it responsible, is thus acknowledged; and the mode of this application only remains to be considered. This ought to be accommodated to the policy of the country. It is the policy of England to consider the government as invested with all political power; hence the principle of division could reach no farther, than a distribution of power among the departments of government. It is our policy to consider the people as retaining a vast share of political power, and as only investing their government with so much as they deem necessary for their own benefit. Admitting, therefore, that it may be consistent with the English policy to mould executive power, by a computation of the portion of power possessed by the Lords and Commons; it would be inconsistent with our policy to mould it by any similar computation. We do not balance power against power. It is our policy to reduce it by division, in order to preserve the political power of the people, by forbearing to excite the ambition and avarice of individuals.

This new application of division, to an allotment of political power between a nation and its government, was suggested to us, by its inefficacy if confined to an allotment among departments of government; it was seen, that omnipotent political power in a government, however theoretically divided, would become practically consolidated. The people, after this species of division of power, retain the importance and sovereignty of Lear, after he had divided his kingdom among his three daughters.

To preserve our unexampled division of power between the nation and the government, a multitude of other divisions became necessary, and these were intended to be made, not for the purpose of a balance of power between departments, but by preventing such an accumulation as to awaken ambition, to defend the sovereignty of the people against all.

The insufficiency of election to prevent great power from awakening evil qualities, has induced the people in their state governments to superadd many auxiliaries drawn from the principle of division. Rotation, plural executives, frequency of election, and a limited patronage, are among them. The efficacy of these auxiliaries, having been evinced by more than thirteen states for thirty years, is equivalent to an experience of one nation for four hundred years. Before an experience of twelve years had passed over, in the case of the executive power of the union, under a relaxation of our principle of division, a majority of the United States have agreed in perceiving in it, an inclination towards principles inimical to our policy. It follows, that the state mode of forming an executive power, will uniformly bring into publick use man's good moral qualities for at least four hundred years; and that the mode adopted by the general constitution, will awaken his evil, in twelve. Division of power, is the cause of one effect, and its accumulation of the other.

History or fact corroborates this estimate. Compare two hundred successive emperours or kings, with the two hundred state governours who have probably existed since the revolution. Fewer tyrants will be found among the governours, than patriots among the monarchs. If a solitary royal patriot should occur, not a single tyrannical governour exists to contrast him. The principle of a division of power has been applied to the governours, and neglected in the case of the kings. Do these facts prove the wisdom of deviating from the precedent of American governours, and inclining towards that of English kings, in moulding executive power, or demonstrate its consequences?

The extent of this inclination in the executive power of the United States, will result from a comparison between a king of England and a president. This king cannot create offices, inflict taxes, pass laws, or raise armies; neither can the president. This king can appoint officers, disburse taxes, recommend laws, and command armies; so can the president. This king can make treaties under the check of two legislative branches; the president can make treaties under the check of one. This king can appoint the members of the legislature to lucrative offices; so can the president: and in both cases an appointment vacates the seat. This king appoints the judges, and the officers who appoint the juries; so does the president. Executive power in the English form, has sufficed to introduce and establish the political elements of fraud and force. But the king of England is not elective. The inefficacy of election, to prevent the abuse of accumulated power, has been shewn; we see its inefficacy in the House of Commons, to shield the people against the oppressions of the English executive power. But the king of England, in the exercise of his patronage, is not checked by a senate. The corruption of two wealthy and numerous legislative bodies in England, is no proof, that a small and poor one in America can repel the addresses of an executive, glittering with prerogatives similar to those which have dazzled all the English patriots for a century past.

Both the English king and our president are the exclusive managers of negociation; and secrecy is their common maxim. By negociation, foreign governments may be provoked; by secrecy, a government may delude and knead a people into a rage for war; and war is a powerful instrument for expelling the element of self government, and introducing that of force. This has been recently demonstrated in France. By negociation, secrecy and war, traitors convert a national detestation of tyranny into a tool for making tyrants.

The assembly of Virginia, in their resolutions of December 1798, after stating 'that *a spirit* has in sundry instances been manifested by the federal government, to enlarge its powers,' concludes 'so as to consolidate the states by degrees, into one sovereignty, the obvious tendency and *inevitable* result of which would be, to transform the present republican system of the United States, into an *absolute*, or at best a mixed monarchy.' The resolutions of the Kentucky legislature of November 1798, after stating a similar *spirit* in the federal government, observe 'that these, and successive acts of the same character, unless arrested at the threshold, may tend to drive these states into *revolution and blood*, and will furnish new calumnies against republican governments, and new pretexts for those who wish it to be believed, that man cannot be governed but by a *rod of iron*.' *

The *spirit* which produced these tendencies towards *monarchy, revolution*, and an *iron government*, could only have been infused into the federal government by some principle of the general constitution. It was an evil moral spirit, and must therefore have proceeded from an evil moral cause. The concurrence of Congress in the measures charged with this spirit, is a proof of the great advances already made by executive influence, and the confidence of monarchists in executive power. And as a spirit propelling us towards *monarchy, revolution* and *an iron government*, appeared only after the great accumulation of executive power by the general constitution, the magician who raised it cannot be mistaken.

We have endeavoured to prove, that the elements of every government consisted of good or evil moral principles; and that the shock received by superstition from knowledge, and by feudality from alienation, has reduced the political competitors for human preference to the system of division and responsibility, or to that of paper and patronage; the first suggested by self government, the second by the elements of fraud and force.

The measures arising from the spirit early infused into executive power by its American form, were, armies, war, penal laws, and an increase of executive power by law, loans, banks, patronage and profusion. These are English effects, and evil effects. Do they proceed from no moral cause, or is that cause unlike the cause of the same English effects? or, is it good, though its effects are evil?

They are the genuine issue of the elements of force and fraud, but infinitely exceeding in malignity the ancient effects of these

* The Virginia resolutions were drawn by Mr. Madison; the Kentucky resolutions, by Mr. Jefferson.

elements; because the modern struggles of reason and self government compels tyranny to drive her screws deeper into the bowels
of society, for the purpose of retaining it in bondage. If knowledge
has taught tyranny new devices, without suggesting to liberty new
defences, mankind will have to regret the loss of an ignorance,
which cheapened the price and diminished the weight of their
chains. It is infinitely less excruciating to be governed by imposture,
than by armies, taxes, patronage and paper.

The new defences, suggested by knowledge, against these modern
devices of tyranny, were zealously enforced by the United States
in their separate governments, and in their first general government. The old Congress held the executive power of the Union. It
was a plural executive, annually appointed, liable to recall, ineligible after three years, incapable of holding any other office, of
little civil patronage, and extremely limited in military patronage;
the states being invested with the appointment of all the officers of
an army, except generals; and it successfully surmounted a period
of war, longer, and attended with more difficulties, than is recollected to have occurred to any monarchical executive. All these
defences, suggested by division and responsibility, were surrendered
in the formation of the new executive, and many new powers were
conferred upon that branch of government. They were overlooked,
because we were dazzled by the prospect of permanent union. The
sponsors for liberty, were forgotten in the general joy; and a president of the United States was invested with far greater powers than
sufficed to Cæsar for enslaving his country. Patronage, negociation,
a negative upon laws, and a paper system, render some of those
talents which Cæsar possessed, unnecessary to enable a president
to perform what Cæsar effected.

The sufficiency of the means, at the disposal of executive power,
to produce a revolution, will induce people to look out sharply for
the event; many will hasten to abandon old principles, and court
the favour of new; and a monarchy may suddenly start into existence, even by the acclamation of a multitude, who will sacrifice
their principles to their hopes or their fears. By weakening these
means, republicanism and loyalty to our political principles will be
invigorated.

Election, instead of being any security against accumulated
power, derives its efficacy from an union with division of power.
Certain metals, compounded in due proportions, produce by
fusion a more impenetrable mass, than either separately; so elec-

tion and division of power, politically mingled, are mutually rendered more effectual. An accumulation of executive power is precisely the contrary principle to that, which alone bestows efficacy upon election. The influence of this accumulation is already so visible, that candidates canvass, not upon the ground of knowledge, virtue and independence, but of devotedness to a president.

Election and constitutional precept, are both a species of didactick sanction, only to be enforced by a division of power; not by its division or balance among orders, but by preventing such an accumulation in the hands of an individual, an order, or a department, as will awaken man's vicious qualities, and through them cause election to be converted into an instrument of fraud and oppression. The division of power among three orders, has failed in every instance to bestow efficacy upon election; first, because, by that system, a government is invested with every conceivable political power; and secondly, because in a division of this endless and enormous mass into three parts, the portion assigned to each order, must unavoidably suffice to awaken ambition and avarice both in the order itself, and in those who seek its favours. If, therefore, in assigning power to the president, the general constitution has deviated in any degree from the idea of dividing power, for the purposes of keeping it manageable by the publick will, and of preventing an accumulation, sufficient to excite man's evil qualities; or if it has inclined in any degree towards the idea of dividing it by the scheme of a balance among orders of men, or orders of power; experience proves that the efficacy of election will be correspondently weakened. The English example proves, that election, united with a division of power, according to the balancing scheme, is even capable of being converted into the most powerful instrument for tyranny. It is our policy so to divide power, as to place every publick officer, isolated in the midst of the publick will; and not to provide for him the support of corruption, of an order, or of a faction, to weaken the utility of election.

An army and patronage enables a president to provide a faction. An army is the strongest of all factions, and completely the instrument of a leader, skilful enough to enlist its sympathies, and inflame its passions. It is given to a president, and election is the only surety that he will not use it, as armies have ever been used. The precept, 'that money should not be appropriated for the use of an army, for a longer term than two years,' is like that which forbid Cæsar to open the treasury.

The other precept, 'that the military shall be subject to the civil power,' would have superseded the principle of division, if armies could have been controlled by precept, or if precept could have been enforced by election; and if precepts had sufficed to restrain an ability to violate them, it would have superseded a necessity for civil government. The army is the creature of law. So were the armies of Cæsar, Cromwell and Bonaparte; and so, at this moment, are the armies of all existing governments, of which force is an element. The banner of usurpation and tyranny is usually hoisted by a legal army; a legal army is the instrument for giving permanency to the evil political principles, fraud and force; and at no time, has a standing mercenary army been the steady auxiliary of national self government, or obedient to election. It obeys its leader.

An army constitutes a mass of power, which has frequently proved too hard for the whole residuary power of a government. Military power, is at least as able to enslave a nation as civil power. To civil power our policy has copiously applied the principle of division; to military, two precepts. Civil power is distributed into a multitude of hands; military is condensed and accumulated in one. The patronage of civil offices is divided among the people, the general and state governments, and many sections of these governments; the entire patronage of military offices is bestowed on the president. To civil power we have applied the principle of division, to military that of accumulation.

A distribution of military patronage, would be some impediment to executive usurpation; but the only effectual mode of rendering military power subordinate to national will, is precisely analogous to that used for rendering civil power subordinate to national will. The latter is effected by dividing political power between the nation and the government, so as to invest the nation with a portion sufficient to control the government; and the former can only be effected, by dividing military power, so as to invest the nation with a portion, completely adequate to the coercion of an army. A nation, unable to control either its government or its army, is not free, nor is self government the element of its policy.

Arms can only be controlled by arms. An armed nation only can keep up an army, and also maintain its liberty. The constitution of the United States, overlooking this undeniable truth, has placed both the raising an army, and the arming of the militia, among the potential attributes of the general government; whereas the first belonged to the principle of accumulation, and the latter to the principle of division. One, therefore, is a power, and the other a check upon that power. One is a foe, the other a friend to liberty. One strengthens the government, the other the nation. And a sound militia makes a govenment dependent on the nation; a bad one, a nation dependent on a government. An armed militia divides the power to raise mercenary armies; wherefore governments, which can raise armies, will seldom be inclined to arm the militia; and the general government has expended its praises on a militia, and the publick money on an army, to an amount, sufficient to create the strongest militia, and the weakest army in the world. What stronger proof can exist of an affection for power and a dislike to duty in human nature, than a preference of the weakest army to the strongest militia? The president is a secret negociator with foreign nations; his monopoly of military patronage, impels him towards war, because war extends his patronage, and patronage is power. A strong solicitation, addressed to the passions of avarice or ambition, is an evil principle. He who could gratify ambition, by involving a nation in war, may be confided in as a negociator, precisely in the same degree, as he who could gratify avarice by conveying taxes into his own pocket, may be confided in to impose them. By removing from the publick negociator, the excitement of military patronage towards war, integrity of negociation would be obtained, and fraudulent pretexts for war avoided.

The imbecility of the precautions against military power, is a chasm in our policy, which jeopardises every precaution we have invented to prevent usurpation and tyranny. Military power awakens and excites man's evil qualities, more than any other species of power, because it is less resistible; hence its malignity to good moral principles and the element of self government.

The regulation of religion, and the establishment of nobility, are among the powers prohibited; the military power is not even divided, and is only subjected in a state of complete accumulation, to the suffrages of an unarmed people. Religion and nobility, as state engines, might have been more safely left to the restriction of election, than an army, because they are thoroughly at enmity with publick opinion, and unpossessed of physical force. By resting for security against military power, upon the naked force of election, all powers, (including the cases of religion and nobility) whether prohibited or limited, are in fact deposited under the same naked security. Military power being capable of destroying constitutional precepts, the security of all such precepts depends upon the precautions used to secure the responsibility of military power. ·

· Had the constitution secured the responsibility of an army to the national will, by requiring the duty of arming the nation to be fulfilled, before the power of raising an army was exercised; the freedom of the press and of religion, would have been safer without a prohibitory clause, than with one, accompanied by an undivided military power. By rendering an army responsible, election is free; and whilst election is free, no security for religion and the press can be better than elections; but it is no security against the will of an army, fettered with precepts, and unfettered by arms. The constitution even neglects the least precaution, for preventing an army from being used against the government; a case entirely beyond the compass to which the most enthusiastick theory can extend the force of election.

An armed nation only can protect its government against an army. Unarmed, and without an army, a nation invites invasion. Unarmed, and with an army, it invites usurpation. All nations lose their liberties by invasion or usurpation. The elective franchise of an unarmed nation, lies between these alternatives. How mercenary armies protect liberty, has been recently demonstrated in France; and how they defend nations, all over Europe.

Division can only be brought to bear upon military power, by a ·compulsory constitutional mandate for arming the nation, and by scattering military patronage. For the latter, the former confederation affords one precedent, and another appears in the prudence even of the phlegmatick Dutch, who had foresight enough, in the early dawnings of civil liberty, to withhold from their stadtholder the appointment of generals.

The military power and patronage of the president, is formidable; united with his treaty power, it becomes more formidable; but to determine whether the principle of division or accumulation prevails in the structure of our general executive, it must also be recollected, that the president appoints judges, ambassadors, and ·a multitude of other civil officers, grants pardons, governs the treasury, convenes congress, recommends and negatives laws. Let it be also kept in mind, that a division of power chastens, and that its accumulation excites our evil moral qualities.

·· Having attempted to shew that this accumulation of executive power ought to be diminished, by a division of the military article, it will further be contended, that the publick good dispenses with the president's judicial power.

It has been a favourite maxim with the Americans, that legislative, executive and judicial power should be lodged in separate hands. And though it must be confessed, that no very visible lines have been drawn between these powers, yet the maxim is evidence of national attachment to the principle of division.

This maxim is violated, under any construction, by bestowing on executive power the appointment of judicial power; precisely as it would have been, had judicial power appointed executive. Had judicial power appointed presidents for life, would the duration of the office, and its independence of the government and sovereignty, have secured executive integrity? Or would it have been secured by an additional power in the judiciary to bestow more lucrative offices dependent on its will, upon presidents? The executive power appoints judges, and by two precedents it is declared, that it may bestow other lucrative offices upon them. The subject is farther illustrated, by supposing executive power invested with a similar right of appointing legislative.

Many truths are interspersed among Mr. Adams's remarks, from which we draw conclusions very different from his. For instance, he observes that 'these principes may say, with as much arrogance and as much truth, as it was ever said by Charles or James, "as long as we have the power of making what judges and bishops we please, we are sure to have no law nor gospel but what shall please us." '* Again, 'our author forgets, that he who makes bishops and judges, may have what gospel and law he pleases; and he who makes admirals and generals, may command their fleets and armies.'†

The president makes judges and generals. This power awakened and put in motion the evil qualities of Charles and James; the effects of the cause in these cases, and indeed in a thousand others, prove that the cause will produce evil effects.

So certain and inevitable was this, that Mr. Adams states it as not requiring proof. He considers it as sufficient barely to bring to our recollection, that he who appoints judges, has what law he pleases; and that he who appoints commanders, determines the conduct of fleets and armies.

Is this compatible with our maxim in relation to legislative,

* Adams's Def. v. 3, 358.   † Adams's Def. v. 3, 383.

executive and judicial power? is it compatible with the system of a
division of power? in short, is it compatible with the principle of
self government? Such an accumulation of power, is as strictly the
attribute of monarchy, as it is obviously the bane of self government. Weak and vicious presidents will play the small arms of
judicial and military power upon individuals and factions; but·an
enterprising and ambitious president, will play the artillery of both
upon the nation.

'He who appoints the judges may have what law he pleases.'
Wherefore then elect a legislature? The right of suffrage and the
efficacy of election, are destroyed or hazarded by an executive
power to make law through judges. Innumerable instances might
be collected, to prove that judicial power is an instrument with
which law can be made; in England, the judges made a law for
docking estates tail, under the influence of the crown, in order to
weaken the power of the very order, designed to balance the
power of the crown; in America, it has been said that the judges
have made a whole code of laws, by declaring the common law of
England in force; and also constitution, by declaring the sedition
law constitutional.

It is inconceivable, that an appointment of a legislature during
good behaviour by executive power, will produce bad laws, and
that such an appointment of a judiciary will produce good; that
the same means will both purify and corrupt the same being. So
flat a contradiction justly excites a suspicion, that its origin is to be
formed in habit or errour, and not in principle or reason.

The influence of executive power over legislative, was considered
as an evil, because it violated the English theory, and had excited
the animadversions of many able writers; but the influence of
executive over judicial power, was overlooked as an evil, because
it was a principle of the English theory, and had failed to attract
the animadversions of political writers, under its present form. Had
the people elected the judiciary in England, and the crown appointed the legislature, we should have contended for the frequent
election and responsibility of judicial, and the independence of
legislative power. It would have been said, that the tenure of good
behaviour was essentially necessary to produce pure laws; and that
as the judicial power was to give what construction and effect to
the laws and constitution it pleased, it was more necessary to make
it elective and responsible than legislative power, which could
neither construe nor enforce them.

The habit, opinion or prejudice, which obtained for executive power the patronage of judicial, in the constitution of the United States, appears however to have been rather forensick than national; and our executive seems to have been enriched with it, rather in consequence of the publick decision upon the constitution, in one mass, than from an approbation of this particular detail.

Nine states continue to appoint their judges by the legislature; the rest, New York excepted, remove them by the will of two thirds of the legislature; and New York appoints them by a council annually chosen by the legislature. Not a single state has copied the general constitution in moulding judicial power, and every state has laboured to place it beyond the influence of executive power.

In forming state constitutions, publick opinion decided upon each detail separately; in adopting the general constitution, it was compelled to decide upon a mass of various details. To this cause it is owing, that violations of several essential principles adhered to by all the state constitutions, have been suffered, rather than adopted in the federal constitution. Every such contrariety is an irrefragable argument to prove, that one end of the oppugnancy ought to be suppressed by a constitutional amendment.

A degree of military power is conferred upon a president, which, when augmented and ripened by pretext, conjuncture or audacity, has alone sufficed, in every instance, to destroy national self government. To this instrument of destruction is subjoined a mass of civil power. The last refuge of self government is the legislature; in the purity of which resides its solitary hope of existence.

The executive power possesses the prerogative of conferring lucrative offices upon members of congress; the senators not excepted, though relied on as a check upon executive power. In England, this prerogative has utterly disqualified the House of Commons, as the organ or guardian of the principle of self government, for the democratical order. It will operate in America as it has done in England. Is a legislature, courting the patronage of a man who commands an army, a pledge or residence for the principle of self government? Is this secured by enabling a man who commands an army, to corrupt the legislature by perpetual and brilliant hopes? Was Swift inspired in describing the difference between the corruption of hope and of prompt payment?

'Sid's rod was slender, white and tall,
Which oft he used to fish withal;
A *Plaice* was fastened to the hook,
And many score of Gudgeons took;
Yet still so happy was his fate,
He caught his fish and saved his bait.'

Is not a president, thus enabled to influence the legislature, exactly a Lord Bute hidden behind the throne?

Mr. Adams converts the American maxim, 'that legislative, executive and judicial power should be seperate and distinct,' into the idea 'of independent orders of men and of powers.' And his theory, though destructive of national self government, acknowledges the fatal consequences to be expected, if one order or one power, should become dependent on another. Will our policy admit of an influence, which will corrupt his?

His theory is contrived to preserve certain factitious rights of these orders; this is only to be effected by their independence of each other; because, if two should be influenced by the power or patronage of one, that one will invade, abolish or modify these factitious rights. Our policy is intended to preserve the natural right of national self government; for this purpose we create three chief organs of national will; now if we enable either of these, by force or fraud, by armies or patronage, to influence the others, the natural right of national self government is lost, with as much certainty, as the factitious rights of orders are, by one order thus influencing two others, or their representatives.

The effort of the general constitution, to say the least, is greater to secure the independence of executive, than of legislative or judicial power; neither of these can appoint a president or enrich him by office. Neither, nor both, can select a president of political opinions similar to their own, or mould his tenets by patronage into such conformity. Was it believed, that numerous bodies would be more likely to corrupt one man, than one man would be to corrupt numerous bodies? Or was it believed, that a single executive was a safer depositary of self government, than a legislative assembly? That he should be enabled to influence them, and that they should be cautiously prohibited from influencing him?

In that part of our policy called the state constitutions, principles, the reverse of these, prevail. Executive power is made dependent on legislative in some way, and vast care is taken to keep legislative and judicial power beyond the influence of executive. In fact, it was and still is the general opinion, that the independence of legislative and judicial power, of the influence of one man, constitutes an indispensable requisite for the preservation of national self government; and that an influence of one man over the legislature, constitutes a substantial monarchy, and is the harbinger of its form. If then executive influence over legislative and judicial power, is a monarchical principle, the president's appointment of one, and his patronage over both, ought to be removed, or we violate the principles by the details of our constitution. It is a principle, that the legislature should utter the will of the nation; the detail, exposing it to executive influence, may cause it to utter the will of a president. The principle and the detail admit of no reconciliation, and therefore the only question is, which ought to be abolished, the influence of the people, or the influence of the president over the legislature?

The elective quality of the presidency, aggravates the errour. It procures a confidence which has no foundation, because election is no security against great power conferred by it on one man; and this confidence, by lulling publick suspicion, will mask the progress of executive influence. A suspicion, both of its progress and the cause of its progress, is suggested by the facts, that in those states where governours have no patronage, no state factions have appeared; and that upon the erection of a general executive, having a patronage previously unknown, national factions, previously unknown also, suddenly started up.

As civil and military patronage, the command of fleets and armies, the direction of a treasury, treaty-making, and a negative upon laws, condensed in one man, constitute a power evidently monarchical, it is important betimes to consider how the elective principle, and the monarchical power are like to work upon the same person; the nature of one, being to draw him within the pale of responsibility, and of the other, to excite him to overleap it.

We ought not to shut our eyes upon the history of elective monarchy, but to discern and avoid the cause of its invariable catastrophe. Orders have never been able to work well with election, nor election with them. If a good government cannot be made of orders, by the help of election, still more discouraging is the experiment of making a good government of monarchy, one order only, by its help. This project requires one man to constitute or represent two orders. He must be a monarch in power, but a plebeian in temper. No instance occurs in which monarchical power, responsible and periodical, has not struggled for insubordination and permanence; and no remedy for this evil has ever appeared; but the experiment in the case of state governours proves, that the evil may be avoided, by bestowing and dividing executive power so judiciously, as that projects to acquire independent and permanent power, may be made inconsistent with common sense. Power in certain masses, is a moral cause which naturally produces certain effects. Kingly power, though conferred by election, constitutes the cause, and consequently produces the effects: even excessively aggravated by the natural indisposition to part with it.

If it is true that aristocratical power, hereditary or not, will suffice to destroy election, responsibility and self government, can it be false, that monarchical power, hereditary or not, will suffice for the same end? No instance occurs in which either aristocratical or monarchical powers have been peaceably and regularly managed by election or national will, or in which they have not destroyed the principle of self government. Names constitute nothing. Monarchical powers constitute monarchy, and though monarchy is elective, it is still monarchy. If monarchy and aristocracy are moral principles productive of evil effects, election cannot change their nature, and force them to produce good effects. As we have a multitude of elective publick officers, without aristocratical powers, we may also have an elective chief officer, without monarchical powers. But if by law, avarice and guile, the aristocracy of paper and patronage is created; and if the mass of monarchical powers, held by the president, remains undivided; this real aristocracy will have a real monarch at their head, who upon the first conjuncture, which enables him to raise an army, will step upon a throne. A system of paper and patronage, and our executive powers, bear an astonishing resemblance to sundry principles of the operating English policy. The detachments of barbarians voluntarily introduced into the Roman empire, was the cause of its destruction.

Mr. Adams abounds in citations to prove, that election is not a sufficient security against great power. We accord with him, and deduce from this acknowledged fact the foregoing observations. His remedy is to make monarchical and aristocratical powers hereditary; ours, to divide them, until they are brought within the coercion of the elective principle fairly exercised, which is the exact test, of their ceasing to be monarchical or aristocratical. He deduces his remedy from the experience of dark ages, in which he says it was never tried; we deduce ours from the experience of the present enlightened age, in which it is tried before our eyes. Governours are completely manageable by the elective system, because they do not possess monarchical powers. From the same cause, state legislatures elect them without disorder or difficulty. At some future day, on an election of a president, it will be found that the hopes and fears inspired by monarchical powers, will light up the brand of civil discord, and visit us with an experimental knowledge of the effects of these powers, first as elective, and then as hereditary.

The question is, whether the experience of all ages, that great power cannot be controlled by election, shall induce the Americans to accumulate power; or whether our own existing experience, that divided power may be controlled by election, shall induce us to divide the mass collected in the national executive.

The evidence on both sides yields exactly the same conclusion. All ancient experiments, to control undivided or great masses of power by national will, failed; our modern experiments, to control power in a state of considerable division, have succeeded; the first demonstrated the evil, the second demonstrates the remedy.

This conclusion cannot be weakened by urging the efficacy of the elective system hitherto, to manage the executive power of the United States, if its early inclination towards monarchy existed. The nation testified to the fact. Will they not believe themselves, until it is too late? A blow cannot be avoided, which is not foreseen. On the very first presidential election, which crossed the progress and projects of monarchy, patronage and paper, a disloyalty to election or national will, was distinctly seen. A disloyalty, disclosed by a power in its infancy, will be carried into effect, when that power is matured by war, fleets, armies, stock and patronage. Perhaps the corruption of another individual at the juncture alluded to, would have demonstrated the argument.

Abbreviation of the time of service, and rotation in office, are auxiliaries in unmonarchising executive power, called forth by the state constitutions, and abandoned or relaxed by the general constitution. Our policy will not be made to flourish by inconsistent principles. Its two parts can only act with effect by acting in concert. The temptation to form factions and perpetrate usurpation, is graduated by the chance of reaping the contemplated fruit. A long time of service, connected with rotation, is an inducement to obtain influence by corruption, in order to destroy rotation; and a short time without rotation, is an inducement to use the same means to secure a re-election. Rotation, and the annual power of the Roman consuls, united, prevented consular usurpation for centuries; annual appointment of proconsuls, without a strict rotation, produced proconsular usurpation in a few years.

All mankind do in fact believe, that a short duration of delegated power, is the best security for its continuing a delegation. In every delegation made by an individual for himself, he adheres closely to this opinion. And though universal experience concurs with universal opinion, both are violated by nations. It is because governments are always formed by those who expect delegations.

Not so will one of these politicians act, should the lot of empire fall on himself. He would frequently change his generals and governours. The more powerful the office, and the more meritorious the officer, the more uniformly would the security of a short term and rotation be resorted to. What nation is enslaved by a fool? Oh people! do not be deluded to pay away your liberty for talents and merit. By rewarding them with great power, or great wealth, or long duration in office, you will lose the power of rewarding them at all; and these rewards, by destroying your liberty, will destroy publick merit and talents, and put an end to the objects of your bounty. It is only by withholding rewards, destructive both of the power and the objects of reward, that nations will be able to evince their gratitude to benefactors. A tyrant would only have kept Cæsar proconsul in Gaul for one year, and would have thus secured his tyranny; the people continued him for seven, and by that means lost their liberty. Their bounty to one man, closed its stream for ever, and annihilated the race of heroes.

Equally unanimous are men of all principles, whenever the delegation relates to their own exclusive interest, that it is dangerous to delegate so much power, as to place them at the mercy of the delegate. Here too every despot discloses his subtlety, and his conviction of the necessity of division to defend his despotism. He carefully divides his provinces, his armies, and his powers, so that no one divided should be strong enough to dethrone him. If he is so imprudent as to place his army and his treasury under one man; and irrevocably to invest him with the command of them for four years, with a power of appointing and removing all officers civil and military, he is dethroned by his first able, artful and ambitious general. He places his sovereignty in the situation of an unarmed sovereignty of the people, and his general in that of the president.

All despots, monarchical and aristocratical, uniformly and strictly practice the principles of division and rotation, as the best means to defend their monarchy and aristocracy; and as uniformly assure the people, that these same principles are the worst means to secure liberty or self government. It is simply because they are friends to their own sovereignty, and enemies to the sovereignty of the people. As countries are divided into provinces to secure kings, power ought to be divided into provinces to secure nations; and as each geographical division is subject to the monarch, each potential division should be subject to the people; great provinces in both cases produce the same consequence. Even rival orders never fail to use innumerable arts to divide each other's power. At one period in England, the other two orders united to weaken the aristocracy, by enabling it to break entails; at another the nobility and commons united to weaken the power of the crown, by depriving it of the prerogative of removing judges at will, and fixing that right in all three; at a third, the crown and nobility contrived to weaken the power of the people, by joining with the commons to extend their time of service.

Power changes moral character, and private life regenerates it. The children of hereditary power are not tyrants from a procreative cause. They are made such by the contemplation of the power to which they are destined.

If the prospect corrupts, will the possession cleanse? It is not in a natural, but a moral birth, that the defect of the hereditary principle lies. Great power, or a long possession of power, changes a man's moral nature, whether it is derived from inheritance or election. Patriots, as well as princes, become tyrants from being steeped in the same menstruum, and yet nations are still to learn, that its intoxicating qualities are the same upon both. They consider its effect as natural in one case, and monstrous in the other; as if both princes and patriots were not men. Revolution fails, because its usual remedy is only to draw the menstruum from election instead of inheritance, into which to plunge the moral qualities of human nature. Even a hope of office corrupts eloquence. It ceases to be the animated auxiliary of truth, and becomes the mercenary ally of interest. Honesty is exchanged for art. An artificial character is formed by a possibility of continuing considerable power. It assumes different principles with different persons. It gilds its baits with patronage, contract and charter, at the publick expense. And the varnish it assumes is to conceal the foulness of the stuff it hides. Whereas a portion of power, insufficient to arm treachery, and limited to an unalterable period, being chastened of the excitements to fraud and force, leaves the mind open to virtue, and the certainty of returning to a private station, settles its bias.

From the foundation of Rome to the accession of Augustus, was above seven centuries; and from thence to the termination of its empire, less than five. The first was a term of growth, the second of decline. The first of progressive prosperity; the second of oscillations depending upon the change of character. The first was a term of rotation, the second of permanent or hereditary power. The corruption or errour of electing the same man a second time to the consular office, was a symptom and became an instrument, of the destruction of the republick, except for which, we can only compute the probability of its duration, by an inference from the long term of its existence under the auspices of the annual rotation of executive magistrates, and a division of power.

The same period demonstrates the errour of the objection, that rotation causes a loss of talents to the publick. It would have been most likely to produce this loss in military affairs. For seven centuries Rome applied the principle of rotation to her generals, and conquered; for five, she trusted to experience, and was subdued. The rotary generals and statesmen of the little Athenian republick, destined it to live for ever in the annals of fame, and most of its contemporary governments are for ever dead. As to civil affairs, the claim of experience would probably be answered by the old adage, but the burst of talents in both cases which blazes forth whenever the monopoly of experience is destroyed by rotation, is accounted for by the fall of the monopoly. The trade being laid open, the wares increase, and are made better by competition. Talents, civil and military, are created by the prospect of employment, and smothered by the monopoly of experience.

A strong and independent executive power, has only been contended for by Mr. Adams and political writers, as a counterpoising weight in the system of balancing orders. There being no orders in the system of the United States, the only reason for a strong executive, does not exist; and a conformity in that department to the theory of a sovereignty of orders, unquestionably proved by Mr. Adams, unquestionably also discloses its nonconformity, to the theory of a sovereignty of the people. A strong executive is the more dangerous, where there is no political order to balance it. By creating an executive with monarchical powers, without the check of an aristocratical order, this monarchical order, is either enabled to assail the liberties of the nation, or the nation are driven to erect an aristocratical order to balance it. The proof of this remark exists, in the ease with which an elective executive in France, with monarchical powers, unchecked by an aristocratical order, has made itself despotick. And Mr. Adams both strenuously urges the necessity of an aristocratical order to balance monarchical powers, and plainly intimates that we shall be speedily compelled, first to extend the term of delegation, and then to adopt the hereditary principle. It is admitted, that the existence of one order, furnishes a reason for another. Monarchical powers can only be assuaged by an aristocratical order. Were the former given to the president, to create a cause for the latter? The alternative for the United States is obvious; it is, either to pare away executive power, below monarchy, to a standard not requiring an aristocratical order to check it, or to adopt Mr. Adams's system of orders. Monarchical executive powers being monarchy in substance, will beget aristocracy, just as a system of paper and patronage, being aristocracy in substance, will beget monarchy. According to Mr. Adams's system, monarchy ought to produce aristocracy, and aristocracy monarchy. The presidency, gilded with kingly powers, has been tossed into the constitution, against the publick sentiment, and gravely bound in didactick fetters, like those which in England and France have become political old junk. Between these, and our principle of self government, there can neither be friendship nor compromise. Either our kingly powers, or the sovereignty of the people, are by the laws of nature destined to perish in their warfare. The first will be suppressed by amendments to the constitution, or the last, lulled by the narcotick, corruption, will be murdered in its sleep.

The people and the legislative bodies of the United States shrink from this honest confession, whilst they are making it in their actions. They will not see the monarchy they court, and expect safety whilst feeding an enemy, from denying his existence; whilst even the European habit, of referring every thing to executive power, prevails. Epochs and measures are ascribed to presidents. Legislative power solicits a state of degradation, by descending to the indignity of pleading a subserviency to them, as a passport to popular favour, and condescending to become the satellite of one man. State legislatures, parties and individuals, enlist under candidates for the presidency, as they do in England under candidates for the ministry; and the nation itself, forgetting their representatives, contemplates the dazzling executive power of their own creation. The phenomena attending it are the same here as in England, and this coincidence demonstrates an identity in the causes; but we fall into the errour, of contemplating the same thing as a mighty substance and an empty shadow, without reflecting that the danger lies, not in the feeble body of an ignorant man, but in an accumulation and concentration of active powers. For a century past, executive power in England, has had the address to change its ministers as they became odious, and to replace them by popular adversaries; retaining the encroachments upon the rights and purses of the people, which produced the odium, and using the popularity of its new ministers, to make new encroachments: who, having lost it in performing this work, make room for others. Thus executive power, working with popular agents, and armed with gold and iron, has long gained ground with undeviating regularity in England. It pursues the same system here. Our presidents are its ministers, suffered only to remain in office whilst popular; encroaching in favour of executive power whilst this popularity lasts; bearing the odium of mischiefs which ought to light upon our accumulation and concentration of powers; leaving encroachments behind them for the benefit of executive power, to be extended by popular successors; and organizing a body of outs and ins, alternately demagogues and tools. These outs and ins are equally proper to delude a nation, and to exalt executive power, which sits in proud superiority, looking down upon the fraud and oppressions caused by itself; whilst the people dare not look up to it as their cause, but will be taught the forlorn hope of redress from a change of ministry, as in England. Hence, both in England and America, executive power obscures legislative to such a degree, that even popular favour is only obtained by an avowal of subserviency or hostility to its prime minister; and we compel our popular representatives gratuitously to become the tools of the same principle, to which the members of the British House of Commons sell their services.

A nation which requires its representatives to become the avowed advocates or accusers of the prime minister of religious or civil power, whether he is called a pope or a president, has an equal prospect for civil and religious liberty. Civil and religious preachers and reformers, marshalled into opposite parties, in all times and countries, are the same sorts of patriots. Representation limited to the alternative of enlisting under one of these parties, ceases to be an instrument of national self government, and dwindles into an instrument of oppression for the prime minister or his antagonist. We see and despise the old whig and tory farce, or the new farce of ins and outs in England; we hold in detestation the corruption which enlists the representatives of a rich and wise nation under the minister of executive power, or his expected successor; we deplore the contempt for publick characters, the apathy towards publick interest, and the surrender of the mind to selfishness, which this foolish imposition generates; and yet we insist that our representatives shall sacrifice their honesty and independence at the same shrine, and make themselves knaves in order to make us dupes.

The struggle for our presidency, like the struggle for the English administration, is the concurrent verdict of the contending parties, that executive power has already obtained the ascendancy. When it depended on a Dionysius or a Timoleon, whether monarchy or republicanism should reign at Syracuse, monarchy was established. It is a government according to the will of one man, not the mode in which that will operates. If it operates by means of a patronage able to influence popular representatives, or by a national humour compelling its representatives to enlist themselves for or against one man's will, it is as much monarchy as if it operated in a different mode. No writer describes a republick, guided by the will of one of its officers, and depending on the chance of that officer's possessing republican or monarchical principles.

We see that an administration majority, will attend successive presidents, as it attends successive premiers in England. Whether it is called whig or tory, federal or republican, high church or low church, causes no difference in the operation of the fact. The discovery we are in pursuit of, is the cause of this fact. Wherefore is it, that in both countries, factions or parties are seen, having executive power for its object, and none paying court to or condescending to be the blind partisans either of legislative or judicial power? It is because one man in both represents the entire undivided mass of executive power, and many men represent legislative and judicial. The two latter powers, being considerably divided, cannot feed mercenary factions; and the former is able to feed them, out of the abundant granary of its monopoly. The same remedy which prevents legislative or judicial power from begetting factions able to make either despotick, will have the same effect on executive. The ability of state governours to create executive factions, is graduated in the United States, by the portions of power which they represent. If a single individual represented the entire mass either of legislative or judicial power in the United States, it would become a power capable of creating factions and undermining the rights of the people. Suppose that one man possessed the legislative power, and that what we call executive power was divided by representation, equally with legislative at present; would not usurpation invariably proceed from legislative, as it now does from executive power? If a division of legislative power, prevents it from becoming an usurper and a tyrant, will not division have the same effect on executive? Republicanism, like a mercantile company, perishes, whenever one man by any means whatever has obtained the direction of the common interest. It is not her motto that 'safety lies in the counsel of one man.'

The people of the United States and of Great Britain, have been frequently censured for a corrupt or absurd exercise of the right of suffrage; and their want of virtue or understanding in the discharge of this function, has been forcibly urged against the right itself. An accumulation of power in the hands of one man, bears a strong similitude to its accumulation in a single chamber. The latter, says Mr. Adams, will diffuse vice and folly throughout a nation, and corrupt election. Will the same cause purify it? It is true that the ruin of election proceeds from this cause, and not from an innate disposition in the people to do themselves an injury. An accumulation of power and patronage in the hands of one man, causes candidates for popular favour to corrupt the people, in order to bring themselves within the notice of this dispenser of wealth; and candidates for executive favour to infuse into them the fatal idea, that they ought to demand of their representatives an accordance with executive will. If such effects do flow from this cause, the people are unjustly accused of a deficiency either in virtue or understanding; and the just conclusion only is, that they are not able to control the moral law of nature, which has irrevocably pronounced, that evil moral effects will flow from evil moral causes. Had we emigrated from Turkey, we might have been wedded to the opinions, that legislative power could be safely represented by one man, because it possessed but few of the means of usurpation; but that executive power ought to be very much divided, because it possessed many of those means. And if ambition is more likely to be excited by a considerable than by a slender capacity to gratify itself, the idea, though brought from Turkey, would not have been so unfavorable to civil liberty, as its converse, which has constituted executive power, the general or universal usurper of the rights of mankind.*

Lord Bolingbroke observes, in his Patriot King, that the management of parliament by undertakers, was one of the most pernicious violations of the whig portion of the English form of government. It converts representation into vassalage to the leaders of parties, disciplined, not by the comparatively honourable infliction of the lash, but by the base and wicked sophism, that it is honourable to stick to a party, and treacherous to adhere to conscience. The disciples of this infamous doctrine are forged into tools for ambition and tyranny by praises and rewards, whilst honesty is discouraged by base epithets, as a foil to the varnish with which the decoys are painted, designed to deceive and enslave the multitude.

The pendulum of power long vacillated in England between whig and tory undertakers, and a gallant nation is the victim of an evil principle. Walpole, a whig undertaker, erected the tory stock system, and wafted power on the pinions of law, from fruitful land to the voracious paper kite. And to this hideous principle of gaining honour and profit by slavery to leaders or undertakers in parliament, it is owing, that the fluctuations of parties have produced more harm than good to the English nation.

The principle is derived from executive power, which infuses and rewards the base subserviency, founded in nourishing hopes capable of being gratified, either by the possessor of that power, or by some leader of an opposition, when he shall attain it. And the rewards are paid at the publick expense for betraying the publick good.

A reformation of the executive power of the general government, sufficient to prevent the custom of managing congress by undertakers from creeping into our policy, would probably contribute more to the safety, prosperity and happiness of the United States, than any other amendment of the constitution, a reformation excepted, capable of producing a real militia. Only two modes of effecting it suggest themselves; one to reduce the patronage of a

* The president of the United States is considered as an elective monarch in God. Po. Jus. v. 2, 77.

president beneath a capacity for creating these undertakers; the other, to shorten the time of his service, and make him for ever ineligible to the same office, to diminish his motives for doing it. This latter mode would rapidly provide an excellent fund for members of congress in a body of ex-presidents, under no temptation to become undertakers themselves, able from their experience to detect other undertakers, and shedding upon congress the knowledge, integrity and independence, derived from its consular members by the Roman Senate, which, whilst the rotation of the consular office lasted, was able to render even an aristocracy illustrious.

Executive secrecy is one of the monarchical customs, plausibly defended, and certainly fatal to republican government, either in an aristocratical or democratical form. Had the senate of Rome suffered their consuls to hide the foreign negociations under secrecy, or legislated upon the credit of their recommendation, without thorough information, even aristocratical wisdom would sooner have fallen under executive prowess. The essential principle of our policy being the division of power, whatever shall convert one primary division of power into an instrument of another, unites and consolidates the means of usurpation in exact violation of it, and substitutes the evil moral principle of an accumulation of power, for its division. The president, who shall be able to bring congress into the practice of legislating upon a confidence in his recommendations, without a thorough knowledge of the subject, will extend the custom of managing congress by undertakers, exercise by their aid the legislative power, and gradually provide the most ample funds for rewarding their services; a British end, to which executive secrecy inevitably leads. How can national self government exist without a knowledge of national affairs? or how can legislatures be wise or independent, who legislate in the dark upon the recommendation of one man?

Executive secrecy furnishes double means for corrupting, nor are the offerings to vanity less greedily accepted, than those to avarice. Intoxicated by the incense of the one, men are prepared for the seduction of the other; nor will they hesitate to extend executive patronage at the national expense, when they consider the wisdom and discrimination in the disposition of secrets, as a pledge for the same degree of wisdom in the disposition of money.

It is in vain to expect civil liberty from the principle which has universally destroyed religious. Benefices are the cause of political as well as of religious factions and parties, and if one man distributes them, he becomes a pope or a monarch. These plunge hereticks into flames, and patriots into prisons; these beget the persecutions of sectarism and the intolerance of faction; and both the holders and seekers of these universally resort to reason or sophistry, to truth or falsehood, not to advance the publick good, but for selfish ends and private emolument. If a handful of guineas thrown among a mob, or a mountain of dollars exposed to be scrambled for by a nation, would produce good order and secure a respect for the rights of others, then happiness and liberty may be reasonably expected from a mountain of executive patronage. Divide this mountain, and it becomes a wholesome circulating medium, doing good like a divided priesthood; undivided, like an accumulation of the whole national coin by one man, it falls upon and crushes popular rights.

I have not entered into a discrimination between executive and legislative powers, because I know of none such, nor any reason why war, peace, appointments to office, or the dispensation of publick money, should have been counted in the catalogue of the former, except the efficacy of these powers in one man, for begetting tyranny; or except an imitation of the English government derived from former habitual opinions. In Europe we find executive power, at all places and periods, legislating by proclamations; in the government of the United States the European allotment is frequently departed from, and in many of the states entirely disregarded. The remark is made merely to suggest to the reader, that it is not an element like water, naturally returning by fluidity or evaporation to a homogeneous mass, but capable of being divided and assigned in such manageable allotments, as society may determine to be best for its liberty and happiness. Filmer's divine origin of kings, Mr. Adams's natural origin of noble orders, and the doctrine of judicial independency (on God and conscience excepted) are equally pious, equally wise, equally in concord with the qualities of human nature, and equally calculated to secure human liberty. Each goes as far as possible towards making Gods of men.

A period existed in the progress of the English government, during which an effort was made to diminish the power of the king. Judicial power was in the list of feudal usurpations. The king, having the right of judging, exercised it by a deputy, dependent on his will. But the other orders stript the king of this branch of feudal power, and succeeded in transferring the dependence of the judges from one order to three.

The term 'independence,' as applied to judges in England, cannot refer to the sovereign power, because they are dependent on the will of the parliament. The doctrine it inculcates, therefore, does not extend beyond the idea of their independence of any power inferior to the sovereignty. The sovereignty in the scheme of balanced orders, as in England, does not rest in one order, but in three; the judges were considered as dependent, whilst they were exclusively subjected to the will of one order, the king; and as independent, when subjected to the will of the parliament, the sovereignty itself; because an exclusive subjection to the will of the sovereign, is the highest state of independence, of which a subject or agent is capable. In an equivalent sense the term is used by our policy. The legislature and executive shall be independent, not of the sovereignty, but of any other agent of the sovereign's.

To effect the English judicial independence, the judges, though named by the king, are removable at the pleasure of the parliament; and our imitation of this policy, destroys the subordination of judicial power to the sovereignty, and bestows a considerable influence over it on an agent or subject of the sovereignty. The president creates judges, and may corrupt them by additional offices; and the sovereignty cannot displace them.

Several political caricatures arise out of these facts. Responsibility is an essential principle of representative government; the English monarchy enforces it on judicial power, and the representative policy of the United States dispenses with it.

Division of power is a republican, and not a monarchical principle. The English policy divides and diminishes the power of the king to appoint judges, by investing the parliament with a right to remove them; our constitution magnifies the power of appointment, by withholding any correspondent mode of removal.

Self government, by responsible representation, is the essence of our policy; the sovereignty of orders in England, preserves its self government, by the responsibility of its judicial organ; our national sovereignty renounces self government by renouncing a similar responsibility. It renounces sovereignty itself, which cannot exist in association with a superior or an equal. Ancient hierarchy and aristocracy, never claimed the privilege of independence of the sovereignty, except under the sanction of a commerce with Heaven, and a descent from the Gods. Are the integrity and wisdom of

judges also of divine right, and entitled to exaltation above nations?
Or, are they subject to frailty, and liable to prejudice and errour?
Political offences have, I believe, been generally decided conformably to the political complexion of the bench.

The people were supposed to be the only source for altering the
constitution, according to our policy; but it is exposed to a power
of construction, not responsible to the people.

Legislative, executive and judicial powers shall be separate and
distinct; yet the judges can abolish or make law by precedent.

The president has a negative; it shall however be controlled by
two thirds of congress; but the negative of the president may be
revived by a control of the judges over the control of two thirds.

'All legislative powers' are given to certain functionaries; the
extent of this power, has suggested the propriety of making them
responsible; yet the judicial power, in its capacity to disallow or
repeal the acts of the legislature, is made a greater legislative
power: has the extent of this power also suggested the propriety of
making judges irresponsible?

'Congress may from time to time' establish new courts: can the
old supreme court abolish them, by declaring the law to be
unconstitutional?

Enforcement of law is the judicial province; every new law is an
accumulation of duty; refinements of the new invented idea of
judicial independence, demand protection co-extensively against
an accumulation of duty, as against a diminution of salary; it is a
principle, therefore, capable of putting a sudden stop to legislation, unless new courts are regularly created, to encounter the
burden of enforcing new laws.

But if judicial power may assail legislative, by disallowing laws;
legislative power may revenge itself upon judicial, by impeachments and convictions; and the station of executive power between
these combatants, contains an ability to keep up the war, until
both are worried and discredited, so as to thrive upon their ruins.

Under the English monarchy, this species of responsibility, impeachment, also exists; but a joint parliamentary vote contains
another species of responsibility, infinitely more valuable; yet both
have been unable in England to shield judicial against the influence of executive power, arising from its patronage in appointing
and promoting judges. Here, the same patronage is created, and
the strongest of these securities against its effects, abolished.

Had the responsibility arising from impeachment been found

sufficient in England, the tenure of royal pleasure would simply have been exchanged for that of good behaviour; but its insufficiency, suggested an exchange of a complete dependency upon the will of the king, for a complete dependency upon the will of the sovereignty.

The reason is obvious. The functionaries in every considerable branch of government, may innocently injure a nation. Erroneous opinion is not less injurious because it is honest. Impeachment is a remedy for crime; the will of the sovereignty, for errour. The English sovereignty has a resource both against crime and errour; the sovereignty of the United States is content with a bad remedy against crime, and no remedy against errour.

A defect of talents disclosed by trial; imbecility of mind or body produced by age or malady; a construction of the constitution favourable to a gradual revolution; might each produce great evils: but impeachment could not remove them. If an indefinite adoption of the common law of England should contain a magazine of tools, for working gradually towards the English policy, impeachment is insufficient to countermine the work. For although the judges should deem it criminal in private citizens, to express honest apprehensions of a tendency towards monarchy; yet the injustice and impolicy of considering honest judicial opinion as criminal, although infected by that tendency, might still be demonstrated.

Opinion, which makes, disallows or construes law, in pronouncing judgements, may be excessively injurious to nations and individuals, and perfectly innocent; or it may conceal criminal designs under an appearance of innocence, beyond the possibility of detection and punishment.

Is a national subjection to opinions, innocent but mischievous, or criminal but apparently honest, consistent with national sovereignty or self government? If so, self government must hereafter be defined 'a submission to fraudulent or erroneous opinions.' A subjection to one of these classes, is a subjection to both, because there is no test for separating them.

Legislative and executive opinions, neither claim or possess this pre-eminent state of insubordination. Though innocent and honest, though delivered on oath, they are controlled by national will. But the instant an individual is removed from the legislative or executive departments into the judicial, his nature is supposed to have been regenerated, his errours are sanctified, his intrigues are overlooked, and his responsibility commuted for the universal refuge of imposture, 'God and his own conscience.'

And yet history abounds with the political intrigues and oppressions of judicial power, in favour of revolution, usurpation and tyranny. These display the insufficiency of impeachment for the correction of crimes, to be almost equivalent to its incompetency for the correction of errour. Judicial power is placed beyond the reach of prosecution from an individual. It can ally itself with a branch of government. And impeachment is in practice more frequently a weapon with which factions assail each other, than the avenger of crimes.

Law is nearer to the sovereign will, than the construction of law, and is therefore more likely to correspond with it; but admitting that a power of construing is nearly equivalent to a power of legislating; why should construction of law be quite independent of sovereign will, when law itself is made completely subservient to it? In England, if judicial power opposes the will of sovereign power, by its power of construing laws, the sovereign power can change its organs. In America, judicial power is increased, and its responsibility, compared with a monarchical standard, diminished. Our constitutions and sovereignty as well as laws, may be moulded or undermined by an immoveable power of construction. Here the power of construction is a supremacy over the legislature and the sovereign; in England, the power of removing judges by the parliament, is a supremacy of the sovereign and the legislature over the power of construction. A right to legislate, subject to an insubordinate right to construe and apply, inverts responsibility, by creating an allegiance of law to judgement, in place of an allegiance of judgement to law.

But judicial power, being in its nature didactick and imbecile, is incapable of constituting a sovereign; and is uniformly induced by a consciousness of this incapacity, to ally itself with some other power. The executive, which appoints, promotes, and patronises judicial power; which wields the sword, and keeps the key of the treasury, is unexceptionably that ally. The necessity for this alliance is demonstrated in the consideration, that legislative power must be in collision with judicial, because its territories only can be invaded by construction. An alliance is not formed with a natural enemy. In alliances, the weak party, submits to the strong one; whatever share of power an insubordinate judiciary may acquire, will therefore become subservient to executive designs.

Judicial power has universally been considered as belonging to municipal, and not to political law. Its functions relate to individuals, and not to nations. In the principles of governments, it is not assigned a place. Mr. Adams compounds his political system of the principles of monarchy, aristocracy and democracy; and perfects, as he imagines, his checks and.balances, without making the least use of judicial power. And that this idea is correct, its subordination to law, and its being invariably the instrument of political power, held by a nation, a government, a faction, or an individual, are strong illustrations. In revolutions it follows, but never leads.

It is questionable, therefore, whether it was the intention of the general, or any state government, to erect judicial power into a political department, by inferences to be ingeniously drawn from the ideas of its independence, and the dependence of legislatures upon constitutions. The lines of a power to mould laws and constitutions without responsibility, into the endless forms within the reach of construction, would have been distinctly expressed, and not left to be traced from a single word of hieroglyphical obscurity.

But judicial power has seized upon a quality peculiar to the American policy, to transform itself into a political department, and to extend its claims far beyond precedent. All our governments are limited agencies; others are universally or generally unlimited sovereignties. Legislation, under our policy, is subject to constitutional restrictions; according to the policy of other nations, it is the expression of the sovereign's will. In one case, legislation, which exceeds its agency or violates constitutional limits, is void; in the other, such an excess cannot happen. Being void, no publick functionary or private citizen ought to execute it; therefore judges, jurymen or officers of any other description, are bound to determine whether the instrument exhibited to them as law, be law.* But all these descriptions of persons are bound by the laws of sovereign governments, and have no power, direct or indirect, to determine upon the validity of a law. None of them, therefore, can become a political department. Whereas, if the judges of the United States can acquire the exclusive right of declaring a law void, without any responsibility or mode of defeating the declaration, they must become a political department of great importance. An in-

* If this reasoning is correct, the courts erred in forbidding juries to consider the constitutionality of the sedition law. It was not a question as to the construction of the law, but whether it was really law or not.

tention of creating judicial power into a political department, as a barrier against legislative usurpation, is the inference drawn by itself, from its right to refuse to execute unconstitutional laws; but this right belongs to juries, to officers, and to every citizen. It flows from the limited nature of our governments, contrived, not to increase the power of judges or juries, but to secure the sovereignty of the people. This would not be secured, by inferring from the limitation of legislative power elected by the people, an unlimited judicial power not elected by the people. To distrust and limit responsible and removable agents, and trust without limit irresponsible and immoveable, could never have been intended.

In the states, judicial power is secured against executive influence in several modes. In two only, can a single will appoint judges; in these, they are removable by an address of two thirds of the legislature, and the governour is elected only for two years immediately by the people; in the others, judges are appointed by numerous and popular bodies, which can plant republican principles on the bench, and invigorate them after they are planted. This fact, both demonstrates the publick disapprobation of the judicial system of the general government, and discloses a remedy against its becoming an executive implement.

And this remedy is sufficient, if we exclude the idea of converting judicial power into a political department. This is only attainable by bestowing publick confidence upon judicial power, and publick confidence can never be purchased, except by actual responsibility. We here detect the false construction of the term 'independence.' The independence, dignity or power of an agent, is reflected from the confidence and power of his principal. By depriving the agent of this confidence, you rob him of his independence. No sovereign will confide in agents, not responsible to him; and therefore judicial independence of sovereign power, is the destruction of genuine judicial independence.

In England, the independence of judicial power was produced, by delivering it from the influence of executive power, and exalting it to a dependence upon the will of the sovereign; in the United States, the independence of judicial power is destroyed, by delivering it from the will of the sovereign, and degrading it nearly to the level from whence it was raised in England; it will therefore become the implement of executive power, for want of the confidence and support, begotten by a dependence on the sovereign, as it was in England on account of the same defect.

Thus we are conducted to the only mode of exalting judicial power into a political department, which would be conformable to our principle of division. It can only be effected by bestowing upon it the publick confidence, and that can only be bestowed by responsibility to the publick.

Disunited from the sovereign power, by the appointment and patronage of one of its creatures, it will reap the distrust and contempt of the nation, who will never transfer to judicial power, thus degraded or corrupted, any portion of their confidence, from a legislature, elective and responsible; just as the Lords and Commons of England suspected and despised the judges, so long as they were under the influence of the king.

Dependence upon the sovereign power, is the only species of independence, of which judicial power is capable. If it is deprived of this species of independence, it invariably becomes a dependant or instrument of some other power. Deprived, under our policy, of a dependence on the nation, judicial power has no other alternative, but to become a dependant of legislative or executive power. It is too weak to set up for itself. In the states, it has been subjected to legislative power; under the general constitution, to executive; and if ever a president should attempt to acquire monarchical authority, judicial power must therefore second his designs.

The independence and strength of power, in every section of our policy, is in proportion to their dependence on the people. This term, being applied indiscriminately, to legislative, executive and judicial power, does not admit a contradictory construction in relation to either, so as to have the double effect, of admitting the dependence of two departments or two objects of the same word, on the sovereignty, and denying it as to the third.

Out of the principles of division and responsibility to the nation, has arisen the idea of one political agent being independent of another. Dependence of one agent on another, would be an accumulation, not a division of power, and power is not made responsible, by its accumulation. Independence of the nation, is at least equally inconsistent with the principles of division and responsibility. It is the same craft which once defended judicial dependence on a king, which now defends judicial independence of the nation. The end of both doctrines is to destroy the best pledges for civil liberty, namely, division of power, and responsibility to nations.

Independence of one agent of another, was not invented to

strengthen, and so render power insubordinate to the national will; but to weaken it, for the exact contrary purpose. To glide the judicial power, under a misapprehension of this single word, into a state of insubordination to publick will, into a sovereign power over law and constitution; and into a dependence on executive power, contrary to the policy the word has been used to impress, is one of those errours, overlooked on account of its excessive visibility.

A sovereignty over the constitution, objectionable as it would still be, would be safer in the legislature, than in the judiciary, because of its duennial responsibility; and because it would not naturally devolve from the legislature upon the president; but an excessive power in weak hands, inevitably becomes vicarious.

But if judicial power can be erected into a political department, capable of restraining deviations from the constitution by the legislature, it would probably contribute towards the preservation of our policy. Publick opinion is now the only legitimate guardian of obedience to the constitution; its sloth and inattention, invites and overlooks aberrations from it, amounting to a tendency, which a watchful political judiciary would detect and control; whilst public opinion would still retain its sovereignty unimpaired, and act as forcibly as at present. And a division of the national confidence between the legislature and judiciary, would carry a degree farther the principle of dividing power; but this can never happen, so long as one is subordinate, and the other insubordinate to national will.

There is a manifest distinction between a political and municipal department; and judicial power, to constitute either, must have its attributes. An origin from the sovereignty and independence of any other department, are attributes of a political department; but a municipal department, is a mere detail of law; and a strict submission to law, its inseparable quality. The attribute of a political department is destroyed, by an origin from or an influence by another department; and the quality of a municipal department is destroyed by an independence of the legislature and sovereignty: a judiciary thus situated, is a nondescript legal or political being. The independence of a political department, cannot exist in an executive creature; nor can a genuine and useful enforcement of law, flow from an independence of the sovereign power.

Let us illustrate the idea by a supposition. The English sovereignty is lodged in the parliament. The sovereignty and the legislature is the same. Judicial power is considered as a mere municipal detail. It is therefore subject to the will of this sovereign legislature and has no power to disallow a law, or change the constitution. Here is consistency. But suppose this sovereignty and legislature could neither appoint nor remove judges; that they were approved and tried by the House of Commons, being nominated by their speaker; and that they could repeal or make law and constitution by precedents: are not the consequences apparent? The English parliamentary sovereign would lose the power of self government; the judges would cling to the commons, they would undermine the sovereignty of orders, and would gradually convert it into a representative democracy. Such is our case. Neither national sovereignty, nor legislative power, nor popular representation, appoints, has a power over, or influences the judges. They are under no responsibility to act according to the will of our sovereignty, or of our legislature. They are nominated by the president, and approved and tried by the senate; and they make or repeal law and constitution by precedents. Therefore they are under the same influence to undermine the popular sovereignty, as the supposed judges would be to undermine a monarchical sovereignty, or a sovereignty of orders. Can a judicial independency of the American sovereignty, prevent the introduction of monarchical principles, because a judicial dependency upon the English sovereignty, prevents the introduction of republican?

Judicial power has never appeared in any political system, completely independent of the sovereign power, except under the constitution of the United States. Sometimes it is dependent on a monarch, at others, on a government or on the people; in England, it is controllable without delay or trial by the sovereign will. In our state governments its tenure is various; but these varieties unite in the common end, of some species of responsibility to the sovereign. In Connecticut, judges have been elected by the legislature for very short periods during two centuries, and their integrity or responsibility has never produced mischief. And a spacious field of comparison has appeared between judges appointed by a single will, and those chosen by popular bodies. The latter are not thrown into the back ground, in point of talents, integrity or republicanism.

A single will, is more likely to be seduced by dogma or ambition, and to overlook virtue in search of engines to advance selfish designs, than the people or their representatives. If this is not true, why do we erect republican governments? if it is true, why is it not applicable to judicial appointments?

Where is the difference in the application of republican principles, between legislative and judicial power?

If the office and powers of a judge are important, so are those of a legislator. If one may injure the publick, by crime, incapacity or errour, so may the other. If time and trial may disclose defects in a legislator, so may they in a judge. If there is a hardship in dismissing one without trial; the same hardship reaches the other. If the tenure of good behaviour, or a right to persevere for life in conscientious errour, would destroy the responsibility of a legislator, it will destroy that of a judge. And if legislative integrity and virtue are only to be obtained by election and responsibility, judicial integrity and virtue can never be expected from an insubordinate power for life. The power of construing the constitution and disallowing law, possessed by our judiciary, being functions of unexampled judicial power, and approaching nearer to sovereign and legislative power, than in any former instance; are considerations which bestow great weight upon this parallel.

Judicial responsibility 'to God and conscience,' is a counterpart of the 'divine right,' cheat, resorted to by innumerable kings, nobles and priests, to delude and oppress mankind. Our system renounces this species of responsibility, and is founded upon the principle of responsibility to the nation. Is this political principle to be lost, and the hostile principle of superstition substituted for it, by the cobwebs of inference and construction? Responsibility to God is the sanction of religion; what would be the influence of religious precept, if this sanction was dissolved? Such as will be the influence of political precept, unattended with responsibility to the sovereign.

Practice, as well as theory, sheds light upon this subject. It affords endless materials to prove the usefulness of judicial responsibility, and to display the force of habitual prejudices; but we will compress an idea of this fruitful argument into the following paragraph.

In England and America, the permanency of some judges, and the fluctuation of others; and the appointment of some by the people or the legislature, and of others by the executive; are positions contended for by the same persons, and the same societies; and habit and prejudice can supply the firmness with which these contradictions are defended. 'Judicial independency' and 'chartered rights' are the sounds which induce us to fall into them. Corporation judges are elected by the people and periodically changed; national judges are appointed by the king, and hold at the will of the parliament. Charles the second destroyed charters, for the purpose of transferring from corporations to himself the appointment of judges and other officers, as a prelude to despotism. The judges of the union are appointed as Charles designed to appoint corporation judges. His mode for assailing liberty, is ours for defending it. As a monarch, he wished to destroy the republican corporation mode of appointments; as a republick, we adopt the mode, which Charles conceived to be monarchical. A million of souls in London, and possibly nearly half that number in our towns, consider their elective judges as the best guardians of liberty and property; and the dismay of corporations, if deprived of this ·chartered right, would be equal to that of the friends to monarchy, ·if national judges were made elective and responsible. A furious zeal will often exist in the same state and in the same person for elective, or periodical, or responsible state or corporation judges, and for executive, permanent and insubordinate federal judges. The case occurs among the states of elective and periodical chancery judges; the habit and prejudice of England and of such states, are both portrayed in this imitation; property is as deeply affected by chancery judges as by law judges; and their power is uncontrolled by juries. To such habits and prejudices, and not to reason, a few of the states have surrendered our foundation principle of responsibility, in constituting state judicial power, and all of them in the case of federal judicial power. Reason is an umpire between contradictions, but she cannot reconcile them.

Names cannot change man's nature, and cure him of his passions and vices; if they could, this discovery would have superseded the necessity of all our inventions for curbing the passions and vices of ·publick officers, by calling them judges. An experiment somewhat like this was tried by the Jews, but they gave it up for monarchy.

It is objected, that a responsible judge may be intimidated or seduced by a faction. Why is not the same objection advanced against a responsible legislature or executive? Because the confidence begotten by responsibility, protects these characters. Impeachment, it is said, will restrain the judge; will it also protect him, and purchase national confidence? A faction must rule the government, before it can intimidate or corrupt a judge; and will judges appointed by it, patronised by it, and tried by it, be safe against its influence? They are placed within the power of alternate factions, lest they should be influenced by factions; and without the power of the nation, lest they should be influenced by the nation. They fear party vengeance, and cannot expect national confidence or protection. If they were responsible to the sovereignty, they would expect its protection against demagogues and factions; but if they are independent of the sovereignty, they must depend on the faction which can try and condemn them. A paper, theoretick, didactick independence cannot shield judges against the influence or corruption of a man or a faction, possessing an intimidating or corrupting degree of power or patronage. If the cause of the terror or treachery exists, the terror or treachery naturally and inevitably ensues. Which is the best remedy against the evil; to create the cause, and to underwrite the 'judges shall be independent of this cause of terror or corruption,' or to forbear to create it? If the national confidence and protection through the medium of responsibility is added to this forbearance, it is probable, that judicial integrity, the object in quest, will be well secured. If a liability to impeachment is a security for this integrity, why is it not exclusively relied on to produce legislative integrity? If a responsibility to the sovereign power, exposes integrity to the influence of an individual or a faction, why is the legislature thus exposed?

A deviation from one principle is the road leading to another. Being taught that the insubordination of judicial power, will wash away human vices and passions, and that national opinion will corrupt it; we shall no longer consider this opinion as the most incorruptible species of political jury, and the only safe guardian of liberty and property. And our respect for the basis of our policy being once weakened, it will be gradually undermined, by diminishing the responsibility of legislative and executive power, until we come to Mr. Adams's republick, composed of a hereditary executive and senate, and of septennial election.

The absence of responsibility is an evil moral principle, from which it is impossible that good moral effects can flow. And the consequences to be expected from an insubordinate power, able to knead and mould a constitution by construction, disallow indigenous law, introduce foreign law, fine, imprison and hang; and which in the struggles of avarice or ambition for wealth and power, must become their instrument; forcibly illustrate the correctness of our political analysis.

If, by the intervention of electors, or in any other mode, judicial power could be made responsible to national sovereignty, as are all our political departments, it is highly probable that it might be raised to the quality of such a department, with powers defined and limited; and that its elevation might become an important improvement of the principle of division. But a judicial sovereignty over constitution and law, without responsibility to the national sovereignty, is an unprincipled and novel anomaly, unknown to any political theory, and fitted to become an instrument of usurpation.

If judicial power was intended to be advanced from municipal to political quality, responsibility ought to have followed the advancement according to the elements of our policy; if not, its quality is merely municipal, and its claims of political rights, usurpations drawn from the limited nature of our governments, by which judicial power has constituted itself the guardian of all the rights retained by the people.

It resembles a legislature compounded of two branches, chambers or benches. The upper bench can pass no judgement, unless it has been previously passed by the lower; nor can it alter the judgement or verdict as passed by the lower; like the case of money bills in England and Virginia. Their separate functions bear a close analogy to the mode of legislating in England about the thirteenth century, when the parliament prepared the abstract and the judges dilated it into technical form. If the matter of the parliament was of more importance than the form given to it by the judges, juries are not the least important judicial bench. By adhering repeatedly to the same verdict, they can force the upper bench to pass judgements against their opinions; they can impose both law and fact on the upper bench, which can impose no fact or law upon them; and they judge really and substantially in every case, whereas the judgement of the upper bench is in most cases a mere formulary prescribed by their verdict. What better title has one judicial bench or chamber, and that the least powerful too, to the epithet 'judicial,' than the House of Lords in England, or the Senate of the United States, to the epithet 'legislative?' Was it intended to erect less than a moiety of judicial power into a political department, and even to endow this fragment with an irresponsible supremacy over the entire legislative and executive departments, by giving it an exclusive power to construe the constitution and annul laws?

Our aukward imitation of English policy, and misconception of its phrase, 'judicial independence,' is displayed in our lower judicial bench, as well as in the upper. We have made one dependent on a creature of our sovereignty, to avoid the old English errour of its dependence on a portion of theirs; and the other on the president through his marshal, in imitation of its English dependence through the sheriffs. In striving to exalt, we have degraded the judicial character, if it is more honourable to be dependent on the third part than on no part of a sovereignty. This degradation as to juries arises from our having overlooked them as composing a portion of judicial power, because the English overlooked and left them under the influence of the crown, when they placed the judges under the influence of the sovereignty.

We contend, that adequate salaries, not to be diminished; a tenure for life, only to be lost by crime or death, and not by folly, ignorance, incapacity, lunacy or idiocy; and a complete exemption from the influence of the sovereign, are all necessary to secure the independence of judges, and we expect the independence of juries, from no salary, an ephemeral tenure, and the culling of an administration party spirit for each particular case.

It is evidently of equal or superior importance to life, liberty and property, that juries should be independent of kings, presidents, factions, and demagogues, as that judges should be so. The verdicts under the sedition law were the ground work of the judgements. Judges were made independent of the crown in England, because judgements were made instruments of tyranny. Verdicts of juries may become such instruments. A president can select juries of his own faction, by his officer, the marshal, and infallibly mould political verdicts.

The king of England often influences verdicts by means of a sheriff, less dependent on him, than a marshal on the president. The office of sheriff is both less lucrative than the office of marshal; one is rotary, and the other capable of continuance by the will of the president. The continuance of a great income tempts; and the certainty of returning speedily into private life, does not deter, in the case of the marshal. Accordingly we meet with many acquittals in England, and with few or none in the United States, in prosecutions under sedition laws.

The dependence of one judicial branch on the sovereignty of the country, is some security against the dependence of the other on the crown; for in England we find judges sometimes deciding contrary to the will of executive power, since their dependence on the sovereignty of the country.

Here, a security against executive influence over juries, is rendered more necessary, by the irresponsibility of the judges to the sovereignty, and none is provided. The dependence of judges on the sovereignty (the security against packed juries, and the source of all those acts for which English judges have been celebrated) is both relinquished in the United States, and a provision is also made for corrupting or influencing them by an additional office from executive power, in lieu of the parliamentary vote. .

By using English words, and subverting English principles, we have made a judicial power independent of the sovereignty, and almost entirely dependent on executive will. The jury branch is unequivocally so; and the upper branch is rendered more so than in England, by its independence of the sovereignty, and capacity to receive executive patronage. And if executive influence in England over judicial power, sheds the blood of patriots, it is improbable that in America it will turn its fury against traitors to patriotism.

. In showing that by some strange fatality, the constitution of the United States had abandoned the precedent it intended to copy, and violated the principle it intended to establish, namely, 'that judicial power ought to be independent of and unbiased by executive power,' no use has been made of the remedy by impeachment, because it is nearly equivalent in both countries, but somewhat worse in the United States. Neither the Senate nor the House of Lords constitutes the sovereignty; one represents a factitious being, called states, the other is itself a factitious being, called a privileged order. The Senate of the United States is a branch of executive power, which is not the case with the House of Lords. It is a party in the appointment of the judges, it has the exclusive privilege of trying, which is not the case with the House of Lords. Judicial responsibility to the House of Lords was not a sufficient security for the national interest, because it was only a portion of the sovereignty; and therefore a responsibility to the entire sovereignty is provided. The objections apply with five-fold force to the Senate of the United States. 1st. The whole body is an executive order, participating in all important executive functions. 2dly. The whole body is an order as representing the factitious portion of the sovereignty of the United States, called states, which from its nature can only act by representation, and not in person, like the factitious portion of the English sovereignty, called nobility. 3dly. One section of the Senate is composed of an order or separate interest, representing large states. 4thly. The other section, of an interest representing small states; and lastly, the Senate constitutes no portion of the sovereignty of the United States. As the House of Lords would be partial to judges who had sacrificed the publick interest, to the interest of the noble order; so the Senate would be partial to those who had sacrificed the popular interest, to the interest of the state governments. So far the insufficiency of impeachment to secure responsibility to the publick interest, is equal; but the four other objections to the Senate, render the insufficiency of judicial responsibility by impeachment, greater in the United States than in England, where experience disclosed the necessity of an additional responsibility to the whole sovereignty. There is very little difference between making judges responsible to the functionary who nominates or who approves. They form in union the executive power which appoints. They never thought in England of trusting to an impeachment before the king, for judicial independence and integrity. In England, the effort has been to prevent judges from being responsible to the power appointing them; here, to make them so. Against executive influence over the upper judicial branch, we have only the security of impeachment before a section of executive power; and against the same influence over the lower judicial branch, we have no security at all. The expression, 'reserved to the states or to the people,' implies the dual nature of the general government, and each portion ought to possess some security over judicial power for the preservation of its reservations. The latter has none. The former, one mingled with executive influence, party spirit, and a remediless contumacy of individuals for six years.

The inefficacy of impeachment from its own nature, to produce the contemplated responsibility, has not been stated. In all political cases, it is guided by party, faction, revenge or prejudice. Sentences flowing from these sources, are neither sustained by publick respect, nor calculated to produce judicial integrity. Judges, to escape the vengeance of impeachment, must appease the passions which inflict it, in place of consulting the publick good. As integrity is no protection, and guilt no prognostick of conviction, this vengeance excites commiseration, and procures respect. And yet, at an epoch when the impeachment of judges has fallen into disgrace and disuse in England, where it was invented; it is exclusively relied on in the United States, as the remedy against the influence of executive over judicial power. A remedy, in which conviction will seldom be thought a proof of guilt.

It is a policy founded in an obvious contradiction. The judges for trying ordinary and private cases, are instituted for life, and absolved from a subjection to the silent suffrage of the whole sovereignty, which might send them quietly into retirement, without throwing the firebrand of impeachment amidst the worst passions with which society is afflicted. But the judges of the highest officers of government, and the most important publick cases, are instituted for only six years, and subject to dismission by a silent vote of representatives of sections of the sovereignty. If a responsibility to one of these sections by election, will secure judicial integrity and independence in these major cases, where it is most likely to fail; a responsibility to the whole sovereignty or its representatives, will secure it in the minor cases, where it is less likely to fail. And if the independence and integrity of the senatorial judges is not secured under their periodical election by state legislatures, then impeachment before judges without independence and integrity, is no security for the independence and integrity of the judges to be impeached.

To determine the propriety of leaving in the hands of executive power, its influence over judicial, it is necessary to comprehend what is meant by judicial independence. If it means that judicial power ought to be independent of the sovereignty and the government, and constituted into an umpire between these parties, to administer the constitution to both; then the price paid for it would be the dependence of the nation and the government, upon judicial power. But this construction is violated by making it responsible to a section of one. If it means, that the judicial section of government ought to be independent of any other section, a responsibility to the sovereignty is consistent, and a responsibility to a section of the government inconsistent with this meaning. To one of these interpretations, the idea of judicial independence must be confined. By the first, judicial power would be made despotick; by the second, a responsibility to a section of the government is forbidden, because it makes judicial power dependent on that section, if a responsibility to the sovereignty would make it dependent on the sovereignty. No mode exists to avoid the dilemma of one of these constructions, but that of making judges responsible to the sovereignty or its representative, but independent of every section of the government.

Legislative power could not be independent, if legislators were liable to impeachment before a court for legislative acts; yet it would be equally so with judicial power, liable to impeachment for judicial acts before the senate; and legislative power is considered as independent, though it is dependent on the sovereignty; demonstrating that the term only implies, an independence of other branches of the government. The independence of judicial power is intended to prevent its being made an instrument of tyranny by another branch, not to make it a tyranny itself. If it is placed beyond the coercion of sovereignty, and made responsible to another branch of a government, it is forged exactly into the instrument intended to be avoided. Its responsibility to the English king, and independence of the parliament or sovereignty of the country, made it such an instrument. Had this responsibility been transferred from the king to the House of Lords, it would have remained such an instrument.

It has been heretofore denied that the judicial power possessed an exclusive privilege to determine the constitutionality of a law; and asserted, that juries and private individuals participate in this right, upon the ground of the nullity of every act by a delegated authority, not warranted by the delegation. In support of these opinions, we must again recollect, that judges constitute but one judicial bench or branch, and that a verdict must be sent to them by the jury bench before they can make a judgement; just as a bill must be sent by one legislative branch to another, before it can be made a law. Are the jury bound to draw and pass this verdict without even considering its constitutionality? What would be the complexion of a legislature, with one branch under such an obligation? Suppose the constitution had expressly invested the court and jury with a power to disallow a law by proclamation as void, and that the court had proclaimed to that effect, but the jury oppositely. Even if an individual is tried for violating a law, because he judged it to be unconstitutional, he is acquitted if he judged right; proving that he had a right to judge.

But although judicial power has no right to enact or repeal law, yet it can effect both ends to great extent by its judgements in private cases; and it has often done so for the purpose of making political or revolutionary law. The English judges destroyed the law of entails, to weaken the power of the nobility, and strengthen the power of the king. The same judges affirmed a law for extending the power of the House of Commons from three years to seven, and thus made the only fragment of the government, over which the people had a feeble power, independent of them. And the judges of the United States have declared an entire code of laws, passed in a foreign nation some centuries before the union, to be laws of the union; although the constitution is literally prospective both as to legislation and the organs of legislation. Had our judges decided differently, their decision would have repealed the common law code. Without inquiring whether their decision is right or wrong, it suffices for our argument to shew, that such is the connexion between legislating and judging, that one may be easily run into the other; and that it is impossible to keep these powers separate and distinct, as our theory requires. If this is true, where is the consistency of concluding that one species of legislation ought to be independent of the sovereignty and another responsible to it? If congress had by law declared the common law of England to be in force, the people could by election have enforced a repeal of this law, but a similar law is passed by judges whom the people cannot compel to repeal it.

The treaty making power is purely executive, or at least the entire natural sovereignty of the country, is excluded from sharing in it. By 'natural,' I mean the people. State governments are artificial beings, and nearly the whole treaty making power is the creature of these artificial beings. It is not meant to discuss the propriety of making law by treaties, without the assent of the natural sovereignty or its representative, and by a moiety of a legislature, but this mode of legislation is exhibited to illustrate the defectiveness of judicial responsibility to the sovereignty. In this mode, the sections of the government which appoint and try judicial power can make laws. These laws may have great political influence and gradually change our policy; and yet the sections of the government which make them, are only responsible to their own creatures and dependents. Had judges and juries been responsible to the sovereignty, it might more safely have established a species of legislation, in which it does not participate. Treaties may more easily and plausibly extend executive and senatorial power, than the time of service of the English House of Commons was extended; and judicial power might be the instrument for enforcing such laws and subverting our policy. It is as easy to pack laws by means of treaties, as to pack juries by a different executive engine. The question is, whether a judicial power, responsible to the executive branches, which branches have an exclusive right to legislate through treaties, is a sound check upon the constitutionality of this species of legislation? Executive power is the universal destroyer of every sovereignty like ours, and our sovereignty invests its natural enemy with an exclusive power of legislating, empanelling juries, and appointing and trying judges.

Our first criticism of the legislative principles of the United States, is directed of course to the sexennial election of senators. The degree in which an independency of publick opinion for six years, is able to efface legislative integrity, and excite disloyalty and avarice, beyond an annual responsibility, by figures and theory, is as six to one. By experience, it is nearly demonstrated in the British House of Commons. The maxim 'that tyranny begins where annual election ends,' subscribed to by Mr. Adams in the prime of life, and copiously applied by the people of the United States, is deserted and reversed in the cases to which politicians have thought it most applicable; where the power delegated was most dangerous. And the reversal of this maxim in the tenure of the president and senators of the United States, may possibly be as mortal to our policy, as the desertion of that so nearly allied to it, which dictated consular rotation, was to the policy of Rome.

The long official tenure of the Senate of the United States has been unwarily suffered, from mistaking it for an aristocratical balance, whereas it is a body organized upon democratical principles, to equalise the rights of states, great and small, rich or poor; and to prevent aristocratical privileges or powers from being usurped by superior strength or wealth. The United States, far from intending to introduce an aristocratical principle by the senate, submitted to this equalising democratical regulation, for the same reasons that rich and strong men submit to an equality of rights with the poor and weak. In considering therefore the Senate's time of service, we ought to be guided, not by a false, but by the true motive for its form; and to discern that the question is not whether a long or a short official tenure is best to sustain an aristocratical balance, but which is best to sustain a democratical equality between unequal states. Which is best to sustain a democratical equality of rights between men unequal in wealth or strength, is exactly the same question. A long official tenure will produce in both cases the same effects. If an independence of the will of constituents, for a period almost amounting to the probable duration of the incumbent's life, would instil aristocratical principles into the functionaries substituted to preserve democratical

215

rights between individuals, the same cause will instil the same principles into those constituted to preserve the same rights between states. The infusion must be healthy or poisonous as to both objects, or as to neither; and the question simply is, whether it is good or bad; and not whether it is of the singular quality, to cure, drunk out of one cup, but to kill from another; just as the same popish relict will draw down blessings upon the orthodox, and curses upon the heretical.

But the exposure of legislative power to executive influence, is unquestionably the heel of Achilles, omitted to be immortalized by an ablution in good moral principles, and left exposed to the poisoned shafts of corruption.

The division and responsibility of power, and the independence of political departments of each other, are the vital principles of our policy.

The legislature, as the most powerful political department, ought not to be influenced by one less powerful, because a weaker power able to make a stronger subservient to its views, acquires an unconstitutional force. What can exceed the absurdity, of considering the principle of separating departments, and delegating different powers to each, as essential to a free government; and yet providing an influence for executive over legislative power, which enables it really to legislate, contrary both to the theory and letter of the constitution? The king of England would be a weaker power, than an independent House of Commons fairly elected; yet, the influence which annexes their power to his, makes him irresistible. Congress, as constituting a complete legislature, was intended to be placed in a state of far greater independence of the president, than the lords and commons were of the king.

He who can apply fear or hope to the human mind, obtains subserviency to his designs. A president may bestow offices and contracts upon members of congress, which excite the fears and hopes of all men; therefore he may obtain an influence over their minds, and destroy or lessen the independence of the legislature. His gradual progress in this work, and not the constitution, will become the thermometer of his power, in which the mercury may rise and fall, until war and debt shall fix it at the English standard. And the lines drawn by the principle of a division of power may be gradually effaced, by a commerce between the departments of government, without the concurrence of the sovereign power. These lines were intended to be fixed by the constitution; and their fluctuation is as inconsistent with common honesty, as with any definite form of government.

The effect of executive influence, interwoven by law with a form of government, although it is disowned as one of its principles, is before our eyes in England; its effect in the United States may be estimated, by comparing the means by which it is worked there, with the means by which it may be worked here.

The chief circumstances in which the cases disagree, are the elective and hereditary qualities of the two executives; the influence of a senate over the president in the exercise of his patronage, and of a council or ministry over the king; and the ineligibility to the legislature of all officers appointed by the president, whilst a part of the officers appointed by the king are re-eligible. They agree in a common capacity for directing the artillery of executive patronage, against legislative integrity; both bestow offices created and continued, and both dispense money raised by law.

We have shewn that an annual power, by means of the disbursement of a nation's money and offices, has often enslaved it. The uncertainty of its tenure, whets its inclination to use the opportunity of acquiring one more permanent. And therefore it is more dangerous to entrust periodical than hereditary power with the means of acquiring undue influence. It has less to lose and more to gain. A king, though limited by orders as in England, would have weaker motives to impel him towards usurpation, than a president, liable to become a private citizen at the end of four years. Yet this king has been induced to corrupt the legislature for the sake of getting more power. When we entrust the same means to stronger motives for using them, the moral consequence is, that they will be used.

The ineligibility of an officer appointed by the president, is an addition to his influence. Pictures of an office, coloured by the imagination, will be contemplated and admired by many members; and whilst one office in England can only corrupt one member, because it is to be paid for after it is received; here it may corrupt several, because it must be paid for before it is received.

These trivial varieties constitute all the additional security for legislative independence here, whilst the plain coincidence in the decisive fact, of an ability in both executives to bestow office and money upon members of the legislature, demonstrates the certainty of a concurrence in effect. From the period in which Philip destroyed the liberties of Greece, by corrupting her orators, down to the present moment, at which we are hearing the groans of England, produced by the corruption of her orators; there is no instance of national safety or happiness, having been produced by a power in one man to corrupt eminent legislative talents.

It is better for a nation to have no elective legislature, than one which can furnish an individual with money and offices, and receive them from him; because this commerce requires more money and offices, than executive power would need without a legislature; and because the abuse would be more clearly seen, if the executive power created the national oppressions, which it dispensed in patronage. The English patronage produces heavier burdens to the nation, than it would do, if there was no House of Commons. A poor effort to meet this enormous evil, is made by our constitution, in an inhibition on the legislature to take new offices created by itself. It acknowledges the evil by an insufficient attempt to prevent it. The remedy does not pretend to provide for the case of money, to be gotten by contracts; insuffices for the case of old offices unnecessarily retained; and may be wholly evaded by transplanting officers.

Suppose the constitution had contained the following article: 'The legislative, executive and judicial powers shall be distinct and independent of each other; that is to say, the president may influence the judges, by appointing and preferring them; and he may influence the legislature by means of offices and money, created, and raised by the legislature.' Would this plain language have obtained the publick approbation?

It is admitted by Mr. Adams and all who defend the system of limited monarchy, that the safety of the plebeian order, rests upon the independence of its representatives of the other two orders. If either of these orders can influence these representatives, the limitation is abolished, and the plebeian order is enslaved. Integrity and fraud will share equally in the suspicions excited by a power to corrupt; and a want of confidence in popular representatives, will work in concert with bribery and corruption, to destroy the liberty which these representatives were instituted to defend.

An opinion, that the confidence of the people is lost, or a conviction that it is not merited, will eradicate from the mind of the representative a reliance upon the people, and plant fear and hatred in its place. This fear and hatred, combining with the influence of office and money, will produce an alliance against the people, between their own agents, and the power these agents were designed to control. If this reasoning is justified by the test of moral cause and effect; it is also justified by the experience of England. Theoretically and practically it results, that a power in one man to bestow offices and money upon a national legislature, is an evil principle; that it is an evil principle, so malignant as to eat out the best qualities of limited monarchy, and strengthen the worst; and that being homogeneous with the worst qualities of limited monarchy, it cannot be so, with the best qualities of republican government.

The system of a balance of orders, is bottomed upon the idea of some natural or political enmity, between the one, the few and the many. A power in the one, to corrupt the representatives of the many, is a mode of protecting the many against his enmity, inconsistent with the understandings of all mankind. No people can confide in representatives whom a king can influence; no king will confide in ministers whom the people can influence; and no individual would trust his liberty and property to an arbitrator, who expected from his antagonist a good office. As an executive power, to bestow offices on the representatives of the plebeian order, overturns all the principles of the system of balances; so executive power to bestow offices upon the representatives of a nation, will overturn all the principles of national self government; because there is so little difference between a plebeian order, and an entire nation, that the representative corruption, capable of subjugating the one, may be safely considered as capable of subjugating the other.

If the principle of executive patronage over the legislature, under the constitution of the United States, is calculated to produce all the evils which the same principle produces in England, and an additional number, springing from our policy, to which the English policy is not exposed; nothing can more justly merit constitutional extermination. An additional malignancy flows from the temporary and elective qualities of our executive power.

A president will be reduced to the alternative of using his patronage to corrupt the legislature, or of losing his office. By withholding from leading members, what they desire and he can give, a president purchases their enmity; if they could receive nothing from him, there would exist no cause for this enmity. With this legislative patronage, reputation and re-election will depend upon a crafty management of money and office; without it, both would depend on merit. In the first case, legislative testimony will be nothing but the tricks and artifices of rapacity and ambition;

and sedition laws for locking up both truth and calumny, would be preferable to these tricks and artifices; under an exclusion of executive patronage, legislative testimony as to the conduct and character of a president, would be unsuborned.

A president, with a patronage over the legislature, must have a sort of prætorian cohorts. They will appear, and force themselves into employment, wherever an individual exists who can pay them. If a president disappoints the expectations of these legislative cohorts, he dies to the presidency; they can more safely attempt the political life of a good president, than disappointed military cohorts could the natural life of a good emperour. The motives are the same in both cases, and exactly those which draw forth from men their worst vices. Nor is there any difference between the largesses from quaternial presidents, and successive emperours under the Roman system of military murder and election, with respect to a nation, except the result of a calculation, whether quaternial election, or irregular periodical murder, will have most effect, in exciting and spreading the corruption of executive patronage.

It is so vicious, as to deprive the patron of the power of remaining virtuous. Hence good men were suddenly changed into wicked emperours. An ability in elected emperours to corrupt an electing army, destroyed their virtues. An elective president will be himself corrupted by an ability to corrupt a legislature. Importunity will assail him. Opposition will excite him. Ambition will entice him. Avarice will harden him. Driven on by his faction, and his passions, his virtue will seldom make any resistance; its struggles will be speedily suppressed by the host of foes, with which his power of patronage over the legislature, will cause it to be assailed.

It is a political drum beating for recruits, notifying where the bounty for taking the field against virtue, is to be had; and as the way to this bounty lies through the legislature, it draws the most impure qualities of human nature into the field of election, where the purest are necessary to sustain republican government. By invigorating and exciting the activity of our worst qualities to obtain popular favour, Mr. Adams's charge against election, of an insufficiency to select virtue and talents, may be made true. These evil qualities will not in the legislature forget the motives which drew them thither; they will not forget that legislative hands can reach the richest coffers of executive patronage. But they will forget that it is the duty of legislators to advance the publick good, and their worst vice to sacrifice it to their own avarice or ambition.

It is essential to the purity of our policy, that the legislature should be unable to translate or prefer executive and judicial agents to more desirable offices; upon what ground is the translation or preferment of legislative agents to more desirable offices, by executive or judicial power, unessential to its purity? Is it less dangerous to society, that the legislature should be corrupted or influenced by the executive or judiciary, than that these departments should be corrupted or influenced by the legislature?

A prohibition upon the legislature to influence members of the executive and judicial departments by office, proves that this identical species of influence was considered as destructive of the principle of division of power. An allowance to these departments to influence the legislature by office, will destroy the principle of division, or what some may call the independence between departments, precisely in the same mode, as it would have been destroyed, by allowing the legislature thus to influence them. The whole difference is in the effect. The prohibited legislative patronage, might have worked slowly towards aristocracy; the allowed executive patronage, will work rapidly towards monarchy.

Stronger reasons exist for shielding legislative power against the influence of executive and judicial patronage, than for shielding these departments against legislative patronage; the legislature can supply them with money and offices, which they may give back to the members of the legislature; whereas they cannot furnish the legislature with either, to be given back to themselves. Offices and money, created or sustained, and taxed by the legislature, are distributed by the executive; and the bankrupt law endowed judicial power with considerable patronage; so that the legislature can extend, sustain, diminish, or cause to fluctuate, executive and judicial patronage, as it is pleased or displeased with the returns to itself.

It would even have been better, that the legislature should have been allowed to distribute among its members, a portion of the offices and money, produced by its laws, than to take them back from executive power; because thus it would have been shielded against executive or monarchical influence, and a power so direct to patronise itself, would have awakened the publick jealousy; which an indirect mode of effecting the same end, is calculated to lull. Then the evil would have been seen; now, the interlude between law and appointment (the puppets of legislative corruption and executive patronage) may hide the evil. Both modes of patronage are seeds of moral and political evil; one is cultivated openly and directly; it is therefore infinitely less pernicious, as is evinced in the instance of state legislative patronage; the other is cultivated secretly and indirectly, and is therefore infinitely more pernicious, as is evinced in the case of England.

The arguments against shielding the legislature from executive patronage, are, that it may deprive patriots of merited reward, and the community of valuable services. Rewards to be bestowed by executive or monarchical ambition, and services to be guided by executive or monarchical designs.

Political merit, consists in preferring the service of a nation to the service of an individual; individuals consider that quality as merit, which is subservient to their interest or designs; hence monarchs, instead of allowing merit to patriots, persecute them as traitors. A nation endeavours to select the genuine species of merit, an individual, the spurious; one seeks for the means of producing publick good; the other, for the means of advancing selfish designs. National patronage is applied with a view to national self government; individual patronage buys talents, or pacifies enmity, for the purpose of destroying national self government. Therefore popular patronage strives to reward such merit and to procure such services, as will advance republican principles; and individual patronage, strives to reward merit and procure services, for advancing individual interest.

The English example and universal experience prove, that the patronage of an individual corrupts what nations consider as merit and patriotism. To bestow on one man a great patronage, from a hope that it will reward the virtues which it destroys, is founded upon a probability, that a moral cause will produce a different effect here, from that which it has constantly produced elsewhere, and is now producing in England.

By detaching the patronage of one man, into elective legislatures, to select talents for publick service, the nation will reap a harvest of services, as abundant as the harvest of rewards, which virtue and patriotism will reap. When one man dispenses the rewards to merit, merit will consist in our attachment to the interest of one man. When the legislature is converted into a school for those intrigues and artifices, begotten and nurtured by the admission of executive patronage within its walls, the antipathy of the mind against fraud and deceit will be gradually erased; politicks will be converted into a science, too mysterious and complicated for popular comprehension; and the diploma of proficiency will constitute the worst evidence of a title to national rewards, but the best, to executive.

If the publick good requires, that members of the legislature should be incapable of receiving offices and contracts, from executive power, it would be immoral and wicked to betray it, for the sake of gratifying individuals. To elude this truth, the necessity of recurring to the talents assembled in legislative bodies, adequately to fill other offices, is suggested. If this argument has weight, national self government cannot exist. It is simply Mr. Adams's idea of a natural aristocracy in a new form. Men are unhappily inclined to be disrespectful to themselves, by admitting the idea of a monopoly and rareness of talents; and although the delusion is known to vanish, whenever it is examined, yet it continues to govern half the world, who only believe the fact, because they have never looked into the evidence. Thus they are willing to suffer the evil of executive patronage over the legislature, to gain for society the benefit of these unseen talents; as men have been willing to suffer the evil of a corrupt priesthood, to gain for society the benefit of unfulfilled oracles. Whilst philosophy boasts of having exploded one species of idolatry, she falls herself into another; and having delivered mankind from the invisible agency of false gods, she subjects them to the invisible talents of false patriots.

Above two thousand years past, the Romans annually found new talents in new consuls, capable of conducting publick affairs, with unexampled prosperity. The French revolution has proved, that even military talents are scattered every where among men. All civilized nations, must have abundantly more men fit for office than offices to give them. No nation can support any form of popular government, where this is not the case. If then the United States have sent executive patronage into their legislature for officers, from a supposed deficiency of talents without its pale, it is done upon a calculation which acknowledges their unfitness for any species of popular government.

Had nature been accustomed to produce occasionally rare and extraordinary talents, it is highly questionable whether they would have been beneficial to mankind. Shall we believe erroneously that she visits us with one calamity, in order to fix upon ourselves another? Shall we corrupt the legislature, to come at rare talents which do not exist, and which would, if found, be a calamity; or be contented with such talents as nature does create, and with legislative integrity in the bargain? If such men as Alexander, Cæsar or Cromwell are examples of this vast superiority of talents, it would be better to let them remain unknown, than to awaken them by executive patronage over legislative power.

The truth is, that rare talents, like a natural aristocracy, are created by ignorance, and that cunning takes advantage of the opinion to scourge mankind. Ignorance is the source of slavery, and knowledge of liberty, because the first begets, and the other explodes the errour, 'that some men are endowed with faculties, far exceeding the general standard.' In thinking it necessary to send executive patronage into legislative bodies to fill offices, lest the publick should lose the benefit of these imaginary faculties, we have adhered to one preceptor, who teaches nothing but slavery; and rejected the admonitions of another, who alone teaches liberty.

It will be admitted that virtue and talents are as necessary for legislative, as for any other kind of publick servants; and that these qualities, transplanted by executive patronage into other departments, ought to be replaced by a full equivalent. If this reimbursement can be made, the pretext that a dearth of qualification for office, makes it necessary to corrupt legislatures, in order to obtain incorrupt officers, is false; if it cannot, the exchange must be injurious to the nation. In England, this argument would be less conclusive, on account of the eligibility of most of the great executive officers to the House of Commons, and the session of all in the House of Lords. There the idea of a dearth of qualification for office, is countenanced by heaping offices, civil, military, legislative, executive and judicial, upon one man. Here, we admit its truth by exposing the legislature to executive patronage, in imitation of the English precedent; and assert its falsehood, by prohibiting accumulations of offices. And though the president remains isolated between our affirmative and negative, we have copied it in a mode excessively increasing its malignity, first by the ineligibility which loses the purchase the instant it is paid for; secondly, by the necessity for fresh means to corrupt or influence such talents, as may appear after the best are transplanted; and thirdly, by the removal of the highest virtue and the best talents from the department, upon which the liberty and prosperity of nations must for ever depend. Ingeniously providing both a constant drain for publick treasure, and a constant drain of talents and virtue from legislatures; and managing to extract from the evil principle of exposing them to the patronage of one man, the evil effects both of stupifying and demoralizing them, one of which has sufficed for the nation we have imitated.

Let us consider the following extract from a late English author. 'But the history of this reign,' that of Henry the 8th, 'yields other lessons than those of a speculative morality; lessons which come home to the breast of every Englishman, and which he ought to remember every moment of his existence. It teaches us the most alarming of all political truths. *That absolute despotism may prevail in a state, and yet the form of a free constitution remain.* Nay, it even leads us to a conjecture still more interesting to Britons, that in this country an ambitious prince may most successfully exercise his tyrannies *under the shelter of those barriers*, which the constitution has placed as the security of national freedom. Henry changed the national religion, and, in a great measure, the *spirit of the laws* of England. He perpetrated the most enormous violences against the first men in the kingdom; *he loaded the people with oppressive taxes, and he pillaged them by loans*, which it was known he never meant to pay; *but he never attempted to abolish the parliament, or even to retrench any of its doubtful privileges. The parliament was the prime minister of his tyrannical administration. It authorised his oppressive taxes, it gave its sanction to his most despotick and oppressive measures; to measures, which of himself he durst not have carried into execution; or which, if supposed to be merely the result of his own arbitrary will, would have roused the spirit of the nation to assert the rights of humanity, and the privileges of a free people.* Our admirable constitution is but a gay curtain to conceal our shame, and the iniquity of our oppressors, unless our senators are animated by the same spirit which gave it birth. If they can be overawed by threats, *seduced from their duty by bribes, or allured by promises*, another Henry may rule over us with a rod of iron, and drench once more the scaffold with the best blood of the nation. The parliament will be the humble and secure instrument of his tyrannies.'* Henry's influence made 'the parliament the prime minister of executive tyranny, and an instrument of the most despotick measures.'

Compare this influence of Henry's, with the present influence of the crown in England, and consider, which possesses in the highest degree, the properties of bribery, alluring by promises, perma-

* Modern Europe, v. 2, 294, 295.

nency, and capacity to convert a parliament 'into the humble and
secure instrument of executive tyranny.' Were Henry's parliaments more subservient to the crown in money matters, than those
subjected to the modern species of influence? Were his pecuniary
oppressions more intolerable, than those which modern parliaments sanction without difficulty? Or was his influence more
systematick and regular, than that of the crown for the last century? If not, the modern system by which executive power influences legislative bodies, is more dangerous than Henry's; and his
sufficed to make him a tyrant.

Executive patronage over legislative bodies, is the essential
quality of this modern system, and the only quality by which
'parliaments can be made the prime ministers of tyrannical ad-
ministrations.' By its means only, can 'absolute despotism be
introduced whilst the form of a free constitution remains.' This
alone is able to convert the only barrier against the usurpations of
executive power, into a shelter for its intrigues, a sanction for its
oppressions, a 'secure instrument' for its ambition, and a vehicle
for revolution to be effected 'by changing the spirit of laws.'

Had our constitution been formed exactly upon the English
model, that experiment would have been a map, upon which the
progress of a government, guided by the vicious principle of executive patronage over legislative power, could have been exactly
traced. Is a principle, too vicious and corrupt for limited monarchy,
sufficiently pure for a republican government? Will limited monarchy exist only in form, and be converted in fact by this principle
into a despotism; and will republican freedom exist in fact, exposed to the same legislative corruption, which has reduced
limitations on monarchy to form?

Why should we conceal from ourselves the plain truth? Representation is either the best security for a free government, or the
best instrument for the most oppressive. Influenced by one man, it
is an instrument; uninfluenced, a security. Need we reason upon
the question? Has not England a House of Commons, and France
a tribunate?

In England, executive patronage has left the entire form of the
constitution standing, and annihilated two thirds of its substance;
it is formed of orders, and two of the three are reduced to cyphers
or instruments. Here, though our constitution is not formed of
king, lords and commons, or of any classification of men, but of the
principles of division, responsibility, and national self government,

226

yet executive influence over judicial and legislative power, can also destroy its substance and leave its form standing, by converting the sentinels of the people into the instruments of ambition, and demolishing the efficacy of division by a corrupt unanimity.

It may fall upon the house of representatives to elect a president, and each candidate may promise, and if he is elected, bestow an office upon every elector. The same effects will follow, as if the parliament was to elect a king. Executive patronage, in the real and supposed case, constitutes the utmost temptation to be treacherous to a nation, exactly where the publick good requires the utmost integrity. It is impossible to contrive a better scheme than this for exciting the virulence of faction, by the goadings of ambition, avarice, self interest, and all the most violent passions; or to take a better chance for producing a civil war.

Since oracles were exploded, no mode has been discovered for deceiving and oppressing nations, equally treacherous and successful with that of corrupting their representatives. Confidence, inspired by religion in the first case, and by election in the second, is the mantle for fraud in both. The influence of one man over a nation, fraudulently or forcibly exercised, is the essential principle of monarchy; as a monopoly of wealth by an exclusive interest at the publick expense, is of aristocracy. In a former part of this essay, an attempt was made to prove, that a mixture of monarchical and aristocratical ingredients in democratical systems, caused those disorders, ascribed by Mr. Adams to inaccuracy in balancing them; and that however commixed, their natural enmity would continue to produce pernicious effects, as in all former experiments. If executive influence over legislative bodies, is a monarchical ingredient; and if a paper system is an aristocratical ingredient; all the horrours of a warfare among orders must ensue, either on Mr. Adams's principles or ours; because, according to him, it cannot be prevented, except by an accurate balance of orders; according to us, it cannot be prevented on account of their natural enmity to each other.

The prospect of victory is on the side of executive power. The code of its political tacticks, lies open in the example of England. That example may accelerate its success, by causing it to be expected. A president, by the legislative instrument, may provoke war, introduce funding and banking, raise armies, increase taxes, multiply offices, and commit the freedom of the press to the custody of penal laws, with as much certainty and system as a British king;

and add to his own power, by throwing the odium of his ambitious practices upon Congress; although, to borrow the words of the last quotation, 'he durst not of himself have carried such measures into execution; or which, if supposed to be merely the result of his own arbitrary will, would have roused the spirit of the nation to assert the rights of humanity, and the privileges of a free people.'

If a president should, by an army, be rendered insubordinate to the legislature, and able to terrify them into his measures, all would agree that neither free or republican government could possibly continue; yet its manifest atrociousness would be some check upon the deed. If a president is not enabled to terrify, but only to bribe or influence a legislature into his measures, what would be the difference? That between having one's wife ravished or seduced. Are not men safer against the first evil, and more frequently rendered miserable by the second?

These criticisms neither impeach the general structure of the government, nor impinge upon any local interest. No doctrine is advanced, not adhered to by state constitutions, and none condemned, to which the people have separately assented. Had they approved of bestowing monarchical powers upon an elective magistrate; of a judicial power insubordinate to the sovereignty, superior to the legislature, and subject to executive influence; or of admitting corruption into the legislature by some crooked path; an adherence to contrary principles would not have remained visible in these constitutions.

To bring the general and state governments under similar principles, would contribute to the security of the union. Hostile elements will ultimately go to war. Hence the experiments of orders in all forms have failed. Their adverse principles have never been able to subsist peaceably together for any considerable time. Influence and insubordination are the contraries of division and responsibility; and the same effects are produced by compounding a government of opposite and hostile orders of principles, as of hostile orders of men; because a contrariety in principles causes the hostility among orders.

This contrariety is the test to establish the sufficiency of our analysis for defining governments by moral principles, and enabling us to foresee effects. We have, for instance, considered division of power, responsibility and legislative purity (one side of a contrariety) as good, and as producing good effects; and monopoly, insubordination and corruption (the other side) as evil, and as producing evil effects; and deduced from these considerations the reasoning of this part of our essay. The mode of applying our definition to particular cases consists merely in stating plain questions. For an instance. Is the power of the president to influence the popular representatives, or the power of the government to neglect the militia, and use standing armies, good or evil, monarchical or republican, or congenial with the policy of the United States or of England, or of both? Is the policy of these countries the same?

Section the Fourth

FUNDING

In a former part of this essay, a promise was made to consider the effects of funding and banking, in relation to the principles and policy of the United States; that promise shall now be complied with.

No form of civil government can be more fraudulent, expensive and complicated, than one which distributes wealth and consequently power, by the act of the government itself. A few men wish to gratify their own avarice and ambition. They cannot effect this without accomplices, and they gain them by corrupting the legislature. Still the faction is too feeble to oppress a nation. Vice looks for defence, because it expects punishment. The legislature must corrupt a party in the nation, and this is effected by the modern invention called a paper system, with a degree of plausibility and dispatch, infinitely exceeding any ancient contrivance. Executive patronage corrupts individuals; legislative, factions; the first by office and salary; the second by law charter and separate interest. Fear and avarice combine to secure implicit obedience from these purchased engines of power, and an inexorable fulfilment of the corruptor's purpose. Accordingly, a paper system will cling to a government, as closely as an army to a general, or a hierarchy to a pope.

An executive power to bestow offices and contracts upon members of a legislature, resembles the idea of procuring talents, and rewarding merit; but a legislative power to buy a faction by loans and charters, cannot crouch behind this subterfuge; it literally displays, and openly practises the same species of corruption, which executive patronage endeavours to hide.

A paper system belongs to the species of patronage which we have called legislative. It is introduced upon various pretexts; but its true ends are simple. These are to enrich individuals, and at the national expense, to corrupt a faction, which will adhere to a

230

government against a nation. Such a system may subsist in union with election, but the principles of our policy cannot subsist in union with such a system.

Its practicability in union with election is ascertained in England, and by widening the distance between individuals in wealth, it has detached the mass of talents from the service of the publick, to the service of a faction; and changed election from a shield for liberty, into a keen and polished instrument for her destruction. This abuse is a refinement upon a late quotation emphatically proving, that the system of balancing or checking monarchy in England, is capable of producing more tyranny and oppression, than simple or pure monarchy would dare to attempt. A monarch, shielded by a corrupt parliament, may adventure upon measures, which he would otherwise shrink from. And a legislature, shielded by a paper faction, may adventure upon measures which they would otherwise shrink from. Election is made the instrument of legislative patronage, and a nation seems to be the author of its own ruin, whilst that ruin proceeds from the operation of a paper system, corrupting talents, enriching a faction, and impoverishing the mass of the nation; yet the people will be kept patient by election itself, from an erroneous opinion, that the government is administered according to their will. Against this species of tyranny there is no remedy, except that of preventing its cause, as the people have no mode of discovering the individuals corrupted by legislative patronage; other forms of tyranny are seen in the persons of kings, nobles and priests; executive sinecure and patronage, are visible; and a visible enemy may be subdued; but an invisible enemy cannot even be assailed.

The possibility of that species of tyranny, arising from an union between an elective legislature, and an interest different from the national interest, was contemplated by all our constitutions; and the whole fund of foresight then existing brought to bear against it. For this precise end, innumerable precautions were used, to subject law-makers to the national will; to prevent them from getting wealth from the nation by their own laws; and to expose them equally with other citizens, to oppressive laws. But all these precautions are destroyed by the legal inventions of funding, banking and charter, more effectually than the liberty of the press was destroyed by a sedition law. The reader will not require a catalogue of cases, to prove how deeply laws can wound constitutions, after this reference has awakened his recollection.

Admitting that the power of creating debt, must necessarily reside in a government, yet, next to the power of raising armies, it is the most dangerous with which it can be invested. Mankind may be governed by money or arms. Both these powers admit of checks, and required them, as being more dangerous than any others. An armed nation would have been a check upon the one; and an effectual exclusion from the legislature, of any participation in the profits of debt, created by funding or banking, would have been a check upon the other.

But a borrowing power itself is rendered questionable, by considering its origin and effects. We possess a correct history of two paper systems only; those of England and America. The first was produced by the personal hatred of William of Orange for Lewis the 14th, the rapacity of Marlborough and Eugene, and the need of a disputed title to a crown, for partisans. The second also followed a revolution, without having contributed towards it; compensated publick services by the tax of appreciation, after they had paid that of depreciation; and transferred much of the reward for which an army bled in defence of their country, to those who had shed that blood. To gratify a king's hatred, enrich rapacious generals, and transfer a crown from one family to another, were ends of the English funding system, not much more just or useful, than those experienced here. This system or policy, therefore, has very little to boast of for its exploits in these two eminent cases.

But there is a theory in favour of funding systems, artfully suggested to cover their practical evils. Nations are persuaded that they can anticipate the riches of posterity and bequeath it their misfortunes; seduced by this glittering temptation, they have forborne to look through its gilding, in order to discover what it conceals.

Could one generation thus have plundered wealth and leisure from another, each would have preferred certain victories costing neither blood nor money, to murderous, precarious, and expensive wars; and though the wisdom and justice of the Deity might have been rendered questionable, by the subjection of unborn innocence to the tyranny of existing vice, yet the crime would have been perpetrated in security, and the magnitude of the acquisition would have varnished over its flagitiousness, in the eyes of the perpetrators.

The propensity of nations to molest their contemporaries for the sake of wealth, is recorded in innumerable examples; and as the same passion would with additional strength have incited them to invade the rights of the unborn, an existing generation would have wanted motives for self-molestation, if these motives could have been appeased by calling forward into their own pockets the inexhaustible wealth of time to come. It is therefore probable that such an operation is physically impossible, because the treasures of anticipation have not suspended for a moment the disposition of existing nations to plunder and oppress each other, or of existing governments to plunder and oppress the people.

But an opinion that it is possible, for the present generation to seize and use the property of future generations, has produced to both the parties concerned, effects of the same complexion with the usual fruits of national errour. The present age is cajoled to tax and enslave itself, by the errour of believing that it taxes and enslaves future ages to enrich itself; and future ages submit to taxation and slavery, by being seduced into an erroneous opinion, that the present age have a right to inflict upon them these calamities.

It is to such national errours, that mankind have been indebted for most of their miseries, and for having fallen a prey to avarice and ambition in all ages of the world. Idolatry was concealed behind an erroneous veneration for those who fed upon its victims. Monarchy and aristocracy are skilfully fenced round by the insidious and erroneous arguments of the mass of talents, interested in their cause. Crusades, in the opinion of several generations, led the way to Heaven, whilst the monks used them to acquire wealth. And the errour of an opinion, that one age can seize upon the wealth of another by anticipation, is no less ruinous to nations, and enriching to individuals and orders or separate interests, than the errours which have supported idolatry, monarchy, aristocracy and crusades.

It is however the most recent, the most plausible, the most seducing, and the most dangerous invention, to which self interest and cunning has ever resorted, for moulding man into coin; and will probably keep its ground, until such calamities as have exploded other errours, shall disclose to an existing generation that it was born free. A truth, which they will then clearly discern to have been revealed to man, in withholding from the dead a power to govern the living, and from the living, a power to govern the dead. It will then be seen, that moral rectitude does not impose upon a living nation the duty of submitting to tyranny and oppression, because a nation, which is dead, chose to gratify the hatred of one king against another, or the rapacity of generals; or to corrupt a party to support or produce a revolution in the government. Evils, controlled by such an opinion, and encouraged by one, that posterity ought to suffer their effects, rather than the generation which caused them.

It would be superfluous to prove that unborn generations are injured by anticipation; it is taxation, by persons, not elected by the payers, nor participating in the tax, but enriched by it. If the laws of nature are so partial and unjust, as to allow one generation to rob another with impunity, the crime will be perpetrated. It will only be prevented by a conviction that punishment follows vice, in this as in other cases; and that the malice of the attempt regularly receives its due vengeance, without a possibility of obtaining a benefit; or by the same disregard of the living to the mandates of the dead, as to the happiness and liberty of the unborn.

Let us consider how anticipation bestows wealth. It does not conjure into real existence, the commercial, agricultural or manufactural products of futurity. It does not add to the corn or to the coin. It only conjures the wealth of existing people out of some hands into others; and the credit with which to buy property of the living given by the certificate, constitutes all the solid wealth gained by anticipation. It is a pretext for taxation, and a mode of changing property among individuals, but produces nothing for nations.

War is among the most plausible means used to delude a nation into the errour of anticipation. Yet it cannot bring up from futurity a gun, a soldier, a ration, or a cartridge. The present generation suffers every hardship and cost of war, although anticipation pretends that it is suffered by future generations. And this delusion is used to involve nations in wars, which they would never commence, if they knew that all the expense would fall upon themselves. It is twice suffered; by the living, who supply all the expenses of war; and by the unborn, who supply an equivalent sum, to take up certificates of the expenses paid by the living.

No item of the expense of war is more transferable from the living to the unborn, than the blood it sheds. Money buys this blood and every other expense of war; but it is neither blood nor bread, and only a collector of them. These realities, not the signs or tokens, supply the war; and after they are expended, their shadows are made by anticipation, to consume the same amount of realities which the war devoured, even that of human life, if death by oppression is equivalent to death by the sword. Thus one war is converted into two, and every period of natural, begets an equal period of artificial war. The same ingenious contrivance, by the help of compound anticipation, converts about fourteen years of war, into a perpetual war. If a million annually comprises or represents the utmost efforts in realities, which a nation can make in war; and the realities represented are expended annually, leaving behind them annually the million of stock or certificates at compound interest, produced by the anticipating mode of calling these realities into use; then a war of about fourteen years continuance, places the nation in a state equivalent to perpetual war; because the stock or certificates will devour in peace, precisely the same amount of the realities represented by money, which the war did. Nor can this nation be ever relieved from a state equivalent to perpetual war, whilst the stock preserves its value, and the national resources are the same. If there are fourteen intervals between the fourteen years of war, the same result will ultimately occur; whence it has happened, that peace has been seldom able to repair the errour in a mode of making war, so calamitous as to double the duration of short ones, and to produce a perpetuity of its evils in the space of fourteen years. A maniac, whose income in kind is just sufficient to support him, takes it into his head to give his bonds to sundry people annually for its value, whilst he is consuming it. At the end of fourteen years his whole income is gone, though he has only expended its annual amount. Such is anticipation to nations. But those who use it to deceive, plunder and enslave them, artfully liken it to the cases of a man who buys an estate on credit, or who gives bonds to himself. One would think that the impossibility of finding any such estate thus obtained by nations; and the possibility of finding the taxes, the poverty, the splendour, and the political innovations it produces, would detect the falsehood of these pretended resemblances; and sufficiently convince nations that they are not one homogeneous mass of matter, but capable of a thorough divisibility into individuals, and into a multitude of separate interests (such as payers and receivers, masters and slaves, impostors and dupes) to disclose to them the folly of transforming themselves into the resemblance of the maniac.

But the fact is, that nations are seldom allowed to look at their interest except as it is reflected by living political mirrors, such as kings, ministers, demagogues or stockjobbers, so contrived as to make deformity exhibit beauty, and poverty wealth, to the infatuated people, for the sake of advancing their own views and projects. Had the representations of these false mirrors been true, all nations would have enjoyed the highest prosperity. The United States are tempted to plunge into anticipation by the funds of back lands and growing population; the first pronounced by twenty years experience, to be insufficient for the sustenance of a single Baring;* and the second unable to protect the existing generation for a single year, against the drafts from their liberty and property which the system inevitably produces. If we are thus seduced into the snare, in which the ambitious and mercenary of the present age involve their prey, our population and lands, are destined to feed the two most insatiable and worst passions which afflict mankind, and our vacant territory will only be a fund for enslaving our children.

Anticipation is at best a mode of putting the energies of present time in motion, without any powers of calling up a single energy of future time. Other modes have operated more powerfully, without being considered as blessings to the age which felt them. Those by which Xerxes, Alexander, Cæsar, Peter the hermit, Tamerlane, Cromwell and Bonaparte were enabled to lead millions to victory or defeat, were more successful in arousing the military energies of the present time, than the anticipating mode.

Nothing exposed the American and French revolutions to greater danger, than the attempts to use this delusion. Anticipation was tried, it taxed the existing generations by depreciation, it superseded the cultivation of other modes of putting existing energies in motion, it failed, the failure almost obliterated the memory and suspended the use, of the real means of war, and a dangerous crisis in both cases was produced. The errour in these instances was surmounted by the good sense which necessity so often teaches.

Political and religious opinion, and a love of country, are stronger excitements of existing warlike energies, than anticipation. They cannot be stolen or hoarded; but war carried on by paper, is starved by peculation, and produces the utmost degree of publick expense, with the least degree of publick spirit. An excitement of the militia of the United States by arms, training, equipments and eulogy, would probably have created a stronger military force, at an inferior expense, than all the efforts of anticipation have been able to produce. Can the most expensive, the least suc-

* A rich English stockjobber.

cessful, and the most corrupt mode of exciting the energies of war, be the best?

If anticipation cannot create, but only excite, it follows, that there is a deception in the idea, that it can postpone the expense of war to a future time. The expense of war really consists of men, food, raiment, arms and ammunition, and not in a juggle of signs; anticipation therefore is a phantom, incapable of alleviating the miseries of war, whilst it is a harpy, able to devour the blessings of peace.

The Romans carried on long and expensive wars without the aid of anticipation, and it failed before the end of our short and cheap revolutionary war. Yet the whole of the paper money was paid, or sunk by depreciation whilst the war was going on; a mode of taxation so excessively unequal, as to ascertain, both the ability and necessity of every existing nation to bear the expense of its own war; for if war could be maintained by a tax excessively unequal, it follows, that the energies of war, are within the reach of an equal tax.

After this unequal tax was paid by the United States, and the war had been finished successfully by patriotism and bravery, anticipation, which had fled disgracefully from the contest, returned to reap the best fruits of the victory; and though a traitor, found means to supplant and plunder the heroes who had won it. This success was more wonderful, from the reason which caused it, than in itself. That a few people should be willing to enrich themselves at the expense of a multitude, is far less wonderful, than that they should succeed by persuading this multitude, that anticipation, which had recently deserted them, was a better defender of nations, than patriotism and bravery, which had recently saved them.

National defence, was never the true cause of any funding system; and no funding system ever defended a nation. It was invented in England to prop a revolution by corruption; extensively used to sacrifice the nation to German interests; and it has been continued to feed avarice, and silently to revolutionize the revolution. It was introduced into America, after the nation had been defended, to enrich a few individuals, and also to revolutionize the revolution.

In England, the advancement of the Hanoverian family to the throne, was disagreeable to the landed interest, of which the tory party at that time chiefly consisted. This compelled George the first to use the whig party. And Sir Robert Walpole, who belonged to it, pushed a paper system to enrich his partisans, and to balance the superior wealth of their political opponents. The artifice completely succeeded; the rich tories were impoverished; a vast change of wealth took place;* an irresistible whig party was formed, and gradually transformed by the same paper system into tories. As a whig party it placed a family on the throne, and then converted itself to toryism with zeal and rapidity, by fraudulent laws to enrich itself.

In America also, a paper system followed the revolution produced by the present form of our general government, and operated upon the landed whigs here, exactly as it had done on the landed tories in England. It taxes them, enriches a credit or paper faction; changes property; forms a party; and transforms its principles as in England. But the American whigs are blind to the ruin which the English tories saw.

Henry the 7th broke the power of the barons to strengthen the monarchy; Sir Robert Walpole destroyed the power of the landed interest, and compelled it to contribute to the formation of a monied interest, to establish a disputed title to the throne. The capacity of the latter invention has probably exceeded what was foreseen. It is found able to seize and to hold the reins of government. It is found able to erect a stupendous fabrick of factitious wealth, and to compel land and labour or real wealth, to become its humble and obedient subject.

The importance of these truths is not diminished, because the monied interest in England happened to start as whigs, and the landed as tories. They shew that a paper system was not introduced for national defence, and that it can transfer property, transform parties, and change the nature of governments. Avarice, and a conviction of its power as a political engine, suggested its introduction; and events have proved that this conviction was correct. It is an engine which is able to usurp and hold a government; therefore it will contend for dominion. As it will contend, it must experience defeat or victory. It is also an engine having no resemblance in interest to land, labour or talents; therefore it cannot be a friend to either.

It was necessary to premise a short history of these two paper

* There is only one title in England which goes with the lands; that of Arundel. Did Henry the 7th or Walpole's paper system, operate most effectually towards this circumstance?

systems, to introduce the following argument, as to the reality or delusion of an idea usually annexed to anticipation. If it did not powerfully and instantaneously enrich and impoverish existing people, how could Walpole so suddenly and effectually have debased a landed, and exalted a monied faction, by its means? The capacity of anticipation to act suddenly upon an existing age, manifests both the delusion of considering it as an engine for drawing up wealth from futurity, and also, that as an engine for producing an oppressive government, it is no delusion. All paper systems, are in fact, indirect laws of confiscation, used for the purposes which induced the French revolutionists to transfer more directly, a great mass of landed property from their antagonists to themselves. These purposes simply were to enrich themselves and establish their power. It was to enrich, and establish the power of the whigs, at the expense of the tories, that Walpole used a paper system. In America, a paper confiscation system, conferred wealth and power on a monarchical party at the expense of the whigs. In both countries, those who furnished the riches, lost much of their power and property; and those who received them, gained it. The French confiscations went boldly to their object, like a direct tax. The English and American confiscations, secretly and circuitously effected their design, by the complication of a paper system; like an indirect tax. One seized and transferred the land itself. The others, mortgaged it; artfully leaving to the owner an appearance of property, whilst he is only a receiver of the profits for the benefit of the mortgagee. Is one mode of confiscation reprobated, because it is an open robber, which quickly ends the pain of its victim; and the other suffered, because it lies hidden under deceit and complexity, and inflicts slow and lasting tortures? Or is one reprobated like a small criminal who robs an individual; and the other flattered, like a great one who plunders a nation? Can violations of private property be rendered just or unjust by their modes? Between the modes we have been comparing, there is one difference. Direct confiscation is always pretended to be a punishment of guilt; indirect, by paper systems, is only used to punish innocence. And yet these indirect confiscations talk finely about forfeitures, and private property; they pretend to protect that which their only effect is to transfer; they pretend to reprobate that which is their own quality; just as a tyrant, in the midst of spoil and carnage, will boast of his justice and clemency.

The appearance of anticipating the resources of future ages, is artfully extracted from the simple idea of borrowing upon interest, to raise up for paper systems a sufficient degree of popularity to support the craft. If the interest, which is the price paid for a loan, is adequate to the value of its use, that use is sold and bought, and not loaned. And such must be the case, as the interest or price is taken or refused at the option of the lender. A nominal borrower is therefore a real purchaser of this use at value, which value he must pay as long as he holds the purchase; nor does he by the purchase of money for interest, differ from a tenant who purchases land for rent, in point of being able to anticipate the wealth of futurity. A new tenant or a new generation may succeed the old, and each may continue to pay the same rent for the land or money, but their predecessors paid it also, without getting any thing out of time to come. This observation applies with still more particular accuracy to funding systems, in that branch of their policy, never to redeem the principal, but to receive a perpetual rent for it.

An individual who borrows money, like one who rents land, does not bring forward for his own use, the least portion of the wealth of time to come. Could he do this, borrowing would make an existing individual wealthier; but as it generally makes him poorer, it seems evident, that he pays himself the value of the use of the money he borrows. If A, having land worth ten thousand pounds, borrows that sum of B, A does not become worth twenty thousand pounds at the expense of his posterity. He has only sold his land to B, and turned his fortune into money; but B indulges A with cultivating the land, and paying its rent under the name of interest. So if a nation, whose lands are worth one hundred millions, borrows and funds that sum, it has only sold or mortgaged its lands to stockholders up to their value, who receive the rent in the name also of interest or dividends. It has not added to its wealth, or drawn any thing from futurity, but only turned its land into money. And between the nation and a private debtor is this difference; that an individual who sells his estate, receives and uses the purchase money; but a nation which turns its estate or any portion of it into money by borrowing, loses both the money and estate.

But the evil is not terminated with this loss. If an age is supposed to consist of twenty years, and it borrows at five per centum, it loses the principal, first by its perversion from publick use to the gratification of private avarice or ambition: secondly, by its entire repayment during the borrowing age; and moreover all individuals who exist above twenty years, pay their proportion of the principal borrowed for each cycle of additional existence. Many will pay three hundred per centum for anticipation in this way only, but few will receive any thing from it, and all subject their descendants for ever to a repayment of the whole principal for every revolution of the stockjobbing orb, without a possibility of their deriving any benefit from it. To these requitals of an existing generation, for attempting the impossibility of enriching itself at the expense of its posterity, a long catalogue of the same complexion might be added; such as the number and expense of new offices, produced by borrowing, not only to expend the principal, but to collect and pay the interest; and the oppression inevitably resulting from dividing a nation into inimical interests. These arguments are bottomed upon the concession of a similitude between renting land and borrowing money, whereas the true similitude from which we ought to draw our conclusions in regard to funding systems, would be one between paying rent for the picture of land, and interest for the picture of money.

If the borrowing age, far from enriching itself, is a sufferer; a system, by which each succeeding age, undergoes the same or greater evils, must be vitally malignant to human happiness.

We have been unable to deduce any paper system, from the origin of honest intention or national defence; but as such an origin, would not alter its effects upon human happiness or liberty, or upon the civil policy of the United States, it is fair to conclude, that as the effects of funding or anticipation will be evil, though the motives which gave rise to it should be honest, so the system is incurably erroneous, even under its most upright application.

Of our civil policy, division and responsibility, are the chief pillars. An accumulation of wealth by law, is the counter principle to that of division. And out of this accumulation will grow an influence over the legislature, which will secretly deprive the people of their influence over it.

This principle of division has been applied to the laws of inheritance in every state in the union; to divide land and accumulate stock, exhibits a political phenomenon, worthy of an attentive consideration; because its consequences must be new and curious. If an accumulation of landed wealth, by the narrow and limited efforts of talents and industry, is an object of jealousy to our policy; an accumulation of paper wealth by the extensive power of law, cannot be an object of its approbation. Land is in some degree a representative of every man's interest, as being the source of human subsistence, and a landed interest cannot tax without taxing itself. Out of paper stock nothing grows. It only represents the interest of its holder, and it can tax, without taxing itself. It must do this, because it can only subsist upon the subsistence it can draw from land and labour; and as an imposer of taxes it is strictly analogous to a legislature of officers receiving legal salaries. If a landed interest, though naturally friendly to man, may be corrupted by moulding it into a separate order; and rendered malignant and oppressive in a considerable degree; it is extremely improbable, that a paper, stock, or taxation interest, can be changed from a foe into a friend, by the means which convert a friend into a foe. The English have paid some regard to their principles of checks and balances, by leaving primogeniture, or an hereditary landed political order or faction, standing, as an offset against their monied faction; the American legislatures have paid no regard to their principles of division and responsibility, and more entirely partial to a monied faction, of their own architecture, have destroyed this offset, alone capable of holding a monied faction in some state of responsibility; and secured agricultural subjection to their off-spring, by charters for accumulating one, and laws for dividing the other.

It is a plausible consideration against this conclusion, that the laws of distribution reach and scatter paper wealth, as laws of inheritance do landed. The following fact, settled by experience, is a conclusive answer to the objection. The English laws of distribution, by which paper wealth is divided upon principles similar to our laws of distribution, have been unable to prevent the existence of a separate, stock, paper, or taxation interest, or the ruinous effects of that existence.

Such is the fact; let us search for its cause. It presents itself in the consideration, that corporations, or factitious separate interests, neither live nor die naturally; they only live or die by law. An established church for instance, is a factitious separate interest, not of natural, but of legal origin, and by law only can its existence be terminated. By increasing the number of priests, and dividing the income of this separate interest among more members, the interest itself is not divided; and instead of being weakened, it is strengthened. So in a separate, stock, paper or taxation interest of any kind established by law. It is an interest one and indivisible; and though the laws of distribution may occasionally add to the numbers benefited by it, these additions are recruits similar to new levies added to an army, or new priests added to an established church. In all three of these cases, an interest, created by law, and subsisting upon a nation, becomes stronger, by multiplying the individuals united to it with a participation in its income; and weaker, by diminishing the number of these individuals. Such interests are incapable, as will presently be proved, of including the majority of a nation, or of a general division among its members; the cement of fear, excited by a perpetual danger of the stroke of death, from their creator, law; and a consciousness of physical imbecility, distinguish them from the object of their apprehensions.

None of these causes will prevent a landed interest from being weakened by a division of lands. Land is not created by law; therefore it is under no apprehension of its death stroke from law. It does not subsist upon other interests; therefore it is not beset by an host of enemies, whose vengeance it is conscious of deserving. By the operation of laws adverse to its monopoly, it quickly adjusts itself to the interest of a majority of a nation; thenceforward it is incapable of the avarice and injustice of a factitious legal interest, because no temptation to seduce it into either, exists. To this point of improvement, a landed interest will invariably be brought, by laws for dividing lands; nor can it be corrupted, except by laws which confine lands to a minority. Then it becomes in a degree a factitious legal monopoly, capable of being favoured by law, and infected with a portion of that malignity, which constitutes the entire essence of a minor separate interest purely factitious.

A paper, a military, or an established church interest, cannot, it has been asserted, include a majority of a nation, as may a landed; because a majority cannot live upon a minority, but a majority may live upon land. Let us take a paper interest of any kind to illustrate this assertion. It is simply debt, in all its forms. If I give a bond to myself, it does not add to my wealth, or create a new interest. If a nation should create any portion of debt, and sustain it in a state of equal distribution among all its members, no separate interest would thence arise. Creditor and debtor are characters essential to the existence of a paper property or interest; if these characters are united, the quality of value flees from paper. Imagine a nation consisting of one million, having paper stock of one million, each person holding one share, and equally taxed to redeem this stock. The principle of division obviously annihilates in this stock, the quality of value or property. But give ten shares

243

each, to one hundred thousand of the same nation, and these qualities are instantly annexed to the stock. But land neither loses its value by division, nor is that value enhanced by accumulation. It is therefore capable of escaping the infection of monopoly, whilst a paper interest cannot exist without it; of this interest, monopoly being the vital principle, the laws of distribution cannot destroy it, without putting an end to the system itself.

The gradual progress of the laws of distribution, must aggravate the evil of a paper monopoly, until the very moment at which they might be made to produce its destruction. As a paper interest draws its subsistence from the residue of a nation, an increase of the number to be subsisted, will add to the burden of furnishing this subsistence; just as an increase of soldiers or priests, will add to the burdens of the nation which maintains them. So long as the increase of an army or priesthood is attended with national ability to maintain them, the effect of bringing more soldiers or more priests to share in a religious or military monopoly, is an aggravation of national oppression; but the very instant a distribution of a religious or military monopoly is extended to a majority of the nation, by making them soldiers or priests (as in the case of a national militia) the ability in the residue to maintain it would cease, and with it, the oppression would cease also. In like manner, the laws of distribution are only capable of affecting a paper interest in two modes. By aggravating its mischief, or producing its destruction. And they must of necessity operate in the first way, until they terminate in the second. Their first effect is certain, and must continue for a long space, to produce a chance for the second; and it is after all highly improbable, that the second will ever happen.

The laws of distribution therefore aggravate the evils of a paper monopoly, whereas those for dividing lands diminish the evils of a landed monopoly. The fact in England and the United States, exactly corresponds with these arguments. The distribution of a paper interest to greater numbers, has strengthened the paper monopoly in both countries. A landed monopoly in England, though supported by the law of primogeniture and a legislative order, is hardly felt as a political principle. There, the mere right of alienation has produced a division of lands, sufficient to destroy a landed aristocracy, and enfeeble a landed interest; and laws for dividing or distributing paper stock, have created and strengthened a paper aristocracy. The latter have the same effect as laws for multiplying offices, in order to cure the ill effects of patronage; or for increasing a nobility or clergy for the purpose of abolishing an order.

Having proved that laws of division or distribution, will counteract landed and aid paper combinations for usurping a government; we will proceed to subjoin a few of the effects which will result from the destruction of a landed, and the creation of a paper monopoly.

As landed possessions are divided, the leisure and income of the proprietors will be diminished; and as paper property is accumulated, the leisure and income of the holders will be increased. The weight of talents will follow leisure and wealth; and these will gradually acquire a locality, corresponding to the abodes of the receivers of stock taxation. This superiority of talents and wealth will invest individuals, and the cities in which they will chiefly reside, with an influence, well calculated to acquire an ascendant over the landed interest, gradually impoverished by division. And though this landed interest may not suddenly sink into an ignorant, scattered, disunited peasantry, taxed by paper operations, to enrich, instruct and elevate a new species of feudal capitalists, yet the tendency of the system is exactly to that point, and the arrival of an unobstructed tendency, is inevitable.

If the division of landed property has a tendency to increase the ignorance of the numerous and valuable portion of society which cultivate it, a defect of the American policy in not providing some remedy to meet this evil, is disclosed. From preventing an accumulation of landed wealth, and providing for a monied or stock monopoly of knowledge, a reason arises for placing the best educations within the reach of that great mass of people, called the landed interest; instead of which its inability to purchase knowledge is studiously increased, by a division of inheritances, and by the annual draughts upon it for the interest and dividends of debt and bank stock. The ignorance of land holders will thus in time be brought to a standard exactly sufficient to render them tame, and subservient to the interest of a stock aristocracy; an event which may even be accelerated, by taxing them for the purpose of diffusing a knowledge of the vulgar tongue, and vulgar arithmetick. These laws for dividing landed property, and levelling landed knowledge, form a striking contrast with those for accumulating stock wealth, and of course stock knowledge. Are both consistent with the principles of our governments? If I wished to level a field, merely preserving that degree of inequality, necessary to prevent the effects of stagnation, ought I to rear a mountain in the midst of it? Is an accumulation of wealth and knowledge by law in a few hands, to be found in any recipe for making a free republick?

The errour of landed wealth, in favouring a paper aristocracy, because it is friendly to a landed one, rises into view at this moment. It does not perceive that even in England, a landed aristocracy has been vanquished and is governed by a paper or stock aristocracy. It does not perceive that a landed aristocracy cannot exist, under our laws, the extent of our country, and the multitude of proprietors; majority is not a quality of aristocracy. And it will not perceive that the landed interest is under our circumstances, irretrievably republican. Being so, the preservation of principles adopted to its nature, or a sale or mortgage of itself for the maintenance of a stock aristocracy, is evidently its solitary alternative. Our landed interest is incapable of forming the aristocracy required by Mr. Adams's system of limited monarchy. In England, the aristocratical power which now props the throne, is compounded of arms, paper and patronage; not of the landed interest. Will a paper system, which has destroyed the power of a landed interest in England, revive it here? Has a landed aristocracy existed, or can it exist, in community with alienations, commerce, the division of inheritances, and the absence of perpetuities?

Perhaps an imaginary apprehension may have suggested the idea, that the mode by which Walpole fixed a tottering throne, was necessary for the establishment of our union. But such an idea is a traitor to that union. Principles can never be established by their contraries. Monarchy may corrupt a faction to support itself, consistently with its principles; but national will cannot corrupt a faction to guide national will, without perishing at the instant of success. Had the proposal been made, it would have been reprobated by every individual friendly to the union. Is the attempt less to be reprobated, than the proposal?

The English have been made to pay hundreds of millions for the Hanover family; but why should the Americans buy the union at the same price, of any party, whether whig or tory? No one has a claim to it, as Stuart had to the throne of England, therefore we can keep it as our own undisputed right. It may be retained by virtue, moderate government, and easy taxes; but it dies under the influence of paper stock. And out of this dissolution the resurrection of Mr. Adams's theory of three orders cannot arise. There can be but two under the system of paper, namely, creditor and debtor, patricians and plebeians, or masters and slaves. We agree with Mr. Adams that two orders will render a nation miserable, though we have denied that three, or even a number equal to the castes of India, will restore it to happiness.

The orders of creditor and debtor, make the system of Spartans and Helots. One will live in idleness upon the labour of the other. But the luxury of the present age, and the effeminacy of modern Spartans, doubly aggravate the malignity of the theory in our imitation. Infinitely more income is required for the paper Spartans, and labour from the free Helots, without the retribution of national defence. But if our modern Spartans are not heroes, they have disclosed an inimitable portion of dexterity, in prevailing upon the order of Helots to buy heroes to knock their fetters on and not off; and to defend, not the nation, but the income of the Spartan order.

It is believed by the intelligent writer of the life of General Washington, that the United States were divided into two parties and brought to the brink of ruin, soon after the peace with England, by the struggles of creditors and debtors. If he is right, he cannot be just or wise to create by legal artifice the two characters to an extent, beyond that which then threatened them with ruin. Paper stock forces every individual into one of these parties, without leaving in the nation a single disinterested umpire, to assuage the passions inspired by a belief, that we have a right to receive what the law gives, and a right to withhold what it unjustly transfers. These will not be the parties of private contract, restrained by the voice of conscience, and moderated by the decrees of impartiality; but of fluctuating interested faction, legislating to get or to keep wealth, and looking only into its own law for justice and judgement.

Paper stock, patronage, and sinecure, profess an affection for commerce, because she is a convenient cord or tackle, to draw out of land and labour, the money which bestows on them wealth and power. For this purpose has English commerce been used, by paper stock, patronage and sinecure, and the maritime force necessary to sustain, is an evidence of their latent hostility towards it.

Dazzled by the splendour of English commerce; shall we forget that we cannot conquer and keep both the Indies, nor compel the world to obey a navigation act for laying it under contribution, by the prowess of stock? Force, conquest, and colonization, furnish the food to English commerce, which it disgorges to be again swallowed by paper stock. Should our commerce mistake this devourer for nourishment, unpossessed of the power of forcing its liver to grow as it is eaten, it will soon cease to excite the jealousy of English commerce. The prosperity which has awakened that jealousy, was produced by its freedom; and the vigorous health hence derived, will speedily be exchanged for the hypochondriacal, and convulsive fluctuations of law, war, and stockjobbing, if it is placed under the patronage of paper stock.

Charter, monopoly and aristocracy in their several forms (those of funding and banking excepted) have been considered by commerce as her foes. She will not even own for her friends, monopolies bestowed on merchants; and although, under the delusion of containing within herself qualities for constituting separate orders or interests, she has sometimes obtained them, yet she has universally upon trial found them unnatural to her constitution.

Adverse to this idea is the paradoxical opinion, that commerce may be made to flourish, by a paper capital, local, fictitious, and oppressive to land and labour. An opinion, contradicted by the commerce of Carthage, under a defective navigation; and by the inability of English commerce to meet its rivals with the advantages of the greatest stock capital in the world, a superiority of manufactures, geographical advantages, and an irresistible navy. She doffs the habiliments of a peaceable trader, cases herself in armour, and kills or maims her relations, to support that life and rivalry with foreign nations, to which her stock regimen renders her unequal.

If these reasons are insufficient to prove, that paper stock is inimical to commerce, the next question is, whether it is able to bestow upon her benefits, which will counterpoise the advantages she derives from a free government? Upon this question she will still find her interest united to her old friends, land and labour. If paper stock will destroy the sound principles of governments, by corrupting their administrators, will it compensate land, labour and commerce, for enslaving all three? Agriculture, manufactures and commerce, are indigenous, as it were, to human comfort and happiness; paper stock is a foreign invader, whose object is to subdue these close friends and natural allies, by instilling an opinion, that one of them will be benefited by deserting to the common enemy.

An association of casualties, frequently begets very whimsical associations of ideas. The rare casualty of despotism and national prosperity, existing together, has begotten an opinion, that despotism would make a nation prosper. And the commerce of England, made up of a complication of circumstances, has begotten an opinion, that the system of paper stock was favourable to commerce. That the opinion flows from this source, is undeniable, and that it is a source producing only a medley of errour, is equally so. It would be as correct, to pick out of this complication, any other circumstance, and to ascribe to it the state of the British commerce, as to paper stock; and many might pretend to such a distinction with far greater plausibility.

Commerce, monarchy, paper stock, legislative corruption, privileged orders, charters of exclusive commerce, and hierarchy, exist together in England. Is there an affinity also between paper stock and monarchy, legislative corruption, privileged orders, exclusive charters for commerce, and hierarchy, because all exist with it; · the reason supposed to prove the affinity between this stock and commerce; or is the simultaneous reason sound in one case and unsound in all the others? Or if the combination of paper stock with commerce, monarchy, legislative corruption, exclusive charters and hierarchy, proves its affinity to all, would it be best to take all for the sake of commerce, or to eject all for the sake of liberty?

The dilemma is avoided, by exploding the errour of considering paper stock as favourable to commerce, because they exist together in England. That one is the bane of the other, we have already inferred from the necessity of England to resort to war and conquest to cultivate her commerce. That one could acquire opulence without the other, is proved in the experience of Carthage. And the early dismay with which England beheld a commercial competition with America before her introduction of paper stock, is a modern concurrence with ancient experience.

The commerce of the United States commenced its operations unconnected with paper money, and advanced for many years without acknowledging its aid; it was obliged to travel from one hemisphere to another, before it could enter into competition with its rivals; it was unprotected by fleets; it traded on the funds of four millions only of people, cultivating a soil, poor in comparison with many countries to be rivalled; and it possessed no foreign dominions to fleece. Yet it suddenly aroused the jealousy of the most extensive commerce in the world, by outstripping all others. These effects appeared either before it was possible for it to owe any obligations to paper money, or whilst such obligations must have been inconsiderable. But our commerce was free. Will it not act precipitately in deserting a career so happily commenced under the auspices of freedom, to enlist under those of paper stock, from an opinion that its rival derived opulence from that source? It may by the experiment enslave itself without enslaving India; it may oppress its land and labour associates by a fleet, without acquiring the empire of the sea; it may guide crowds of people by monopoly, into a willingness to exchange a moderate climate and fertile soil, for torrid and frigid zones; and to snap all the ties of the human heart, in an eagerness to flee from the direct and indirect taxation of paper stock; without possessing a Botany Bay to hide the crimes, which oppression will beget; and having at length lost its original vital principle, it may in its last agonies deplore the . infatuation, which dazzled it with the unattainable and transitory expedients of English force and monopoly.

Paper money is precisely as unable to draw up out of futurity, the commodities of commerce, as the energies of war. The stock in trade of an individual may consist of signs or representatives, but the stock of commerce consists of the things themselves; namely the products of the earth, and manufactures. Specie cannot draw forward any of these things from the next century into the present; it can only draw them from one country into another; even this cannot be effected by local paper money; its office is to transfer real wealth from man to man, not by commerce, but by a juggle in legal and local signs of property. This is effected by monopolies for uttering, and regulating the quantity of paper money. It has been a general opinion that monopoly was a principle, unfavourable to commercial prosperity. Commerce struggled to destroy perpetuities, and monopoly to prevent alienations. In the distribution of wealth, commerce is active, unwearied and useful; devoted to its monopoly, she becomes speculative, voluptuous and pernicious; under the latter employment she sickens; unnatural as it is to her, it is the essential quality of paper systems. Whilst the office of one is to distribute and of the other to monopolize, a natural enmity is strongly to be apprehended.

That paper stock will have the effect of accumulating wealth in the hands of individuals, is admitted by its friends and foes, and confirmed by experience. This effect is the exact reason felt in its defence. It can only be produced by thievishly taking from some to enrich others; or by miraculously drawing up out of futurity the commodities of commerce, as it pretends to do the energies of war; or by propelling and exciting human industry: it remains to consider, whether, in this last character, it acts as a goad or a reward; and whether any more effectual, permanent, and upright mode of excitement is practicable.

Several ideas occurring here, will be postponed until the subject of banking is considered. At present, however, it is necessary to remark, that stock, created for war or commerce, will equally excite either as a goad or a reward, and that if it acts as a goad, it behoves us to consider whether industry, like bravery, may not be excited in some better mode.

Any species of paper stock, which is a debt upon national industry, is taxation. Taxation is not a reward. It belongs to the tyrannical class of excitements. If such excitements have a stronger influence over the human mind, than those arising from the principles of social liberty, the governments of the United States are founded in an erroneous policy. They have all conceived that industry would be better excited by justice, than by taxation; that commerce to flourish, needed only to be free; and that by freedom, the supplies of land and labour would be increased. By free and moderate government, our constitutions have expected to excite a military spirit to defend, an industrious spirit to improve, and a commercial spirit to enrich our country. Neither the monopolies of standing armies, hereditary perpetuities, or chartered currencies, were considered as the best excitements for defending, cultivating, or enriching it.

A feudal or landed monopoly starved commerce, because it tended to discourage industry, by which commerce is supplied. This effect flowed from the injustice of enriching by legal monopoly without industry. A monopoly for the regulation of a paper currency, far more exceptionable, enriches by law without industry; and in producing the same effect, discloses that it is the same principle. If this monopoly was guided by a noble order, unconnected with commerce, she would exclaim against it; and guided by her, she is able to use it to oppress agriculture and labour, just as the feudal monopoly was used to oppress labour and commerce. That she would diminish her own prosperity, is an insufficient security against the abuse of such a monopoly. The landed interest diminished its own prosperity, by the oppression of commerce and labour. By justice, as to all three, a nation will prosper; by enabling either to draw wealth from the other two, by

251

law, without industry, the common good or general interest is invariably wounded.

Equally remediless is the evil of corporate bodies for regulating commercial currency, by the expedient of forming them with land holders, merchants, and manufacturers. That a land holder will not oppress a landed interest, is a stale and exploded idea. If he receives the tax or the office in which the oppression consists, although he contributes towards it from his land, the security vanishes. The whole catalogue of tyrants have been land holders. If a bank currency is a tax upon land labour, and commerce, as will hereafter be demonstrated, stock holders, even composed of land holders, merchants and manufacturers, will for ever remain willing to receive the whole tax, though they may contribute a proportion of it. Nor will it follow, that bank or funded stock is beneficial to the landed, commercial or manufacturing interest, because we see several land holders, merchants and manufacturers enriched by it; any more than that sinecure offices would be beneficial to these interests, were we to see several land holders, merchants and manufacturers enriched by them. It is the income drawn from land and labour, and not any benefit rendered to commerce by stock, which causes its wealth. And this fact is the true reason, why stock transplants men from the natural interests of society, into the artificial interest of paper and patronage.

To buy cheap, and to sell dear, is admitted to be the object of commerce. The English mode of effecting these objects, is to compel labour to sell, and foreign nations to buy, at the prices which paper monopoly shall settle. If the code of pillage contains a law, allowing one nation to pilfer another, that of social justice contains none, by which the idea, of enabling an artificial interest, directly or indirectly, to force down or regulate the prices of the natural interests in the same community, can be defended.

No benefit arises to a nation from such an operation. It merely creates a rich order, by creating a poor order. The wealth obtained from the foreign nation by the reductions imposed upon the price of labour at home, is only taken by force or fraud from that labour, and given to stock capitalists. This is precisely the species of excitement produced by the English, and all other paper systems. National, social and moral law unite in pronouncing it to be unjust.

And however it may enrich a few, it impoverishes and oppresses a multitude, and changes commerce into a national curse. It becomes a blessing, whenever one nation can undersell another; not when an order or several merchants, are enabled to undersell foreign merchants, at the expense of fellow-citizen manufacturers. It is no benefit to the plundered, that the robber can undersell a fair purchaser.

The rival modes for enabling one nation to undersell another, are, the English, composed of force, fraud and paper, and calculated to render labour subservient to avarice, by bestowing on the latter the power of regulating wages; and that, which acquires the same advantage from the moderation, freedom and cheapness of the government. By this system the United States have successfully rivalled Europe, and obtained a degree of prosperity not embittered by the reflection of having killed and plundered foreign nations, and oppressed fellow-citizens, for the sake of commerce.

If paper systems are in their nature suitable to legislative corruption, aristocracy and monarchy; and if the momentum they bestow upon commerce, will enrich a few and impoverish a multitude of the same nation; yet, it is still said, that paper stock or national debt is an augmentation of national property, in addition to its retributing a nation for the taxes it inflicts, by the industry it excites.

The 5th chapter of Sterne's posthumous works, gives an account of a pamphlet written by himself in defence of Sir Robert Walpole, and contains the origin of this doctrine. He proved, says he, 'that the accumulation of taxes, like the rising of rents, was the surest token of a nation's thriving; that the dearness of markets, with these new imposts of government, necessarily doubled industry; and that an increase of this natural kind of manufacture, was adding to the capital stock of the commonwealth.' He subjoins, 'that his book had been the codex, or ars politica of all the ministerial sycophants ever since that æra; and that he had scarcely met with a paragraph in any of the state hireling writers, for many years past, that he could not trace fairly back to his own code.'

If American commerce, dazzled with the glare of the English, produced by consuming great masses of domestick and foreign happiness, is insensible to the prophetick satire of Sterne, and the catastrophe hovering over her rival, we must intreat her to have recourse to her own skill in calculation, and to estimate political consequences, with only half the attention she would devote to a trading voyage.

Mr. Adams has told her, that three orders, two of them hereditary, are necessary to create a limited monarchy, a monarchical republick, or the English form of government. We remind her, that orders appear in every monarchy, limited or despotick. The nobility of Germany, France and Spain, the Mandarins of China, the Nabobs of India, the Bashaws of Turkey, and the military order in every form, are proofs, that monarchy, mixed or pure, can only be supported by orders.

If we have proved, that paper systems lead to the establishment of orders; and if those which are guilty of oppression, or those which suffer it, are naturally driven to monarchy for defence or protection; orders or separate and inimical interests, are universally to be considered as the prelude to monarchy. And whether they will terminate in a limited or absolute monarchy are the events to be calculated. The probability of either is only to be inferred from experience. And the evidence of experience is found, by counting the cases wherein orders or separate legal interests, have resulted in absolute despotism or limited monarchy. The catalogue of the first class, is almost coequal with the number of governments, which have ever existed; and one case exists, or in its purity has existed, according to Mr. Adams, of the other.

This is the adventure, upon which American commerce is embarking her freedom and prosperity. By favouring the English paper system, she endeavours to introduce separate and inimical interests; these will beget monarchy; there is a thousand to one, that this monarchy will be absolute, even supposing that one case does exist, wherein orders have protected liberty by checking monarchy. If no such case exists, she exchanges her freedom and prosperity for slavery; if it does, she takes the chance of one against a thousand, of exchanging it for limited monarchy, in preference to a free republick.

But commerce will exclaim that she is an enemy to orders or separate interests, that she is a republican, and in favour of equal rights and privileges. We shall believe her if she unites in the expulsion of a separate interest; but if she craftily turns her eyes from the quarter, on which it is advancing, however vociferously she may call our attention to a feint, she will be suspected of a confederacy with the enemy.

Nobility and hierarchy are not the only modes of constituting orders, proper for fomenting national discontent, and introducing monarchy, if it is true, as Mr. Adams asserts, and as all mankind allow, 'that wealth, is the great machine for governing the world.'

Hence wealth, like suffrage, must be considerably distributed, to sustain a democratick republick; and hence, whatever draws a considerable proportion of either into a few hands, will destroy it. As power follows wealth, the majority must have wealth or lose power. If wealth is accumulated in the hands of a few, either by a feudal or a stock monopoly, it carries the power also; and a government becomes as certainly aristocratical, by a monopoly of wealth, as by a monopoly of arms. A minority, obtaining a majority of wealth or arms in any mode, becomes the government.

Nobility and hierarchy cannot acquire in the United States the article of wealth, necessary to constitute a separate order or interest, and therefore they can only be used as feints to cover the real attack. It cannot be forgotten, that aristocracy is a Proteus, capable of assuming various forms, and that to make these forms appear in that natural hideousness common to the features of the family, it is necessary to touch it with some test. An accumulation of wealth by law without industry, is this test. In our situation and temper it can only be effected by patronage and paper, which now bestow monarchy and groans upon England. Title without wealth is the shadow; an accumulation of wealth by law, is the substance. We have only to determine which is the feint, and which is the foe.

We hear indeed of the aristocracy of the first and second ages, from the repinings not the efforts of hierarchy and title; whilst paper systems and patronage, the aristocracy of the third, are using force, faith and credit, as the two others did religion and feudality; and these new artifices cloak themselves under the smoke produced by the explosion of the old.

Against one shadow of aristocracy, the general constitution provides in these words, 'no title of nobility shall be granted by the United States.' Suppose, as a provision against the other, some member of the convention had proposed, 'that the reinstatement of Jupiter, and the convocation of Olympus should be prohibited:' Ought he not to have been seconded by the inventor of the security against aristocracy, contained in the prohibition of titles? The people of England were taught to believe, that they had nothing to fear except from the pope and the pretender, by the ministers who mortgaged them irredeemably to oppression.

Imaginary Gods and empty titles, are in the United States equally to be dreaded, and are equally able to erect the aristocracies of superstition or feudality. A pecuniary interest, quartered on nations by law, is here the engine of power and oppression.

Unnecessary office, sinecure income, stockjobbing by the law-maker, a legislative patronage of separate interests or factions, and a concentrated power to tax, to incorporate, to borrow and to receive, make up the convolutions of a serpent, which is silently and insidiously entwining liberty; and to divert our attention from the operation, we are terrified by the dead skeletons of the two ancient aristocratical mammoths.

Superstition has received its death blow from knowledge; a landed aristocracy, from commerce, alienation and the division of inheritances. Against the dead, liberty is safe; from the living aristocracy of paper and patronage alone, she can receive a deadly wound.

A man, being informed that three assassins had determined upon his death, but that two of them had suffered the punishment due to other crimes, solemnly anathematizes the dead bodies, and takes into his bosom the living murderer. Liberty is the man; superstition and title her dead enemies; and the system of paper and patronage her living foe.

But we are blinded by names. Hierarchy concealed its malignity, by usurping the name of religion. The new system of oppression conceals itself, by calling patronage, necessary office; a funding system, faith and credit; and a banking system, an encouragement of commerce. Mankind have discovered the difference between religion and hierarchy; they must also discover that between useful and pernicious offices, between genuine and spurious faith and credit, and between commerce and monopoly, before they can maintain moderate and free governments.

The system of paper monopoly deceives no less by rejecting, than by assuming names. It renounces titles, that it may be thought to have renounced aristocracy. And it renounces disorderly government, that it may be thought to have a regard for private property. But titles are inconsistent with its species of aristocracy, and property is more securely and permanently invaded and transferred, by a regular and orderly system, than by occasional and disorderly violations.

This love of property is artfully seized by the system of paper and patronage, as a handle with which to guide human nature. Whilst superstition was its strongest passion, that was the handle used for the same purpose. But this system, discovering that a love of superstition has given place to a love of property, and concluding that mankind are fated for ever to be traitors to their reason and dupes to their passions, moulds them to its purposes by the same means which superstition used successfully for ages.

Had the system of paper and patronage, proposed to give property in Heaven for property on earth, the countless profit of the exchange might have reasonably attracted the passion of avarice, and in some measure varnished over the imposture; but when it imposes on a love of property, by pretending to revere and protect, that which its only employment is to violate and transfer, we cannot forbear to exclaim, that avarice is a greater fool than superstition; we are dismayed at discovering that a stronger engine for manufacturing tyranny exists, than superstition itself; the mind startles at its own imbecility, and shudders at its visible love of imposture.

A love of property, under which the system of paper and patronage crouches, is the very passion by which it ought to be assailed. All frauds pretend to be founded upon the principles, which apply most forcibly against them; just as superstition pretended to be religion. So this system uses the passions of avarice in others, to gratify its own. By pretending to protect property, it acquires property. It ingeniously persuades us, that it can effect the first object, without possessing a single quality adequate to it; and that it does not effect the other, with qualities competent to no other end. And it gravely and loudly proclaims its love of good order, but conceals that its motive for such apparent integrity, is the perpetuation and security of its own unjust acquisitions.

A love of good order, is a publick virtue. It is more useful the wider it is diffused. Is it good policy to bribe a minority into a profession of this virtue, by suffering it to pillage a majority? Is good order secured by rendering the mass of a nation discontented, to content a few? Let us inquire whether such a policy is wise. No one will assert that it is just.

The love of property is now the second basis of civil government. The question is, how a wise statesman should avail himself of this passion. If he forcibly or fraudulently takes wealth from a multitude, and gives it to a few, these few, it is confessed, will support all his projects, bad or good; and call his government orderly, and a protector of private property. But if he forbears to take directly or indirectly from the multitude, in order to corrupt a faction, he acquires the affection and support of this multitude. The difference between the acquisitions is this. The corrupted faction will adhere to the vicious as well as just measures of our statesman; the

I   257

majority, treated justly, will condemn his vices, and only applaud his virtues. That government or party therefore which designs to do wrong, will resort to one policy; and that which designs to do right, to the other.

It is a falsehood, that the policy of enriching a minority at the publick expense, is ever resorted to, for the purpose of protecting property; or that it is capable of any such effect. The idea of hiring a minority in civil government, to protect the property of a majority, is visibly absurd. Both from its physical inability, and also because all minor interests invested with political power, have universally violated property. That they shall necessarily do so, is therefore a settled moral law.

Our policy and constitutions rigidly distinguish between good and evil moral principles, upon this subject. The love and protection of property was one of those good moral principles which caused the war with England. In a government, it is only a virtue, so long as this love and protection shall be impartially extended to every member of the society. Of this virtue, avarice is the correspondent vice. It loves and pilfers the property of others, and protects what it gets. Does the system of paper and patronage correspond with the virtue or the vice?

The force of this reasoning is sometimes eluded, by charging it with assailing the propriety of taxing, for the support of civil government. This is an artifice to hide the iniquity of taxing for the benefit of the aristocracy of paper and patronage, under the justice of taxing for the common good. To infer that we are inimical to needful taxes, from our endeavouring to display the principles and effects of the aristocracy of the third age, is only a repetition of the artifice, which induced the aristocracy of the first age, to accuse a man of irreligion, whenever he reasoned against superstition.

Despotick power strives to blend itself with legitimate government, as paper stock does with private property; both endeavouring to sanction the evils they dispense, by the blessings which flow from the resemblances they falsely assume; and private property, the earning of labour, the reward of merit, the almoner of age, and the soul of civilization, is transformed by stock into a political monster, as hideous as government transformed by tyranny. It becomes the right of fraud, the scourge of industry, and the instrument of despotism. Stock private property, can condemn the seventh part of the most industrious and ingenious nation in the world, to poverty and vice, or to hospitals and prisons. When freedom and tyranny are both called government, and rightful acquisitions and paper stock both called private property, it can only be, to say the most for such denominations, as Gabriel and the Devil are both called angels.

Mankind have suffered nearly as much from confounding natural with fictitious property, as from confounding legitimate with spurious power. If the acquisitions of useful qualities are genuine private property, can the crafty pilferings from useful qualities under fraudulent laws, to gratify bad qualities, be genuine private property also? If the fruit of labour is private property, can stealing this fruit from labour, also make private property?

By calling the artillery property, which is playing on property, the battery is masked. Tythes and stock, invented to take away private property, are as correctly called private property, as a guillotine could be called a head. The system of Mr. Adams and Lord Shaftesbury, is founded upon the principle of applying the guillotine of law, to property instead of heads, to keep wealth, to which they both correctly annex power, balanced among three orders; the stock system is founded in the same principle, with this difference, that it takes away the entire property or its profit from majorities, whereas the system of orders is content with two thirds of it.

There are two modes of invading private property; the first, by which the poor plunder the rich, is sudden and violent; the second, by which the rich plunder the poor, slow and legal. One begets ferocity and barbarism, the other vice and penury, and both impair the national prosperity and happiness, inevitably flowing from the correct and honest principle of private property.

When it is proposed to tax stock or tythes for the support of civil government, they claim the stipendiary character to procure an exemption from taxation; but when it is proposed to abolish them, because the services under which this stipendiary character is claimed, have become useless or pernicious, they as loudly claim the character and the rights of private property. Feudality, hierarchy, and paper stock, have each successfully resorted to these subterfuges to keep justice at bay; and had the English House of Commons been open to the clergy, as all the departments of the American government are to stockjobbers, the former would probably have still maintained the same invaluable exclusive privilege, which the latter now enjoy.

The American constitutions are equally opposed to invasions of property by fraudulent and swindling laws; or by impracticable, dishonest and ruinous equalising reveries of political enthusiasts. They pursue the idea of securing to talents and industry their earnings, and not of transferring these earnings to others. Therefore they have rejected an equality of property, standing armies, hierarchies and privileged orders; and had they foreseen, that their principle in relation to property, was capable of being undermined by paper magick, that also would have been specifically guarded against.

Accumulations and divisions of property by law, simple or complicated, are equally adverse to our policy, and to moral rectitude. Both will excite hatred, discourage industry, and infuse knavery into the national character, by dividing it into factions, perpetually striving to pillage each other. Whether the law shall gradually transfer the property of the many to the few, or insurrection shall rapidly divide the property of the few among the many, it is equally an invasion of private property, and equally contrary to our constitutions.

If equalising and accumulating laws are the same in principle, it is inconceivable how the same mind should be able to detest the one, and approve the other. Integrity is compelled to reject both, and spurning at doctrines, calculated to incite the few to plunder the many, or the many to plunder the few, leaves every man under the strongest excitement to labour for his own and the national prosperity, from a conviction, that the laws are a mantle of justice, and not an intricate net to fish for his earnings.

Our policy is founded upon the idea, that it is both wise and just, to leave the distribution of property to industry and talents; that what they acquire is all their own, except what they owe to society; that they owe nothing to society except a contribution equivalent to the necessities of government; that they owe nothing to monopoly or exclusive privilege in any form; and that whether they are despoiled by the rage of a mob, or the laws of a separate interest, the genuine sanction of private property is equally violated. Are these the principles of our policy? Do paper systems correspond with these principles?

If legislative patronage enriches a portion of society, that portion is necessarily converted into an order, possessing the qualities of an aristocracy. It is placed between the government and the nation. It receives wealth from the one, and takes it from the other. This ties it to the government by the passion of avarice, and separates it from the nation by the passion of fear. And these two passions, annexed to any separate interest, have unexceptionably converted it into a political order, and forced it into the ranks of despotism.

War, in former times, enriched and aggrandized by conquest; in modern, by loaning. Titled orders, in the first case, usurped and monopolized what the nations they belonged to, conquered from their enemies; and by means of this usurped wealth, enslaved the conquerors. Paper orders acquire wealth in modern wars by loaning, although nothing is obtained by conquest. Now, a nation, by war without conquest, is made to furnish the means for its own subjection. The enemies of the Roman people, supplied the means for enslaving the Roman people. The English pay for their slavery themselves. An interest enriched by war, successful or unfortunate, must be separate and aristocratical.

Nations have effected an improvement in universal law, or the law of nations, without deriving from it the greatest advantage it is calculated to produce. Conquest respects private property; hence a nation can no longer conquer for itself. Formerly, every individual of a conquering army, got some share of the plunder; if his officer obtained a palace, the soldier got a cottage; if his officer obtained an house, the soldier got a cow. Then, one nation might be said to conquer another, although the spoil was unequally divided. But now the expression has become inaccurate, because there is precisely that degree of protection allowed by conquest to private property, necessary to the interest of the modern aristocracy of paper and patronage. As therefore, under the modern law of nations, no nation can gain any share of the booty, or conquer another nation, it is strange that nations should still go to war, when they can only conquer themselves; and that this propensity apparently increases.

In the solution of this enigma lies a proof, that paper stock is a separate aristocratical interest. Titled orders fomented war, as in the case of the Roman patricians, because they obtained the best share of the spoil. The nobility in England no longer foment war, because they are not aggrandized by it. And war has been still more ardently fomented in that country than ever, because their system of paper and patronage gain spoil by it in any event. Conquest furnishes it with funds on which to bottom more stock, and the war which made the conquest, with a pretext for quartering more patronage and paper on its own nation. Is not that a separate aristocratical interest which gains more by war and conquest, than orders of titled nobility formerly did? Those got most, this gets all.

The Roman aristocracy engaged the nation in war to aggrandize itself; but it entertained the people with shows, feasts and triumphs, and allowed them some small share of the booty. The English aristocracy of paper and patronage, engages the nation in war for the same purpose; and entertains the people with heavy taxes, hard labour, penal laws and Botany Bay.

Ancient and modern wars between civilized nations, have chiefly originated in the avarice and ambition of individuals, orders, or factions. A propensity for war, is evidently a separate interest inimical to a nation; and if this interest is contrived to derive vast accessions of wealth and power from every war, fortunate or unfortunate, from victory or defeat, it must be driven into a propensity for war, by an influence, exceeding in power, that which was sufficient to drive feudal barons into war, for their own advantage, and the oppression of mankind.

These barons were in some measure checked by the fear of danger. Their lives were risked in battle, and their possessions lost by defeat. But bank or debt stock shed no blood in war. To them it is a sure game. Hazarding nothing, a chance for winning of their foes, and a certainty of winning of their friends, must inspire them with principles more inimical to friends and foes, than even those of the separate feudal interest.

This system exhibits a new mode of enslaving nations infinitely more powerful than any heretofore invented. It can conquer a nation, whilst that nation is in a career of victory. Marlborough's victories created more debt, and of course destroyed more liberty in England, than any previous war. It places governments beyond the influence or scrutiny of the people. Two governments may engage in war for the purpose of obtaining power and wealth, each from its own nation. The cause of quarrel, the battles, the sieges and the peace, might be all amicably arranged before the declaration of war; and a complete victory infallibly secured to both the governments, without the transfer of an acre of territory. The system of paper and patronage would be the key to such a war, as it is to the history of England for the last century.

This evident propensity for war, arising from the strongest conceivable excitement, of itself suffices unquestionably to establish the enmity of paper systems to our policy, if our policy is friendly to liberty. To that, every species of war is dangerous; and one, fed by paper systems, fatal. The princes leagued against France, though beaten in the field, obtained a victory at home by paper and patronage, and by the effects of war, destroyed republican opinions in France. War, in this one operation, has, before our eyes, diminished the liberty of about twenty European nations.

Not the titles of orders, but a separate interest from the rest of a community, has induced them to harass the human race with war. Are the privileged titles of England, able to govern or control its system of paper and patronage? If not, these titles have long ceased to be the cause of her wars. They have neither motive nor power to produce them. But the system of paper and patronage has power to produce war or peace, and war is produced. This hungry calculator does not go to war out of chivalry, but from interest. Its propensity is proved in this evidence; its enmity to all majorities in society is a consequence of this propensity; and its aristocratical spirit, of that enmity.

A perpetual increase of taxes, is a constant effect of paper systems. Being essential to their existence, the consequences only are to be considered. Mankind have talked and written for ages about liberty, and yet the world is as far from agreeing in a definition of it, as Europe is from settling a balance of power. It is because liberty is made to consist in metaphysical dogma. As a thing of real substance and use, taxation, unmetaphysical taxation, is able to supply us with a correct idea of it. Heavy taxes in peace are unexceptionably political slavery. Liberty and slavery are contrary principles, and therefore liberty does not produce heavy taxes. Suppose, however, a conjuncture can be conceived, of liberty and heavy taxes in union; yet a free form of government cannot last, if heavy taxes continue until the poverty of the payers, and the wealth of the receivers, have separated the nation into two orders far apart. Heavy taxes are both an effect and a cause of tyranny, and cannot therefore be admitted in a substantial definition of liberty; being an inevitable consequence of paper systems, these also must be substantially inimical to liberty, however consistent they may be with her metaphysical definitions.

Taxation, direct or indirect, produced by a paper system in any form, will rob a nation of property, without giving it liberty; and by creating and enriching a separate interest, will rob it of its liberty, without giving it property. Taxation, for the maintenance of civil government or national defence, will also take away property; but then it may bestow liberty. The slave, who receives

263

subsistence from a master, may advantageously compare situations with the vassal of the first species of taxation; he gets something for his liberty and property; he gets subsistence without care: his compeer loses his liberty and property, and only gains an augmentation of the anxieties of life. To the second species of taxation, mankind are indebted for social liberty. How have these opposite principles been blended and confounded with each other? Merely by the avarice and ambition of orders, separate interests or aristocracy. How cautious and circumspect ought nations to be, when they discover, that the most inimical moral principles are hidden in one term. One species of taxation destroys; the other, preserves their liberty.

Barbarism thirsts for blood; civilization for wealth. To defend men against these propensities is the legitimate end of civil government. A government, administered so as to expose property but protect life in a civilized nation, is equivalent to a government, contrived to protect property but to expose life in a savage one; and the barbarian, whose property was safe, whilst his life was defenceless against the passion of blood-thirstiness, might as justly boast of his freedom, as the civilized man, whose life was safe, whilst his property was exposed to appease the money-thirstiness of paper and patronage.

If that species of protection to property, afforded by paper systems, operated in an invasion of the principal instead of the profit, it would be universally assailed as a robber. How thin is the veil by which we are deceived! We are content to lose the profit for the sake of the occupation. We forget that the safety of property consists in the enjoyment of its profits; and that the utmost permanent violation of which it is capable, is consistent with occupation and subsistence.

The history of Villeinage illustrates this idea. Villeins were nominally emancipated for the interest of the masters, not of the slaves. With subsistence and the occupation of property as tenants, they were more profitable to the barons than in a state of direct slavery. Paper systems, taking the hint from this history, have artfully placed themselves in the predicament of the feudal lords; and nations, in that of emancipated villeins. The profits are taken, the occupation left, and this is called freedom or protection of property.

These systems, being simply compounded of debt and taxation, must divide a nation into annuitants and labourers, engender want and luxury, reduce each individual to the alternative of oppressing or being oppressed, and cultivate avarice and rapaciousness both by the gain they bestow, and the loss they inflict. Divines and philosophers may possibly have erred in omitting hitherto to recommend such principles, as promoters of virtue, religion and national happiness. Whether politicians have found out, that a power in legislators to enrich themselves by stock of their own creation, will perfect the system of election and representation, is hereafter to be considered.

A nation is never conquered by an army, or enslaved by a faction, so long as it is willing to defend itself. The concentration of wealth in a few hands, obliterates this disposition. The disciplined Romans were subdued by raw barbarians, when the lands of Italy were held by less than three thousand proprietors. The feudal nations were weak, whilst a few nobles held the property of the nation; and their petty wars were rendered less destructive by this national imbecility. The same consequence resulted from the possession of one third of the property of a nation by the priesthood. And stock in England, which covers and transfers property to its amount, is so well convinced that the motive exciting nations to self defence is thereby impaired, as to resort to the alternative of a standing army, and to stake the national existence upon a battle, to be fought by mercenaries. The people and armies of the Roman empire frequently preferred a coalition with Scythian invaders, to the danger of resistance, or the calamity of victory; and twelve millions of people are apprehending or invoking conquest, on account of an unanimous opinion, that paper stock has incapacitated a great nation for defending itself against a single army.

Oppressive taxation is the effect of standing armies, noble orders, hierarchies or paper stock. A similarity in moral effects, demonstrates a similarity in moral causes. All of these have pretended to defend nations at different periods. England possesses all these defenders. The first and the last are the modern champions of nations; if she had possessed neither, she never would have gained sundry victories, but she would have possessed a gallantry which burthensome taxes never inspired. And what conqueror can be more oppressive than two mercenary armies, one of soldiers, and another of stockjobbers? Besides, funding never fights for a nation in imminent danger; its wars are guided by other calculations, than those of publick safety; and the moment of peril is the moment of its flight.

If posterity could pass a law, for imposing heavy taxes on the present generation, the entire universe of existing progenitors would exclaim, 'if you can rob us of property, we can rob you of life. It is better that you should never exist, than that we who do exist, should be the prey of your avarice; than that a series of generations should be sacrificed to one unborn and unsympathising.' In the character of sufferers, the parties concur. Progenitors would destroy posterity, and posterity would destroy progenitors, rather than submit to unlimited, unfeeling and unconsented to taxation.

Funding, by growing too rapidly in the Mississippi and South Sea cases, inconsiderately disclosed its real character; it has since distended itself to a degree of magnitude and mischief in England infinitely exceeding those detestable frauds. An ugly cur, suddenly bursting upon a company of children, inspires them with horrour; and they get a young tiger, caress, feed and rear it, without a suspicion of its furious and bloody nature, until it devours them. But it is not the office of truth, in distinguishing between good and evil moral principles, however the deluded may believe that there is no generical affinity between a pug and a mastiff, to represent the same thing as a vice or a virtue according to its dimension; and therefore it seems impossible to transplant funding of any size or age from the place in the moral world assigned to it by its own nature, or to expect good moral effects, from a moral cause, fruitful of evil beyond most of its kindred.

Between the two items of paper stock, the similitude is such, that, though this section is here concluded, the reader will discern in the next, many observations applicable to its doctrine.

Section the Fifth

BANKING

I SHALL now proceed to the examination of banking, in the face of a prepossession, which has seized, like a panick, upon the publick mind. If it is a limb of the aristocracy of the third age, it cannot be attached to the body of our policy without some dismemberment to make room for it. We know that banking made no part of this policy, state or continental, originally; and that now, like the tail of a Cape sheep, it constitutes its most conspicuous member.

Priests have at all times performed acts, which enrich themselves, and are by the laity believed to be miracles. Had it been your lot, reader, to address an audience composed of these priests and their laity, to prove that such acts were not miracles, what would you have considered as the most stubborn obstacles against success? You answer, the interest of one party and the superstition of the other. And yet neither this interest nor superstition, furnish fact or argument as to the truth or falsehood of these miracles, or the justice of the tax they inflict. Ought either then to suffocate inquiry and truth; and would you not pity the unhappy blindness or vice capable of fostering an errour so gross?

Reader, I only ask you not to become yourself this object of commiseration. Neither prejudice nor avarice will conduct you to truth. Refute the arguments which are refutable; but yield your conviction to those which you cannot refute.

Premising, that all the objections against debt stock or paper systems, apply with equal, and often with accumulated force against banking; and that the latter subject is considered separately, not as being of a very different nature, but for the sake of perspicuity; we will enter directly upon it.

Had banking been called 'a paper feudal system,' and had the barons proposed to take it by that denomination as a reimbursement for their abolished tenures, it might have been fairly weighed against the landed feudal system, to estimate the effects of the exchange. In that event, it would have been clearly seen by the people, that the money to be collected by 'a paper feudal system' for their lords, was the representative of the services rendered under the landed feudal system; and that whatever convenience they might derive from altering the mode of payment, the payment itself would remain. Money, or a circulating medium of any kind, in its quality of representing property and labour, conveys property and labour to its possessor; and if A, entitled to the menial services of B, contracts to receive of B their value in money, though B may prefer this mode of payment, he must still perform the same value in labour to acquire the money it is commuted for. Such bargains were often made between the kings and the people of England, in the sale and purchase of vexatious prerogatives. If then a nation bestows a pecuniary income on an order of nobles or of bankers, it conveys so much of its services to this order as the money represents; nor is there any difference between rendering the services in kind, and in the pecuniary commutation, except in the superior convenience of the latter mode; since the services must be still performed. If a great nation owed its personal labours to one thousand individuals, so much excepted as might afford a bare subsistence, it would mend its condition in a small degree, by purchasing them out for an annuity in money; but not in a great one, if it paid to the order the full value of them. As money is a vehicle for retaining, it is also one for conveying the most oppressive usurpations, and possesses a complete capacity for re-enslaving nations indirectly, after an accession of knowledge or a division of property, has liberated them from the direct feudal slavery. This treacherous quality of money was perceived by the Spartan legislator, without discerning any remedy for it, but that of destroying its inestimable benefits. It is clear that nations, by giving any species of currency to an order or interest, will give it a title to every species of service from the multitude; that the revival by law of a title to such services through the intervention of a currency, is a substantial revival of the feudal system; that a legal currency possesses a power of destroying, with wonderful rapidity, the division of property which destroyed that system; and that without a very considerable division of property, a free government cannot exist. The remedy for these evils, which Lycurgus did not discern, is to prohibit legal distributions of money or currency, those excepted rendered unavoidable by government, and to leave their distribution to industry.

Even the precious metals have furnished to the contrivers of pillage and oppression a medium for extracting indirectly from nations, a far greater proportion of their labour, than they could ever be made to pay directly by the feudal or any other regimen: but the impossibility of multiplying these metals at pleasure, inflicted a considerable check upon this fraudulent perversion of so useful a representative of property. An artificial currency is subject to no such check, and possesses an unlimited power of enslaving nations, if slavery consists in binding a great number to labour for a few. Employed, not for the useful purpose of exchanging, but for the fraudulent one of transferring property, currency is converted into a thief and a traitor, and begets, like an abuse of many other good things, misery instead of happiness.

Mankind soon discovered that money was easily converted into a medium for oppression as well as for commerce, and hence arose nearly as strong a dislike to heavy taxes in money as in kind; it being clearly seen that labour and property were transferred by money. This plain truth, awakened the exertions of avarice and ambition, to deceive the vigilance of labour and industry: the objects of pillage. The first intricacy with which they endeavoured to hide their design, was woven of indirect taxes travelling in mazes; the second, of loaning obscured by the mist of futurity; and the third, of an artificial currency or banking, complicated by the crookedness of its operation, flattering to industry, and restrained by no natural check, as a medium of fraud and tyranny. The defence of banking, 'that its enormous annual acquisitions travel to it from some terra incognita, and are not drawn from the labour and property of a nation,' shall be first considered.

The common nature of bank debt and funded debt, has attracted the common appellation, stock. Existing together, their price will fluctuate in relation to national adventures, because the national ability to pay, is coextensively the sponsor for each. Peace and prosperity, cause bank and funded stock to rise in price; war and adversity, cause both to fall. Both are heroes and patriots in safety, and cowards and traitors in danger. As the state of the nation affects both in the same way, both must affect the state of the nation in the same way. If stock did not act upon the labour and property of nations; their adventures or wealth, could not react upon stock. The reaction is the same as to both funded and bank stock.

If national adventures or measures can raise or diminish the value of bank stock, it is under the same inducement as debt stock to influence a government. Therefore one hundred millions of bank stock, will acquire as much of this influence, created by laws and not by constitutions, as one hundred millions of debt stock. Its sole object is to induce a government to enable it to tax the nation, in an indirect and complicated mode, to enrich itself; whereas the chief design of our constitutional policy, is to subject the government to the national influence to prevent this wicked deed. Had there been no debt stock in England, but an equal value of bank stock, that alone would have influenced the government to govern in the same mode, as bank and debt stock united induce or compel it to do. The same interests which now exist, would have existed in that case, namely, the stock interest, the government interest, and the national interest; and the same union between the two first, would have produced the same effect to the last.

Debt stock could not permanently receive its interest, where there was no labour; if bank stock could not permanently receive its dividends, in the same case, those dividends, however indirectly collected, must also be paid by labour. As the fund necessary for the subsistence of the one, is necessary for the subsistence of the other, it follows that they are of the same nature, and must subsist by the same means; and that neither debt stock nor bank stock can be fed, except by taxation, direct or indirect, simple or complicated.

The degree of taxation produced by these engines, is capable of being ascertained with considerable correctness. Debt stock gives to a nation or its government, one hundred pounds of money, for an annuity of five or six pounds. Bank stock receives an annuity of ten or twelve pounds, including dividends, expenses and perquisites of directors, for keeping its hundred pounds. Which is the highest tax upon a nation—five millions annually for one hundred millions received; or ten millions annually on one hundred millions of bank stock, for nothing received? Can the latter tax be concealed by its enormity, as a high mountain is hidden by clouds?

The custom of buying the privilege of banking, is an evidence of its nature. Unless it had been a tax, it could not be bought, nor could it be sold. The title by which a government sells, is that of national agent, selling national property; and the purchaser is enabled to buy, by a reimbursement of his purchase money with a profit. Sale and profit imply property; how is it reached in this case, except by taxation?

The ingenuity of beguiling a nation, by bribing it with a part of its own, strengthens this observation. Suppose a thousand stock-jobbers, with the munificence and patriotism of stockjobbers, should say, 'Society, create ten millions of stock; you may keep one fifth of it, as payment for four fifths which you shall give us.' The property of stock being to tax, the proposition simply is, 'Society, if you will permit us to tax you at eight hundred thousand dollars a year, (computing bank dividends at ten per centum,) you may tax yourselves at two hundred thousand.' As bank stock holders retain their stock, they do not lend it to a nation as a compensation for taxing it by means of that stock. These two hundred thousand dollars, are ingeniously used to dazzle the multitude, so as to conceal from them, that they pay eight hundred thousand to individuals, for the privilege of taking two hundred thousand from themselves, and bestowing it on the government. To be gulled by false prophecy or pretended miracle, is known to be within the capacity of human ignorance; but a national inability to count is a real miracle. Corporate rights to tax the nation in a great sum, for the sake of that nation's exercising the right of taxing itself in a small one, are like bribes to a government for permission to plunder the people, as practised under the Turkish policy.

The fact 'that bank stock is a tax gatherer,' is only controverted by the assertion, that its dividends arise from the voluntary acts of individuals. 'Voluntary and individuals.' Precisely the terms invariably resorted to, whenever the object is to varnish over tyranny, pecuniary or personal. Innocent men are imprisoned for life by tyranny, and a nation is fleeced by monopoly and indirect taxation; ought the indignation of justice to be quelled by being told, that these calamities only fall on individuals?

Most taxes, by which nations have been enslaved, are voluntary. By forbearing to drink liquors of any kind, or to make a deed, will, bond or bill of exchange, several taxes in England may be avoided; strictly then, their payment may be called voluntary; yet by these and similar taxes, England is made the property of a monied aristocracy; and such taxes were felt in the United States as a regular progression towards the same system. Did neither of these countries sustain an injury, because the injury was inflicted throughout the medium of voluntary taxation? Is the sale of church paper, for enriching a clergy in this world, under pretence of excusing the sins of the buyer in the next, innoxious to mankind, because the traffick is voluntary?

Whether the ignorance of the payer that he is taxed, so as to diminish or destroy the responsibility of a government to a nation, is a good or a bad argument in favour of indirect or voluntary taxes; it does not at least justify the imposition of such taxes for the sake of the argument: it does not prove, supposing it is a good stratagem to keep the people ignorant of the amount paid, that this amount ought to be given to corporations or private individuals; it does not justify the establishment of chambers of taxation, entrenched in impenetrable secrecy, with power to commission and scatter tax gatherers wherever they please. Whatever therefore can be urged in defence of indirect taxation for the benefit of a nation, leaves the collections made by banking for the benefit of a chartered company, as defenceless as before.

Admitting then, that the tax paid to banking, arises from the voluntary acts of individuals, it is by no means an argument in its favour, stronger than the voluntary purchases of church paper or indulgences, in favour of that practice. The question would still remain, whether it is wise or just to suffer the passions of individuals to be used as channels, for drawing the wealth of a nation into a few hands.

But it is denied that the profit of banking belongs to the voluntary class of taxes; and in the course of the following observations, we shall urge sundry reasons to shew, not only that it is a tax, but an inevitable tax.

A, whom we will consider as representing the whole class of borrowers from a bank, must acquire a profit upon the use of the paper, equivalent to the interest he pays; otherwise he could not borrow. From his continuing to borrow, it is evident that he only advances the tax, and that it is reimbursed. This regular result is of the nature of fate or necessity, and not of free will or discretion. The residue of a nation composes the class, throughout which, A, the borrowing class, circulates the paper, and it is unable to exercise any volition, adequate to the avoidance of his reimbursement.

Excluding the idea of the class of borrowers, the certainty and simplicity with which a bank inflicts and collects its profit, becomes still more visible. The operation is carried on between a nation and a banking corporation. The nation, through the channel of its members, exchanges a thing called credit, reduced to the form of bonds or notes for the payment of money, with the corporation, giving a boot, profit or difference, of about eight per centum per annum, which the bank bond, note or credit, is arbitrarily made by law to be worth, beyond the national bond, note or credit. This effect is produced by subjecting the members of the nation to the payment of a compound interest to the corporation on their bonds, notes or credit, and absolving the corporation from the payment of any interest to the members of the nation, on its bonds, notes or credit; and exhibits both the inevitability of the tax, and a mode of its collection.

It is asked, whether the borrowing class, may not forbear to borrow, and whether this power of forbearance, is not an evidence, that the profit or income collected by banking, proceeds from the voluntary act of individuals. Should bread and water be placed in abundance, before a hungry and thirsty multitude, could their eating and drinking be fairly said to be merely voluntary? Currency is the medium for exchanging necessaries. If gold and silver, the universal medium, are legislated out of sight, all human wants unite to compel men to receive the tax collecting substitute. This is banking. By the help of law it creates a necessity for its own currency; and this extreme hunger is misnamed volition.

The coin currency being expelled or drawn out of circulation, to an extent sufficient to create a necessity for some substitute, the power possessing the right of supplying and regulating that substitute, can inevitably so manage it, as to enrich itself by means of that necessity. It can supply the needed currency upon the terms, and in the quantities it pleases. And if fluctuations in currency, produced and managed by chartered monopolies, can affect price or value, it follows, that through his income, his money, and his property, an individual is reached by the tax of this currency, although he never borrowed or used it. Such sufferers do not exercise the least formality of volition.

That the profit of banking is both a tax and an inevitable tax, is asserted by stockholders themselves, and the legislatures which grant charters. The wealth collected from a state by bank paper issued without it, is called a tribute; and the remedy resorted to is to establish the tribute at home. Tyranny, and especially pecuniary oppression, has been generally most tolerable, the farther off. It is certainly true as bankers assert, that a banking corporation in Maryland can tax Virginia by circulating its paper within that state, and of course it is also true, that a banking corporation in Virginia, can tax Virginia by the same means; the questions are, which can carry the oppression to the greatest extent; the domestick or foreign corporation; and if the former, whether a greater, will remedy a less evil?

The argument in favour of repulsive banks, coincides in other points with the ideas we have expressed. Few or none of the notes coming from distant banks, admitted to have collected a tax in Virginia, were borrowed by the citizens of that state. Therefore, not the borrower, but the nation in which the notes circulate, pays the tax. If the borrower does not pay the tax, his will or pleasure that it shall be paid by others, does not make it a voluntary tax; nor entitle it even to that unsubstantial defence. As the circulator of the paper, he inflicts and enhances the tax for his own benefit. And the payer, not being the borrower, has no check over, or volition in relation to the tax. It will even be collected from individuals whom the paper never reaches, by its capacity to cause the value of property and even of coin itself, to fluctuate.

Those who create new banks, to protect one state against the calamity of bank paper, coming from another, also assert that bank paper is a blessing. Bold contradictions sometimes hide truth, as vehemency does cowardice. Will climate, or the names of stockholders have the effect of making bank paper sometimes a curse, at others a blessing? Then a tribute; now a mine of wealth? Sincerity, as a citizen of Virginia, wishing to introduce banks, after having truly urged that Virginia paid a tax to stock holders in other states, would have simply requested that the same individual tax might be transferred to Virginians. This would have brought the question fairly before the publick. Shall a tax be created for the sake of its expenditure at home? Shall we foster separate sinecure interests at home, because a contribution towards their support abroad, is an evil? And even these questions would have resulted in a very simple numerical calculation; namely, whether it would be wise to extract a revenue from the state, payable by all its citizens except about one thousand, who should receive it; in order to save half the sum, collected by citizens of other states, towards the payment of which these thousand also contributed? This degree of sincerity might reasonably have been expected of stock itself; but disinterestedness would have added, that the idea of one tax driving out the other, that is, of domestick bank paper, driving out bank paper issued without the authority of the state, was delusive. The extraneous paper, being possessed of the quality which collects the tax (currency or circulation) would continue to circulate and tax; and the remedy would therefore simply amount to an addition of a new tax to the old. Such will continue to be the effect of this remedy of opposing state paper to extraneous paper, until a state is saturated with the tax. A country is saturated with debt stock, when it can no longer pay its interest, and with bank paper, when it can no longer pay its dividends. Whilst Virginia is able to pay the dividends of her domestick stock, and the same contribution heretofore collected from her by extraneous paper, one payment will not abolish the other, but both will be made; and the creation of a bank tax to expel a bank tax, only amounts to the ingenious idea, that one lash will cure the smart of another.

The real remedy against strange bank paper is as visible as, light; but it would lead to discussions, which native stock feared to encounter. If bank paper is a tax gatherer, one state may prohibit the circulation of another's paper, with as much propriety, as it could expel tax gatherers in the shape of men, commissioned by another. No disguise, change of shape, or new dress, can bestow a right to tax, where no such right exists. But native stock felt its dilemma; an expulsion of strange paper by law, because it was a tax, would have told the people by law, that native paper was also a tax. It preferred therefore the delusion of an opinion, that one tax would diminish another, as the basis of its own existence, to an inquiry, which might have terminated in the conclusion, that no legislature in the United States have a better right to tax their constituents for the benefit of banking corporations, than one state has to tax another state for the same purpose.

Into this inquiry, let us proceed; beginning with the right of Congress to tax the Union for the benefit of a bank corporation. Our arguments will be founded upon an opinion, that bank paper collects a revenue. Supposing its payment to be unavoidable, an apportionment by the census is required by our constitutional policy; allotting it to any other description of tax, a bank in each state, or some distribution of stock, is equally required by the mandate of uniformity; and both these constitutional principles are grossly violated, by a bank so located, as to enrich one state, and tax another. Considered as a non-descript species of revenue, no power to inflict it on the publick, or to bestow it on private people, is given to Congress.

In the appropriation, as in the apportionment or uniformity of revenue, will be found a limitation of the power of Congress. An unconstitutional mode of taxing, may inflict partial injuries upon particular states, but an unconstitutional application of revenue, may be ruinous to all. It is inconceivable that the constitution, whilst so cautiously providing against the first evil, should have overlooked the second. The loosest security against it, is deposited in a limitation of the revenue collected, to the 'common defence and general welfare of the United States;' and the right of Congress to appropriate a revenue collected by bank paper, for the defence or welfare of a corporation, is visibly beyond this wide definition.

Under the idea 'of carrying the powers given into execution,' could Congress have invested the parliament of England, with the privileges granted to the bank of the United States? Such a charter would have bestowed on England the object of her war upon us, revenue. In what part of the constitution is to be found a prohibition upon Congress to bestow a revenue upon the British parliament, or a power to bestow one on chartered companies? A construction necessary to invest Congress with one power must include the other.

Testimony applicable to the question exists without and within the constitution. A rejection of a proposal for empowering Congress to establish a bank by the convention, is the evidence without the constitution; and a special power to grant charters 'to authors and inventors,' is the evidence within it, uniting in a condemnation of the construction, which claims for Congress an unlimited power of bestowing revenue upon corporations, and literally forbidding that mode of doing it called banking. A special and limited power excludes the idea of a general and unlimited power, which includes the special one.

In most or all of the state constitutions, diploma, charter and corporation, are condemned as inimical to liberty, and as usurpations upon man's natural rights. In none, is a power given to the legislature, to bestow a revenue of any kind at the national expense upon corporations.

The constitution of Massachusetts declares, that 'no man, or corporation, or association of men have any other title to obtain advantages or particular and exclusive privileges distinct from those of the community, than what arises from the consideration of services rendered the publick;' and that of Virginia, 'that no man or set of men, are entitled to exclusive or separate emoluments or privileges from the community, but in consideration of publick services.'

The words 'common defence and general welfare,' twice used in the constitution of the United States, contain the principle advanced in the two last quotations. They are the exact contraries to 'particular, exclusive or separate privileges or welfare.'

The constitutions quoted, literally enrolling 'exclusive privileges and emoluments' in the list of tyrannies, proceed to expound the words 'publick services.' These only are admitted to possess a legitimate title 'to exclusive privileges and emoluments.' Had legislators been left at liberty to extend these words to whatever they should deem to be publick service, they might have created and endowed with exclusive privileges and emoluments, a corporation for introducing monarchy, as well as for introducing the aristocracy of paper stock, under the idea, that it would serve the publick.

But their constitutional exposition is unequivocal. The privileges and emoluments allowed to publick services, are neither 'inheritable or transmissible to children, descendants or relations,' because 'publick services' being 'in nature' neither hereditary or transmissible, so exclusive transmissible privileges or emoluments were incompatible with the principles of liberty. This construction of the terms, by the instrument in which they are used, restricts legislative power by a definition, far short of an unfettered imagination, licensed to pronounce whatever comports with its fancy, its interest or its plots, to be serviceable to the publick. It unequivocally dissevers the privileges or emoluments allowed to publick services, from whatever may be sold, or transmitted to relations, like bank stock. And expounds these terms, as well as their equivalents, 'general welfare,' according to their original unsophisticated intention.

The governments of the union, Massachusetts and Virginia, have granted banking charters, conveying saleable, transferable and descendible exclusive privileges and emoluments; and have thus opened by precedent a way to every conceivable power, by usurping the mother of all powers, that of distributing wealth. This may be given to foreigners, whether plebeians, nobles or kings, and held both in peace and in war, as rewards 'for publick services' or 'for common defence and general welfare,' by bank 'exclusive privileges and emoluments.' The word 'common,' requires a membership with the community, and the king, nobility, clergy and paper aristocracy of England, holding bank stock in America, in a war between England and the United States, must therefore be considered, as rendering publick services, and advancing our defence and welfare, to bring the appropriation of money to their use by the bank law, within the meaning of this expression. If such fictions are able to overturn constitutional principles, the idea of a constitution capable of restraining legislatures, is itself a fiction.

It is admitted that this part of our reasoning is of little weight. If banking is a publick benefit, constitutional prohibitions ought not to deprive the publick of that benefit; only the constitutions ought to be amended to come at it. Banking ought therefore to be considered, as it affects nations morally and politically, and not by any verbal test. But it cannot be overlooked, that although banking was rejected and excluded by the framers of the general constitution; and although many eminent and learned men long denied to congress a power to incorporate banks; yet it has never been judicially questioned; and all the state legislatures have found it in the words 'publick services,' after congress discovered it lurking under the expression 'general welfare.' Individuals and entire parties, to a vast extent, have loudly reprobated, and calmly defended this power; and the folly or knavery of those who first represented it as an usurpation dangerous to free government, and afterwards seized upon it, ought to be a memorial to nations against reposing an excessive degree of confidence in parties or individuals; in judges or legislatures; in governments or patriots.

The history of man proves that all will often avail themselves of the precedents established by their predecessors, and reprobated by themselves. Every precedent, however clearly demonstrated to be unconstitutional and tending 'towards monarchy and an iron government' by a party out of power, will be held sacred by the same party in it; and those who clearly discerned the injustice and impolicy of enriching and strengthening federalists by bank or debt stock, at the publick expense, will seldom refuse to receive a similar sinecure. In short, a power in the individuals who compose legislatures, to fish up wealth from the people, by nets of their own weaving, whatever be the names of such nets, will corrupt legislative, executive and judicial publick servants, by whatever systems constituted; and convert patriots from the best friends, into the most dangerous foes of free, equal and just principles of civil liberty.

Let us return more particularly to our subject. It will be remembered, that we have endeavoured to prove, that a revenue is collected from nations by banking. Our knowledge of that currency, called paper money, will suggest new arguments to this point. Long experience has demonstrated to America, that a paper currency will never retain its value, unless it is attended by a tax adequate to its redemption. We will suppose, however untrue it may be, that every bank contains coin to the amount of its capital. Yet this is a sum, inferior to the aggregate of its stock, its notes, and its dividends. If the coin is only mortgaged for the two last items, yet these greatly exceed its amount, and this excess forms a mass of paper currency, for which the coin is no security. Without a security adequate to its redemption, we know it to be a law of paper currencies to depreciate; and as this surplus of bank paper beyond the ability of the deposited coin to redeem, does not depreciate, its credit must be supported by some other security; that security is the tax, which banking collects; a tax, not only sufficing for the redemption and credit of this species of paper currency, but supplying a redundancy, sufficient in some cases to add one half of its numerical value to the coin deposited as stock.

Of the correctness of this reasoning, and of the nature of banking, an ancient practice in Pennsylvania, furnishes a demonstration. That state, whilst a province, became a banker. It made and loaned a paper currency, at a moderate interest. The interest paid for it to the state, was a tax, applied to publick use. This is banking, stript of its ambiguity. Simply an indirect mode of taxation, successfully used to raise national revenue. The idea that it was not a tax, because individuals borrowed the money, and collected and paid the tax, would be an assertion in every view less tenable, than that an impost upon ordinary licences was not a tax, because such licences were voluntarily taken and confined to a few persons; the reimbursement derived from the privilege in both cases, transfers the tax from the individuals to the publick.

The differences between the Pennsylvanian and the present mode of banking, are, that then the tax was paid by individuals to the publick; now it is paid by the publick to individuals. Then it was paid to assist industry, and defray publick expenses; now to enrich idleness, and supply the means of luxury to a separate interest. Then the publick required a knowledge of the amount paid, from its own representatives; now it pays an amount unknown, to corporations in which it is not represented. Then the publick received five or six per centum of individuals for paper currency; now it pays ten or twelve per centum to individuals for the same currency. That species of paper currency could not corrupt legislatures or nurture aristocracy; this must do both. That being dealt out by the publick interest, and not by the interest of monopoly, circulated through a nation like coin, liable to no artificial fluctuation, and begat fair, useful and honest competition; this being regulated by a separate interest, is made to cause prices to fluctuate with a view to personal and local emolument. That did not monopolize and expel specie; this commences with the first measure, and terminates with the second, so as to make itself indispensably necessary.

But it is said that the Pennsylvanian species of bank currency will fail in its credit. It is never to be forgotten, that credit is an ally of safety and factions, and not of peril and nations. That it is bold and flourishing in security, and fearful and withering in danger. A small degree of danger being about to assail the credit of the bank of England, the corporation influenced government to protect it against the payment of its debts to the nation; a protection, which would not withstand the shock of war, invasion, superior force and disaster, as long as did the currency of national credit in France and America.

National credit includes the credit of every individual; a part cannot be more solid than the whole; and if the whole is lost, the parts must also be lost. A calamity which threatens to overwhelm a nation, destroys confidence among individuals. Bank credit depends upon bonds given by individuals. Pennsylvanian credit was supported by the same pledge, and by the additional guarantees of landed security and national faith. A calamity, capable of destroying the bonds, mortgages and national faith, three sponsors for Pennsylvanian bank currency, will destroy the single sponsor for chartered bank currency. And a nation will defend its own credit with more animation, whilst it diminishes their taxes, by bringing them revenue; than it will bank credit, which increases their taxes, without bringing them revenue. National credit would arouse bravery, interest and patriotism, like other property; but bank and funding credit, cannot inspire a nation with patriotism, because it is a tax gatherer, which zealously engages in the wars of ambition, avarice and orders, and flees from imminent national danger. A rapacious coward cannot make a nation brave.

If the credit of a whole nation is perfidious, it only aggravates the absurdity of purchasing a portion of its own perfidious credit, at an enormous price; and of expecting to cure the perfidy of the whole, by attaching to a part, the additional excitements towards treachery, arising from exclusive privilege and separate interest. These never had any business in society, but to corrupt governments and plunder nations. They are exactly the remedy, universally proposed by the enemies of the principle of self-government, for this imaginary evil of national perfidy to itself. National credit, say they, is perfidious. Resort therefore to corporation, vendible, monopolized and successional credit, as a much better shield for liberty. Equally perfidious, in their opinion, is national wisdom, and therefore they recommend titled, hereditary and successional wisdom, as also a better shield for liberty. Such opinions are consistent. But how can those be reconciled, which assert, that treachery to liberty forever lurks in hereditary, successional and monopolized wisdom, and that her safety consists in vendible, successional and monopolized credit?

Pennsylvanian credit, produces the benefit of a revenue, as national wisdom does that of freedom; and corporation credit produces taxation, as hereditary wisdom does tyranny. As credit can produce revenue, it is property, and it will be considered, whether as such, it can under our policy be thrown into a state of monopoly, or disposed of by exclusive charter, as districts and inhabitants are in Russia, or branches of commerce in England. If a monopoly of the wine trade, cannot be chartered to a corporation, will credit, which covers every branch of commerce, admit of a state of monopoly?

The value of credit, as property, appears evidently in the price it sells for. A nation, by giving away its credit, loses what Pennsylvania sold at six per centum. By erecting corporations to monopolize or expel its specie, to make room for their credit, it loses the use of this specie worth six per centum more. And necessity then compels it to buy of these corporations the credit it gave to them, at the price of ten or twelve per centum upon their stock. These items shew that credit is either property, or a machine for transferring property, more effectual than that made of hereditary. and exclusive wisdom. Both machines have been invented for this purpose. The hereditary magnifies the defects incident to human government in its best form, to hide its own greater vices. The credit machine, in strict imitation of this example, seizes upon the errours of paper money, as reproaches against national credit; and hides under them its own greater aptitude to shrink from danger, and also its capacities for corrupting governments and plundering nations. Of the bad features in the face of paper money, corporation credit makes two masks, one to hide its own hideousness, the other to hide the benefits of national credit.

If all the banks in the United States circulate fifty millions of paper dollars, five millions of real property will thereby be collected. And if national credit, instead of corporation credit, had issued the same sum in the mode successfully practised in Pennsylvania, a revenue of five millions would have been received instead of being paid, making a difference of ten millions annually to the nation. Are these great sums of wealth no property? If they are property, to whom do they belong? If they belong to any body, can they be transferred by laws and charters, under a policy, which considers property as sacred?

This plain fact enables us to compare accurately, our system of monopolized and transmissible credit, with a system of monopolized and transmissible wisdom. By this comparison it will be divulged, that the pecuniary oppression of privileged credit, is far greater than that of privileged wisdom; and hence it is a just inference, that its avarice is also greater. Avarice breeds the treacheries of privilege against liberty. Unprivileged or national wisdom is its friend, because such wisdom can see no object to betray, for the gratification of avarice or ambition; privileged or corporation wisdom is its foe, because the species of wisdom can see such an object. We will select an expensive system of monopolized wisdom, to illustrate these ideas. The king of England receives for his wisdom, one million of pounds sterling, equivalent to the annual labour of fifty thousand men. The labour of fifty thousand men, is equivalent to the subsistence of two hundred thousand people. For the subsistence of two hundred thousand people, this man renders the 'publick service' of a king, and pays also the salaries of sundry other publick servants. His exclusive emolument therefore, however exorbitant, is within the principle of the constitutions lately quoted. The banks in the United States receive for their credit, at least five millions of dollars annually, equal to one million one hundred and twenty-five thousand pounds sterling; to the annual labour of fifty-six thousand five hundred working men; and to the subsistence of two hundred and twenty-five thousand people. They are neither publick servants, nor do they pay the salaries of publick servants. Confining the payers for the king's wisdom to Britain, the expense is divided among twelve millions, and extending the computation to all his dominions, it may possibly reach to twenty. Therefore the proportion of subsistence drawn by the king's privileged and monopolized wisdom from labour in England, is less than that drawn from labour by privileged and monopolized credit in America.

When we behold an honest indignation against the system of privileged and monopolized wisdom, and an honest approbation of the system of privileged and monopolized credit, existing in the same mind, why should we be proud of the human intellect?

The pecuniary sufferings of nations from banking may be exhibited with some accuracy by figures, and though figures cannot exhibit its drafts upon their political principles, we may conclude with almost equal certainty, that a separate factitious interest, will not preserve a free government in America, because it has never done so in any other country. Monopoly, like other evils, takes refuge under some good. It attempts to include within its scope, the acquisitions of talents and industry, and to confound them with those of legal fraud; and to consider private property, roads and canals, whence arise good effects, as of the same nature with hierarchy, nobility, banks, or any species of legal separate interest, though productive only of political oppression or pecuniary fraud.

Admitting private property, however incorrectly, to be a species of monopoly, its effects, such as subsistence, comfort, and a multitude of physical benefits, draw a distinct line between it and the fraud or force of hierarchical and feudal usurpations. These, instead of possessing a common nature with private property, diminish or defeat its benefits.

Government, considered as a monopoly, has also been called a necessary evil, because it has been almost universally planted in its evil and not in its good qualities. A monopoly is erected, calculated to awaken the avarice and ambition of its members; these evil qualities are accordingly awakened; they resort to force and fraud for their own gratification; and such monopolies beget the civil tyranny, denominated a necessary evil.

But as private property may be planted in the good or in the evil qualities of monopoly, so may a government; by banishing fraud or force, as means of acquiring private property, its protection begets beneficial effects; and by forbearing to excite avarice and ambition by fraudulent laws and separate interests, government will produce human happiness and comfort, and be considered as a necessary good.

It has been our policy, so to divide power, and diminish the excitements of avarice and ambition, as to wring out of its soul the poisons arising from the evil qualities of monopoly; laws to foster these qualities, labour to revive what that policy labours to destroy.

If monopoly is made up of good and evil qualities; and if our policy has planted our government in its good qualities, a revolution is effected by transplanting it into its evil qualities. The constitutional corporation is endeavoured to be cleansed of avarice and ambition, the scourges of mankind; and legal corporations, having the first, which begets the other, breathed into them, as their vital principle, cannot constitute the same species of government.

These inimical principles cannot in nature subsist together; one must subdue, reform or contaminate the other. In England a paper system has contaminated the government; here, the only argument which can be urged against the same process and result, is, that the pure principles of our constitutional corporations, will reform the vicious principles of our legal corporations, created by themselves.

Towards this experiment, the constitutional and legal corporations are mixed up together. The constitutions and laws then begin to solicit the suffrages of this compound. 'Adhere to us,' say the constitutions, 'and we will take care that neither your ambition nor avarice shall be gratified.' 'Come over to us,' say the laws, 'and we will gratify both.' Will the audience make a separate interest, which bestows on it exclusive wealth and power, subservient to the general interest, which rigidly refuses to feed it with either?

If it is a moral truth, that mankind prefer themselves to others, then it is a moral certainty, that members, both of the government and of the corporation, will prefer the interest of the corporation to the interest of the nation. As a member of the government, I am met constantly by division and responsibility; the money I collect from the people, must be accounted for and applied to their use; and both my power and compensation is dependent on their will. As a member of the separate interest, I tax without limitation; I receive without account; I apply to my own use; I am dependent only on my own pleasure; and I acquire the power following wealth, unsubjected to the publick suffrage. By taking the side of my own interest, I influence the government in my own favour. By taking the side of the national interest, I sacrifice my own. As all separate interests prefer themselves, and bend governments into a subserviency to their designs; so one neither responsible, nor weakened by division, nor made up of distinct independent interests, by means of different departments and unconnected offices; will act with a degree of concert and force, for its own aggrandizement, which would be impracticable to the several governments in America. The banking power is therefore a stronger, as well as a richer power, than the civil. The holders of both will use the latter as an ally of the former; the two powers will unite in one, and all the checks invented to control the civil power, will be silently lost in the illimitable influence of the stock power. A power of regulating property is engendered, of a capacity to enslave nations surpassing a power to regulate the press, as far as an influence over a whole nation, or great factions, exceeds one over a poor author.

There is no occasion that one should be a political Linnæus, to discover the class of political systems, to which orders or separate interests belong. When such influence a government, publick opinion cannot also influence it. They do not belong to that class of political systems, which they destroy. Their essence is minority, and their principles must participate of their essence; and if it is good government to consult the national interest, they must uniformly be opposed to good government, because they constantly consult their own interest.

Without closely estimating the political influence of the species of separate interest called banking, we can at a glance discover, that a power to give and receive charters, to draw wealth from the people, and to share in it, and to obtain adherents at the publick expense, is a great power. It is that which I have called legislative patronage.

This excessive power, like all others, will act upon the moral qualities of human nature. Its pecuniary seductiveness, is exactly opposed to the policy, supposed by all our constitutions to be most likely to awaken the good moral qualities of human nature; and exactly such, as have constantly awakened its evil. Nations, resorting to elective and representative forms of government, consider a strict similitude between the interest of the legislature and of the people, as the chief security for fidelity. They have never divided these interests, by establishing a difference, to the extent of five millions annually, to be paid by the one, and received in money or power by the other: no free constitution has ever declared, that a legislator might legislate wealth to himself, and taxes to the people; and no man in his senses ever thinks of securing the honesty of an agent, by a powerful temptation to betray him. Even the king of England cannot himself pass a law, to inflict the million he receives; whilst the legislators of these states might receive the five millions they inflict by banking, and do receive a considerable portion of it. On the contrary, all our constitutions consider it as a sacred principle, that legislators should really, and not nominally, be affected by the good or evil dispensed by law, as the nation is affected. As a majority of a nation cannot be bankers, the opening of a subscription to all is a formality, the futility of which is demonstrable in the certain and necessary result of this formality. That, invariably places the legislator-stockholder in a minority. And of course he must be affected by every law which may affect stock; not as the nation are affected, but as this minority is affected. Executive patronage would become similar to legislative, if the president could both create offices, and bestow them on himself or his creatures, as the latter bestows charters.

Whenever legislatures, or men in power of any denomination, can receive charters, exclusive privileges or emoluments which they create, they will incline to make them good gifts. Accordingly, bank stock is so manufactured as to sell at an advance, often as high as fifty per centum. Thus a legislator who creates, subscribes for and sells stock, converts by his own legal magick, every dollar he can raise, into nine shillings. This is undoubtedly a good thing for himself; if a miracle can be performed, and if laws for enriching orders, without labour or industry of any kind, will enrich the rest of the people, then it may be a good thing also for his constituents.

If it is, let nations rejoice, and look for the speedy accomplishment of their hitherto frustrated hopes, that oppression would cease. It will be both useless and absurd, that avarice should any longer pursue its tyrannical measures, after a mode is discovered of gratifying its lust, without putting the rest of a nation to any expense. Still more wonderful is this discovery; better than costless; it is sold to enrich a nation, by enriching a paper interest. Oh happiness unlooked for! No longer remains then a motive for that mass of patronage and taxation, by which nations are enslaved. This beautiful system of banking enriches stockholders by dividends and the people by bank notes. Patronage is received and returned with mutual civility and profit. And avarice is at length converted into a blessing for industry.

Every word of this reverie must be credited, to justify banking. But although we may wish that it was as true as it is pleasant, yet it requires a very strong faith indeed to believe, that this political alchymy is less fraudulent than the chymical. One proposes to make gold out of something; the other out of nothing.

If England held all the bank stock of the union, the furnace of this new species of alchymy would burst, 'as if a bolt of thunder had been driven through' the states, and all its promises would vanish, 'in fumo,' not before the refined satire of Ben Jonson, but before common sense. It would be instantly seen, that England, the stockholder, was enriched by the dividends, and America taxed and impoverished by the notes. By filling the place of England with three or four thousand native and foreign stockholders, the place of the people is not altered. Such of them as are legislators, will vote upon political questions, exactly as England would, if she held our stock and could legislate for us. The ground which sustains this argument, is that upon which banking has spread from state to state; namely, that taxes, and not gold for publick benefit, are forged in the furnace of this new alchymy. Whether taxes are repealed by transferring their appropriation from A to B, from a foreign country to a native legislator, is left to the sagacity of the reader.

Patronage is an instrument by which governments corrupt a faction to take part with them against nations, and thus gradually acquire more power than the people ever gave. If this instrument is obtained by foreign conquest, as in the acquisition of India by England, the people still suffer by the unconstitutional power it confers; it is infinitely more calamitous to a nation, when gotten by domestick operations.

Had the governments of the United States, bestowed upon themselves and their partisans, offices to the value of five millions annually, the patronage would have been the same with that created by banking; which welds the corporation to the government, and the government to the corporation, against the people, like sinecure offices to the same amount. For this vast and boundless mode of acquiring power, there is no allowance in any constitution. It is a great weight, which was never thrown into the scales, by those who made them; can it be thrown in by law, and leave the division of power between a nation and its government, unaltered?

In another view, the patronage created by banking, spreads out in the United States, far beyond any influence capable of being produced, by creating offices of the value just mentioned. The general government may influence the whole fabrick, by means of a power to regulate the places of deposit of the general taxes, and by regulations as to the paper which may be received in payment. This influence may reach state legislatures as stockholders, and convert the best barrier devised by the principle of division, against usurpation and consolidation, into an insidious and secret instrument, for the ends it was intended to obstruct.

A slight interest is a bad mirror for reflecting justice, but a great one is a camera obscura inverting right and wrong. Through this medium, stockholding legislators will discover, that it is just to retain their annuities, by any compliances for which the people, not themselves, suffer; and a silent revolution, which will secure or increase these annuities, will appear to them to be necessary for the publick good.

Against this obvious danger, we are consoled by being told, that the separate banking interest, is not a titled order; that if titles were added to its wealth, our constitutions, like the walls of Jericho, would be overset by the noise; but that unless the aristocracy shall discover its progress by its shouts, they are safe.

On the contrary, a separate interest is more dangerous, if it can create, sustain and enrich itself without being designated, than if it cannot; if it assails by mine and sap, than if it assails by the sound of drums. If Lords could create and enrich Lords by law, the government would soon become a feudal aristocracy. If bishops could create and enrich bishops by law, the government would presently become an hierarchical aristocracy. So if stockholders can by law make and enrich stockholders, the government of course becomes a paper aristocracy. It was the title or badge of the hierarchical and feudal orders in England, which by designating the members, afforded the means of limiting their progress; and if either of these aristocracies could have possessed itself, unseen, of legislative power, it would have legislated itself into permanent tyranny. If our constitutions required that every stockholder should be clothed in a surplice, that he might be known and excluded from legislative power, or only allowed a portion of it, as belonging to a separate aristocratical interest, he would, like the lord or the bishop, be thereby rendered less dangerous. Thus checked or balanced, these orders are considered by republicans as a bad political system; unchecked or unbalanced, even monarchists allow them to be execrable; they admit of no control without a title or badge; and the paper interest is designated by neither.

That a separate untitled interest is more powerful and dangerous than a separate titled interest, is a fact so notorious as to supersede an occasion for argument. The untitled paper interest in England, has made prisoners of the two titled orders, uses them sometimes as clerks in its counting house, at others' as jackals to hunt its prey, and at all times to pronounce its will for law; this it has gradually effected, because it could act secretly; it is a warriour invisible to his adversary, or a conjurer invisible to the crowd he defrauds.

In the history of our forefathers, we recognise three political beasts, feeding at different periods upon their lives, liberties and properties. Those called hierarchical and feudal aristocracy, to say the worst of them, are now the instruments of the third. Protect us, Heaven! we exclaim, against these monsters, inert, subdued and far away from us! Oh what a beautiful creature is here! we add; upon beholding a whelp of the third, so strong as to have swam into our country across the Atlantic; and the infatuation concludes with a sincere commiseration of the people of England, on account of the misery with which they are loaded by the mother of this identical whelp. Our mistake in estimating titled nobility and paper stock, is exactly that of the mouse, terrified with the cock and charmed with the cat.

Representation ceases to be an effect of election, whenever a representative can draw wealth from his own laws, by means either of office, sinecure or monopoly. His income under the law, being greater than his expense, his interest is adverse to the interest of the people, who pay the tax or income which he receives. A power to take from a nation and give to itself, is a strict definition of civilized tyranny. A legislator cannot be guided by the interest, both of the minority and majority; of the exclusive and general interest; of the receiver and payer of the tax. He will be guided by the interest to which he belongs; if he is a receiver of the tax, he will tax.

Established banks exclaim that others would be pernicious; just as one established or chartered religion exclaims against chartering another; or as patricians disapproved of ennobling plebeians. But though the established bank contends that others would be pernicious, an application for a new bank, as loudly insists that the old one is a hateful monopoly, which a new one will destroy. Destroy in the same manner, as a noble order of fifty members would be destroyed, by creating fifty more, and as the oppression resulting from one titled sect, would be destroyed by titling another.

This falling out is managed with mutual embarrassment; the parties are obliged to conceal the true cause of quarrel, and to put it upon the ground of partialities to individuals in loans of bank currency. As if the new bank was not as capable of partiality as the old. The evil of bestowing on the quality, partiality, the distribution of national currency, is proposed to be remedied, by extending the power of partiality. Not this partiality, but the dividends or tax, is the real object of dispute. The old bank knows that its paper is a tax, subject, like other taxes, to the limitation of national ability, and it wishes to exhaust this ability itself; but the proposed bank wishes to come in for a share of it; yet neither, even when under the obligation of legislative responsibility, is ever heard to make to the people these honest confessions.

This true ground of quarrel between established and proposed banks, confesses the correctness of the opinion, which supposes that funded stock and bank stock, are both national debt; and that interest and dividends are both paid by taxing the nation. By new stock, the evil in both cases is cured in the same way. So long as national ability to pay interest or dividends suffices to meet the new stock, it is an additional tax upon that ability; whenever either species of stock exceeds this ability, either will depreciate. Both, therefore, equally imply a debtor and creditor. But in a legislature made up of old stockholders, and intended stockholders, such an idea of the subject will be suppressed, and a compromise effected between the parties upon selfish grounds, not upon principles of national interest.

It is easy to comprehend the possibility of a form of government, capable of being correctly denominated, an elective aristocracy; and to predict, without much foresight, that the decay of the principles of our policy, will commence with that form. It is produced by whatever will defeat an honest and faithful sympathy between a nation and its representatives. Such a case is illustrated by the house of commons of England. That house gains a power by its paper system, which is able to proclaim its corruption, and to defy reform. Such a case is the natural offspring of an union between an elective legislature and a separate interest. Can a stronger cement for this union than banking be discovered? It gratifies the avarice and ambition of the confederates, without expelling from the senate house, disclosing acquisitions, or attracting punishment.

The division of powers is an essential quality of our policy and constitutions. That between the people and the government is destroyed, by a power in the government to increase its share, by its own laws; as is that also between the general and state governments, if either distributee can increase its quota of power by law. By banks, governments may create factions, which will adhere to them against the people, or to one section of our policy, against another. With these instruments, the general or state governments might disorder the distribution of power between themselves and the people, and between each other. To both, enlistments by lucrative charters will furnish mercenary troops, and mercenary troops, wielding either stock or swords were never considered as good guardians of liberty. Charters and banks will become the chief objects of state legislation, and if twenty legislatures can outstrip one in this manufacture, the general government may lose its power, and the calamities of a dissolved union will follow. These will ravage the states, until they ripen the publick mind for the introduction of a steady tyranny by some military adventurer; and the catastrophe of the drama will be the effect of exchanging our system of genuine representation, cautious division, and effectual responsibility, for the monopoly and corruption of a system of banking, charters and paper.

There is utility in these baleful auguries. They may induce the nation to examine omens, and enable it to defeat fulfilment. They deserve in this view, all the indulgence of honest intention.

States may see an advantage in excluding the currency of banks created by Congress. Large states may exclude that of small. Exclusions of this kind will enhance the value of state stock. This will be just, because no equality in the profit made by bank paper, can exist between states of an unequal size, with an equal and unlimited right to send out this tax-gatherer. The collections under the laws of each state, ought at least to correspond with the domestick fields for circulation. The same reason which induces a large state to emit rival paper, may induce it to expel rivalry from its own dominion. It would be evidently unjust that Delaware should be enriched by taxing the union with a mass of bank paper; therefore it will be prevented. The bank tax of Virginia, has the same motive for driving away any interloping bank tax, as for introducing itself; money will be made by it. Cannot you discern, reader, stuff for weaving a tissue of avarice, ambition, rivalry and hatred, which has no ingredient for allaying human passions, restraining human vices or preventing human slaughter? View it steadily, and you will behold our inestimable state governments, shrinking into charter traders; and contriving paper navigation acts to plunder or repel plunder, by means of paper currency, with the same spirit and intention in regard to other states, which the trade navigation act of England breathes, in regard to other countries.

To avoid these calamities, our hope rests upon the moderation of charter and monopoly. The extent of this moderation, is equivalent to that exhibited by the invocation, required of their subjects by Persian monarchs. Charters command their subjects to exclaim, 'Oh monopoly! live as long as the law pleases.' If the law can bestow existence for one year, it may for a million. It may give perpetual life to whatever metaphysical being it can create; and charter is so moderate, as to claim a right to live out the whole life allowed by law. Once created, it pretends to independence of its God, law; to independence of law's God, constitution; and to independence of constitution's God, the nation.

These pretensions are not extravagant; for if a government is so contrived, as that its members can take the charters which they make, these charters will live as long as the government lives. A maker of laws, to enrich himself, which cannot be repealed, is a far greater power than a maker of constitutions. Constitutions are tenants at will; the tenure of charters is not even limited by good behaviour, or liable to be annulled by impeachment and conviction of treason. A legislator, by charters here, and charters there, can so wedge up present or future ages, that the long possession of these tenants for years will become a settled right, and the remainder-man will forget his reversion.

A power to make irrepealable law charters, is above responsibility, and independent of its constituent. The correction of a corrupt or ruinous measure, comprises all the essence and benefit of responsibility. A change of representatives, without this correction, is a barren formality. It is even impolitick, unless followed by a correction of the mischief which suggested the change. New representatives will be incited by the preservation of a pecuniary abuse, to repeat it for their own emolument; if they are not permitted to destroy it, they will think it right to reimburse themselves by a new charter, for their sufferings under the old.

The infatuation opposed to the reasoning, which discloses the destruction of responsibility and legislative integrity, lurking in the system of charter and banking, is an unexamined idea, that our constitutions contain some charm, some magical influence, which will preserve liberty, by the agency of avaricious charter-making and charter-taking representatives. History produces no instance of national happiness, under a legislator, corrupted by the most sordid passion, of which human nature is susceptible. Legislative purity might preserve liberty and happiness, under constitutions otherwise defective; but the most perfect constitutions otherwise, could not preserve liberty and happiness, with legislative corruption.

In all ages legal beings have been invented, which contend that man was made for them, and not they for him. Having both escaped from his service, and converted him into their servant, they invest themselves with a drapery of glittering fictions, to dazzle him into submission. Hierarchy, though always defended by whatever could inspire reverence, and often dressed in the robes of religion, has at length fallen before the solid principle, 'that civil institutions belong to nations and that nations do not belong to civil institutions;' whilst avarice presumes to assert the reverse of this doctrine, which religion was unable to defend. It pretends that man was created for law charters, tho' not for law churches; and that it is equally a sacrilege to discontinue the former, as to revive the latter. Thus parties and factions measure their principles by their interest, and assert or deny the same proposition, like lawyers for fees. Hence they censure their predecessors for obtaining wealth, in modes which they use themselves, and pretend to be guided by different principles, whilst they worship at the same shrine. Just as a Pope, had the conversion of Rome to christianity failed, would have become the high priest of Jupiter, and practised the idolatry he had loudly condemned, to increase his revenue, splendour and power. Or does this charter doctrine advance the designs of the leaders of opposite parties, as a good revenue might have done those of the leaders of opposite religions?

The ability of a corrupt legislature to make a form of government or constitution worse, and finally to overturn it, is illustrated, not only in England, but in the history of Rome. Two of the means used by the patricians to effect this end, were usury and an usurpation of national conquests. Compound usury and an usurpation of national credit, are two of the means used by the system of banking. The dexterity of the present age, has sharpened the edges of these patrician weapons, and varnished and lengthened their blades, so as to dazzle and to strike a whole nation. The patricians enslaved individuals with usury; banking, nations. The patricians usurped and drew wealth from foreign conquests; banking usurps national credit, and draws wealth from domestick territory. The patricians by their means, gained wealth so slowly, that it required an operation of several centuries to corrupt and destroy the government; stock can collect wealth by credit so rapidly, as to shorten the process to a few years.

Five millions drawn annually from a nation itself by a separate interest, will with more certainty enervate and enslave it, than if the same sum was drawn from their conquered enemies; because toiling for others, and receiving the earnings of others without toil, is a double momentum towards these results; whereas a tribute paid by foreigners, as debasing only by luxury, and not by tyranny also, is a single one. Profit without labour, will be preferred to labour with loss. The effort of the best informed will be to get out of the nation into the separate interest, to avoid the labour with loss, and to gain the profit without labour.

Nations have for three thousand years been doomed to oppression, by an opinion that they had not capacity to govern themselves; are they doomed to suffer it for another three thousand years, from an opinion that they are unable to give themselves a paper currency, if it should be useful? In the first case, the nation is persuaded that it is a fool, but that a few individuals are wise; in the second, that it is a pauper, but that a few individuals are rich. The last idea is even ludicrous, as the sole object of banking is to tax a rich nation to enrich poor individuals.

After a patient trial of charter privilege and monopoly for three thousand years, almost at the moment they are rejected as poison to civil and religious liberty, we are told that they are wholesome aliment for commerce. It is not surprising that self-interest should tell us this; but it is, that self-interest should believe it, and recommence the fairest, most patient, and most expensive experiment which was ever made. After another tedious term of rueful experience, monopoly will again exclaim, that it confesses itself to be pernicious, when applied to commerce and credit, just as it now confesses the same thing, in relation to religion and civil power, but that in some new form it is a blessing; and the experiment ought then, with as much reason as now, to be recommenced.

It is to elude the discovery of its enmity to civil and religious liberty, that monopoly confesses the charge in its old forms, hoping under the candour of this confession, to get into operation in a new form. Admitted in the stupendous form of a paper currency, it becomes instantly connected with civil government, and civil and religious liberty is settled by experience, to be uniformly the victim of a connexion between a lucrative monopoly, and government in any form. It is not a new experiment, therefore, which we are trying. It is only charter and state instead of church and state. Even supposing the principle of monopoly can be introduced by banking without its infecting the civil government; the wisdom of planting some parts of our policy in a monopoly of civil rights, and others in their freedom, is still questionable. These principles are irreconcilable enemies. Mr. Adams's history of orders abundantly proves that they are never found in the same community, but in a state of war; and that the war never terminates, but in a victory on the side of one of the combatants.

If it would be dangerous to republican government, for the President to make officers of monarchists, is it safe for legislatures to make monarchists of citizens by debt and bank stock, or by any species of monopoly? Republicans, turned into kings, bishops, lords or stockholders, are no longer republicans. Neither bishops nor bankers are exempted from the physiological qualities of man. Less than a million annually received by the officers of government, is supposed to expose them to the effect of these qualities, and excludes them from legislatures; five times as much received by bankers, is supposed to exempt them from the effect of the same qualities, and conducts them into legislatures, where they shield themselves from taxation; and from one exclusive privilege, extract another. Yet banking creates treasuries for usurpation; a division of wealth is a necessary auxiliary to a division of power; and an accumulation of the former, a stride towards rendering the latter useless. That it can also create treasuries for national defence, is the countervail urged in answer to this argument. And this countervail itself encourages the dissipation of governments; endows them with a dangerous degree of pecuniary independence of the nation; stakes the national safety upon the capriciousness and selfish views of every predominant party; involves the necessity of nurturing at the general expense a minor interest, and terminates in the state of England. The quackery of defending nations by banking, is a mine of wealth to an order of bankers, as the quackery of defending them by feudal tenures, was to the order of nobles. Give us all the land, said the feudal barons, and we will defend you. Give us all the money and credit, say the bankers, and we will do it. In both cases, nations pay the hire, and do the work themselves. Just as the quackery of salvation was a mine of wealth to the priesthood, and purchased nothing for the laity. What mystery can be more absurd, than the doctrine that an entire nation cannot defend itself, but that it can be defended, by the device of converting a few of its members into bankers?

Mr. Adams asserts, and republicans admit, that a policy which confers civil power on one separate interest, is more imperfect than one which divides it among three. It is better to have no predominant separate interest, or more than one. None is freedom, one is tyranny, and several may be a mixture of both. If the king and the house of commons, were cut out of the English government, the nobility would be tyrants. By aggrandizing the nobility with a certain degree of wealth, the king and the house of commons would be nearly or entirely expunged from the English form of government. By aggrandizing a banking interest co-extensively, the same result ensues. The history of feudal barons and religious titularies proves, that wealth, and not title, conveys power.

Election advances and rivets the power of a wealthy order. In England, election, so far from producing an order or interest to counterpoise the stock order or interest, produces the most effective instrument for advancing its wealth at the expense of the nation. Could any better means have been devised for increasing the income of the stock order, than a house of commons? If the eligibility of the king or the nobles to the house of commons, would have destroyed the theory of checks and balances, although these interests might be avoided by the people in elections; we cannot fail to discern the reason, why the eligibility of the stock interest to that house, (which cannot be avoided by the people) converts it into an instrument for effecting, what it was intended to prevent; namely, the predominance of a separate interest over the national interest. Is a corruption, poisonous to the British theory, salutary to the American?

Though an order or distinct interest is compounded of many members, it constitutes only one body, guided by self-interest. Whenever in a combat between two men, a leg or an arm of one shall desert to the other, then a member of the stock interest may be expected to desert to the national interest. Add to the cement of wealth a mass of political power, gotten by election, and a Colossus rises up, animated by one mind, who easily makes the havock of the national interest required by his own, because its members are never united by one mind, and lie about, so scattered and dis-jointed, that he picks up and uses them as weapons for assailing the body they belong to. The capacity of a paper interest in England, to make instruments of orators, kings, lords and commons, evinces its gigantick power.

What! exclaims both the friend and the foe, to publick good; shall we have no corporations, no colleges, no turnpikes, no canals; because they are separate interests? Do not charter and privilege strew the face of a country with palaces and plenty? Yes, and with huts and penury.

With equal propriety it might be asked, if we can have no magistrates, unless these magistrates are kings or nobles? The assertion that these beget liberty, made by the admirers of mon-archy, is equivalent to the assertion, that paper orders beget national prosperity, made by the lovers of stock. As the first is asserted of the most inveterate enemies to liberty, the other is asserted of an inveterate enemy to property. Magistrates may be so moulded as to turn out despots: charters, as to turn out thieves; oppression, under pretence of protecting; and fraud, under pre-tence of enriching, are not novelties. Magistrates and separate interests, moulded to advance the publick good, are blessings; but for gratifying ambition or avarice, are curses.

Although the king of England has but few domains, yet the English civil power, is that generated by a rich government and a poor people; whilst the reverse is superficially the case. The phenomenon is resolved by considering the power carried by wealth to the paper, patronage and church separate interests, as given by the government to itself, at the expense of the people; and demonstrates by experiment a mode of usurpation. Walpole strengthened the English government by stock and taxes. Five millions annual income to bank stockholders, create a more alarm-ing degree of power, than if the five millions had been given to one man; it makes a multitude ardent in the cause of fraud and oppres-sion, instead of one; therefore Walpole, to strengthen a king, made a faction by stock, in preference to enriching the king himself. If our government (including the state sections of it) had given five or six millions annually to itself, every man would have per-ceived its accession of power; but when it dispenses the same sum in the mode thought by Walpole to obtain the most power, the

K*   297

accession is hardly seen by any, and is utterly imperceptible to the receivers.

It being unquestionably true, that an organization of property by law, is equivalent to an organization of power by law, as Mr. Adams and Lord Shaftesbury assert, it follows, either that the governments of the United States have not a right to exercise the first, or that they have a right to exercise the second. If it is not our policy that a government can increase its own power by its own will, and if laws for enriching factitious interests will increase its power, by bribing partisans, such laws are subversive of our policy.

This indirect mode of stealing power from nations, compensates them with vices for the wealth it purloins. It corrupts a passion to which mankind are indebted for the most perfect state of society, and its blessings, namely, a love of property. In either extreme, like many other passions necessary to our happiness, it becomes pernicious. Enthusiastick philosophers, falling into one, by attempting to eradicate a love of property, have laid the axe to the root of society. Such attempts, though always unsuccessful, are always mischievous. By covering a love of property with odium, it unfits inexperienced young men for an association, of which this love is the chief ligament. By depreciating the motive of the sanction, the sanction itself is weakened. Accordingly, having rooted out a love of property from the mind, law and contracts lose their influence, and a community of goods, unsuccessfully attempted even by religious zeal, terminates philosophical fanaticism. Before the catastrophe arrives, pecuniary distress, begotten by a contempt of property, prevents men from being good, and is active in forming bad citizens; and not unfrequently converts a metaphysical saint, into a practical devil. He arraigns justice of avarice; he adjudges it to be sordid and base in a creditor to demand payment; he breaks contracts, because they are to be fulfilled by money; and as most civil rights are measured by money, he tramples upon most. His theory being repugnant to the principles of society, he violates them at every step; he cannot live by rules he hates and breaks; and he is gradually moulded by the bitter expiations to which he has condemned himself by a contempt of property, into a malignant misanthrope, an abandoned scoundrel, or an unprincipled and ferocious demagogue. He who dissipates his property, dissipates also his virtue and honour.

This extreme however is so far outstript by its opposite, in generating human misery, that language recoils from the horrour of a just description. Separate interests, goaded on by an avarice, awakened by unjust laws, and rendered unconscious of guilt, by the sanction of the statute book, have filled the old world with crimes, and perverted the primitive end of society to secure property, by making it the instrument for its invasion. Is the new world destined to copy this old process, and suffer its dispensations?

This essay has been written for the purpose of inquiring by what interest mankind ought to be governed, natural and general, or artificial and particular. It considers industry, effort and talents, as constituting the first class, and law and charters, for enriching individuals or factions, as constituting the second. Without pursuing the details to which the subject would lead, it has selected a few of the latter, to illustrate its reasoning, but not as containing a history or exhibition of the whole class of artificial and particular interests, by which mankind have been oppressed. In this selection, feudal, hierarchical and stock, are the particular interests, of whose history most use has been made, as they have succeeded each other in England. The stock tyrant, the present metropolitan of the benefice called Britain, is said to be fair and just, because those who chose to do so, might subscribe to banks or loans. To the arguments used in another place for detecting this fallacy, the following are added. The mode by which a tyrant succeeds to his tyranny, cannot convert oppression into justice. If offices, productive of mischief to a nation, were like bank shares exposed to sale, could the purchasers justify the mischief, by urging, that any one who had money, might have purchased? Several Romans purchased the empire. Could they justify a right to tyrannize, because any other person, rich enough, might have also purchased? Could a lottery for distributing the titles and privileges of an aristocratick nobility be fair, because all those of a nation able to pay for them, might buy tickets? Did the neighing of Darius's horse make his government legitimate, because seven persons possessed tickets in the lottery, or would it have been legitimate, if seven thousand had shared in the chance?

Among the instruments of oppression, the hereditary are most excusable and least oppressive, and those bought the least excusable and most oppressive. The former are thrust by birth into tyranny; the latter purchase it with a deliberate malice against justice and liberty. The mischiefs of the hereditary tyrant are limited by his physical imbecilities; those of a bought separate interest, are extended by a boundless moral energy. If a title by birth, by lot or by purchase, would not have justified or softened the tyranny of a Tiberius, a Caligula, or a Nero, how can a title by either justify or soften the tyranny of the more lasting and extended feudal, hierarchical or stock tyranny?

One tyrant may thank God that he is not another tyrant. Banking may say that it is not a hierarchy or noble order. It will admit that charters for establishing such orders are criminal, and contend for the innocence of its own; just as the nobility and bishops of France, once held mercantile charters in the highest contempt, and their own in the highest respect. When Europe was torn to pieces by the principle of bestowing exclusive wealth and privileges on religious sects, each sect contended that the remedy for the evil, lay in its own possession of this wealth and these privileges. It was found however by the United States, to lie in the abrogation of them all. Mr. Adams's book, by changing a few names, might be easily converted from a system for balancing civil orders against each other, into one for balancing religious sects in the same way; and when the most powerful of these sects, were intriguing, fighting and negociating to find out this balance of wealth and power among themselves, those who expected to gain by the doctrine, would allow it to be classical. The balance of religious sects, however, could never be found, and the privileges bestowed upon them by law, charter or treaty, were only apples of discord thrown into society. Such apples are the privileges of civil sects. These inflame the zeal for wealth, as those did the zeal for religion. The former zeal burns now, as did the latter some centuries past; and civil privileged sects will regard the publick happiness, as religious did then. The principle, universally agreed in the United States to be inconsistent with religious happiness, cannot advance civil. On the contrary, civil privileges are likely to produce religious misery, as religious privileges have produced civil misery, and we must probably have both privileged, civil and religious sects, or neither.

Wealth, religion and truth, as by law established, compound a political system, of strict Athanasian orthodoxy; it does not contain three principles, but only one. And wealth, religion and truth, established by industry, conscience and free inquiry, is the opposite system, founded also in one principle.

Wealth, established by law, violates the principle, which induced the American states to wage war with Britain. It separates the imposer from the payer of taxes. No nation would tax itself to enrich an order or separate interest. When therefore a nation is so taxed, it must proceed from the power of the order itself, which is invariably the imposer and receiver of the tax; whilst the rest of the nation is the payer.

No interest, whose acquisitions are the effect of law, and not of labour, can pay any portion of a tax. Publick officers, who receive salaries, pay no taxes, and therefore are not allowed to impose them. If one half of these salaries were taken from them by the name of a tax, they would neither be taxed, nor entitled upon that ground to participate in the imposition of taxes; because the law only resumes what it gave, and takes nothing which it did not give; it would only be a diminution of salary for services. In like manner, bankers ought not to inflict the payment of the wealth they extract, and if this wealth given by law, was resumed by law, it would only be a cessation of a naked benevolence; and a worse ground for claiming a right to impose taxes, than a diminution of a salary for services.

Mankind are united by the necessity for subsistence in a common interest. Those who furnish the subsistence, pay all the taxes. As subsistence flows from the earth, that may be called the mother of men, liable to make all the disbursements they need. Hence, all, or nearly all taxes, must be ultimately paid by agriculture, and ought of course to be inflicted by her, if the doctrine is true, that the payer is the only just imposer of taxes. Agriculture cannot be partial, because she cannot shift the tax from her own shoulders. From her other interests diverge, like rays from the sun, but she is the centre of them all. If one of these rays usurps from the parent sun, the distribution of his light, it may be induced to darken another, for the purpose of increasing the splendour of its own; as a child who makes the will of a parent, disinherits his brethren for his own advantage. And so legislation flowing from, or influenced by any particular interest, in whatever form, has never failed to rob other interests.

Perhaps no separate interest would constitute a less exceptionable legislator, than commerce, on account of its close connexion with agriculture and manufactures; and yet, without considering the complicated means she could practise, to make other interests, and even that of agriculture, subservient to hers; a simple power of converting all other interests into insurers of her adventures, giving them the losses, and keeping herself the profits, would be sufficiently tyrannical.

BANKING

If commerce would be the least exceptionable separate interest, as a legislator, or as influencing legislation, because of her connexion with agriculture and manufactures, paper stock must be the most exceptionable, because it has no connexion with either. It is not one of those rays diverging from the sun, or one of those interests arising from the earth, capable of being softened by the affinities of a common ancestor. Belonging to the family of cunning, it is inexorable to the family of the earth, and favorable to its own relations. These two families, in all their branches, are natural enemies. Whenever any member of the family of artificial interests gets into the camp of the other family, it lets in its comrades, and plunders to the uttermost. Among them, paper stock has been most conspicuous for such feats. In England, it has allied itself with its kindred, gotten into the camp, and plundered the nation in the last century beyond the magnifying conception of lunacy itself. Above ten hundred millions of pounds sterling are now supposed to be due to loan and bank stock, to which the payments made during a century must be added, to find the amount of which the family of the earth, has been stript by the family of law. In the United States, speculation, as it was called, bought of the family of the earth an hundred millions at one shilling in the pound, and then compelled it to re-purchase it at twenty. This family of the law soon disclosed its affection for its relations, monarchy and aristocracy. Here too bank stock is already annually extracting from the family of the earth, of labour and of property, five times as much as the civil government of the United States costs. Already, like the ancient hierarchy, it pretends that to tax it would be sacrilege. And already, like a tyrant preparing punishment for treason, it has proposed to inflict death upon forgery, where the system of mildness has been carried so far, as to subject murder in the second degree to imprisonment only. Fear for its wealth will induce this branch, like all of the same race, to let in its kindred.

The revival of the charter of the bank of the United States, was denied upon the ground of the political power conveyed by bank stock to the subjects of England; and the highest authority declared in this denial, that less than ten millions of it would invest foreigners with a pernicious portion of such power. Natives will derive still more power from stock, because their whole mass of social rights are enlisted as its ally and partisan. There is no provision in our constitutions, for a legislative conveyance of power by bank stock, either to citizens or foreigners. This decision, and the talents which

302

produced it, proclaimed, that bank stock conveys political power. It proclaimed, that less than ten millions of it made a few foreigners, under all the disadvantages of that character, dangerous; but the same authority is silent as to the danger to be apprehended from an hundred millions of bank stock, in the hands of people to whom every branch of the government is open. The United States bank stock held by the English possessed the usual transferable quality, but no one contended that this quality was any security against the pernicious political power annexed to bank stock. If the United States had originally created a government of bank stock, and annexed the entire political power to an hundred millions or any other amount of it, a transferable quality in this stock, would not have expunged the aristocratical qualities of such a government. Had A assigned a share of this stock to B, the latter would have occupied the place of the former in this government, just as a feudal son did that of his dead father. Nor is a transfer of the power annexed to bank stock, from one citizen to another, a better security against that power, than was a transfer of the stock of the . United States' bank, from one Englishman to another, against the political power derived from stock by Englishmen.

The similitude between a stock and a feudal aristocracy is perfect. Money is made the basis of political power in one; land, in the other. The power is not annexed to money in general, but to a portion of it, moulded by law into stock; as in the feudal form it is not annexed to land in general, but to a portion of it, moulded by law into lordships. Those having money but no stock, are excluded from political power in a stock aristocracy; as those are, having land but no seigniory, in a feudal one. In both, though money and land possess the same intrinsick value by whomsoever held, portions of each are by the artifice of law, made more valuable than other portions naturally of the same value; and of course more powerful. This identical essence of monopoly, and sole cause of aristocracy, is the same in both cases. If there are two portions of people, each possessing a million of dollars, and one has its money converted by charter into stock, whilst the same favour is refused to the other; the difference between them as to social influence, power or rights, though less visible, is really the same, as between the same portions possessing an equal quantity of land, after the lands of one portion are moulded by law into lordships, whilst no favour is granted to those of the other. However such monopolies may be decorated by the trappings of ingenuity, the artifices of fraud, or the oblations of folly, both exhibit the simple case of endowing by law a selected portion of property, either money or land, with a better income and more social power, than is derived by its holders from a far greater portion of both, not so endowed.

This argument suffers no injury from the consideration, that our constitutions have not expressly annexed political power to bank stock; because, if it naturally imbibes political power, such indirect acquisitions derived from ordinary and not conventional legislation, however tortured, can never be reconciled with the policy of the United States, if it is founded in good, just and equal moral or political principles; as to that, the difference between the treason of the sword or of the pen by which it is destroyed, will merely consist in the degrees of pain inflicted by the respective operations. Banking has only appeared to any extent in Genoa, Venice, Holland and England. Does it bring its letters of recommendation from these monarchies or aristocracies, because it has homogeneously coalesced with them? Yet, these experiments, by disclosing the fatal truth, that banking could enrich an order, awakened an order here to be enriched. It advertised itself as a talisman against poverty, and obtained proselytes both of clergy and laity, or of those to whom its promises were truths, and of those to whom they were falsehoods. Fraud ever promises riches in heaven or upon earth, and hence it has been necessary in this essay to trace it through the chief forms it has assumed, in the first, the second and third ages, to shew the innate similitude of these forms to each other, and the inconsistency of all, with the civil policy of the United States. The subject ought to be fairly explained, that the nation may judge whether monopoly shall destroy its constitutional principles, or these principles, monopoly. If circumstances propelled the United States, like France, into a form of government too free or too honest for the national character; or if the wages of banking, like the pay of armies, have already moulded our legislatures into mercenary troops, it may be best to avoid an unavailing contest by a tacit submission; but if a publick exists in the United States, able to sustain a publick interest, a greater quantity of human happiness will be produced, by preferring that interest, to a monopoly in the hands of a very few.

This essay does not aspire to the honour of proposing a new political system. It only endeavours to ascertain the principles of old ones, and to shew that the publick will and publick interest, and an exclusive will and an artificial interest, cannot possibly constitute a governing power, in union. That these moral beings, are the only natural political enemies capable of existing, and are doomed by the author of human nature to eternal warfare. That no artificial balance can appease this eternal hostility, any more than it could reconcile good and evil. That hence, and not from a defective balance, Mr. Adams has never been able to find these opposite principles quietly poising each other. And that the United States, by creating a pecuniary separate interest, capable of entering the list with publick interest, have proclaimed a warfare precisely of that nature, which has demolished human liberty universally. In this age of avarice, a nation which creates paper stock and monied monopoly, but guards itself against feudal tenures, secures its liberty as wisely, as one would have done in the fourteenth century, by creating feudal tenures, and guarding itself against paper stock.

The gross and humiliating delusion by which banking lives, is 'that the family of industry, are enriched by the idle family of artifice.' England displays the profound wisdom of land and labour in outwitting stock, in this trial of skill. Stock now receives from them nearly double the amount of the whole price of all the exported labour of the nation; that is about forty millions, for enhancing the value of its exported labour, which sells for twenty. The United States will not yet supply us with this perfect demonstration, but the progress towards the same point has been as rapid as was the progress of England, from the commencement of her stock career. In debt and bank stock we only pay about ten millions of dollars annually, to obtain the enhancement of price or value, which we are taught to expect from stock, on about forty millions worth of exported labour. If stock benefits land and labour, then it is a misfortune to us only to pay it twenty-five per centum on our exports, and we ought immediately to create a sufficient quantity to acquire the English blessing of paying it two hundred. An exact statistical knowledge of the enemy's country, being disclosed by the unerring medium of figures, we must resort to fate to account for the blindness of mankind.

All separate factitious interests pretend that they benefit nations in some mode, too intricate to be investigated by the mass of mankind. Thus hierarchies and noble orders yet retain a spacious existence. Of all such pretences, banking resorts to the least intricate. It gravely tells nations that it enriches them by taking their money; that by emptying a quart bottle of half its contents, the residue will become three pints. If a nation possessed a certain quantity of bread, would it be increased by depositing it in the hands of a corporation, and paying ten per centum for receiving the residue on the credit of the corporation bread notes? Would an annual deduction of one tenth part of the bread, increase the quantity, and make the nation more secure against famine? Will an annual appropriation of one tenth of its money to the use of a similar corporation, increase its wealth and secure a nation against poverty? The first species of fraud would be reprobated with universal indignation; the second is deliberately practised. Is the belly wiser than the head? A monopoly of money reaches all human wants, comforts, luxuries and passions. Every oppressive government is produced by some of the progeny of monopoly. If an individual of this family, has too often enabled tyrants to oppress nations, can the genus, covering, corrupting and commanding the whole species, enrich them?

If the monopoly of banking will rob a nation of its liberty, by corrupting or usurping the government, it is almost superfluous to prove, that it will rob it of its property also; because every separate interest acquiring one, has uniformly gotten the other. To the latter inquiry we shall however more particularly advert, since the pecuniary effects of banking will admit of reasoning so nearly connected with figures, as to exhibit mathematical certainty. The truth or errour of the assertion, 'that banks add to the price or value of the product of labour,' is capable of being exhibited to the eye.

The reader will recollect the difference between price and value. Local price will settle its own level, in relation to local currency. If the price of agricultural products, consumed at home, had been increased by banking, home manufactures so consumed, would have experienced a proportional increase. No species of labour, will suffer itself to be sacrificed by bank currency, for the benefit of another. Each will compensate itself, by enhancing its price up to its natural level. If therefore bank paper could produce local disorders, in the balance of labour against labour, the effect could not be permanent; and a re-adjustment of the level of price, would place the several departments of labour in the same relative situation, as to value, even if the price of each had been doubled. To disarrange the natural relation between the value of labour, ascertained by fair competition, would wickedly oppress, unfairly to enrich; and damp the spirit of industry. And an advancement of the price of labour, pari passu, would produce neither gain nor loss. It follows, that if bank paper did advance prices, nothing would be gained by a nation, in regard to its domestick commerce; and of course, that it can gain nothing by banking, except through the medium of its exported labour.

All the ground therefore upon which banking can operate, as to an increase of value, lies between the domestick and foreign price of exported labour. If wheat is worth eight shillings here, and ten shillings in the foreign market, the influence of bank currency upon the price of wheat, would be limited to two shillings. Beyond these confines, its power to enhance price by exciting competition, cannot extend; and therefore an enhancement within this narrow restriction, comprises the entire retribution within the power of banking to make, for the revenue it extracts.

Supposing there exist banks in the United States, operating upon a capital, real or imaginary, of fifty millions of dollars, and receiving a revenue, including dividends, perquisites and expenses, of ten per centum, or five millions annually; this five millions is the sum paid by the United States, for the supposed benefit of having the price of exportable labour enhanced within the limitations just stated. We have before proved that an evil and not a benefit, is conferred on a country, by disordering or raising the prices of labour consumed at home.

Supposing the exportable labour of the United States, to be forty millions annually, then they pay five millions or twelve and an half per centum to banks, upon the total of the subject, the real value of which can possibly be effected by banking; and if the difference between the value of this subject, here and abroad, should not amount to twelve and an half per centum, as is generally the case, it is evident, that a pecuniary loss results to a nation b banking, because the price paid for it, exceeds any possible enhancement of value within its power.

Out of the same fund, that is, the difference in a specie value, between the price of exported labour here and abroad, the whole amount of mercantile profit is to be taken; because competition cannot be so excited by banking, as to destroy this profit, without destroying commerce; nor is it conceivable that mercantile calculation could be so deceived, as ardently to patronise a system productive of such a consequence. If this mercantile profit amounts also to twelve and an half per centum on exported labour, it raises the deduction under a bank currency, upon forty millions of this subject, to twenty-five per centum, or ten millions annually. From this expense, there is no deduction pretended, except the enhancement of value by exciting mercantile competition. To reimburse it, banking, through this boasted competition, must save to the nation five millions annually, out of a mercantile profit of five. At whatever rate mercantile profit is computed, the advantage of mercantile competition must come out of this fund. Would an able calculator give six per centum for bank paper, if it was true that it deprived him of one, two, three, four or five millions annually, and bestowed it on labour?

The difference between the home and foreign price, as the ground for banking to operate on, is yet farther narrowed, by the deductions of freight, commission and insurance. These cannot be destroyed by any competition it may excite; on the contrary, if banking did increase the price of labour consumed at home, it would increase this deduction, and narrow still more the ground for its operation, on exported labour.

In fact, banking, instead of exciting competition, must, like duties, fall on the commodity, and fail to lessen mercantile profit. The merchant advances the price paid for its currency, as he advances duties. He must not only be reimbursed the one, in the price of the commodities he buys, as he is reimbursed the other, in the price of the commodities he sells, but he must also gain a profit on both his advancements, otherwise he would be as inimical as he is friendly, to imposts and banking. Duties add to nominal price; do they also enrich nations?

The inefficacy of banking for enhancing the value of the products of labour, was demonstrated in the United States by an embargo. The exportable, instantly lost two-thirds of its price, without any change in the bank currency. And the price of the consumable, was instantly regulated by the home demand, just as the demand of foreign markets, when these markets are open, regulates the price of exportable labour. Could banking have regulated value or even price, the exact regulation of both, by need, would not have appeared in this complete experiment, of an intercourse between its currency and the products of labour, upon a theatre, isolated by this embargo against every species of foreign influence.

Its impotence for enhancing value, between the people of the same country, is not however conclusive evidence of its effects between distinct nations. Seeing that price and value are regulated at home by the market or need, we may certainly conclude that products consumed abroad, will be regulated by the same stan-dard, and therefore the only question is, in what mode banking affects these regulators. This is done by increasing or diminishing the labour of a country, employed in providing for human wants. If it increases this labour, it diminishes; if it diminishes this labour, it increases the price of its products. It is certain that banking pro-duces the latter effect, to the extent of the labour employed in its operations, and of that enabled to live in idleness upon the income of its stock. So far as it thus enhances the price or value of labour at home, it is a mode of doing it, precisely equivalent to effecting the same end by neutralising an equal portion of labour, with use-less offices, endowed with unearned income. But so far as it thus enhances price abroad, it is a solid enhancement of value in favour of the nation which has the understanding to avail itself of the circumstance. The enhancement of the price of wheat in England, for instance, so long as its bank stock maintained its equality with specie, was a real enhancement of the value of labour in the United States, but not in England, by reason of the equalising powers of native labour; and the whole effect of our own bank paper, was to render some part of this real benefit merely nominal.

We now arrive to a conclusion of a formidable aspect. If bank currency cannot benefit a nation, through the medium of domes-tick commerce; because every species of labour consumed at home, will equalise its price in relation to a local currency; and if it can-not destroy or even diminish mercantile profit upon exported labour; it follows, that it does not reimburse a nation for the tax it collects; and at best only raises prices and excites industry, like· taxes and useless offices.

A bank currency may therefore, in its domestick operation, both increase price and diminish value. The first by neutralising a por-tion of labour; the second, by burdening the same country with its maintenance, against any reimbursement for which the equalising nature of native prices, is an effectual obstacle.

But specie rather excites than neutralises labour, and draws little or no tax from a nation. The possessor can part with it at a small profit, or even at none, without ruin, because he pays no interest for it; and it is his interest to take any profit in preference to its lying inactive. But the borrower of bank paper, cannot part with it, without making a profit equal to its cost. He cannot afford to take a profit even of five per centum, as a buyer with his own money may. He must consider himself in the lights of both borrower

and merchant, and feel a necessity of making profit in both characters. The owner of specie considers himself as a merchant only. The
first is under a necessity of uniting in a tacit combination, compounded of bankers and borrowers, to depress prices, that one may
get interest, and the other profit; these ends must be effected, or
borrowing and lending bank paper would cease; they are only to
be effected by a depression of price. And thus a field of competition
to the vast amount of six per centum, is shut against bank currency,
and open to coin; of course coin will produce better prices than
bank currency, unexceptionably according to the criterion of
value, and generally according to a nominal computation. Whenever it has hoarded or banished specie, it has gained the exclusive
regulation of prices, as there does not exist a specie currency able
to rival corporate currency; and then it becomes so powerful a
regulator of prices, as to produce most of the effects of an exclusive
privilege.

After the banishment or incarceration of fifty millions of specie,
and the substitution of one hundred millions of bank currency, the
latter would render all the commercial duties, previously rendered
by the former; but as it could not render more than all, so it cannot perform more duty than the preceding sum of specie; if it was
miraculously turned into specie, half of it would fly away into
other parts of the commercial world, because half could perform
the whole duty. Still the hundred millions, though half of it is useless, cannot afford to give as good prices as the fifty, because the
hundred millions is burdened with the payment of eight on ten
millions annually to the bankers and their officers, whereas the
fifty, like an owner of land in fee, has no such rent to pay. Whence
it happens that the price and value of the products of labour is
higher in South America, than in England and North America,
although the latter countries have a greater quantity of circulating
currency in proportion to population; but then the former has
more specie currency.

Bank currency, being in its nature a monopoly, must inevitably
be governed by the innate law of monopoly. This is to enhance its
own value, by diminishing value in some other quarter. It cannot
otherwise subsist. If bank currency gave a better price than coin,
the coin would be drawn from the bank for the purpose of buying
cheaper, and the moment it performs its promise of outbidding
coin, it perishes by depreciation.

. So long as it operates as specie, an influx of bank paper into this country, produces an efflux of specie, which departs to raise the real value of foreign labour, whilst the remaining local currency, can at most bestow only a nominal increase upon domestick. Bank currency, passing as specie, is embodied with the general business of commerce, and like specie, is governed by the principles of commerce. These have declared, that even a redundancy of specie itself, cannot be made to render permanent local benefits. If bank currency is inextricably interwoven with and influenced by the principles of commerce, it is simply a redundancy of specie, under a prohibition against exportation. It will enhance the value of the commodities, bought by the banking nation of another, periodically, by producing a redundancy of specie; and permanently, by a diminution of labour. Whilst a country can give high prices in specie, for foreign manufactures, on account of a redundancy of money caused by bank currency, foreigners will prefer them to high-priced commodities. After the specie is gone, the price of the same commodities, as to foreigners, will be fixed by the markets abroad, and not by the paper at home.

But reasoning upon the question, whether bank currency will enhance or depress prices, is superseded by experience. The philosophers no longer debated whether a monster was in the sun, after they saw the fly in the telescope. Through the experience of England, we are presented with the disputed fact. England has the most paper currency of any country of the commercial world, and the price of her manufactures is the lowest.

In contemplating the example of England, we must discern compulsion at the beginning, as well as at the end of her commerce. Her labour is compelled to sell low to her mercantile interest, and foreign nations or her colonies are compelled to purchase high of the same interest. Her maritime power is the instrument of the latter compulsion, and her bank currency of the former. This bank currency cannot force up the prices in foreign nations, as her fleet does by vexing and crippling competition; but it can force down the prices of labour at home. By taxing labour to maintain this fleet, that commerce is enabled to sell high abroad; and by a monopolized currency, regulating the prices of domestick labour, she buys low at home. She draws wealth and opulence from two sources, knavery and violence. To maintain the oppression over foreign nations and colonies, she frequently involves herself in war; to maintain the oppression over home labour, she is forced to use the penalties, corruptions, and mercenary armies, forming the code of all despotisms. But she is enriched, because labour is her slave, goaded by a paper system, and she makes competition shrink by a fleet.

Lord Sheffield lately observed in debate, that 'money was the medium of commerce in France, and credit its medium in England.' And he supposed, that hence arose the advantage possessed by English commerce over French. It is true, that this cause does constitute a portion of that advantage. Specie, the national currency in France, allows labour a competition with commerce, in fixing prices; but paper currency or credit, guided by the spirit of monopoly in England, enables commerce to settle the prices of labour. Commerce and productive labour are dealers; with a national currency they bargain on equal terms; with a corporation currency, governed by commerce, on unequal. Hence the price of labour being higher in France than in England, France shuts her ports against English manufactures: Yet English credit or paper, far exceeds French coin; therefore less coin gives better prices, than more credit or paper. If France and England should exchange situations, the prices of home labour would be raised in England by a less amount of national currency; because it would consist of specie, and force commerce to deal with labour on equal terms; and in France, these prices would be depressed, by a greater amount of national currency, because it would consist of corporation paper, and enable monopoly to regulate the prices between labour and commerce.

A circulating medium, measured out to a nation by corporations, or even by the commercial interest, will certainly enrich and strengthen the measuring interest, but is there a single circumstance tending towards publick happiness or virtue, in this effect? The acute bishop Tillotson has said, 'If the appearance of any thing be good for any thing, the reality must be better.' The appearance of virtue may be useful to the guilty; but it is less useful than virtue itself, and is frequently a snare to others. The appearance of money may be used to transfer property, like the appearance of virtue; and to an interest which monopolizes this appearance, it may be, according to Lord Sheffield, more beneficial in a pecuniary view, than the reality; but to a nation, the money itself, or a national currency, will, in conformity to Tillotson's maxim, be better than credit or 'an appearance of money.

The design and nature of money or currency, confirms the

superiority of coin to credit. Money is not intended to create wealth, or the objects of commerce; nor is it able to do either. Its office is to represent and exchange them. Such being the limited power of specie, paper, its shadow, cannot do more. Specie can transfer wealth from one country to another. If the United States could at pleasure create specie, they might, by a prudent use of such a monopoly, enrich themselves considerably at the expense of the world. It is not the office of paper currency to transfer wealth from one nation to another, because of its locality; but to transfer wealth from man to man, or from a nation to a corporation. Its design is to enable individuals to imitate nations, in the science of overreaching. So long as it represents wealth, corporations, able to create it, can more effectually draw wealth from the rest of a nation, by its means, than one nation could from others, by a power to create specie; because it can transfer land from man to man, whereas specie can only transfer moveable wealth from nation to nation. Paper money or credit, within the sphere of its currency, is more able to transfer property, than specie, within the sphere of commerce. A chartered power of creating it will therefore be used, as would be an exclusive national power of creating coin.

If a paper currency increased the price of exports, England could not export. This idea is repeated for the sake of examining a difficulty which it suggests. Although the price of English exportable labour is kept lower than the exportable labour of other countries, by the means to which the United States have resorted, to raise the price of their exportable labour; how happens it that England must moreover resort to war and fleets to force her commerce, and that she shrunk from a competition with the United States, even when our currency was specie, and the price of our labour higher?

The fact shews, that a nation, after having submitted to the evil and injustice of diminishing the price of its own labour, by a paper currency, was yet unable to rival a country without a paper currency, and where the price of labour was higher; and therefore that its commerce was in some way injured by the monopoly prescribed for its benefit. The solution of this enigma requires a knowledge of English commerce, the want of which confines me to surmise. Foreign nations and colonies, would as probably take advantage of the low price of labour in England, as her capitalist or commercial interest does, if they could enter into a competition with that interest. This is prevented by a navigation act, contrived to secure the benefit of the low price of labour, to an order of citizens; and to exclude foreign participation. And the spirit of monopoly, which levelled this instrument against home labour, levels it also against the world, to enhance the value of exportable commodities, after they have passed from the workman to the capitalist or merchant.

But the fact, without any explanation, suffices for our argument. It proves, that bank currency will have the effect of diminishing the price of exportable labour to the workman, and that it must be raised in favour of the merchant, by the means used in England, namely, war, fleets and navigation laws.

It is as a general position true, that the interest of commerce and agriculture are the same; and we are seduced by the truth of this maxim, to neglect an examination of our subject; concluding, from the great opulence evidently drawn from corporation currency by commercial individuals, that agriculture must be correspondently enriched. The real opulence bestowed by banking on one interest or one place, we see with the eye of the body; the supposed opulence bestowed on the other, we imagine is to be seen by the eye of the mind, through the mirror of a general maxim.

The maxim might be greatly extended. All human interests are the same. Nothing which is vicious or wrong, can be really beneficial to any. The interest of governments and nations is the same. Yet tyranny, mischievous as it is to both, is common. False and factitious interests, are eternally seducing men from true and natural interests; and alliances, intended by nature, are often broken by law. A monopoly of commerce, or of a branch of commerce, would enrich the monopolist, but injure the agriculture or manufacture, which supplied the commodity. A monopoly of commerce before the revolution, enriched Britain; the merchant of America; but it was injurious to our agriculture. To bestow opulence upon an American city by a commercial or paper monopoly, would be merely as oppressive to agriculture, as to bestow it by the same means on Glasgow. Washington might be enriched by settling there a vast stock income, or sinecure offices to an equal amount; but would this enrich the nation? And if commerce and agriculture may commit hostilities against each other, it would be still more erroneous to cover a monopoly of national currency, by a maxim, which only supposes that commerce and agriculture have the same interest, whilst they pursue their true interest.

Agriculture, formed into an aristocracy by the feudal system, being guided by a false interest, became infinitely less beneficial to commerce, than it would have been, uninfluenced by the spirit of monopoly; and commerce, moulded into a paper aristocracy, will thence also become less beneficial to agriculture, because it will be influenced by the same spirit. That it can breathe its pernicious errours into the one, wide as it is spread, is evinced by its capacity to corrupt the other, which spreads wider; unless the monopoly of national currency, is an organ of political respiration, less powerful than feudal monopoly. A close affinity is perceivable between the operations of a feudal and paper aristocracy; and if commerce could justly complain of the one, agriculture must suffer by the other. Labour needs land to produce, and money to transfer agricultural products. A monopoly of the necessity, land, or a monopoly of the necessity, money, are equivalent modes of extorting from labour. A vassalage, inflicted by means of the necessity, money, is not more voluntary than a vassalage inflicted by means of the necessity, land. Borrowing is as unavoidable, as leasing for rent or services. The collection of the interest or dividends by a stock aristocracy, is as certain as the collection of rents and services by a feudal; and the superiority of one over the other, for effecting the end of every aristocracy, rests upon the superiority of the sum collected. This estimate is left to the reader.

We will proceed to another. As we all know that a regular influx of wealth, from a majority to a minority, is a regular influx of power, the United States ought to estimate the quantity of each, they are pouring into a banking interest. If no new banks should be created after 1808, nor the acquisitions of the old increased, the five millions annually collected by the existing banks, at compound interest, carry from the publick to the corporations, in twenty years, above one hundred and eighty-four millions of dollars. Here is already a vast current of money and power running one way; will those check it in whose favour the current sets? Are the receivers, as regulators of power and wealth, of undoubted confidence?

In the same twenty years, the United States lose the use of fifty millions of specie, or national currency, expelled or locked up as bank stock, to create a demand for bank paper. At compound interest, (specie being equal in value to bank paper) this use is worth above one hundred and ten millions, exclusive of the sum exported. Thus, by being deprived of its specie, for which it paid nothing, and supplied with paper at the price it costs, the difference to the nations in the present state of things, will amount in the next twenty years to near three hundred millions of dollars.

If stock should cease to accumulate, such will be its operation; but as history, both here and in England, ascertains its fertility in devices for its own increase, our calculation is probably too low. Let us however fix the amount at three hundred millions. The reader will recollect, that in treating of debt stock, we endeavoured to shew, that its interest was equivalent to the rent of land, and that to borrow was to sell. In that case, the nation is supposed to receive a price for itself or its land; in this, it pays the rent, interest or dividend, but receives no price. And it enhances the price of bank stock, for which it receives nothing, by subjecting itself to pay double the interest paid for debt stock.

That a banking system does amount in several views to a national sale of itself, the history of its infancy here, furnishes strong apprehensions. Church stock, and feudal stock, formed parties, which trafficked in publick rights; and parties have grown up with paper stock here. It has been said in the publick prints, that banks have already become instruments for influencing election, and that the Manhattan bank could have defeated Mr. Jefferson's. If one bank could deprive the publick of any degree of patriotism and talents, the whole system could expose it to any degree of vice and ignorance. Whilst I am writing, prices are offered to legislators for charters. What can be sold for these prices, except the people? What else have legislators to sell? It is admitted, however, that it is as well to sell them, as to bestow them gratuitously.

. In Rhode-Island, bank stock, to the amount of four millions, is said to have been created. She has near seventy thousand people. Allowing her eighteen thousand actual labourers, and her stock to collect in expense, perquisites and dividends, ten per centum, her labour pays a capitation tax of above twenty-two dollars annually to banks. If the union contains six millions of people, it can bear, by the ratio of Rhode-Island, four hundred and twenty millions of bank stock, which would inflict upon the people an annual tax of forty-two millions. There is nothing extravagant in this calculation; England has far oustript it in stock accumulation; Rhode-Island has already realized it.

If the stock interest in Rhode-Island, draws more nett profit from banking, than the Virginia masters do from eighteen thousand Negro slaves, banking approaches in substance to a mode of selling freemen. Arthur Young calculates the profit of English West-India slaves, at five pounds each. The banking mode of converting the labour of one to the use of another, is more profitable than this personal slavery.

We cannot omit here to remark a difference between the pecuniary interest of wealthy classes. Where monied capital or stock constitutes wealth, its interest points to land and labour, as the only objects able to satisfy its purpose and trade; but where land and labour constitute it, income and accumulation can only be drawn out of itself by the creations of industry; for the utmost oppression of real over factitious wealth, is limited to a forbearance of its own bounty. This suggests a question of worldly wisdom. It is left to the reader to decide which is the dupe. The stock interest, in supposing that it enriches itself by banking, at the expense of land and labour; or the land and labour interest, in supposing that banking will enrich that. One is inevitably mistaken.

The efficacy of stock, as a mode by which governments sell or give nations to minorities, of which they may constitute a portion themselves, is capable of arithmetical certainty. A debt of four hundred and twenty millions sterling covers twelve millions of people at thirty-five pounds sterling a head. This is about the average value of all the people in Britain, including every age and sex, considered as personal slaves. Britain owes several hundred millions of debt stock, beyond this sum, and nearly as much more to banks of all descriptions, besides her East-India debt. Ireland has an equivalent debt of her own. This valuation is regulated by the value of the West-India slaves; but as the people of Britain supply a double capitation income to stockholders, a better mode is disclosed of making some men profitable to others, than the West-Indian. This enormous mass of stock for transferring the profit of labour to idleness, has been compiled with about twenty millions of specie; evincing, that governments can make stock out of stock, and that debt stock, like bank stock, is capable of being indefinitely multiplied without money. It has been often said, that poor labouring people in Europe, encounter more penury and distress than the Negro slaves in the United States. The profit extorted from the Negro slave is moderated by the immediate interest of his master in his existence. It is moderated by the master's benevolence, and by his respect for his own reputation. But the slave of stock enjoys none of these ameliorations; and therefore it is not surprising that he should be more miserable than the personal slave. The several descriptions of stock in Britain already require a far greater profit from the people, than can be paid by twelve millions of personal slaves. The paying class, is also diminished by the receiving and unproductive classes. Excessive labour, poorhouses, penury, prisons, famine, crimes, must follow. Let not the advocate for enslaving freemen by means of stock, venture to compare his system with personal slavery. It will be found that indirect slavery, like indirect taxation, is capable of being carried to greater excess than direct.

It is proper to examine arithmetically also, the progress of stock in America. Our supposed fifty millions of bank stock, being a sum beyond the deposited and existing coin, fixes the capacity of our stock like the English; to multiply itself without specie. It circulates, we will suppose, eighty millions of paper, costing the country above six per centum; adding these eighty millions to as much debt stock supposed to exist, and the grapples of stock to about thirty-two dollars a head, appear already to be thrown over us. Shall we disentangle ourselves from them whilst we have it in our power, or defer the effort, until we are irretrievably entangled in the intricacies of indirect slavery? A slavery, in which the sufferer is ignorant of his tyrant, and the tyrant is remorseless, because he is unconscious of his crime.

By bank stock, unless all our reasonings are erroneous, and our examples inapplicable, a government may subject a nation to the payment of a capitation profit, to those to whom it shall be conveyed by charter, exceeding any profit extracted from personal slaves; and political principles may be corrupted. Are there any greater temporal calamities? Are there any temporal blessings capable of balancing them? Weigh the terrifick duumvirate, oppressive taxation and a corrupt government, against the benefit proposed by banking. All it proposes, its total advantage, lies in the simple space of substituting some millions of bank currency, for some millions of specie currency.

We have endeavoured already to prove, that the substitution is an evil, supposing it to cost the nation neither money nor principles; if we have failed, it may yet be an evil, on account of the loss of money and principles it requires. We will add several observations upon these points.

The freedom of our commerce, and the tendency of money to find a level in the commercial world, furnishes a well founded belief, that specie had arrived, or was hastening from all parts of the commercial world, to render us all the commercial services capable of being rendered by money, when banking checked its career.

The sudden diminution of specie upon this event, is an evidence that we had enough for our wants. Had we needed more currency, specie would have continued in circulation with bank currency. But that currency, by producing a redundancy of circulating medium, became an ostracism against the innocent and patriotick specie.

It follows that bank paper is an operative agent in the adjustment of the level of specie, throughout the commercial world, though local itself; because the specie it banishes from one country, goes off to another. Hence a country, by confining her currency to specie, will receive remittances in coin from all others resorting to bank currency; by resorting to it, the same country sends such remittances to other countries in coin also. Banking therefore effects two ends completely: it enriches other countries by the expulsion of specie; and it enriches stockholders by the price paid for their paper, to supply the place of the expelled specie. Do we incur the first misfortune, for the sake of the second?

The disappearance of specie, ascertains that its quantity sufficed to render every commercial service which currency can render, and no amount can render more service than a sufficient amount. But though no amount of currency, can perform services for a nation, beyond the national demand for such services, yet an artificial bank currency may be thrown into circulation, capable of taxing, but incapable of serving a nation. Supposing that fifty millions of specie have been taken out of circulation by banking, and that this sum sufficed to meet all our demands for a currency, we now give five millions annually to get too much of that, of which we had enough for nothing; and with which we were regularly supplied, by the equalising nature of universal currency; just as Virginia, by an utter exclusion of paper, would have been supplied with specie. The single quality of universal currency, possessed by bank paper, consists of a detrimental capacity to expel specie, whilst it is unable to go abroad itself, to remove the evils arising from a redundant currency. Of these qualities, a state of the Union, or the whole Union, may avail itself, as a means of turning the paper systems of other states, or of the commercial world, to advantage. Their influence in adjusting the distribution of money, would ensure to the forbearing country its allotment in specie, whilst the inability of paper currency to fly abroad, condemns the banking country to the two evils of a redundancy of currency, and of receiving its allotment in local paper purchased by an annual tax.

It would be endless to enumerate all the effects of this condemnation; a few, serving to illustrate the scope of our reasoning, and the imbecility of all attempts to prevent the natural flux and reflux of specie, cannot be omitted.

There is certainly a measure, beyond which a nation cannot be benefited by money. Its redundancy being an evil, the political or commercial body instinctively labours to expel it, as the natural body does a disease. But if a nation entrusts to a college of political doctors, the power of dosing it with money, whilst they are enriched in proportion to the physick they administer, their fees will be their guide, and not the health of the patient. A redundancy of local currency, produced by doctors hired to keep it up, cannot be disgorged by the efforts of nature struggling for health.

Money (like prices, trades and manufactures) regulates itself better than it can be regulated by the doctors, despotism, monopoly or banking. A regulation of money, is always a regulation of prices, and an interposition by law, in the economy of individuals. It covers effort and competition in every shape, and combines in a mass the several evils which would flow from distinct legal prices, for each separate object of human industry. Such an interposition with a single article of industry, has invariably terminated in mischief; it is therefore probable, that the power of measuring out currency, placed in corporations, which is an interposition with all prices, and all objects of human industry, will not produce good.

A providential scarcity of the metals, devoted to become the medium of commerce, prevents the evils of pecuniary redundancy, and this utility is destroyed by an unlimited power of multiplying paper currency. Overflowing mines of these precious metals, would destroy their utility as a medium of exchange; and confined to one nation, would diminish rather than increase its happiness. Paper money enables avarice to inflict the misery of this redundancy, whilst not even the refuge of forging it into ploughshares is left to the nation. Corporations are solicited by the most fascinating orator to deluge a nation with a flood of currency, no part of which is subject to be drained off by the ebb natural to specie. Is that commerce free, the currency of which is regulated by a corporation?

It is because no single government is able to regulate universal currency, that it cannot raise the value of exportable by local currency. It is, however, able to diminish the profit of this labour, by quartering upon it the dividends of this local currency, as we have ° endeavoured to prove. Supposing that it may also produce the effect, insisted on for its defence, namely, that of enhancing local prices or home subsistence; it then combines the two operations, of diminishing the value of exportable labour to the labourer, and of enhancing his expenses.

An effect, extremely similar to this, is produced in England by paper currency and excises. The first keeps down in a degree the prices of exportable labour or manufactures, and the second enhances the expenses of subsistence. A redundancy of bank paper here, which shall enhance expenses, operates as excises do in England, except that the excise there goes to the government, and here to corporations.

And a consequence of placing the exportable labour of that country, under the regimen of a currency regulated by a corporation, illustrates both the mischief of such a power, and our whole scope of reasoning, by a very striking fact. It is by this means deprived of a share in the government. The manufacturers are subject to capitalists, and regulated for their benefit. We have endeavoured to prove, that the paper system would impoverish the agricultural interest, which produces our exportable labour, worm it out of the government, and reduce it to subjection. Let the fate of the English manufacturers, from a paper regimen, point to our agricultural fate, under a similar regimen. Let their fate also display the justice dispensed by a power to regulate currency. It is the justice invariably dispensed under the seduction of avarice. But seduction is unnecessary to produce an adherence to one's own interest. A power to regulate currency for the agricultural, or manufactural interest, and to enrich itself thereby, will rapidly acquire the weapon which governs the world. In pursuance of its separate interest, it has usurped the government in England, under the name of the monied interest: reader, which is the preferable substitute for our constitutional policy, the Emperour of France, or the monied interest of England?

The power of substituting a factitious local currency, for one naturally universal, is a handle, stronger than that of superstition, with which to manage nations. Allegiance to the faction, is secured by the fear of losing this artificial money. Specie is independent of a faction, and able to become a patriot. It can attend us in our flight from tyranny, and travel over the world, to feed, clothe and arm patriots; but paper chains to the sod, and remains at home to tax for party or corporation benefit, and not to cherish liberty. But let us leave the goddess to take care of herself, and look a little farther after our money. Although we have seen separate interests enslaving nations from the beginning of the world, it is still a very difficult thing to make mankind believe, that corporations for gathering money, do really take that which they were instituted to take. They are now convinced, that the separate interests of super-stition and title, had their money in view, under other pretences; and to save it, have expelled them. But they will not believe, that a pecuniary order, which avows the design, denied by these detected orders, is in earnest. No, this order, unlike others, intends to enrich nations, not itself. Let us count these riches in other modes.

Supposing about fifty millions of stock to exist in the United States, and that about eighty millions of bank currency are circu-lated, it follows, as before observed, that the nation pays at least five millions annually for the bank currency, and loses the use of fifty millions specie, worth annually three millions more.

These eight millions are annually paid by the nation, to gain thirty millions currency, more than it set out with. The price paid for this additional currency amounts to about twenty-seven per centum per annum. Which is the better policy; to give eight per centum for money, for the purpose of attacking France or England; or twenty-seven, to raise up a separate interest to attack our form of government?

But if the fifty millions specie performed more useful services than the eighty millions bank currency, the computation settles in the fact, that we pay a difference of five millions annually in favour of an evil. This is an errour still more egregious. It is taking up sorrow upon interest. A nation which can count, will see that direct pecuniary orders operate as their indirect predecessors have done.

Our calculation goes upon the favorable ground for banking, that the stock is in specie, ready to meet the notes, or to come forth upon a national emergency; but if this stock was never real, or if the specie is banished by a redundancy of currency, so as gradually to reduce the supposed specie stock to paper credit; the total loss of so much coin, and the possible misfortunes which may arise from an inability to meet the debts of banking by real money, would constitute no inconsiderable items of additional evil bought by the nation.

The evils bought with debt stock, have been often compared to those obtained by banking. Compare also the riches they bestow on a nation. One does not expel specie, the other does. One collects five or six per centum interest, the other ten or twelve per centum charges and dividends. Ah! but these dividends cost nobody a farthing. Well! let us call the interest of national debt a dividend, and the debt is no more.

Their political and physical similitude, breaks in upon us at every step, abstractedly or experimentally considered. Funded stock, when proposed for national consideration, was announced as a blessing; this blessing was said to be comprised in its increase of capital and industry. The same mantle, stript by publick sagacity, from funded stock, has been with wonderful ingenuity, thrown over bank stock. That also is gravely announced by its inventors as a publick blessing; and why? It will increase capital and industry. The United States detected the shallow artifice under which the designs of funded stock were hidden, because it was moreover defended by pretexts, said to be necessities; they cannot see the same artifice spread over the designs of bank stock, because it has no auxiliary; or because we sometimes search in vain for that which lies directly before our eyes.

This common and solitary refuge of our twin namesakes, is simply that of all orders enriched by law and oppression. 'It is their opulence,' say they, 'which gives employment to labour and excites industry.' Thus have all such orders concealed the wealth they extract, and the poverty they inflict. As a justification of banking also, this old mode of concealment requires attention.

Does banking increase capital? It does, if real capital is increased, by increasing paper currency; but if paper currency can at most be considered as capital, when balanced by property and labour, an additional quantity can no more increase capital, than blowing up poor mutton can increase meat. A redundancy of specie would not form a stationary capital. As birds of passage travel in search of food, specie travels in search of the real capital it represents; and if the food or employment is insufficient for either concourse, the overplus flies away. If specie could create capital, it would find stationary employment every where. From these facts we infer, that money is not capital, but the representative of capital; and that it is inverting the true and genuine relation

323

between capital and money, to suppose that money produces national capital, instead of national capital producing money. The value of labour is real capital. If a nation had an hundred millions of money, but did not labour, it would presently be without capital; but if its labour was worth five millions annually, though it had no money, it would have an hundred millions of capital, which would soon attract money. The introduction of bank paper is uniformly the epoch from which the diminution of specie is dated. If specie therefore is capital, bank paper diminishes capital; if not, neither can its representative be capital. It is by real capital, that specie is equalised among commercial nations. As a representative, it is subordinate and responsible to its principal. Bank paper cannot possess an intrinsick value, if the value of specie is representative; therefore it cannot increase capital; and a surplus, beyond a necessary currency, far from falling within any idea of the term capital, can only exist by feeding on capital, the principal of currency. If bank paper was new capital, so far from expelling the representative of the old, it would require more representation, and attract specie. Or if, like specie, it was the responsible representative of capital or property, it would be subordinate to its principal. On the contrary, it is made by law, an irresponsible representative of capital or property; and a currency converted from the servant into the master of property, necessarily becomes a tyrant, to secure its power.

The advocates of banking admit this doctrine, by contending that it is beneficial to a nation to expel specie by paper; as it causes an exchange of the representative of capital, for the thing itself. If the capital, thus gotten from foreign nations, by the expelled specie, would produce a permanent profit, superior to the annual cost of the substituted paper, this would be true; but the difficulty of discovering any such profit, and the visibility of the cost, are strong evidences that it is false. This stratagem for enriching a nation can be practised but once, whereas the cost of bank paper substituted for expelled specie is annually repeated. Besides, a redundancy of specie for exportation, produced by the creation of bank paper for home use, diminishes the value of that specie; and this depreciation both causes its flight, and constitutes an actual loss to the stockjobbing nation. Again. If an increase of currency, was an increase of capital and industry, the stratagem of sending abroad the specie or universal currency by the stockjobbing nation, defeats the end proposed; both by the amount of the money exported, and also by increasing the capital and stimulating the industry of rival nations, to whom the specie is exported.

When we see gold and silver fly away from a country, because it is unable to create capital, and because capital can only retain a competent representation in currency; an opinion, that bank currency will create it, undoubtedly contains more of credulity, than one, that any other metal can create gold. It affords matter for another alchymist. The drama might again exhibit cunning preying upon the avarice it pretends to feed. But a stage would be too small to contain the two orders of character; that of Epicure, Mammon, Ananias and Tribulation on one hand, and of Subtle and Face on the other.

Bank paper, not being capital, or able to create capital, it is to be further examined, whether it encourages and creates labour and industry, as it also pretends. If it did, the new created industry, would retain the specie it expels. This inquiry lies in a comparison, between a legal institution for acquiring wealth to an enormous extent, without talents or industry; and leaving its acquisition to the regulation of talents and industry. Wealth in both cases is supposed to be the spur to exertion. By a laborious cultivation of my talents and persevering industry, I acquire a moderate degree of wealth; by banking I acquire infinitely more, without labour or talents. Why should I subject myself to the fatigue of becoming learned and useful, to become the scoff of a rich, idle and voluptuous order? Their abundance, to which I must contribute, will diminish my competence, in the eye of comparison, almost to nothing; and of course in my own eyes. No, I will go into the lottery where there are no blanks; where every ticket draws annual prizes; and where, as a stockjobber, I may be as rich, as idle, as ignorant, and as useless, as a bishop, nobleman or king. What will the world say of our experiment to establish a free government, if an epithet, universally considered as far more humiliating than those of bishop, nobleman or king, should become the title of a separate order or interest in the United States?

This mode of encouraging industry, by creating rich and idle orders to give it employment, has been practised in various forms, but all contain the same principle. Hereditary and hierarchical orders, encourage industry in the same way as stock orders do; by taxing it to maintain themselves in idleness and affluence. The lash is applied to slaves, and taxation to freemen, to encourage industry. Masters and orders praise the effect of both causes, to gain wealth and leisure for themselves. If one evil has been imposed by a foreign nation on this country, should it therefore impose the other on itself?

When debt stock boasts that it is an encourager of industry, it refers to the stimulus of taxation; yet it attempts by every artifice, to conceal from the people the cause of this vaunted effect. Bank stock also boasts of the same merit, but it pretends that an abundance of money, and not the goad of taxation, is its cause. The first, by hiding the cause of the effect it claims, confesses its treachery not more conspicuously than the second, by pretending that it encourages industry by a superfluity of money. Are extortion and donation, a robber and a prodigal, equally encouragers of industry? I, says debt stock, encourage industry, by taking away your money; and I, says bank stock, by pouring money into your pockets. When, by theory or experience, has it ever been said, that either the redundancy of money, or the loss of earnings, was an encouragement to industry? If the inculcation of a false opinion, that industry enjoys her own earnings, is the best mode to which all orders, titled or stock, can resort for her encouragement, it is evident that the mode would be improved, by making the opinion true. Fulfilment would be a stronger excitement to industry, than disappointed hope.

The true sanction of private property, consists in its effect to stimulate men to industry, and the improvement of the understanding; from the consideration that they will enjoy whatever their knowledge and industry may gain. Exactly the reverse of this sanction, and this effect, is the doctrine, that knowledge or industry will be excited and increased, by transferring a portion of their gains from themselves, to orders, hereditary, titled, hierarchical or stock. Although all such orders profess themselves to be encouragers of knowledge and industry, and friends to private property, it is hence evident, that they either deceive themselves, or attempt to deceive others.

An idea, heretofore suggested, seems of sufficient importance to be again brought to mind, for the sake of arguments, which have since occurred. It is that which supposes the credit of nations to be property, of a species, as far beyond the power of a government to give away to corporations, as any other species.

Currency and credit are social rights, in a state of appropriation, and not a species of wild game, to be seized and bestowed by governments, any more than other social rights. To save, not to sell or give away such rights, constitutes the utmost power of free governments. To bestow on corporations, by charters, an exclusive right of uttering currency, is more exceptionable, than to give or sell to them an exclusive right of uttering new patents for land, because every individual owns a share of the national credit, which is not the case as to land. Or considering the nation's land, in a territorial view, as equivalent to the nation's credit, the dismemberment of one, would be a question equivalent to the dismemberment of the other.

The term 'national,' applied to currency and credit, furnishes an argument in favour of these positions. The use of a term descriptive of appropriation, proves that currency and credit are appropriated. All property is under the sanction of a twofold species of appropriation in society. It is appropriated to the use of the nation, for publick defence, and the administration of the government. After this object is satisfied, it is appropriated to the use of the individuals composing the nation. But there is not in free countries any appropriation, to the use of a government, called party or administration territory, commerce or credit, to be chartered by it to individuals or factions. On the contrary, this third kind of appropriation, constitutes a violation of publick and private property, and the difference between free and despotick governments.

The right and property of national credit, territory and commerce, are of the same nature; and it equally violates a policy, founded in the principles of liberty, for a government to charter away portions of one, as portions of another. Those minor appropriations of credit, land or commerce, produced by the talents, labour and industry of individuals, or by the municipal law which embraces every member of a society, are of the second species of appropriation, and distinct from the third.

The principles of political morality admit only of the appropriation of property, in the two first modes, and reject the third, as unnecessary for a government, inconsistent with the ends of its institution, and the ground work of civilized tyranny.

A transfer of private or publick property, or both, from individuals or nations, to orders, corporations or to other individuals, is the evil moral principle, in which all hereditary and hierarchical orders have been founded, and of course, in plain hostility with any principles, capable of being assigned as the ground work of the government of the United States.

That government could not by its laws or its power, enrich

corporations at the publick expense, nor touch property, except for publick use, was so well understood as a principle, essential to liberty, as to have been unequivocally expressed in most of our constitutions, by inhibitions of 'exclusive emoluments,' except for such publick services as were not transmissible. Our governments are not allowed to invade that appropriation of property called private, by bestowing emoluments which some portion of it must pay, upon any occasion, except such as is covered by that appropriation called publick. They are therefore prohibited by the written rule, as well as by the moral principle, essential to free forms of government, from invading or transferring property for private or corporation emolument. And lest a government might call a violation of private property, a publick benefit, as it has uniformly done in every species of monopoly, the constitutions quoted have provided against this evasion, by limiting a power in the governments to bestow emoluments, for the compensation of personal and unalienable publick services.

That credit and currency are, in society, property, both publick and private, is demonstrable from other considerations. Talents and industry will divide and distribute credit and currency, as they do land. A species of wealth which talents and industry can distribute, is property. What is the distinction, allowing our governments to take away the whole, or any portion of this species of property, and to give it to corporations, which must not admit a power of chartering away the lands of individuals, and the national territory? If both land and credit, or currency are distributable by talents and industry, then, to distribute either by law, is fraudulent and oppressive.

If it be said, that credit and currency cannot be considered as property, publick or private, because they cannot be divided by metes and bounds, like land; it is answered, that an incapacity for a similar division is common to sundry social rights, such as the freedom of religion and of the press; and that the sanction of the right, not the marks of the division, being the basis of property, this sanction must be equally strong in relation to land and credit or currency, if it can reach both, and must be equally violated by distributing either by law.

Commerce is called national, like credit and currency. It is less capable of a division among the people than credit, or currency. Is it not a species of property, both publick and private? As publick, it is an object of taxation. As private and publick, our government cannot charter it entirely or in portions to corporations, because in our society, there exist only two appropriations of property, publick and private; the first as payment for publick services, to be made by law; the second, the acquisition of private people, which no law can transfer to other private people.

There is no distinguishing between commerce, credit and currency, as objects of social property. This indelible similarity admits only of two inferences; either that our constitutions have surrendered both to be appropriated to individuals or corporations, by the charters of our governments, or that they have surrendered neither.

Knowledge, at first view, seems to possess less of the nature of property, than lands, commerce, credit or currency; yet a legal monopoly of knowledge, is inconsistent with our principles. The compulsion to buy corporation currency, produced by banishing national currency, greatly resembles the compulsion to buy hereditary knowledge, by banishing national knowledge. To buy corporation currency to carry on trade, seems as absurd as to buy hereditary knowledge to carry on government. The Chinese monopoly of knowledge, is an illustration still stronger than the hereditary. An order, by prohibiting the use of an alphabet (the coin of knowledge) produces national ignorance, and thence draws with its exclusive knowledge, exclusive wealth and power. By the banishment of specie (the coin of fair and free commerce) and the substitution of hieroglyphicks confined to a species of mandarin, the privileged individuals, will also, like mandarins, draw exclusive wealth and power. If this Chinese monopoly of knowledge, sensibly affects private property, is it inconceivable that a monopoly of credit or currency will also sensibly affect it?

Credit or currency, is unquestionably of the nature of private property, so far as it is able to transfer it. If a government should allege against a charge of having invaded private property, that it only furnished the instrument for taking it away, the charge would be acknowledged. There can be no honest difference between transferring property from private people, to a corporation, directly or indirectly. The moral and constitutional principles, which condemn the one, condemn the other. Not the process, but the injury, constitutes the violation of these principles. Will it be said, that although our governments cannot directly take away publick or private property, and give it to corporations, that they may give them the power of expelling specie, and of transferring property indirectly by corporation currency? Any portion of bank paper, thrown into circulation, represents and transfers some portion of private property, from individuals to corporations or to other individuals. If it becomes the only currency, its effect in this operation is constant and great. And the limitation of this transfer, depends on the will of the corporation. Although we have avoided the details of banking as much as possible, it cannot be overlooked, that the liability of the stock only, the unlimited power to issue notes, and the capacity of those notes to transfer property, constitute temptations, which human nature has never been a match for. The nation possessed a national currency; after the complete introduction of a corporation currency, it no longer possesses this species of property. If the national territory was as effectually thrown into the form of a feudal monopoly, as its currency is thrown into that of a banking monopoly, the national territory would be covered by the term 'seigniory,' as the national currency is now covered by the terms 'bank notes,' and the suppression of the term 'national,' in both cases, is an equal evidence that an order had obtained, what was previously the publick property.

Let us suppose that a legislature had in the publick treasury half a million of dollars. Could it make a bank by charter, and give it this money? Why not? The money belongs to the nation; and it would be a transfer from the nation to a corporation, of so much publick property, for no publick object.

If national currency is suppressed, and corporation currency interpolated, it will have the effect of transferring from the nation to the corporation, a much larger portion of private property, than this unjust and unconstitutional donation of half a million of the publick money. Is a small transfer of publick and private property to a corporation, contrary to our policy, but a great one consistent with it?

This argument cannot be eluded by the fact, that bank corporations supply their own stock or capital. It is not the property covered by that capital, supposing it to be specie, which is transferred by governments from nations to banks. That capital covers as much of the property of other people, without the help of law, as it ought to cover; and can only transfer the amount it represents. To this amount, and to no more of the property of others, are the holders of this specie capital, justly or constitutionally entitled.

But the law steps in, unites these holders into a bank, and empowers this bank to issue twice as much currency as its capital, actually retained to meet its notes. Thus the effect of transferring property from the people at large to the bank must inevitably follow, by deranging so egregiously the fair and equitable value or level of national currency, as to make a portion of it in the hands of corporations, of double value to that which remains in the hands of the nation. And this enormous and exclusive appreciation of the value of specie or national currency, is gained by the privileged sect; whilst the money held by all not of the corporation, is in fact depreciated by the fraudulent donation.

Let us throw this argument into figures, as the only mode of making it perfectly plain. Half a million, in a fair and just state of the partnership, called society, represents and entitles the holders to only half a million's worth of property; and those who hold the property of this partnership, owe to its holders, and must relinquish so much of their property as the currency represents, and no more. But a few individuals of this partnership or society, have prevailed upon the government to grant them an exclusive charter, to issue a whole million of currency, upon the credit or opinion that they possess half a one. Is it not evident, that these members of the society have gained an advantage over those not sharing in the privilege; and that so much of the property of the rest of society, as the whole million of bank currency will cover, beyond the half million of specie, is thereby inevitably taken from the partnership called national or social, and transferred to the minor partnership, called corporate or banking? If so, the principle of an equality of rights is violated, by making the money of a few men, more valuable than the money of the people at large; and by the indirect, but certain mode thence arising, of transferring the property of those who have the least valuable money, to those possessing the most valuable. Nor can a species of exclusive privilege be conceived, capable of producing greater pecuniary loss and gain. Accordingly, banking, in gathering wealth, travels with a rapidity unattempted by the most able hierarchical collector.

We have supposed, merely to simplify the argument, that specie stock emits double its amount in bank currency. This is precarious and fluctuating; and therefore the reader is reminded, that although a precise sum is mentioned for the sake of perspicuity, yet that the argument applies to the surplus of bank currency issued, whatever it be, beyond the actual specie deposited in the bank. The portion of society privileged to issue two, three or four dollars for one, becomes one order, and the unprivileged, another. The dollar which can multiply itself, is more puissant, than the dollar which cannot. One is a patrician, the other a plebeian. These dollars will represent their owners, or the owners their dollars.

But to prevent any mistake, it is necessary more particularly to explain the mode or process, by which the enhancement of the value of an incorporated dollar, beyond an unincorporated one, is effected. It consists chiefly of two items. First, the surplus of notes circulated, beyond the amount of the stock or capital, produces a surplus of interest, beyond what the stock or capital could produce; the whole of which is an addition to the value of incorporated, beyond that of unincorporated specie; and will transfer a correspondent surplus of property. For instance, if a capital of half a million stock, can circulate two millions of paper at six per centum only, one-fourth of the paper produces the whole interest which unincorporated specie can produce; therefore the other three-fourths are additional value given to the incorporated specie by an exclusive privilege, destroying an equality of rights in the national pecuniary partnership, and transferring unjustly all the property covered by such additional value. The second important item of this process of appreciation, consists of the artifice of taking out a portion of the stock or capital, and acquiring with it the whole property it represents, and ought in justice to transfer; and of circulating paper currency, upon the credit of an opinion, that the stock thus used remains deposited. It is obvious, that the interest of the whole of the paper, circulated upon the basis of ideal stock, is an addition to the value of the specie, which has in person transferred all the property it ought to transfer; and that this unjust enhancement arises from the exclusive privilege. If it is recollected that there are about fifty millions of bank stock in the United States, and that even a moiety of it could not possibly have been deposited in specie, the great effect of artificial stock, in transferring property will at a glance be conspicuous.

The example of a commercial partnership, consisting of one thousand persons, supplying different quotas of stock, will still illustrate the argument. We will suppose that the stock of the wealthiest individual of the partnership, amounted to one thousand dollars, and of the poorest, to one; and that the intermediate space, was occupied by a great variety of sums, constituting the stock of the other partners. The profits are the property of the partnership, and ought to be proportioned according to the stock of each individual. The partner entitled to one thousand dollars, ought to have one thousand times more than the partner entitled to one dollar of the stock. But if you give him two, three or four thousand times more, than you give to the partner having one dollar stock, you rob this poor partner, and all the intermediate partners, of a portion of their property, and give it to the rich partner. By suffering the rich partner to take his thousand dollars out of the partnership, and leave only his credit behind, he acquires its value in property, besides retaining the double interest to acquire more property. Society is this partnership; bankers, the partners who draw more property than their money or that of others represents; cunning and rich bankers, those who take away their stock, or a portion of it, and continue to draw this overplus of property; and the poor partner represents those, not bankers, and limited to draw property in strict proportion to the value of their money.

National currency is the stock representing national property, as mercantile capital represents partnership profit. This stock is unequally divided, but it is entitled to a proportional value in property, as mercantile capital is in profit. Banking enables about one in a thousand of a nation to draw out of the national stock of property, considerably more than his share of national currency entitled him to, which unjust overplus is a deduction from the property of the other members of the society; just as any mode, direct or indirect, by which one partner could get more than his proportional share of mercantile profit, transfers to him the property of others. And as the acquisitions of banking, from the nature of the institution, must settle in the hands of the wealthy class, it is of course a mode of adding to the wealth of that class, by taking from all others; similar to the enrichment of the rich mercantile partner, and analogous in its effects to every exclusive order, which has heretofore deluded and enslaved nations.

The injustice of appreciating partially and exclusively the money of a minor order, or of any portion of society, is yet further illustrated, by recollecting, that appreciation is necessarily attended by its correlative, depreciation; and that the effects of the one in moral geometry, are an exact mensuration of the effects of the other. Value is relative. If the money or property of one portion of the society, is made by law to be worthless, the money or property of those not thus oppressed, will consequently be worth more; if the law adds partially to the value of the money or property of some, it correspondently diminishes their value as to others.

The funding system illustrates both positions. First, by funding without providing for the interest, the certificates were depreciated, and other money or property appreciated, because two shillings of it would buy twenty shillings of the certificate. Secondly, by providing for the payment of the interest after the depreciated property had been purchased by the appreciated property, an appreciation of certificates took place, which lessened the value of all property subjected to make the appreciation good, even of those who had suffered the depreciation. This appreciation of certificates tenfold beyond their current value, is the literal case of appreciating specie by banking beyond its current value; except that the appreciation of specie does not visibly appear to be so exorbitant. Although, if banks have resorted to paper to make up capital, as is unquestionable, the difference between the legal appreciation of monopolized certificates, and of bank stock, in point of exorbitancy, will be inconsiderable. Whatever it is, the moral injustice of making a currency, worth only twenty shillings in the pound, of the value of eighty or forty shillings, in favour of a few corporations, is founded in the same principles of monopoly, partiality and violation of property, in which the depreciation and appreciation of the certificates was founded; except that for this, no pretext or nominal reason existed. It is a plain continuation of that system. The depreciation of certificates, enabled a few to get them at one-tenth of their nominal amount. Their appreciation invested the holders with an enormous pecuniary advantage. Banking appreciates money incomputably, especially where bank paper has made bank stock. It is the second great movement of an enormous and crushing monopoly.

To display and compare with our policy and constitutions, the abuses which have successively destroyed liberty and happiness, it was necessary to prove the distinction between these abuses and our political principles, and their irreconcileable enmity to each other. This part of the essay, is devoted to the consideration of a system of partiality and monopoly, introduced by law, because we conceive it to be as inimical to our policy and constitutions, and more dangerous than Mr. Adams's system of orders; or than the aristocracies of nobility or hierarchy.

Aristocracy is forever adapting itself to the temper of the times. In those of ignorance and superstition, it pretended to be the sanctified herald of the gods. In warlike times, it glittered in armour, and boasted its prowess. And now, it dazzles avarice with such riches as we see in dreams, whilst it is building up for itself a tower with cent per cent, from whence it can scale and conquer our constitutions.

Against that portion of the system of paper and patronage, called funding or anticipation, none of the American constitutions have provided a check. If borrowing and funding can enslave nations, our governments possess a despotick power, without any control, that of election excepted. It ought therefore, if it can be effected, to be placed in a state of division, between the general and state governments, to prevent either from destroying the other by this instrument; or to be subjected to some other check. Armies will enslave their country, after they have bled for it; therefore they must be checked by an armed nation; funding systems bleed their country, and unless they are more patriotick than armies, they seem to be an object of equal danger.

The army mode of enslaving the nation, is not left to the exclusive control of election. Military men are excluded from legislatures, and whilst the general government may raise an army, the states may arm, officer and discipline the militia.

If banking is inconsistent with the positive rules of our constitutions, or adverse to their general principles, the laws upon the subject are void. But supposing it only transfers property unfairly, and to be as dangerous to liberty as funding, it cannot plead national necessity as a subterfuge against annihilation; and what friend to free government would hesitate to annihilate the power of borrowing, if there was a certainty that the national defence would never render it necessary? But it can plead charters; the Lord deliver us from charters! Admit that the banking system ought not to have existed, yet these sanctions for evil say that it shall continue to exist.

A history of charters would afford vast amusement and instruction to nations; it would terminate in ascertaining, that orders have practised as insidiously behind these, as behind altars. Such as are improvidently granted by nations, or corruptly by governments, are said, like the oracles, to be sacred; but those obtained by nations or individuals from orders, are disregarded or destroyed, as interest or ambition dictates. English municipal law, applies to the charters to be revoked in favour of orders, the term obreptitious, implying, that they were obtained by surprise, or by a concealment of their effects; in which cases they are to be vacated. But it has no term or process, recognising a right in nations to resume improvident grants, or to annul those made by the government, contrary to national rights or publick good. Admitting, however, that the people of our Union have no right to save their liberties against an host of charters, unless a precedent to justify it can be found (a doctrine as correct, as that they have no right to the Union or their policy, because they are unjustified by precedent) this English law furnishes such a precedent.

Orders in England constitute the sovereignty; the people, in the United States. The sovereignty of orders annuls charters for sundry causes; the sovereignty of the people may therefore, even according to precedent, annul them for the same causes. No cause could be more completely within the reason and scope of the English doctrine, than one, which would tend to the destruction of the sovereignty of orders in that country; whatever tends to the destruction of the sovereignty of the people here, is equally within its scope and meaning. And the right of the sovereignty here to annul obreptitious charters, is stronger than it is in England, because there the charter may be the act of the sovereignty itself; here it can only be the act of the agents of the sovereignty, responsible, of limited powers, and having no power directly or indirectly to change the nature of the government by obreptitious charters.

Bank charters, in a vast variety of views, fall within this English law doctrine, unless the reasonings of this essay are incorrect. Who, for instance, was aware that this was a mode of indirect taxation? And who believed, that at this moment the United States were paying five millions worth of their property, annually, to a small portion of their people, for a fictitious currency?

These law charters, however sanctioned by legal forms, are never genuine national law. National will, in free governments, is the only genuine sanction of law. The will of the legislature, is the instrument for proclaiming this sanction. If a legislature should pass a law charter, for advancing the exclusive interest of the legislative body, or of some other combination of men, at the expense of the national interest, both moral and pecuniary, it obviously makes a false proclamation, and the question is, whether the genuine sanction of law, or this false proclamation, ought to be most sacred. Without leaving our subject to consider the device of consecrating these spurious laws, beyond the genuine, and even beyond constitutional law itself, it falls within it to consider the character of a separate or exclusive interest, which invariably dictates them.

It is happily hit off unintentionally by Mr. Addison in his third Spectator, where he personifies publick credit, by a virgin, enthroned on gold in the hall of the bank of England; surrounded by funding laws; delighted with contemplating them; timorous; a valetudinarian; suddenly withering; suddenly reviving; converting whatever she touched into gold, which would as suddenly vanish or become tallies, if she was affrighted; fainting and dying at the sight of a commonwealth; and revived by monarchy.

By mistaking the exclusive interest called funding, for publick credit, Mr. Addison has described the character of paper stock. Gold, and not virtue, is the terrestrial deity of this allegorical being, so improperly represented as a virgin. She admits promiscuous and loathsome embraces to acquire it. Wealth rises as if by magick around her, as around fraud and theft. It disappears upon the least rustling of danger; as a robber hides his booty. She is timorous from conscious guilt. She is a sickly moral being, because she is formed of bad moral principles. She faints and dies under a commonwealth, because she cannot live within the pale of common interest, and can only subsist on its destruction; and she is revived by monarchy, a congenial being, which aids this fearful, sickly, fainting, reviving, magical and wicked being, by surrounding her with consecrated law charters.

Contrast genuine and honest publick credit, with this thievish spectre, and assign the privilege of consecrating law, to general or exclusive interest, as the result shall indicate which of the two is the purest legislator.

Genuine publick credit is enthroned, not upon gold gathered by law into a bank, but upon property distributed by industry. It is greatest, where national debt is least. It flows from national wealth and prosperity, not from the wealth of corporations enriched by exclusive privileges. It creates gold by industry, not by magick; and saves it by valour, not by hiding; it is a healthy moral being, because it is formed of good moral principles; and bold, because it is honest. It flourishes under a commonwealth, and dies under a monarchy. Hostile principles cannot live in union and friendship. National credit and corporation credit must consort each with its like. They are respectively killed and revived by monarchy and a commonwealth, because a government founded on the principle of minority accords with one, and that founded on the principle of majority, with the other. Corporation credit, artificially created by law and orders, unite and cohere, from an identity of origin and nature. National credit, arising from fair industry and national wealth, can only unite with a free and equal government.

All partial interests, capable of procuring or sustaining a law, belong to the family of this virgin described by Mr. Addison. Of the two sisters of this family which have appeared in the United States, funding and banking, one only is now heaping up gold by magick, and figuring in legislatures. She is adored as a beauty, and the other execrated as a hag; although the family likeness is so strong, that they pass for twins. As the fate of the general interest, depends upon this amour between the government and the twin sister of Mr. Addison's virgin, the consequences of endowing her with the privilege of passing consecrated laws or law charters, as her English sister has been endowed, are referred to the reader's consideration. Liberty was nearly smothered in the embraces between our government and Mr. Addison's virgin; the amour going on with her sister will hardly revive it. But let us return from the political features of the subject, to calculation. The annual exports of the products of the United States, have been supposed to amount to about forty millions of dollars, and the bank capital to about fifty; and we have endeavoured to prove, that the five millions paid annually for bank paper, cannot be reimbursed by any additional price bestowed by it on our exports. This glimpse of the manner in which banking, in its infancy, enriches agriculture and manufactures; in its maturity, becomes a clear light. By the return of 1803 to the British parliament, the official value of British manufactures or exports, was less than twenty-four millions sterling, but their real value was estimated by the minister at forty millions. Suppose the quantity of bank paper, publick and private, circulating in England, to be about five hundred millions. It receives between twenty and thirty millions, for enriching those, who export forty millions worth. The agriculture and manufactures of England, are enriched also in the same mode, by the sister of banking, so recently eulogised in this country for possessing these qualities. Above five hundred millions of debt stock, receives annually more than bank stock. Of what is paid to two other members of the same family, named patronage and hierarchy, we have no account; but exclusive of the sum paid to hierarchy and banking, by manufactures and agriculture, to get rich by the bounty of this generous family, the supplies of the same year exceeded seventy millions sterling; so that the scheme of paper and patronage, when matured, takes from a nation about one hundred

millions sterling, to enrich agriculture and manufactures, by enhancing the price of forty millions worth of their commodities.

And after paying all this money, it remains a question, whether
bank currency does not moreover diminish prices, to enrich capitalists, at the expense of agriculture and manufactures. In 1803, the
United States contained something more than one-third of the
people of Britain, and exported much more than a third of her
official exports, and nearly that proportion of her estimated exports. The exports of Great Britain were swelled by the estimate of
the minister, very far beyond the official returns; and those of the
United States, are rigidly confined to them; therefore it is highly
probable, that the value of exports, from the two countries, in relation to the number of people, did not fall short on the part of the
United States. Britain then, with a vastly greater proportion of this
stimulating and enriching stock, exported the same or a less value
of commodities, in relation to the number of people, than the
United States. This is only to be accounted for, by balancing the
exclusive advantages she possesses in fertility of soil, in manufactural perfection, in machinery and in rich provinces; with a drawback, arising from paper currency. Except for some drawback,
these immense advantages, ought to have been accounted for in
the comparison, by an immense superiority of exports in relation
to the numbers of people in the two countries. As they are lost, it
affords the strongest evidence against the assertion, that paper currency will excite industry, enrich manufactures or agriculture, or
even benefit commerce.

How can it do either, when paper stock draws from the national
labour, more than the whole value of what it exports? How can it
fail to be the most oppressive tax gatherer, when it is able to take
from a nation more than it sells? If it is admitted to be a tax when
it takes all, does it cease to be a tax, when it takes a part? The ten
hundred millions of bank and debt stock, has made every soul in
England worth to paper alone, eighty pounds sterling. Adding to
the drafts of paper, those of patronage, civil, military and religious,
the value of each soul to the system of paper and patronage, is
about one hundred and fifty pounds sterling. The American and
West-India slave owners are not task-masters, if this system, which
has made freeborn Englishmen of threefold value to itself beyond
African slaves, to their master, is not a task-master.

This stupendous mass of paper has been raised from a foundation as imaginary, as that of the earth in Indian cosmography. A

339

man, by becoming a law-maker, contrives to make the reputation of wealth more profitable to him than wealth itself. If a true opinion as to one's wealth, ought not to plunder a nation, the rights of falsehood are thus made greater than the rights of truth. The means used by the credit men in England, to lay industry under contribution, are used by the men of actual property in the United States, to lay themselves under contribution. The richest interest in the United States, is the agricultural. It does not hold by the tenure of its land, a shilling of the credit which sustains banking; and the small portion of bank stock it possesses, bears no proportion to its landed property. Yet it first mortgaged itself to enrich a poor speculating interest by the funding system, under the delusion of supporting a false national credit; and it again mortgages itself to enrich a banking interest, under the delusion, that it receives, and does not pay the profits of appreciating paper in the last, as in the first form.

In other countries, if the rich are knaves, they are not blind to their own interest. They inflict taxes, direct, indirect and intricate, of which they pay a part; but they take care to receive most or all. If these taxes are paid to armies, churches, navies, pensions or sinecures, they are received by the rich or their children. The paper interest in England, is willing to pay a small part of the enormous tax, drawn from the nation by paper stock, because it receives all; and the landed interest of the United States, is willing to introduce this fathomless mode of taxation here, because it pays nearly all, and receives a small part.

In the United States, the civil offices cost but little, and do not exceed the legitimate necessities of civil government. We have no armies, churches, navies, pensions or sinecures, contrived for the purpose of conveying to the richest class of citizens, the money drawn directly or indirectly from the nation. Stock, bank and funded, are the only modes hitherto used for drawing money from the many for the few; and the rich agrarian law-makers have most unskilfully suffered the money thus drawn to pass into the pockets of fallacious wealth. It is nearly true, that the rich class in England pay some and receive all; and that the rich class in the United States pay all and receive some. The first, fleece labour and industry for themselves; the other, fleece themselves for paper craft. Had the landed interest of the United States, laid out the nine millions a year, which it gives to bankers and certificate buyers, in a church, an army and a navy, it would have made a provision for its younger sons, like the rich classes of other countries, according to the wisdom of this world; all other rich classes combine their own interest and prosperity with high taxes; but to combine its own decay and ruin with taxation, by paying to paper stock nine millions a year, of which it receives but a trivial proportion, is a species of acuteness in the landed interest of the United States, according to the wisdom of no world that I know of.

It is true, that if the landed interest, in creating this annuity, had kept it for itself, corruption, oppression and party spirit would have been the consequence; such being the unavoidable effect of giving away by law, a sum of money annually, eighteen times more valuable than the Yazoo speculation; but as the landed interest pays the chief part of this annuity, it had the best right to receive it; and its sons, crowned with mitres or with laurel, might have cultivated virtues which adorn or benefit society. In how many revolutions of Mercury, would stock beget subjects for a Plutarch?

Had the nine millions been laid out in official patronage, instead of stock patronage, the amount paid by the nation might have terminated there. But banking, besides its dividends, possesses a power of causing the quantity, and of course the value of currency to fluctuate, by which it may impoverish and enrich, or tax and patronise, to a vast amount beyond its dividends; of this the nation can get no account. It is a power equivalent to incessant adulterations and purifications of specie, by an absolute monarch. Coin adulterated, or paper multiplied, buys less. Coin purified, or paper diminished, buys more. It would be dangerous for the strongest despotism to gather wealth, by causing gold to fluctuate, between twelve and twenty-four carats, several times a year. If this despotism was a merchant, it could by such a power, buy and sell the commodities of its subjects at what gain it pleased. The carat of paper money, fluctuates with its quantity, and this fluctuation is at all times within the power of banking, and frequently produced. Being capable of greater repetition, it can enrich and impoverish, beyond any practicable alternate adulteration and purification of coin, for the benefit of a corporation or a despotism. Paper currency can be made better and worse more frequently by the magick of a bank, than specie by the furnace of a monarch; but although the banking adulterations can do so much more work, yet we do not believe it because we do not see the process, and only see the effect, in their amassing wealth with a rapidity and duration, far beyond adulterations of coin in any mode hitherto discovered. If a king of England should call in forty millions of specie, and pay it back in adulterated money, so as to rob the nation of twenty; that freeborn people would probably cut off his head; and the same wise-born people, are quite contented to be robbed of a larger sum annually, by the same principle.

To illustrate the facility with which this may be done with paper, in a stockjobbing way, better than with specie, in a despotick way (as a chymical process, in the moist and dry way, can produce the same result) let us suppose the managers of banking to be buyers of the staple of a country; wheat for instance. When the crop comes in, the price will be kept down, by appreciating or purifying paper currency, by lessening the quantity. Under this influence, those who work the furnace, buy. The loss, like adulterations of specie, falls upon ignorance and industry. It is a law of maximum, or for fixing prices, except that an interested party regulates them, instead of a government.

This incessant fluctuation, in the intrinsick value of bank currency, is at least more likely to favour cunning, knavish, calculating speculation, than simple, honest, thoughtless industry. Those who settle the carat of this currency, are buyers; upon what principle to be found in human nature by the grossest credulity, can they be possibly induced to use this power, for the purpose of enhancing the value of the commodities they buy?

If the government of the fluctuation or carat of bank currency, was in the hands of a native mercantile interest, such an interest would undoubtedly endeavour to gratify the love of gain, by using it to buy as cheap, and to sell as dear as it could; and it would be to a considerable extent successful; but although it would appropriate to its own use, the whole mass of gain transferred by this fluctuation from the other interests of society, yet the nation would possess the consolation of reflecting, that its loss remained at home, and would return to it, the species of retribution, arising from individual splendour, munificence and luxury. But if a foreign capital should acquire an influence over the quantity, fluctuation or carat of bank paper, the wealth collected by it will be drawn to a foreign country. This is not all the calamity. If such a foreign capital or interest, should be the buyer of our exports, a power over the quantity or carat of bank paper, will enable it to diminish the exportation price, for the benefit of itself, and its own country. The degree of influence held by British capital over American banks, cannot be estimated. Whatever it is, a correspondent degree of effect must follow. It can diminish the prices of our exports both here and in Britain, and increase the English profit on re-exportation. The whole diminution it can cause, in the price of any article, is its gain and our loss. If in the article of tobacco, for instance, this gain is made on re-exportation to other countries; if on that of cotton, on its return, in a manufactured state, in a large amount, to this.

A variation in the value or carat of money, defeats its genuine end, and usefulness. It is the measure of all property, as the bushel is a measure of grain. Permanency makes measures the vehicles of justice; fluctuation, of fraud. If a fixed measure for some articles of property, will dispense justice and discourage fraud; a fluctuating measure for all articles of property, must dispense fraud and discourage justice. False weights and measures will corrupt morals, and a corruption of morals, will overturn governments founded in good principles. If such is the effect of a fraudulent mode of weighing and measuring property, by scales and measures, capable of being examined by the senses, and easy of detection; what will be the effect of measuring property, by a fraudulent mode, beyond the reach of the eye, and only to be detected by patient and deep investigation? Fluctuating money makes all weights and measures false. By extending and diminishing price alternately, the utmost evil of false weights and measures is produced. A few men, whose interest it is to do so, can cause the carat of bank currency, to fluctuate without control, account or punishment. When it diminishes the price of property (wheat for instance) twenty-five per centum, the effect to the seller is the same, as if the buyer had secretly added one fourth to the capacity of the bushel; when it increases the price co-extensively, the effect to this buyer, now the seller, is like cutting off one fourth of the same capacity. And the managers of the fluctuation, or carat of the measure, may thus gain twenty-five per centum, unjustly, by each operation.

A fluctuation between the two steadiest measures of property, gold and silver, has at some periods trenched considerably upon fair dealing, and produced oppressive consequences; adulterations of coin, are partial and temporary aggravations of these consequences, which are never long endured, because the process is physical, and easy to detect; and fluctuations of bank paper, from which the same effects in their utmost malignancy and permanency must follow, are endured, because the process of detection is metaphysical.

If the senses cannot perceive, that the same moral cause will produce similar effects; and that if a fluctuation in the measure of property, by the two first modes, brings oppression, its fluctuation by the third will also bring it; let the mind reflect upon the following supposition, congenial with this third mode. Suppose a corporation, exclusively possessed of the knowledge of assaying metals, to be endowed also with the right of coinage, without check or control, or any knowledge in the nation, as to the quantity of money made, or what it was made of. This corporation would resemble banking in all its aspects but one. A banking coinage, by managing fluctuation, or frequently changing the measure of property, may sell dear and buy cheap; it can throw alloy into paper, by the medium of quantity, and take it out by the medium of scarcity, at the national expense; but the coining corporation have no means of extracting the alloy thrown into gold or silver, without suffering themselves. Herein the cases differ. The coining corporation, can only fleece the nation by putting in the alloy, but the paper corporation can fleece it by taking out as well as by putting in the alloy. This power is an invisible agent, who pares, clips or sweats property at every contract, by making its measure contract or dilate according to his interest.

A nation must have permanent standards for measuring power and property, and perfectly understand their capacity, or cease to be free. If a legislature, though annually elected, can invent a measure, for transferring either to themselves or their faction, they will make it as capacious as they please. The office of our constitutions, is to take this identical power from our legislatures. A bushel of money absorbs power, or a bushel of power, money, as a bushel of sand does water.

By fraudulent modes of measuring property, nations are universally enslaved. Thus the feudal system enslaved. The fraud consisted in accumulating land in the hands of a few, under pretence of compensating these few for defending a multitude. The papal hierarchy became a tyranny from a fraudulent mode of measuring property on earth, by the artifice of selling heaven. Patronage generates despotism, simply from being a fraudulent mode of measuring property; it is not an empty office, but the wealth which it transfers or measures out from the many to the few, in which its tyranny consists. All these are modes of oppression, only because they are fraudulent modes of measuring property. They are indirect, but money is the direct mode of this mensuration. Though money is limited to specie, and should possess the steady value of a known and fixed carat, yet these indirect modes enslave nations, by measuring out property unfairly. But if money, the direct mode of measuring all property, can be made to fluctuate in value or capacity, by a few corporations, the operation in transferring and accumulating property, must be infinitely more rapid, than the operation of any indirect mode; and the effect infinitely more certain. It is this operation which terminates in tyranny, whether it is produced, directly or indirectly, by fraud, accident or pretended necessity. By ending in accumulation, sufficient to beget a separate interest, the tyranny follows of course. Whether banking therefore is founded in fraud or honesty, in deception or sincerity, is unimportant to the inquiry. So long as it is a mode of measuring property unequally by law, and not by industry, capable of begetting a separate interest in a nation, it must produce the effect produced by the feudal, hierarchical and patronage systems; because the effect of all three flowed from their being modes of measuring out property unequally by law, so as to beget a separate interest in a nation. Throughout the history of the civilized world, the admeasurement of property by industry, has bred patriots; by law, traitors to the liberty and happiness of nations. Will the form of a caliber, render a ball propelled by the same force, harmless? Principle is the powder which produces the effects of moral artillery. The powder of banking is precisely the same, with that used by the feudal system, hierarchy and patronage, to batter human liberty; namely, a distribution of property, not by industry, but by law. Wherein consists the oppression of monarchy and aristocracy, except in being such modes of measuring property? Wherein consists the fraud of these modes, except in making this distribution, by the unjust measures, law, and fluctuating adulterated money, instead of leaving it to be made by the just measures, industry, and money of a steady and known carat?

We have supposed the case of one state, erected by congress into a corporation, with the exclusive power of supplying the others with bank currency. Let us subjoin to the supposition, the idea of the incorporated state being mercantile, and the others, agricultural. How forcibly are the effects illustrated, of a power in one dealer, to regulate the value of the currency, or the capacity of the measure, by which the price of property is regulated for both. The whole agricultural interest, unadulterated by any commixture with the banking interest, occupies the precise place of the unprivileged states. In the case supposed, the oppression would not be borne for a moment; because the suffering being would be equal in union, sagacity and power, to the inflicting being. It is borne in the case existing, because the suffering beings, are unequal in union, sagacity and power, to the inflicting beings. Individual ignorance, passion and folly, is no match for corporate knowledge, calmness and cunning. To let loose upon a nation, a faction, enlisted and disciplined by charters and avarice, for the purpose of gathering money of individuals, is a project, equivalent to that of letting loose a veteran army upon an undisciplined militia.

Banking exclaims, let individuals shift for themselves. A band of conjurers or robbers, requires only that individuals should be left to shift for themselves. Individuals can never defend themselves against associations. The design of government, is to protect individuals against these very associations. The tyranny of fraud is not less oppressive, than that of force. All national grievances act upon individuals. A redundancy of circulating paper stock, collecting an enormous tax, must act upon individuals, like other national grievances. If the ten hundred millions of such stock in England, was suddenly converted into specie, whatever would fly away to other countries, would be the portion of currency, useless, and therefore oppressive to the extent of the tax it gathered. The specie expelled by bank paper from the United States, was made by that paper a redundancy of currency, useless, or it would have remained; the tax paid for a paper redundancy, which cannot follow the specie, is an oppression similar to the English. We see in the example of England, the errour of an opinion, that the quantity of a paper currency will be regulated by national wants; we see in America, that bank currency soon expels as redundant, a sum of specie currency, and takes its place to a far greater amount; we see that this redundancy, though unnecessary and pernicious, can gather wealth for a separate interest; to what amount, England has laboured in vain to discover, for a whole century. What expedient can individuals use to avoid these calamities?

Let individuals shift for themselves. What is this, but to exclude them from the benefits of government and society? Unassociated, the bitter beverage, prescribed by the paper capitalists to the English manufacturers, must replenish their cups. There, capital thrives, and labour starves. Here, industry has hitherto regularly gained from capital possessed by idleness. This wholesome operation will be reversed, as in England, by factitious capital, able to tax and out-thrive industry. It can as easily become the master of the industry applied to the earth, as of that applied to the products of the earth. The portion of a nation subject to supply the income of a paper capital, is not in fact in a state of society. Union or association implies equality. But what equality exists between in-fliction and suffering, between extortion and payment? Can a society or association be formed of a party of masters and a party of slaves? Those associated by law, cry out, 'let those out of this legal society shift for themselves.' Gentlemen, our policy intended to give an equal chance to us all in shifting for ourselves. Throw away the law charter tubes, contrived for sucking subsistence from those at work, as the vampire sucks blood from those asleep. How-ever insensible we are of the operation, as you distend we contract, and must dwindle into your slaves, if the process continues. If it is right that individuals should be left by government to shift for themselves, why is the enchanted mantle of law charter drawn over you, which makes those under its cover flourish, and withers all within the reach of its shadow?

When Walpole and the whigs invented the paper system of England, the increase of nominal price it promised, pleased the nation, and established the party. Inquire now of the nation, what pleasure the system gives them, and you are answered with groans. A party, called federal, in the United States, repeated Walpole's experiment with some success, by exhibiting to the nation the phantom of additional price, and giving to stockholders real wealth and power, at the national expense. And a party, called republican, incited by the pecuniary and political success of these progenitors, are repeating the same experiment, to gain the same substances, by an exhibition of the same phantom. Yet it is notorious, that it is the circulator, and not the receiver of bank notes, who grows rich. No corporation even asked a legislator, for the privilege of receiving paper. The British nation belong to paper stock, and not paper stock to the British nation. The whole juggle is managed according to the arithmetick of Laputa. Suppose a nation raises a certain quantity of exportable commodities, measured by the universal standard, gold or silver, bank projectors pretend to increase the quantity to what extent they please, by substituting a paper measure. And if they can increase them a jot, by altering the mode of measuring them, it is confessed that they can increase them without limitation. For this project, the nation at first pays the projectors five millions worth of the commodities measured by the

347

old standard. Thus the nation lose, and the projectors gain already an eighth part of these commodities. As the paper is increased, the opulence of the projectors and the impoverishment of the nation, correspondently follow. When the projectors gain twenty millions annually, the nation loses half its exportable substance, for a numerical phantom, by which to measure the other half. England gives the whole substance for this phantom. It is Wood's project in a worse form, as his half-pence contained some copper.

The engines of Archimedes destroyed the Romans, whilst they could not see from whence their fate proceeded. Moral engines are for the same reason concealed from those on whom they play. And these moral engineers, more skilful than Archimedes, often persuade their victims, joyfully to stretch out their necks to the stroke, like Turkish fanaticks, under a persuasion that it will waft them to paradise.

Taxation is a power, infinitely dangerous, and liable to abuse in the hands of a separate interest. In England, the noble interest cannot even propose a money bill. In America, the banking interest taxes, raises or diminishes these taxes, and publickly divides its collections, of about five millions annually, under charters for long terms, without the knowledge or control of the people, or their representatives. Patriotism is even more fusible than conscience, in money. We know that those who rob nations, do really feel as if they were virtuous and honorable men, and would scorn to steal a shilling. Hence the danger of exposing ourselves to be taxed, directly or indirectly, by an individual or a corporation. Feudal barons were liberal, and hierarchical dignitaries, charitable. Yet they oppressed nations by their privileges, with a good conscience. This is the best morality to which banking can aspire. Our policy has exploded it, by considering the criminality of injuring a nation, as amplified beyond that of injuring an individual, by the whole additional extent of the mischief.

Between accumulation by banking, and division by excluding perpetuities and promogeniture; between exclusive chartered interest and general social interest; between publick and corporate, or party influence over legislatures; no resemblance in principle, no sympathy exists. They are all contraries and antipathies. A republican will deride Mr. Adams's idea, of forming a quiet, permanent and happy government, with contrary and unfriendly principles; and attempt himself to reconcile enmities, inspired by clashing pecuniary interests, at least as malevolent as those inspired by orders. Exclusive privileges, for gathering money, produce parties more hostile to each other, and consequently to human happiness, than exclusive honorary titles. From the spirit of discord and injustice, infused into nations by titles, arise the objections to Mr. Adams's system. Is this spirit most malignant whetted upon the warm and flexible bosom of honour, or upon the cold and hard liver of avarice? In what unexplored depths of intellect, is to be found the patriotism and consistency of zeal, against and for the same evil principle, selecting its most aggravated forms both for reprobation and eulogy?

Wealth, it was observed, absorbed power, as sand does water. Another figure may place the idea in a stronger light. It attracts, contains and discharges power, as clouds do the electrical fire. Nothing can withstand its bolts. Wealth accumulated by legal means is here spoken of; that within the reach of human industry, being like genial clouds, as incapable of attracting a dangerous surcharge of the moral, as such clouds of the subtile physical fluid. Can Congress and the state legislatures, consistently with our policy, create by law, this electrical machine, able to shock or destroy our constitution?

Words hold principles, as sieves do water. In the words therefore, and not in the principles of our constitutions, parties seek for the chartering power. There, although a power in Congress, to bestow an exclusive banking charter on all the citizens of one state, could not possibly be found, all parties have found a power to bestow it on a few of them, or on a few aliens. And under this construction of the words of constitutions, not containing a single word relating to banking, people are fined, hanged and imprisoned with the common consent of judges, juries and lawyers, out of imitation to the English stockjobbing system. If legislatures can destroy political law or constitutions, by any mode not verbally prohibited, the exclusive right of the people to pronounce this law, or to establish constitutions, is a shadow; as a specification of every mode for destroying constitutions by law, is impossible. In this right consists their sovereignty. The people may call as many conventions as they please for fixing the principles of their government, but these principles can never be fixed, if legislatures can destroy them in any mode not verbally prohibited. All our constitutions, recognise and labour to fortify this right of the people; therefore an indirect legislative mode of destroying it, must be equally unconstitutional, with a positive law for that purpose.

349

If banking charters, like all other modes for measuring wealth by law, will change the nature and principles of governments, they are as unconstitutional, and as subversive of the sovereignty of the people, as a law for creating a king or an order of nobles. The five millions at this time taken annually from the people by these instruments, have already begotten a political power able to influence governments. This magnet for attracting power, grows daily. Anticipate its effects, by contrasting the accumulation it may end in, with an equal division of property. Would the political effects of the two measures be the same? Would these contraries generate contrary forms of government? If they would, then both are in substance, political or constitutional law, and legislatures have as little right to pass banking laws, for the accumulation, as agrarian laws, for the division of property.

If it is contended, that the state and general legislatures, cannot pass laws for dividing property, but that they may pass laws for its accumulation in the hands of a chartered interest; or that laws either for the division or accumulation of property, are of an honest and genuine municipal nature, without possessing a capacity to model power, and change governments; and if these assertions can be proved, we must proceed to the following argument.

The formation of society, and the alteration of its constituent rules, are admitted by our policy to be rights exclusively lodged in the people, in which rights the government they establish have no share. It is also admitted, that the rights subsisting previous to the compacts called constitutions, all remain, except those relinquished for the sake of forming the government. Banking diminishes these remaining rights, by transferring a portion of them to a new society, not formed by the people. But the government has no power to touch rights, not surrendered by the people for its formation. It was lately stated, that if a legislature can by law form a new society, to draw money artificially from the rest of a nation, that the residue of the old society was no longer in a social state. By the association of the people, the principle of an equality of rights may be asserted and established. By the association of the government, the contrary and artificial principle of exclusive privilege, may be asserted and established. Property, by the association of the people, may be placed under the protection of the first principle; by the association of the government, it may be exposed to the depredations of the second. The first association makes an entire nation; the second divides that nation into two, privileged and unprivileged. The object of one, may be the general good; of the other, to make the general good subservient to private avarice. Both their principles and ends may be precisely opposite. Suppose this new-formed little nation, had been invested by government with a power of waging war, against the lives of the associates under the old compact; would it not have violated the rights never surrendered by the people to the government? Do charters to a few, for waging war against the lives or against the property of the rest, differ in principle? Do not both equally violate the rights never surrendered by the people of the United States in forming governments? Where is the difference between taking away the arms or the wealth of the great nation, and giving them to the little nation? Is it not obvious, that a new association, by which either is affected, however called, overturns the old association? From that moment, no association but the new exists; because its operation makes the old association inoperative. The government which contrives, will adhere to the new compact, against the old, contrived by the nation. Those without the new society, to which the government has deserted, belong to no society; and those within it, belong not to the old society formed by the constitution, but to the new one, into which they are formed by law.

To illustrate the ease with which the principles of the society, established by the people, may be destroyed by a banking fabrick, reared by law, let us suppose Congress to create a bank, in which the state governments should receive allotments of stock, equal or superior to the state expenses. As it would be easy, by such an institution, to suppress all other banks, the capacity of this engine to produce an income adequate to the end, is unquestionable. Would it not commute the constitutional policy established by the people, for a new policy growing out of such a law? All the old checks and divisions of power would be overthrown. The pecuniary dependence of the state governments upon the people, would cease. The independence in their allotted spheres of the state, on the general government, would also cease. The state governments would become wholly dependent on Congress for money, by the disuse of the people to their taxes, which like poison administered in honey, would be too pleasant for ignorance to resist. Congress would see and use the influence thence arising, and the state governments would be such checks upon the general government, as those receiving salaries at his will, are upon a king. A charter of the general government would give money to the state governments, to gain a power inconsistent with the charters by which both were created. The political consequences of a proposal to subject the state governments to a pecuniary dependence upon the government of England, would be at once perceived. Is there more danger that they will merge into the English government, than into the general government? Would political or constitutional changes grow out of the remote cause; and none out of the near one? Let us suppose that the general government should be made dependent for revenue upon bank stock under state law charters, and the people to be thereby trained into the habit of paying nothing towards its support. Would it have an influence upon our constitutional policy and endanger that government? If such would be the effect of placing the general government under a pecuniary dependence upon state charters, the effect of the converse of the proposition is certain.

If a foreign government should acquire such a pecuniary influence over the state governments, the considerations, that no political or pecuniary connexion existed between it and our people, and that it did not procure money for the state governments at their expense, by spreading a corrupted faction among them; would present a feeble resistance to its destructive effects upon our policy; but no considerations equally consolatory occur in the case of a similar influence, possessed by the general government. The state governments being bribed to favour the minority nation created by the general government, a triple combination necessarily becomes the real government, and representation would be used as its instrument, just as it is used in England. Corruption would settle down from the head to the foot of the nation.

If banking would change our form of government in the supposed mode, it demonstrates the capacity of law for that end. If it could thus influence legislatures, it demonstrates its capacity to form individuals into corrupt factions. And if it would be dangerous to any society, should a foreign nation create a corrupt faction by a pecuniary influence within its bowels, it is more dangerous to it that its own government should do so, for the reasons by which the danger of an influence, foreign or domestick, over the state governments, is graduated.

The course of reasoning pursued by this essay, results in the definition, that *a transfer of property by law, is aristocracy, and that aristocracy is a transfer of property by law.* Mr. Adams's book is eminently instructive, by proving that aristocracy has every where generated calamitous struggles between those who gained, and those who lost property. Besides the unavoidable atrocities of enriched and impoverished factions, Mr. Adams proves by a multitude of examples, that the same aristocratical policy, will induce one or the other of these factions to destroy every vestige of free government; the enriched, to fortify their fraudulent wealth and power; the impoverished, to flee for refuge against many tyrants, under one. It is true that the banking mode of introducing these mischiefs, like the balancing, will ascribe them to an inartificial texture of the machine, but it will not gain the long credit of other aristocratical principles, because its superior rapacity will hasten it on towards the usual catastrophe of political fraud.

Section the Sixth

THE GOOD MORAL PRINCIPLES OF THE
GOVERNMENT OF THE UNITED STATES

By understanding the defects of our policy, we are enabled to correct them; by understanding its beauties, we shall scorn the delusive attractions of its ostentatious rivals. Its actual dispensation of more happiness than any existing competitor, demonstrates its superiority to the existing world; and testimony gathered from tombs, by title, orders and exclusive interest, or fashioned for the purpose which induced priests to fashion oracles, is not equally credible. The Augustan age itself, invoked by monarchy to confront with republican government, is like the golden one, a fiction. It was moulded by those who received, not by those who supplied the exactions of monarchy. A despotick and artful man, did not corrupt the talents of one age, to buy truth for the use of another. Truth is never disclosed, except by talents which are independent, and inquiries which are freer. Augustus was the monarch of the whole learned world; Lewis XIV was the monarch of France. Had France contained the learning of the world, the age of Lewis, would have furnished the same evidence in favour of monarchy, as is furnished by the age of Augustus. We only know that the reign of Lewis exhausted the adulation, the purses and the liberty of his subjects, because it is described by persons, neither his sycophants nor slaves. Of the Augustan age we now judge from such materials, as posterity would have done of the reign of Lewis, upon the exclusive evidence of his venal panegyrists or dismayed dependants.

It is by travelling from the court to the cottage, that the effects of political principles upon human happiness, can be computed. Hence, existing nations, can only confide in existing cases. The cottager has no historian to commemorate his misery, and the historian of the prince is bribed to hide it.

Soldiers and statesmen think the French and English forms of government the most perfect, because they are the most partial to their own professions; and strive to bend all freer forms towards these models best contrived for their own gratification, because that effect is the logician which defines their patriotism. The policy of the United States was contrived for advancing the prosperity of an entire society; but it cannot be preserved against the power and arts of soldiers, statesmen, or separate interests of any kind, except by discovering the principles of government calculated to dispense general good, with the same acuteness by which the creatures of legislative partiality, discern whatever will transfer wealth and power from nations to themselves.

The moral, like the physical world, is subject to system and regularity. It is not left by Omnipotence in a state so chaotick, as that the same moral cause, should now produce good, and then evil. Men do not entrust their sheep to wolves, because it is fabled that once wolves were not carnivorous. The description of monarchical governments, by the minions of its frauds, or the candidates for its treasures, is entitled to the same credit as the description of the wolf in the fictions of poetry.

The fact we have assumed, lies before the senses of the reader. Let him look at the monarchies of the present age, and then at the United States. Let him listen to the groans of other regions, and the exaltations of America. Let all his senses go in quest of comfort and wretchedness. Each on its return will testify 'that the effects of our policy are infinitely better, than those of any other.' The comparison at this time spreads over a vast variety of governments, founded in force or fraud, but exhibited in sundry modifications of factitious orders; it therefore brings the whole group to the test of one, founded in a selection of good, and an exclusion of bad moral principles. The success of our experiment, confronted with an host of miscarriages, bestows upon its title to pre-eminence, the utmost degree of demonstration, of which the case is capable.

The grateful task of ascertaining the principles, which have produced effects incomparably beneficial to the United States, is left by Mr. Adams to be discharged. Instead of their vindication, promised by the title of three volumes, he casts a glance towards the contour of our governments in one volume, leaves them in repose throughout two, and defends contrary principles in all. Compelled directly or indirectly to assail the principles of our policy, because they lay in the way of his system, a caricature or travesty appeared, when we expected a defence.

Mr. Adams considers our division of power, as the same principle with his balance of orders. We consider these principles as opposite and inimical. Power is divided by our policy, that the people may maintain their sovereignty; by the system of orders, to destroy the sovereignty of the people. Our principle of division is used, to reduce power to that degree of temperature, which may make it a blessing and not a curse; its nature resembling fire; which uncontrolled, consumes; in moderation, warms. The principle of its division among orders, is to erect an omnipotent power, able, like an irresistible conflagration, to consume every thing in its way.

This radical errour forced Mr. Adams to overlook the prime division of power, between the people and the government; the federal division of power between the general and state governments; and that beautiful division of election, by which an ochlocracy or mob government is prevented; and to convert the subordinate divisions of power, which are only details of these superior principles, into sovereign orders and virtual representation.

Without either stating or discussing the principles of our policy, Mr. Adams concludes, that they ought to be changed, *because commotions and revolutions perpetually attend factitious orders or ranks.* To ascertain this fact, he cites all the memorable forms of government, comprising the principle of factitious orders, furnished by the history of mankind; and having indubitably proved it, he infers that our policy is bad, because it has rejected that principle.

The surprise which such an inference would naturally excite, is assuaged by the address of substituting a theory of the British system of government, for its real operation. The sophistry of reasoning from a comparison between theory and practice, is obvious. The most perfect operating government, may be made to look defective, compared with a fabrick, reared by the imagination. And by calling this imaginary fabrick, the British government, all the old prejudices in its favour are ingeniously ensnared, by the Aristotelian artifice of hypothetical systematizing. The mind can only be freed from these fetters by comparing realities.

The history of ancient times is hardly more weighty, opposed to living evidence, than the wanderings of fancy; it is invariably treacherous in some degree, and comes, like oracle, from a place into which light cannot penetrate. We are to determine, whether we will be intimidated by apparitions of departed time, frightfully accoutred for that purpose, to shut our eyes, lest we should see the superiority of our policy displayed, not in theory, but in practice; not in history, but in sight.

Mr. Adams reasons from hypothesis and theory, in his defence of factitious orders. He establishes by complete testimony, the fact, that political evil has been universally their associate; but instead of suffering this effect, to lead him to such orders as its cause, he attributes it to their inartificial adjustment. Such reasoning is the errour of ancient philosophy, exploded by Bacon. Rejecting hypothesis and theory, he travels by effects to causes, and from causes to effects. To the use of this correct mode of reasoning it is owing, that other sciences have advanced so rapidly since the time of Lord Bacon; whilst political philosophy remained unimproved until the American revolution, because it assumed ancient theories for settled facts.

The basis of our policy, like the basis of modern philosophy, is the constancy of nature, in her moral, as well as in her physical operations. A frequent or long concomitancy between cause and effect, establishes a particular fact, from which we are enabled to infer a general law. A concomitancy between hereditary orders or exclusive factitious interests, and political misery, has constantly apppeared throughout the annals of human nature; and a concomitancy between political equality and political happiness, has endured in America, for the space of thirty-five years in above thirteen separatè governments, making an experience equal to four hundred years, to which ought to be added near two centuries previous to the revolution, not in theory, but in fact. Hence necessarily results a general law, unless nature, in her moral operations, pursues principles the reverse of those, to which she strictly adheres in her physical; and is capricious, arbitrary and inconsistent. If the fact we contend for is ascertained, and if from this fact a general law is discovered, it then becomes as certain and inevitable, that political misery, will be an effect of hereditary orders or factitious interests, as that light will be the effect of the rising of the sun. Let the intellectual, like the material philosopher, reason from facts, and the phenomena of mind will become as well understood for temporal purposes, as those of body.

A law of nature constitutes truth. This would suffice for human use, if we were unable to discover how it became a law, as is frequently the case. If these orders or interests tend to excite, not the good, but the evil qualities of man; the moral power which enacts the law, and thè impossibility of its abrogation, both become manifest. It is as unnatural to expect, by artificial means, to cause such orders or interests to produce peace, justice and happiness, as that any artificial arrangement of a society composed of lions, wolves and bears, would prevent the effects of their natural qualities; because the natural qualities of moral beings (if the expression is allowable) such as hereditary orders and separate factitious interests, are not less certain and unchangeable, than those of these beasts.

The inability of mere form or artificial arrangement, to defeat a natural law, even of the moral kind, is demonstrated in the experience of the United States. These forms or arrangements have been frequently changed, and are different among the states. But the irresistible power of the moral principles common to all, compels every modification to be subservient to its will. And the good effects under different forms, produced by the good moral principles of all, are an evidence, that evil moral principles cannot be made to produce good moral effects by the force of form or artificial arrangement; it would be as possible, that a less mechanical power should control a greater.

A theory or hypothesis, cannot pretend even to plausibility, unless it is deduced from some general law of nature. One which sets out upon the foundation of hereditary orders or alienable exclusive privileges, violates the law, which has determined that talents shall not be inheritable, nor merit transferable. Let us endeavour further to apply this observation to Mr. Adams's system, by comparing it with the agrarian theory.

The idea of Lord Shaftesbury, adopted by Mr. Adams, is, 'that the political balance of orders cannot be adjusted or maintained, without a balance of property.' The perpetual changes among the holders of land, the most permanent and unchangeable species of property, render this ingredient unattainable. And yet its attainment is obstructed by fewer difficulties, than a permanent and equal distribution of power and mental capacity, necessary to perfect the system of orders. As the system proposes to produce good effects, upon no other condition than that of violating and controlling several irresistible laws of nature, it is invariably unsuccessful.

A political equality of rights among men, on the other hand, is founded in a general law of nature; and yet even this simple and natural system is declared to be unattainable, by those who contend for the possibility of a political equality of rights among orders. That which they assert cannot be effected between two individuals, though it naturally exists, is proposed to be accomplished between orders, composed of multitudes.

The ingredients of Mr. Adams's theory, consist of an equality or balance of property, power and understanding, between orders comprising a nation. And yet all the disciples of the theory, will exclaim against the mischief, folly and impossibility, of levelling or balancing property among individuals.

I agree with them in a disapprobation of levelling property by law; but the difference between us is, that I object to the levelling principle itself, whilst they approve of its application to effect their theory. I contend that the folly and mischief of enriching orders, such as the feudal and the paper, at the expense of a nation, is at least equal to that of levelling property among individuals; and that the impossibility of maintaining the equality they approve, is as great as that of maintaining the equality they condemn.

Now if Mr. Adams's theory of a balance or equality among orders, consists of three ingredients, neither of which is attainable, according to the laws of nature, it is itself a phantom of the imagination; and yet the imagination which fosters it, asserts that the system of an equality of rights, naturally existing, and actually operating, is impracticable. The hypothesis of orders, to exist itself, resorts to one fiction, 'a king cannot die;' and to destroy a successful rival, to another, 'an equality of civil rights cannot live.' But several complete experiments, as effectually overturn the latter fiction, as a multitude have the former.

The excellencies of our civil policy, and the defects of all others, cannot be estimated, unless the language used to explain them is well understood. To the efforts already made for impressing a correct perception of the principles on which the reasoning of this essay is founded, we will therefore add another. To understand, we have analyzed the intellectual world into two classes, good and evil; and to discover the members of each class, we fix their qualities, not by the hypothetick, but the practical mode of reasoning. If the fact appears by a satisfactory experiment, that the political moral being, called hereditary order, or that called exclusive privilege, begets the evil effects of avarice, ambition, faction, commotion, tyranny, or any others, we assign them to the evil class. And if by the experience of America, the fact appears, that an equality of civil rights, produces moderate government, or any other national benefit, we assign this moral being to the good class. Having discovered by their phenomena the classes to which these beings belong, we conclude, that no human ingenuity can change the class or the nature of any individual, any more than it could change the nature of a physical being. And that it is as obviously erroneous to assert, that hereditary order, or exclusive privilege, will bless mankind, as that water will burn them.

The possibility of effecting a classification of the beings or individuals of the moral world, and of assigning each to his proper class, by an impartial and careful investigation of phenomena, with a degree of accuracy, exceeding even the classification of the vegetable kingdom, is not incomprehensible. And its importance seems to have been suggested by divine intelligence, in having implanted in every breast, an auxiliary for the head in the prosecution of this science, of acute discernment, and instinctive integrity.

Such a work, however, was neither within my powers nor design. To arrange a few of those moral beings, called political, by the test of facts; and particularly those of which the American policy and Mr. Adams's system are compounded; to ascertain the difference and the preference; and to detect any fugitives from one class to the other, is the utmost I propose.

Besides hereditary order, and exclusive privilege, placed at the head of one class, we have swelled it by the moral beings, called legal religion, legal freedom of inquiry, accumulation of power, patronage or corruption, ignorance, virtual representation, judicial uncontrol, funding, and political families, or an oligarchy of banks.

In the opposite class of moral beings, we have placed an equality of civil rights, freedom of religion, and of inquiry, division of power, national influence or sovereignty, knowledge, uncorrupted representation, and actual responsibility. This enumeration of a few individuals is used to explain our reasoning, and not as including entire classes.

We have attempted to prove, that the evil class, cannot be made to produce good effects, nor the good class, evil; and the superiority we contend for, on behalf of the policy of the United States, consists in this, that it is compounded chiefly of the good, whilst all other governments have been compounded chiefly of the evil class; so as to account for the blessings of the one, and the mischiefs of the other; and to produce both a shining pattern and a shining beacon.

The same mode of reasoning appeared calculated also to awaken publick vigilance, against the most dangerous means of changing the nature of a government. It may have been compounded of moral beings, selected with integrity and wisdom, from the good class; but by transplanting into it by law, individuals from the evil class, these exoticks must change its nature. For instance; let us look at our own policy, as it stood immediately after the adoption of the present general government, and contemplate the features or moral beings, to be seen in the faces of the several constitutions, of which it was compounded. Transplant into it a sufficient portion of executive patronage to influence Congress; a banking oligarchy without a distinguishing badge, influencing election; judicial irresponsibility; religion, printing and speaking, regulated by law; an unarmed militia and a standing army; or any system of legislation congenial with monarchy or aristocracy; and say if our policy would be unaltered. The change would be owing to an interpolation of political moral beings into it, taken from a class opposite to that which furnished its original materials.

It is necessary to keep in sight our policy, Mr. Adams's system, and the actual English government, to illustrate or explain the principles contended for. In all Mr. Adams's authorities, we find orders, titles or exclusive privileges in some shape; but in none, the exact and permanent balance, without which Mr. Adams's admits them to be a curse. Vicissitude, and not permanency, is their essence, as determined by experience, and a constant succession of revolutions is the dispensation they yield. The alternation was rapid among the Italian republicks. The aristocratick scale, whilst loaded with wealth, talents, perpetuities, and superstition, preponderated against the democratick, lightened with ignorance. In England the first being unladen by alienations, and the second rendered more weighty by wealth and knowledge, an approach towards a balance begat evils, which drove that country for refuge into the aristocracy of the third age, composed of paper, patronage and armies. Experience declares, and Mr. Adams acknowledges, that the theory of balancing orders, has never generated the effects which Mr. Adams thinks it capable of generating; whilst the theory of a division of power, for the express purpose of subjecting governments to nations, has unexceptionably succeeded in the practice of each of the states, and of the United States. This double experience defines the nature of the moral elements, both of the American and Mr. Adams's policy. Ours, by suppressing the evil principle of privileged orders, begets none of those calamities, swarming about every experiment founded in his. His, taking the balancing principle for its basis, has laboured in vain to draw good out of it, by the artifice of measuring out power, or the excitement to tyranny, equally between orders. Ours does not trust to evil for good; his admits each order, separately existing, to be a political devil; but asserts, that three devils, may by the menstruum of mutual jealousy, be turned into one God. Ours conceives that a political deity ought to be made of eternal moral virtues, and not of fluctuating human vices.

The only use which the theory of ranks or orders has been pleased to make of the laws of nature, is drawn from the existing inequality among the talents and qualities of men. Enough has been heretofore said upon this subject; and it is only mentioned to suggest, that the degrees of this inequality, are compressed by this theory into three, not by the suggestion of nature, which with the intervention of education, displays them at this day, as numberless, but by the arbitrary will of hypothesis. The magick contained in the number three is the magick of habit, not of nature. Human qualities are infinitely more divisible. In England, a triple natural division is said to exist. There they have a king, lords, commons, judiciary, army, paper system and hierarchy. In India, titles and tribes are endless. In Rome, the first theory consisted of a king, patricians, knights and plebeians. In America, we see power, legislative, executive and judicial; but these are so far from comprising the mass of political power, created by our system, as to be themselves subordinate to a division of power, between the people and the government; to a division of power between the general and state governments; and to the sovereignty of the people. Hence this number is no less arbitrary and unconnected with any principle in nature, when applied to power, than when applied to orders.

The more power is condensed, the more pernicious it becomes. Divided only into three departments, such as king, lords and commons, it can easily coalesce, plunder and oppress. The more it is divided, the farther it recedes from the class of evil moral beings. By a vast number of divisions, applied to that portion of power, bestowed on their governments by the people of the United States; and by retaining in their own hands a great portion unbestowed, with a power of controlling the portion given; the coalescence of political power, always fatal to civil liberty, is obstructed. Small dividends are not as liable to ambition and avarice, as great dividends. Self interest can only be controlled by keeping out of its hands the arms with which it has universally enslaved the general interest. But it universally gets these arms by persuading mankind, that the danger is imaginary, and the remedy useless; and hierarchy, feudality, hereditary orders, mercenary armies, funding and banking, have successively inflicted upon them, the expiations of an opinion so absurd.

Nature, says Mr. Adams, suggests, nay dictates, the system of three orders. As to the United States, he satisfies this natural law, by legislative, executive and judicial orders; as to England, by king, lords and commons; making judicial power a natural order here, but not in England. The natural right of self government and natural orders, cannot associate. Our policy is erected upon one principle; Mr. Adams's upon the other; and a defence of his, cannot be a defence of the policy of the United States.

By contrasting the division of power resorted to by our policy, with Mr. Adams's idea of a triple division by nature, a wide difference will appear. By our policy, power is first divided between the government and the people, reserving to the people, the control of the dividend allotted to the government. The dividend allotted to the government, is subdivided between its two branches, federal and state. The portion of this subdivision, assigned to the federal government, is again subdivided between two legislative branches, two executive branches, and two judicial branches; judges and juries; all enjoying specified powers independent of each other. The portion assigned to the state governments, is distributed in quotas still more minute, many of which will be omitted, because of the various modes pursued towards this end, by different states. We find two legislative branches, two executive, and two judicial. A power of such magnitude, as to be relied on for national defence, immediately dependent on the people, and generally removed far from a subserviency to any other division; this is the militia, officered by the people, or by the county courts; trying offenders by its own courts, or holding commissions during good behaviour. Patronage, a formidable power, is divided in a multitude of ways, the chief of which consists of portions exercised by the people, by legislative bodies, and by a variety of inferior courts. Ineligibility is a species of division of power often resorted to. And throughout the whole distribution, our policy, as if on purpose to subvert the hypothesis of a triple natural division of power, has in a multitude of instances, invested the same organs with different powers; such as legislative branches, with judicial and executive powers.

· As the government is divested by a multitude of divisions, of the ability and inclination to tyrannize; so by the multitude and variety of its elections, our policy cleanses the sovereignty of the people of those defects incident to its aggregate exercise; concluding that power, untempered by division, exercised by nations or their governments, is invariably the scourge of human happiness.

What do we discern in this system of division to justify the hypothesis of three natural orders, or three natural classes of powers? To which of these classes can the division of election be assigned? But if a doubt should remain, let the reader reflect upon the inconsistency between natural powers or orders, and their responsibility. In providing for the responsibility of political power of every complexion, our policy denies the truth of the position, which asserts, that political power is created by nature.

It establishes, with unexampled ingenuity, a double responsibility; of the people to the government, and of the government to the people; the division of election, is the basis of the one, and the division of the powers of government, of the other; by the first, the danger of a physical accumulation of power, and by the second, the danger of its moral accumulation, is obstructed; to prevent the people from acting in mass against the government, under the impulse of passion; and the government from acting in mass against the people, under the impulse of avarice and ambition. The division of election renders it difficult to turn the people into an ochlocracy; and the division of the powers of government, renders it difficult to turn the publick officers into an aristocracy.

Political errour contains two extremes, both of which are happily guarded against by the principle of division; and it would make but little difference to the nàtion whether it was plunged into one, by abolishing the responsibility of the people to government; or into the other, by abolishing the responsibility of the government to the people. Just as the devastation of a furious torrent, and the exsiccation of a vertical sun, are both destructive, and both prevented by the divisions of a stream, according to the ingenious system of irrigation.

It is important to inquire, whether the right of instruction is attached to the right of election. Neither the moral right of any species of principal to employ agents, nor the moral duty of agents to conform to the instructions of principals in discharging agencies, is denied. Obedience to monarchical, aristocratical, military, legislative, judicial, and all individual instructions, from principals to agents, is universally enforced by dismission, sentence, fine, imprisonment and death; and disobedience is considered as illegal, immoral and void. It is also agreed, that the duties of agency, implied or expressed, allowed to kings, to conquerors and to beggars, and enforced by the axe, the musket and the forum, belong also to the species of sovereignty existing in the United States.

A constitutional declaration, that duty was an adjunct of agency, would have been as absurd, as that heat was an adjunct of fire. The qualities by which a thing is defined, must be included in that thing; and an assertion, that an insurance against fire, did not include an insurance against heat, would be equivalent to an assertion, that an agency did not imply an obligation to fulfil its duties; or a right to raise armies, a right to arm them. Political law could not have deprived agency of its attributes, without extinguishing it; because, stript of its duty to its principal, its nature is as completely changed, as the nature of despotism, stript of its power.

The sovereignty of the people arises, and representation flows, out of each man's right to govern himself. With this individual right, political structures are built. Individuals, ·in forming a society, may arrange their rights in such forms as they please. They may, like the Greeks, lodge legislation in the society collectively; and they may, in that case, allow a representative to an absent individual. Would this representative be the agent of the individual who deputed him, or of the rest of the society? Would those personally present enjoy their shares of the legislative power, and absorb as a majority the shares of those represented; or would each legislator be the agent of the majority of the society? Neither of these intentions could, consistently with the supposed policy, exist, because the majority could not be ascertained, except by counting the individuals of the society. The English house of lords, with the right to vote by proxy, is such a nation. The proxy is subject to the instructions of his principal, and owes no duty to the majority.

Or suppose a society constituted in imitation of the Roman model, with legislation condensed into centuries, each entitled to vote personally, or by its representative. Would the representative of a century, be the agent of the majority of centuries, by which he was not deputed, or of the century by which he was; and how could this majority be known, except by ascertaining the opinion of each century? If no century could vote by representation, each century in voting would be exercising not a trust but a right; nor could it be the agent of a majority, because in every question the majority could only be ascertained by the votes of the centuries; and an agent cannot exist before a principal. If all the centuries legislate, not in person, but by representatives, the representative could not owe the duties of agency to the majority of centuries, both because his principal did not, and also because it is as impossible to ascertain this majority, as in the last case; this can only be effected by counting the votes of the centuries, personally, or by representation. Thus a duty to obey the instruction of an ideal majority, would divest the representative of the character of agent, and transform him into a despot, at liberty to pursue his own ambition, interest, caprice or vanity, without regard to any principal; and under pretence of loyalty to a nonentity, convert representatives into a succession of despots over real majorities.

Societies may give legislation whatever form they prefer. They may legislate by the majority of individuals. They may allot themselves into centuries or districts, and legislate by a majority of sections. Or they may legislate by representatives deputed aggregately or by sections. If they legislate in person, aggregately or in sections, this real nation cannot be considered as the minister of an ideal nation. If they legislate by representatives, chosen aggregately or in sections, the members of the society, are as much principals, whilst acting as electors, as they would have been acting as legislators, had they not resorted to representation. The idea that the whole society, acting aggregately or in sections, exercises only a ministerial authority, and not an inherent right, is not sustainable; because self government cannot be the donation of the society which it creates; and if election is a resource for exercising a natural right, and not the author of that right, this resource for preserving, could never have been intended to destroy the right, whether it was exercised individually or in sections. Voting in sections is as compleat an exercise of the natural right, as voting individually. Election by sections, is equivalent to aggregate election. And by dividing election into sections, the rights and duties of principals and agents are also divided, because there is no other social principal to depute or to instruct. Laws made by centuries or districts, each having a vote, or by the agents of each, are binding, because the society has adopted such modes of ascertaining the social majority; and the adoption of one mode, proves that no other exists. A division of the mode of exercising the natural right of self government, is extremely different from a division of the right itself. The first is indispensible in a large territory, from the impossibility of assembling the nation at one place, for the preservation of the right. But to cut the right itself asunder, and to lodge only half, or less than half, with the divisional mode for exercising and saving it, would certainly kill the whole. It is compounded of the powers of naming and instructing its agents. The instructing moiety is better than the naming moiety, as the right of naming an agent is no security if we cannot influence him; nor is it of much consequence who names him, if we can. If the divisional mode of exercising the right of self government, can only contain its form, but not its substance; and the aggregate mode has been determined by experience, to be unsuccessful in small, and impracticable in large countries, the conclusion is, that the right itself must die. It can be held but not exercised aggregately, and it can be exercised but not held divisionally.

The objection to the district right of instruction, is founded upon the idea, that a nation, though it divides election, retains aggregately the right of instruction. But all natural rights are individual, and this individuality is the substratum of our policy. It has not moulded this individuality into an aggregate right of instruction but it has moulded it into a right of district election, without committing the errour of withholding the natural appurtenance of election, and breaking up the relation between principal and agent, to bestow on itself the following hideous aspect. If the electing, punishing and rewarding district, and this national majority, under which rebellious agency pretends to take sanctuary, should give contrary instructions, the chastening provision of our policy, according to the idea of an aggregate right of instruction, would have been an alternative between committing a crime with impunity, or suffering a punishment for patriotism. The aggregate majority would hold a right without the remedy, and the district the remedy without a right. But it is overlooked that majorities and their rights are creatures of social compact, and not endowed by nature with political power. They are compounded of men, excluding women; of adults, excluding minors; of landholders, excluding those who have no land; and in a multitude of ways. However compounded, they are a social being, and no social duty can accrue to any majority, but to one established by social compact, because no other majority exists possessed of any political right. Admitting then the right of the majority to instruct, the right accrues to the social majority, and wherever that exists in the form of sections or districts, the mode by which it can exercise its power, must be through the form in which it exists. Thus only can it elect, and thus only instruct. Any other species of instruction, instead of a social, would be revolutionary or rebellious. An appeal by the representative from the organized majority, to an ideal disorganized majority, is therefore a violation of the duties of agency. And instruction from such a source, would be contrary to the social compact; inconsistent with the moral relation between agency and duty, and between crime and punishment; and as impracticable as aggregate election. It is, however, necessary to consider, whether a right in the social majority to instruct its agents through its moral, covenanted and practicable channels, is necessary to preserve the sovereignty of the people, or of a republican form of government.

Out of the natural right of self preservation, sovereignties of all forms have collected the same right, as inherent without the formality of a positive stipulation. There never has occurred the least occasion to convince an aristocratical or monarchical sovereignty, that periodical agents, above their immediate control, would speedily subvert their sovereignties. Who ever thought of preserving life, by a perpetual obligation to swallow all the drugs administered by a periodical succession of doctors? Would not free nations soon die of their doctors, when the highest fees are gained by the most poisonous prescriptions? And to what purpose would the epoch of election return, after freedom was dead? It is a question of fact precluding argument. History abounds with the treasons of agents towards nations. Denmark recently, and France before our eyes, were betrayed to tyranny by elected legislative agents.

Without denying to our species of sovereignty the right of self preservation, we are perplexed as to the modes of exercising this right by blending sovereignty with agency; and the demonstration of the integral sovereignty of districts, as to legislation, is somewhat obscured by the idea of degrading them into agents, without discerning that it would exalt lower agents into sovereigns. Like the electors of the president and Maryland senators, once accoutred in the garb of agency, districts become subordinate, and evanescent; and our sovereignty is dissolved, or embalmed by verbal syrup into a mummy, retaining only a periodical nomination of sovereigns. No species of sovereignty can subsist, without subsisting attributes equal to its preservation. I am speaking of social sovereignty, and not of the natural right to resist oppression; of organi-

368

cal, not of irregular remedies. The natural right appears throughout history, to be the least successful guardian of liberty, and as
frequently the author as the destroyer of tyranny.

An independency of district instruction, is assumed upon Mr.
Adams's doctrine of virtual representation. That doctrine recognises hereditary usurpers, as national representatives; the British
parliament as representatives of America, and each district agent
as the representative of an entire nation. Virtual representation
and a balance of orders or powers, are twin labourers for transforming our division of election and of power, into instruments for
working ends contrary to those they were intended to produce. In
search of power, it destroys subordination and social order. Every
civil functionary, starts up into a representative of the entire
nation, none owes obedience to any other superior, and the general
and constable, have an equal right with the district member, to
assume the independence it bestows.

An incapacity of political law for producing the subordination
of its agents to the sovereign power, would produce the same
effects, as an incapacity of civil law, for producing the subordination of individuals to the government. Murder, rapine or theft,
would be but badly restrained, by an advertisement to culprits,
that they might wallow in wickedness for four or five years with
impunity, after which the power of committing further crimes
should be taken from them. Kings, though not among the wisest of
sovereigns, never thought of this species of civility to deputies as a
security for sovereignty. A chain of subordination from sovereign
power downwards, is necessary for its preservation; and instead of
snapping asunder the link between sovereignty and its highest
agency, it ought to be the strongest, because that agency is
uniformly its destroyer, whenever a new sovereignty is erected
upon the ruins of the old. Otherwise the sovereignty in its interval
of torpidness, must submit to behold its agents, like Persian satraps,
go to war with each other for itself. What, for instance, can preserve
the rights and duties attached to the presidential agency, against
Congress, but the sovereign of both? If the sovereign is unable to
protect some agents against the usurpations of others, the powers
of all will gradually fall under the regulation of force and corruption, and ambition or casualty will supplant compact. Even
mutual corruption might cement legislative and executive power,
in a league to destroy the popular sovereignty of our system, if it
cannot act constitutionally at all times for its own preservation.

Publick opinion is felt even by despotism. The best eulogy of printing, is its facility for applying it. Election by districts is selected by our policy as the cleanest channel for conveying it. If party gazettes were more chaste vehicles of public opinion, why were they not entrusted with the selection of legislative agents? If they are less so, why is election to be stript of the appurtenant right of instruction, except to contaminate and discredit publick opinion, and to convert representation into a despot? The best channel for electing publick opinion, must also be the best for instructing publick opinion. And if popular sovereignty is even limited to that definition, the best mode of destroying it, would be to destroy, one after the other, the best channels by which it can be conveyed.

If state legislatures are to be considered as holding each a dividend of an aggregate sovereignty, their right to instruct their senators in Congress, would be equal to the right of a district to instruct its representative. But if each state constitutes a distinct sovereignty, its right of instruction is equal to that of an entire society. It being admitted, as its form demonstrates, that this senate was created for the purpose of preserving state sovereignty.

Oaths of agents are prescribed to enforce, not to destroy the duties of agency. If a popular sovereignty, and its appurtenance, instruction, exists in our policy; and if no such sovereignty can be found in it except in the district form, the fidelity required by oaths must be due to that form of sovereignty, and not to one which only exists in the imagination of the swearer. Because, if the swearer could fashion the oath to his own conscience or judgement, under the pretext of its binding him to pursue the publick good, as indicated by these guides, instead of conforming his conscience and judgement to the established policy, the oath would not perfect, but dissolve the obligations of agency, and leave him at liberty, if he supposes it will benefit the nation, either to disregard instructions, or to legislate for the introduction of monarchy. If the oath is only a pledge of loyalty to pre-existing duties, these duties thus confessed by the oath are evidence of principal and agent, insisted upon by the imposer, and admitted by the taker, which suffices to refute the idea borrowed from monarchy, that our government is our sovereignty; and also to demonstrate that our sovereignty resides elsewhere. The punishment of rejection on a new election, is an additional proof that our policy by the oaths of fealty, so far from contemplating the idea of a loyalty of the swearer to himself, recognises a superior invested with power to apply a remedy for the insufficiency of the oath. And though the insufficiency of this remedy itself to compel obedience to instructions, is urged as an argument against their force, yet it is of the same weight with the assertion, that these oaths also are without obligation, because the mode of compelling obedience to them, is as imperfect as the mode of compelling obedience to instructions. The imperfection of a remedy, is no argument against the right. The Saxon weregild, of fifty shillings, was a better security for the right of living, than an empty periodical election would be for the right of living free; yet the ability to pay the fine, so far from justifying the right to murder, suggested the necessity of a better remedy. A moral code, can only be perfected, by providing new remedies against crimes, when old ones become insufficient. The right to life is not destroyed, by an imperfect remedy for its preservation; and if the oath of loyalty to our sovereignty, with the punishment of rejection on a new election, are imperfect remedies for preserving the sovereign right of instruction, new remedies, and not an abandonment of the right, can only preserve our moral code, called political law.

As representation was intended to express, not to subvert publick opinion, our policy resorts to sundry expedients for making representatives the genuine organs of certain districts, and for preventing them from degenerating into representatives of themselves, or of their own consciences, vices or follies. This degeneracy is a subversion of the republican maxim, that the right of national self government rests in the majority; and transfers that right to a very small number of individuals, by using the maxim itself as the instrument for its own destruction. Representation by districts, being the only social mode of ascertaining the will of the majority, and each district exclusively possessing the means of infusing its will into its own representative; an end which our policy every where labours to attain; the will of a majority can never be constitutionally ascertained, except through the regular organized channel for that very purpose; for if instruction by districts, is not a pure indication of the publick will, neither can election by districts be so; and no genuine mode of ascertaining it exists.

Let us now compare our beautiful system of dividing election, agency and power, with the multitude of forms of government quoted by Mr. Adams. Where do we see in it the aristocratick and plebeian castes of Rome or Florence, arrayed against each other by trivial accidents, by the vile arts of factitious demagogues, or by the viler dishonesty of separate interests or exclusive privileges? It is in vain that Mr. Adams is forever quoting the mischiefs produced by any system of government, having factitious orders, armed with the motives and passions which murder and burn; or separate privileges, armed with statutes to plunder and tax; or national mobs, under the lightning of an orator's eye, within the melody of his voice, and drawn into ruin by all the chords of sympathy; unless he can make us discern these orders, privileges or mobs, in our policy. These must be created, before his cases or his inferences will apply. Shall we create orders and exclusive privileges, to discover the accuracy with which Mr. Adams has described their effects?

It is the absence of these political causes, and an ignorance of their effects, which has constituted a degree of political happiness, throughout seventeen nations, unexampled in history, and unequalled in duration; adding together the space of each experiment. So that Mr. Adams's very language is new and strange to us. He talks perpetually of the aristocratick and democratick interest. An use for this computation will be the era of those calamities, which have constantly attended it; and of the application of Mr. Adams's precedents.

To the regularity of the phenomena, reducing these conclusions to moral certainties, for the sake of those who love authority, we will subjoin one of an eminent English author. Russell, in his Modern Europe, observes, 'But an equal counterpoise of power, which among foreign nations is the source of tranquillity, proves always the cause of quarrel among domestick factions.'* This counterpoise of power, among three domestick factions, is the only basis of Mr. Adams's hopes; if he should succeed, it is, says Russell, a constant prelude to a warfare between these counterpoised factions; if he fails, Mr. Adams acknowledges, that the predominant faction becomes a tyrant. Was it the accomplishment of the counterpoise in Mr. Adams's numerous cases, which regularly produced Russell's consequence?

Had a balance of power, among orders or factions, caused tranquillity, its absence would have caused broils and tumult. Tranquillity is one of the phenomena, arising from the unbalanced sovereignty of a single order; and broil and tumult are phenomena, which have ever attended a division of power among orders. Democracy was quiet under the feudal aristocracy, the church estates under the popes, the plebeians under the late government of Venice, and the peers of England are quiet under patronage,

* Modern Europe, v. 2, 410.

paper and armies. But whenever an equipoise of power, or an approach towards it has existed, as among the Grecian states, at Rome, among the Italian republicks, and formerly in England between the king and the nobility, civil war and bloodshed ensued.

It is impossible, that a balance of power among orders, should produce the same effects, as the preponderance of one. As the causes are widely different, so will be their consequences. And it is unphilosophical to conclude, that the moral beings, ambition, avarice, rivalry and hatred, breathed into orders, by an equipoise, will, like the fear breathed into the people by despotism, beget political tranquillity.

Between the noxious alternatives, a warfare of orders and the quietism of tyranny, antiquity could discover no resource. The oscillations, both of political philosophy and vulgar prejudice, have been perpetual from one to the other, because miseries which have passed away, are gradually forgotten by miseries which are endured. And science, in this case, has been welded to ignorance, by the anguish of a common feeling, without searching for a remedy in the resources of intellect.

The new idea of rejecting both alternatives, was reserved for the new world. Instead of being a pendulum swinging between two curses, and capable of no enjoyment, except that which a change of pain may afford, the United States have rejected both the calm despotism of one order, and the turbulent counterpoise of several. Oppression, rivalry, civil war, ambition, and the whole tribe of moral effects, incident to these alternatives, will either disappear with their causes, or tinctures of such effects will be so many intellectual beacons, notifying to the nation of good moral beings, that their natural enemies are about to invade them.

It was reserved for the United States to discover, that by balancing man with man, and by avoiding the artificial combinations of exclusive privileges, no individual of these equipoised millions, would be incited by a probability of success, to assail the rest; and that thus the concussions of powerful combinations, and the subversion of liberty and happiness, following a victory on the part of one, would be avoided.

How fortunate it is, that the two systems are so visibly marked by distinct principles, that wilfulness only will be able to view encomiums on one, in any other light than as censures of the other.

It must however be admitted, that in our constitutions and political disquisitions, a struggle between the light of our revolu-

373

tion, and the clouds of previous habits, is also discernible. The numerical analysis, a balance of orders or of powers, and a social compact between nations and their governments, often bewilder us, so as to exhibit reason and prejudice, striving for a reconciliation. Our policy, says one, abhors and rejects orders of men; but, replies the other, it loves and creates orders of power; as if power could exist abstractedly of men. The didactick, dependent, subservient judicial power, is blown up to occupy a niche, in imitation of the English balance, as children imitate cannon, by the help of bladders; and Lepidus is associated with Augustus and Anthony, for the sake of a triumvirate of orders of power, though he never can become a candidate for empire. Thus judicial power may be debauched without tasting the pleasure of sin; and the nation is seduced into a reliance upon one balance against oppression, as heavy as the thunder of the Vatican and the terrors of excommunication, opposed to the power of Bonaparte. And for the imaginary social compact between the king and the people, one as imaginary, is also conjured up, to shoot other old errours into our new system of policy, by the shuttles of old phrases.

The balancing system arose out of the ancient opinion, that the power of a government was unlimited. The American revolution, in exploding that opinion, subverted its consequences. The discovery of limitations upon the power of government then made, was improved to great extent in the establishment of the general government, and demonstrates, that the two modes for preserving a free government, are distinct and incompatible. Unlimited power could never be estimated or balanced, because the human mind cannot embrace that which has no limits; but specified and limited power, can easily be divided, and its effects foreseen. A nation, possessed of a mountain of gold, which should bestow the whole upon three ministers, trusting to their broils for its liberty, would pursue the old policy; by keeping the mass of its mountain, and entrusting agents with occasional sums, to be employed for its use, the new. The property in power, claimed by orders, causes their efforts for its increase; and these efforts constantly produce the incurable defect of that system, by proving the point upon which it rests its value to be unattainable. Agents, pretending to no such property, are not exposed to the same temptation; nor can their frauds and usurpations avail themselves of specious but spurious pretensions. The abuses of the old policy will therefore often find refuge in honest opinion; the inexorable and patriotick

374

adversary of those committed under the new. Every deduction of power from a compact between a nation and its government, is incompatible with the right of self government; nor can a policy which admits the first, be founded in the same principles with that which asserts the second. No contractor, with the right of self government, can exist. A social compact, which is only an union of individuals, for the end of creating a government, ceases on the accomplishment of this end. The political society created by a constitution, is the only existing society, and the government is its agent; but under the natural individual right of self government, this political society itself may be dissolved. Until dissolved, it is the master of the government, or the real political sovereignty; but the natural right of self government, is superior to any political sovereignty. The ancient notion of a social compact between nations and their governments or monarchs, alone sufficed to corrupt them. A right of construction being involved in the character of a party to this imaginary social compact, it might easily be modelled into an inexhaustible treasury of power, by the party always active and able to mould it into any form; whilst the party always sluggish, could never find it a powerful champion for liberty. For this ancient species of compact, our policy has substituted a chain of subordination, suspended from its principle of the right of self government. Our political sovereignty is the first link, and our government the second. The original right exercised its superiority over the social sovereignty previously existing, and over the whole herd of fictitious compacts between the people and the government, or between the states, or the states and the Union, at the last establishment of a general government; none of these governments had any agency in their own creation, or in that work. The state governments did not surrender, but the people transferred a portion of power, without their consent, from them to the general government, from the plenitude of the right of self government. Had any social compact existed, to which government was a party, it would by this transfer, have been violated. If these governments should frame compacts between themselves, even for self preservation, it would violate our policy, because it would impugn the sovereignty of the existing political society, and also detract from the national right of self government. Our political legislation depends upon the same plain sanction with civil legislation; superiority and subordination. Uncorrupted by imaginary compacts, the right of the general or state governments to break the Union, though by mutual consent, disappears; nor can the interpolations of these imaginary compacts or balances into our policy, whilst the national supervision of its governments and armies, by election and a 'well regulated militia' remains, have any effect but to countenance the errour, that the government of the United States is a monarchy in disguise.

. Religion, like politicks, has been inclosed within certain dogmas, out of which the human mind was long unable to push its operations. The contest between the grossest errours and the plainest truths, was long and doubtful, after its first glances. Guile and treachery, which constitute the philosophy of errour, caused an English archbishop to resort to mimickry, relicks and ostentation, under pretence of perfecting a religious reformation, just as the political reformation of the United States will be perfected, by the doctrines we have been contesting. Doctrines, which would conduct our civil reformation almost back to the errour it destroyed, as happened in the case of the English hierarchy. A comparison between these revolutions would furnish to our subject many illustrations, but we must content ourselves with that between our policy and Mr. Adams's theory.

One commences its justification in the language of paradox, by asserting 'that separate interests beget an union of interest.' The other uses that of common sense, 'a common interest is union.' One boasts of an ingenuity, capable of equalising political weapons among orders, with such dexterity, as to tempt them into hostilities, without end and without object. The other thinks it better to exclude the combatants themselves, because their battles add nothing to human happiness; and because the boasted skill in measuring the weapons, has in no instance produced the miracle (like the suspension of Mahomet's coffin) of a perpetual battle and never a victory.

Contrast and superiority, were so visible in a comparison between these ultimate principles, as not to escape. Mr. Adams's penetration. Foreseeing that an opinion might prevail, unfavourable to the idea of producing a common interest by dividing a nation into sects, or a good sailing ship, by cutting her into three pieces; and to the project of perpetual hostilities between factions without mischief or victory; he assails our policy at its root, for the purpose of proving it defective, at the same place where he sees an incurable defect in his own.

Nedham's doctrine 'that the people were the best guardians of their own liberty,' presented Mr. Adams with an opportunity to try this experiment. He therefore replies, 'that the people are the worst enemies to themselves.' Hence, though warring or conquering orders, should appear to have been enemies to the people in all ages, still they might be an alleviation of the superlative enmity.

This idea of justifying a system upon the argument of a natural self enmity in man, is as strange as that of producing unity of interest by division. The surprise it excites, is not diminished, by supposing that the enmity meant by Mr. Adams, was the result of errour or ignorance. In the present state of mankind, no arrangement of orders, could produce a freedom from errour, or an exclusiveness of knowledge. The aristocratick order, therefore, whether this enmity is deduced from a supposed self hatred in human nature, from errour or from ignorance, would as probably constitute 'the worst enemies to themselves,' as the popular; and hence this argument against one order, applies with equal force against another. The application theoretically is equal, but practically unequal. If the calamities aristocracy has drawn upon itself in all ages, by crimes and vices, have been more voluntary than the sufferings of the people, this order is more justly chargeable with self enmity.

The mode by which Mr. Adams provides against this self enmity in the people, is no less pleasant and paradoxical than the enmity itself, or the idea of uniting a nation by dividing it into orders. Having contended for a natural aristocracy, as strenuously as old Filmer (whose notions Mr. Adams calls superstitious and absurd) did for natural or divine kings, but being unable to say 'lo! it is here, or lo! it is there,' he is at length obliged to have recourse to a convention, to come, artificially, at a natural aristocracy. He draws a veil over the self hatred, folly or ignorance of the people, (whichever he means) and allows them self love and wisdom for one occasion only, provided that occasion be an establishment of his system of orders. After which, self love, wisdom and capacity to take care of themselves, are, like the bones of Lycurgus, to be considered as lost for ever; and as nature has decreed that they cannot be recovered, the system of orders is ingeniously furnished with a sanction for its perpetuity, infinitely stronger than the spartan oath. Does reason or zeal dictate this project?

Our policy does not conceive that nature will sometimes create an aristocracy, and at others, by refusing to do so, leave its creation to the people. It does not believe that she deprives mankind of the

377

qualities necessary for self preservation, and yet enables them to judge correctly of Mr. Adams's intricate theory. Nor that she qualifies nations to erect governments for the purpose of establishing their liberty and then disqualifies them for keeping these governments to their duty. The idea, that the people may be once friends, but ever after enemies to themselves, is as remote from our policy, as from nature.

The reader is warned not to misunderstand the application of the principle of division, as used by our policy and Mr. Adams's theory. Our policy divides power, and unites the nation in one interest; Mr. Adams's divides a nation into several interests, and unites power. By our policy, power having been first sparingly bestowed on the government, is next minutely divided, and then bound in the chains of responsibility. This discloses its opinion, that each part of political power is dangerous to liberty; and because the whole is of the nature of its parts, the entire government is subjected to the right, asserted by our policy, and admitted by Mr. Adams to be capable of once doing good; the right of the nation to influence or change its government.

Our policy does not confide the powers withheld by the constitution, to the protection of any theory of balances. The government is not made amenable to itself. If it usurps a power withheld, by whom is it to be restrained? 'Not by the people, (says Mr. Adams) they are no keepers at all of their own liberties.' And upon the credit of such an assertion, he contends for a government of orders, as if power would be a safe centinel over power, or the devil over Lucifer. But our policy considers the physical force of an armed nation, and the moral force of election and division, as better centinels. Both arms, and the right of suffrage, ought however to be taken from the people, if they are their own worst enemies. The hypothesis which rejects the idea of a moral gravitation, and asserts that parts of the same entity naturally repel each other, is thought by our policy to be unphilosophical. Hence it infers, that it would be as wise and prudent to entrust national liberty to the exclusive care of three guardians, all composed of political power, as a bag of money to three thieves. According to Mr. Adams's system, three thieves can never carry off the bag of money, because they can never agree about its division. Parts of power and of knavery, attract each other and coalesce like drops of water: drops, however, may be kept asunder, but rivers will soon form a sea.

To excuse this striking defect in the system of orders, Mr.

Adams produces their virtual responsibility. This acknowledges the defect. The question therefore is, whether the remedy is sufficient. Virtual responsibility (as it was termed by the British parliament) can only be enforced by civil war; whilst actual responsibility may be enforced without it. Their difference is demonstrated in the cases of Lewis XVI, and the second President of the United States; and the preference, in relation both to the nation and the magistrate, is obvious.

Against the oppressions of Mr. Adams's hereditary representatives, nations have no remedy but physical strength; against those of temporary representatives, the moral force of opinion suffices. The first remedy can never be legally exerted, because no government will make laws to punish itself; to avoid which, these hereditary representatives invariably disarm the people, and so make the remedy for the coercion of this virtual representation quite nominal. Its use is moreover prohibited by the dreadful avenger of rebellion. Restrained by the dangers which beset it, the physical strength of a nation moves only in the paroxysm inspired by long suffering or extreme peril; and it is to the overthrow of reason, by this paroxysm, that the frequent disappointments of national exertion, to enforce virtual responsibility, are to be ascribed.

By our policy, actual responsibility is preferred to virtual, or to speak correctly, nominal. Conscious of the danger arising from the physical force of mercenary troops, it insists upon the necessity of securing to the nation the only safe protector of moral or political power, in an armed militia; to prevent responsibility from rebelling against nations, by the same means used by monarchs and orders, to prevent nations from rebelling against them. Under the protection of the physical power of a militia, the moral or political power reserved by our policy to the people, acts legally and peaceably, by opinion and election; and the reason of the nation can have recourse to a degree of reflection and deliberation, unattainable during the confusion, the dangers, and the crimes of civil war. Without a sound militia, all popular rights, including election itself, must become tenants at will, of monarchical or aristocratical landlords.

Of the nature both of virtual and actual responsibility, no nation ever experienced evidence equally complete with ours. The multitude of cases, in which the states have enforced the latter, has given them infinitely less trouble, than any single enforcement of the former. When it shall require as much blood, treasure and misery, to remove a bad president or a bad governour, as to remove a bad king, we shall have exchanged our actual, for Mr. Adams's virtual or hereditary responsibility.

The doctrines of Mr. Adams, which have suggested several of the preceding remarks, are exhibited in the following quotations, that the reader may determine whether their construction is correct.

'It is agreed,' says he, 'that the people are the best keepers of their own liberties, and the only 'keepers who can be always trusted; and therefore the people's fair, full and honest *consent* to every law, by their representatives, must be made an essential part of the constitution: but it is *denied that they are the best keepers, or any keepers at all* of their own liberties, when they hold collectively or *by representation,* the executive and judicial power, *or the whole uncontrolled legislature.'* *

'An hereditary monarch is the representative of the whole nation, for the management of the executive power, as much as a house of representatives is, as one branch of the legislature, and as guardian of the publick purse; and a house of lords too, or a standing senate, represents the nation for other purposes.'†

It is impossible to utter a more positive censure of the policy of the United States than the first quotation. It asssails the doctrine of conventions, which invests the people, by representation, with unlimited power. It assails all our constitutions, under which the people, by representation, possess an uncontrolled legislative and executive power. And instead of the sovereignty fully, fairly and honestly allowed to the people by our policy, it limits their rights to the subordinate privilege of consenting to law. A law is irrepealable by consent, and one, obtained by surprise, manacles a nation forever. This forlorn privilege of consent, accords with the English system, and beyond it all ought to be passiveness on the part of the people, according to Mr. Adams; if the polite concession of a nominal responsibility to them, does not in reality soften the assault upon the sovereignty of the people, as being only a naked compliment of a right without a remedy.

That Mr. Adams meant no more, results from a slight comparison of the two quotations. By one, it is said, 'the people are no keepers at all of their own liberties when they hold by *representation* the executive and judicial power, or the whole uncontrolled legislative.' By the other, that hereditary monarchs and a house of lords, are in their functions, *representatives of the nation.'* It is extremely

* Adams's Defence, v. 3, 293.   † Ibid., v. 3, 367.

difficult to discern a valuable representative quality in a king and house of lords, which the people cannot hold, without losing themselves the quality of being 'keepers of their own liberties.' And yet the whole drift of Mr. Adams's reasoning goes to prove, that this aerial responsibility, which is so thin as not to be discernible between the assertions of the two quotations, is preferable to solid and real responsibility.

But the theory of orders neither promises nor owes any species of responsibility to the nation. It literally claims an uncontrolled executive power. This is a manifest difference between that theory, and our policy. Ours proposes an union of interests among equal citizens, and subjects the government to the will of such an union; that, a disunion of interests among equal orders, and subjects the nation to the will of this disunion. One looks for freedom and happiness, by making it the interest of the controlling power to be free and happy; the other expects freedom and happiness, from a controlling power, compounded of ambition, jealousy and hatred, the gratification of which is the interest and aim of each part of the composition.

This moral being, jealousy, is magnified by the theory of orders, into an excellent and safe political principle, for its own use; and reprobated with equal zeal, whenever it is used by a nation. Nothing more strongly marks the character of the system than such language. Conscious that it owes no responsibility, it forbids the nation to be jealous of the government, and requires it to confide in the jealousy of the government of itself.

The jealousies of nations and factions are however different passions. The first is inspired by a love of liberty; the other by ambition and avarice. The first is extinguished by the virtues of justice and moderation, and returns love and respect; the other can only be gratified by power and pillage, never can be extinguished, and returns hatred and contempt. The first is demonstrated in the existing relation, between the united nations of these states, and their governments; the other, by the eternal discord among orders. That discord breeds malignant, treacherous, and violent tempers to fill the magistracy. Are men, rendered miserable, by such evil moral qualities, the best agents for rendering a nation virtuous and happy? Is the school of dissimulation, the school of liberty?

The history of England itself, is as fruitful in the effects of a jealousy among orders, as any other example quoted by Mr.

Adams. It exhibits a series of efforts on the part of the nobles, to become independent of the crown; on the part of the crown, to become despotick; and on the part of the commons, to subdue the king and nobility. And we see that gallant nation, after toiling for centuries in the cause of liberty, take refuge from a system, founded in a jealousy of orders, to one, founded in the corruption of its representatives. The most perfect experiment, hitherto made, (as Mr. Adams believes) of balanced orders, is deserted for a system of force and fraud, as an amelioration of its malignity. And the issue of the system of orders in this celebrated experiment, simply is, that whilst these orders are guided by jealousy, the nation is distracted, and when united by paper and patronage, it is plundered.

The constant termination of the system of orders elsewhere, and its catastrophe in England, proves that a balance of power among them, is an unnatural speculation; it is invariably disordered by a tendency towards some one simple principle of government. The question with the United States, was, whether they would try the mixed system of orders, and be conducted by this medium to one of these simple forms; or whether, instead of committing their fate to accident, they should plant it in good moral principles.

They saw that the mixtures of orders, without any exception, after suffering the most agonizing throes, had brought forth monarchy, the ancient aristocracy, ochlocracy, or the modern aristocracy of paper and patronage; and that it had in no instance produced national self government. They preferred that simple principle, which the system of orders has never produced. And our computation lies between the preservation of this principle, and a painful travail, through the organ of orders, to one of the principles it generates.

Because certain publick functionaries, convene in different chambers, or are invested with different powers, for the purpose of preserving the principle of national self government, Mr. Adams concludes that we originally adopted a very different one. An errour, which forcibly displays the power of opinion over maxim and precept. Self government, a maxim of nature, and a precept of our constitutions, has seen opinion, under her banner, bringing up the troops of contrary principles, to effect her destruction; whilst she was told to her face, that she did not exist, and could only be created by a balance of power among three orders.

When she sees an ambitious and mercenary army, possessing the exclusive military power of a nation, converted into patriots by metaphysical lines, for dividing it into three detachments; then let her believe, that three orders, exclusively possessing civil power, may also become subordinate to national will.

Unity, harmony and proportion, are as necessary in politicks, as in the drama, musick or architecture. A tragi-comical government, a Corinthian capital over a Dorick column, jarring dissonances, mingled with soft notes, an aristocratick democracy or a monarchick aristocracy, destroy sympathies, proportions and melody. It is consistency which produces perfection in arts and sciences. Let us proceed to inquire, whether it is to be found in either of the two rival systems we have frequently compared. And first, we will look into that composed of orders.

It charges human nature with an insubordinate mass of evil propensities; thence it infers a necessity for vast power to curb them; and it bestows this vast power upon human nature. Great power often corrupts virtue; it invariably renders vice more malignant. Is human nature made worse, a good corrector of human nature? Is vice cured by the strongest temptations? History every where contributes evidence, distinctly replying to these questions. In proportion as the powers of governments increase, both its own character and that of the people becomes worse.

Our system does not attempt to restrain vice by provocatives to vice. In destroying the evil principle, inordinate power, it has destroyed a cause of more vice, than human nature has ever perpetrated from any other cause. Having cut off the most copious source of vice, by disabling a government from committing more iniquity than it can prevent, it finds no difficulty in curbing the petty class of municipal offences. It has not been induced by the fact, that one individual will sometimes injure another, to establish the cause of all those dreadful atrocities, which sweep away the liberty, the property, the virtue and the existence of nations.

The project of hereditary systems, is to destroy the morals of one part of a community by power, in order to preserve the morals of the rest, by despotism. Hence it is compelled to multiply punishments for crimes which it causes; and to defend itself against punishment, for having caused the crimes which it punishes. It corrupts the morals of the few, under pretence of restraining the vices of the many; and this corruption is a source of more vice than it restrains.

Our policy takes a wider range. It is not so miserably defective, as to make one part of a nation worse, for the sake of making another better. It considers government as intended to improve the manners and happiness of the whole nation; and instead of leaving half its work undone, proposes to finish it, by providing for the manners and happiness of those who govern, as well as of those who are governed. It applies the reason for civil government, not partially, but generally; not to particular orders, but to nations; not to individuals, but to totals. This reason simply is, that the restraint of accountableness, improves the manners and happiness of mankind. Unable to see a distinction in nature, between man and man, our system has made that happy discovery, by which the salutary restraint of accountableness, may be extended to every individual of a nation. Instead of leaving some men to the guidance of an uncontrolled will or in a state of nature, it subjects all to law; and instead of sublimating the evil qualities of human nature, to their highest degree of acrimony, by power unrestrained, it subjects it in as well as out of office to government. It does not attempt to prevent a viper from biting by irritation.

Whether man is naturally virtuous or vicious, is a question, furnishing, however determined, no just argument in favour of hereditary systems. If the most transcendent virtue is hardly proof against the seduction of exorbitant power, these systems, in their own defence, ought to prove, that mankind are by nature virtuous. If he is vicious, his restraints ought to be multiplied in proportion to his power to do mischief; if virtuous, it strengthens the reasons derived from self love, for leaving moral power, where nature has placed physical.

Estimated by its sympathies, human nature discloses a vast preponderance of virtuous sensations. It spontaneously shrinks from an expression of rage, and is drawn towards one of joy; whilst ignorant of the cause of either; because one is an emblem of vice, and the other of virtue.

Horrible or impious, as the atomical philosophy may be, it cannot be more so, than the idea of a natural depravity in man, rendering him unfit for self government. One doctrine assails the existence of a God; the other, his power or goodness. If man, the noblest creature of this world; if mind, the noblest attribute of this creature; are both incorrigibly imperfect; the inference that the world itself is a bad work, is unavoidable. Man's case is hopeless. If he is the creature of malignity or imbecility, and doomed to be governed by fiends, naturally as bad, and artificially made worse than himself, where is his refuge? Shall he fly to the hereditary system, which teaches him to despair; or adhere to one, which inspires him with hope? The hereditary system! which having almost exclusively exercised the office of forming the human character since the creation of the world, very gravely urges as a reason in favor of its regimen, that its work is detestable.

Upon this wretch, man, however wicked he may be, nature has unequivocally bestowed one boon. This blessing, the hereditary system proposes to deprive him of; our policy uses it as the principle of civil government; it is the right of self preservation. No other government, ancient or modern, has fairly provided for the safety of this right. In all others, it is fettered by compounds of orders or separate interests; by force or by fraud. Between governments which leave to nations the right of self preservation, and those which destroy it, we must take our stand, to determine on which side the preference lies. A coincident view of happiness and misery, will presently transform this line, into a wide gulf, on the farther side of which, we shall behold the governed of all other nations, expressing their agonies. Shall we go to them, because they cannot come to us?

The restraint of governours, or the laws impressed on them by the nation, termed political, in this essay, constitutes the essential distinction between the policy of the United States, and of other countries. Machiavel, in deciding that a 'free government cannot be maintained, when the people have grown corrupt;' and in admitting monarchy, 'to be the proper corrective of a corrupt people,' has reasoned from false principles to false conclusions, because he had not discerned this distinction. He supposes orders proper to maintain liberty, whilst the people are virtuous; and that they are hurtful, when the people become corrupt; and taking it for granted, that liberty cannot exist without virtue, nor without orders, he dooms all nations to orders or to monarchy. If virtuous, he saddles them with political orders; if vicious, with an avenger instead of a reformer. History has neither related, nor fable feigned, that monarchs or demons reform the wicked committed to their durance. His errour lay in an utter ignorance of restraining governments. He never considered whether a corrupt nation might not establish a free political system, as avaricious mercantile partners establish just articles of partnership; and that it would be the interest of the majority to do so, because slavish political systems, inevitably prey upon majorities; nor whether this interest, united with common sense, would not induce majorities, since they cannot be lasting tyrants themselves, to absolve themselves from tyranny. Orders and national virtue united, says Machiavel, produce liberty; but if virtue disappears, liberty ceases. Others, split up this dogma. Virtue, say they, will produce liberty; and without it, liberty cannot exist. Orders, says Mr. Adams, will produce liberty. If in the case of the compound dogma of Machiavel, virtue and liberty disappear, whilst orders remain, the orders were not the cause of the liberty. If the virtue and liberty remain, after orders disappear, as in America, the orders caused neither the virtue nor the liberty. And if orders will produce liberty, according to Mr. Adams, the necessity for virtue to preserve liberty does not exist.

This confusion arises from the substitution of moral artifice, which may be good or bad, for good moral principles. Virtue, or moral goodness, may overpower an evil moral artifice, and for a short space preserve national liberty, against the assaults of a bad form of government. National virtue, pervading both the governours and people, like individual virtue, is a sponsor for happiness; and whilst political writers tell us that an assembly of good moral principles, embraced by the term virtue, will produce their natural effects, they say nothing in favour of evil moral artifices. The general acknowledgement of the capacity of good moral principles to correct a bad form of government, is a vast encouragement to expect from them a capacity to correct bad governours; and hence our policy has resorted to the good and virtuous moral principle of responsibility, or a strong code of political law, which can exist and operate upon governours, if the nation understands its interest, at whatever degree of virtue or corruption it may be stationed, in fact or in theory.

If orders (a moral artifice) should become corrupt, they are then, says Machiavel, hurtful to liberty; and he recommends one of these corrupt orders, a king, as a cure for the hurt. Bolingbroke observes, 'Instead of wondering that so many kings, unfit and unworthy to be trusted with the government of mankind, appear in the world, I have been tempted to wonder that there are any tolerable;'* and 'a patriot king is a kind of miracle.'† If the moral artifice, 'orders,' should become corrupt, Machiavel's remedy is Bolingbroke's miracle. These are ranked among the first class of political writers.

* Patriot King, p. 88.   † Ibid., p. 117.

'Nothing can restrain the propensity of orders to hurt liberty, but virtue,' says Machiavel. 'Good kings are not to be expected by the laws of nature,' says Bolingbroke. Yet they concur in favour of orders. Each decides against his own reasoning, because both being enslaved to the old tenet of the one, the few and the many, neither contemplated the abolition of orders or monarchy, nor the invention of a sound restraint upon the vices of governments, now practically illustrated in every state of the Union. In fact, neither of them saw the difference between a moral artifice, and a moral principle. Bolingbroke's alternative, of an elective or hereditary monarch, is unnecessary, because both are evil moral artifices, which may be superseded by a political system, founded in good moral principles. If inconveniences appear in the United States on the election of presidents, it will only demonstrate that we have approached too near to the moral artifice, called an elective monarchy, and that we ought to recede from this bad moral artifice, nearer to the good moral principle of a division of power. Neither of these writers entertained the least idea of a policy founded in fixed and good moral principles, and have only laboured like Bayes, in his dance of the sun, the moon and the earth, to invent new postures for the triumvirate of the old political analysis.

Bolingbroke says, 'that absolute stability, is not to be expected in any thing human; all that can be done, therefore, to prolong the duration of a good government, is to draw it back, on every favorable occasion, to the *first good principles* on which it was founded.' Does he mean by carrying a government back to *good principles*, to carry it back to monarchy, aristocracy, democracy, or to some mixture of them? Such was not his meaning, because these human contrivances are not principles themselves, but founded in, or deduced from principles. And whether either, or any mixture of two or all, is founded in good or bad moral principles, is the immemorial subject of political controversy. If he did not mean that a decaying government should seek for regeneration in some one of these human contrivances, the moral nature of which remained to be tried by the test of principles; or that the test was its own subject; he has explicitly admitted the existence of a political analysis, both the ancestor and judge of the ancient analysis of governments, and also of every conceivable form which can be invented. Upon this anterior analysis, the policy of the United States is founded. We resort to it as the test by which to discover whether either member of the old forms of government, or any

mixture of them, is good or bad. It is not a fluctuating, but permanent tribunal. Its authority is divine, and its distinctions perspicuous. And if it shall supersede the erroneous idea, that mankind are
manacled down to monarchy, aristocracy or democracy, as the
only principles of government, the effect of diminishing the instability of human affairs, by a resort to unchangeable principles,
may be fairly anticipated.

Without considering 'good principles,' as distinct from forms of
government, a return to them, for political regeneration, could not
convey a single idea. A government may commence in monarchy,
aristocracy or democracy, and degenerate from either to another.
Recessions to and from all forms of government may take place,
and therefore these forms could not be intended by 'good principles,' because these fluctuating recessions would, under that idea,
make all forms good, and all bad.

The inability of the old analysis to define a good form of government, and its destitution of some beacon by which to steer back to
the harbour of safety, from an ocean of corruption, is thus apparent.
It only tells mankind, when unhappy under monarchy, aristocracy
or democracy, to go back from one to another, or to some mixture
of them. Whereas the analysis of this essay, by arranging governments according to the principles in which they are founded,
discloses the mode of their preservation in a state of purity, and
also the way to restore that purity whenever it is impaired.

Although the idea of going back to *first good principles* has been
repeated into a maxim, it is seldom honestly explained or applied;
nor has it ever been confessed, that the phrase explodes the old,
and suggests a more correct analysis of governments. Its correctness
and power is illustrated, by supposing that sedition laws, or a
chartered stock aristocracy, are deviations from our *first good
principles.* How is the deviation to be discovered? By launching into
the ocean of the old analysis and its mixtures? No. By bringing it to
the test of the new analysis, founded in moral principles. If it is
thus discovered, how are nations to return to their *first good principles?* By taking refuge in monarchy, aristocracy, democracy, or a
mixture of them? No. By repealing laws deviating from its *first
good principles.* One of these illustrations will also serve to display
the errour and fraud of the artifice, by which mankind have been
persuaded to subscribe to the following syllogism—'Man cannot
possess free government, unless he is virtuous; but he is vicious;
therefore he cannot possess free government'—so ingeniously in-

vented, and so comfortably recommended in all ages, by patriotick kings, ministers and nobles. Now if the banking system is a mode, however ingenious, of oppressing a majority, that majority, however corrupt, may remove the oppression. And if the corruption itself, shall have been chiefly produced by the oppressing system, as is generally the case, then the removal of the oppression, is the true remedy for the corruption. Not so, say Machiavel and Montesquieu; virtue being gone, freedom has fled beyond the reach of a nation, and oppression or monarchy is the remedy.

The interest of a vicious majority to remove oppression from itself, is as strong as if it was virtuous; and the coincidence between its interest and reformation, is a foundation for an honest politician to build on. If avarice and fraud are propagated by laws for amassing wealth at the expense of a majority, the pecuniary interest of this majority to destroy these laws, is the strongest ground for effecting a reformation of the corrupt manners they have produced. And the just laws of a vicious majority, in self defence, will have a wide influence in the re-establishment of virtue; whereas no corrupt minority whatever, composed either of orders or separate interests, can be actuated by self interest to enact just laws, the best restorers of good manners.

There are two considerations which sustain this reasoning. First, that man is more prone to reason than to errour. Secondly, that he is more prone to self love than to self enmity. Notwithstanding the first propensity, every man, however wise, is liable to err; and an occasional errour of a wise man may ruin a nation. The general propensity of the whole species, will usually impress its own character, upon a general opinion, and is undoubtedly less liable to errour, than the conclusions of an individual. It is safer to confide in this propensity, than in individual infallibility. One exists, the other does not. One is ever honest, the other often knavish. The force of self love, is as strong in majorities, as in an individual, but its effect is precisely contrary. It excites one man to do wrong, because he is surrounded with objects of oppression; and majorities to do right, because they can find none. Their errours of judgement are abandoned, so soon as they are seen, whilst the despotism of one man is more strongly fortified for being discovered. The old analysis intrusts great power to individuals and minorities; and provides no mode of controlling their natural vicious propensities. Our policy deals out to them power more sparingly, and superadds a sovereign, whose propensity is towards reason, and whose self interest is an excitement to justice. Such is the competitor of the sovereign of the old analysis, of which even its advocate, Bolingbroke, admits, that a good one would be a miracle. To avoid reasons, so strong in favour of our species of sovereignty, kings, nobles, and even mobs, have claimed a divine right to govern, because there existed no ground between the right of self government and authority from God. It was obvious, that a nation, like an individual, could never become a tyrant over itself, and therefore all abuses of good moral principles, whether in the form of the ancient analysis, or of the modern aristocracy of paper and patronage, find means to control and defeat national self government, either by the impiety of fathering tyranny upon God, or by the fraud of admitting but evading its pretensions. And though it is at length confessed, that nations have a right to destroy tyrants, the difficulty of finding a tyrant willing to be destroyed, remains. Monarchy, aristocracy, hierarchy, patronage, and ambition, still urge every plea, however false, which transient circumstances may render plausible; even the paper aristocracy of the United States, though constructed of republicans, would surrender the sanctity of tyrannical kings, to secure a sanctity for tyrannical charters; and whilst it strives to find refuge for the latter, under some good word, joins in dragging the former from under the throne of God himself.

Although there is no middle ground between national and divine civil government, Montesquieu's position, 'that virtue is necessary for the preservation of liberty,' has long deluded the world into a state of indecision. If it means that the members of a society cannot form equal and just laws for self government, unless these members are virtuous, it is false; but if it means that liberty cannot be preserved without virtuous laws, it is true. That vicious men can constitute themselves into a society by laws, free, just and virtuous respecting themselves, is proved by the associations of nobles, priests, merchants, stockjobbers and robbers, which are contrived, whether the members are virtuous or not, to preserve individual social rights. And that virtuous men cannot constitute themselves into a free society, by oppressive, unjust and vicious laws, is obviously true. As fraudulent laws enslave a virtuous nation, just laws will preserve the liberty of a vicious one. It is in the governing principles, and not in the subject to be governed, that the virtue or vice resides, which causes the freedom or oppression. But kings, nobles, priests and stockjobbers, have transposed this idea, and insisted upon the necessity of virtue in the subject to be governed, to create pretences for vicious laws to feed their own appetites.

A nation cut up into orders or separate interests, cannot exert national self government, because the national self no more exists, than a polypus, after being cut into four or five pieces, which forage in different directions or upon each other. Suppose it dissected into four, the ennobled, military, hierarchical and stock; which of these could pronounce any other opinion than its own? Each would constitute a distinct moral self, and could only entertain opinions, naturally flowing from its own moral nature; the ennobled, military, hierarchical and stock selves, must as necessarily have opinions, distinct from each other, as the English, French, Spanish and German nations. And these opinions would be more frequently contradictory, than the opinions of those nations, because the interests of domestick factions would more frequently clash.

The experiments for balancing power among the nations of Europe, produce effects analogous to those for balancing power among orders. Europe cannot be formed into one quiet government, because the different nations, having different interests, cannot form one political being. The supposed project of Henry IV. of France, for moulding Europe into such a being, was therefore chimerical. Political orders, are as distinct and as inimical nations, as those of Europe. Of course they have never been compressed into one nation, having one interest, one will, and one self, all indispensable to self government; but like the scheme of balancing power among the European nations, that of balancing it among privileged orders, produces plots or wars without end, until they end in a conquest and tyranny by one.

A nation cut up into separate factitious moral beings, is compelled to use the means for enforcing municipal law, used by France and England to enforce European law. The contest for predominance among privileged orders, can only be restrained by standing armies, and these at length determine it, by declaring for one. Constitutions are only treaties between orders, where they exist; and these treaties, like those between nations, are broken or evaded, whenever it is the interest of any party to break or evade them. Accordingly, the history given by Mr. Adams, and by all others, of these orders or artificial nations, proves, that they are constantly making and breaking treaties, and that they have universally been more treacherous, cruel and malicious towards each other, than natural nations.

Mechanical or habitual applause, cannot preserve the policy of the United States. It can only be saved by thoroughly understanding wherein its excellency consists. If it does not consist of a common interest, let any other eulogist point out its distinction from the policy under which men have hitherto groaned. If it does, and if its capacity for preserving free and national self government, is thence derived, it follows, that laws for cutting up the nation into distinct interests, will essentially destroy, without changing a letter of our constitutions, or a shadow of our forms of government.

But having discovered, that the superiority of our policy consists of an exclusion of separate interests, able to create factions; that the good or the detriment of the community, may be the subject of inquiry in the several departments of governments; it will be easy to detect laws, appearing in the questionable shape of deserters from the region of evil moral principles, and fraught with separate interests, or contrivances for distributing wealth.

Of this nature, we have considered banking laws. They create an order, having above fifty millions capital, most of it consisting of nominal stock, called credit; a privilege of emitting national money; and the power of banishing national coin, of governing commerce, and of deciding the fate of mercantile individuals; it draws five millions annually from national labour; and is able to influence elections, and to corrupt legislatures. Is it for the good or the detriment of bankers, borrowers, creditors or debtors? are questions, which pilfer nations, and stain the statute book; whereas it is our policy to keep it clean, because upon its purity depends the national freedom and happiness.

The history of Lacedemon exhibits a correct idea of a distinct order; that of England, of a distinct interest. The order of nobles, was the master of the order of Helots; not individually, but as an order. From one order, the other drew its subsistence directly, because it was ignorant of the ingenious paper mode of taxation. The paper interest of England, is also the master of property and labour, not individually, but as an order; from these it draws its subsistence, not directly, like their Spartan prototype, but indirectly. Both end in the same results; each bestows leisure and plenty on one order or interest, and labour and penury on another. But the latter operates the most powerful effects. It outstrips its compeer. In a former part of this essay, a calculation was made of the hold it had gotten upon the people of England, which is left behind whilst I am writing. The growing taxes, sinecures and dividends, will probably make each free born Englishman, worth three or four times as much to the stock order, as each base born Helot was to the Spartan, by the time this essay shall be read, if it ever is read.

Let us return from this digression, if it be one, to the comparison we have undertaken. Mr. Adams's system is incapable of a division of rights between a nation and a government. This idea is incompatible with hereditary, but conformable to responsible power. It is incompatible with natural orders, but conformable to natural rights. And it is incompatible with the opinion, that the people are no guardians, but conformable to the opinion, that they are the best guardians of their own liberty. Therefore his system annihilates that sacred effort of our policy, to withhold powers useless or pernicious; and to secure rights necessary for the preservation of liberty, or without the office of governments. Among these, the rights of bearing arms, of religion, and of discussion, constitute of themselves a measureless superiority in our policy, over any other, unable, by reason of different principles, to place them beyond the reach of government; as we shall presently endeavour to prove.

If a nation surrenders all its rights to a government, it cannot be free. Freedom consists in having rights, beyond the reach and independent of the will of another; slavery, in having none. The form of the master, or his having three heads or one head, does not create the slave. It is on account of the opinions; that nations might be made free by the form of the master, and that the powers of a government are incapable of limitation; that they have been so universally enslaved. From this point, a glance discerns the wide difference between our political system, and the British or Mr. Adams's. The parliament, or orders, are theoretically and practically omnipotent. Such is the doctrine of the British government and of the British lawyers. The government possesses unlimited power, and the nation has no rights independent of the government. The reverse is the principle adopted by our policy. It contends, that the power of a government may be limited, and that the people may have rights independent of the government.

To assert, without enforcing this doctrine, would be equivalent to its relinquishment. Even Mr. Adams is willing nominally to admit it, in his virtual representative quality of hereditary orders. This idea is an admission of national rights independent of government; but it confides them to the custody of the idea only. How far

N*   393

they have been actually secured by hereditary power, in discharge of its supposed representative duties, depends upon a fact, to which all history testifies.

Our policy, dissatisfied with an unfruitful intellectual acknowledgment of the theoretical truth of this doctrine, has sought for the means of making it practically useful. It does not rely upon the most positive verbal renunciations of absolute power, or acknowledgments of national rights, without means in the hands of the nation, adequate to their enforcement.

Here the attention of the reader is requested. We believe that one mode only of limiting the power of governments, and securing the rights of nations, within the reach of human nature, exists. To this, our policy, and no other, has resorted. Its abandonment, would be a surrender of the doctrine, and the erection of a despotism, however the government is formed; if a nation without rights, and a government without restriction, constitute a despotism. Therefore, the only existing mode of preventing it, deserves a more attentive consideration than any other human invention.

It consists simply in uniting the sovereign, physical and political power in one national interest. If any uncontrollable political power is held by a government, it will instantly seize upon an equal physical power by means of mercenary armies. But by combining the supreme political power with the natural physical power of a nation, seasonable exertions of the first, will peaceably prevent the ruin of the other. This union is effected, by a sound militia and elective systems. The sovereign, physical and political power, being thereby inseparably united, national self government is perfectly secured. If one half of this sovereignty is transferred to mercenary armies, and the other half to balanced orders or separate interests of any kind, they unite for mutual safety against the nation, from which both moieties are taken. Election, without her ally, a national militia, and united with standing armies, hereditary orders, or separate interests, such as banking, becomes an instrument to inflict their will. Equally unavailing to preserve liberty, is a militia, made subject to a political power beyond its influence, because such a power can disarm, neglect, and subject it to an army of its own.

A nation is both a natural and a moral being. Its natural powers we call physical, its moral, metaphysical or political. If it is deprived of its physical power, it is like a man possessed of reason, bound; if of its intellectual only, it is like a maniac, unbound. If a nation is allowed the uninterrupted possession of either, it will get the other. Yet if it loses one, it will lose both; because usurpation is never safe with one only. Therefore an attempt to deprive it of either, confesses an intention to deprive it of both. If the attempt begins with an army, it ends with destroying the political power of a nation; if it begins by assailing its political power, with orders, separate interests or corruption of any kind, it ends with an army. A man who surrenders his reason or his body to another, is soon forced to make both conformable to that other's will. To prevent mental slavery, our policy reserves to the nation intellectual rights, or the use of its reason; and to prevent physical slavery, it reserves to the nation, the military power, in an armed and organized militia; knowing that it must retain both or neither. By retaining both, a nation is a physical and intellectual being. By losing one, it becomes a being quite anomalous to human nature; physical, and not intellectual, like a corpse; or intellectual, and not physical, like a ghost. By losing both, it is annihilated, as having neither a physical nor intellectual power.

We cannot condescend to enter the lists with the wicked artifice of destroying nations, by a fraudulent use of words and phrases; such as licentiousness, sedition, privilege, charter and conventicle; because a nation, capable of being subdued by these feeble instruments, is incapable of liberty, as a man is of long life, who can be persuaded to hold out his throat to the knife of an assassin, lest he should cut it himself.

It would swell this essay beyond the contemplated size, to enumerate and explain all the rights held by the people of the United States independently of their government. Such a work would however be extremely useful, for instructing us in the principles of our policy, and for demonstrating that these rights are so linked together, that not a single link can be removed, without materially impairing the strength of the chain.

But the dexterity of the artifice, which inculcates an opinion, already contested, that if the link of election remains, it will alone constitute a security for liberty, as strong as the entire chain of these rights, induces me to select the rights of a real national militia, and of a freedom of religion, of speech and of the press, both to display the vast superiority of our policy over any other, in their recognition; and also to prove that the strength and efficacy of the right of election, is itself dependent on the real operation of other rights.

395

It is a principle of our policy, that the military should be subordinate to the civil power. Why was this subordination required, and how is it to be enforced? It was required on account of the universal insubordination of mercenary armies, to every species of civil power, not their accomplice in oppression. Not that soldiers are more cruel, avaricious or tyrannical than priests, stockjobbers or nobles, for the contrary is the fact; but because a military is a separate interest, subsisting on the nation. The militia being nearly the nation itself, is the solitary appendage of civil power by which this principle of our policy can be enforced. If it is rendered incompetent to this end, election, a mere moral power, has no remaining ally able to save it, and hence almost every composition, constituting the code of our policy, has asserted the indispensable necessity of a well regulated militia.

The supremacy of civil power over military, is a stipulation in vindication of national self government, or a sovereignty of the people. We know that from the beginning of the world to this day, the military sovereign has universally been the civil sovereign, and therefore our policy never intended to sever civil and military power, so as to invest the people with the first, and to divest them of the second moiety of sovereignty.

Let us suppose a nation to have held both a civil and military sovereignty, one by election, and the other by an armed and trained militia; and that the latter was at length transplanted into the hands of its government, by disarming and disorganizing the militia, and raising a standing army, under any pretence whatsoever. The people retain the civil, and the government has gotten the military sovereignty. Is election without its ally, what it was with it? A nation voting under the protection of an army raised by its own government, is not a new spectacle. We see it in France. A protector is unexceptionably a master. A naked permission to keep and bear arms, is an insufficient ally of election or civil sovereignty. Doctor Franklin indeed used it as a resource for evading the religious scruples of a Pennsylvania assembly, but found it an inadequate defence against the feeble incursions of ignorant savages; and it would be infinitely less adequate to restrain the daring usurpations of an artful government. Without a 'well regulated militia,' the military sovereignty of a nation, exactly resembles its civil sovereignty under a government of hereditary orders. Hereditary kings and nobles, says Mr. Adams, are civil representatives of nations; well, let standing armies become their military representatives, and both their military and civil sovereignty will stand on the same ground, and reap the fruits of the same species of representation.

Neither the British nor Mr. Adams's system provides for any species of military sovereignty in the people. The English orders disarm the people. Mr. Adams acknowledges their sovereignty, is silent as to a militia, and gives them hereditary representatives. Our policy endeavours to combine a real militia with an elected temporary representation. It is whimsical to hear the British system talk of the sovereignty of the people. A lunatick only, can be persuaded that he is a king, by a crown of straw.

It is remarkable, that almost all governments, having a power to raise and pay standing armies, have neglected a militia. A power of resorting to the first mode of self defence, has created insurmountable objections to the second. Congress has power 'to raise and support armies,' and 'to organize, arm and discipline the militia.' Like other governments possessing the first, it has been unable to discover any mode of executing the second. The profound wisdom and admirable foresight of our policy, in providing a remedy for this indisposition to create a sound militia, merits an encomium, in which none other, ancient or modern, can pretend to any share. Other systems of government, in bestowing a power to raise mercenary armies, have bestowed an indisposition to cultivate a militia; ours has left with the state governments a power to cultivate a militia, and withheld from them that of raising mercenary armies. As no governments can exist without military protection, and as a militia constitutes that, to which alone the state governments can resort, they must make it adequate to the end or perish. Viewed as rivals, the general government seems to have possessed a distinct, and the states an obscure idea on this subject. By protecting them with a mercenary army, and neglecting the establishment of a sound militia, the general government would inevitably become the judge and jury of the state governments; because they have no mode of effecting a subordination of the military to their civil power, except by a well regulated militia. The history of the world exhibits but a single nation which has maintained its independence against conquerors. It was inferior to its enemies in number, possessed a worse country, and is imprisoned by the ocean. But being unable to maintain mercenary armies, and forced to resort to national self defence, the twin brother of national self government, its militia won the crown of bravery by a long course of splendid actions, and the nation, the exclusive honour of never having been subdued.

The ability of our policy, to leave to men a perfect right to conscience, is an advantage which the system of orders has never been able to reach; and when we see that system unable to secure this right, so extremely foreign to the office of governments, and so extremely valuable to the happiness of men; the conclusion, that the theory itself is unable in its nature and principles, to secure to nations or individuals any rights whatsoever, which the government cannot invade and destroy, is unavoidable.

By our policy, mankind possess the right of worshipping the Creator of the universe; by the English, they are compellable to worship the God by law established. By one, revelation is assigned to the paraphrase of the head and the heart; by the other, to that of pains and penalties. By one, an expectation of individual retribution, is considered as a good reason for leaving each man to work out his own salvation; the project of the other, is to take a chance for national salvation, by compressing a whole people within the pale of one faith. It is unaccountable, that the same system, should with equal zeal exert itself against the division of national interest, as to eternal concerns, and against its union as to temporal. If a common interest in the next world is so desirable, why is a nation to be cut up in this, into orders and exclusive privileges?

An idol of metal or stone, differs from an idol of the imagination, in being more permanent and comprehensible; and its worshipper possesses an inestimable advantage over the worshipper of an idol of the imagination, in being able to convert it into an emblem of any object of adoration he pleases. Dogma, more cunning than wooden gods, deprives the conscience of this resource. The Pagan mythology was ingeniously rendered a complete liberty of conscience, by considering each idol as emblematical of some divine attribute; and he who worshipped all, only paid his adorations to all these attributes. Neptune was an emblem of the Deity's power over the ocean; Minerva, of his justice; Ceres, of his bounty.

Hence arose the difference in temporal consequences, produced by solid and imaginary images; namely, festivity and mildness; bloodshed and persecution. The fancy is unable to adorn hideous tenets, with the agreeable illusions inspired by the Venus of Praxiteles, nor can the mind evade their recognitions by mental substitutions. We can substitute a supernatural being for a solid image, but we cannot substitute an abstract proposition, for a different abstract proposition; therefore the moderns have endured death in every form, rather than render homage to the idols of the imagination; whilst the ancients yielded to the illusions of art; or exercised the resource of converting the idols of the hand, into types of whatever supernatural beings they chose. Hence the ancient solid images or idols, were easily admitted and adopted, without embroiling nations or exciting malevolence among individuals; whilst metaphysical images or idols, engender remorseless hatreds, incessant persecutions, and sprinkle the earth with human blood.

Ancient atheism, or God as by law established, required only an external or ceremonious worship of a visible idol; modern atheism, or God as by law established, requires an internal or conscientious worship of an invisible idol. 'Bend your body,' said one tyrant; 'Bend your mind,' says the other. 'I will punish you,' said one, 'if you do not perform certain gestures which you can perform.' 'I will punish you,' says the other, 'if you do not believe certain dogmas, which you cannot believe.' One said, 'I have with my hands made a God, you shall see him, and externally worship him.' The other, 'I have with my fancy made a God, whom you cannot see, or a tenet which you cannot believe, which you shall worship internally.' Modern atheism is incomparably the most tyrannical, and has accordingly provoked incomparably most resistance. It requires of man to mould his mind and annul his convictions.

It can also manufacture instruments for effecting its ends, infinitely more destructive than the ancient. Zeal is whetted by the imagination into the utmost keenness. Praxíteles would more easily be persuaded, that his statue of Venus was not a goddess; than Origen, that his dogmas of the pre-existence of souls, and that Christ was to be again crucified to save the devils, were errours. The stuff of which physical idols are made, may be analysed and comprehended; but that which is the basis of metaphysical idols, is always beyond human understanding, whilst it is still liable to greater agitation by the idea of a ghost, than from a real stump.

The art of governing the deity is cultivated for the sake of governing men. If a government or a church should by its mandates directly regulate the temporal and spiritual dispensations of the Almighty, the burst of derision would be universal; but laws establishing tenets, tones, gesticulations and ceremonies, for the purpose of indirectly regulating these temporal and spiritual dispensations, are slyly resorted to, because they gratify man's lust of power, and flatter his aversion to a reliance on a life of moral rectitude for salvation. Laws, dictating the mode of influencing the deity, are declarations, that the deity shall be influenced by law. And the conspiracy between the priest and the proselyte, is founded in the compact, that the priest will learn the proselyte to govern the deity, if the proselyte will suffer the priest to govern him. Besides, true religion will not do the work of tyranny, like an heated and beguiled imagination. Tyranny wants persecutors, not advocates of truth and virtue; to gain these, it makes gods and religions. Is tyranny able by its laws to bring the King of Heaven down to earth, and convert him into its instrument? If tyranny cannot coerce the true God, into an instrument of its vices, then the gods it uses must be false.

The same governments and hierarchies, which eulogize Daniel in their prayers, imitate Nebuchadnezzar in their actions; they set up dogma for his image; and pains, penalties or tythes for his furnace. The Spaniard who reads of this furnace with horrour, dances at an auto de fe with transport. And the governments which erect the modern furnace, contrived to consume without fire, believe the dogma, for the sake of which they harass and torture mankind, as faithfully as the Babylonian did the divinity of his image.

Although the atheism of images, has been less mischievous than the atheism of dogma, the additional malignity of the latter, is only an exacerbation of the same principle. It is as presumptuous in you, to require me to worship the manufacture of your head as of your hands; your imaginary or solid idol; and it would be wicked in me to do either. But there is less tyranny and impiety in worshipping the solid image, because the mind has a refuge in its emblematical nature. Had Henry, Mary and Elizabeth, set up solid images, by a Babylonical proclamation, containing a disclosure of the power of mental substitution, many martyrs to polemical dogma, would have escaped the flames.

When a government usurps a power of legislating between God and man, it proves itself to be an atheist. If it believed there was any God, it would be conscious of the vice and folly of making one; if it believed there was any revelation, it would see the vice and folly of construing it by laws, which are not revelation; if it is believed that God made man, it would acknowledge that man could not make God.

Religion is God's legislation. He alone dispenses its sanctions, and these sanctions are mostly of another world. Were the governments of this earth, to legislate for the inhabitants of the moon, the absurdity and inefficacy of such laws would be less, than laws for taking care of human souls, by settling the rights of God, and the religious duties of man. If man, by his laws, can regulate his duties to God, he can increase, diminish or expunge them; and has more power over the deity, than Canute had over the ocean.

This aggravated species of sacrilege is perpetrated by governments to gratify ambition or avarice; but they endeavour to hide their true design, under the pretence that it is good policy to make a vulgar, that is, a false religion by law. It is but a vulgar kind of veneration for the deity, which supposes, that the bulk of mankind can be better governed by man's frauds, than by his truths. The idea, that God made a true religion only for a few learned men, and gave them a commission to make false religions for the vulgar, from time to time, supposes that the deity was unable to legislate for the great mass of his creatures. By reserving truth for the learned, and cheating the ignorant into virtue, religion is considered as necessary for the first class, and superstition as sufficient for the second, without any divine authority for the discrimination. But governments do not perceive the high encomium they thus pass upon the people, by admitting, that the light of religion is necessary to check the propensity of the wise for vice, and that the blindness of superstition is unable to corrupt the propensity of the vulgar for virtue. And thus discover that they foster a delusion incapable of making men better in this world, or happier in the next, from their own secret avarice, ambition and atheism.

Governments and hierarchies have annexed a sanctity to the utensils of religion, which they will not allow to religion itself. To protect these utensils, artfully blended with their usurpations, they have invented the term, 'sacrilege.' They are too holy and sacred to be altered, taken away or applied to any temporal purpose. Less delicate with religion, they form and transform it, for wicked temporal ends; and the only good one they pretend to expect from the trade of religion-making, is, that the veil of a treacherous or deluded concurrence, drawn by law over a nation, will produce good order and morality. Are deceit, purchased by office, or imposed by fear, and ignorance produced by fraud, good nourishers of moral virtues? Will habitual insincerity to God, habituate us to sincerity in our commerce with men?

A new species of political atheism or polytheism is making its
·appearance, and gradually gaining ground among mankind, more
specious, insidious and dangerous than the old. It is that of making
government the patron of the whole tribe of tenets or metaphysical
idols, existing, or capable of being invented. We will suppose only
an hundred of these in a nation, each pronouncing the rest to be
damnable errours. You shall adventure your soul, says a government, upon a lottery, wherein the chances are an hundred to one
against you. Why are men driven by law into this injudicious
species of gambling? Because governments believe in neither of
these metaphysical idols, and gain power by patronising all. Had
they believed any one to be the herald of salvation, they would
have exhibited some preference for truth, or at least have forborne
to coerce men by penalty into an election, deterringly fortuitous.

A polytheism of tenets would probably have appeared as ridiculous to the ancients, as their polytheism of wooden idols does to
us. Without settling the point of plurality, between physical and
metaphysical polytheism, they might have considered it as more
likely that all their gods existed, than that all our contradictory
tenets were true; and they might have urged the emblematical
nature of their system, to shew that it was less polytheistical, than
a political patronage of a pantheon of tenets. A government which
assumes this patronage, is less theocratical, and more atheistical,
than one which assumes the patronage of a polytheism, composed
of solid images of various divine attributes. Its object must therefore be power and not truth.

This new species of atheism or polytheism (for the patron of
many contradictory tenets or religions, must either believe that ·
there are many gods or no god) under the garb of toleration or
liberality, conceals a political instrument of tenfold malignity to
human happiness, beyond the ancient. Ancient governments, by
the aid of one superstition and one priesthood, were able to destroy
civil liberty; what then will not modern governments effect, by the
aid of many contrary tenets, and many priesthoods? By the ancient
polytheism, the people were united, by the modern, they are
divided. Under the ancient, governments destroyed civil liberty,
by corrupting one priesthood; under the modern, a patronage of
many priesthoods will produce the same effect. The power of
governments, arising from the corruption and influence of many
priesthoods, produced by its patronage of a polytheism of metaphysical deities, will infinitely surpass any power, arising from a

polytheism of physical deities; because of the rivalry among these tenets and their priests. This will render each separate priesthood more influential over its sect, and more subservient to the pleasure of the government. Whereas Jupiter, Mercury, Diana, and the rest of the heathen deities, in the shape of images, to the learned were emblems, and to the vulgar appeared as friends; exalted by the imagination into intellectual beings, united in convocation, and arranged in subordination, whose little disputes or amorous adventures never destroyed the peace or good humour of mankind.

The union of the priesthood under ancient superstitions, formed a powerful, and occasionally, an useful check upon the government; and although like any other order, it was prone to coalesce itself with it, to deceive and oppress the people; yet an ancient priesthood constituted a balance conformable in principle to Mr. Adams's system, and productive of similar effects.

All the controversies between hierarchies and governments and their several fluctuations of power, are witnesses to the truth of this observation. A balance of power between a government and a hierarchy, produced with critical exactness, the same effects as its balance between other orders. The two orders were constantly in a state of war, for the purpose of subjecting each other; or united, for the purpose of oppressing the people; and their warfare produced occasional ameliorations of the hard and regular tyranny arising from their union.

No such amelioration can occur, from a priesthood and a nation, cut up into jealous and inveterate religious orders or castes, by a multitude of tenets; when patronised and managed by a government. These divisions would in time constitute so many castes of China or Indostan, over which, western, like eastern governments, would preside with absolute power; because they will be made to deprive a nation of its unity or self, and destroy the idea of a common or publick good, as effectually, as its division into civil orders or castes. Such a divided priesthood, instead of a check upon tyranny, would become its instrument. And under pretence of impartiality between God and Baal, the government would draw inexhaustible recruits from both.

The oppression resulting from a mass of legal pecuniary religious rights, orders or privileges, will ultimately become the same as that which would result from a mass of legal pecuniary civil rights, orders or privileges. Mercenary armies, and most corporate bodies, belong to the latter species of moral beings; and a patronage of government over the whole priesthood of a nation, composing one church or many churches, to the former; but both are of the same moral nature, and will operate the same moral effects.

The denunciation of exclusive privileges, titles, and an interposition with religion, by the policy of the United States, was suggested by the consideration, that such rights or powers, commence or terminate in despotism. One of the reprobated powers is exercised by charters, and another is advocated by the doctrine, that government ought to patronise all metaphysical idols. But neither the perpetrated nor intended violation is chargeable to our constitutional policy; that labours to leave wealth to be distributed by industry, and salvation by God; and abstains throughout from the idea of a power in government to regulate either by law. By leaving to every one a fair chance to work out his temporal and eternal welfare, it excites merits called forth by no motive, when governments assume the dispensation of both.

The constitutions of the United States, have renounced the practice of creating by law, moral duties, temporal or eternal, in the shape of exclusive privileges or religious tenets, because they deemed it equally oppressive to enrich the priesthood of fraud as the priesthood of superstition. Had they been formed by atheism, they would have seen no objection to one species of manufacture; nor to the other, had they been formed by paper systems, patronage or orders.

From an opinion, that there is really a God, our policy has inferred, that he has established some mode of inculcating virtue, preferable to human frauds; that there is no occasion to kill or persecute one another on the score of religion, because God needs no champion to assert his honour or to avenge his quarrels; that at this time of day, martyrdom would be lunacy, and saintship, under the banner of a dogma, intolerance; and that it is a profanation of religion, to make it an instrument, to gratify avarice or ambition.

Governments have almost universally inculcated opinions contrary to these, and irreligion and insincerity have been the fruits of their policy. If we see governments making gods of wood or of dogma, or settling revelation by law; if the people see them coining religion into power and money, under pretence of coining it into good morals; it will teach them also atheism and deceit. As a cunning government uses religion to cheat a nation, a cunning man will use it to cheat his neighbour; and in place of its being a bond of love, a preceptor of virtue, and the refuge of hope, religion would be thus made an engine of publick oppression and private fraud.

Atheism forbids men to look into the book of nature for God, and asserts its fluctuating fables to be better evidence of his existence, than his own permanent creation. And it forces men to see God, not in the sun's light, but in some dark tenet, adapted to a temporary market.

It is to this hour unknown, whether established or legal religions have ever carried a single soul into heaven; but there is no doubt of their having carried millions out of this world. Yet it is under pretence of making men extremely happy, after they are dead, that these religions make them extremely miserable, whilst they are alive; and the compensation for the promised happiness, is always estimated upon the supposition of its being as certain, as the suffered misery. Can honesty or virtue have contrived a lottery, from which men draw oppression in this world, and blanks in the next; or can impiety exceed the presumption of selling or bestowing heaven? The polytheism of tenets, or a political patronage of the whole tribe of fanatical follies, entangles men more inextricably in this lottery, than the establishment of a single religion; one may be true; many, contrary to each other, must all be false except one. To be oppressed by the whole tribe, to pay the whole tribe, and to strengthen a government against a nation, by recruiting its power with the patronage of the whole tribe, merely to take the chance of being jostled into that, which really bestows what they all promise, is the speculation proposed by a polytheism of tenets.

Warburton is the only bishop who has disclosed a religious candour, equal to Mr. Adams's political honesty. In the first volume of his Divine Legation, he defines an established religion to be 'a league between a civil and religious society for mutual defence and support; to secure the obedience of the people to the government, in which it is so efficacious as to gain reverence and respect for tyrants; for giving to a church a coactive power to punish intentions by spiritual courts, and thus supply a defect in civil society, which can only punish acts; as an engine bound to render its utmost services to the government for its wages; as a means to prevent the rivalry of sects, by admitting one only to a share of power and emoluments; as a compact founded in reason and nature, equally with the original compact between the government and the people; as one to be made between the government and the largest religious sect in society; as entitled to a test law for its security against the tolerated sects, now inflamed by the advantages of the established sect; as giving no cause of umbrage to other sects by its exclusive privileges and emoluments, because rewards are not sanctions of civil law, wherefore a member of society has a right only to protection, and magistrates an arbitrary power to dispose of all places of honour or profit; as preventing the persecutions, rebellions, revolutions and loss of liberty, caused by the intestine struggles of religious sects.' And he concludes, 'in a word, an established religion, with a test law, is the universal *voice of nature.*'

Nature, according to the bishop, dictates an establishment of one religious sect; according to Mr. Adams, of three civil sects; and according to both, for the purpose of preventing persecutions, rebellions, revolutions and loss of liberty. She dictates, according to one author, that no regard is to be paid to truth in the selection of the established religion; according to the other, that no regard is to be paid to talents, in selecting kings or nobles; preferring the size of the sect to the one, and lineage to the other. Warburton utters the religious policy of the system of orders, and that system adheres to the religious policy of Warburton. A complete parallel would disclose an indissoluble affinity, but as the reader knows, that though God has made a diversity of opinion a quality of human nature, the bishop says, that nature dictates the establishment of one religion, or a repeal by man of this diversity; and that though nature appears to take very great care, not to signalize particular families with royal or noble marks, Mr. Adams says she dictates an establishment of orders; he will need no assistance in discovering the indissoluble union between a political system, comprising orders, and a religious system, comprising an established sect; nor in estimating the value of the policy of the United States, from its not requiring any association with political atheism.

The world is indebted to Mr. Jefferson for an argument, condensed into a law, and recorded for the use of posterity in the statute book of Virginia, which political atheism has never yet adventured to face. Like the serpent, uncovered in its lurking place, it indeed hisses at the hand which removed the concealment. But the long acquiescence in the principles of this law, may be fairly considered as having ripened them into maxims, asserted by our policy, and established by experience.

The religious policy of orders considers man as a perishing physical being; and treats him with errours and idols, as a savage is amused with beads and trinkets; that of the United States, considers him as a moral being; and inspired with a hope that his attainments are not concluded in this world, encourages him to look towards truth and God. The old theory believing there is no God, usurps the regulation of the intercourse between its phantoms, soul and deity, by laws operating upon body; because it discerns no danger in using religion to bribe, deceive and oppress; the new, believing that there is a God, shrinks from the impiety of thrusting laws between God and spirit, which neither can be made to obey; because it expects retribution in another world, for its doings in this. Such laws, by the old system, are called pious, by the new, impious frauds. The old system pretends to govern God and spirit; the new humbly subordinates itself to God; the old, because it believes in neither; the new, because it believes in both. In short, the deity of the old political theories is admitted by themselves to be 'a pious idol;' whereas the deity of the policy of the United States is the eternal God.

And yet this old atheist, the universal advocate of an opinion that a pious fraud is a deputy for God, capable of managing men better than God himself, exclaims, that a new atheist has risen up in the new political theory; just as exclusive privileges accuse equal rights of an enmity to private property. The priests of the idol and the privilege are equally clamorous to transfer their own guilt to innocent avengers, for the same reason; atheists and invaders of private property themselves, they endeavour to repel truth by odium. Savages deify the author of evil; but they do not demonize the author of good. If neither of the combatants should be furnished with an army of mercenary troops, we may certainly foresee on which side victory will fall; but if we seduce from their principles, the honest proselytes of our policy, by offering them bribes to enlist under the banner of the old atheist, one other demonstration will be added to the fate of Socrates, of the insecurity of virtue and innocence exposed to fraud or folly.

A belief in a deity and in the existence of the soul, is consistent with the religious policy of the United States; and a disbelief in both, with the religious policy of almost all other governments. The reader will recollect, that we arranged governments into two classes; as being universally founded in, or drawn from good or evil moral principles. Theocracy must be the creed of one class, and atheism of the second. The advocates of good moral principles such as truth, freedom of religion, knowledge, limitation of power and equal rights, cannot be atheists; and the advocates of evil moral principles, such as fraud, force, ignorance, despotism and exclusive privileges, cannot be believers. By their fruits ye shall know them.

The infidelity, in which the old political theories are all founded, is visible both in their formation and practice. They commence with forming religion, in a mould constructed by politicians. And they practise fraud and force, because politicians never believe religions constructed by themselves. Freed from responsibility by atheism, oppression and blood are ordinary items of their operations; and they use religion as a cold tyrant to inflict the one, or a fanatical butcher to shed the other.

Not less visible is the faith of the political theory of the United States. It was that faith which placed religion above the reach of the politician, that it might not by his arts be transformed from a consolation into a scourge. By the same faith, was our theory guided to associate itself with a catalogue of moral principles, precisely contrary to those used as accomplices by the old theories. It would be doubly inconsistent to allow faith to political theories, which make religion a pander for avarice, ambition and tyranny; and to deny it to one, which rescues it from this shameful servility. False religion, like false honour, is easily detected by discovering its source in prejudice, passion or fraud, and not in moral rectitude. Both, goaded on by an ignorant infatuation, or a wicked pride, expect heaven and fame for inflicting evils on mankind or on themselves. Both profess, boast, destroy and dissemble. The fanatick and the duellist are the same characters; devotees of vice or errour, and contemners of morality and truth; who pervert honour and religion into cabalistical terms, to bewitch, deceive, and torment themselves and others. How wonderfully astonished must these characters be, after a life of mutual contempt and execration, to discover their exact identity?

Mr. Adams has omitted to contrast the American and English systems, in relation to religion; and to acknowledge, that the freedom it enjoyed under the one, was incompatible with the principles of the other. The English, is one of those old theories, which makes gods or religions by law; and it is essential to this, as well as to all governments composed of orders, to coerce the mind into one opinion, religious and political; these orders being equivalent to a set of anatomists, for carving the faces of all mankind into one shape; except that the instruments which cut the mind, inflict more pain than those which cut the flesh; and that it is easier to mould matter than spirit. The necessity of a system of orders for the mind-carving policy, is as demonstrable from their nature as from experience. Such systems can only operate according to the minds of their component orders. The operation of these three artificial minds, must control the minds of individuals, or these orders would cease to govern, and the system terminate. Its essence consists in substituting three artificial minds or interests, for a natural mind or interest. If a government is founded in the first, it destroys the latter; if in the latter, it destroys the first. The natural mind and interest must of course be carved into a shape, suitable to the artificial mind and interest. The necessity of this substitution to the system of orders, for the sake of existence, is the true parent of its double-faced idols, called church and state. And hence religion in England is contrived for the temporal salvation of three artificial minds, neither of them existing after death, instead of the eternal salvation of the souls of men.

Orders seldom admit that their powers are deduced from the people; they deduce them from inheritance, unwritten compact, or time immemorial. The rights of man being thus lost in the rights of orders, it is obvious that an individual cannot retain any species of right, not even the right of conscience, because it is the principle of orders, that nature gives man no rights at all; and that all his rights are conventional or legal. Such being the case, if it is the will of a government of orders, that the conscience of an individual should be cut into any shape whatsoever, it would be preposterous for him to assert that it ought not to be done, and that he ought not to be punished for having a conscience which he was obliged to take from an almighty power. He would be silenced by learning, that under the theory of orders, there are no natural rights.

Religious freedom, or the right of keeping our consciences, is compatible with the policy of the United States, because the natural mind or will of man is not controlled by the artificial mind or will of orders; and because it admits man to have derived rights from nature, as well as from law. Having rights, men, when forming governments, may relinquish or retain such as they please; and by so forming a government that the natural mind of man, shall not be controlled by the artificial mind of orders, this natural mind will be able to preserve the natural rights connected with it;

whereas if this natural mind is controlled by the artificial mind or will of orders, no natural right whatsoever can remain, because there cannot exist together, a natural and an artificial sovereign.

It is important to discover the reason, why the system of orders, in every form, has invariably moulded religion into an engine for its own purposes, lest it should be imagined that this feature of that policy, might be obliterated by Mr. Adams's new idea of the responsibility of orders, as hereditary representatives.

A nation is no more a nation, after it has lost its unity, than a man would be a man, cut up into pieces. Divided into orders and interests, it is turned into several nations, separated, not by geographical boundaries, but by legal lines drawn between different privileges, or between privilege and degradation. The nations residing on each side of these legal boundaries, will hate each other far beyond any degree of animosity, which can exist between nations geographically divided; because the legal boundaries must benefit and injure; whereas the geographical may do neither. The former create in some proportion the relation between master and slave, and excite correspondent passions; the latter are perfectly consistent with the relation between equal friends. Accordingly, nations or individuals living on different sides of geographical lines, may sometimes love each other; whilst orders on different sides of legal lines, always hate each other.

How then can Mr. Adams's idea of the responsibility of orders, save for a nation the freedom of conscience? There is no moral being, after it is divided into several moral beings of distinct interests, to enforce this responsibility. The natural mind, acting by election, is superseded by a legal mind, guided by the interest of orders.

Suppose he intends that the rights and privileges of these orders shall be settled by a constitution. This is no more than a treaty between these artificial and legal nations. And if such nations hate each other more sincerely and constantly than natural nations, treaties between them will be more frequently violated. In fact, orders never make such treaties, without instantly commencing their violation; and it is owing to the impossibility of forming a treaty which they will observe, that Mr. Adams throughout his erudite researches into their history, has found them constantly at war. It is not unnatural that he should be inflamed by the ill success of all others, to evince his diplomatick skill in forming a new treaty; but a nation is under no such emulative impulse to become the subject of the experiment.

410

If orders cannot be kept from hostilities, secret or open, by didactick stipulations, can it be expected that they will forbear to use the most powerful political weapons? They are political beings themselves, and no political being, having a power to use religion as an instrument, has ever failed to exert it. The only security consists in withholding this power from political beings; but this cannot be resorted to in the case of orders, because they are sovereign themselves, and disclaim the idea of allegiance to any superior.

There being several nations intermingled together, under a treaty for securing to, and excluding privileges from each, the defence and enlargement of these privileges will be their first interest; every means will be resorted to for these ends; and the more absurd and oppressive the privileges are, the more violent and wicked will these means become. A noble nation and a plebeian nation, or a banking nation and an unprivileged nation, will necessarily terminate in an oppressing and an oppressed nation. These legal nations hate each other as mortally as white and black nations mingled together. One of them will constantly endeavour to plunder another. Robbery is the invariable design of a confederacy of legal privileges, and the retaliation it finally provokes is still more heinous. The wars between the whites and blacks of St. Domingo, being transitory, were inconsiderable in point of mischief or horrour, compared with those between legal nations, called orders, detailed by Mr. Adams. To make inimical interests friendly to each other, by the theory of balances, is more difficult than to establish harmony between different colours, because men will contend more malignantly for substance than for shadow.

Under the policy of the United States, the moral individuality of the nation being preserved by the elective mode of giving effect to its will, by an unity of rights, by its sovereignty over the government, and by the militia system, such a moral being may retain for the members which constitute itself, the liberty of conscience; but this becomes impossible after separate interests are substituted for united; after the government becomes the sovereign of the people; or after a mercenary army becomes the sovereign of the militia.

Freedom of religious opinion, is another link of the chain of rights, necessary to preserve election. If a government is invested with a power to inflict on the mind religious coercion, it will add political. And if it can mould opinion by force to suit its interests or designs in one case, it will do it in the other. The freedom of opinion is an indivisible right. If a government can split it at all, it may by frequent divisions destroy its strength. And as this freedom is the essence of election, whenever it is impaired in the case of religion, election itself receives a wound; which again illustrates its dependence for efficacy, on the preservation of other rights. Good and evil principles attract or gravitate towards each other, and are as incapable of exchanging places as matter and spirit. Political orders are therefore naturally unable to associate with religious liberty, because this instils brotherly love; those, brotherly hatred. Indians imagine that a Deity and a devil unite in the government of the universe. And a union between the good principle of religious liberty, and the evil principle of sovereign orders, in the government of a nation, would exemplify this savage philosophy.

Upon none of this important ground has Mr. Adams ventured to tread. As to the freedom of conscience, the dearest right of human nature, he is silent. Silence was less injurious to his theory, than a confession, that religious liberty could only exist with the principle of national self government; because a sovereignty of orders annihilates a real national mind, and substitutes for it three artificial minds.

Before this subject is concluded, it is suggested to the reader, that rights retained by nations, as unnecessary for governments, constitute our most useful division of power. The rights of conscience and of the press, deprive governments of much power, to be otherwise drawn from superstition and ignorance. Besides these, the people of America have endeavoured to keep in their hands a great extent of political ground, forbidden to government. All this territory is lost at once by introducing the sovereignty of orders. It will also be lost by laws gradually encroaching upon it; such as laws for cutting off the provinces of free inquiry and militia defence; by regulating the press, and by standing armies. The first mode of getting rid of the whole catalogue of human rights, is not less certain than the second; it drives men gradually towards slavery, by law, as the Indians are driven towards the ocean, by encroachment.

From among the rights retained by our policy, we have selected those of self defence or bearing arms, of conscience, and of free inquiry, for two purposes; one, to shew the vast superiority of our policy, in being able to keep natural rights necessary for liberty and happiness, out of the hands of governments; the other, to shew that this ability is the effect of its principles, and beyond the reach of Mr. Adams's system, or of any other, unable to reserve to the people, and to withhold from governments, a variety of rights. Of the three selected as illustrations, the right of free inquiry remains to be considered.

Caligula's appointment of his horse to the consulship, is both an illustration and a mockery of the idea of national sovereignty, without the freedom of utterance; and a nation, the members of which can only speak, and write as government pleases, is exactly this consular sovereign.

But although the rights of the horse and the nation may be equal, their happiness will be unequal. The thoughts of the horse being under no legal control, he retains this natural source of pleasure. Man's thoughts, suffered to flow, furnish the purest streams of human happiness. Dam'd up by law, they stagnate, putrify and poison. To his characteristick qualities of speaking and writing, all man's social discoveries and improvements are owing. Qualities which distinguish him from the brute creation, must be natural rights; and those which are the parents of social order, must be useful and beneficial. Why should governments declare war against them?

Expression is the respiration of mind. Deprived of respiration, the mind sickens, languishes and dies, like the body. It flourished in the climates of Greece and Italy, whilst it could breathe freely; it has decayed in the same climates, according to the degrees of suppression it has suffered. Wherever it can breathe freely, mind seems to begin to live; swells, as if by enchantment, to a sublime magnitude; and suddenly acquires wonderful powers.

The objection against a free respiration of mind, is, that it may occasionally emit from its lungs (according to our metaphorical license) noxious vapours. The same reason is infinitely stronger for smothering body; its lungs constantly emit noxious vapours. If we deprive mind of health or life, because its breath is sometimes noxious, let us adhere to the principle and finish the work, by smothering body also. Had they so existed, as to be capable of separate destruction, which species of murder would have been entitled to the first degree of guilt? Estimate mind without body, and body without mind. Behold an idiot! Let not those pretend to religion, who would poison or murder mind, but not poison or murder the body of an idiot. Do they perpetrate the first crime, to prove that they will abstain from the second?

The long stationary state of political science, previous to the

American revolution, must have been owing to some peculiar cause, which enabled other sciences to outstrip it. And there is no cause so peculiar to political science, as a legal prohibition of discussion. Mind, as to this science, was fettered; as to others, free. The commencement of the American revolution, knocked off these fetters, political science bounded forward, and a government was formed, which is at this moment the solitary political object of universal commendation. Few prefer even the government under which they live, to ours; none, any other.

The opinions in several state constitutions, in favour of mental emancipation, being so construed as to expose mind to legislative fetters, the good sense of mankind had in this as in many other instances, preceded precept in exploding errour. Political prosecutions for opinion had become as obsolete as those for witchcraft, before the general constitution obeyed publick opinion, by declaring their inconsistency with free government; and before the sedition law endeavoured to drive political science into a retrocession of centuries, for the sake of reviving them.

The third section of the third article of the general constitution, had been deeply rooted in the natural right of free utterance, before the public solicitude required its farther security, by the third amendment. The utterance of any opinions could not constitute treason. Irreverence expressed for our constitution and government; falsehood or reasoning to bring into contempt and overturn them; were not thought politically criminal. Instead of being condemned to punishment, they are shielded against prosecution. What could the constitution do more, for the vindication of an unlimited freedom of utterance, than expose itself to this license? Could it have intended to defend one officer of the government by criminal prosecutions, against the freedom of opinion, after having subjected the whole government to its inspection? We should, under an ignorance of its source, have attributed the constitution to beings more inconsistent and romantick, than those whose errours were limited by human folly, had it exposed its own life to preserve an indispensable principle, and relinquished the same principle, to preserve the reputation of an individual. If such is the text of the constitution, three volumes written by a president, for the purpose of destroying our policy by hereditary orders, and laws for prosecuting sarcasms against the same president, may both be justified by its construction.

The criminality of bringing a president into contempt, consists of its indirect tendency to destroy the government; a direct attempt to destroy the same government cannot be less criminal. If an indirect attempt by writing or speaking was punishable, a direct attempt of the same kind would not have been shielded against punishment. He who reads Mr. Adams's sarcasms upon election, and eulogies upon hereditary orders, will confess, that they are as well calculated to bring a government, founded in one principle and reprobating the other, into contempt, as those uttered against one of its temporary officers.

Reverence for a magistrate, is frequently contempt for a constitution. The contempt of the English nation for James II. arose from a reverence for their form of government. A contempt for principles, and a reverence for men, conducted the French nation to the issue of that revolution. It is the policy of all despotick governments, enforced by sedition laws. In Turkey this policy is perfect. In England, where this policy is less pure than in Turkey, to assert that the king, by corrupting two branches of the legislature, was destroying the principles of the government, would be morally true and legally false; and to assert that each order maintained a constitutional independence of the others, would be morally false and legally true. Legal truth, by the sedition law policy, is moral falsehood; the alternative lies between betraying the principles of a good government, or submitting to be considered as libellous, seditious and traitorous. It proposes to us to wound our consciences, by becoming traitors to our constitutions; or to be rewarded with bodily punishment for constitutional loyalty. Truth and falsehood under such laws, unexceptionably mean praise and censure of men in power.

These murderers of discussion, knowledge and patriotism, engrave upon their tomb, 'that private citizens have neither the right nor capacity to canvass the measures of government.' Men are advised to institute governments to secure their rights, not to destroy them; for this purpose, they are allowed to possess all the rights and talents of human nature; and the ministry who preach this doctrine, no sooner climb by it into power, but they very gravely tell the same men, that they have neither talents nor rights; that they cannot distinguish between pleasure and pain; and therefore that there is no occasion for them to write or speak either truth or falsehood, upon a subject which embraces all their rights, and regulates most of their pleasures.

Such is the language of orders and privilege in every form. Into such politicians, orders and privileges transform patriots. They assail truth and knowledge, because truth and knowledge assail them. They stigmatize discussion, because it leads to discovery. They foster ignorance, because it is blind.

Every attempt by a government to control free discussion, indicates fear and jealousy. Jealousy by a government of a nation, is always criminal, because a nation cannot usurp its own rights; but jealousy by a nation of a government, is always laudable, because a government may usurp the rights of the nation.

Criticks, to good writers, are friends; to bad, foes. Bad writers call them malicious demons; good, court their examination, because they consider the praise of ignorance as ridicule. Good and bad governments, regard free discussion, as good and bad writers do criticks; being the only impartial judge of governments which can exist, one kind preserves, the other destroys it, for the same quality.

Some governments which do not avow despotism, are not so hardy as to deny the right of free discussion; they only defeat it. They allow or punish criticisms upon themselves by their own will and pleasure. A criminal who makes the law, selects the jury, settles the evidence, and pronounces the judgement, may safely come to trial. A subordinate member of a government, cannot be made an impartial judge of his superior's merits. A king of England boasted, that he could have what law or gospel he pleased, because he could appoint, promote and translate judges and bishops. Would these judges and bishops impartially try such kings?

A judge of the United States, possessed of an embassage, or capable of receiving one, would be an English bishop holding in commendam, or expecting translation. An instance of such a bishop, uninfluenced by the government, is regarded with admiration. Sedition laws subject publick discussion to this species of holiness; are its decisions infallible, because they may be always foretold?

It is obvious that nations are the only juries qualified to try governments. Can they decide justly without discussion, and without facts, except those admitted by the culprit? Will the ambition and avarice of factions be recited in their own laws? or will these factions enact their frauds into justice, as they do idols into gods? When laws pretend to make gods or truth, we may certainly expect idols and falsehood. Factions will never make truth by law, for the sake of detecting or punishing themselves. The instant a government is guided by avarice or ambition, it degenerates into a faction, which makes laws to punish the opinions of others, and to hide its own crimes. Vice is even less likely than errour, to subject itself to punishment.

The chains which bind nations to the block of slavery, have been forged of such strength, that it is a prodigy to break them without calamities almost as terrible. Between these chains and such calamities will continue to lie the election of mankind, unless a force sufficing to break the former is discovered, capable of effect without begetting the evil of civil war. No such force has occurred to the mind of man, except the freedom of discussion. If power shall seize on the press also, what will men gain by the art of printing? This noble art itself, will rivet and not break the bonds of despotism. Under the direction of a government, it will operate upon civil liberty, as oracles did upon religious. The press will lie like the oracle, when a government directs its responses; and the success of falsehood, protected against investigation, is illustrated by the influence of oracles for centuries.

The preservation and use of language, are the benefits gained by mankind from the art of printing. Refined and fixed, religion and science need no longer be stored under locks, liable to rust, and keys perpetually changing their shape. Hieroglyphick, sanscrit and corrupted latin, the only previous depositaries of both, have been superseded by printing; and rivers of truth and reason began instantly to clear away the dust and cobwebs in which they were involved. Religion, as most important, preceded the sciences in extracting truth and reformation from the art of printing; and when we see her no longer like a blood stained fury, we almost lament that this soul and body saving discovery, had not been revealed with the gospel. Why should the science of government be retained in the bondage, which for ages could demonize religion, and obstruct knowledge? and are not the fetters of sedition laws, as strong as those of latin, sanscrit or hieroglyphick?

An argument used against free discussion by governments, was first used by the Pope of Rome. It would excite sedition and civil war. A world of experiments have ascertained, that the propensity of mankind is infinitely stronger to bear bad governments than to subvert good. This propensity for politicial obedience, is strengthened by free discussion, on behalf of good governments, by the influence of the merit it discloses; and weakened under bad, by disclosing their vices. On behalf of which will its suppression operate?

· Suppose, both that the people are inclined to turbulence, and governments to tyranny. Yet, for one evil inflicted by turbulence upon governments, one thousand have been inflicted by tyranny upon nations. To suppress free discussion from an apprehension of an evil, rare and temporary; for the sake of fostering one, frequent and durable; would be obviously unwise. But when we find religion cured of its fury by free discussion, may we not confidently consider it as a cure also for political rage; and the true panacea both for the tyranny of governments and the turbulence of the people; and that to surrender its benefits for fear of its evils, would be like surrendering the benefits of the sun, because of its noxious exhalations?

Such a surrender would be a substitution of the correlative vice for the opposite virtue. Resistance and submission to tyranny are relatively contraries. Resistance is a generous and active principle, inspired by a love of mankind, which makes all the efforts designed to advance the publick good; it is the sole defender of human liberty, and reasoning is its best and safest weapon. Ought the patriot, resistance, to be disarmed, and metamorphosed into the slave, submission? This patriot never draws a sword, unless he is robbed by law of free discussion. Compare the erect, open and manly countenance of one principle, with the downcast, gloomy and fearful visage of the other; and use the limner, free discussion or sedition law, to paint your own face, according to your own ideas of beauty.

Free discussion will instruct the publick mind, in what is just or excellent in government, as it refines the taste and judgement of mankind in relation to other sciences. And publick officers will be compelled to conform their characters, as authors do books, to this refinement. The license of the press, like the license of the stage, will be corrected; and even the frauds and tyranny of news-papers, will at length be resisted by this correct, trusty and inexorable tribunitial power; which will learn to pronounce its veto against deviations from the principles of free government, with the same skill it discloses in detecting deviations from the principles of other sciences. Without it, the best principles may slide into the worst; the liberty of the press itself might be perverted; and printers might become tyrants under the cap of liberty. This might be effected by extracting from the liberty of the press, the right of producing condemnation, by withholding the means of defence, or of killing unheard. But this species of tyranny too enormous for ·

governments to claim, would be soon detected by free discussion, as a fraud upon principle, to which it would at length bring back culprits, by opening to defence the channel of accusation.

God has not by sedition laws, prohibited to man the free examination of his works; but man 'cloathed in a brief authority,' arrogantly extorts a species of reverence, which the deity disclaims. 'Consider my works; I have given you reason and left it free.' Such is the law of the creator. 'Reverence my qualities; presume not to consider my works; use your reason according to my will.' Such is the law of a creature. It is a law which idols in every shape enact, because free inquiry would never mistake them for gods. Governments resort to sedition laws, for the same reasons which induce many dealers in newspapers to obstruct free inquiry; to hide their frauds, and make themselves idols.

When a fraud commences its operations, it is annoyed by truth and knowledge. To meet these enemies in the open field of fair discussion, would be its ruin. It therefore avoids this species of combat, by calling it sedition. This misnomer parries detection, by persuading mankind that the only mode of making it, is a greater evil than the fraud itself. And by ingeniously drawing the alternative between the fury of sedition and the good temper of knavery, the latter is placed in the most favourable light. Whereas, had fraud confessed, that knowledge could never abound without free inquiry, and that ignorance invited imposition and tyranny with inevitable success; it would have been obvious, supposing that free inquiry tended to beget both knowledge and sedition, that a good and an evil were preferable to two evils, ignorance and tyranny, the fruits of its suppression. Fraud strives to hide the long chain of moral effects attached to each of the principles; knowledge and ignorance; because it would find sedition an appendage of the latter. During above thirty years, since their independence, less mischief has been done in the United States by sedition, than frequently in Turkey, during the same period, in one day.

Free inquiry, national interest, and national power, united, can seldom produce sedition, because it can have no object. Power, united with these associates, never thinks of entrenching itself behind sedition laws, whilst united with orders or exclusive privileges, it flees to them for refuge. Therefore the policy of the United States both permits and requires free inquiry, by which knowledge is advanced, whilst the system of orders permits and requires sedition laws, by which knowledge is suppressed.

If free inquiry or discussion may be abused, so may religion and the power of speech. Ought religion and speaking to be suppressed, because an abuse of one, produces idolatry, and of the other, lying? Every good has an alloy of evil. It is the case with life itself. Shall we destroy social freedom, for the sake of destroying its alloy, calumny? We can destroy this and all other temporal evils by death; and we can increase them by an enslaved press. What is the wisdom of that policy, which brings upon men an host of foes, in order to destroy one?

The only abuse pretended to be checked by sedition laws, is the promulgation of falsehood. Their efficacy for attaining this solitary end, is questionable. An exclusive privilege of lying in a predominant party, is a premium for its encouragement; and an equality in the right between rival parties, may produce a reciprocal check.

Detraction and flattery also afford some correction to each other, and diminish the mischiefs produced by the exclusive agency of either. The zeal of governments against detraction has caused them to overlook the malignity of flattery without its check. The falsehood of one, deducts from the falsehood of the other. Leave flattery without the subtractor, detraction, and the quantity of falsehood is increased, both by the natural disposition of flattery, and also by an artificial excitement of that disposition. Thus also sedition laws create more falsehood than they destroy, and of a more pernicious nature. If they destroy the species of falsehood, which calumniates individuals, they create that called adulation to governments; and to destroy a small evil, foster a great one. The delirium provoked by the sweet poison, flattery, is often assuaged and even cured by the bitter antidote, detraction. The medicine, however acrimonious, may not be invariably useless to individuals; and it invariably, as to governments, produces the wholesome effect of causing them to turn their eyes upon themselves; a spectacle which the mirror of flattery never justly reflects.

Sedition laws are as often suggested by a love of truth, as religious laws, by a love of God. The former enlighten men politically, as the latter do religiously. Civil liberty flows from one policy, in streams as copious, as religious does from the other. A restraint of religious discussion by law, is exploded in the United States, because idolatry, fraud and oppression, are the fruits of this restraint. Will a restraint of political discussion, produce knowledge, truth and liberty? Have we torn this mantle of imposture from false gods, wherewith to enrobe false patriots?

Having submitted to the consideration of the reader a few general arguments to prove, that for the preservation of civil liberty, sound policy dictates an unlimited freedom of discussion, concerning magistrates and their measures; and that if the magistracy can restrain discussion, human reason, instead of being a check, will be made an accomplice of usurpation; it behoves us now to view the question under the particular policy of the United States.

Without stopping to explain the consequences of a common power in the general and state governments to make and modify sedition: to declare the same words to be false and penal there, and true and meritorious here; and without anticipating the mutual reprisals to be expected, from these pretended cruisers after truth, detached by aggression or defence into their respective territories; let us come at once to the fundamental principle of our policy and constitutions, and consider whether it can be sustained, under a government regulating publick opinion, by law, judges and juries.

A nation, to retain rights, or exercise self government, must be an intellectual and political being. Thinking is as necessary to a body politick, to enable it to shun evil and obtain good, as to any other reasonable being. If a monarch, an aristocracy, or a parliament, possess the sovereignty of a country, a doctrine that these sovereignties should not think, speak or discuss, except according to such rules as should be prescribed to them by the people, would be equivalent to the doctrine, that a nation possessing the sovereignty, should not think, speak or discuss, except according to such rules as should be prescribed to them by a monarch, an aristocracy or a parliament. In both cases the sovereignty would be transferred from the automatical to the prescribing power.

Suppose an aristocracy to hold the sovereignty, and the rest of a nation to assemble and prescribe to it rules for thinking, speaking or discussing, enforced by punishments to be inflicted by judges of national appointment; if such a regimen would transfer the sovereignty from an aristocracy to the people, it follows that the same, only reversing the case, will transfer it from the people to any political power, however composed, which can thus prescribe and enforce, as to them.

This demonstration is ingeniously evaded, by resorting to the representative quality of our policy, and thence inferring, that such rules or laws are to be considered as the act of the people, or of the sovereignty itself, by its representatives; or as restraints imposed by one's own will, upon one's self.

Under this decoy, every measure of the government, intended directly or indirectly to transfer the sovereignty from the nation to itself, might be hidden. There can hardly exist a degree of sagacity, unequal to its detection.

Election and representation may be united with a sovereignty of orders; it cannot therefore of itself constitute a sovereignty of the people. Election and orders act together under the English policy; there, election disavows the existence of a sovereignty of the people; here, to cover assaults upon this sovereignty, it is said to be constituted by election, and exercised by representation. In England, say the disciples of the same political system, representation helps to take sovereignty from the people, and bestows it upon the government; but in America, representation takes it from the government, and bestows it upon the people. In England, suffrage and sovereignty are considered as distinct, and suffrage is allowed no portion of sovereignty; here they are considered as one and the same, by those who are for giving the sovereign power to the government, merely to amuse the people with its shadow,

By allowing to the people that species of sovereignty, which can be found in suffrage and representation, and no other, it results, that the people may be deprived of free discussion without injuring their sovereignty; according to the facetious corollary: that if I choose a sovereign, I am myself a sovereign. But, rejecting this mode of reasoning, and allowing to nations a right of self government or a national sovereignty, anterior to suffrage; the primitive of suffrage itself and the antecedent of law; it realizes a national free right of discussion, as radical as the right of self government itself, because the one cannot exist without the other.

Illustrations of this reasoning may be drawn from the English parliament. Though the house of commons is the creature of suffrage, this very house denies to its elector, any portion of sovereignty, and constitutes, with the other orders, the sovereign power. In its character of sovereignty, it exercises the right of free discussion, because this right is essential to sovereignty. Deprived of it, the house of commons would constitute no portion of a sovereignty. Deprived of the same right, the people can constitute no portion of a sovereignty. The people have suffrage and representation in England, but not free discussion; and the parliament without the two first, and with the last, possesses the sovereignty. It is thence evident, that the sovereignty of the parliament arises from the right of free discussion, and the want of sovereignty in the people, from the loss of that right. Parliamentary will, opinion and sovereignty, is of course substituted for national. The parliament restrains individuals by sedition laws, upon the same principle that the people of the United States restrain governments, political departments and publick officers, by constitutions. The English nation suffer, what the American people inflict; namely, political restraints; because that nation is the subject of parliamentary sovereignty, and our government is the subject of national sovereignty. Sovereignty only is competent to inflict, and subjection to suffer, political regulations and restraints. Monarchs never think of imposing these regulations and restraints upon themselves, by constitutions or sedition laws, because sovereignty is unable to restrain sovereignty. My will to-day, cannot bind my will to-morrow. If the prior will should resolve to punish the posterior, the resolution would be abrogated by the posterior will, whenever the period of punishment should arrive. If an absolute monarch should by election constitute a power, and invest it with a right of inflicting upon his intellects, whatever political restraints and regulations this elective power pleased, the destruction of his sovereignty would follow. The fallacious idea, that election will secure sovereignty, has cheated many nations of liberty, but not a single monarch of despotism.

We must stop for a moment to explain to the reader what is meant by 'political rules and regulations.' If he should recollect a distinction formerly stated, between political and municipal law, he would presently discern the force of our reasoning. By one, it was said, governments are regulated; by the other, individuals. The latter species of law, comprises the whole scope of legislation, which a free nation can part with; the former, it must forever retain and pronounce, or cease to be free. The treacherous art of blending these objects is exercised by sedition laws. They profess to regulate individuals, but design to regulate the form of government. They are nominally municipal, and operatively political law. The dictator over discussion, is a dictator over decision. Volumes of cases might be cited, in which nations have gradually lost their liberty, by an insidious introduction of a political regimen, under a municipal title; and these cases forcibly recommend to the United States a wakeful memory of the solemn truth, that every government which can innovate by civil upon political law, is despotick.

The opinions under discussion, are, that the elective policy transfers sovereignty from the electors to the elected; that every act of a representative government is an act of the nation; and that the nation possesses only that imperfect and evanescent species of sovereignty, the right of suffrage.

If representation destroys that which it implies, namely, subordination, then it can annul or alter constitutions; and if the act of their representatives is the act of the people, representation constitutes a sovereignty incapable of limitation. Necessity compels us to consider our policy or constitutions upon a supposition, that these opinions are true or false. If they are true, these constitutions are subject to the sovereign representation. If they are false, then the existence of a sovereignty over representation, is demonstrated.

The imperative style of our political decalogues called constitutions, implies the existence of some superior power, whose organs they are; whilst the doctrine, that this power, by having thought and spoken once, had lost the right of thinking and speaking forever, is equivalent to an assertion, that the Deity, by prescribing the Mosaick dispensation, had forfeited the right of prescribing the Christian.

If a sovereign power, by one declaration of its will, does not lose its sovereignty, it must retain also an unlimited freedom, in whatsoever is necessary towards any future declaration of its will; otherwise its first will, must be its last will.

An intellectual political being, differs essentially from an intellectual physical being. The first can only think by speaking and writing, as it is compounded of many individuals. If it is not allowed to think freely, it can never decide or act according to its own will, since its will can only be discovered by freedom of expression. This position is demonstrated by considering the process, necessary to form the opinions of a body politick and of an individual. A comparison of ideas is necessary in both cases. The body politick being composed of many distinct minds, cannot compare its ideas, except by collecting them through the external mediums of speaking and writing, or by free discussion; whereas an individual can compare his ideas, by the internal operation of thought. An individual may therefore decide, or discover his opinion, because no human law can prevent him from thinking or comparing his ideas; but a body politick may be prevented from knowing or exercising its opinions, because human laws can prevent it from thinking, by free discussion, either to fix or to discover them.

Sovereignty is an intellectual political being. In Britain, it is parliamentary; in America, national. Publick opinion, ought to rule, according to our policy; parliamentary, according to hers. Had the English king possessed a power, to regulate by penalties, the discussions in the house of commons, its freedom of opinion would have been equivalent to the freedom of national opinion here, under such a power in the government. If each individual of the parliament, was confined separately in a dungeon, and brought out once a year to give a silent vote, parliamentary opinion and sovereignty would be, what national opinion and sovereignty becomes, under an inhibition of free discussion. Conferences by stealth, would be modes for discovering publick opinion in a wide territory, even less effectual, than the echo of those groans, which would resound among the cells of these incarcerated parliamentary sovereigns.

The argument for depriving nations of the right of thinking, by speaking and writing, is, that a nation may have bad thoughts. An individual may also have bad thoughts, and the same argument would, if it could, put an end to his thinking. Members of the British sovereignty, may also have bad thoughts, but they are supposed to be overbalanced by the good. Imperfect man's best prospects, must be confided to a preponderance of good thoughts, in respect to sovereignties, governments and individuals; and to deprive either of thinking, lest the thoughts should be bad, would cut off the prospect of deriving any good from the subject of this deprivation. It is moreover an ineffectual remedy for the evil, because no prescribing power can be found, which may not itself have bad thoughts. Governments must have infinitely more bad thoughts than nations, because they can acquire wealth and power by their bad thoughts; whereas nations, by theirs, can only gain misfortune or despotism. Nations err undesignedly. Governments are liable to the same source of errour, and it also pours in upon them through the sluices opened by ambition, avarice, and a great variety of human vices, which sleep least under the strongest incitements to awake. To cure the propensity of human nature for vicious projects, by constituting a dictatorial power over the right of thinking and discussing, in which the same propensity exists, in its most aggravated state, is plunging into the ocean, for fear of being drowned in a bucket of water.

We have been endeavouring to illustrate the defect of Mr. Adams's system, and of all others constituted of orders, by shewing

o*   425

the inefficacy and ambiguity of the sense annexed by them, to the expressions, 'national rights and national opinion;' rights, supposed to be secured by an incapacity of acting from intellectual conviction; and opinion to be formed without thinking by a free comparison of ideas.

National rights and opinions, held or moulded at the pleasure of governments, are the creatures of a species of political transubstantiation, which declares it to be heresy, not to believe, that the opinion and will of a government, is the opinion and will of a nation. That bread and wine, are indeed flesh and blood.

National rights and national opinion, cannot really exist, without powers for defending the one, and organs for expressing the other. The system of orders must shew these or confess that they have provided for neither, and that it uses the terms as decoy phantoms to delude nations within its grasp. The policy of the United States, exhibits its militia, its right of bearing arms, its rights retained, its right of instruction, and its inclusive right of abolishing the entire government.

Our policy, considering a nation as possessing rights it cannot alienate, secures its will and ability to protect them, by moral and physical means. It provides election, attempered by free discussion, as a moral mode of subjecting governments to the sovereignty of the nation, and not to subject the nation to a sovereignty of the government. And it provides a militia, as the physical mode for securing obedience to the moral means by which the will of the nation is disclosed. Like twins growing to each other, either of these guardians of national sovereignty perishes, if the other ceases to exist. Sedition laws destroy one, and standing armies the other. Either, therefore, terminate in despotism; a militia deprived of its intellectual associate, presently becomes a maniack, who must be disarmed and guarded by a mercenary army, which confines him to a bed of straw, and feeds him upon bread and water. And intellectual freedom, severed from its physical friend, is John the Baptist preaching to a wilderness. United, they are the body and soul of popular government, just as free will and a standing army, are the body and soul of monarchy. Destroy the body or soul of either, and the whole being dies.

If these reasonings are correct, the inconsistency between a sovereignty of the people, and a power in government to regulate the thoughts or discussions of this sovereignty, is such, as to render it impossible that both qualities can subsist in one government.

426

One of them must be unequivocally surrendered by a candid politician, unless he can devise a species of dual sovereignty, upon the principles of the Athanasian creed. Even then his political creed would fall short of the perspicuity of its model, if he allowed the sovereignty of government, to regulate by sedition laws the sovereignty of the people. He would have to prove that a political almighty, could beget a more potent almighty.

The existence of national sovereignty is asserted every where by the policy of the United States, and under its auspice the general constitution sought for a sanction by the terms, 'We the people.' Rob it of this sanction, and what is its obligation? Or suppose the people had as unequivocally relinquished, as they have exercised their sovereignty by that instrument, still the question would have turned upon the power of one generation, to surrender a natural right of another.

Admitting this power to exist, and admitting also that the establishment of a government is a virtual surrender on the part of the people of their sovereignty, according to the ideas of Mr. Adams, and of all those who assert, that on this event, sovereignty deserts its old habitation, and transfuses itself into a new one; just as some conjurers can shoot their souls out of one body into another. Allowing these concessions to be true, a new dilemma arises from an idea heretofore suggested. The people had established governments previously to the erection of the general government; and if this act causes a transmigration of the soul of sovereignty from a nation, the people had no remaining sovereignty to transfuse into the general government. This doctrine would make the state governments sovereigns, over which the people could not more rightfully place a sovereign, than they now can over the general government. Thus the only sanction of the federal government, consists in the doctrine of popular sovereignty; or that governments are agents, and not masters. Deprive it of this, and it becomes a rebel against the sovereignty of state governments. Mr. Adams both laboured to plant state policy in British principles, which deny any species of sovereignty to the people; and testified in favour of the sovereignty of the people, by allowing the federal to be a legitimate government.

As the federal government cannot legitimately exist, except by admitting that the people are the sovereigns of governments; so the system of orders, or checks and balances, cannot exist, except by admitting it to be the sovereign of the people. National sovereignty

427

would throw into confusion all the weights, and unhinge the whole architecture of the checks and balances. Accordingly, no instance has occurred of orders, admitting themselves to be bound by popular conventions, as did the state governments in the case of the federal constitution. Thus we discern, that sedition laws are consistent with the system of orders, for the same reason which makes them inconsistent with the policy of the United States. The sovereignty of orders being maintainable, only by reserving to itself free discussion, and imposing restraints upon the people, it follows, that national sovereignty is only maintainable, by reserving free discussion to the people, and imposing restraints upon the government. The rapture with which we contemplate the exclusive ability of our policy to subject government to limitations, would excite ridicule, united with the doctrine, 'that the power upon which the enforcement of these limitations depended, could be bound in legal chains, by the power upon which they were to operate.' These beacons, erected in our political territory, to warn us of an enemy's approach, would be dead lights, if law should prohibit the only mode by which they can be kindled.

If our constitutions admit the sovereignty of the people; if the federal government is erected on that foundation; and if no species of sovereignty can exist without freedom of will and of discussion; it follows, that laws for restraining or regulating discussion, are axes which cut up our policy at its root.

Had national sovereignty been a splendid phantasm, as its enemies contend, it could neither have been seen, assailed or defended. Without adverting to its works in the United States, it is sufficient to inquire, why its grave and learned enemies, have engaged so earnestly in a warfare with an unsubstantial spectre. The renowned knight of La Mancha himself, was unable to make giants out of nothing. A dream of infatuation, does not possess the power of creation, nor can a shadow overturn a tree.

Many political writers, including Mr. Adams, assail the principle of national sovereignty, by paying it obeisance, not for the purpose of yielding to that, but to induce that to yield to their systems. As a phantasm, a dream or a shadow, they do it homage; they only object to it, as a being of substance, efficacy and activity. It is said, that publick opinion will have its weight even in despotick governments, merely to prevail on it to submit to them.

The slow and whispered admonitions of publick opinion, to tyranny, are struggles of nature for her rights, excited by acquisitions of knowledge; like the efforts and uneasiness of a strong man, long confined in darkness, excited by a ray of light. Upon every appearance of these struggles, orders and exclusive privileges cry out, that kings, aristocrats, priests and privileges ought to unite, and confine her in stronger bonds. What is thus feared, flattered and fettered, cannot be a shadow. Had it been a shadow, it would not have been regarded and treated like a strong man in pursuit of his rights, by those who withhold them.

If national sovereignty may be assailed, it may be defended. Said an American general to his men, 'you see those fellows yonder, if you don't kill them, they will kill you.' By the same terms, the attention of national sovereignty or publick opinion, would be correctly and emphatically directed to orders and exclusive privileges. This would be incorrect, says Mr. Adams's system; orders and exclusive privileges do not kill publick opinion, they only gag her with law, and point at her breast the bayonets of a standing army, lest she should use force to free her intellects. Still this system asserts, that publick opinion will have an influence over despotism itself. Stephano gags Trinculo, lest he should speak; cuts off his fingers, lest he should write; and imprisons him for groaning; yet Trinculo retains an influence over Stephano, arising from an apprehension of his escape. But an image, sometimes worshipped and sometimes whipt, by its savage subjects, is a less miserable sovereign than Trinculo.

The effects of a sovereignty of law over discussion and opinion are multifarious; all of them are sappers of the principle of national self government. A few more will be adduced.

It begins, by making it criminal to calumniate a form of government; it proceeds, to make it criminal to calumniate those individuals invested with most power, and most subject to the crime of usurpation; and it ends by making every species of writing and speaking criminal, tending to obstruct the avarice or ambition of the power which legislates, or which can influence legislation. Thus governments make of calumny a sponge, to expunge their own crimes. They affect to take the side of truth to hide falsehood, as they do the side of religion, to hide the frauds of hierarchy. An attempt to aid by penalties the cause of religion and truth, is a proclamation of imposture. These champions have ever found them their enemies. The penalties which extorted Galileo's renunciation of his discoveries, attempted to fix and flatten this earth for truth's sake. Laws for regulating truth and religion, like

Samson's hair, strengthen as they grow; and governments not being blind, are at length enabled by them to pull down the fabricks, election and militia; and instead of being buried in their ruins, to convert them into castles for oppression.

Suppose such laws should make it criminal to calumniate some officers and not others; will not those unprotected by the law, be more responsible to publick opinion, than those it covers? Will not election operate more forcibly as to those whose qualities it can sift by free discussion, than as to those whose qualities cannot be canvassed with equal safety? It might be made as dangerous to speak irreverently of a president's posteriors, as it was of old to look upon the Ægis of Minerva.* Every one can correctly estimate the value of a right of discussion, free in relation to a constable, but restricted in relation to a president.

The pleasure of the government may leave those officers exposed to free discussion, or amenable to the sovereignty of the people, who can do no mischief; and cover those against it, who can overturn our policy. This pleasure may allow this sovereignty, more freedom of discussion as to the same officers in one year than in another, in imitation of the suspensions of the habeas corpus act in England. In short, this pleasure may diminish or increase the information and power of this sovereignty, according to its own views; and if there should be factions, it may easily allow more freedom to one faction or portion of this sovereignty, than to another.

Such a subject sovereignty or counterfeit republicanism, is precisely that held by the people of England, France and Turkey; and that conceded to all nations by the theory of orders. Wherever such a theory becomes a government, the sovereignty of the people becomes a theory. Whether national sovereignty or self government is converted into theory by parliaments, judges, juries, prisons and Botany bay; or by national assemblies, soldiers and Cayenne; or by the koran and the sabre; all are equally the instruments of usurpation and tyranny used to repel the lashes of publick opinion in proportion as they are merited. The English government can inflict perpetual imprisonment, in defiance of their boasted habeas corpus, without trial, upon any member of Mr. Adams's theoretical national sovereignty it pleases, should he

---

* The case of Baldwin in New Jersey, here alluded to, ought to be preserved as a monument, to remind the United States, of the short work of sedition laws, in destroying the freedom of speech.

endeavour to exercise his sovereign function, by proving, that the government was oppressive and ought to be changed; whilst his species of the sovereignty of the people, and their species of habeas corpus provision, would lie in his book, and among their statutes, as pictures of lifeless and forgotten rights.

Usurpation, perpetrated or designed, invariably resorts to sedition laws, because by suppressing discussion, it defends itself against suppression. What! Are these laws also defenders of national sovereignty or self government? Will they, like Swiss soldiers, fight equally well for spurious or for legitimate sovereignty? Will a suppression of discussion, be equally serviceable to a sovereignty which lives upon free discussion, and to one which cannot live, until free discussion is dead? Can an usurper and a nation secure sovereignty by the same code?

The friends of sedition laws will not be able to answer these questions, without first proving that freedom of writing and speaking is unfriendly to every species of sovereignty, whether of the people or of orders, whether spurious or legitimate; and its suppression co-extensively favourable to all, however dissimilar in principle. It will be impossible to do this, so long as the relation between cause and effect shall subsist in the moral world.

Sedition laws have been used in all ages to defend governments, because the idea of the sovereignty of the people, or of national self government, was never well understood, unequivocally asserted, or successfully practised, except in the United States of America. This old way of maintaining forms of government, would be more likely to renovate them, than to invigorate our new policy. By transfusing it into their body politick, the United States will practise the Medean method of changing their age, ingeniously reversed; they may suddenly transform their political youth, health and vigour, into the old age, infirmity and decrepitude of some ancient policy.

The idea of a sovereign subject to law; the idea of a responsibility, which can impose penalties on an investigation of its acts; and the idea of a publick opinion, whilst every member of the publick is liable to be committed to prison for expressing an opinion; a publick opinion buried in the grave of silence; these ideas must be found in our constitutions, to empower our governments to govern the right of free discussion, by armies or laws; by generals or judges. That the people never entertained them, is demonstrated by dissolving and creating constitutions, with a deliberation enlightened by discussion, for the purpose of discovering publick opinion.

These conspicuous proofs of national capacity to express an opinion, and the supreme authority of that opinion, undeniably demonstrate that our policy is founded in the idea, that national sovereignty is either a natural or social principle, and our constitutions unequivocally assert allegiance to be due to it, both from their creatures, governments; and even from themselves, the creators of governments. It follows, that the amendment to the general constitution, respecting the freedom of religion, speaking and writing, or any other part of it, cannot be so construed, as to bestow upon government a power inconsistent with its elementary principle. Such a mode of reasoning, would only be a repetition of the idea of cutting off a king's head, by virtue of his authority; and if a stagnation of free discussion will as effectually kill the moral being, national sovereignty, as a stagnation of blood would the physical being called a king, then sedition laws are as favourable to national sovereignty, as the decapitation of kings to monarchy. The circulation of rational ideas by free discussion, is as much a vital principle of the one, as the circulation of the blood of kings is of the other.

There is a strong resemblance in some measures taken against each other, by contrary political principles. The head of Charles was assailed by the axe, under his authority, under protestations of loyalty to monarchy, and under the pretext of reforming abuses. National sovereignty, the head of our policy, has also been assailed even by opposite parties, acting under its authority, under protestations of loyalty to this sovereignty, and under the pretext of preventing sedition. It is wiser to strike at the head than at an inferior member, when a revolution is contemplated. A proposition to put out one of Charles's eyes, or to change the ratio of representation here, would probably have excited greater opposition than more deadly measures. By striking at a vital part, success ends the war. As republicanism aimed at the vital part of monarchy when she struck Charles's head, monarchy aims at the vital part of republicanism, by striking at free discussion. Deadly enemies strike at mortal parts.

If the third amendment to the federal constitution, was not intended to destroy the elementary principle of our policy, an effort to place that policy beyond the reach of the imperfection of language, and the sophisms of construction, is the only remaining intention, which can with any colour be ascribed to it. Religion, speaking and writing, were placed beyond the power of law, because the first appertained to the sovereignty of the deity, and the two last to the sovereignty of the people. Why does not the constitution reserve a right to think? Because that faculty could not be taken away, and it was reserving a national and political faculty, which could be taken away; being that, by which alone nations can supervise governments, retain sovereignty, or perform political functions.

A political national mind, required a protection against the usurpation of governments. The mind of an individual was beyond its reach; but a congeries of expressions constituting national mind, was within it. If the latter species of mind does not exist, how inconsistent are those, who talk of national opinion. Where does it reside? It is not the opinion of an individual. It is not the opinions of any number of separate and solitary individuals. If it can exist without discussion, it cannot without disclosure; and the freedom of speech and of the press, is as necessary for the latter purpose, as for the former.

An objection is urged against the idea of national sovereignty, with a degree of plausibility, unable to avoid the detection of a degree of consideration. Are not the people, it is said, subject to law; and is not their sovereignty inconsistent with this subjection?

The repetition necessary to answer this objection, is not painful, because it will impress a principle of the last importance to the policy of the United States.

The people, by our policy, are considered as possessing two capacities, political and civil. Under one, they are susceptible of the rights which nations can exercise; such as those of forming, reforming and supervising governments. Under the other, they are susceptible, individually, of such rights and duties, as an individual may hold or owe. As an individual cannot hold or exercise the first class of rights, a nation must be considered in the light of an associated, political and moral being, or these rights can neither exist, be held, or exercised.

The first species of capacity we assign to the people, operates between them and governments; the second, between governments and individuals, and between citizens. It is our policy to subject the whole field of this second capacity to legislation, and to exclude it from the whole field of the first. Law is allowed to regulate right and wrong in the latter cases, but not between the nation and its government. It cannot form a new government. The right to do this being held by nations, and not by governments or individuals, is evidence that nations hold rights in a moral and social capacity, not subject to law. A form of government being anterior to law, cannot be created by it; and the social rights of nations, cannot be destroyed by political laws, concealed under municipal titles, if law cannot create a form of government.

An unsubjected sovereignty, composed of subjected individuals, is the supposed inconsistency upon which the objection rests.

And yet the same inconsistency, if it be one, exists in the system of government, chiefly admired by the objectors themselves. The British sovereignty is unsubjected, and is composed of subjected individuals. Every member of the parliament of which this sovereignty is composed, including the king himself, is subject to municipal law. Where then is the absurdity, inconsistency or impolicy, of composing a sovereignty of subjects? It is, in fact, the common and plain case, of an individual, holding corporate rights, and owing corporate duties; or of a corporation, which governs its members, and yet is governed by them.

The idea, that a nation must necessarily be divided between sovereignty and subjection, to form a government, allotting one or a few to the first principle, and the mass of the people to the second, is precisely the barbarous opinion, which has always made tyrants and slaves. The whole merit of the British system, consists in a partial refutation of this opinion. That this refutation did not go as far, whilst it acknowledged the principle of ours, arose merely from the orders and separate interests in which the nation was split, some of whom used it to gain the substance of liberty for themselves, and to amuse the people with its shadow.

The English system captivated the nation, in disclosing the borders of republican principles, by lodging sovereignty in orders; ours has only passed these borders, and gotten into the country itself, by lodging it in the nation, instead of orders. Both orders and nations are composed of subjects.

The repetition with which we threatened the reader, consists of the illustration furnished by this reasoning, to the distinction formerly taken between political and municipal law. The power possessed by its members over a corporation, represents one; that possessed by a corporation over its members, the other. If a minority of this corporation, invested with limited powers to transact certain special affairs for the whole, should restrict or

destroy the right of the majority to discuss and censure their conduct, it would be exactly a sedition law under our policy, and from
that moment the nature of the corporation would be changed.

The chief beauty of the English system, is said to consist in the
restraints of orders upon each other, by mutual jealousy; but the
animosity inspired by it, has disfigured the national good by many
a scar. The chief beauty of our policy, consists of a mutual power
in the people and government, to restrain each other, by political
law on one hand, and municipal on the other; these powers do not
clash; the first is influenced by national good, and the second by
private justice; and neither by the ambition, jealousy or hatred of
orders. These two systems are clear mirrors reflecting their effects;
it is only necessary to look into them, to decide the preference.

The affinity between the freedom of religion and of discussion, or
between the right of an individual, to provide for his eternal, and
of a nation, to provide for its temporal welfare, has coupled them
in one sentence, and confided both to one security; so that the
government possesses an equal right to regulate religious and
political discussion,·by fine and imprisonment. Glance your eye,
reader, at courts and juries, composed of opinion, religious or
political, to try opinion. Do you not see hierarchy or faction, ambition or avarice, superstition or tyranny, invariably pronouncing
sentence? A trial of opinion can never be fair or just. Whoever is
of my opinion, acquits, of an adverse, condemns me. Where nature
disables us from judging impartially, it forbids us to judge at all.
The right of A to condemn B, is no better than the right of B to
condemn A; and a clashing right cannot be a right in either.
Monarchy, aristocracy, democracy, and sects, religious and political, judge of each other's opinions, as the Pope judged Calvin;
Calvin, Servetus; the independents, Charles; and Cromwell, the
independents; the precise species of judging at which the sacred
prohibition discloses itself to be levelled, by its reference to the
probability of retaliation—'Judge not, lest ye be judged.'

Whether any consanguinity originally exists or not, between the
freedom of religion and of discussion, the similarity between the
moral effects of such freedom in relation to both, is evident.

Wherever churches regulate religious opinion, and governments,
political, persecution rages, pecuniary burdens multiply, blood
flows and wretches burn. An abandonment of the regulation of
religious opinion, discloses the effects of a similar policy with regard
to political. Both species of regulation are exterminated by our

435

policy, and we happily know only from books, that both prefer flattery to truth, persecution to liberty, and the money of the people to their happiness.

In the execution of religious sedition laws, each sect, when in power, appeals to its own party to determine, whether the complaints of their opponents are not excessively unreasonable. 'They are allowed,' says the law-maker, 'to preach freely, provided they will preach truth, and they ought not to preach falsehood.' 'Nothing can be more reasonable,' is the response of the law-maker's party to the law-maker's appeal.

If the abolition of religious sedition laws has abolished religious wars, why may not the abolition of civil sedition laws, abolish civil wars? Admitting a similarity in their nature and consequences, a discovery by which the tongue and the pen are made to fight all the battles of religion, will probably be able to confine political combatants to the same weapons.

The experience of the United States furnishes a multitude of precedents in favour of this opinion. Constitutions and governments have been frequently made and destroyed, without war, commotion or inconvenience. But it was done in the absence of sedition laws, standing armies and rich monopolies.

These moral beings are generally contemporaries; either is soon followed by the others. The climax of their appearance in the United States has preserved its uniformity. A funding system, a sedition law, an army. So unfounded is the idea, that authors of sedition laws design them to preserve publick tranquillity, that they never fail to provide armies to quell the commotions, which they foresee that these laws will excite.

If it is true, as we have hitherto contended, that free discussion is the creator, the preceptor and the organ of publick opinion; the guardian of national sovereignty and of religious freedom; the seedsman of political knowledge, and the guarantee of moderate government; this precious jewel in our policy is rendered inestimable, as another link in our chain of national rights, necessary to bestow efficacy upon election. Our policy and experience, must either overturn Mr. Adams's system, or be overturned by it. To his system, armies, patronage, paper and sedition laws are congenial, because sovereignty is lodged in orders. These, consisting of a minority, and possessing only a factitious and fraudulent sovereignty, need such auxiliaries. They must of necessity resort to armies, patronage, privileges, corruption and sedition laws, or surrender the sovereignty. These are suitable to a sovereignty of orders, because they impair or destroy the sovereignty of the people. But our system renders armies, patronage, privileges, corruption and sedition laws unnecessary, by placing sovereignty in a majority, which needs no auxiliary, can find none, is able to defend itself, and attracts no enmity from a better title. A transition from the sovereignty of the people to the sovereignty of a government, is a revolution only to be effected by artificial accumulations of power or wealth, by armies, patronage, privileges, paper or sedition laws; of course these instruments are mortal enemies to our policy.

We will take leave of this subject with the following observation. The design of substituting political for religious heresy, is visible in the visage of sedition laws. A civil priesthood or government, hunting after political heresy, is an humble imitator of the inquisition, which fines, imprisons, tortures and murders, sometimes mind, at others, body. It affects the same piety, feigned by priestcraft at the burning of an heretick; and its party supplies such exultations, as those exhibited at an auto da fe, by a populace; and the same passions and interest which furnish cruelty to fraud and superstition, banish commiseration from avarice and ambition, towards those guilty of the unpardonable heresy of opposing their designs.

It is remarkable that the individual, so instrumental in disclosing the wickedness and folly of the notion, that the reputation of the deity needed the protection of heretical laws, became also an example to prove, that the reputation of governments and publick officers, did not need the protection of sedition laws. Whilst we see the shafts of calumny falling harmless around human integrity, we conclude, both that they can never reach celestial perfection, and also, that human virtue ought to recoil from an ally, whose resemblance to the ugliest foe of religion and piety, is so exact.

We now proceed to the consideration of two features of the federal constitution, which have been claimed by the theory of orders, and even renounced by that of self government. If either of these opinions are correct, then this essay incorrectly maintains, that the will of a majority is our elementary principle. It is said, that the form of the senate, and the rule, that three-fourths of the states should concur in amending the constitution, are violations of that principle; and that aristocracy is interwoven with our policy, in the power of a minority through the states or the senate, to arrest amendments and to pass laws. Had this assertion been true, our system of reasoning would have required the arrangement of these features among the defects of the general constitution; on the contrary, we shall arrange them among its beauties, and endeavour to prove their strict conformity with the policy of the United States.

Let us first consider, whether the senate is in fact deformed, as some think, or embellished, according to others, with aristocratical qualities.

The federal government is the creature of two kinds of beings, which I will call physical and moral. Meaning by physical beings, the individuals of the United States; and by moral, the state governments. Our elementary principle in forming a government compounded of both, was equivalently used as the best resource for preserving the rights of both. Accordingly, both popular majority and state majority are resorted to by the constitution of the United States, upon similar principles and for similar ends.

The principle of equality was applied to strong and weak states, as it was to strong and weak men, because each was free; and that freedom brought all to a level in treating or confederating, just as freedom levels individuals of unequal size, in associating. But its beneficial effects outstrip those produced by its application to individuals, because of the wider range of social happiness arising from a society of nations, than from a society of individuals. And this principle has effected the supposed project of a French king to unite or associate Europe, as to more nations, and over a wider space, without war, expense or force; although a love of the union and a hatred of political equality often meet in the same breast, because it is not perceived that the object of our affection was begotten and subsists by the object of our abhorrence.

Without a federal will, to be ascertained by a majority, peace could not be preserved among the confederates, no separate existence of states could have been retained, and our new and efficacious division of power, between the general and state governments, must have been abandoned. And without a popular will, to be ascertained in the same mode, the natural right of self government would have been lost.

The senate being formed for the first end, its democratick complexion is equivalent to that of the house of representatives, constituted for the second. Both the wills provided by the constitution to operate upon the general government, are intended to produce the government of a majority, to be determined by the principle of equality; and the state governments being of unequal strength, democratical and popular, it could not have been intended, because it was not possible, that they should infuse aristocratical opinions into the senate. Just as an assent of the people to constitutions by conventions, cannot be considered as flowing from an aristocratical source, although given by a few persons. A nation has been considered as a moral or political being, capable of opinion, will and sovereignty. States, are nations. When several of these are associated for some ends, and unassociated for others, distinct orders of political beings exist, created by distinct associations. Our policy provides organs to bestow efficacy on the opinions of both, because their existence itself can only be known or preserved by their opinions; and the senate was made the organ of those moral beings called states, to prevent the separate social existence of each, from being swallowed up by a society of all. The people have constituted themselves into two associations; of states and of their union. As these moral or political beings, infuse into our government its spirit, one for some purposes, the rest for others; and as all of them are composed of the same intellectual beings; a construction which supposes, that our policy expected both democratical and aristocratical influence to proceed from the same intellectual source, is as unphilosophical, as to expect hot and cold breath at the same time, from the same nostril. Separate interests only, and not national opinion, can furnish a government with opposite and contending impulses. If the states are not aristocratical beings, how can they produce an aristocratical being?

It is as foreign to the intention of our policy, to create a monarch as an aristocracy. The president is the compound creature of the equality of states and the equality of man, both of which are infused into the mode of his election, for the purpose of preserving both; and in his legislative capacity, he is equally exposed to the control of the popular and state representatives. Thus doubly subjected to the principle of equality, by which both these bodies are constituted, it would be doubly inconsistent with our policy, should he imagine himself to be a king.

This idea is in some degree violated, by the practices of district or legislative electors; the latter of which makes state will, and the former, general will, the electors of a president; and it is observed with great accuracy, by that of choosing electors by the people of a state, in the mode of a general ticket. This mode compounds and blends both the will of the people and the will of the states, and confers an influence in the election of an officer, who has most power to assail or defend both, upon the principle of equality as applying both to the states and to the people. Whereas this union of influence between state equality and human equality is defeated, by state electors which exclude the one, and by district electors which exclude the other, from a share in the election of the president; and the exclusion of either from an influence over the officer, by whom it is most endangered, will weaken its means for self preservation, and create means for severing the union between friends, neither of whom can probably exist without the other.

But the district mode of election, is far more inconsistent with the principles of our Union, than that by state legislatures; because, in that mode, state will, though one of the parties to the union, loses its whole influence; whereas, in an election by state legislatures, popular will retains an influence upon the election of a president, equivalent to its influence over these legislatures. And as a state influence in this election, is a great security to the division of power between the states and the general government, the loss of it would endanger all the securities for a free government, arising from that division.

The importance of this subject will justify an effort to explain our meaning by different language. It has been invariably contended, that the people are the source of all the sections of our government. They have formed themselves into two societies, state and general. In establishing a general government, they have defended both these associations of their own, by constituting that government of three organs; one appointed by themselves in their popular capacity; another appointed by themselves, by representation, in their state capacity; and the third, appointed by themselves, partly in their popular and partly in their state capacity. If the responsibility of the third organ to the nation, in each of its social characters, is equal, the end of our policy is perfectly attained; if unequal, it is in a degree defeated. By legislative elections of electors, the state association, by district, the general popular association, acquires an unequal share of influence over a president. Either is a tendency adverse to our policy; the first, towards disunion, the second, towards consolidation. An election by a general ticket, blends, unites and reconciles these two capacities or associations, more completely than either of the other modes.

If it is proved, by the division of the legislature between general and state will, and by imparting to each species of will an influence over executive power, that the intention of our policy was to preserve and defend both the state and general associations; how can the opinion, that the senate was modelled upon aristocratical principles, be maintained, except by shewing, that an aristocracy is calculated to preserve the democratical state associations?

The ingenuity with which state and general will is blended in the construction of the general government, displays an intention of preventing the evil of a rivalry between the two orders of governments; would the introduction of an aristocratical order into one, have been consistent with that object?

A short comparison between the aristocracies of the first, the second and the third ages, and the senate of the United States, will convince us, that as the senate possesses no quality common to these aristocracies, so a common epithet cannot be applied to both. Superstition, title and paper; consecration, inheritance and fraud; sacrilege, irresponsibility and stockjobbing; and a corporate or party interest feeding upon the people; constitute the characters of these successive aristocracies. It cannot be imagined that the constitution discloses an intention of copying some one of those originals by neglecting to preserve a single feature of either in the formation of the senate. With less foundation still, has Mr. Adams maintained the existence of the aristocratical principle, in state senators.

If it is proved that the senate of the United States, neither is nor was intended to be, an aristocratical body, but the representative of the political beings called states, as parties to the general government, upon democratical, equal or self governing principles; it follows, that it is organized upon the selfsame principles of equality, democracy, representation or self government, which pervade our whole policy. It is the representative of the moral or political beings called states, as the other branch of the legislature is, of the people; and it votes by the rule of majority. It is the band of the union by preserving equal rights to great and small states, as a fair government does to rich and poor men; and it so far receives our eulogy.

But so far from intending to weaken the objection against the long period for which its members are chosen, the considerations which entitle the senate to our approbation, shed new force upon it.

If the senate is the representative of the beings called states, why should it not be at least as amenable to the will of its constituents, as the representatives of the people? The publick good is as deeply involved in the rights of states, as in the rights of individuals. The states have been made parties to the Union by the people; and power necessary to preserve the rights with which they are intrusted for the publick good, could not have been designedly withheld.

Those most strenuous for the aristocratical complexion of the senate, are most deeply impressed with the fear of frequent elections; and yet they are willing to allow to the people a frequency of election, which they deny to the state governments. What! do they confess that governments are worse electors than the people? Or if they deduce the supposed aristocratical spirit of the senate, from a supposed aristocratical spirit in its electors, is the danger three times greater from aristocratical, than from popular electors? If to the simple computation of time, we add the difference of responsibility, between a gradual and an entire change of a representative body, the rates of confidence in the people, and diffidence in the state governments, as electors, are still farther increased. It will be also seen from such a computation, that it is infinitely easier for the representatives of the states, than for those of the people, to betray their constituents to a consolidating principle; and that the responsibility of the senate to the states, though the chord by which the union itself is intended to be secured, is too feeble to inflict any considerable degree of stricture upon human conduct.

A still stronger view of this subject exists. The popular and the federal, are the principles of the general government. The federal principle is not allowed the intellectual or moral means for self preservation, of frequent election, or of recalling its deputies, or of an entire change of them at one period. By weakening the means of confederation to defend itself, this chief principle in the structure of the general government, is particularly exposed to the frauds of its natural enemy, consolidation; because its means of defence are merely moral, and ought of course to have been at least equal to the moral means of its co-principle, supported by the physical force of the people.

As the responsibility of their agents, is the only means whereby the federal parties to the government can enforce their will, or defend their rights, there is no danger in making it effectual. An intellectual control over federal deputies, may be safely entrusted to state governments, unarmed and influenced by the people, as the best mode of counteracting designs to destroy the union; designs, which these governments will most effectually detect and defeat.

We may take stronger ground yet. Hitherto we have chiefly exhibited the states and the people in a kind of contrast, in order to make our reasoning understood; but by forbearing the distinction, the argument becomes more forcible. The general government is the creature of the people only, established to preserve their rights in their double capacity, as the state and federal sovereign. Responsibility is therefore equally due to them in both these capacities. If it is less in one case than the other, one class of rights are safer than the other. And if one is left to depend on the qualities of individuals, whilst the other is secured by placing these qualities under the discipline of the sovereign power, then one is hazarded upon the old principles of government, and the other secured by the new. Is it the interest of the people to lose either the state or the general government; or do opposite principles produce an equal degree of security?

The more a nation depends for its liberty on the qualities of individuals, the less likely it is to retain it. By expecting publick good from private virtue, we expose ourselves to publick evil from private vices. This miserable tenure which has scourged the world, has been exchanged by the United States for the restraints of political law, among which an effectual responsibility is the strongest. Is not this as necessary for men in power, called senators, as for men called representatives? The world has been enslaved by depending for liberty on the uncontrolled passions of individuals; we have enjoyed freedom, by controlling these passions. Every body makes good state governours where executive power is most restricted. Will the state rights of the people be best secured, by committing them to the custody of the passions of such individuals, as may form the senate, or to an effectual responsibility to the guardians of the rights themselves? To the ancient system of confiding in human vices, or to the modern, of confiding in strong political law to control these vices?

If the moral principle of equality, was intended to exist among the states, an effectual mode of securing it, accords with this intention. Whether a seven years' independency of electors, secures the faithfulness of representatives to good, or exposes them to evil moral principles, is demonstrated in a branch of the British government. Are the people of that country made free and happy by representatives, as responsible as those the states elect here? The effects to be engendered here by a moral cause, such as exists there are there demonstrated. If the degrees of responsibility are the same, the effects must also be the same; and supposing a septennial power to change an entire chamber of representatives at one period, to be one year more valuable in point of responsibleness, than a sexennial power of changing it at three equidistant periods, these degrees are the same.

The opinion, 'that the mode prescribed for amending the constitution of the United States, does not pursue the principles of democracy, self government or majority,' is met and contested by the arguments used to explode a similar objection to the structure of the senate. States being considered as entitled to equal rights, and the people of the United States having rights also independent of state governments, it was necessary to obtain the consent of all these rights to amendments, in pursuance of the principles said to be violated by the mode adopted. Amendments, inflicted by a majority of the people and a minority of states, or by a majority of states and a minority of people, would have violated the natural or political equality, either of individuals as members of the general national society, or of the same individuals, as members of the state national societies. To violate neither was the object of the constitution, and therefore a mode of amendment, sanctified by the consent of a majority of both of these free, equal and independent parties to the union, was adopted.

The people of the states, treated and united as independent of each other, surrendered a portion of their independent rights, into a common treasury, and retained another portion. The contract derives its force, not from the consent of a majority of states, but from the separate consent of each. If the moment the contract was signed by these independent parties, it had been subject to modification by a majority of states, the common treasury of rights, might have been plundered; if by a majority of people, the state rights retained, might have been invaded. The first would have erected an aristocracy, by making a majority of states and a minority of people, masters of the majority of the people of the United States. The second would be the case of a minority of the strongest men joining together after forming a society, to compel a majority of weaker men, to submit to such alterations as they chose to make. The destruction of popular government, was not the

444

motive for the confederation. The federal and popular expressions abounding in the constitution, prove it to be a compact, both federal and popular, requiring the happy expedient of securing a concurrence both of the federal and popular will, to amendments for self preservation; had popular will dictated these amendments, state self government, the federal ingredient of the constitution, would have been destroyed; and had federal will dictated them, national self government, the popular ingredient of the constitution, would have been also destroyed.

But if the senate are not responsible to the publick will through the medium of the states, they may defeat by less than a majority, the united will of three-fourths of the states, and a majority of the people, to amend the constitution; and drive them to the resource of calling a convention; the result of which any one state may refuse to concur in, because then each state will resume its original right to refuse or consent, as being independent of each other in negociating the terms of a new union. The concession by each state of this independency to three-fourths, suffices to shew, that a majority of states had no claim over the rights of each state, except from concession; and that each state might annex such terms to its concession, as it pleased. A power over the independence of each, is by each conceded to three-fourths. A quadruple alliance might, upon the same principles, be made amendable by three of the parties.

To the exclusive power of the senate over the president, to its being a sublimated medium of popular will, and to its being the guarantee of state rights, is to be added its power over the concession of each state's independency to three-fourths of the states, as a new and weighty reason for its being more responsible than a British house of commons. If an abbreviation of representative tenure, would be a wholesome emendation under a monarchical policy, a republican policy, seconded by considerations arising from the peculiar structure and powers of our senate, must loudly demand it. By frequent election or a power of recal, publick opinion will be breathed into the senate, through the lungs of state societies; and then publick opinion, and not the private opinion of thirty or forty individuals, will constitute as it ought and alone can, the restraint of executive power, the protector of state rights, and the judge of amendments to the constitution. These are functions belonging to nations, and to the discharge of which, individuals are incompetent, having a capacity only to convey the publick opinion, which is itself the real power. A body of men, upon which publick opinion cannot effectually stamp its impress, never fail to pass off the false political coin of private opinion, under the forged name of publick. The forgery is discovered, and the counterfeiters are compelled to use armies, superstition, penal laws, and paper corruption, to make the base coin pass. The publick can only become the tutelary guardian of the senate, and the senate the genuine organ of the publick, by means of the power and confidence which an effectual responsibility to the nation, through its state sections, will create.

Section the Seventh

AUTHORITY

CONFIDENCE is a substitution of the understanding and honesty of others for our own; authority, the understanding and honesty so substituted. Whether this substitution belongs to the good or to the evil class of moral principles, is the same question in another shape, with the controversy for preference between the policy of the United States, and that of every other country. Monarchy, aristocracy, hierarchy, privileged orders, and all parties and factions, political or religious, being founded upon the substitution of the understanding and honesty of others for our own; and the policy of the United States, upon the use of one's own understanding and honesty.

From the fact, that the inducements of nations to defraud or enslave individuals, are infinitely fewer than those of individuals to defraud or enslave nations, our policy has inferred, that the judgement and honesty of a nation, is more likely to produce its own liberty and happiness, than any other judgement or honesty which can be substituted for it, either of a king, an order, a patriot, a party, a demagogue or a faction. Authority asserts the contrary.

Authority is subject to fraud and errour; national judgement, to errour only. Nations have no motive for deceiving or injuring themselves; authority, so many for deceiving or injuring nations, that it seldom or never fails to do both. A nation never knowingly adopts or adheres to an oppressive measure; authority is so entirely addicted to this vice, that it is constantly its original design, or final effort; and the first pretension to the dictatorship it usurps, is an advertisement that it is already a knave, or will finally become a tyrant.

If authority should miraculously possess integrity, it is more liable to capricious errours and absurd prejudices, than national judgement. The wisest man is never free from these humiliations of human vanity, but he can never convince the majority of a nation, that his humours are wise. National opinion shields mankind against the afflictions arising from individual caprice and prejudice, to which authority exposes them; and therefore it is a wiser, besides being an honester standard of truth.

We may without much difficulty discover our own opinion, but not one in a thousand can possibly know the opinion of the authority in which he confides. Like a river, it commences in a diminutive rill, which is swelled in its course by innumerable turbid and nauseous additions, until not a drop of the original fountain, can be obtained; whilst confidence must still swallow the contaminating compound, and allow its impurities to be transubstantiated into holy water. The supposed fountain is even often quite dry; and a river wholly deceptious is formed, without containing a single drop from the source it claims, to raise an artificial current, for conveying, not the nation, but demagogues or knaves, into a good harbour. It is not therefore matter of any astonishment, that most publick measures derived from authority, end in repentance.

Wherever authority guides a nation or a political party, there cannot be a national or party principle, opinion or measure. It converts nations into the engines of an aspiring individual or a faction, for enslaving themselves; and parties into beasts, to be ridden by a few artful men into office. To this surrender of national and party principles and opinions to authority, is to be superadded, the stupidity of corrupting the object of confidence itself, by assuring it of indiscriminate support. Propelled by this preposterous admonition towards its natural bent, authority very soon abolishes the distinction between principles, parties are converted into mere ladders to power, and election is restricted to the barren right of saying which ladder shall be mounted; so as to produce, not a check, but an excitement of the authority to make the most of present power. Authority moulds men into the same kind of moral beings, whether it is bestowed by a free or an oppressed nation, by a patriotick or a slavish party, because the same moral effects proceed from the same moral causes; and hence, however derived, its apprehensions of the alternation to which it is exposed by election, produce to confiding nations the same misfortunes.

All the truth in the opinion 'that knowledge is the best security for liberty,' lies within its capacity to detect the fraud of authority, and to retain the contrary principle, self government. Our policy draws the liberty we enjoy from one principle; authority is the source of the present state of other countries. The comparison would at once awaken the credulity, by which nations are induced quietly to put on the yoke of authority, were they not perplexed by its false and constant claims to national gratitude. Would to God some standard could be established to detect the fraud of magnifying publick services, up to the value of national liberty. When were those rendered by George Washington exceeded by any individual? Yet if the publick services of all other citizens during the same period, were poised against his, the disparity would satisfy every future patriot, that he ought to submit to an example, which graduates the highest publick services, by a scale, far short of justifying bad precedents and sacrifices injurious to nations.

Authority is similar to monarchy or aristocracy, in preferring the abilities and interest of one or a few, to the abilities and interest of all, as the ground work of government. It is similar to an elective monarchy or aristocracy, in being the creature of national or party confidence. But it is more pernicious to good government than elective monarchy or aristocracy, in being more mortal; it cannot outlive the man to whom it is attached, and may die before him. The struggle to depose and transfer it is so perpetual, that an interval of repose can seldom occur; and the permanent state of a nation guided by it, resembles the temporary state of an elective monarchy at the epoch of election. Successions of authority, like the waves of a troubled ocean, perpetually roll along over each other, and the instant one is buried, another rushes into its place, and speedily follows on to the grave. The excessive mortality of authority demonstrates its incompetency for the government of a being, which seldom or never dies. The longevity of a principle, ought to be equal to whatever is entrusted to its care. Can a living nation secure its liberty and prosperity by confiding it to a perishing authority? The vital defect of hereditary monarchy, is the mortality which exposes nations to the fluctuations in the characters of men, and deprives them of the benefit of unchangeable principles; and the vital remedy for this defect, is still more adverse to the greater degree of fluctuation in the principle of successional authority. It lies in fixed good moral principles, and genuine self government, capable of living as long as the nation, and wisely confiding for happiness in that which can live as long as itself.

The whole moral world cannot afford so perfect a coincidence of phenomena, for ascertaining the true value of any moral principle, as in the case of authority. Cæsar, Cromwell and Bonaparte obtained degrees of democratick authority, never reached by others. The parties which bestowed them, by substituting confidence for judgement and conscience, were of the highest democratick orders, and proved to be the completest instruments for tyranny. The whig and tory parties of England in possession of authority, uniformly pursue the same measures; and unpossessed of it, uniformly avow patriotick opinions, for the sake of obtaining an opportunity to violate them. The republican and federal parties of the United States, are evidently clambering towards the system for consigning a nation to the constant spoliation of a successive authority, more aggravating to vicious passions, because more unsettled than monarchy itself.

Far from correcting the abuses with which they charge each other, their leaders, trusting to the pernicious doctrine of confidence and authority, will convert their mutual abuses into mutual precedents. Neither parties nor individuals will voluntarily diminish power in their own hands, however pernicious they have declared it to be in the hands of others, because if they are vicious, they are willing to abuse it, if virtuous, they presumptuously confide in their own moderation; therefore abuses can never be corrected, where confidence and authority have subverted national principles.

As authority generates the same effects upon all men, the men are not blameable, because it is obvious from the constancy of the effects, that the force of authority is irresistible by human nature. If a physician mingles poison with wholesome food, not he who is poisoned, but the physician who poisons him, deserves punishment. If a nation poisons parties or individuals, or its own government, with confidence and authority, the nation which applies the poison, and not those who cannot avoid its effects, is blameable; and therefore the moral law is strictly just, which recompenses with arbitrary sway, those poisoned by confidence, and punishes the poisoners themselves with slavery. The same inexorable moral law brings similar private guilt or folly to the expiation. Individuals, like nations, who substitute in the management of their servants, confidence and authority for an inquisitive scrutiny and a strict responsibility, are exposed to pillages, which justly transfer their estates to those whom they have thus corrupted.

As the guilt of nations in betraying posterity to oppression by yielding to authority, is inevitably punished by their own subjugation, the severity of this punishment constitutes a proof of the badness of the principle, satisfactory to all who believe in a superintending providence. Parties who corrupt their leaders and subject themselves by the same evil principle, are punished with still greater severity. Like herds of swine, they are fed with grain or garbage, until they are fit for slaughter; this is never deferred a moment after the conjuncture is ripe, lest they should escape; and without remorse, they are always put to death by the tyrants of their own creation. Thus the great democratick leaders, Cæsar, Cromwell and Bonaparte, dispensed justice to their stupid parties. Cæsar, a courtier, originally raised them for their end. Cromwell, a fanatick, was stubbornly honest, but authority melted that honesty, because human nature cannot resist the moral law which imposes new opinions with new circumstances; and he served the party he adored, as Cæsar served the party he despised. Bonaparte, originally neither a statesman nor a fanatick, happening to float upon accident up to a momentary authority, demonstrated by the use he made of an unpromising conjuncture, how fatal a heedless though trivial confidence may be, to the nations and parties by whom it is bestowed.

It is wonderful that the human mind should have been able to detect the impostures founded in the authority of Gods, and remain blind to those founded in the authority of men; that it should despise oracles pretending to inspiration, and surrender its judgement and conscience to authority pretending to none; and that it should worship dying men, after having ceased to worship living spirits. An hundred volumes might be filled with the fatal effects to nations and parties, in ancient and modern times, from sacrificing their own principles, consciences, judgements and interests, to authority; but leaving them to the recollection of the reader, we will proceed to quote a few cases to shew the influence of circumstances upon the soundest heads and the purest hearts; those best grounds for any pretensions which authority can advance.

Almost every eminent man who has appeared in governments tinctured with liberty, might be quoted as an authority against the opinions by which he was raised; but the habit of setting out with free and proceeding to slavish principles, is so common, that a contrary case, rare, if not singular, is first exhibited to the reader. Dean Swift, in his prime, was a tory, a statesman, a priest of the high church party, and a violent opponent of the whig principles. .In his retirement, uninfluenced by ambition, this profound politician sent to his friend an abstract of his political opinions, to be

451

found in Pope's works, vol. 6, p. 120, which is transcribed as an evidence, both of the force of passions and circumstances upon our current opinions, and of a concurrence between this able man when uninfluenced by these passions and circumstances, and several important doctrines of these essays.

'I had,' says Swift, 'a mortal antipathy against standing armies in times of peace; because I always took standing armies to be only servants hired by the master of the family for keeping his own children in slavery; and because I conceived that a prince who would not think himself secure without mercenary troops, must needs have a *separate interest* from that of his subjects. Although I am not ignorant of those arbitrary necessities which a corrupted ministry can create, for keeping forces to support a faction against the publick interest.

'As to parliaments, I adored the wisdom of that Gothick institution, which made them annual; and I was confident our liberty could never be placed upon a firm foundation until that ancient law was restored among us. For who sees not, that when such assemblies are permitted to have a longer duration, there grows up a commerce of corruption between the ministry and the deputies, wherein they both find their accounts, or to the manifest danger of liberty? Which traffick would neither answer the design nor expense, if parliaments met once a year.

'I ever abominated that scheme of politicks (now about thirty years old) of setting up a monied interest in opposition to the landed. For I conceived, there could not be a truer maxim in our government than this, *that the possessors of the soil are the best judges of what is for the advantage of the kingdom.* If others had thought the same way, *funds of credit* and South Sea projects would neither have been felt nor heard of.'

Further to illustrate the force of passions and circumstances upon current opinions, and to recommend the work of an author of no fame, by exhibiting its concurrence with one other of high reputation, the following dissertation, the original of which is now before me, written by Mr. John Adams during the revolutionary war, is exhibited to the reader. As correct extracts not taken from this copy have occasionally appeared in the newspapers, its diffusion as a model for government, is a proof both of care in the composition, and of its great credit with the author and the patriots of those times.

'If I was possessed of abilities equal to the great task you have imposed upon me, which is to sketch out the outlines of a constitution for a colony, I should think myself the happiest of men, in complying with your desire: because, as politicks is the art of securing human happiness, and the prosperity of societies depends upon the constitution of government under which they live; there cannot be a more agreeable employment to a benevolent mind than the study of the best kinds of government.

'It has been the will of heaven, that we should be thrown into existence at a period, when the greatest philosophers and law-givers of antiquity would have wished to have lived; a period, when a coincidence of circumstances, without example, has afforded to thirteen colonies at once an opportunity of beginning government anew from the foundation, and building as they choose. How few of the human race have ever had any opportunity of choosing a system of government for themselves and their children! *How few have ever had any thing more of choice in government than in climate!* These colonies have now their election, and it is much to be wished that it may not prove to be like a prize in the hands of a man who has no heart to improve it.

'In order to determine which is the best form of government, it is necessary to determine what is the end of government. And I suppose that *in this enlightened age*, there will be no dispute, in speculation, that the happiness of the people, the great end of man, is the end of government, and therefore that form of government which will produce the greatest quantity of happiness is best.

'All sober inquirers after truth, ancient and modern, divines, moralists and philosophers, have agreed that the happiness of mankind, as well as the real dignity of human nature, consists in virtue; *if there is a form of government whose principle and foundation is virtue*, will not every wise man acknowledge it more likely to promote the general happiness than any other?

'Fear, which is said by Montesquieu and other political writers, to be the foundation of some governments, is so sordid and brutal a passion, that it cannot properly be called a principle, and will hardly be thought in America a proper basis of government.

'Honour, is a principle which ought to be sacred: But the Grecians and Romans, pagan as well as christian, will inform us, that honour at most is but a part of virtue, and therefore a feeble basis of government.

'A man must be indifferent to sneer and ridicule, in some companies, to mention the names of Sidney, Harrington, Locke,

Milton, *Nedham*, Neville, Burnet, Hoadly; for the lines of John Milton, in one of his sonnets, will bear an application, even in this country, upon some occasions.

> 'I did but teach the age to quit their cloggs,
> By the plain rules of ancient liberty,
> When lo! a barbarous noise surrounded me
> Of owls and cuckoos, asses, apes and dogs.

'*These great writers, however, will convince any man who has the fortitude to read them, that all good government is republican; that the only valuable part of the British constitution is so*; for the true idea of a republick is, an empire of laws, and not of men; and therefore as a republick is the best of governments, so that particular combination of power, which is best contrived for a faithful execution of the laws, is the best of republicks.

'There is a great variety of republicks, because the arrangements of the powers of society are capable of many variations.

'As a good government is an empire of laws, the first question is, how shall the laws be made?

'*In a community consisting of large numbers, inhabiting an extensive country, it is not possible that the whole should assemble, to make laws. The most natural substitute for an assembly of the whole, is a delegation of power, from the many, to a few of the most wise and virtuous.* In the first place then establish rules for the choice of representatives: agree upon the number of persons who shall have the privilege of choosing one. *As the representative assembly should be an exact portrait, in miniature, of the people at large, as it should think, feel, reason and act like them,* great care should be taken in the formation of it, to prevent unfair, partial and corrupt elections. That it may be the interest of this assembly to do equal right and strict justice, upon all occasions, it should be an equal representation of their constituents, or in other words equal interests among the people, should have equal interests in the representative body.

'That the representatives may often mix with their constituents, and frequently render them an account of their stewardship, elections ought to be frequent.

> 'Like bubbles on the sea of matter borne
> They rise, they break and to that sea return.'

'These elections may be septennial or triennial, but for my own part I think they ought to be annual, *for there is not in all science a maxim more infallible than this, where annual elections end, there slavery begins.*

'But all necessary regulations for the method of constituting this assembly, may be better made in times of more quiet than the present, and they will suggest themselves naturally, *when the powers of government shall be in the hands of the people's friends.* For the present it will be safest to go on in the usual way.

'But we have as yet advanced only one step in the formation of a government. Having obtained a representative assembly, what is to be done next? Shall we leave all the powers of government to this assembly? Shall they make and execute, and interpret laws too? I answer no; a people cannot be long free, and never can be happy whose laws are made, executed and interpreted by one assembly. My reasons for this opinion are these.

'*A single assembly is liable to all the vices, follies and frailties of an individual.* Subject to fits of humour, transports of passion, partialities of prejudice; and from these and other causes, apt to make hasty results and absurd judgements: all which errours ought to be corrected, and inconveniences guarded against by some controlling power.

'A single assembly is apt to grow avaricious, and in time would not scruple to exempt itself from burdens which it would lay upon its constituents, without sympathy.

'A single assembly will become ambitious, and after some time will vote itself perpetual. This was found in the case of the long parliament: but more remarkably in the case of Holland, whose assembly first voted that they should hold their seats for seven years, then for life, and after some time, that they would fill up vacancies as they should happen, without applying to their constituents at all.

'The executive power cannot be well managed by a representative assembly, for want of two essential qualities, secrecy and dispatch.

'Such an assembly is still less qualified to exercise the judicial power, because it is too numerous, too slow, and generally too little skilled in the laws.

'But shall the whole legislative power be left in the hands of such an assembly? The three first at least of the foregoing reasons, will shew that the legislative power ought not to be wholly intrusted to one assembly.

'Let the representative body then elect, from among themselves

455

or their constituents, or both, a distinct assembly, which we will call a council. It may consist of any number you please, say twenty or thirty. To this assembly should be given a free and independent exercise of its judgement, upon all acts of legislation, that it may be able to check and correct the errours of the other.

'But there ought to be a third branch of the legislature: and wherever the executive power of the state is placed, there the third branch of the legislature ought to be found.

'Let the two houses then by joint ballot choose a governour. *Let him be chosen annually. Divest him of most of those badges of slavery called prerogatives.* And give him a negative upon the legislature. This I know is liable to some objections, to obviate which, you may make him in a legislative capacity only president of the council. But if he is annually elective, you need not scruple to give him a free and independent exercise of his judgement, for he will have so great an affection for the people, the representatives and council, that he would seldom exercise this right, except in cases, the publick utility of which would soon be manifest, and some such cases would happen.

'In the present exigency of American affairs, when by an act of parliament we are put out of the royal protection, and conse-quently discharged from all obligations of allegiance; and when it has become necessary to assume governments for immediate security, the governour, lieutenant-governour, secretary, treasurer and attorney general should be chosen by joint ballot of both houses.

'The governour, by and with and not without the advice and consent of council, should appoint all judges, justices and all other officers, civil and military, who should have commissions signed by the governour and under the seal of the colony.

'Sheriffs should be chosen by the freeholders of the counties. If you choose to have a government more popular, all officers may be chosen by one house of assembly subject to the negative of the other.

'The stability of government, in all its branches, the morals of the people, and every other blessing of society, and social institutions, depend so much upon an able and impartial administration of justice, *that the judicial power should be separated from the legislative and executive, and independent upon both*; the judges should be men of experience in the laws, of exemplary morals, invincible patience, unruffled calmness, and indefatigable application; their minds should not be distracted with complicated jarring interests; they should not be dependent on any man or body of men; they should lean to none, be subservient to none, nor more complaisant to one than another. To this end they should hold estates for life in their offices, or in other words their commissions should be during good behaviour, and their salaries ascertained and established by law.

'If accused of misbehaviour by the representative body, before the governour and council, and if found guilty after having an opportunity to make their defence, they should be removed from their offices and subjected to such other punishment as their offences deserve.

'*A rotation of offices* in the legislative and executive departments has many advocates, and, if practicable, might have many good effects. A law may be made that no man shall be governour, lieutenant-governour, secretary, treasurer, counsellor, or representative, more than three years at a time, nor be again eligible until after an interval of three years.

'A constitution like this, of which the foregoing is a very imperfect plan, naturally introduces general knowledge into the community, and inspires the people with a conscious dignity becoming freemen. A general desire of reputation and importance among their neighbours, which cannot be obtained without some government of their passions, some good humour, good manners and good morals, takes place in the minds of men, and naturally causes general virtue and civility. That pride which is introduced by such a government among the people, makes them brave and enterprizing. That ambition which is introduced into every rank, makes them sober, industrious and frugal. You will find among them some elegance, but more solidity, a little politeness, but a great deal of civility, some pleasure, but much business.

'Let commissions run thus, "Colony of North Carolina, to A. B. greeting, &c." and be tested by the governour.

'Let writs run "The Colony of &c. to the sheriff &c."

'Let indictments conclude "against the peace of the Colony of North Carolina, and the dignity of the same" or if you please "against the peace of the thirteen united colonies."

'We have heard much of a continental constitution. I see no occasion for any but a Congress. Let that be made an equal and fair representative of the colonies, and let its authority be confined to three cases, war, trade and controversies between colony and colony. If a confederation was formed, agreed on in Congress, and

p*   457

ratified by the assemblies; these colonies, *under such forms of government and such a confederation, would be unconquerable by all the monarchies of Europe.*

'This plan of a government for a colony, you see is intended as a temporary expedient under the present pressure of affairs. The government once formed, and having settled its authority, will have leisure enough to make any alterations that time and experience, and more mature deliberation, may dictate. Particularly, a plan may be devised, perhaps, and be thought expedient, *for giving the choice of the governour to the people at large, and of the counsellors to the freeholders of the counties.* But be these things as they may, two things are indispensably to be adhered to; one, is some regulation for securing forever an equitable choice of representatives; another, is the education of youth both in literature and morals.

'I wish, my dear sir, that I had time to think of these things more at leisure, and to write more correctly. But you must take these hints rough as they run. Your own reflections, *assisted by the patriots of North Carolina*, will improve upon every part of them.

'As you brought upon yourself the trouble of reading these crude thoughts, you can't blame your friend.'

Principles and convictions are expressed in this dissertation, in ideas and language, as strong, as plain, and undoubtedly as honest, as in the book of the same author upon the same subject; his mind must have attained to its maturity at the time of the first composition; and the force of the difference between a struggle for liberty, and an enjoyment of a rich executive office, only remains to account for the different appearance of the same principles and the same words to the same mind, at different times. A few remarks will sufficiently display this difference.

In the dissertation, the sovereignty of the people is unequivocally asserted, as the basis of society and civil power. Representation is made its *substitute*, from the impossibility of holding national assemblies. And being drawn from this origin, its perfection is made to consist in *thinking, feeling, reasoning* and *acting* like, and being an *exact portrait in miniature, of the people at large.*

Mr. Adams's later system is bottomed upon orders, two of them hereditary, incapable of thinking, feeling, reasoning or acting like the people at large; and yet exercising a complete sovereignty, as in England.

The dissertation contends for the frequency of election, its application even to executive power, for securing its responsibility;

and the infallible truth of the maxim, that 'where annual elections end, there slavery begins.'

The system renounces two thirds of the principle of election for hereditary orders, and advocates the idea of unelected virtual representatives, never *to mix with the people, account for their stewardship, or be,*

> 'Like bubbles on the sea of matter borne,
> To rise, to break, and to that sea return.'

And asserts that elections ought to be rare; that they produce every vice; and that they bring the worst men into power.

Both in the dissertation and the system, the impolicy of accumulating all civil power in one assembly is justly insisted on. In the first, election is considered as sufficient to produce a division o power; and the people, as being able to split their agencies, and not compelled to consolidate them into one mass. In the second, hereditary orders are eulogized as the only remedy for such a political evil. The argument used against a single assembly is, that 'it is liable to all the vices, follies and frailties of an individual.' Or, in other words, like a king. Then a king or an individual must be liable to all the 'vices, follies and frailties' of a single assembly. Mr. Adams was forced to use one of these political beings, as a mirror to reflect the deformity of the other. But forgetting their similitude, he becomes in his system the admirer of that, selected in his dissertation to exhibit a single assembly in an execrable light.

The dissertation urges an annual election of an executive or governour, as the means of securing his 'affection for the people, the representatives and the council.' The system recommends an hereditary executive or a king, as the means for securing his affection for the people. One recommends a rotation in offices; the other that they should be for life and inheritable.

The dissertation asserts, that the constitution it proposes, would introduce knowledge, inspire the people with dignity, good humour, good morals, good manners, virtue and civility; that it would make them brave and enterprising, sober, industrious and frugal; and that if a confederation was formed only for the cases of war, trade and controversies between the colonies, they would, under such forms of government, be unconquerable by all the monarchies of Europe.

The system transfers these eulogies to the English form of government; and recommends that monarchy, as particularly well contrived for war, although it was one of the European group of monarchies, defied by the dissertation, with an unarmed American democracy, not containing one-twentieth of their number.

In advocating the doctrine of compounding a government with orders, Mr. Adams has omitted to consider the moral principles of such forms. Except that he insists upon the evil principle, jealousy, as an effect of these forms, likely to produce harmony and peace. The moral principles, fear and corruption, are not more sordid, base and brutal, than jealousy between political orders. Fear, corruption and jealousy, are essential principles of every hereditary system, past and present. In his dissertation, Mr. Adams indignantly rejects the idea of founding a government in a principle, sordid, base and brutal, and considers virtue as the 'principle and foundation of government most likely to promote general happiness.'

Two ideas are suggested by his considering virtue as a principle of government. One, as requiring a virtuous nation; the other, as only requiring a virtuous government, or one founded in good moral principles. The former idea is most common; the latter, most correct. The principles of a society may be virtuous, though the individuals composing it are vicious. Vicious beings may severally wish for security against vicious beings, and this can only be obtained by good moral principles. The moral being called government, is instituted to restrain the vices of man, as a moral being also. Its morals must be more perfect than the morals of man, or it can never make him better. And although man is its author, yet an author can compose a better system of morality, than his own example exhibits.

At this era of the world, avarice is man's predominant vice. It can only be gratified at the cost of man, and of the major number of men. These majorities have an interest and a power to defend themselves against it, by virtuous, just or equal principles of government; and societies composed of avaricious members must be founded in these principles, to afford the utmost gratification to the avarice of the majority, because it cannot gain so much by unjust laws for pillaging a minority, as by just laws for suppressing pillage. In all partnerships for gain, banking or commercial, care is taken to prevent one or a few of the members, from gratifying their avarice at the expense of the rest. Avarice propels the partners towards this precaution. The same principle, the same interest, and the same motive, propels nations to save their liberty and property from ambition and avarice. By the cases quoted, we see that an avaricious society can form a government able to defend itself against the avarice of its members. It requires such a government more than a benevolent society. Thus men can form a government, able to restrain the vices of man. The more vicious he is, the more he needs a virtuous government. Cities being more vicious than the country, require a more virtuous form of government. Accordingly, they are generally obliged to ask, and monarchy to grant, charters for civil government, founded in republican principles; because the necessity for a good government, becomes more urgent as the people become more vicious; just as the worse the partners, the better must be the articles.

It is a consolation to observe, as a vicious majority can only defend itself against vicious minorities, by founding society or government in good, just and equal moral principles, that the interest of vice is enlisted on the side of virtue; and suggests the establishment of such forms of government, as will produce a benign influence on private morals. It would be as foolish in a national majority, to enable one or a few of the members to defraud or oppress the others, as in a banking or commercial majority.

Mr. Adams, in the dissertation we have copied, by contrasting virtue and fear, as principles of the moral being called government, discloses a correspondence with the doctrine of this essay; which is, that a government and its laws, ought to be founded in good moral principles, to advance the interest of a vast majority of mankind, however vicious they may be.

If virtue, as a basis of government, be understood to mean, not that the principles of the government, but that the individuals composing the nation must be virtuous, then republicks would be founded in the self same principle with monarchies, namely, the evanescent qualities of individuals. But interest is a better and more permanent basis. Its wonderful capacity for concretion bestows on noble orders, hierarchies and stockjobbers, power for oppression, and loyalty to each other in defrauding; and why may it not also secure the fidelity of nations to themselves, though composed of people equally as vicious? Mankind being now too wise to suffer governments, founded in superstition or fraud, to go on undetected, must either submit to an armed force able to defy knowledge and protect guilt, and become less free as they grow more wise; or use their knowledge, to discover and secure their interest. Because the speculations of errour, and the tongue of flattery, have assigned to republicks, the virtue of the people, and to monarchies, honour, as necessary principles; are we to believe that tyranny causes the human mind to sparkle with more brilliant honour than freedom; and that freedom teaches the catalogue of humble and meek virtues resulting from oppression, better than tyranny? Or surmounting an authority, overturned by every day's experience, conclude, that bad men may take care of their interest as well as good men, make as good social bargains, and as success-fully apply virtuous principles to forms of government?

Mr. Adams's expression is, 'that virtue must be the *principle* of a republican government.' Of the government, not of those who live under the government. He means that the government must be constituted upon virtuous or just principles, and not upon fraudulent or unjust. In conformity with this idea, in his dissertation, he calls executive prerogatives 'badges of slavery;' and yet by his system he considers them as bulwarks to defend the people.

In his dissertation, Mr. Adams utters a panegyrick upon several authors, who had written against the English monarchy. He pronounces with asperity the full competency of those writers to convince any man, 'that all good government is republican;' and he removes every doubt, as to the sense in which he uses the term, by observing, 'that the only good part of the British constitution is republican.' And yet a great portion of one volume of Mr. Adams's work, is dedicated to the refutation of Nedham, one of the eulogized authors, in language nearly as rough, as that applied in the dissertation, to those who would not be made republicans by Nedham's arguments. In defence of his dissertation, Mr. Adams relies upon Nedham; in defence of his later system, he endeavours to confute him. In his dissertation, he deduces a form of government from Nedham's position 'that the people were the best guardians of their own liberties;' in his book, from the position, 'that the people are their own worst enemies.'

Mr. Adams's idea of judicial power, as expressed in the dissertation, accords with the principles of this essay. The judges, says he, 'should not be dependent on any man or body of men; they should lean to none, be subservient to none.' For this end, he proposes to give them commissions during good behaviour, and to subject them to the judgement of one branch of the legislature, on the accusation of another.

We agree in the utility of judicial independence and impartiality. The independence meant by Mr. Adams, and by all other politicians, in speaking of judicial departments, never refers to a sovereign power, but to a *man or body of men*, clothed with some political function. The end of judicial independence, is to shield the judges against the influence of the creatures of the sovereignty, and the sovereignty against the evils of this influence, and not to supersede the sovereignty itself by one of its creatures. Not partiality to a nation, but to a faction or an individual, is the evil to be prevented by judicial independence.

As partiality to a nation, on the part of judges, is not the evil; independence of the nation, is not the remedy. The evil, partiality, and the remedy, independence, both refer to delegated power, and not to national sovereignty; and are converted, by transferring their allusion to wrong objects, into a political caricature. Judges, independent of nations, lest they should be partial to delegated power; and subject to the appointment, patronage and removal of delegated power, lest they should betray nations!

Upon this ground, it has been urged, that judicial independence of a nation, will not shield judges against partiality for a man or body of men in power, or against becoming instruments of usurpation in the hands of governments; and that trial by impeachment, was not calculated to suppress the passions of men, to ensure an impartial judgement, or to allay in the minds of judges every apprehension of a man or body of men.

On the contrary, it was contended that a judicial responsibility to the nation, could only obtain for judges, independence of a man or body of men clothed with power. And that the want of publick confidence, naturally attending an absence of responsibility, with executive appointment, promotion and patronage, and legislative accusation and trial, would produce the dependence and partiality, deprecated by Mr. Adams, and too often displayed by experience. It is in the mode only of obtaining the same end, that the dissertation differs from this essay.

After all it is admitted, that Mr. Adams's change of opinion, can have no influence upon the argument, except to remove the obstacle of his authority, against an impartial consideration of the question. It was a weight too heavy for a subordinate rate of talents to bear, and therefore recourse was had to a powerful auxiliary.

But facts are not altered by a change of political opinion. They continue immutable. Those asserted in his dissertation by Mr. Adams, are as true now as they were then; and they were then true, or he would not have asserted them. As they cannot be retracted, one, subversive of the ground work of his reasoning in favour of orders, is a fair and powerful argument.

'How few (says he) of the human race, have ever had any thing more of choice in government than in climate!'

If this forcible exclamation is true, as it undoubtedly is, it follows, that few governments, if any, except those of the United States, have been the result of national will and intellect; and that his mountain of quotation cannot be applicable to our governments, which were produced by national will or intellect.

A transition by the United States, from force, fraud or accident, to human will and intellect, as the source of government, was the event which justified Mr. Adams in applying the terms 'enlightened age' to the era of our revolution; and in felicitating himself upon existing, at the period 'when the greatest philosophers and lawgivers of antiquity would have wished to have lived.' Had they risen from their graves at that time, they would have joined their labours to his, in drawing government from this new source; at least it was this unprecedented event which caused Mr. Adams to think, that the sages of antiquity would, if they could, have lived altogether in the United States, at the era of the revolution.

But if they could now rise from their graves, how sorely would they feel the mortification of finding, that Mr. Adams himself had given up national opinion as a source of government; and had gone back in search of political improvement to forms, with which it had as little to do, as with climate!

The discovery, that the moral effects of accident, fraud and force, were better than the moral effects of man's free intellectual powers, would either have exceedingly humiliated these sages, or they would have denied the fact, and have placed before the United States a picture of all the governments, not the result of free intellect, to compare with the only government which is so.

Orders would be the most prominent feature in the whole of these arbitrary or accidental governments; and no instance would appear of their having ever been created by free national intellect. Mankind have been scourged for ages by these self created beings; the United States have preferred free will and intellect to this scourge; and the question is, whether they will revolt from their own understandings, for the sake of having as little choice in their government as in their climate.

If the circle of ages has exhibited all polished nations, except one, without choice as to their forms of government; and if most or all of these disinherited nations, contained noble or separate orders; can time make stronger the evidence, to prove, that these orders were in reality the usurpers of the birthright belonging to nations, and that the solitary nation, so fortunate as to preserve it, owes its prosperity to their absence?

It thence follows with a degree of certainty, seldom attainable in argument, that the United States, once seduced into the establishment of a limited monarchy, or a monarchical republick; or suffering a paper order or interest to acquire an influence over their governments; would, thereafter, like other nations, find government as imperious as climate, and never more exercise a right of choice.

Although Mr. Adams's dissertation is replete with sentiments adverse to his system of orders, and concurring with the principles of this essay, one more only will be particularly quoted.

America, says he, has been *favoured by heaven* with the power of choosing, changing and building government from the foundation; and in this *enlightened age* the happiness of the people is allowed to be the end of government.

If this power is really a favour from heaven, it would be no proof of the wisdom or piety of the present age to return it to the state of abeyance, in which it resided, until the United States obtained the possession and benefit of it. A successful vindication of the right to draw government from the sources of intellect and will, is the proof adduced by Mr. Adams of the light of the present age; remnants of feudal darkness will obscure this light; because it is impossible for a nation divided and distracted by orders, peaceably and deliberately to make, mend, destroy and renew forms of government, as intellect and will may dictate. And if Mr. Adams's rapture and adoration were proper, in contemplating the blessing of self government, so new and wonderful that he ascribes it to the immediate interposition of heaven, ought the present generation to conclude their thanksgiving, by requesting the deity to resume his benefaction?

The next instance of the force of circumstances on the human mind, to which we will advert, for the sake of ascertaining the value of authority and the folly of confidence, results from a short comparison between an address to the people, gratuitously proposed by Mr. Jay whilst president of Congress, on the 13th of September, 1779, and unanimously adopted by that body, with a

465

passage in the Federalist or Publius, a book partly ascribed to this gentleman.

The indignation against the British form of government, and the ardent affection for ours, which the first breathes, are not considered as of much weight, except to prove that their principles were different; because, although Mr. Jay's conviction at the time is evinced by his resorting to the deity as a witness of it, yet conviction may be certainly raised and lowered by zeal, as well as by circumstances.

Without availing ourselves therefore of Mr. Jay's eloquence, we shall only draw out of it a few cool opinions and simple facts. He considers 'equal liberty as our principle of government, our rulers as the servants and not the masters of the people, and our governments as founded in freedom; the British monarchy as crumbling into pieces, the parliament as venal, the country as oppressed, the people as destitute of publick virtue, and the government as violating the rights of mankind.' And after contrasting the English and American forms of government, in his forcible style, he emphatically concludes, that one is the tyrant, the other, the servant of the people. It was the object of the address, to inspire the United States, by this fact, with perseverance in the prosecution of the war. Therefore, both Mr. Jay and the Congress must have disagreed with Mr. Adams, in the similarity between the two forms, for which he so laboriously contends; or in his opinion, that the people addressed were enlightened.

The Federalist contains an eulogy of the English form of government, infinitely transcending the compliment paid to it by Mr. Adams and incapable of augmentation. Mr. Adams's similitude between ship-building or navigation, and this complicated moral machine, allowed to it only a comparative degree of excellence, which might have been extended by substituting a watch, or at least a spinning machine moved by fire, as the object of comparison. But the Federalist, by an ingenious use of Montesquieu, exalts it to the station among governments which Homer occupies among poets.

If the invective in Mr. Jay's address, and the eulogy in the Federalist, flowed from the same pen, the subjection of the human mind, in its highest perfection, and utmost maturity, to circumstances, is here again demonstrated; and in this demonstration, is exhibited the folly of expecting to find a steady patriot in a slave to uncontrollable events.

The same book has furnished us with the finest definition of that species of patriotism, imbibed or bestowed by confidence and authority. The allegiance of its supposed authors to its tenets was destroyed by circumstances, upon the very heels of promulgation; and they arranged themselves in political opposition, whilst their tenets, through the blind submission of confidence, and the despotick power of authority, acquired the singular felicity of maintaining an orthodoxy with hostile parties; each of which assailed their antagonists from the same quiver, and as ardently believed in their own patriotism, as inimical fanaticks who are the dupes of leaders, do in their own sanctity.

Though integrity, talents and elegance of style, were unable for a moment to retain, against the force of new circumstances, the adherence of only three political doctors to their own prescription; yet fidelity to our constitution was mutually allowed by opposite parties to this fortunate composition; each only claiming for itself an adherence to the constitution and its paraphrase, and charging its antagonist with a violation of both. Either this fidelity or one of these accusations is necessarily unfounded; yet confidence has hitherto been unable to discern its errour.

To me, this authority for opposite principles, appears to be planted in the ancient analysis of governments, to be neatly cultivated with the English doctrine of checks and balances, and to be highly adorned with all the comely theories of limited monarchy, invented between the accession of Charles I. and the death of William of Orange; but never actually practised; theories, indebted to the corruption by which they are defeated, for the false evidence of their supposed operation. Like a foreign silk, embroidered with flowers of gold and silver, its splendour on one side conceals the defects of its workmanship; and its insufficiency for use and comfort, as well as its hidden deformities, can only be discovered by adverting to the other. The English writers during the specified period, contain whatever is to be found in the Federalist; but all their theories sunk, as soon as they were promulgated, in a vortex of corruption; and the nation has drawn from them an overwhelming addition to its burdens. What is to keep the same doctrines from the same fate, or shield the United States under their guidance, from the same effects? Our genuine native policy, being woven with strong homespun threads of plain principles, undarned by a fragile foreign glossy manufacture, more likely to ruin than to improve its texture, exposes us to none of those calamities drawn by England from a system, resorted to by the Federalist for the explanation of this policy. By its capacity of operating without the help of bribery and corruption, it discloses its radical difference from a system, so universally allowed to require such assistance, as to have inspired its votaries with a notion, that this bribery and corruption constituted its chief excellence; in truth, there lies no medium between this opinion and a surrender of the system itself. To avoid a dilemma so unpromising, the wide difference between a derivation from fixed moral principles, or from fluctuating mixtures of monarchical, aristocratical and democratical orders or powers, is contended for throughout this essay.

The truths, with which the book we are speaking of abounds, have probably so far covered the errour of deriving the general constitution, from the idea of the old analysis, commingled in imitation of the English system, as to have infused some drops of this foreign poison into the laws of the United States. It considers a constitution as defective, where the whole power is lodged in the hands of the people *or their representatives.* * It represents the British standing army as harmless.† It calls a distinction between a confederacy and a consolidation of the states 'more subtle than accurate.'‡ It asserts that English liberty by the revolution of 1688 was '*completely* triumphant.'§ It ingeniously defends mercenary armies,** and it declares 'that in the *usual* progress of things, the necessities of a nation *in every stage* of its existence, will be found *at least* equal to its resources.'†† These, and a multitude of similar doctrines, swallowed by both the parties which have divided the nation between them, in the sweet but poisonous pill of confidence, must necessarily have bestowed upon legislation, a tone not perfectly in unison with the genuine policy of the United States. What, for instance, could a nation suffer, or tyranny extort, between an eternal payment and dispensation of resources equal to its ability?

It was unfortunate that so great a mass of zeal, integrity and talents, should have been expended at the juncture of a controversy, calculated rather to inspire the ingenuity necessary to win a victory, than the cool inquiries necessary to discover truth; and that party collisions should subsequently have deprived it of the liberty of applying to this controversial composition, the test of a candid revision. I believe that one of the supposed authors at least

* No. 8, p. 43.   † No. 9, p. 51.   ‡ No. 11, p. 65, 67.—No. 24, p. 154. § No. 29, p. 187.   ** No. 47, p. 93.   †† Vol. 2, No. 41, p. 40. Tiebout's edition, 1799.

does not approve of all its doctrines; and the occasion which produced them having passed, neither the feelings of its authors, nor the gratitude and applause of the publick, ought to undergo any change, from an effort to preserve the policy of the United States, which this book so eminently contributed to introduce; suggested by a conviction, that however it may abound, like Mr. Adams's, with republican principles, these, mingled up with the principles of the British form of government, constitute such a picture of our policy, as Christian precepts mingled with the fictions of Mahomet, do of Christianity.

The safest repository of the authority created by political confidence, would be a philosopher, abstracted from the influence of station, of party, of avarice, and of ambition. But even this rare character, seduced by genius, excited by a love of literary fame, or inebriated by hypothesis, is often the author of splendid errours, destined, however they may be admired by a taste for elegant composition, to be detected by common sense. If the scrutiny and wisdom of publick opinion is necessary to restrain the honest flights of imagination, can its application to the corrupt artifices of self interest, and the stubborn prejudices of station and power, be safely dispensed with? If the general good sense, is necessary to correct disinterested individual capriciousness, can this unhappy quality be sanctified by an union with irresistible temptations?

Godwin and Malthus, philosophers of talents, accomplishments and integrity, unsurpassed by any of their contemporaries, supply us with illustrations of this best title to political confidence and authority.

Godwin, by equalising both knowledge and property, proposes to remove every obstruction to population; and Malthus demonstrates that this effect would destroy the design of Godwin's system. And from this demonstration he draws the conclusion, that population can only be kept within the capacity of the earth to feed it, by positive laws or by misery. These are probably among the best written books which have ever appeared, and both authors retain the fairest reputations; yet one is a text book for mobs, and the other for tyrants. Both the systems of these adversaries, are built upon fragments of human nature. Godwin's, on its good moral qualities, exclusive of its evil; Malthus's, on a single animal quality, exclusive both of its other animal qualities, and of all its moral qualities.

The arguments used by Malthus to destroy Godwin often recoil upon himself. Your moral system, as we both confess, says Malthus, will place human nature in a state extremely favourable to population. Wherefore? Because population is regulated, as Godwin contends, by moral causes. If this unqualified admission destroys Godwin, it must also destroy a system built upon the contrary idea, that human population is regulated by food. By your division of property and knowledge, says Malthus, you will remove want and misery, the checks upon population, which must of course become redundant, because these checks are removed. But I propose to remove want and misery by a law to prevent procreation. Well, does not the redundant population as certainly follow, whether want and misery are removed in the mode of Godwin or of Malthus?

It is true that Malthus, aware of the objection, whilst he allows to man's moral nature a great influence upon population to destroy Godwin, so blends this admission with the entire dependence of population on food, as to support the latter idea throughout his book. And as one system considers mind as the despot of matter, the other considers matter as the despot of mind. Whereas the fact is, that with or without civil government, population has never been able to overtake the capacity of the earth to yield subsistence; and therefore it is probable, that all the operations of food and population, or of mind and matter, upon each other, are regulated by some unalterable natural law. At both extremities of man's moral state, the urban and the savage, we find its traces. Rather an excess than a want of food, is generally met with in cities; and where a want of food is produced by a savage state, it is never owing to an incapacity of the country to produce it. The checks upon population in both states are therefore moral. Countries, in which a few savages starve for want of food, afford abundance for an hundred fold population, of a different moral character, as has been demonstrated in North America.

The cases of a rapid population after plagues, are weaker than those of a rapid population, after the expulsion of savages, by all the difference between gaining the possession of an improved and an unimproved country. Both cases are regulated by the different moral impressions of wealth and poverty upon human nature. A colony from London, settling in America on its first discovery, and the remnant of a plague, would both lose and acquire many moral qualities deeply affecting population; and in both cases the moral character which excites the population, flows from a multitude of causes independent of food. If there are human situations which suspend the moral qualities calculated to impede population, and others which awaken them; and if a certain degree of populousness never fails to awaken them; then population being graduated by a natural moral law, there is no need of the artificial laws proposed by Malthus to check it; nor any grounds for an apprehension that Godwin's system could have overturned this natural law. It could only come at it by effecting several impossibilities; but Malthus, alarmed, brings into the field a new impossibility to arrest a foe who can never appear. Godwin proposes to equalise wealth and knowledge among all men; Malthus to equalise food and procreation almost as extensively; and Mr. Adams to equalise wealth and power between three political orders. Thus we see at one view three great authorities, agreeing in principle, at war in fact, and each proposing to effect similar impossibilities. One offers to root out self love and all evil human qualities, and to plant equal and universal knowledge and benevolence where they grow. Another offers to control the least governable human passion at the most inauspicious epoch; and the third offers to maintain an equality of wealth and power between jealous rival parties. It is as practicable for mankind to change, as to suspend their nature for twenty years. The human qualities proposed by Malthus to be subdued, are undoubtedly as unconquerable, as those proposed by Godwin to be subdued. Indeed, these authors seem to agree that they are more so. Godwin, by relying on reason for suppressing selfishness; Malthus, by resorting to law for suppressing love.

It is more likely that man's errours should overlook nature's powers, than that his wisdom should outstrip her foresight. All her resources are not explored, and it assails a sound maxim, to expect the invention before the necessity. The recent use of cotton, improves upon wool in economy, far beyond the improvement of wool upon skins. And until we see the improvements of agriculture exhausted by population, a system of inexorable oppression to prevent men from starving, will by its elegance, only more forcibly display the insecurity of resting upon authority.

This authority bursts upon the poor of England with a new oppression. To the system for distributing wealth and poverty by law, an exclusion of those to whom the latter is assigned, from the pleasures of relationship, friendship and love, lest they should be starved by this artificial poverty, is an admonition, both of the end to which that system leads, and of the coldness with which even philosophy can look upon such an end. The more eminent a political authority becomes, the more awfully it operates as an admonition. Malthus teaches us, that the English system of distributing wealth and property, in modes which the United States have begun to imitate, instead of leaving that distribution to industry, will devote one part of a community to death by famine, or to the necessity of living above half their lives, without affections and without mind.

The creation of a poor class by law, and a refusal of alms from law, to prevent a redundant population, would very forcibly illustrate the difference in point of benevolence, between indirect slavery to a separate interest, and direct slavery to an absolute master.

The terror of a plethora of population, and the hope of obtaining wealth by a plethora of paper stock, concur in defrauding man of his liberty and property. By the first, he is represented as sailing in an ocean of atmosphere, with a limited stock of food on board, and he is told that nothing can save him from famine, but a power in a few of the crew, to regulate the births and deaths. The second asserts, that the same minority, by modifications of rage and ink, can multiply wealth or the means of supplying his wants, without limitation. It happens, not unfrequently, that the same individual believes, both that the earth is inadequate to the production of bread sufficient to meet population, and that paper can produce endless wealth. As if nature had forgotten to provide subsistence for her creature, man; and remembered to provide it for his creature paper stock. Nature! who like the fates, is ever spinning and cutting, whose business is production and destruction, and who has worked equally hitherto, with both her hands.

The first of these chimerical systems, by infusing a feverish zeal for educating a whole nation, has rather checked than encouraged the progress of knowledge. Projects for turning all men into philosophers, advance knowledge, as those for turning all metals into gold, advance wealth. Godwin's system is an enchantress; Malthus's, a gorgon. But it is equal to mankind, whether they are enticed into ignorance and slavery by the captivating imagination of equalising knowledge and property, or terrified into it, by the dread of a redundant population.

A theory built upon the whole, and not upon a part only, of man's moral character, can constitute a real foundation for a government; just as earth, not vapour, must be a foundation for a house. Mr. Godwin deserts the practicable remedies of division of power and responsibility, by which the evil portion of man's nature may be controlled, for the impracticable idea of rendering this control unnecessary, by changing that portion of his nature. Mr. Adams insists, that this portion of the human character will forever adhere to man; but rejecting, with Mr. Godwin, the use of a division of power and responsibility for its control, he proposes a balance of wealth and power, among inflamed orders. And Mr. Malthus founds his moral theory upon a single physical quality, to regulate which, a stronger government would be necessary, than any which has yet appeared. He proposes to introduce the papistical system of celibacy, without the wealth or the concubinage, by which it was made practicable.

Mr. Godwin's and Mr. Adams's systems have yet a further resemblance to each other. The first author proposes to render responsibility for restraining the evil portion of human nature unnecessary, by curing selfishness with a balance of knowledge and property among men. The second, to render it unnecessary, by curing selfishness with a balance of wealth and power among orders. One nostrum, is a cure for all mankind; the other, for the few composing governments. The only difference between them is, that one balance has never succeeded, and the other has never been tried. Our policy, differing from the projects of curing all men of the evil qualities of human nature, by a balance of property and knowledge, according to one philosopher; or of curing only governing men of these evil qualities, by a balance of wealth and power among orders, according to the other, proposes to subject this bad portion of human nature to a strict discipline, by civil and political law; or a code of laws, able to reach the delinquencies of those imperfect beings who govern, as well as the delinquencies of those who are governed. Godwin's system proposes to render accountableness unnecessary. Mr. Adams's applies it partially, ours universally. They resemble religious systems, declaring that all men, a few, or none, ought to be exempted from the sanctions of religion. Our policy is bottomed upon the old idea that men had two souls, one good the other bad; Mr. Adams's, upon the idea of forming a government of three souls, all bad, as being inspired with jealousy and hatred against each other. If one good and one bad soul make a being, requiring all the varieties of legal and political responsibility, what is to be expected of a being compounded of three bad souls, without any responsibility? Or how can the favourers of the system of balances justly ridicule Godwin, on account of his project for casting out man's bad soul by reason, when they propose to neutralise or destroy the good one by hereditary power and jealous orders?

Mr. Adams, in availing himself of the authority of Aristotle, as being 'full of the balances,' furnishes us with another illustration of the subject we are discussing.

That ancient philosopher assigned the legislative power to the people at large; the executive, to the magistrates; and the judicative, to the tribunals of justice. These magistrates and judges were to be appointed by the people. This species of mixt government, he supposes to be adapted for one city; and he adds, that the government of an agricultural people, ought on the other hand to be popular.

The inconclusiveness of these ideas is obvious. They propose that magistrates should be magistrates; and judges, judges. They suppose a more popular government, than one wherein the whole people legislate and appoint all publick officers; and they are destitute of any artificial arrangement of power, either by balancing co-ordinate bodies of men, subjecting all publick officers to national control and sovereignty, or dividing it into manageable sections.

The idea of a political trinity, coequal, could never have entered into the head of Aristotle, because his magistrates, being elective, were not co-eternal with the people; and being artificial, the architect might demolish as well as build. He would as soon have imagined, when a statuary had finished three statues, that these statues naturally swallowed up the statuary, as when a nation had created three orders of power, that these orders naturally swallowed up the nation.

Aristotle, being ignorant of Mr. Adams's idea of making a government out of three repellant principles, or compressing three such principles into an unity (a doctrine infinitely more miraculous than an unity among three homogeneous principles,) literally states the sovereignty of the people, as the source, creator and master of every species of check and balance, capable of being extracted from his garbled sentences by amplifying construction.

The gravity with which this authority is urged by a gentleman of Mr. Adams's erudition, shews the rashness of confidence, and the following quotation will fix its value. Aristotle's Rhetorick contains this passage. 'Minerva preferred Ulysses; Theseus, Helena; Alexander was preferred by the *Goddesses*, and Achilles by

Homer. If Theseus did no injury, neither Alexander. And if the Tyndaridæ, neither Alexander. And if Hector equalled Patroclus, Alexander equalled Achilles. There are persons against whom no judgement is to be given, as princes.' The Goddesses were the virtues, supposed by the mythology of the times, to be the makers of Gods.

Authority is frequently corrupted by a subjection to authority, and the influence of Alexander must have operated as strongly upon Aristotle in favour of monarchy, as that of a wealthy and powerful banking aristocracy all around him, undoubtedly did upon Adam Smith. These ingenious men, in labouring both to satisfy the mandates of authority, and to save their own opinions, have spread obscurity and indecision over the latter, as the plainest declaration of war, upon which a philosopher could adventure, against the military conqueror of ignorant nations, or the paper conqueror of an enlightened people. Could influence re-absorb what it has infused into the writings of these great men, one would probably appear to be an enemy to monarchy and the other to aristocratical establishments, in all their forms. Aristotle himself says, 'those who are constrained, speak far more untruths than truths.' And he countenances our conjecture, by a definition of law, in which, distinguishing between common law and prescribed law; meaning by the first natural justice, and by the other human institution; he defines the latter to be 'the common consent of a city,' instead of referring to monarchy, or a sovereignty of balanced orders, as its source. And (agreeing with Mr. Adams in the dissertation we have transcribed) he says, 'For thus the people being able to confer honour on whom they please, will not envy those who receive it; and eminent men will exercise probity and sincerity, to gain the esteem of the people.' The people, not privileged orders, are to draw eminent qualities from eminent men. How? By election and responsibility, or by rejecting the government of authority, and exercising self government. A monarchy made out of Aristotle, as girls make a peacock by patching together shreds of silk, in the face of his unequivocal preference of a popular government for an agricultural people, would be a perfect emblem of authority.

Religion or patriotism by deputy, is the cause of the errours and mischiefs of both; and parties or individuals, pretending to be pious or patriotick, because they believe another to be so, are universally knaves or fools. The most ignorant, unenslaved by authority, discerns goodness by the light of his conscience, and distinguishes between an easy and a hard government, by the light of his senses. But authority, by depriving us of conscience and sensation in religion and government, causes such calamities as are encountered by a blind man who is a lunatick. It assures us that human reason can neither select a religion nor a government, for the sake of making a tyrant of this very reason. It confines us to revelation and to nature, as the authors of its dogmas, but refuses to our human reason a capacity to construe either, that it may construe both by its human reason, to enslave and defraud ours. And being in its own essence a tyrant, its followers, whether prompted by knavish zeal or pious folly, are as really the slaves and instruments of tyranny, and will as certainly degenerate into the vices and baseness of slavery, as the followers of Peter the hermit, or of Bonaparte the conqueror. Parties are unwarily admitted to be natural and wholesome to republicks, though republicks are constantly destroyed by parties. Without the debasements of confidence, and the frauds of authority, their existence would be seldom felt, and the slavery they draw upon nations, would be never suffered.

If men will plant liberty in individual imperfection and mutability, instead of planting it in the permanency and perfection of principles, it must perish. The tools of patriots frequently become the authors of more evils, than the slaves of tyrants. A republican government cannot live upon monarchical diet. Free governments are destroyed by confidence and authority. Can a more dangerous habit befal the people or parties of the United States, than one which is the constant prelude of slavery?

We have suffered authority to call forth in self defence her stoutest champions. She has summoned to her assistance, an orator, a saint and a hero; the English and American parties of whig and tory, federalist and republican; and six philosophers of unsurpassed integrity and talents. Yet these formidable auxiliaries only serve to rivet the conclusion, that the common sense and common honesty of a nation, is both a wiser and honester source of government than the authority of saints, kings, philosophers, heroes, orators, parties, factions or separate interests in any form. Nor do I know a maxim, the belief of which would be a better security for liberty, than that *no nation can long preserve a free government, if it is guided by the caprices or frauds of authority in the enumerated shapes or in any others; nor can it be enslaved, except by commuting national understanding and honesty for a dependence upon this humoursome, fickle, selfish, ambitious, and dishonest moral being.*

Section the Eighth

THE MODE OF INFUSING ARISTOCRACY INTO THE POLICY OF THE UNITED STATES

AMONG civilized people, no species of tyranny can exist, without the help of aristocracy; because intricacy must keep pace with knowledge, to conceal or defend oppression, to which no nation ever submits knowingly and willingly. The weakness of simple monarchy is so extremely visible, that upon the first emergence of a nation from profound ignorance, it is compelled to call in the help of aristocracy. It has never been able to find any other ally, because it can have no common social interest; and being therefore forced to purchase allies with property and privileges taken from the rest of a nation, these allies must of course be aristocracies in fact, under whatever form they are reared. Aristocracy existed without monarchy, in Greece, Rome and Venice, by the help of superstition, bravery and a complication of contrivances; but at present, it appears every where, though in different shapes, as the engine of monarchy, because of certain changes in man's moral character. In France and Turkey it is military; in Spain it is made of a superstition so powerful, as to have exposed the nation to the loss of its independence, for the shadow of monarchy; in China, it is made of superstition, civil privileges and military power; and in England of paper stock, military power and patronage. Aristocracy is no where agrarian. And wherever it has taken deep root in any form, an agricultural interest has ceased to be known or even spoken of, as having any influence in the government.

Whenever the lands of a country are so divided, as that the weight of a few landholders is not perceivable in the government; or so that the majority of the nation belong to the agrarian interest; no species of aristocracy, partaking in the least degree of a landed interest, can possibly be introduced.

Minority is an ingredient, without which no aristocracy can exist. A feudal king and his barons, possessed of nearly all the lands of a country, were a minority, constituting a landed aristocracy, living upon the rest of a nation. But this species of aristocracy being destroyed in England by a division of lands (though individual landed fortunes there, still greatly exceed any here) a new species of aristocracy became necessary to sustain monarchy in that country, in which a landed interest has been so far from keeping an ascendancy, that it has been unable to get a just share of representation.

The crown, aided by the remnant of the feudal aristocracy, after contending against the principles of civil liberty, introduced by the Puritans into the English policy, being defeated, abandoned this prop of monarchy in that form; and revived it in the form of paper stock and corruption, so as to have undermined all the fortresses erected against its power, and made itself stronger than it was before it was reduced.

A minority capable of subsisting upon a majority, being an essential quality of aristocracy, the landed interest of the United States, so far from being susceptible of any portion of aristocratick power, is precisely that interest which must inevitably furnish subsistence and privileges for an aristocracy here in any form; because it is a majority, and incapable of subsisting upon any other interest.

The fœtus of aristocracy here, can therefore only consist of the same qualities, which have grown up into a giant in Britain. These are paper stock, armies and patronage. The question is, whether the landed interest of the United States, as it cannot constitute an aristocratick order between a king and the people, had not better unite with the other popular interests, to strangle in its cradle any infant visibly resembling this terrible giant?

The modern species of aristocracy neither wants nor fears titles. In their absence or presence, in France and in England, its operation on the side of executive power, is the same. It can operate in the United States, as it does in France, without titled orders; and Mr. Adams's project of the balances is unable to prevent it from operating, as it does in England with them. A didactick aristocratical body, is no check, without solid power. If the power is derived from representation and responsibility, it is not aristocratical; if from corruption and patronage, it is the tool of a. monarch. And a naked constitutional precept would be as strong a check upon actual power, as a naked didactick aristocracy. A French senate, an English house of lords, and the conscript fathers under the Roman emperors, are examples of these assertions.

These examples display the justness of Lord Shaftesbury's and Mr. Adams's opinion, as to the necessity of a balance of property among orders, to enable one order to balance another in power. The nobility in England can no longer balance the crown, because its property is lost. The senate in France cannot balance the emperor, for want of wealth. The Roman emperors succeeded the conscript fathers as plunderers of the provinces. It results, that a noble order here, could not balance executive power or the people, unless endowed with the same ingredient. Money and arms are the instruments of power. Mr. Adams's system, without its means or principles, could never work according to his hopes. Its essential principle or means is, that the noble order must be endowed with wealth. Mr. Adams ought to have told us from whom this wealth is to be taken, and of what it is to consist.

Let us suppose that it is to consist of land, for the sake of flattering the errour of some landholders in the United States, who conceive that their interest leans towards an aristocracy. It will require one-third of the lands of the Union, to give a landed aristocracy weight or power sufficient to answer its purpose. Suppose also, that the zeal of landed men in favour of a landed aristocracy, should induce them to part willingly with one-third of their lands to obtain it, and consider what retribution would be made for the sacrifice.

The late aristocratical order of France was a landed one. It derived its power from possessing a third of the lands. And it used this power to shelter its own lands from taxation, and to shift the publick burdens from its own shoulders, upon those of the rest of the people. Even a landed aristocracy must possess the essential quality of feeding upon all except itself. Besides, every landholder, in nurturing the errour that his interest leans towards a landed aristocracy, has many computations to make; such as, whether it is likely that all considerable landholders will be made lords; or in case of a selection of two or three hundred individuals to constitute a noble landed order, whether it is likely that he will be one. Whether such a body can be any thing but the infamous instrument of a tyrant, unless it is endowed with sufficient property to give it weight; and whether he is willing to give up one-third of his lands for that purpose.

If it would be improvident in the landed interest of the United States, to part with one-third only of its lands, to gain the benefit of an aristocracy capable of some agrarian sympathy, what must be

THE MODE OF INFUSING ARISTOCRACY

the foresight of mortgaging the whole, to rear up an aristocracy of stock corruption and patronage, capable of none? England answers the question. But undeterred by her cries to forbear, the landed interest of the United States, with exclusive skill or folly, is moulding heavy ordnance to play upon itself, and whittling down its own armies into pocket pistols. Perpetuity and primogeniture are its heaviest artillery against stock monopoly. With these, the English landed interest has fallen before it; and the American, without either, provokes the combat. The landed interest of England foresaw its disaster, and fell against its will. The singular management has been reserved for the landed interest of America, of cherishing contrary principles, both tending towards its own subjugation; one, a division of lands; the other, an increase of stock, armies and patronage. And whilst it would grudge one-third of its lands to create a sympathizing aristocracy, it subjects the whole to be for ever fleeced by law, without stint, to create an inexorable one.

The favourers of monarchy, are so entirely convinced of the in-efficacy of a didactick king or nobility, that they will never attempt to introduce either. They will make these orders with solid and not with imaginary materials. With wealth, armies and patronage. These are the trees, which, when planted and suffered to grow, will produce the fruit of course. They are exceedingly difficult to eradicate, after they begin to bear. And when mature, upon touching the bud, the fruit bursts forth in its highest flavour.

The policy of the United States must see, and not wink upon this reasoning, if it expects to last. The landed interest being incapable of becoming an aristocracy itself, must unite with the other natural interests of society in maintaining a republican government, or submit to an aristocratical monarchy of which it cannot constitute a part. It can possess no essential weight or power, except under a form of government which shall exclude orders, because it cannot become an order itself; and because it must pay and not receive the corruption, found by experience in England, necessary to keep a government of orders together. It is yet able to make a master for itself in any shape it may fancy; or to pluck the mask from the Proteus, aristocracy, whether it lurks under a coronet, a mitre or paper stock.

It is hidden so artfully under the last, that it is hard to exhibit it in bodily shape. No escutcheon is hung out. No ensigns are un-furled to mark its march and its victory. And we must resort to Mr.

Adams's book to find a badge, designating stock aristocracy with as much correctness, as a crown designates a king.

This badge he affixes to it in the following maxim: 'Money, which all people now desire, and which makes the essential instrument for governing the world.'* By bestowing on a banking interest 'the essential instrument for governing the world,' you enable it to govern. Every separate interest, able to govern, does govern. And every separate governing interest, being a minority, must also be an aristocracy.

Let the landed interest compare Mr. Adams's maxim and his system with each other, and it will see the force of this reasoning, and his inconsistency in proposing to make orders by conventions, in the face of his own maxim. What could these orders effect without 'the essential instrument for governing the world?' Would the landed interest supply or receive this essential instrument? and will not this instrument make governours of a stock order, as it does of others? Suppose two orders, one poor and didactick, the other possessing the instrument for governing; where would the power settle? The system of dividing lands and amassing a paper interest, creates these orders. Titles and superstition have ceased to constitute aristocracy, among commercial and enlightened nations. Are we not in this class? Shall we then expose our policy and freedom, to the only instrument which creates aristocracy, among enlightened nations, and be content with defending them against title and superstition, which are no longer instruments of tyranny?

The landed interest of the United States, being indissolubly betrothed to commerce, has been considered as so completely covering the interests of the society, that it is used in several states as a substratum of civil government, recognised as republican, by the guarantee in the federal constitution. And where the range of suffrage is wider, but attended either by a greater portion of bank stock or executive patronage, the tendency towards monarchy or aristocracy is more visible, than where suffrage has been in some degree limited to land, but attended with less stock or patronage.

Popular governments and popular principles could not thus flow from the landed interest, if it possessed aristocratical qualities. Majorities only sustain such principles and governments. By sustaining them, the landed interest appears to cover a majority. Because it covers a majority, it does sustain them; it being impos-

* Vol. 3. p. 360.

sible for a majority to maintain itself by oppressing a minority. Even the Goths and Vandals, sought for plunder among great nations, not among little clans less wealthy than themselves.

The extent of our country would alone suffice to prove, that our landed interest cannot be an aristocracy or a monarch. Had the whole earth formed one nation, with the lands divided as they are in our portion of it, such a landed interest would have been as capable of constituting an aristocracy, as the landed interest of the United States. It would have been the world itself; where would there have been other worlds, to bear its oppression or obey its power? Here it is the nation; where could it find subjects upon which to exercise an aristocratical spirit? If any species of master interest should be interpolated upon our policy, it cannot therefore be the landed; the alternative of which is limited by the laws of nature, to equal rights in a free government, or passive obedience under an arbitrary one.

We lose truth in names and phrases, as children lose themselves in a wood, for want of geographical knowledge. Because titles have been frequently annexed to aristocracy, it is erroneously imagined to be made by titles; and the thing dreaded can creep in, under an imagination, which cheats us into a belief, that its road lies through titles only. Lords without wealth, are an aristocracy, exemplified by the hierarchical power of American bishops. Individual wealth, not derived from an exclusive interest, is so far from participating in the spirit of aristocracy, that its contributions must at least be equivalent to its ability, and its interest is therefore repugnant to every pecuniary oppression.

Even its disbursements through the medium of tenants, would operate as diminutions of rent, and form deductions from its income. And this species of individual wealth, constitutes the whole mass of power and talents, by which the poor and uninformed are secured in their rights and liberties, under the bond which unites all persons having the same interest. The prejudices arising from words, darken the mind so generally against a perception of real qualities and principles, as to justify us in recalling to the reader's recollection, a few cases to expose the frailty of such precipitate conclusions.

The Lacedemonians had two kings; but the government was aristocratick. The Athenians had a king archon; but the government was democratick. The Roman government was called indiscriminately a commonwealth or republick, whether its complexion was aristocratick, democratick or monarchical. In all its stages, the English government has been called a limited monarchy, whether the barons were masters of the king and people, the king of the people and barons, or a paper fabrick of the rest of the nation. The words 'king or republick,' do not make a monarch or a free government. Nor do the words 'duke, marquis, bishop,' make an aristocracy. It is made by principles and qualities. A separate interest in a minority, is one principle or quality, which makes an aristocracy; and a mode of extracting wealth by law from the rest of the nation, another. Neither riches without a separate interest, nor a separate interest without riches, can in the present state of things make an aristocracy.

Mr. Adams has cautioned us against the abuse of political phrases, whilst he reiterates the expressions 'a mixed government; checks and balances; middle orders,' without explaining the qualities or principles necessary to make those checks, balances or middle orders; or considering the influence upon this theory, from armies, patronage, corruption, the poverty of a nominal middle order, or the enormous wealth of a separate interest. Had Tacitus undertaken to recommend the government of the Emperors to the Romans, he would in like manner have used the terms consul, senate, patrician, plebeian; and by suppressing the qualities of these orders, he might have easily proved, that a limited monarchy existed under the Roman emperors, as well checked, balanced and provided with middle orders, as that existing under the corrupt system of England.

As governments change, names represent different things, but are often retained to gull prejudice and varnish tyranny. For this end, the names of senate, consul and patrician remained in Rome. For this end, the name 'parliament' remains in England. In neither case, was 'free and moderate government' preserved; and in both, oppression was the effect of real changes under old names.

Mr. Adams has even called the English form of government 'republican;' but if the United States should slide into it for that reason, they would act as the Athenians would have acted, by giving to Clitomachus (who had been branded with infamy) the command of an army, because his name signified 'illustrious warrior.'

The hooks of fraud and tyranny, are universally baited with melodious words. 'Passive obedience' was a bait sacrilegiously drawn from scripture. 'Church and state,' from a fear of popery. 'Checks and balances, and publick faith and credit,' are still more musical baits, and however harshly 'patronage, corruption, paper stock and standing armies,' may at first sound, even these words are at length thought by some to contain much secret harmony.

Fine words are used to decoy, and ugly words to affright. 'Security to private property' is attractive. 'Invasion of private property' deterring. The invader of course devoutly uses the first phrase, and indignantly applies the second to those who oppose him. Where is there an instance of an invasion of private property, equal to that effected by the paper system of England? As its greatest invader, it has of course been the loudest advocate for its safety.

'Energetick government' is a phrase happily chosen to please honest men, and to beguile nations of unmanageable power. Under the agreeable jingle in the antithesis, between 'protection and allegiance' was long hidden a large reservoir of arbitrary power. Of the same family is the ancient idea of 'a contract between the king and the people.' Implying equality, either party might construe this contract, and the active power of construction being in the hands of kings, they made all their own actions, fulfilments, and such actions of the people as they pleased, breaches.

There is edification and safety in challenging political words and phrases as traitors, and trying them rigorously by principles, before we allow them the smallest degree of confidence. As the servants of principles, they gain admission into the family, and thus acquire the best opportunities of assassinating their masters, should they become treacherous. That useful and major part of mankind, comprised within natural interests (by which I mean agricultural, commercial, mechanical, and scientifick; in opposition to legal and artificial, such as hierarchical, patrician, and banking) is exclusively the object of imposition, whenever words are converted into traitors to principles.

The good words 'order, a sacred regard for private property, national credit,' have made the British government bad; and the good word 'truth' makes sedition laws. The same words, faithful to principles, would protect private property against stock, keep a nation out of debt, destroy sedition law, and, in short, be the allies of honest and moderate government.

Thus the word 'energy' may be an ally of freedom or despotism. The energy of monarchy is distinct in its qualities and end from the energy of republicanism. One is made of orders, stock, patronage and armies, to maintain the power of a government over a nation;

the other of equal rights, taxation for national use, division of power, publick opinion and a national militia, to maintain the power of a nation over a government. Monarchical energy, is a Delilah, knowing that the great strength of free government lies in republican energy, and omitting no opportunity of shaving it away, to make room for itself. When it has once bound or blinded the popular Samson, however he may chance to take vengeance of his enemies, he is generally crushed in their fall.

Between the introduction of aristocratical, and the expulsion of republican energy, there is an interregnum of principle, which requires great acuteness for the preservation of property. Aristocratical principles favour artificial property, such as paper stock, office, and corporate privileges; republican, substantial property obtained by industry and talents, and not by law and sinecure. One species of this property preys upon the other. And it requires some judgement to change property, as the nature of its protection changes; to escape from the drudgery of industry and talents, and to share in the luxury of stock, office and privilege.

Principles, congenial to aristocracy (among which monopolies of wealth by law have been universally esteemed) are huntsmen in pursuit of republicanism, to strip her of her plumage. Will she turn and defend herself, or like a foolish bird, expect to escape by shutting her eyes upon her enemy?

It is extremely important that private property should be clearly ascertained, to withstand the assaults both of those who would abolish it by mobs, and of those who would defraud it by law to create an aristocracy. Civilized society is dissolved by the enthusiasm of one party, or corrupted by the knavery of the other; and it is the policy of our system to guard against both. To apply this policy to the preservation of the ligament upon which its own preservation depends, the nature of that ligament ought to be thoroughly understood.

The fruit of labour or industry, is an unequivocal species of private property; is that also an unequivocal species, which takes away this fruit? If a law, which enables A to transfer to himself B's unequivocal private property, may boast of the protection it gives to property, by securing B's to A, oppression and fraud may upon the same ground justify their most atrocious actions. And if laws for bestowing wealth, may be permanent, rigid and insatiable extortioners, they cannot be also guardians and protectors of private property.

485

THE MODE OF INFUSING ARISTOCRACY

Such laws succeed, by seizing upon the passion of avarice, and bewildering computation. Although a vast majority of mankind universally lose property by these laws, each individual is at a loss how to class himself. Deluded by the hope of gain, he submits to an immoral mode of enriching some, at the expense of others; and yet by considering whether he is a member of general and natural, or of exclusive and factitious interests, the difficulty would vanish. It is easy to determine, whether we subsist by labour, industry or talents; or by patronage, privilege, sinecure or stock. True private property, is a political being permanently guided by good moral principles, because its interest is to do right; spurious, one as permanently guided by evil, because its interest is to do wrong. The enmity between them is exactly that between religion and idolatry. Laws may be either the accomplices of spurious, or the protectors of legitimate private property. And the principle by which they are stampt with one or the other of these characters, ascertains what private property is. Laws to enable men to keep their property, stand exactly opposed to laws for transferring it to other men. Governments are instituted for the first object, but they strive to acquire the second. And no government of any form did ever acquire this second power, without using it to impoverish a nation and enrich an aristocracy, titled, hierarchical or stock.

A has inherited or earned 'a sum of money; B, being more cunning than A, obtains a law enabling him to get A's money, directly or indirectly; and after he has gotten it, the law guarantees it to B. Was this money private property in the hands of A? Is the social sanction which secured it in his hands, less sacred or just, than the legal sanction which transferred it to B?

If property is admitted to be a social right, it does not follow that society gives an absolute power over it to governments. Upon this ground however, sovereigns ingeniously invented forfeitures for offences, and applied them to their own use. By this feudal fraud, privileged orders were nurtured. Our policy detected and abolished this fraud. An invention for the benefit of society, ought not to be used to its injury. It followed the same principle in a denunciation of the whole tribe of exclusive privileges, which like forfeitures, would all serve to feed some order or faction. And having thus disposed of forfeitures, and privileges, it never could have intended to invest law with a power to apply private property, to a use, to which it refuses to condemn fines for crimes.

All societies have exercised the right of abolishing privileged, stipendiary or factitious property, whenever they became detrimental to them; nor have kings, churches or aristocracies ever hesitated to do the same thing, for the same reason. The king of England joined the people and judges, in abolishing the tenures and perpetuities of the nobles; the king and nobles united in abolishing the property of the popish clergy; the consistory of Rome suppressed the order of Jesuits and disposed of its property; and several of these states, have abolished entails, tythes and hierarchical establishments. What stronger ground can be occupied by any species of law-begotten wealth, than by these?

Poverty is justly exasperated against the wealth which caused it; but it temperately contemplates wealth, flowing from industry and talents, and not from fraudulent laws. It knows that as one man's industry, cannot make another man poorer; so wealth gotten by legal means, without industry, must. And if aristocracy is introduced into the United States by legal modes of dividing property, violent animosities between the rich and poor will attend it, to a greater extent than in other countries, because the means for controlling them are less.

From the legal frauds by which property is transferred and amassed, human nature has derived most of its envy, malice, and hatred. And if the acquisitions of hierarchy, privilege, patronage, sinecure, bribery, charter and paper stock, have been but seldom able to inspire it with a sufficient share of these passions, to assail fraudulent kinds of property; what danger can be apprehended by genuine private property, defended by all the sanctions which defend the spurious, with the addition of justice?

The only danger of innocent, arises from an alliance with guilty property. Such an alliance is assiduously sought for, and artfully supported, by its pretended friend and real foe. A knave will strive to associate himself with an honest man, and the latter must dissolve the connexion, or risk his reputation. Thus honest property is exposed to danger by an association with fraudulent property; and its safety is ensured, by dissolving the connexion. Honest property, disunited from a system which deeds away a nation to individuals or factions, by offices, privileges, charters, loans, banks, and all the variety of incorporations, will have nothing to fear, whenever publick indignation and justice awake. It will both escape and inflict the fate of its natural enemies, by disdaining to serve under their banners, or to become the dupe of their frauds.

To the indignation inspired by the fraudulent legal modes for acquiring wealth, mankind are indebted for the pernicious and impracticable idea of equalising property by law. This speculation has been considered by philosophers, in contrast with its opposite. It seemed to them more reasonable and just, that property should be made equal, than unequal by law. Destroy the alternative, by assailing both its branches with the benefits arising from leaving property to be distributed by industry, and the argument would assume a new aspect. It would be discovered, that arts and sciences, peace and plenty, have never been found, disunited from metes and bounds. And that hence mankind have preferred that branch of the alternative which required, to that which rejected them; considering a system of property, compounded of honesty and fraud, as preferable to its abolition.

By artfully drawing the question to this point, legal, factitious or fraudulent property; comprising every species resulting from direct and indirect modes of accumulation by law, at the expense of others; has been able in all civilized countries, to unite itself with substantial, real or honest property; comprising accumulations arising from fair and useful industry and talents. The equalising speculation, by proposing to destroy both, united these two opposite moral beings in a defensive war; just as a good and a bad man would unite against an assassin, indifferently determined to murder them both. Had philosophers wisely avoided this snare, and confined the discussion to a discrimination between the useful and pernicious kinds of property, they would never have given to the latter the benefit of an alliance by which it is sustained; and might have long since settled some definition of private property, sufficiently perspicuous, to defend mankind against the pecuniary oppressions they are forever suffering for want of it. Instead of associating honest and fraudulent property in one interest, by the chimerical and impracticable equalising project, they would have established a rational and practicable distinction, between that species of private property founded only in law; such as is gained by privilege, hierarchy, paper, charter, and sinecure; and that founded also in nature; arising from industry, arts and sciences. And they would have proved, that the two species constituted two principles in the world of property, as strictly opposed to each other, as the two principles in the moral world, one of which is worshipped and the other execrated. Blended, they make up a system of property, similar to a system of religion, compounded of theocracy and demonocracy.

488

Nothing is more remarkable in their contrariety, than that fictitious property is founded in the principle of agrarian laws, which it reprobates. The simple objection to these is, that they take away a portion of one man's property, and give it to another. How otherwise can the balance of property between orders be effected, as contended for by Mr. Adams and Lord Shaftesbury? Does it alter the principle, to transfer the property by means, avowed and direct, or insidious and indirect? However indirect, yet privilege, hierarchy, office, paper, charter, and sinecure, are means, by which the property of some is taken away, and given to others. All the difference is, that in agrarian laws, or laws for an equal division of land, the principle is applied between individuals; and in laws for nurturing separate interests, between orders.

A single effect, observable wherever Mr. Adams's and Lord Shaftesbury's system exists, of a balance of property between orders, is quoted to illustrate this reasoning. It is attended by a multitude of poor rates, work houses and hospitals. Why? Because many individuals of the most numerous order, being excessively impoverished by dividing or distributing property among orders, would perish, unless provided for by those legally enriched. The right of the poor to require subsistence from those who have made them poor, is so strong as to be admitted by the authors of their impoverishment. An agrarian law, or an equal division of property, would not be equally attended by poor rates, work houses and hospitals, because it would not equally impoverish individuals. Will it be contended, that laws which impoverish a great number of individuals, are less atrocious violators of justice and private property, than laws which impoverish none? We must now discern that the principle of distributing property by law, is more malignant, when applied to equalise wealth between orders, than when applied to equalise wealth between individuals. A principle, more malignant against social happiness, than a general agrarian division, cannot be the genuine principle which causes society to guard private property. Thence we are necessarily driven in search of some other principle, and if we are right in considering industry, arts and sciences, as its true sources, a correct definition of private property, must exclude all the legal modes invented for its division.

Lord Shaftesbury and Mr. Adams strenuously contend, that a balance of property among orders, is necessary to preserve their freedom. In like manner, a balance of property among individuals, is necessary to preserve theirs. The first species of balance, destroys the second. The legal distribution of wealth, necessary to preserve the balance of property, and its dependant, the freedom of orders, destroys its distribution by industry and talents, equally necessary to preserve the second species of balance, and its dependant, the freedom of men. Thus the attainable object of a free government, is destroyed by the forlorn attempt to keep three orders free, by balancing wealth and power among them. By transferring, an agrarian law, invades property. All laws for this purpose, direct or indirect, are equally its invaders. Those for dividing lands, and for making sinecures, useless armies and offices, bank stock and hierarchies, transfer the property of some to others, and therefore all belong to the same class. If an end of a government is to protect property, it cannot be an end of the same government to make these laws, because the two ends are contrary to each other. It would have as good a right, under a power to protect property, to make an equal division of it by a direct law, as an unequal division of it, by indirect laws. Our policy labours to prevent necessary laws from degenerating into the latter usurpation, by cautiously guarding against excessive expenditures even for publick uses; and it excludes a right of legislation, for the purpose of transferring private property from some to others, or for the sake of creating or balancing orders or separate interests, civil or religious. Laws for maintaining a balance of property among orders, necessary to sustain an aristocracy, however disguised, defeat every such principle of our policy.

By suffering industry to distribute property, industry will be created. It teaches no vice. It bestows health and content. It is a pledge of virtue. It doubles our happiness by enabling us to blend with it the happiness of others. Its benefits reiterate and spread like the undulations of the waves. Yet the hags, feudality, hierarchy, privilege and stock, have successively been preferred as regulators of private property, to this charming goddess. The distribution of property by law, first introduces into a government what I shall call an aristocracy of parties; and an appearance of this species of aristocracy, is a proof that its pabulum exists. The few who contend for prizes, arrange a nation into parties, who zealously plead for and against each set of distributees, both having in view the goods and chattels of the infatuated advocates.

The similitude between party and aristocracy, is explained by Mr. Hume's distinction between an aristocracy of individuals, and one consisting of a separate interest; exemplifying the first by the

Polish, and the second by the Venetian nobility. An aristocracy or party of individuals, consists of a few Polish noblemen, at the head of an ignorant and obedient mass of followers. An aristocracy or party of interest, consists of a conclave of individuals, united for the end of defrauding others to enrich themselves. In the same essay Mr. Hume has said, that free governments are most happy for those who partake of their freedom, but most ruinous and oppressive to their provinces. They dispense ruin and oppression to provinces, as the inevitable effect of a separate interest. The certainty of this moral law, is nearly demonstrated in the relation between England and Ireland, and quite so in India. If a free government is converted by a power of distributing wealth by law, into an oppressive aristocracy of its provinces, every species of aristocracy or separate interest, must be guided by the same moral law.

The United States exhibit four parties, the republican, monarchical, stock, and patronage. The two parties of principle, unsophisticated by the parties of separate interest, would discuss with moderation, and decide with integrity; but the two last, accepted on both sides as recruits, by an ardour for victory, though known to be allies who serve for plunder, empoison them by all the contaminations of an interest, distinct from the publick; and by all the animosities, aristocracies of interest inspire. Aristocracy or separate interest in our case, at present takes refuge under one and then under the other of our parties, because it is not yet able to stand alone; but whilst it is fondling first one and then the other of its nurses, it is sucking both into a consumption, and itself towards maturity.

It is thus that patronage transforms any party into an aristocracy of interest. The money dispensed by the executive power of England, creates a powerful aristocracy of interest, unfriendly to the national interest. The patronage of the President of the United States, is aggravated by the temptation to employ it for his re-election. This aristocracy of patronage, arises from a division of property by law, and the only modes of reconciling it with republican government, are, to settle salaries by a standard, too low to create a party of interest; or to divide patronage so widely, as to prevent it from becoming the property of one man, or of one body of men. People will then cease to enlist under some banner to gain an office, to elect partisans, and to raise by their own suffrages a mercenary civil army for the destruction of their own liberties. The effect of the inconsiderable sum laid out by patronage upon Congress, reflects with fidelity, the fatal aristocracy of interest to be expected from the vast sum, distributed by banking among the people.

The enlightened author of the life of General Washington, ascribes the parties in the United States, to the intrigues of Mr. Jefferson, to French influence, and to other transitory and fluctuating causes. If his opinion had been correct, these parties would have disappeared with the supposed causes. But being in truth produced by the mass of property transferred by funding, banking and patronage, creating (to borrow Mr. Hume's phrase) an aristocracy of interest, they yet exist, because these laws divided the nation into a minority enriched, and a majority furnishing the riches; and two parties, seekers and defenders of wealth, are an unavoidable consequence. All parties, however loyal to principles at first, degenerate into aristocracies of interest at last; and unless a nation is capable of discerning the point where integrity ends and fraud begins, popular parties are among the surest modes of introducing an aristocracy. The policy of protecting duties to force manufacturing, is of the same nature, and will produce the same consequences as that of enriching a noble interest, a church interest, or a paper interest; because bounties to capital are taxes upon industry, and a distribution of property by law. And it is the worst mode of encouraging aristocracy, because, to the evil of distributing wealth at home by law, is to be added the national loss arising from foreign retaliation upon our own exports. An exclusion by us of foreign articles of commerce, will beget an exclusion by foreigners of our articles of commerce, or at least corresponding duties; and the wealth of the majority will be as certainly diminished to enrich capital, as if it should be obliged to export a million of guineas to bring back a million of dollars, or to bestow a portion of its guineas upon this separate interest.

As a separate or aristocratical interest, is the cause of party in countries where avarice or reason prevails over superstition and fanaticism, it follows, that instead of party spirit being natural to free governments, it is only natural to those, where aristocracies or parties of interest are artificially created and combined by law; and that by uncreating these causes, such aristocracies and parties naturally die. Ambition itself, in the present state of manners, despairs of gratification, except by the help of a party founded in interest, which it can create by no mode, except by that of invading property by law or force. It must hire an army or a legislature, or both, to gain power. It cannot hire either without money, and it cannot obtain money, without associates. If ambition is unable to form an aristocracy or party, except by violating and transferring property, it follows, that no other means exist for its formation; and of course, that its appearance is a proof that property is violated and transferred. It follows also, that free and fair governments cannot be subject to party, but such only as have ceased to be free and fair by the creation of aristocracy, or a party founded in interest. If this reasoning is true, there is neither wisdom nor policy, in providing constitutional precepts requiring ambition and avarice to be quiet; and yet to nourish them by law. It makes the constitution a blind, from behind which legal parties or aristocracies strike nations.

Orders enslave nations, by making parties; and they are enabled to make them, by laws for transferring property. If such laws make parties, and if the party spirit of orders, is the cause of their oppression; then, though titles are excluded, yet wherever party spirit is created, the oppression produced by orders is secured. Patrician and feudal parties were made by conquered lands; church parties by tythes, offerings and endowments; military parties, by wages; patronage parties, by offices, bribes and sinecures; and paper parties, by stock, interest and dividends. All were made by laws for transferring or invading private property, all are parties or aristocracies of interest, and all are avoided by forbearing to make the laws which make them, and in no other way.

Two causes are adduced to shew, that property and not title, creates the parties or aristocracies which enslave nations. The whig party was made strong in England, by the paper stock with which it was enriched and united. In spite of its principles, it was forced by the regimen of this legal wealth to enslave the nation, by poisoning the principles it professed to nurture. Hence a modern whig may believe, that it would have been better for the English nation, had success followed the landed tories, who would have strangled the paper system of the whigs in its infancy. If the stock system of the United States proceeds as it has done for fifty years more, it will give occasion for a similar computation. This case proves, that the present state of England, was caused by a party, formed by a legal and artificial mode of distributing property, and not by a titled order; and that paper stock was this mode. Paper stock can therefore make aristocracies or parties, able to overthrow political principles.

The Cincinnati of the United States could never form a faction

493

or party; because title, without fraudulent laws to transfer property, is incompetent to such an end; but the funding and banking system could; because such laws without title, possess this competency. Even at home we have already learnt, that titles cannot' make parties; that laws for distributing property can; and that such laws operate under our political system as they do under all others.

The precise principle we are contending for, is resorted to by the constitution of the United States, to prevent party and faction. But it is applied only to states, and not to individuals. Partialities by law, for increasing or diminishing the taxes of a state, and every species of exclusive privilege, or exclusive burden, between states, is carefully guarded against. This is done, because laws of either complexion, would unexceptionably transfer property from the unfavoured to the favoured states; and would unexceptionably also create the former into an exasperated, and the latter, into a fraudulent party, or an aristocracy. This fraudulent party, could not for a moment deceive states into an opinion, that laws for bestowing exclusive privileges and wealth upon other states, or exclusive burdens upon themselves, would add to their wealth or happiness. A state makes but one moral being; its capacity is equal to the moral beings who would practise this deception; it contains no inimical ingredients, willing to sacrifice it to another state, because of its unity as a moral being; nor has its legislature any interest, to make and hide this sacrifice from the people. It would therefore instantly decide, that all laws for enriching particular states, directly or indirectly, were fraudulent and oppressive.

Do not such laws operate between individuals, precisely as they operate between states? Being fraudulent and oppressive in relation to individuals, as they are in relation to states, they will also generate party, faction or aristocracy. It is less violent than a party of states would be, because the deceptions used to defend the imposition, have some success among individuals, from their ignorance, and from the arts of those interested. These causes of deception do not apply to factitious modes of transferring property between states, and therefore a state is never deceived, and indignantly resists such laws in every shape.

Suppose, for instance, that congress had invested particular states, with the exclusive privilege of supplying the Union with paper currency by banks, and had prohibited the issuing of any other. Could the states, unpossessed of a share in the privilege, have been persuaded that it would add to their wealth, happiness or prosperity? They would, in the supposed case, have occupied the place with all its consequences, of that entire mass of individuals, unpossessed of bank stock. Yet in an eternity, no civilized state could have been made to believe itself benefited, by having the bank paper of the privileged states circulated within it. An exclusive privilege of furnishing the United States with manufactures would have an equivalent effect.

By excluding partial modes of transferring property by law between states, the constitution designs to deprive ambition and avarice of a handle, by which to work up and manage geographical passions and parties, for their own selfish ends. How can it be just and wise, to offer a like handle to ambition and avarice, in a social union of individuals, by permitting them to transfer and accumulate property by law, if it is unjust and unwise to admit of its existence, in the union between the states? If its exclusion in one case, is calculated to counteract parties, factions or aristocracies, formed of states, its exclusion in the other, would prevent parties, factions or aristocracies, formed of citizens. By excluding it in both, the only tool with which ambition and avarice can undermine and destroy a free government, can no longer be forged.

If there exists no mode under the constitution of the United States, by which the government, or some section of it can exercise partialities between states in relation to property, they will probably escape the evil of geographical aristocracy. Should a statesman, an orator, a hero, or a patriot, begin to draw lines of separate or exclusive interest from north to south, from east to west, along a chain of hills, or from the source of a river to the ocean; like all legal frauds for distributing property; they will be merely designed to enrich some party of interest, at the expense of those whose benefit is pretended; and as these lines drawn by civil law, invariably mean fraud and avarice, they only acquire the additional attributes of ambition and treason, when attempted for political revolution. But if the pretext for such an experiment was ever so preposterous, yet if it was connected with a partial distribution of property by law between the states, it would create a geographical party, as was in some degree illustrated by the effects of the funding system, and may be illustrated by the influence of executive patronage. The richer it becomes, the more zealous will districts be, led by the exertions of fraud which hopes of office or contracts will excite, to gain the presidency.

The artifice of enemies, and the credulity of friends, in fostering an opinion, that party spirit was natural to honest and free government, prevents us from discovering that it is invariably produced by dishonest or ambitious designs, and unexceptionably indicates the existence of an aristocracy of interest. Mr. Adams allows that party spirit is a regular fruit of orders, without deducing it from aristocratical laws for distributing property, allowed also by him to be necessary to the existence of these orders. If then party spirit, orders, or aristocracy, flow from the same cause, whatever will prevent either, will prevent all, and whatever will produce one, will produce the rest. As a distribution of property by law is the common cause, an exclusion of such laws, is the common remedy; and as according to our idea of a republican government, it cannot exist in union with these partial laws, the parties they produce are chargeable to a different form of government, partial to a separate interest, and in principle, aristocratical.

Mr. Godwin has said 'that all government is founded in opinion, and that publick institutions will fluctuate with the fluctuations of opinion.' This position assigns the publick approbation to all governments, which have existed or can exist. It bestows upon an aristocracy or party, whose power is planted in self interest, the sanction of publick opinion; and raises the influence of authority to the highest pitch. With equal justice, he might have assigned the same sanction to the power of a disciplined army, over an undisciplined nation. It is never the opinion of nations that slavery is good; yet they are enslaved. Nor is it the opinion of nations that an aristocracy or party of interest is good, but they suffer it, because the individuals of a general interest cannot be cemented in the same way with those of a separate one, as there is none to supply the glue.

Opinion may in one sense be correctly considered as the foundation of all governments. They are all derived from general or partial opinion; from the opinion of the nation, or of some party of interest; but as general and party opinion, are opposite and contradictory sources of government, one must be bad. As moral enemies, they cannot unite. Mingled; commotion or death ensues, as in the case of poison mingled with wholesome drugs. Milton could not bring back Satan to heaven by the benignity of the Almighty, because good and evil are incapable of associating. Even the license of poetry does not extend to a fable contrary to nature. Mr. Adams contends for this mixture, in the very act of proving that it has universally failed.

General, and not party opinion, is the principle of our policy. All our constitutions contain efforts in favour of one, and no efforts in favour of the other. Laws which have the effect of mixing party opinion with general opinion, correspond with Mr. Adams's policy, and have ever been fatal to such a policy as ours. They introduce party interest into the departments of government, and create intrigues against the general interest; exactly as Mr. Adams proves orders to have universally done. A stock or patronage interest will be as selfish, as a noble or religious interest. The publick interest and the party interest, commence hostilities and continue the war, until one of them is vanquished; and as defeat has hitherto pursued the publick interest, it is unaccountable that it should be persuaded to create a foe, before whose prowess it is destined to fall.

A separate interest, drawing wealth from a nation, and able to gain an influence in a government, cannot be a republican, any more than an individual nobleman in the same situation. To the term 'republican,' the Americans have annexed the modern meaning of general good. The opinion, that parties were natural to republicks is the creature of the old idea, that republicks could be constituted of orders or parties. Parties are indeed natural to governments made of parties. But if we reject this old construction of the term, which makes it to mean any thing or nothing; we ought also to reject the old errour, that parties were natural to republicks, as arising from the errour, which considered governments formed of parties or orders as republicks.

The antipathy of party spirit to publick spirit, sophisticated terms, for the purpose of deceiving nations, so that old as the world is, we still want a political word, to express the idea of national self government, unadulterated by orders or parties of interest. If republicanism is allowed to convey the idea of a government guided by publick opinion and operating for publick good, then wherever a legislature is guided or influenced by the opinion of a banking party, the government has ceased to be a republick, as completely as if it was influenced by a king.

Despotisms are more lasting than free governments, because, as they do not suffer an order or a party possessed of exclusive power and privileges to exist, they are not subject to party spirit. By making free governments as little subject to party spirit, they will probably become more permanent than despotisms. It is excluded from despotisms, by excluding separate interests, calculated to plunder, and then dethrone the monarch with his own wealth; and it will be excluded from free governments, by forbearing to create these separate interests, still more dangerous to national wealth and sovereignty.

The appearance of parties of interest under a despotick government, is a proof that a new power has crept in, aspiring to the control of the despotism. A conflict of course commences, which ends in the destruction of one of the combatants. The appearance of such an aristocracy, under a free government, or one founded on common interest, indicates also the existence of a new power, and a similar conflict is unavoidable. Despotism will seldom create and nurture its own foe; free government is frequently seduced to do so. A despotick sovereignty keeps patronage in its own hands, and never confers privileges independent of its own will. A national sovereignty surrenders patronage to an individual, and charters away exclusive rights and emoluments. The consequences which would result to a despotick sovereignty from such a policy, do result to a national sovereignty. Reasoning is at an end, if the same moral causes, are not allowed to produce the same effects. If parties under despotisms are in collision with despotick sovereignty; parties under free governments must be in collision with national. And if the suppression of a party interest, is necessary to save a despotism, it must be necessary to save a free government. The appearance of party is a beacon proclaiming a tendency, which instantly alarms despotism; and it brings back the government to its principle by suppressing the inimical tendency. Free government has only to be equally vigilant against these inimical tendencies, to live longer than despotism; for as party interest is unnatural to one in a state of purity, so is it to the other.

Instances without number might be adduced, to shew, that separate interest is a thermometer accurately disclosing the progress of a revolution, both in property and principles; and that the latter are modelled by fraudulent dispositions of the first. In England, though titles remain, patrician and plebeian parties have yielded to a party or aristocracy of interest. Whigs and tories are melted into one mass, by the same crucible. This crucible is made of paper stock and patronage. The property it invades, plunders, and distributes, has begotten new parties, and abolished old principles. In the United States, no parties of importance have ever appeared, except such as arose from paper stock and patronage; and by this transfer of property, old principles, as in England, will unquestionably be altered or destroyed.

If the term 'patronage' was limited to wages for publick service, legislative, executive or judicial, yet should those wages be made so high as to produce detriment to the publick, the surplus beyond the sum required by publick good is fraudulently transferred by law. In computing them, every consideration in relation to the receiver of the wages, ought to be excluded, because they are bestowed to benefit, not him, but the nation. Even legislative wages, capable of protracting sessions for the sake of transferring a greater mass of property, from the payer to the receiver, or of exciting election frauds may form a secret and mischievous party of interest, under its own patronage.

The argument, by which plentiful wages are defended, is, the tendency of law to expel merit and talents from legislatures, and to throw government into the hands of a wealthy order. This argument can only be of force in countries, where legal means are used to create wealthy separate interests. Where wealth is distributed by industry and talents, and not by law, it will nearly cover the merit and talents of a country, and no wealthy order can usurp the legislative power, because none will exist. And high wages, far from enabling merit and virtue to curb a wealthy separate interest, are only another motive, and new means, for enabling them to gain possession of legislatures, by corrupting election.

It is said that Doctor Franklin, convinced that the evils of patronage outweighed the benefits of wages to publick officers, would not receive any as chief magistrate of Pennsylvania. Nations require civil and military services. Militia services are rendered to great extent without wages, and those paid for them in war, are regulated by the idea of publick benefit, and not of adequate compensation. Parsimony, applied to civil duties, would not fall heavier on the rich, than it does on the poor, when applied to military duties. If the chief burden of military service is inflicted on one class, as a duty, because it is most capable from its number of discharging it; ought not the chief burden of civil service to be inflicted on the other, as a duty also, because it chiefly possesses the talents for discharging that? A standing army of mercenary civil officers, being as fatal to free government, as an army of soldiers, the militia principle may be as useful and necessary in the one case, as in the other.

Wages sufficiently high to protect legislative sessions, are a sinecure paid by the publick to corrupt the department of government, which ought to be the purest. They excite official fraud and artifice, and subject members to executive influence for the sake of re-election; and tend in this way towards an aristocracy of interest, of the species most malignant to free and fair government; namely, that compounded of legislative corruption and executive influence.

We ought fully to comprehend the distinction between a personal aristocracy, and an aristocracy of interest, lest we should be surprised by the one, whilst we are watching the other. Hume's illustration of the latter by the Spartan aristocracy, would have been as apt, had that aristocracy extracted its subsistence from the mechanicks and cultivators, or Helots, by paper stock, as by the mode it pursued. It had no titles, and was one interest living on another. The impossibility of providing a balance of property in the United States, for a personal aristocracy, was explained, to shew that an aristocratical principle cannot be introduced in that mode, and if not in that, it can only be introduced in the mode of an aristocracy of interest. Through principles, and not names, this species of political power, becomes real and oppressive. Was any person ever weak enough to discern hierarchy, aristocracy, or monarchy, in Scotch bishops, the American Cincinnati, or Theodore king of Corsica? Wealth is indispensable to sustain both a personal aristocracy, and an aristocracy of interest. The first can never obtain this indispensable principle in the United States, except they should be subdued by an invading or a native army, and divided among its chieftains. The second may obtain it, by means of patronage, corruption, privilege, and paper stock. It may steal into sovereignty with great rapidity, by selling its influence in society to the personal or disinterested parties alternately. Every aristocracy of interest is ardent in this traffick, and a love of power unhappily induces all political parties (unless they are controlled by nations) to bestow wealth and credit upon this species of aristocracy, until their own principles are lost in the corruption they have countenanced to preserve them, and they themselves sink into a state of subjection to their own instruments.

Section the Ninth

THE LEGAL POLICY OF THE UNITED STATES

Montesquieu's analysis of forms of government, is neither moral nor numerical. He divides them into 'republican, monarchical, and despotick,' and the presence or absence of law constitutes his criterion of liberty and despotism. But having by these definitions disclosed a partiality for his country, he proceeds to truth, by proving that civil laws are the instruments for fostering or destroying both free and despotick governments, and that neither can be preserved, except by an analogy of legal to constitutional principles. Whatever analysis of governments we adopt must also be an analysis for legislation. If we adopt the numerical, the same laws cannot be congenial with the three, nor with any two of its forms; if the moral, it is still more difficult to reconcile the same laws, with both good and bad principles. The necessity of civil law, to foster or impair every form of government, makes it equally indispensable to a free nation and a monarch, to be able to distinguish its character and effects, for the preservation of liberty or despotism. A conviction that republican forms beget the first, and monarchical the second, united with an ignorance of the laws adapted to the preservation or introduction of either, excites the fermentation of mobs, and ends in the tranquillity of tyranny.

An incapacity to discern the difference between a power to divide and to protect property, or between a national militia and a mercenary army, is an incapacity for the preservation of a free government. As the first member of each contrast corrupts or enervates nations, they belong to the evil class of moral principles. Individuals, parties or governments use all the means placed in their hands to obtain their ends; and a dependence for defence upon a mercenary army, renders a nation unable to defend itself. The jesuitical maxim 'that every thing is lawful to effect good ends,' makes every thing lawful in the eyes of governments and

501

parties, which is necessary to effect their own ends; because self love convinces all men that their ends are good. Every principle, bad or good, drawn from the moral qualities of an individual, applies to a multitude. A power making one man a despot, will make despots of a party of men; the only difference being, that one species of despotism resembles a scorching fire; the other, a consuming conflagration. Parties clothed with evil or despotick powers, destroy free governments with a rage and rapidity far outstripping the capacity of individual tyrants, because many men can do more mischief than one. This fact demonstrates the incapacity of the numerical analysis for informing us whether a government is free or despotick, and explodes the hideous doctrine 'that the will of a majority can do no wrong,' under which parties, in imitation of kings, often endeavour to hide atrocious legal violations of good moral principles. Many men can even do more wrong to one or a few, than one or a few can do to many. This analysis is still more defective as a criterion of good or bad laws, because those of its best form are not necessarily good, and no commixture of its several forms can make arbitrary or fraudulent laws, free or just.

The principle 'that a government and its laws must be of the same moral nature to subsist together,' furnishes the only existing security for the preservation both of a free and an arbitrary form of government. Monarchy cannot subsist upon republican laws, nor a republick upon monarchical. The numerical analysis can inform us, whether we are governed by one, a few, or many persons, but its whole stock of knowledge is expended in the performance of this paltry office, and it is utterly unable to give us any instruction as to the mode of preserving the selected form of government. But an analysis founded in moral principles, furnishes nations with constitutional restraints upon governments, and with perpetual sentinels faithfully warning them of the approach of their worst foes; bad laws. It transfers popular attention from the persons composing the numerical analysis, to the principles by which it is itself composed; and settles a wise veneration or a just hatred upon the good and bad divisions of these principles, instead of that ridiculous veneration for a president and a congress, a king and a parliament, or an emperor and a senate, which never discloses the approach of a single foe to liberty. A moral analysis alone can teach nations the only mode of sustaining a free government. It can detect attempts to destroy our moral constitutional principles of a division of power between the people and the government, or between the general and state governments, by political or civil laws. And it can keep us attentive to the fact, that a power in a government of any form, to deal out wealth and poverty by law, overturns liberty universally; because it is a power by which a nation is infallibly corrupted; and the legislature, whose laws caused the corruption, is at length forced by the national depravity, to abridge the liberty of the people; or an usurper makes it a strong argument, even with good men, for erecting a despotick government. A power in Congress, for instance, of influencing the wealth or poverty of states by taxing exports and making roads or canals; or of individuals, by charters; would be used by successive parties for self preservation, with an activity, by which government would exchange the duty of protecting for the privilege of regulating property. The alternative of receiving or yielding the golden fleece, according to the will of these parties, would suddenly excite an equal degree of baleful activity among the people, to gain the one and to avoid the other; and soon overturn the whole catalogue of moral principles, necessary for the preservation of a free form of government. In whatever numerical class a government is arranged, a power of advancing the wealth of one part of the nation, by civil laws, will be used by its successive administrators to obtain a corrupt influence, wholly inconsistent with any good moral principles interwoven in a constitution, and certainly destructive of them.

Every party of interest, whether a noble, a religious, or a military order; or created by a corrupting degree of legislative or executive patronage; or by usurping a power of regulating property by means of paper credit, charters or fraudulent wars; is the instrument and ally of the power by which its interest can be fed or starved. It must acquire an influence over legislation, both to do its own work, and the work of the power it serves. It can by law slip under governments a new substratum, without altering a feature of the numerical analysis. And it will be invariably purchased at the publick expense, by the political party in possession of the government, at a rate proportioned to the service it may be able to render.

This game between political and pecuniary parties, is precisely the cause by which free, moderate, and honest forms of government are destroyed; it inflicts heavier taxation, than any other species of misrule; and it cannot be carried on, except by a legislative power to regulate wealth and poverty. In England this power is complete, and has scattered every where parties of interest of all sizes, and individuals, paid for their services directly or indirectly by the political party in power, at the national expense, and ready to serve any political party whatsoever for pay. Hence arise the excessiveness of taxation, the parliamentary corruption, and the frequent wars of that country. None of our constitutions intended to endow legislation with this power of regulating property, thus exercised in England, because its effects there demonstrated, that the moral principles upon which they were built, could not subsist in union with such a power; and that it would have amounted to a provision in them all, for absolving the government from the moral restraints previously imposed. But political parties have attempted to acquire it in imitation of the English precedents, (which will for ever be admired by men in power) as in the cases of a legal appreciation of paper stock far beyond the price at which it was purchased, of banks, and of the Yazoo report; and if the system of changing the principles of a government by laws is not well understood by the people, they will go on, and at length make sales of national property to stockjobbers, if stockjobbers will sell them support even in the form of a war.

A legislative power of regulating wealth and poverty, is a principle of such irresistible ascendency, as to bring all political parties to the same standard, and to make it quite indifferent to nations, which shall prevail. It is the solution in which is found the political identity of the whig and tory parties of England, in the exercise of power, during their highest state of acrimony; and in which this acrimony was at length lost.

It is matter of surprise that mankind should owe their greatest calamities to the two most respectable human characters, priests and patriots, from a political gluttony, like that of swallowing too much food, however good. If responsibility to God cannot cure priests of the vices which infect legislative parties of interest, what security lies in a responsibility to man? If the love of souls cannot awaken integrity, laid to sleep by this species of legislative patronage, will it be awakened by a love of wealth and power? But nations have no right to complain, because they corrupt their priests and patriots by temptations, which human nature has never been able to resist. Our policy, rejecting a reliance upon either, because they are men, has endeavoured to exalt political law from a numerical form, into a science; and to substitute permanent principles for fluctuating passions. But if laws can distribute wealth and power, among individuals arranged in combinations to acquire both; and if the fashion should prevail of scanning them by party comments, and not by honest principles; our beautiful experiment of confiding for a free government in good moral principles rather than in priests or patriots, will be exchanged for a confidence in stock-jobbers and various other parties of interest.

These parties plead patriotism to ignorance and credulity, and offer wealth and power to avarice and ambition. The most fraudulent is loudest in professions of zeal for the publick good, and like the Mississippi and South Sea projects, is often the most successful; because the vicious principle of creating wealth by law, having debauched the minds of the audience, no dishonesty appears to be attached to any excesses of legislative robbery. Audacity or delusion at length inculcates an opinion, that he who refuses to surrender his conscience and his understanding to some party, is a knave or a fool; a knave, in pretending to honesty under a legislative distribution of wealth; and a fool, for preferring hopeless efforts to serve the publick, to his own aggrandizement at the publick expense. Thus the maxims taught by the legal intercourse between political and pecuniary parties reverse the dictates of common sense and common honesty. Knaves or fools only, surrender their duties and rights to party despotism. Knaves, to get a share in its acquisitions; fools, because they are deceived. Can an honest man of sound understanding think himself bound by wisdom or duty, to give or sell himself to one of two parties, prompted by interest and ambition to impair the publick good? Are men bound by wisdom or honour to take side with one of two competitors, if both are robbers or usurpers? On the contrary, as neither could succeed except by dividing the national force between them, a nation of fools only could be drawn into a division, in which the success of either party, is a calamity to a majority of both. And as civil government affords wealth and power to a very small proportion of a nation, if those who reap neither from it, are seduced into an opinion that they ought to enlist under one of two small parties contending for both, they are only entitled to the same character, as being the instruments of their own misfortunes, in all the fluctuations of victory. Parties, like usurpers, acquire nothing from each other. The rich spoils of a gallant but deluded nation, were the fruits gathered by the whig and tory parties from the opinion—that it is knavery to adhere to the publick interest, and folly to exercise one's own judgement. Thus election, designed to advance this interest, is converted into an instrument for parties; and that which is successful, hastens to reap the transitory harvest by legislative abuses, during the delirium of victory, until its crimes make room for a rival, equally unrestrained, which follows its precedents, repeats its frauds, and experiences its fate. By considering a zeal for party as more wise or honourable, than a zeal for good or bad laws, a nation is thus perpetually suspended in a state of political warfare, pregnant only with aggravations of calamity.

Election in the United States becomes more contemptible than in England, when degraded by a legal power of regulating wealth and poverty, into a whig or a tory, a Pitt or a Fox, if it is seduced by a worthless maxim to commit the crime, for which the English parliament are wise enough to obtain a valuable consideration. It appoints the prime minister of our sovereignty. If like the corrupted English interests, which govern the appointment of theirs, it was well paid for its work; or if like the king by whom this appointment is nominally made, it was lavishly endowed without expense to itself: it might boast of having sold its conscience and understanding for something solid; but to give away both, for a hollow notion of adhering to a party, that it may be fleeced and not bribed, would be an act of self abasement demonstrating that it was unable to distinguish between good and bad principles, and was of course flattered, despised and cheated. A sovereignty, popular or monarchical, ignorant of the principles by which it is preserved or destroyed, is first a cypher, then a tool, and finally the victim of its own servants. The folly both of a foolish people and a foolish king, consists in suffering the attention to be diverted from the moral nature of the acts and laws of their servants, to the frivolous names and treacherous professions of contending parties and rival courtiers.

The evil moral qualities of human nature, as natural to parties as to man, constitute the evidence in favour of restraining them by good moral principles, and evince the absurdity, in every case, of losing these principles in a career after names, to be equivalent to that of shutting the eyes for the sake of substituting confidence for seeing. The political party which brought Charles the first to the block, made sundry good laws for checking the regal, hierarchical, and titled parties of interest, from which the petition of right for repairing the usurpations of his two sons, extracted all its merit.

Yet it soon degenerated into a fraudulent and oppressive party of interest itself. This case teaches us, that legislation can change the nature of a government, without changing its form; that the numerical analysis, being unable to discern such changes, describes a government by the same name, after it has undergone a material change; that without understanding the moral principles of laws, nations can neither foresee nor regulate revolutions; and that neither party principles, merits nor names, are a good security for the continuance of party patriotism.

The pigments of the human character, by which this last fact is exhibited, are so numerous, that the habit of overlooking them is like the simplicity of a child, unable to recognise his own image. Eyes, seeing power eternally corrupting men, and minds, acting upon a supposition that it does not, make up the foolish compound which has legislated for the world; and the world has been enslaved. The patriots Cæsar, Cromwell and Bonaparte, and the parties whig and tory, federal and republican, have acted and legislated alike, because men are influenced by power as all kinds of water are by rum. No name nor badge can enchant a man against a moral law impinging on his nature. If a partridge was called an ostrich, it would not save him from the talon of the hawk; nor can a man be shielded against the effects of power by writing 'patriot' on his forehead. Whenever, therefore, the popularity of parties or individuals, shall free law from a strict examination at the tribunal of moral principles, a revolution is effected or at hand.

The constitutional power of the president to influence the legislature by his patronage, and the unconstitutional practice of its members in influencing the election of a president, might be moulded into a powerful ally of a system of legislation, neither suggested nor examined by good moral principles. Its tendency is to weaken, and at length to destroy, the responsibility of the president to the people; to extend the corruption of patronage in the legislature, and to defeat the good effects designed to be produced by the division of power between the legislative and executive departments. By the constitution of Virginia, a patronage operates visibly upon the independence of that branch of the legislature, numerically inferior, because its members can only gain the best offices in the state by the favour of the other. A cross patronage between the president and congress, more than doubles the operation of this mode of appointment against the principle of dividing power. In Virginia, the evil is mitigated by the absence of any executive patronage over the members of the legislature. But if the president should become the patron of congress, and congress the patron of the president, checks would be converted into accomplices, and a secret and intricate consolidation of those divisions, intended to restrain legislation within the verge of good moral principles, would necessarily ensue. The political sect arising from this commerce, would resort to law to strengthen an evasion of the constitution. The obstacles against the institution of titled orders, would turn its attention towards the creation of parties of interest in other forms, to secure its power and gratify its wishes. And besides, all the artifices for inflaming the passions of the vulgar, and bewildering the understandings of the ignorant; an identification of the government with the nation to free the party in power from responsibility; a national debt to chain the wealthy to the combination by the same strong ligament which binds them in France to Bonaparte; a direction of the publick admiration to military men; to reduce those most likely to oppose arbitrary laws, to a state of inferiority; a neglect of the militia, under the doctrine that it is unfit to resist foreign armies, so as to make it unable to resist domestick; a gradual reduction of the state governments to insignificance; and a perpetual increase of the energy of government, under the pretext of extensive territory; being all within the scope of the powers of the general government, will all be summoned to the aid of any combination between political departments; and a power of regulating property by law would dig the fosse of corruption, and render the circumvallation for its defence, impregnable to its slaves. Against this host of dangers, no security occurs to me, except a strict scrutiny into laws and all the measures of government, by the light of good moral principles.

Our policy has attempted to wrest war from the hands of executive power, lest it should be used as a means of making legislative an instrument for advancing its projects, and representation a mask to conceal them. War is the keenest carving knife for cutting up nations into delicious morsels for parties and their leaders. It swells a few people to a monstrous moral size, and shrivels a multitude to an equally unnatural diminutiveness. It puts arms into the hands of ambition, avarice, pride, and self love, and aggravates these passions by erecting the holders into a separate interest, which without arms has in no shape been made just or honest by the restraints of moral principles or didactick prohibitions. It breeds a race of men, nominally heroes, mistaken for patriots, and really tyrants. It enables knaves and traitors to delude the multitude into a belief that real patriots are knaves and traitors, and thus to force good men to become the instruments of bad, to avoid the persecutions of this delusion. And without a sound militia, it is more dangerous to our policy than superstition, nobility, and exclusive privilege united; because these could only sap it slowly, whilst that can carry it by storm. Hence this instrument, so well adapted for its destruction, is attempted to be withheld from executive power. But no provisions enforce the prohibition, and no precautions against executive intrigues with party spirit, the influence of patronage, nor the precipitancy of passions, are resorted to. The most trivial law is suspended for the president's concurrence, and the most trivial amendment of the constitution must receive a chaste national approbation; but a law for war is absolved from this check, and unsubjected to publick opinion. Party legislation converts the constitutional precaution into an aggravation of the danger, and restores the knife to the president, freed from any responsibility for using it. Twenty six per centum of the legislature, being the dictators of a party predominancy of fifty one per centum, in virtue of the party loyalty spread by fashion over perjury and treason, like embroidery over putrescence, holds in fact the power of declaring war; and political fashion, having thus diminished the work for the blandishments of flattery, the prejudices of party spirit, and the allurements of executive patronage, then covers the real authors of war against responsibility, under the canopy of a fraudulent majority, and the justification of a national concurrence, drawn from a false appearance. The gradation of reasoning, 'that each individual ought to be governed by the majority of some party; that a majority thus obtained, is a genuine republican majority; and that it is both the government and the nation,' seizes upon the amiable and honest respect of the people for their representatives, and rewards them for their virtues by the calamities of a war, entered into contrary to the true wishes of themselves, and of those who have thus sacrificed a virtuous to a wicked allegiance. Other less important consequences of party allegiance might have been cited, to illustrate the impossibility of maintaining a free government, unless the majority of a nation shall continually try two parties struggling for wealth and power in a free government, not by prejudices and delusions, which these parties in their pleadings infuse, but by fixed moral principles. Being as corrupt as hierarchies or noble orders, and struggling for the same objects by which such parties are invigorated, they draw their qualities from the same infusion; and a nation divided between them in a constant political warfare, can only win by their alternate victories that kind of liberty, to be reaped from a similar warfare under the banners of an order of priests, and an order of nobles.

Whilst the preservation of a federal form of government, dictated precautions against its subversion by political law, it is left exposed in a considerable degree to the lever of civil law and party spirit united. Had legislative chastity been secured against the addresses of executive patronage, and laws for making war been subjected to the concurrence of two thirds of the states, precautions better than those existing might have prevented the differences between the states, and alleviated the animosities between the parties, which seem better calculated to foster provincial hatreds, and the gradual approach of burdensome government, than wealth, happiness, and liberty. The didactick state authority is no match for a power concentrated in a few hands, and able by law to make war, and to require 'all the revenue a nation can pay.' Add to this force the power of distributing wealth by law, and the division of might between the general and state governments, would be well represented by a giant armed with a scimitar, and an infant, with a needle. Heavy taxes, loaning, war and legal devices for distributing wealth and poverty, are the modern scalping knives, tomahawks and rifles, used by avarice and ambition, because the more merciful weapons, superstition and nobility, having been broken by knowledge, more cruel became necessary, to intimidate, or more expensive, to corrupt her; and mankind must hence suffer, on account of an accession of knowledge, an accession of oppression, or piously acknowledge the divine favour, by reaping from it the greatest of sublunary blessings. Legislation must either be restrained within the pale of good moral principles, by the exertion of this modern dispensation; or it must more extensively than ever resort to bad ones, to suppress its effects. And neither monarchy, faction, avarice or ambition, will be able hereafter to effect their ends in the mild modes of ancient oppression, until ancient ignorance is restored, as was evinced by the revolutionary struggles and their termination in France.

Constitutions are often converted from tests for law, into snares for ignorance, by the ingenious verbal criticisms, to which the vices, the errours, and the passions of parties will often resort. If the single words 'religion and republick,' are often made to cover superstition and tyranny, what party can fail to find shelter for any law under a long constitution; but good moral principles cannot be made bad by words, nor bad, good. Constitutional powers, being all subordinate and subservient to the end of preserving a free and moderate government, do not admit of any constructions subversive of these ends. If a nation should erect a temple, and bestow on trustees powers for its preservation, no construction of these powers could be correct, by which its pillars would be gradually weakened, and the edifice finally destroyed. Even no power expressly given, can be constitutionally used to defeat the intention for which it was given. Congress are empowered to raise armies and to borrow money; but by using one power to erect a military aristocracy, like the French, or the other to erect a stock aristocracy, like the English, they would be guilty of treason against the constitution, without violating its letter.

In like manner, had an express power to grant charters been given to congress, it could only have been constitutionally exercised for the support of a free and moderate government, if this was the primary end of the constitution itself; and its use for the destruction of this end, would have been a real usurpation, by the help of a legal fraud. If this reasoning is true, all aristocracies of interest, military, stock, ministerial, or party, whether created by laws literally constitutional, by a patronage equally warranted, or by the struggles between the ins and outs under less faithful denominations, for the powers and profits of government, being hostile to the true principles of our policy, are really treasonable, and would at once appear to be so, if they were compared with the moral principles by which the constitution was constructed, and the end it had in view. Upon the same ground, the great legislative power bestowed by most of the state constitutions, would not suffice to justify the destruction of the primary end of these constitutions themselves, by any laws, however justifiable by their letter. The state and the general constitutions form but one system of policy. The spirit of this policy, to be only fairly drawn from an inspection of the whole, is adverse to aristocracy in every form, because it is not itself an aristocratical spirit. All laws driving into our policy any portion of this new spirit, will drive out a correspondent portion of the old. But we are not left to infer from the general structure of those instruments from which we deduce our policy, whether its end was aristocratical or not. Titles, exclusive privileges or advantages, so as to comprise completely the ideas of personal and pecuniary aristocracies in all forms, are every where exclaimed against, for the purpose of closing the legislative door against all such modes of destroying our policy. And the success with which these positive inhibitions have been hitherto gotten over, by the constructions of parties of interest in some form, serves to demonstrate both the inefficacy of political law to restrain such parties, and the necessity for ascertaining the principles which constitute a good or a bad government, as a test to which the people may resort for discovering the tendency of civil law.

The laws for making that which was purchased for one shilling worth twenty, and for making these twenty worth thirty or forty, as stock in the bank of the United States; exhibited so dazzling a degree of success in the legislative mode of becoming rich, that all the objections against them as a mode of poisoning our policy, disappeared; and our legislatures suddenly became staples for manufacturing anew the political wares broken to pieces by the revolution. If the English nation, at the accession of William of Orange, had restored to the crown the fraudulent prerogatives, for exercising which Charles bled and James was expelled, our legislatures would have had a precedent for reviving the monarchical policy of welding aristocracies of interest to our new government in a thousand forms, by legal distributions of wealth at the publick expense. Privileges and monopolies, flowing from law, are of the same nature as if they came from prerogative, like the same poison poured from different phials. The English declaration of rights at the revolution, does not more explicitly condemn the oppressions it corrects, than our state constitutions condemn the principle of creating aristocracies by legal privileges. This declaration is the most explicit acquisition obtained by that nation at the expense of much civil war, in favour of civil liberty, but its benefits have been defeated by making the statute book a receptacle for the same frauds which were formerly recorded in the archives of prerogative. An hundred laws to create an hundred aristocracies of interest, if they collect as much money, are the same to a nation, as an hundred of queen Elizabeth's monopoly grants. These laws require armies and penalties to defend them, live in the United States upon agriculture, and fear a militia.

No government ever commenced its operations with so pliable a people, as that of the United States. Among their most firmly rooted principles, were an aversion for legal privileges, aristocracies of interest and standing armies; and an affection for agriculture, commerce and the militia. By considering the effects of legal patronage upon the first triumvirate, and the effects of withholding it from the second, its force upon national policy, and its capacity to produce one evil as a cause for another, will be seen. A military nation, received from the revolution, has been treated for thirty years with stockjobbing laws; and by throwing away three hundred millions during the same period upon a trifling standing army, without expending a shilling on the militia, an argument has been made against reposing in the latter any future dependence.

The difficulty of proving partial laws to be publick evils, increases as the fact becomes more obvious. As feudal castles and the monkish convents increased, they were thought to yield to nations more defence and more charity, as banks, by an increase of their paper, are said to add to their wealth. The people of England have rejected the defence of the castles, the charity of the convents, and now want bread in the most fruitful of all countries, though tottering under the wealth of paper stock. Such is the effect of enriching capital or cunning by law, of robbing talents and industry of their natural right to divide property, of conveying away national rights by irrepealable laws, and of repealing by laws constitutional principles.

In England the crown lands, though alienated by absolute deeds, have been often resumed, as a publick right, without the power of the king to destroy. Laws for enabling chartered aristocracies of interest to raise a revenue, impair the national ability to defend its liberty; deeds for alienating crown lands, only impaired the ability of a king to maintain his dignity; perhaps his vices. For the first species of right, nations receive nothing; the last was often sold by kings. If the alienation of a fourth of the crown lands was a deduction from the whole, ten millions collected under laws by aristocracies of interest from a national ability to pay forty, must be an equivalent deduction. Can law justly convey publick property to enrich aristocracies of interest or individuals, (publick services being out of the question) though it is forbidden to prerogative, as too fraudulent and oppressive for monarchy? Revenue is more clearly publick property and a publick right, than those crown lands. Unhappily for England, her statesmen discovered, about a century past, that it would sell much better. And after refusing to be defrauded of the crown lands by the term 'prerogative,' in an age more enlightened she has been deluded by the terms 'charter and national credit,' into sales of her liberty and property, under the usual pretexts of statesmen, but really to enrich parties of interest, to sustain ministries, and to feed vices tenfold in number, and similar in depravity, to those which caused the alienations of crown lands.

The practice of legislation, in imitation of queen Elizabeth, of selling charters of privilege, will suggest some remedy against reviving an old evil in this new mode; and though the same applause awaits the repeal of law charters, which has been paid by all historians to her repeal of privilege charters, (because the receivers or purchasers of national rights, if they are excusable for the attempt to acquire, can never be admitted to have effected the acquisition,) yet her precedent will rob it of the honour of first breaking down the barriers of private avarice, to come at the publick interest.

 'Common consent,' Aristotle's definition of law, is only correct in reference to societies actually exercising the right of self government. Force and fraud are in fact more frequently sources of law, than consent. Of this, the argument, that a law should remain against common consent, because it had been enacted by it, is an eminent instance. Does it require a politician as crafty as the English judge who invented the mode of docking entails of land, to teach us how to dock entails of the errours, vices, follies and misfortunes of the dead upon the living? Our common consent is expressed representatively, in a mode of feudal origin, by which dead, often legislates against the will of living consent. If the representative mind consists of three portions, one third can legislate against the will of two thirds; if of two, one moiety legislates against the will of the other. Custom of feudal contrivance, has led us not only into the practice of sustaining law against the consent of two thirds, or a moiety of the legislating mind, but even in the case of the general government, to that of sustaining it against the consent of an entire legislative mind.

The union is a compact between two distinct minds, state and popular. The two branches of its legislature, consist of the separate representatives of these two minds. Its health, peace, and perhaps its existence, depends upon the consent of both of these minds to law. If either could retain a law by which it had acquired an unforeseen superiority over the other, the dissatisfaction of the ensnared party would ensue, and the law itself would be a violation of the federal compact. The constitution provides for the consent

THE LEGAL POLICY OF THE UNITED STATES

of both of these minds to law, and a feudal form has introduced a mode of making it, against the consent of one, and sometimes against that of both; so that a portion of our laws are derived neither from consent, force, or fraud, but from the form of stating a question; a source which Aristotle himself has overlooked.

In a state legislature, composed of two branches representing· one mind or body politick, a concurrence of some portion of this mind must attend the continuance of every law. In congress, the representatives of the state mind may prevent the repeal of law, which will then continue against the will of the entire popular mind, or against the will of the states, if the repeal is prevented by the popular representatives. Or if the repeal is prevented by the president, the law continues, somewhat equivocally on account of his representative character, against the will of both minds.

A perfect consolidated government guided by the popular mind, or a perfect federal government guided by the will of the states, would be very different from the existing general government. To prevent fraud or accident from destroying by means of law, the equilibrium between these contracting minds, as established by the constitution, both should be free, and neither able to retain an intended or accidental legal advantage over the other. If either of the political contracting parties composing the union, keeps the other subject to a law contrary to its will, it is equivalent to keeping the people of a state subject to a law, although the entire organ of their will should dissent therefrom. And if self preservation requires that this entire popular mind, should be able by its whole representative to repeal a law, the reason is equally cogent to prove, that each of the distinct minds composing the union, should be able to exercise the same power by its similar organ. A power which holds another to law against its will, is dominant, and inequality or war must ensue.

The danger from making law by form, contrary to principle, is greatest to the popular mind. It ought to be less; because that is a natural being having natural rights, whereas the states are artificial beings having artificial rights only. But law is the engine of usurpation upon natural rights, to which the factitious beings called aristocracies, constantly resort. The contest between artificial and natural rights is never equal. One band of these combatants may win rich and substantial booty; the other can win nothing. The reciprocity is as unequal in relation to the chance, as to the stake. The duration and small number of the Senate, affords room for more concert and dexterity, in procuring and sustaining laws favourable to factitious interests, than can be practised by the house of representatives against them.

A strict computation of chances is unnecessary to the argument. It is enough to shew, that out of an unprincipled form, the great social evils of disordering the equilibrium of the general government, and of quartering artificial burdens upon natural industry, may grow; and that these evils are unattended by a chance of equivalent benefits.

As law is the machine used by all factions and aristocracies of interest, for boarding and capturing both social and natural rights, an easy mode of recapture will discourage, whereas a difficult one excites efforts, never fraught with good to human happiness. An advertisement informing a nation, that whatever can be gotten by legal frauds shall be sacred, will tend as much to the encouragement of virtue, as one, that such acquisitions from social rights shall be suddenly reclaimed, would to the encouragement of vice.

Let us view this subject by the light of moral and republican principles. One branch of a legislature is not invested with a power of making law affirmatively, in a society exercising self government, because it cannot express the common consent, on account of representing only a portion of it. If the reason for prohibiting it from making law by saying yes, is good, how can the same reason allow it to make law by saying no? Shall a law continue? Shall a law be repealed? are the same questions in substance; but English monarchy and feudality saw the advantages they would gain over the popular interest by the latter form. It would enable both to retain every encroachment upon popular rights, by the affirmative will of either, under the garb of a negative erroneously supposed to be inefficacious. The pretence, that this negative was necessary in a government of orders, for the preservation of each, is exploded by discovering that such an end would have been much better effected by the principle, that no law should continue without the consent of all. This, in a government composed of three minds or three orders, would have been Aristotle's 'common consent.' And whilst such a principle would have produced the common safety of these distinct political beings, it would have repressed the encroachments of either, by affording a peaceable mode of self security to all, infinitely more effectual for the meditated end, than the civil wars produced by the defectiveness of the remedy resorted to.

Republican and moral principles concur with the language of all our constitutions, in the opinion, that legislatures are divided into several branches, not to enable one only to make law against the will of two others, but to obtain a sounder expression of that common consent, which is the basis of law in a free government. Let us imagine these branches to be three, each consisting of an hundred members; why should one hundred be able to retain law against the will of two? Suppose there had been only one legislative chamber of three hundred members; would the negative of one hundred members on the proposed repeal of a law, have controlled the negative of the two hundred as to its continuance?

By our constitutions a power to legislate is bestowed, generally, upon several legislative branches; but the legislature of Vermont consists of a single chamber. Bestowed either upon several branches or this single chamber, it is an affirmative power. What reason can exist why this affirmative power should in substance be acquired by a moiety or a third of the legislature, when it consists of two or three branches, and be yet incapable of being acquired by a moiety or third of a legislature consisting of a single chamber? Legislative power is bestowed on both in the same terms. Yet in consequence of the feudal form of putting a question, this moiety or third of the legislature constituted in the first mode, makes law by retaining it; whereas no such power can be exercised by the legislature constituted in the second mode, although the powers given to both are precisely the same.

Thus a body of men gains out of a form moulded by itself and subject to its own pleasure, a power to legislate, bestowed neither by the constitution, nor by republican principles, nor even suggested by sound reasoning, in a government planted in a compromise between three orders. When the true question is 'whether an old law shall continue,' the collateral question 'whether a new law shall pass,' important only from its incidental influence upon the true question, bestows upon a negative vote an affirmative power, or a substantial legislative power, which it could never exercise by voting affirmatively. And a negative upon a bill by one legislative branch, supersedes negatives upon the continuance of a law by two, in consequence of an arbitrary form, in a country whose policy it is, that law should be the genuine result of common consent affirmatively enunciated.

This invention of the English orders, transplanted by blind imitation into our policy, cannot be favourable to this policy, if it was favourable to those orders. But it may be highly favourable to all the legal aristocracies of interest, which may be created to subsist on the common interest, by impeding the recovery of national rights, conveyed in charters or laws fraught with privileges like those of queen Elizabeth. And if we should even so far violate the principles of our policy, as to reduce the people to the station of a democratick, and to exalt all the charter or privileged men, to that of an aristocratick order, yet self preservation would require a negative in each upon law, as the only security against the disorders, invariably produced in the best constructed species of political balance. It is particularly remarkable therefore, under a system of government, acknowledging the sovereignty of the people, and reprobating privileges and exclusive interests, that laws may be retained against the will of this acknowledged sovereignty, after they have been found to operate to a revolutionary extent, in favour of the reprobated principles. If the form, by which an anomaly so egregious has been ingrafted upon our policy, without the concurrence of the sovereign we acknowledge, was skilfully contrived to yield advantages to the ennobled English orders, its introduction here is no proof of popular acuteness; and if this device is found there to be favourable to the sprouts from the principle of privilege or exclusive interest, in all the modifications produced by modern manners, its partiality to the family of factitious honour, ought not to excuse its partiality to the family of factitious wealth, in the eyes of a sovereign who must supply it.

The numerical analysis is incompetent to the detection of real legislation, by an unconstitutional authority, under a negative ceremony; but the moral will discern with ease, that it is pregnant with effects founded in bad principles, or at least in principles adverse to those of our policy. It invests minorities and parties of interest, with a formidable power of retaining oppressive or fraudulent laws, which the majority and the publick interest, wish to repeal. It corrupts the outs or opposition, as well as the administrators of the government, because the leaders of both are equally liable to be annexed to some part of interest by wealth or ambition. And it combines together these rivals, for self preservation, so as to resemble an army, which the people could not disband except by its own vote, however its officers may struggle with each other for command and lucrative employments.

Hence all aristocracies of interest contend, that it should be easy to pass laws, when we can only conjecture their consequences; and hard to repeal them, when these consequences are known; and the sovereignty of the people, being persuaded that it is impregnably fortified by a negative against unforeseen evils, and an inability to arrest such as it feels is gradually inclosed within a circle of long and perpetual laws, drawn by this negative magician; and finally becomes a pageant as powerless as the grand Lama; whilst factitious interests become oppressors as tyrannical as his substitutes.

Attempts to reconcile opposite principles are causes of party spirit and revolution. To sanction law by common consent or publick will, is one principle; by the will of a combination among parties of interest, another. If the first principle can only prevent, whilst the other can retain fraudulent laws, it is obvious on which side lies the ability to make encroachments. One is armed with a power strictly defensive, and utterly incapable of conquest; the other with a power of retaining every acquisition it can make, by its frequent and sudden inroads upon the territory of its honest and peaceable neighbour.

The unsettled question in relation to the right of instruction, aggravates the evil of minority legislation, and the moral right of self government is defeated in both cases by form and ceremony. In one, the mode of putting a question confers on minorities a legislative power withheld by the constitution; in the other, the mode of giving the instruction, is also used to confer on the representative a power of legislating contrary to the will of his constituents; and yet both the minorities and the representatives acknowledge a moral obligation to be bound by the wills they respectively defeat. Although a nation holding extensive territory, resorts to district election, as the only possible mode of acquiring the benefits of representation, it cannot exercise, it is said, the inherent right of instructing its agents, in the same practicable mode. Had the division of election, heretofore celebrated among the moral beauties of our policy, been rejected, representation must also have been banished from it. Aggregate instruction is as impracticable as aggregate election. But supposing that both or either could have been effected, it was not desirable, if the principle of division is as salutary in restraining the passions of the multitude as the powers of a government. And although it is alleged that the risk of re-election is a sufficient substitute for the right of instruction, it is an argument so analogous to the notion of thieves, 'that the risk of the gallows justifies the theft,' as hardly to deserve refutation upon the still stronger ground, that it would deprive nations of self defence whilst their ruin was effecting, upon a speculation quite useless after it is accomplished. A combination among parties of interest, founded upon the negative mode of legislation, thus absolved from the supervision and restraint of instruction, might continue legal tyranny fraudulently or accidentally introduced, against the will of a nation and of the majority of its representatives, if it possesses no practicable mode of instruction; and its own money would at the same time pay the cost of treason and be used in corrupting election itself.

Liberty, like religion, is lost by planting it in dogma. Roman Catholick christianity was corrupted by heathen ceremonies. The United States have burst through the political superstitions of church and state, and protection and allegiance, into the principle of national right to make and alter national laws; and boast of constitutions calculated to prevent legislatures from introducing legal oppression. Yet we see them suffering law, from a superstitious veneration for a feudal ceremony, highly favourable to the objects of all aristocracies of interest, which will use it to secure the species of property arising from legal frauds, by inculcating an opinion, that it is dangerous to amend constitutions. Such an opinion deserves consideration, as a powerful ally of the two forms, by which the negative of a minority retains obnoxious laws, and the only practicable mode of instruction, is disqualified for restraining perfidious agents.

As the human mind is unable to foresee or to provide against its own devices; a code of political law, is as unable to provide completely for the safety of publick rights, as a code of civil, for private. Perhaps this is making too great a concession to the adversaries of amending constitutions, and that it might with justice be asserted, that it is much more difficult to foresee and restrain the arts of cunning politicians, aided by means infinitely greater, than those of ignorant, disunited individuals.

Suppose a legislature appointed to prepare a code of civil law, to be dissolved upon a supposition that the work was perfected. If crimes and evasions, unforeseen and unprovided against, should occur, who would contend that it would ruin the nation, should it appoint another legislature to correct these crimes and evasions? Criminals and sophists. Ought nations to hallow guilt or errour by suffering the evils they cause?

The temptations to violate political law are greater, and the danger of punishment less, than in the case of civil law. In one case, wealth and power are solicitors for crime; in the other, temptation is comparatively trivial, and the spectre of punishment stares it in the face. Will the terror of the gallows seduce men to violate civil law, and the allurement of wealth and power deter them from violating political, so that the stratagems of theft must be eternally met by new remedies, whilst those of avarice and ambition will never require them? If a party should persuade a nation to make no more laws against fraud, would it not be considered as a band of thieves? The illustration of the opinion 'that it is dangerous to devise new remedies against avarice and ambition,' by the idea of prohibiting amendments or additions to civil law, is too feeble. Individuals would retain the right and the power of self defence, against injuries from individuals, for which the civil code provided no remedy; but all aristocracies of interest, or combinations of avarice and ambition, work their ends with civil law, against which a nation has no remedy, if amendments or additions to political law should fall into disuse. Wherever the idea of political law exists, frequent charges will be laid before the people against those in power, for violating it; and as these charges will seldom want some foundation, they will sometimes cause the nation to transfer the reins of government to the accusers; but they seldom or never produce any effectual new political law, because the accusers, by acquiring power, are converted into an aristocracy of interest; at least to the extent of the universal desire to hold good offices; and instantly become more inclined to extend this power by the help of the precedents of their predecessors, than to contract it, by declaring these precedents to be unconstitutional or fraudulent.

The policy of the United States is attached to the idea of a government contrived for dispensing benefits equally, (the case of payment for publick services excepted) and adverse to all partial dispensations. In an extensive country, conventions (as we understand the term) are the only guardians of this policy, and civil law is every where the chief or only instrument by which it is destroyed. A rejection of its creator and guardian, and a confidence in its destroyer, would be a revival of the policy by which mankind are universally enslaved.

Legal prescience must for ever remain imperfect, because the evolutions of the human mind can never be limited. How can unchangeable constitutions manage this prolifick being? It leaves every thing behind which does not move with it, except mere matter, and hence laws thus forsaken are called 'a dead letter.'

When the mind, upon which a constitution was calculated to operate, is gone, though it may exist embalmed in the statute book like magna charta, it exists in the repose and nullity of a mummy. If a moiety of national moral character is changed, then an unchanged constitution would be half dead, and the remainder would be in the state of a living twin, united to a dead one. A constitution cannot be kept alive, or efficient, except by connecting it with a living national character; this is not to be done in any other mode, than that of extending its remedies to new inventions and living abuses, before they gain strength to defy reformation. A neglect of this precaution by political, and a constant use of it, by civil law, is the cause of the difference between the danger of altering these two kinds of law. Attempts to reform abuses of long standing, generally terminate like those of the emperor Pertinax or of the French jacobins. When civil war is the reformer, it is apt to forget its business, and to create more cause for reformation than it removes. When the funding invention, which has nearly destroyed the political weight of the English nobility, and wholly overwhelmed that of the landed interest, or interest of industry, was in its infancy, this species of revolution, not provided against by magna charta (considering that instrument in the light of a constitution) might have been arrested by an addition to the political code; but now the English nation is forced to live under the oppressions of this modern invention, only to aggravate the evils to be suffered at its death.

The idea 'that it is wrong to correct wrong,' is illustrated by the errours it engrafted on Christianity in the church of Rome, and the injury that church thereby sustained. If revelation can be corrupted and its end defeated by civil laws, how can a constitution, contrived by human wisdom, be safe against the ambition and avarice of parties and individuals? It is better illustrated by the usual coincidence, between an enmity to the idea of the perfectibility of man, and an enmity to a removal of constitutional defects. Those who can see the absurdity of the notion of his perfectibility, can discover the perfection of his foresight. However inconsistent such opinions may appear, both are consistent with their motive. Improvement, the best evidence of man's imperfection, is suppressed, whilst that imperfection is exaggerated, for the purposes of taking advantage of his oversights, and subjecting him to hard government, under pretence of restraining his vicious nature, but really to defend these vicious advantages.

The most immoral motives contend most loudly for the capacity of human nature, to turn out of its hands a perfect moral work. All priesthoods assert the perfection of the dogmas under which they get wealth and honour. Magna charta, that machine for any kind of political work, has been equally praised by a haughty nobility and rebellious mobs; a papistical and a protestant episcopacy; sound and rotten borough representation; annual, triennial and septennial election; a militia yeomanry and a mercenary army; and moderate and stock taxation. Avarice, ambition and self interest, are loud in proclaiming the perfections of the principles of a government, in proportion to their own violation of these principles. A representation in England, designed to shield the people against oppression, has been gradually changed into a representation to shield oppression against the people. Whatever objections, therefore, lie against conventions, they are to be balanced against a tame surrender of the right of making political law, to fraud and corruption. Their certain tyranny is more terrible than this modern experiment, to which we are indebted for all the political good we enjoy.

As good and evil are natural enemies, eternal warfare must exist in the moral world, and the combatant which desists from hostility must be subdued. Good, too often falls into this errour; evil, seldom or never. Hence the first is more liable to lose the fruits of victory. Upon political success, it has hitherto established a wise numerical form of government, as it supposed, formed a didactick lecture for this government to govern itself by, and thrown away its arms. These are seized by the foe, forged into the shape of civil law, and turned against the late victor; and it soon appears that armed sinners are an overmatch for unarmed saints.—The control of nations over governments, can only consist of political law, enforced by good moral principles. A dread of conventions, enables governments to make political law to control nations. They are compelled to do it, if nations will not, to provide for new circumstances. Thus the design of political law is reversed, and its power for preserving a free government, destroyed.

A nation must keep and use an unlimited power over its government, or a government must acquire such a power over a nation. The question in fact lies between the genuine political law of conventions; and the spurious, made by the frauds of parties of interest, aided by the form of repealing civil laws.

It is an old question. Conventions are discredited for the same reasons, which caused kings, courtiers and publick harpies, to discredit parliaments, whilst they checked fraud and oppression. We have seen in Filmer and other court writers, all the arguments against parliaments, or their frequency, now used against conventions. Parliaments were feared, whilst they nurtured liberty and corrected abuses. Their meetings are no longer deprecated, because this fear is removed by corruption. And an apprehension of conventions in the United States is in like manner a testimonial, both of the eminent virtues they have so often displayed, and of the great abuses which have already eluded their authority.

If our allotment of political law to national conventions, and of civil to governments, so essential for the preservation of liberty, cannot be legitimately defeated by an entire government, the enormity, committed by the creature and dependant of a government, must be flagrant. Judicial decisions, in spite of every precaution, might impair and undermine the principles of any constitution, against the will both of the nation and the government, nor is there any sufficient remedy against such an evil, except additional political law. The absence of any check against this mode of changing constitutions, displays the errour of considering election, singly, as a sufficient sponsor for a free government. It is itself the child, the creature and the instrument of political law, amidst whose numerous progeny it occupies but one, though an important station. If self government or political law should yield all its rights and all its power to election, like the parent who transfers his whole estate to a favourite child, it would first become contemptible, and then die forgotten.

An ignorance of conventions and political law, and an unlimited confidence in election, have heretofore defeated the hopes of all the fabricators of free governments. Election, both legislative and executive, has been uniformly corrupted by parties of interest, political or pecuniary. In Rome, and in Italy during the three centuries quoted by Mr. Adams, by patrician orders. In England, first by feudal barons, then by the papal hierarchy, and now by the ministerial and stock parties of interest. These cases shew that aristocracies of interest in all shapes, titled or untitled, can hammer election into a political machine, resembling a curious knife said to have been invented by ingenious thieves, for cutting purses from pockets, without alarming the owners. Whig election passed the septennial law in England, and party aristocracy debauched even Addison into a strenuous vindication of this atrocious usurpation.

Elective responsibility passed a law in Virginia in 1779, declaring 'that it was inconsistent with the principles of civil liberty, and contrary to the rights of the other members of the society, that any body of men therein should have authority to enlarge their own powers, prerogatives or emoluments, and that the General Assembly cannot, at their own will, increase their allowance.' And near twenty years afterwards, in the true spirit of a party of interest, it added fifty per centum to its own wages. This addition, and the recited law, stand unrepealed to this day, as evidences of the feebleness of constitutional or political law, made by governments; and the inefficacy of election, singly, to preserve the plainest principle of civil liberty. But the election of conventions is a different thing. It looks for different qualities; it is not bribed by hopes of money or office; its offspring cannot bestow either on itself, and its life is too short to admit of corruption, or to reap power and wealth from the political law it enunciates, like a government.

It is universally allowed that forms of government are liable to decay. Without repair, decay terminates in destruction. A constitution must therefore die in the common course of nature, unless it eludes the scythe of death, for ever in the hands of fraud and ambition, by occasional restoratives. However proudly the English form of government at one period reared its head above its rivals, patriots now contemplate it, as travellers do the ruins of Palmyra. Its vital faculty is gone, though an interesting skeleton remains; but its resurrection in its purest form would now cause a degree of terror, something like what is expected at the day of judgement.

Mr. Adams's theory, and all others adverse to conventions, must establish the constancy of human opinion, or fail. Was this supposed constancy a fiction whilst he was a disciple of Nedham, and does it become a truth, now that he has changed into an enemy to this author? Can that nature be constant, which is to-day ardent for democracy, to-morrow, for monarchy? Is not a capacity for improvement inconsistent with the attribute of constancy? Can unchangeable constitutions, be adapted for a being changeable and corruptible? Would an entire nation, as accomplished as Mr. Adams, require the same form of government as a nation of savages? If the moral nature of man is inconstant, how is this inconstancy to be controlled or nourished, in order to preserve a free government, except by new political law? It is unavoidable. The only question is, whether it shall be enacted openly by conventions, or covertly by governments.

The whole family of aristocracies of interest, deprecate the frequency of conventions, on account of the imperfections of human nature. 'Man is man,' exclaim they; slyly insinuating, by the manner of the exclamation, that he is nearly a devil. To keep this devil in order, hierarchy contends that he ought to be cheated by superstition; monarchy, that he ought to be lashed by despotism; aristocracy, that he ought to be pilfered by privileges; and parties of interest, that he is fair game for all fraudulent laws. And forsooth, because man is man. And why not lash these lashers of man themselves into the path of moral rectitude, by political law? A good huntsman lashes his worst dogs into the right trail. Why should some men shrink from the mild discipline of justice, whilst they prescribe to others the cruel severities of fraud and oppression? Oh! say all parties of interest, with great solemnity, the laws for gratifying our avarice and ambition, are necessary to make other men good, or to keep them in order.

Thus thin is the delusion under which tyranny is concealed from the good, and perpetrated by the bad. And as Indians assume a new disguise when their prey detects the old, the centuries employed in emptying pockets under pretence of saving souls, may possibly be repassed in the same business, under the still grosser pretence of filling them. Conventions, alarmed by the first fraud, have expelled priests from legislatures; and legislatures, participating in the second through the channels of avarice or ambition, have colonised them with stockjobbers and legal artificial interests of every description. By political law, a paper instrument, to which no income is attached, is supposed to create a dangerous separate interest; by civil, a paper instrument, bestowing an enormous annual income, is supposed to create none. The pretended enemies of Mr. Adams's system of political law separate interests warily balanced, throw open all the avenues to power in favour of civil law separate interests without check, and furnished with the artillery which has demolished even his best conceived balances. A pecuniary separate interest, unchecked by some coequal power to which its growth might be dangerous, constitutes the most oppressive conceivable species of government, because it collects private wealth for itself from the people by its own laws; and it will loudly deprecate conventions, because the abuse admits of no other remedy.

Such arguments as assail conventions, have been suggested by the same motives, against every moral improvement, to which the present age is indebted for all the happiness it enjoys. Christianity was dangerous in the opinion of pagan priests. Galileo's speculations were dangerous in the opinion of the Pope. Toleration is dangerous in the opinion of established churches; and conventions are dangerous in the opinion of every separate interest. Yet Christianity prevailed; Galileo's principles triumphed; toleration exploded persecution; and conventions bestowed upon the United States the best practical government which has hitherto appeared.

All craftsmen, or parties of interest, exclaim 'that human nature is too imperfect to avail itself of the principles of political morality.' Ought idolatry to have defeated christianity by the same argument; or are the principles of christianity less perfect than those of political morality? Or is human nature capable of being benefited by good religious, but not by good political principles? Let prejudice, zeal and interest jointly answer these questions. There is no opinion more injurious to mankind, than 'that virtuous nations only can maintain a free government.' It enlists on the side of despotism all persons of a misanthropick turn of mind, by a computation of the human character, founded in a casual complexion, and liable to be false; and which would not justify the inference, if it was true. It enlists industrious men under the same banner, by terrifying them with the consequences of indulging vicious beings with liberty. It cuts off the hope of improving the morals of mankind, by excluding the most successful preceptor. And it excludes the remedy against abuses, by asserting that it must fail, if the nation is not virtuous. Without losing time in shewing, that the difficulty of ascertaining the prevalence of national virtue or vice; and whether it is natural or artificial; and the want of a standard for fixing the quantity able to maintain good, or requiring bad government, leaves the position in a state of generality, incapable of being proved or disproved; I shall upon other grounds advert again to this doctrine, on account of its special hostility to the conventional mode of preserving good political principles.

Which is the best defender of human rights, virtue or wisdom? Cannot an individual maintain his rights unless he is virtuous? Behold the virtuous fool and the wise knave. If a philosopher should run through the world exclaiming to every vicious man he met, 'Sir, you cannot be free, because you are vicious; the best thing you can do is to become my slave,' would he make one proselyte? Would he be thought a maniack or an apostle? Why has the same egregious absurdity, preached by politicians, succeeded? Simply

527.

because it was favourable to abuses, frauds, parties of interest, and tyranny in every form. All associations, chartered and unchartered for trade, city government, banking, and speculations of every kind, earnestly preach and sedulously in practice, contemn this doctrine. They rely upon wisdom and republican principles for the security of their own rights, and deny the efficacy of the same security in respect to national rights, because of a defect of virtue in a nation, of which they compose a portion, not more virtuous than the rest. They are perpetually calling partnership and separate interest conventions, in order to make use of their wisdom, to defend legal or chartered privileges, to advance private interest, and to annoy the publick; but they will not allow nations to use their wisdom for self defence in the same mode, because they want virtue. If wisdom and strength enables individuals to maintain their rights, why may not social rights be maintained by the same agents? Is it virtue which enables one nation to conquer another, or a treacherous faction to enslave their own country? Virtue could not protect the Roman Senators against the swords of the Gauls, and vice can see that eleven men can control the tyranny of one. If minorities often make themselves tyrants by wisdom, why may not nations preserve their liberty by it? Why do all minor societies find wisdom and republican principles, the best securities against their own vices, if they are no check upon national vices? Why are conventions useful to them, and pernicious to nations? And why are additional conventional laws necessary for the safety of sub-societies, but not for national safety? The solution of these inconsistencies is short and plain. Conventions, wisdom, and republican principles, are the best controllers of vice hitherto discovered. All sub-societies, therefore, use them to restrain the vices of their own members. But they are not willing that nations should use them, for the same reason by which they are induced to do it. Being themselves the least virtuous members of every nation, they are unwilling to suffer the control they carefully inflict. To this cunning and self interest mankind are indebted for the doctrine, 'that they cannot be free unless they are virtuous.' Whereas the fact is, that virtue may be more safely dispensed with in a national convention, than in an inferior association, or in an individual; because wisdom in the first case is exposed to no temptation to vice, as it can discern no object to defraud or oppress; whereas such objects, in abundance, assault the wisdom of exclusive interests. Wisdom is of no use without will, and national will with us can only be expressed by conventions, òr additional political law. By withholding from a nation the use both of its wisdom and will, it must become a statue, and some aristocracy of interest, a Prometheus, who will animate it with such civil law as he pleases, but never inspire it with celestial fire.

Conventions are the remedy against the errour of trusting to some dogma for a free government, and against the danger of despair, whenever this dogma is exploded. That liberty cannot exist without virtue, that it depends upon education, and that it is graduated by skilfully balancing the members of the numerical analysis, are among the most specious and the most pernicious. By making virtue a necessary antecedent to a free government, their natural moral order is transposed, and the prospect for both is diminished. Those moral principles upon which every fair association, political or private, must be built, constitute in their operation a school for virtue, by the restraints or responsibilities of which justice to associates is enforced, whilst morality is impressed by habit. No opinion could be inculcated more fatal to a science, than that it must precede instruction. The second dogma is more dangerous, as containing a greater portion of truth; because education is undoubtedly one of the sources of wisdom, although it might be fatal to a nation, to mistake it for wisdom itself. Comparisons between the Augustan, and some early age of the Roman Commonwealth; between some Gothick age, and that of Lewis the 14th of France; between England and France; and between Scotland and the United States; would demonstrate that free government was not graduated by education. The refutation of the third, as infinitely the most dangerous, has been the chief object of these essays; for although Mr. Adams himself has proved it to have been the most unfortunate of all in practice, he has persuaded himself that it is the most perfect in theory.

Mr. Godwin has said, 'that a scheme of national education is the most formidable and profound contrivance for despotism that imagination can suggest;'* and hence concludes that education ought to be left to itself. The philosophick, as well as the religious fanatick, must be detected, to come at practical truth. If education is this powerful instrument, liberty, by foregoing its use, would experience the same fate, as she would suffer from surrendering to despotism the exclusive use of fire arms. And as these, however dangerous to liberty, united with the invention of standing armies,

* Pol. Jus. vol. 2. p. 298.

may be made subservient to her safety by a good militia system, so a good system of education, would send large contributions into that reservoir of materials, of which knowledge is compounded. The superstitious mode of trial by battle, would have been rendered too ridiculous even for its Gothick æra, by allowing to one, and withholding from the other combatant, the most formidable weapon which imagination could suggest. Neither philosophers nor priests will ever be able so far to change the materials of human nature, as to invest one with the powers of all. It is difficult to form education into a despot by precept; for however undisciplined the militia of man's other powers may be, education will constantly lean towards their regulation. But if a fraudulent system of education and a mercenary army, can bestow long life upon a tyrannical form of government, it is probable that a just system of education and a sound militia, would perpetuate a free one. Why should auxiliaries so powerful to a bad cause, be renounced by a good one? Wisdom will work for vice as well as for virtue. The rulers of the civilized world at this time, possess a far greater portion of knowledge, than the individuals composing a nation could ever acquire; some displaying its effects under the tutelage of political law, and others its effects under no such restraint. And a comparison between these effects is a decisive proof, both that Mr. Godwin's idea of extracting from wisdom unrestrained by political law a free government, is chimerical; and also that this restraint, imposed by national wisdom, causes the wisdom of governours to be infinitely more subservient to publick good. The facts on both sides go to demonstrate the impossibility of national freedom, if nations, by losing the custom of enacting and enforcing political law, should suffer this right to be gradually usurped by their governments. The doctrine, 'that school masters can keep us out of tyranny, so as to enable nations to dispense with political law,' is a dependence like that upon priests, to keep us out of purgatory. But if a mode of education, like a standing army, can change the nature of a government, and constitute the most formidable contrivance for despotism, a nation, to preserve its liberty, must have wisdom enough to influence this moral mode of destroying it, just as it must control a standing army, for the same purpose, by the superior physical force of a militia. Education must be supervised by the same vigilant national wisdom necessary to defend liberty against whatever can be used to destroy it; and the same care must be taken to prevent it from being converted into an instrument by a sect, religious, political or chartered, as to withhold from avarice and ambition the use of a standing army. The benefits derived by mankind from academical institutions, though fettered or corrupted by despotism or superstition, are a pledge for their effect when nurtured by the principles of a free government. How great is our debt to those of Athens only, during a short period! The objection to an expense, of which a proportion falls on those who can receive no part of the education, would be stronger against publick taxes to support government, because many more people participate in the good effects of academical institutions, than in the salaries or benefits of publick offices. An augmentation of knowledge always dispenses some good to the whole nation, whereas the majority frequently suffers much evil from certain modes of civil government. The access to wealth and power is widened by education, and contracted by its absence, because genius, however poor, will acquire knowledge if it is introduced into a country, just as the art of weaving has spread from a few looms throughout the civilized world. A publick patronage of a few good colleges, is therefore a patronage of genius; and as the chance for it is equal among all, the poor, from their superiority of number, will draw most prizes in the lottery of knowledge, established by means of colleges, chiefly supported by the rich. It is only necessary to chasten academical institutions by the same good moral principles necessary to make a good government. To establish responsibility; to make income depend on merit; and to banish offices for life, sinecure salaries, and idle, vicious, or incompetent functionaries.

The difference between knowledge and education is certainly considerable. We often find most liberty attached to the inferior stock of education, but we should be able to discern a more equal distribution of knowledge attached to it. Without attempting to reconcile theory and fact in such cases, it is sufficient to observe, that civil laws contrived to dispense knowledge to parties, sects, or exclusive interests of any kind, and ignorance to the majority, are precisely of the same nature with those contrived to dispense wealth and poverty in the same way. A wise clergy and an ignorant laity, or a wise stock interest and an ignorant agricultural interest, produce the same consequences as any other rich and poor orders or interests. Either molten or printed images can forge and fix fetters. Hence it behoves a nation having wisdom enough to be free, to supervise the conduct of its government by conventions, and to prevent a fraudulent management of education, as well as of property, by civil laws, for the purposes of fostering parties of interest, defending fraud, and maintaining despotism.

In the United States, agriculture covers the interest of a vast majority. Whatever civil laws pass for distributing knowledge or wealth, operate against her; because being the mother which suckles all other interests, her own children cannot suckle her. Our landed interest corresponds with the tenantry of England, being composed, generally, of cultivators. The English landlords are satisfied with a policy which distributes wealth and knowledge by civil laws, because they are themselves the chief objects of its fraudulent bounty, and their tenants the chief assignees of ignorance and poverty. The gross errour of the American agricultural interest, in imagining itself to bear a resemblance to the English landlord interest, may beguile it into the English system of legislating ways and means for extracting wealth from labour, and of course leaving it ignorance; but if it should, our cultivators will voluntarily inflict on themselves the evils, under which the English tenantry unwillingly groan. Laws for dividing landed, and accumulating legal wealth, will also convey mean talents to real, and splendid to artificial property; and the effects of moral superiority inevitably follow. Even laws with the specious object of diffusing education, may be contrived to distribute knowledge and ignorance, so as to establish the power of legal aristocracies of interest. It is easy to educate agriculture and labour at their own expense, sufficiently for submission, but insufficiently to balance or control the high moral accomplishments bestowed upon aristocracies of interest, as an appurtenance of the wealth transferred to them from agriculture and labour by fraudulent laws. Projects of this kind will be used to conceal from the mass of a nation, the undeniable truth, that no such experiments can save its liberty, whilst laws exist for creating factitious wealth; because all parties will use such a legislative power to produce great inequalities of wealth, and this wealth will carry with it those talents which guide all civilized governments, though all the rest of the nation should receive ordinary educations.

The idea of equalising knowledge, is as impracticable as that of equalising property by agrarian laws. Both are extremities of political fancy. But the opposite extremities are unfortunately practicable. Knowledge, and property or wealth, may be rendered extremely unequal by fraudulent laws. And it often happens, that the destroyers of primogeniture, for the sake of dividing lands, are so inconsistent, as to accumulate wealth by laws founded in the contrary principle. A power to distribute knowledge or wealth, is a power to distribute both. One is annexed to the other. A free government cannot subsist with either power, because selfishness invariably patronises itself and its adherents, and allots ignorance and poverty to the mass of people, always necessary to be sacrificed to the legal opulence of a few. If knowledge and wealth are left to be distributed by industry, a beneficial excitement of effort, and a division sufficient to preserve a free government, are produced. By dividing lands, and creating stock of various kinds, drawing twenty millions a year from labour, a double operation to great extent is produced, of enriching and enlightening factitious interests, and of impoverishing the landed and working interests of the United States, both as to their minds and estates. This impoverishment of mind will endow the legal interests with the offices of government, convert representation into a mantle for fraud, and our government into an elective aristocracy. Had these twenty millions remained in the hands of agriculture and labour, they could have annually purchased knowledge to that amount; and the difference between this annual supply, and its transference by law from them to factitious interests, constitutes the pure principle of aristocracy. Common good, is the best principle for industry and majority; partial, for fraud and minority. If the first associates assign their wealth and knowledge to their natural enemies, as they have generally done, the war will terminate in the old way. By cutting up the landed interest into little farms, the interest of industry and majority will gradually lose that dissemination of moral talents, necessary to restrain the frauds of the whole family of legal, exclusive or aristocratical interests. The interest of the majority must perish, unless a sound mind is lodged somewhere within it. To cheat it of the share of knowledge by which it may maintain its rights, under pretence of making it all mind, would be like persuading the other members to cut off the head, and to depend for their future safety on a new contrivance for making all of them heads. Such is the reimbursement promised by a system of general education, for the removal of wealth and knowledge from agriculture and industry to legal interests. It resembles the device of sumptuary laws to hide the cause of luxury. Remove the cause, and the luxury ceases. Remove the frauds which make a majority poor and ignorant, by making a minority rich and wise, and these evils also cease. Sumptuary laws cannot prevent luxury, if its cause remains; nor can the poverty and ignorance of the mass of a nation be removed by any system of education, if laws exist for enriching a minority. The laws enabling individuals to amass great wealth by means of the spoils of conquest, enslaved Rome. Laws for enriching parties of interest, by tythes, offices, sinecures and stock, enslave Europe. A division of wealth, by industry and talents, never enslaved any nation. Some idea of this intelligence from experience, seems by their constant hatred of heavy taxation, to have been planted in the minds of the people, of which ignorance is often cheated by the arts of fraud. Sometimes by charges of sordid parsimony, advanced by avaricious parties of interest; sometimes by means too indirect and intricate to be unravelled by instinct; and at last by pretences of associating it in a plot for plundering and enslaving posterity.

Inferior agents in all wicked plots suffer punishment in this world, whilst their leaders often avoid it until the next. It seems as if these leaders hoped to expiate their own crimes by chastising their instruments, without suspecting that they may be reserved for severer justice. Thus parties of interest universally treat the mass of nations, for assisting them in their conspiracy against posterity. They reap the whole benefit of the fraud, and use it to corrupt and change the existing government. If, however, the fraud of transmitting debt, taxes and tyranny, to posterity, was assented to by every individual of an existing age, to gratify its follies or enrich its parties of interest, the assenting age itself would still be a party of interest or an aristocracy, in relation to its successors. It endeavours to enrich itself or pay its debts at the expense of a vast majority, for which it legislates without any authority. It violates its own principles of representation and taxation far more tyrannically, than was attempted by England against these states. The taxes imposed are infinitely heavier. Not a single cord of sympathy draws commiseration towards the unborn. Their money is spent without a possibility of the reimbursement, whatever it amounts to, drawn by cunning from the vices created by fraud and oppression. The parties of interest who receive the tax by anticipation, avoid the small check of contributing towards it. And the oppressor having enjoyed his spoil, has gotten out of reach, before the oppressed acquires a power of resistance.

The celebrated idea, 'that the people are their own worst enemies,' expressed by Ovid in his assumption of Romulus, and alluded to by Garth in his preface to a translation of the author, in the observation, 'that after a people are preserved from the enemy, the next care should be to preserve them from themselves,' is adverse to the argument against a system of legislation in favour of parties of interest or aristocracy. Romulus himself was the author of the patrician party of interest at Rome, which murdered him, appropriated to themselves the publick wealth, oppressed the people, and drove them finally under the dominion of one tyrant, as a refuge from many. The Spartans never thought of these saviours against themselves. They were a democracy of masters over a democracy of slaves. These masters remained long free, because they trusted to themselves for safety. Nations who receive safety, receive at the same time a master, whether that safety is bestowed by law or by force. If by law, it must be the donation of some party of interest, and as it is of the essence of all such, to elevate without merit, and to enrich without industry, the genuine cements of honest society, and the motives inciting men to good and useful actions, must all be destroyed. By seeking for honour and wealth in title and law, men scatter curses. Left to feed their passions by the help of merit and industry, they scatter blessings.

Mercier, a French political writer, ascribes our constitutions to the wisdom of European philosophers, and foresees our ruin from mercantile guile. If the assertion is true, our gratitude for a policy, which that quarter of the earth has been unable to equal, ought to be measured by their envy; and when this envy shall cease, no reason for our gratitude will exist. His apprehension glances at its termination, but he has contracted a great idea, after he had almost compassed it, down to nothing, by the epithet 'mercantile.' Knowing that guile and venality led the way to despotism, but seeing none established by our political laws, he turned his eye towards the mercantile, and overlooked the capacity of civil law to issue it in copious streams. The mercantile, concealed like guilt in the breast of an individual, bears no resemblance to the political, published like justice in the face of the statute book. One never destroyed a free government; the other never failed to do it, unless the nation destroyed that. When the English clergy owned 28,115 knights' fees out of 60,215 into which the whole kingdom was divided, the guile and venality of this party of interest, made it the pest and the tyrant of the country for five centuries. If our exports amount to $40,000,000, twenty of which are expended in taxes and the sustenance of labour, and the banks have already gotten a moiety of the remaining twenty, they have outstript the monks in availing themselves of the civil law mode of growing rich. The clerical party of interest contended successfully for a long time, that to tax it was wicked; the banking has successfully advanced the same doctrine. The clerical intrigued with kings and beneficed the sons of nobles, to obtain the support of the government; the banking bribes governments, and infuses stock into agriculture. The clerical pretended to bestow heaven on·the laity; and the banking pretends to bestow wealth on labour.

The republican principle of general or publick interest, cannot be successfully assailed by the mercantile guile and venality of individuals. But the guile and venality emitted by civil law in the shape of a party of interest, endeavours by every expedient, to cut up the general interest, for the sake of its own safety or aggrandizement; and soars above little individual frauds in the sunshine of legislative favour. To these parties of interest nations owe the exclamations against a militia, and the commendations of standing armies. The conquest of the Roman empire; the emancipations of Holland and the United States; the resistance of France against a combination of nearly all Europe, aided by her deserted standing army; the resistance of Spain, defrauded of her standing army, against France; and the consequences of a single defeat to countries confiding in standing armies, can never plead successfully for a militia, where the system of rearing separate interests prevails; because a militia cannot exist where its natural ally (the general interest) has been massacred up by civil law, into a herd of parties of interest, actuated by that species of guile and venality by which free governments are destroyed. If men could be made wise as well as knavish, by self interest, the majority would see the same principle in the doctrines of saving nations against themselves, of defending them by standing armies, and of governing them by a knot of parties of interest, intertwined like a knot of serpents for self gratification. A standing army being itself a legislative party of interest, becomes naturally the associate and ally of a policy compounded of such parties. If a militia cannot defend a country, the inhabitants cannot long exercise the right of self government. If it cannot repel invasion, it cannot prevent the usurpation of an army which can. A government at the head of an army able to control the people, will never regard election but as another instrument to rivet oppression.

The events of the revolutionary war are misrepresented by the combination of parties of interest (at the head of which, it is to be remembered, that the existing government by which they are created or sustained, is always stationed) as sufficient to explode a reliance upon a militia. During that war they performed many gallant actions, often gained victories unconnected with regulars, and submitted at least to equal hardships, without bounties, without clothing, without half pay, without donations of land, and without mutiny. A theory of what might have been achieved by a great regular army, is arrayed against a mass of actual services rendered by the militia. But it ought never to be forgotten, that the maladies which swept away the first small army, would have reached a great one; that the inability to arm, clothe, feed and physick it, would not have been removed by its increase; that the small army hardly suffered those unavoidable privations, which a large one would have redressed in its own way; and that this experiment of a militia, was made by a government without resources, without military knowledge, unestablished, and divided into thirteen independent sections.

No department of the legislative policy of the states, separately or united, seems to me to be more defective, than the management of the militia; which, like a government, is capable of being corrupted or destroyed by bad principles. The militia of Virginia, for instance, is commanded by officers holding commissions by a more independent tenure than the judges; namely, during good behaviour, of which they are themselves to decide; and these officers are almost entirely promoted by rank. Responsibility is lost or enfeebled. Successional power, as poisonous to our policy as hereditary, supersedes the qualities fit for office; and patrician notions are infused into those who ought to be the vindicators of equal rights. If civil offices were made successional, if they were held for life, and if the incumbents were only responsible to their own corps, it would beget a political exhibition resembling a militia, moulded by the same principles.

The commendations bestowed by foreigners upon our form of government, are suggested by an inspection of our political laws and the principles they inculcate upon civil legislation. It is probable that a discouragement and neglect of agriculture and the militia, was never suggested by this inspection to the most capricious imagination; and yet it is equally probable, that our legislatures have devoted a thousand fold more time to the single subject of banking, than to both. The maxim, 'that nations cannot be free without a sound militia,' is reiterated by our constitutions; and our legislatures bestow penalties and contempt on this mode of defence associated with the general interest; and pay, clothes, rations, bounties and honour, on a mode of defence associated by its moral nature with legal beings of the same moral nature. Fraud and folly then express astonishment at beholding a good thing uncultivated, less thrifty than a bad one carefully nurtured. Suppose the comparison had been, between a regular army nursed by privations, and a militia fed by money. Let an honest inquirer after truth, ascertain the amount spent on the perishing modes of defence by parties of exclusive interest, military and naval, since the revolution, and estimate the impetus which the same sum judiciously applied, would have communicated to the general and immortal mode of defence.

Perhaps the principles and doctrines of England, for many centuries, in favour of liberty, so incomprehensible to the rest of Europe, and so useful to these United States, arose from her long disuse of standing armies, and her moderate recourse to them, after the rest of Europe had been made subservient to the chiefs of these parties of interest. Providence seems to have raised up another nation in the United States, better isolated against the pretexts under which the military separate interest poison is administered. Oceans in front and rear, on one flank a barren, and on the other an enervating climate, with a vast expanse of territory within these natural circumvallations, ought to enable them forever to reject the bitter potion, so long resisted by their ancestors within the shadow of powerful rivals. The legislative neglect of agriculture and the militia, and cultivation of parties of interest to enrich and for defence, have been selected to shew the necessity of distinguishing between good and bad principles, for the purpose of preserving the loyalty of legislation to the political laws, enunciated by the sovereign national authority.

Rely not upon oaths for this loyalty. They were formerly used to hide treachery by kings themselves, who swore to defend liberty, fulfil treaties, and observe charters. Oaths never stop the current of consequences flowing from laws inconsistent with the principles of constitutions. Prospective oaths may possibly be presumptuous and impious, in promising mental stability, when the Deity has not implanted that quality in man. Being taken according to law, and broken according to nature, the reverence which would have sanctified the obligation, had it been limited to past occurrences, is weakened. As a security for the observance of political law, the sovereign power of construction to heal the most tender consciences, renders them quite insignificant. A thousand instances of this species of party medical skill have occurred. 'The constitution, the laws of the United States, and treaties, shall be the supreme law of the land.' Construction can condemn the second number of this sentence into an allegiance to the third, and open the way for a subserviency of the first to the two last. It can substitute for the responsibility of the house of representatives to the people, a submission to the President and Senate. It can require law unsuggested by discretion, and unexamined by the understanding. And it can invest the President and Senate, having the concurrence of the judges, with a power to impose taxes, incur debts, dismember the territory, and legislate almost without limitation. Let us rather then establish principles, than trust to oaths, for the maintenance of our policy.

Patronage must be recorded among the modes of destroying forms of government; or political, by civil law. It can seduce the servants of God to advocate fraud and superstition. It excites talents against truth. It corrupts by hope, by fruition, and by disappointment. It teases and deceives the people by its contentions for office, into a fatal indifference towards the measures of a government. And its poisonous influence reaches electors, as well as representatives, by a thousand imperceptible channels. A balance of good and evil ought to be struck between patronage, exercised by one man or divided among a multitude. In the first shape, it is able to produce a monarchy in disguise; in the second, its factions are perishing. Exercised by various transitory bodies of men, it produces no fraudulent party combinations, because such bodies escape both from vice and rancour, as a cloud escapes from view; and the happy divisions of our government, bestow an opportunity to disperse a tumour, constituting a species of accumulation of power, of the most acrid nature, in relation to our principle of division, in all its applications. Accumulated, patronage becomes the real legislator of a nation, under whatever forms laws are constructed; and secrecy, both legislative and executive, draws over its operations a dark cloud, through which a combination of intellect and opportunity only can penetrate. Pretexts for this secrecy can never be wanting, when philosophers have represented the principle as a valuable attribute of monarchy, by inventing a theory of its usefulness, without contemplating the real objects exposed to view, whenever time has torn off the veil, under which kings, priests and statesmen, modestly pretend to conceal their virtues. Are these gentlemen less inclined to boast without merit, or to disclose their virtues, than others, because they can pay flatterers without disgrace, and repel contempt by power? If so, there is some reason for bestowing upon their humility that confidence, which consigns the fate of nations to the exclusive custody of governments, and subverts the entire political structure erected upon the principle of self government, and the sovereignty of the people. Secrecy is good for conquest, say its advocates. Let nations who wish to be free, remember that freedom cannot exist, except by controlling the conquests of their own governments at home. Patronage and secrecy united, are daily carrying some of their defences. Conquest abroad is rare, and no compensation for conquest at home. Algernon Sydney (an author, who stands as a witness, that talents and truth may be outfaced by ignorance and errour) has proved that the ardour of conviction, is preferable even in war, to the apathy of secrecy. If this ardour is too strong for discipline, where discipline is strongest, what will be the success of a free form of government, capable of being sustained only by the convictions of reason, if it is confided to the same species of apathy? Conviction built upon secrecy, is religion built upon mystery. Is religion improved or injured, by being purged of this feculency? Will that which purifies religion, corrupt a government? A system of legislation in favour of parties of exclusive interest, influenced by patronage and shrouded in secrecy, constitutes a body politick of thorough putrefaction in the eyes even of an ordinary republican anatomist. He will easily discern, that though a government founded upon a publick opinion, which opinion was to be founded upon secrecy, might rival the Indian cosmography, it could never know the principles on which it stood.

Governments, like persons or poems, ought to sustain a consistent character. Had Homer made his heroes whine in elegy, or chat in pastoral, he never would have been called the prince of poets. If antiquity had transmitted to us two fabulous poems; one, of a king, nobility and house of commons, contending for mastery during several centuries; the other, of a nation which had sustained the calamities of a long war to establish a republican government; both concluding in the catastrophe of swallowing up the long adjusting balances, and the late established republicanism, with the greedy throats of paper stock and parties of interest; would they not have been considered as monstrous violations of probability, well depicted in the first five lines of Horace's art of poetry? Still, either monster, like the God Fo, would be celebrated by its priesthood. A knowledge of principles is as indispensable to a nation, to enable it to sustain a free government, as of plants to a horticulturist. It is as absurd to ingraft aristocratical or monarchical buds upon a republican root, as a brier upon an oak. Those who pretend to this art, design gradually to eradicate the oak, and to plant the brier where it stood. By being able to class principles, we shall easily class laws. Aristocracy, by playing the Harlequin, by Protean transformations, and by its painted draperies, will no longer be able to perplex and deceive mankind. Through the robes of superstition, noble orders, paper stock, and of all the various parties of interest, the same principle will be seen, and whenever it changes its dress, every body will know it to be a new attempt to conceal its deformity.

But our efforts to understand principles, are obstructed by that toad accoucheur, construction, which pretends to draw out of the womb of the term 'republick,' every conceivable form of government, except the solitary despotism of one man; and to require her maternal tenderness and blind affection for the whole monstrous progeny. This skilful operator boasts of the still rarer art of making two beings out of one foetus, in the case of the English government; and of proving that though this republick and monarchy, this piece of hermaphrodite political mechanism, has been born again and again, according to the motley humours of barons, priests, kings, conquerors, mobs and stockjobbers, it has yet the wonderful property of being always the same, or at least, whatever our operator pleases to make of it. By travelling over history, and collecting the fraudulent or erroneous applications of the word republican to reduce it to an equivalency with the word 'government,' it is made like the term 'man,' to embrace all moral qualities, good and evil; and liberty is deprived even of her name. This device can only be eluded by a moral analysis. It will enable us to know good or bad governments, or good or bad laws, in the mode by which we distinguish between good or bad men. Its basis, is a specification of qualities, illustrated by those of our policy; as for instance, 'the sovereignty of the people, an equality of rights, an abhorrence of privileges and sinecures, free discussion, a preference of a militia to mercenary armies, a protection and not a distribution of property by law, an enmity to all parties of interest, and many others;' and not political names, always expounded by interest and party, to mean any thing or nothing. Guelph and Ghibeline, Whig and Tory, Federal and Republican, have all been equally capable of no meaning or any meaning; nor was the name Praise God Barbone, any proof of the piety of its owner. But though the names of men or of parties, are a frivolous definition of such human qualities as are liable to fluctuation, yet it is easy to invent or agree upon some epithet, denoting a definite collection of moral principles, applicable to the formation of a government, having previously arranged such as are contrary to each other in distinct divisions. Freedom of speech or its suppression, responsibility or exemption from control, division of power or its accumulation, defence by a militia or by a standing army, division of property by individual exertions or by fraudulent laws, are instances of the facility with which an arrangement might be made, exhibiting distinct classes of moral principles, capable of receiving a name, or of being used to chasten governments or legislation, without being comprised by any epithetical definition. Either the word 'republican,' may be used to convey an idea of the class of good political principles, or if it be true as is often contended, that like the names Peter and Judas, applied to men, and whig, tory, republican and federal, applied to parties, it can convey no idea of principles, then the class of good principles may be constituted into a band of sentinels, each ready to alarm nations whenever an inroad is made by fraud, avarice, or ambition, upon the quarter where he is stationed. It is true that the names of governments are as unable to convey an idea of the qualities of governours, as are the names of men or of parties of theirs, because men are still the subject named, and therefore, unless we abstract the name of our form of government, from those who may administer it, and consider it as implying a fixed class of principles, for the express purpose of controlling the fluctuating and selfish nature of these administrators, its freedom cannot continue. By relying upon the undulating temper of undisciplined man for the administration of a government, we are brought back to the most artless and savage state of society which can be conceived, and lose all those principles for regulating human nature, to which the world is indebted for its whole progress from a state of barbarity. Government, freed from moral restraints, is the result of the passions of the men who govern. Men, combined in self constituted parties, such as whig and tory, republican and federal, not being exposed to any moral restraints, similar to the political laws of constitutions for disciplining governours, act as governours

THE LEGAL POLICY OF THE UNITED STATES

would do unrestrained by political law. If governours thus unrestrained, would be guided by selfishness, avarice and ambition, all such political parties must by the laws of nature follow the same guides. If governours, at liberty to follow their own passions, would not be constituted into a genuine republick by assuming that name, neither can a name infuse republican principles into unrestrained parties of interest, of ins and outs, struggling for wealth and power. The world has never seen such parties guided by the principles which secure a free government, because they are not tied to loyalty by the ligament of political law in their party proceedings, nor would it have ever seen a republican government, if all governours had been equally at liberty to pursue the dictates of self interest or passion. Nominal republicanism, being spurious and fraudulent, takes every thing it gains from that which is real and true. The penalties paid by nations for an opinion, that good names implied good principles, caused the United States to resort to the expedient of controlling men by political law, to which they have already been indebted for a wonderful number of good governours, whilst few or none have ever been made, even by the good names judge, bishop or nobleman. Whenever they are deluded of this expedient by the artifice of adapting names to a temporary prejudice, they will pay the same penalties paid by other nations for the same absurd idolatry. Government has been called a necessary evil, on account of the propensity of governours to sacrifice the publick good to their own selfishness. Why should nations invent a whole tribe of parties of interest, which are not necessary evils, when it is so difficult to manage one? Their unrestrained vices replenish governours with the bad qualities designed to be effaced by political law; and the loyalty of folly to party names, occasionally releases a government from the wholesome restraints of political law and good moral principles, so as to place arbitrary power within the reach of the human deities of the day.

Let us draw a short comparison between the true legal policy of the United States, according to their constitutions, and that of England. The first is guiltless of making legal virtue and vice, knowledge and ignorance, wealth and poverty; of preventing industry from counteracting pernicious extremes; and of rooting out social order by levelling, or social liberty, by monopolizing laws, to exhilarate transiently mad zealots, or to enrich permanently knavish parties of interest. The disposition of wealth to individuals and parties of interest, is the essential employment of the English legal policy. In such a legal policy is lodged the kernel of every civilized tyranny, however the shells may be diversified. If a nation is wise enough to chase this single political demon out of its statute book, it can hardly lose its liberty; if it is so weak, as to surrender that book to the fiend, it cannot keep it. By leaving property to be divided by industry, the avarice of the majority is engaged on the side of a free government; by legal divisions of it, the avarice of a minority is bribed to destroy one. Nature, cries one philosopher, produces equality; it produces aristocracy or the well born, says another; our policy draws on itself the hatred of both, by refusing to both, laws for effecting that which they assert is produced by nature; and the English obtains the admiration of one, for effecting by law, that which is said to have been effected by nature.

Laws to make men rich, are like those to make them wise. Both cause innumerable evils to mankind. The wise men made by nature, are eternally overturning those made by law; and industry, like wisdom, being unequally distributed, is for ever resisting similar legal frauds against its rights. Nature, by refusing to transmit talents or industry from father to son, frowns both upon hereditary forms of government, and equalising and accumulating laws. The first are the least adverse to her decrees. Individuals of fine qualities may be selected with whom to commence monarchies or aristocracies, and accident or education may possibly cause some succession of these qualities, however certainly fools or tyrants will turn up at last. But laws for enriching, in their commencement and throughout their operation, are regardless of merit; and the equalizing theory pretends both to keep property equal among evanescent beings, and to supersede mental inequalities. The ability of industry to divide property sufficiently to destroy political combinations, was demonstrated in England by the contrivance of the king and the judges, for letting her loose upon entails; and the ability of accumulating laws to destroy this wholesome operation, was subsequently demonstrated, by letting loose funding and banking laws upon industry. The idle, who seek for wealth by chartering laws, are wiser than their equalising brethren. Law has never been able to produce an equality of property, where industry exists; but it can produce its monopoly. Our policy rejects its application to both objects, and our constitutions unequivocally disclose an opinion, that civil liberty depends upon leaving the distribution of property to industry; hence laws for this end, are as unconstitutional, as those for re-establishing king, lords and commons. Legal wealth and hereditary power, are twin principles. These frauds beget all the parties or factions of civil society, such as patrician and plebeian, military and civil, stock and landed. The enmity and contrast in all these cases, arise from a legal difference of interest, and the active and passive members in this fraudulent system, are distinctly designated by the wealth and poverty it diffuses. In England, where it prevails, 'every seventh person draws support from the parish at some period of his life, exclusive of those who submit to misery, in preference to the humiliation of asking charity.'

· It is an unalterable law, that man shall be guided by self interest. Governments, therefore, administered by man, though made by constitutions, are maintained, corrupted or destroyed by laws. Legislation in favour of parties of interest, shews that they govern legislation; and in that case they always cut a new government out of any constitution, by a succession of laws, as a statuary cuts a statue of any form out of a rock. The party of interest created in England by paper stock, moulded the government in a century, into the form most suitable to itself; and the celerity observable in the motions of a similar party here, is an evidence of the advantage it derives from the precedent.

Self interest is so ingenious as to deceive both itself and others, by verbal patriotism and false comparisons. The order produced by hereditary magistrates, is compared with the confusion produced by fraudulent laws; superstition is compared with atheism; a well armed and appointed mercenary army, with an unarmed and unorganized militia; and the freedom with the licentiousness of the press. By such arts and arguments, parties of interest effect their selfish purposes. The two artifices of comparing loans with taxes, and war with a dishonourable peace, are most unhappily adapted for consigning nations to those who deal in credit.

The ancient aristocracy perished with idolatry; the modern, rejecting divine descent as no longer tenable, relies for defence on human laws. It is remarkable that Mr. Godwin, discerning no match for aristocracy but aristocracy, (as if the devil could only be controlled by the devil) should propose a theory bottomed upon its essential principle, for the purpose of destroying it. Can a more wicked association of aristocrats be conceived, than the idle, assembled to enact Mr. Godwin's law, for dividing among themselves the property of the industrious. Proteus, in his ugliest form, does not cease to be Proteus. Considering private property as a natural or social right, the observation is equally just. As nature compelled man to acquire in order to exist, his acquisitions from his own labour are his property, according to the law of his maker; since man must have existed before society. Man's unequal moral and physical powers and wants, further disclose nature's enmity to the equality of his acquisitions. And the pleasures and pains annexed to industry and idleness, strongly prove that they are bestowed by nature, as just rewards or punishments for a virtue or a vice. But both the levellers and monopolists are for destroying nature's or the creator's law, built upon these physical and moral grounds; the first faction, because property is thereby made too unequal, the second, because the same law distributes it too equally; and though inveterate enemies, they agree that this divine errour should be corrected by human laws; only that each contends for an opposite excess, and brands the extremity of its adversary with all the epithets used to define tyranny. But either would be a legal metempsychosis of our policy. The levellers, indeed, by attempting that which is unattainable, betray the principle of leaving property to be divided by industry, and destroy the interest by which they are directed. If the accumulators succeed, the two most remarkable revolutions recorded in history, will terminate at the points they started from; the equality of France, in a despotick hereditary dynasty; and the republicanism of the United States, in the English aristocracy, compounded of a variety of parties of interest.

. This species of confederation, so different from that by which these states are united, has invented a species of law neither constitutional nor legislative; and sought for a new term to gain for it an independency of the nation, who can alter the one species of law; and of legislatures, which can annul the other. Law-charter claims an inviolability beyond all civil and political laws whatsoever. The origin and use of instruments assuming the privilege of violating whatever principles they please, without being subject to any, is worthy of some attention.

Charter was originally a monarchical mode of conveying to towns or mercantile associations, certain portions of civil liberty, considered as valid, upon the ground that the liberties of the grantees belonged to the grantor, and were, therefore, subjects of sale, gift or barter. Upon this stock has been engrafted the idea, that law-charters were irrevocable, without considering that liberty, according to our policy, is not a subject of sale, gift or barter; or the property of the government. Though kings, according to the first opinion, might by charters, sell or give more liberty to some of their subjects than to others; and though such deeds ought to be considered as not within the power of one contracting party to vacate; yet it does not follow, according to the second, that our governments can do the same thing, or that charters made by them for privileges or monopolies, ought to be equally sacred. Liberty, by means of royal charters, crept into cities, and from these diffused many benefits over nations. That aristocracy should make this fact a precedent upon which to creep into our policy, is a striking illustration, either of its own ingenuity, or of its rival's ignorance. To draw a precedent in favorem mortis, out of one in favorem vitæ, and to pass off the deduction, as genuine, upon those to be killed by it, shews that logick itself deserves the character we have heard given to republican forms of government; and that Mr. Locke might have saved himself all the trouble he has taken about the human understanding, by subjecting it to the same definition. The fetters of bondage were gradually broken by the irrepealable charters of kings, and ought, therefore, to be gradually welded by the irrepealable laws of republicks; and frequent elections being necessary to enable nations to preserve liberty, the design ought to be defeated by the irrevocable laws of a single legislature, which may choose to destroy it. What but the corruption of hope, from the dreams of wealth poured by aristocratical artifice into the imagination of ignorance, can make such reasoning current? Thus alchymy is made to appear practicable, and soldiers are persuaded to make conquests. The conquest is made, their leaders are enriched, and the soldiers live in poverty and die in hospitals. And so the people of England have been led to make laws in favour of parties of interest, and to experience the fate of soldiers.

Mr. Adams considers the existing English government, not as a confederation of parties of interest, but as a kind of national confederation, inclosing every individual within its pale, marshalled into three orders. But having exhibited it in a theory to which he allows perfection, he goes over the world in search of its practical existence, exclaiming, 'lo it is not here, lo it is not there, but it would have appeared both here and there, had the balances been properly adjusted.' To me this government seems to consist of a confederation of parties of interest, excluding the majority of the nation. Such as the church of England, the paper stock party, the East India company, the military party, the pensioned and sinecure party, and the ins and outs, once called whigs and tories; each struggling for self interest and self government, but all, creeping forth like caterpillars from the legal nests in which they have been hatched, to feed upon the fruits of the nation. Most of these combinations are republicks, convinced that they are their own best friends, whilst they prescribe monarchy to nations, pretending that national association is its own enemy. The last doctrine is preached to transfer to themselves the property of others. But they prefer republican principles to secure it.

The form of the English parliament was originally fashioned by feudal principles; to give money to the king was its chief duty; and he could garble election to effect his ends. The modes by which its pristine end was effected, are changed, but the end is the same. The king has found rotten borough and septennial representation, with a close union between the crown and the herd of parties of interest, a better system for raising money upon the nation, than even his feudal privilege or power of bestowing or revoking the right of representation; because these parties freely give him the money of the nation for a good share of it. The poverty of the English nobility, compared with its wealth before the abolition of perpetuities, has exposed the house of Lords to the full effect of the modern modes for guiding the house of Commons. Can we more clearly discern Mr. Adams's idea of a beautiful balance of orders in England, either in the original feudal parliamentary constitution, or in its existing modification, than we can Dr. Henry's, of a beautiful English constitution somewhere hidden, in a short, frivolous and dead code of civil laws, called magna charta? If this is a just picture of the English government, with what reason has Mr. Adams eulogized it? With what reason has Publius or the Federalist, assigned to it the rank among governments, which Homer bears among poets? And with what reason are politicians introducing parties of interest, the present poison of that, into our form of government?

Let us count the cost of the modern English system to that nation, to place before our eyes what the same system will cost here. It draws from the nation into its unappeasable avarice, not less than one hundred millions of pounds sterling annually. If the English king was to ask the nation for one third of its lands only, the dullest man would see that despotick power must grow out of such excessive wealth; but an annual receipt by himself and the parties of interest leagued to the crown, of more than the rent-roll of the whole, has hidden the despotism in an aggravated degree, under the various covers these parties of interest are bribed to throw over it. England and Scotland contain about fifty millions of acres of land. It is probable that an average rent of twenty shillings an acre would exceed its value, and certain, that double this rent would do so. Legislation, exercising a power of distributing wealth, has then in England already disposed of all the land of the kingdom, or its income. In the United States, the same system has not yet ripened into equal maturity. But such political arithmetick would probably in a state of peace, exhibit an expenditure of about twenty millions annually, by all our governments, state and continental, partly for necessary purposes, and partly to feed parties of interest; and a gross income to banks of about five millions annually. This total exceeds a moiety of our exports, and yet the system, discontented with this proportion of them, may possibly propose to be let loose upon exports more directly. Twenty five millions of income at six per centum, require a principal of four hundred and fifty millions. Supposing the lands of the United States to be of the average value of four dollars an acre, this income covers above one hundred and twelve millions of acres. If a moiety of it is received by funding and banking, then these two parties of interest, have already attached upon more acres of land here, than the whole family have been able to lay hold of in England.

The question to be determined is, which is best for mankind; a government for advancing the prosperity of an entire nation, or one for selecting, by law, sundry minor nations out of the great one, and extracting as much money as possible, in straight and crooked ways, under honest and fraudulent pretexts, from the entire nation, to enrich these legal selections. If the united interest of the king, nobility, priesthood, stockjobbers, placemen, chartered companies, army and navy, with their associates, governs the British government, then the national association (if there is or ever was one) has no government. There is no British nation, except a combined minority of interests, distinct from the general interest. It might with equal propriety be asserted, that the servants and drudges who enrich the East India company, were members of that company, as that British people, not belonging to the association of exclusive interests, but serving and enriching it, were members of the British nation. The first species of government does good to a multitude of people, without injuring one; the second, does good to a few people, by injuring a multitude. The latter is the principle of every species of political oppression. Can a preference be given to a principle in any form, comprising the essence of political tyranny in every form?

The malignity of monarchy, aristocracy and hierarchy, rests in their disposition to bestow by law, benefits upon some, at the expense of others. It will be curious if the human intellect should be able to see this evil, however disguised by governments thus denominated, and also be blind to it undisguised, when practised by a republican government. When posterity shall compare Europe, plundered by the tricks of popery, with nations plundered without a juggle, its verdict as to the relative state of knowledge between the tenth and nineteenth centuries, may be anticipated. The more pilgrims, the more wealth for the priests of Loretto, and the less for the laity. The more paper stock, the more wealth for stockjobbers, and the less for those from whom it is drawn. Such will be the evidence upon which it must decide.

Doctor Samuel Johnson, who was probably the best informed tory (if despotick principles are meant by that name) who ever lived, has been able to find but one argument in defence of converting civil government into a pecuniary machine; and those who mistake names for principles, or sacrifice principles to self interest, have availed themselves of it in a multitude of modes. Pecuniary extravagance is in his opinion no evil, but a good, as it produces a brisk circulation of money. A sophism which can only acquire credit by proving, that the situations of debtor and creditor, payer and receiver, and rich and poor, are equally desirable. Can the opinions of all mankind upon these contrasts be changed by an author, however famous, who has in a thousand other parts of his writings, discovered, that he himself concurred, unequivocally, with the universe. Nations deluded by it, when reduced to the state of the prodigal son, find prisons and poor houses, in lieu of a father's roof and a fatted kid. If the argument is false in respect to the party of interest exercising a government, it must be equally so, respecting every other party of interest. Kings, hierarchies, noble orders, stockjobbers and chartered companies enriched by law, must either be all blessings or all curses, as the circulation of money is increased in all these cases, first by taking it from the multitude, secondly by giving it to the few, and thirdly by its employment in the purchase of property and the enjoyments of luxury.

In the same ingenious mode a brisk circulation of power is

also produced. Accumulated in a few hands, like money, it breaks down confinement, spreads itself far and wide, and compensates majorities as they are compensated for legal accumulations of money. Doctor Johnson has neglected to tell us, that mankind cannot have one of these blessings without the other; that money attracts power, and power, money; and that by accumulating either for the sake of a brisk circulation, you accumulate and circulate both. The accumulation of power has used two arguments in its defence, infinitely more plausible than any urged by legal projects for accumulating money; namely, the supposed benefits of a uniformity of religion, and the difficulty of governing an extensive territory. Europe, however, renounced a religious monarch, and the United States a civil one; the latter upon principles incapable of being dissevered from those which forbid legal accumulations of wealth. Knowledge and will being considered as the governing agents, it seemed unnatural to contract the agency, as the territory to be governed became more extensive. The sphere of one man's knowledge and will, is infinitely less than that of several millions of men. Each planet, however brilliant, is unable to exceed its limited orbit in the firmament. The knowledge and will of a monarch is limited by this moral geometry, like those of other men. When the territory bursts beyond his orbit, monarchy ceases, and some anomalous government ensues; oligarchical, military, deputy-royal, tumultuous, or infinitely variegated by circumstances. Hence neither the virtues nor vices of a monarch are felt at a distance from his person. Miserable provinces under a good, and flourishing under a bad monarch, are common spectacles; because monarchy ends at the end of the monarch's sphere, and some political anomaly commences. Instead of monarchical or aristocratical accumulations of power, to give it a brisker circulation, the United States have rested their policy upon the two governing agents, knowledge and will, of a capacity or moral sphere commensurate to their territory, and naturally expanding with it. The capacity of this policy beyond monarchy, for the government of an extensive territory, is proved by the equality of liberty or of government, between those who reside near to the capital, and those far from it; an effect of infinite value, which monarchy cannot produce. Near the monarch and at a distance from him, different governments are always found. Monarchy only succeeds in cases where it is not unnaturally loaded; as those of armies, garrisons, savage tribes and private families; and the same cases are found to be below the genius of a policy calculated for a wider sphere. With such experience and without considering that the mind of a nation is spacious, and that of a monarch narrow, the maxim, 'ne sutor ultra crepidam,' is wonderfully violated by the dislocated notions, that monarchy is fitted for spacious, and republican forms of government, for narrow spheres.

A power of changing oligarchs, is the most perfect capable of being exercised by the monarch of an extensive territory; but this change of oligarchs is far from proving that no oligarchy exists, and therefore unless oligarchy is monarchy, the latter cannot cover a large territory.

As election cannot extend the knowledge and will of one man contrary to the laws of moral geometry, the execution of the boundless power of appointment bestowed upon the president, must depend upon the knowledge and will of the very worst kind of oligarchs; such as are irresponsible and unknown. The moral incapacity of one man to legislate, knowingly, for a great nation, is the same in respect to official appointments. Accumulated power to be circulated by one man, bears a close resemblance to accumulated wealth to be circulated by a few men. If merit could arrange its own claims to office, with a degree of justice infinitely exceeding the power of one man, that imperfect mode of appointment would never have been admitted. Industry, talents and labour can arrange their rights to property, with infinitely more justice, than any species of legislative distribution can effect. Election infuses into the legislature a quantity of publick spirit, beyond what it infuses into a president, of numerical proportion; but this spirit commensurate to our territory, is itself altered and narrowed by replacing it with the avarice and ambition of individuals, infused by a power of distributing wealth by law. By superadding this power to the injurious influence of executive patronage, self interest is awakened as far as it can be awakened by any political means, and totally expels from legislatures the publick spirit infused by election, because representatives able to distribute wealth, never forget themselves. Oligarchy and aristocracy are the natural fruits of this legislative patronage, far richer than the president's, and corrupting whole corporations and all legislative personages. And if our policy meditated an elective aristocracy still less than an elective monarchy, any mode of introducing one, must be a usurpation. As money and power accumulate together, laws for introducing one will produce both.

In empowering governments to control the passions which stimulate individuals to injure each other, nations have unwarily by unnecessary powers, stimulated governours to become themselves the wrong doers. The whole preference of the policy of the United States, consists in an avoidance of this errour; by adopting the errour, this preference will be lost; the old system of distributing property by law, is exactly that unnecessary power, by which most or all the governments tried by men, have been stimulated to oppress the people, upon the merit of preventing the people from oppressing each other. Hence has arisen the difficulty of deciding between republican and monarchical forms of government. When both exercise the tyrannical power of distributing wealth, the latter must be least oppressive, because it is less expensive to gratify the rapaciousness of one than of many. Accordingly, spurious republicks, or those exercising this power, universally afflict the people with the heaviest taxes. Life is not without its evils, though spent in the lap of a genuine republican government; but morbid ideas of imaginary perfection, or the disposition of ignorance to encounter unknown evils to escape from present inconveniences, too often draw us out of limited happiness into unlimited tyranny. If we should exchange a bed of down for a bed of thorns, because we sometimes rested badly, we should resemble the nations who have preferred a distribution of property by the will of a government, to its genuine republican distribution by industry, talents and labour.

It was an early discovery, that conscience was an insufficient security for justice between man and man; but the insufficiency of the same security for justice on the part of governments to nations, was never distinctly perceived before the American revolution. Out of the complete discovery then made, arose our political laws for assisting the consciences of governours; and if they can emancipate themselves from restraint by civil laws, sowing cancerous seeds in the body politick, the discovery will probably be lost forever.

If separate legal orders or interests are the causes of social oppression, free government ensues of course, by avoiding them. If a combination among the legal distributees of wealth, generates the kind of government existing in England, then the same kind of government naturally ensues here from the system of distributing wealth by law. Mr. Adams's book contains an extensive collection of the causes which have produced tyranny. These are unexceptionably, the separate interests of legal privileges or emoluments.

As to the evil we agree; in the remedy we differ. Introduce, says he, the cause, to prevent the effect; expel it, say I, for the same end.

There is no difficulty in deciding upon the proper objects of this expulsion. The polarity of the moral is as distinct as that of the material world. A politician as certainly knows the point of the moral compass to which the system of distributing wealth by law, inclines, as the mariner, whether his needle points toward the north or the south. The polarity of the re-eligibility of the president has been seen in the re-eligibility of consuls Augustus and Bonaparte; and that of individual patronage and legal parties of interest, is before our eyes in the present state of Europe. The extent and situation of the territory of the United States, enable them to resist this system more successfully than any other nation. Extent keeps at a distance from the bulk of the nation the calamities of war, and enables it to reflect. Cut up into sections, not a single individual might escape them. Small nations are continually exposed to the artifice of legal wars, from the facilities for them furnished by impinging territories; and are debarred from the use of reason to detect the fraud, by the universality of the distraction they produce. But a nation possessed of extensive territory, happily removed from real causes of collision with other nations, like the United States, is peculiarly favoured by providence for the detection of this artifice (so generally practised by ins and outs, and other parties of interest) both as the pretext for it must be shallower, and the national capacity for its detection by reflection and reason, greater. The pledge for a free government arising from the extent and situation of our territory is so transcendant, that the enemies of a republican form of government craftily inculcate an opinion, that this form is not adapted for an extensive territory; for the purpose of producing territorial divisions to discredit republican systems, by the calamities to which impinging states are exposed from the artifices of parties of interest; or with a design of transferring to their rival, monarchy, the advantage of extensive territory, so important that it is at least doubtful whether a greater portion of human happiness would not result from it, though united to a bad form of government, than from the same region cut up into narrow territories, governed by the best forms.

The United States, under a monarchy, can only retain the advantage of extensive territory, by an oligarchy composed of deputy-kings, bashaws, satraps or mandarins. As a republick, the advantage can only be retained, by rejecting the aristocratical system of feeding avarice by law; because this system, being more oppressive than monarchy, would be exchanged for it. If this errour is rejected, instead of paying the old price for extensive territory, no inequalities of liberty or of government can exist, and the territorial capacity of our policy, will be adequate to the liberty and happiness of the whole, instead of being devoted to the avarice and ambition of parties of interest. Monarchy ties extensive territories together by deputy-kings, fortresses and armies. A numerical but spurious republick, uses for this purpose both armies and laws for distributing property, but soon becomes the victim of the first, because the hatred purchased by the second deprives it of national assistance. But a genuine republick unites the most extensive territories by justice, and is defended by the national affection. It travels over space without bloodshed, advances without conquest, and is only arrested by the ocean. How much more sublime is the idea of forming a great nation, by a chain of republicks, subordinate to publick good, than by a chain of satraps subordinate to imperial will, or of chartered companies subordinate to selfish avarice! Such a system stands upon national interest. No people, except ourselves, have seriously attempted to make this interest the basis of civil government. Sometimes it is lost in the pomp of titles, at others under the cowl of superstition; sometimes it is drowned in the din of arms, at others counterfeited in the garb of patriotism; sometimes it is sacrificed for the bribes of patronage, at others stupified by the promises of stock; but under our policy it can never become completely a felo de se, except it shall submit to the legislative usurpation of distributing wealth and poverty.

A free government, like the trinity, consists of integral qualities. General legislation or legal impartiality is one. Legal dispensations of wealth, being a contrary quality, cannot be also a quality of a free government. On the contrary they enable governours to create factions, feed avarice, and usurp arbitrary power. Perhaps the final success of the revolutionary war, was produced by the depreciation of the paper money, and the other causes, by which government was prevented from creating parties of interest by pecuniary laws; an impotence which guaranteed the patriotism even of both ins and outs. Election, though another integer of a free government, is so far from being a compensation for the errour of distributing property by law, that it is itself corrupted by it. In England it is made the instrument of the will, the advocate of the follies, and the shelter for the crimes of an officer, who is thus constituted a despot, capable only of being displaced by another despot. An alliance between election and a legislative power to divide property, constitutes the elysium of statesmen and the purgatory of labour and industry. There is no other mode by which one party can be induced to pay, and the other can acquire as much money. Hence statesmen will for ever admire and recommend the English form of government. But what answer could they give to the following simple address: 'You tell us that we shall be wonderfully benefited by legal transfers of our income to the creatures of law, in a multitude of modes. As your arguments perplex us, be pleased for one year to transfer the income of these creatures of law to the children of industry, that we may feel the truth.'

The question, 'whether a legal power can be constitutionally used to impair or destroy the principles of our policy,' has been already brought before the publick, in the efforts of the general government to distribute gain or loss between the states by protecting duties, banking charters, making canals and roads, and other legal benefactions. The children of a father who lives for ever, but annually makes a division of their property according to his own pleasure, are his slaves. If the general government gains a similar position in relation to the people and to the states, the principles of a division of power, of its responsibility, of protecting property, of its division by industry, of state confederation, and indeed all other principles constituting a genuine republick, are abolished.

The best restraint upon legislative acts tending to the destruction of a true republican government, consists of the mutual right of the general and state governments to examine and controvert before the publick each others' proceedings. This right is stated in certain resolutions which passed the legislature of Kentucky on the 8th of November, 1798, in the following words, 'Resolved, that the several States comprising the United States of America, are not united on the principle of unlimited submission to their general government; but that by compact under the style and title of a constitution for the United States and of amendments thereto, they constituted a general government for special purposes, delegated to that government certain definite powers, reserving each State to itself, the residuary mass of right to their own self government; and that whensoever the general government assumes undelegated powers, its acts are unauthoritative, void, and of no force. That to this compact each state acceded as a State, and is an integral party, its co-states forming as to itself, the other party. That the government created by this compact was not made the exclusive or final judge of the extent of the powers delegated to itself, since that would have made its discretion, and not the constitution, the measure of its powers; but that, as in all other cases of compact among parties having no common judge, each party has an equal right to judge for itself as well of infractions, as of the mode and measure of redress.'

The style of these resolutions throughout ascertains the author.* Both the parties of the United States have asserted and denied this doctrine, as they happened to be in or out of power; for or against the existing administration. But I am unable to discern any better resource for the preservation of civil liberty, than it affords. The state governments are wise, watchful and temperate sentinels, checks upon each other as well as upon the general government, not dictators armed with force, but advocates armed with reason. Vindications of this salutary doctrine are necessary to save it from the usurpations of precedents, of which parties will even avail themselves in power, although that power was obtained by opposing them. But this mode of extending the powers of the general government, is inconsistent with the principles of our policy. It is restricted by limitations imposed by a superior authority, which it can neither diminish nor destroy by its own acts. It is not a complete government, but associated with the state governments by the same superior authority, which has allotted specified powers to each party, and neither can increase these powers by its own precedents, nor even by its positive laws, without rebellion against this authority. If both should concur in extending or diminishing the powers of one or either, by the plainest precedents or laws, it would still be the same species of rebellion, and unconstitutional. Prescription and precedent, founded upon the acts of an entire government, are extremely different from those founded upon the acts of a section of a government, because the first is a complete political representative of the nation and the second not so. Their authority is also widely different in limited and unlimited governments; if the former could extend their powers by such agents, they could make themselves unlimited. The legislation of congress, contrary to the principles of the general constitution, is in every view similar to the legislation of the senate without the concurrence of the house of representatives, and equally entitled to the authority

* Mr. Jefferson.

claimed by precedents under absolute governments; an authority founded only in unlimited power.

The danger of extending by legislation powers given to powers not given or prohibited, is also exposed to the publick view by the same resolutions, as follows: 'That the construction applied by the general government (as is evident by sundry of their proceedings) to those parts of the constitution of the United States, which delegate to congress a power to lay and collect taxes, duties, imposts, and excises, to pay the debts and provide for the common defence and general welfare of the United States, and to make all laws which shall be necessary and proper for carrying into execution the powers vested by the constitution in the government of the United States, or any department thereof, *goes to the destruction of all limits prescribed to their power by the constitution*. That words meant by that instrument to be subsidiary only to the execution of the limited powers, ought not to be so construed as themselves to give unlimited powers, nor a part to be taken so as to destroy the whole residue of the instrument. That the proceedings of the general government, under colour of these articles, will be a fit and necessary subject for revisal and correction at a time of greater tranquillity, while those specified in the preceding resolutions call for immediate redress.' It is to be lamented that these proceedings of the general government, going 'to the destruction of all limits prescribed to their power by the constitution,' had not been specified by the same able pen. That they could only be of a legislative nature is plain; but whether laws for subjecting agriculture, manufactures, talents and labour to legal capitalists; for rallying chartered and stock feudatories around the general government; or for destroying commerce under the power of regulating it, were meant, is uncertain. The evil however has arisen from a confidence inspired by the numerical analysis. By deluding us to expect from men, that which principles alone can yield, namely, a free government, we are induced to neglect the application of principles to laws. A numerical classification of men, triple, decimal, or centuriate, as imperfectly ascertains their moral qualities, as one drawn from size, meat, bone or hair. An analysis of sheep, founded in moral qualities, is equivalent to the numerical analysis of governments; by the first, we can never discover whether we have good sheep; nor by the second, whether we have a good government or good laws. Had each quarter of the globe adopted a different member of the numerical analysis, supposing it to comprise monarchy, aristocracy, democracy, and a mixture of the three, the whole world might still have suffered oppression. Crimes perpetrated individually or collectively are still crimes; but nations led astray by the numerical analysis, having selected one of its members for their form of government, conclude that they have attained to the utmost degree of political perfection, and cannot do better than to bear its crimes as they do a drought. Hence a disciple of the most republican member of the numerical analysis is induced to bear, defend and applaud the crimes of his selected form, an abhorrence of which when committed by other forms, caused his preference; and hence political parties are equally strenuous for the justification or correction of the same abuses, as they happen to proceed from their own or the leaders of their adversary. Both evils arise from the want of a worthy object on which to bestow our zeal. Having been taught to believe, that the numerical analysis presents us with a complete political pantheon, we are compelled to pay our adoration to some of its deities. Yet we never extend the blindness we attach to the object of our own worship, to the objects selected by others to receive a similar offering. A republick sees very plainly oppressions committed by monarchy and aristocracy, and these two, those committed by republicks; but whilst each sees the vices of the other members of the numerical analysis, the blindness occasioned by the want of a moral analysis, tolerates the same vices in itself. If we would consider, that we discover the vices of the rejected forms of government, by bringing them to trial, without favour or affection, before a jury of good moral principles, we should instantly discern that the same tribunal would detect the vices of the government we have selected; and that an analysis, similar to that formed in our own minds to try supposed culprits, might be perfected into a complete capacity for rooting up as they are planted, those legal scions, which otherwise never fail to grow, until they draw to themselves all the nourishment of a free government.

It is necessary to illustrate these observations by the aid of a familiar fact. The two parties, called republican and federal, have hitherto undergone but one revolution. Yet each when in power, preached Filmer's old doctrine of passive obedience in a new form, with considerable success; and each out of power strenuously controverted it. The party in power asserted, that however absurd or slavish this doctrine was under other forms of the numerical analysis, the people under ours were *identified* (the new term to cog this old doctrine upon the United States) with the government; and that therefore an opposition to the government, was an opposition to the nation itself. The extraction of passive obedience, of all political principles the most slavish, out of the best member of the numerical analysis, as the extractors themselves confess, furnishes a conclusive proof of its insufficiency for teaching us how to preserve a free form of government. This identifying doctrine is exactly analogous to Agrippa's fraudulent apologue, for constituting a government the intellectual dictating head of the whole body politick, and subjecting the members to a passive obedience. It puts an end to the idea of a responsibility of the government to the nation; sameness cannot be responsible to sameness. It renders useless or impracticable the freedom of speech and of the press. It converts the representative into the principal. It destroys the division of power between the people and the government, as being themselves indivisible. And in short it is inconsistent with every principle by which politicians and philosophers have hitherto defined a free government. This ingenious doctrine of identity for justifying tyranny in fact, because a government is free in form; and for defeating the responsibility of the government to the people, because the constitution was calculated to produce it; asserted and denied by both our parties, demonstrates that opinions fluctuate with power. From this undeniable fact it follows, that a nation and its governours can never entertain the same opinions. Nations will for ever wish to be free, and governours to be despotick. Future parties will not be less infected by power than former, and former have successively advanced the doctrine refuted by Sidney.

The parties called whig and tory in England, the first the disciple of Filmer and the other of Sidney, have conclusively settled the fact; and out of the demonstration have arisen the efforts of the United States for securing the general interest of the nation, against the ambition and avarice of the party of interest administering the government, by a string of moral precautions, endeavoured to be explained in this essay; such as responsibility, division of power, a sound militia, and a distribution of property by industry and talents and not by law. And if a nation should sacrifice to any governours whatsoever, these moral precautions for the preservation of its liberty, it is as certainly lost, as are the previous principles of every party by the acquisition of power.

The danger of parties to free governments, arises from the impossibility of controlling them by the restraints of political law; because being constituted upon selfish views, like a set of mountebanks combined to administer drugs for the sake of getting fees, the nature of the poison cannot be foreseen, nor an effectual antidote anticipated. No division of power, no responsibility, no periodical change of leaders, no limitation of 'thus far you may go and no farther,' stops their career. In every form, therefore, they constitute the same avaricious or furious species of aristocracy, which would be produced by a form of government in the hands of a self constituted and uncontrolled body of men. They are universally disposed to persecute, plunder, oppress and kill, like all governments unsubjected to political law; and under the title of patriots, are, like fanaticks under the title of saints, ready to perpetrate any crimes to gratify their interest or prejudices. By melting down the fetters of moral and republican principles in party confidence, we abolish the only known remedy against the evil qualities of human nature, abandon our experiment of political law founded in these principles, and rest for security on ignorant mobs, guided by a few designing leaders, or on cunning combinations, guided by avarice and ambition. The Independents of England and the Jacobins of France, even abhorred the despotisms they introduced, but the results were unavoidable, as the natural effect of the unlimited confidence these parties acquired. This confidence produces an unlimited government, or one unrestricted by the ligatures of a moral analysis; and such a government is despotick. Under a despotism of any form, and in the form of a party of interest more than in any other, bodily safety, the safety of property, and the freedom of the mind, cease. Malice, envy and calumny instantly become the prime ministers of the furious and tottering tyrant. Knowing his doom from the fate of his predecessors, he hastens to glut his appetite for mischief before he dies. No numerical checks or balances can reach this dreadful party tyranny. It is even able to suspend or destroy those solemnly established by nations, and to make the people themselves the authors of their own ruin. A political analysis alone, composed of moral principles, can reach and tame a beast, from which men flee to monarchy, because it lays waste and devours their rights with a thousand hands and a thousand mouths. This can test party legislation and actions. But freed from the rigid control of good moral principles, the professions of parties are like the flattering sunshine of the morning, and their acts like an evening deluge. In legislation contrary to genuine republican principles, sustained by a dominant party zeal, lies, in my view, the greatest danger to the free form of government of the United States; nor can I conceive any augmentation of the danger, equivalent to an exercise of the power of distributing wealth by law. If, therefore, these essays should only prove, that it is the office of a republican government to protect, but not to bestow property, they may protract the period during which our government may remain the servant of the nation. For as worldly omnipotence is annexed to a power of dealing out wealth and poverty, nations are universally retributed for the folly and impiety of submitting to this species of human providence, by a divine decree, that it shall unexceptionably convert these servants into masters and tyrants.